History of Art
for Young People

History

Second Edition
Revised by
Anthony F. Janson

# of Art

for Young People

H.W. JANSON
Professor of Fine Arts,
New York University

With Samuel Cauman

THAMES AND HUDSON

First published in Great Britain in 1973
by Thames and Hudson Ltd, London

Second edition 1982

Printed and bound in Japan

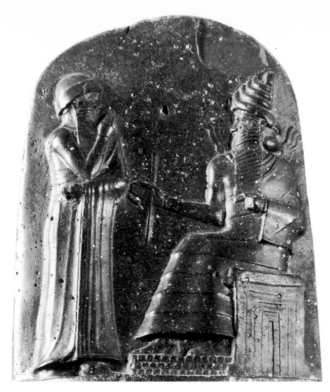

Contents

PART ONE How Art Began

Map   8

Images and Imagination   10

The Magic Art of Cavemen and Primitive Peoples   12
  The Old Stone Age • The New Stone Age
  Primitive Art

Art for the Dead—Egypt   18
  The Old Kingdom • The New Kingdom

Temples, Palaces, and Citadels—
The Ancient Near East and the Aegean   27
  Mesopotamia • Persia • Aegean Art

Greek Art   43
  Painting • Temples • Sculpture

Etruscan Art   60

Roman Art   62
  Architecture • Sculpture • Painting

Synoptic Table I   72

PART TWO The Middle Ages

Map   76

Early Christian and Byzantine Art   78

The Earlier Middle Ages in the West   88
  The Dark Ages • Carolingian Art • Ottonian Art

Romanesque Art   105
     Architecture • Sculpture • Painting
Towns, Cathedrals, and Gothic Art   118
     Architecture • Sculpture 1150–1420
     Painting 1200–1400
Synoptic Table II   156

PART THREE The Renaissance

Map   160
The "New Age"   162
Late Gothic Painting North of the Alps   163
The Early Renaissance in Italy   174
     Sculpture • Architecture • Painting
The High Renaissance in Italy   192
Mannerism and Other Trends   221
The Renaissance in the North   231
The Baroque in Italy, Flanders, and Spain   239
The Golden Age of Dutch Painting   250
The Age of Versailles   256
Rococo   279
Synoptic Table III   286

PART FOUR The Modern World

Map   292
Introduction   294
Neoclassicism   294
The Romantic Movement   299
Realism and Impressionism   315
Post-Impressionism   329
Art in Our Time   339
     Expressionism • Abstraction • Fantasy
     Newer Trends • Sculpture
     Twentieth-Century Architecture
Synoptic Table IV   386

GLOSSARY   390
BOOKS FOR FURTHER READING   394
INDEX   398
LIST OF CREDITS   411

PART ONE
ONE
How
Art Began

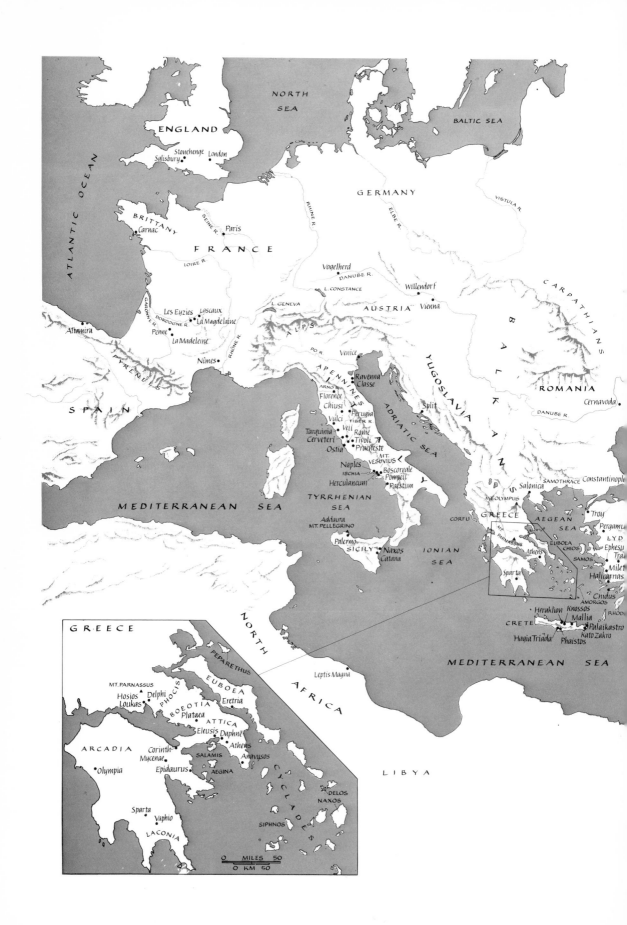

NORTH
SEA

BALTIC SEA

ENGLAND

ATLANTIC OCEAN

Stonehenge
Salisbury London

GERMANY

CARPATHIANS

BRITTANY
Carnac

Paris

SEINE R.
RHINE R.
ELBE R.
VISTULA R.

FRANCE

LOIRE R.

Vogelherd

DANUBE R.

Willendorf

AUSTRIA
Vienna

L. CONSTANCE

L. GENEVA

GARONNE R.
Les Eyzies Lascaux
Dordogne R. La Magdelaine
Penne La Madeleine

Altamira

RHONE R.

ALPS

PO R.

Venice

DANUBE R.

ROMANIA

Cernavoda

PYRENEES

Nimes

SPAIN

APENNINES
ARNO R.
Florence
Chiusi
Vulci Perugia
TIBER R.
Tarquinia Veii
Cerveteri Rome
Ostia Tivoli
Praeneste

Ravenna
Classe

Split

ADRIATIC SEA

YUGOSLAVIA

B A L K A N S

MT.
VESUVIUS
Naples Boscoreale
ISCHIA Pompeii
Herculaneum Paestum

MEDITERRANEAN SEA

TYRRHENIAN
SEA

Salonica

SAMOTHRACE Constantinople

MT.OLYMPUS

CORFU

GREECE

MT.
PARNASSUS

AEGEAN
SEA

Troy

Pergamu

LYD

Addaura
MT. PELLEGRINO

Palermo

SICILY

Naxos
Catania

IONIAN
SEA

Athens

EUBOEA
CHIOS

SAMOS

Ephesu
Tra
Milet

Halicarnas

Sparta

AMORGOS

Cnidus

RHOD

Heraklion Knossos
Mallia

CRETE Palaikastro

Hagia Triada Phaistos Kato Zakro

MEDITERRANEAN SEA

NORTH

AFRICA

Leptis Magna

LIBYA

GREECE

PEPARETHUS

MT.PARNASSUS

Hosios Delphi
Loukas PHOCIS

EUBOEA

Eretria

BOEOTIA
Plataea

ATTICA

Eleusis Daphnē

ARCADIA

Corinth
Mycenae

SALAMIS

Athens

Anavysos

Olympia

Epidaurus

AEGINA

CYCLADES

DELOS
NAXOS

Sparta

Vaphio

SIPHNOS

LACONIA

0   MILES   50
0   KM   50

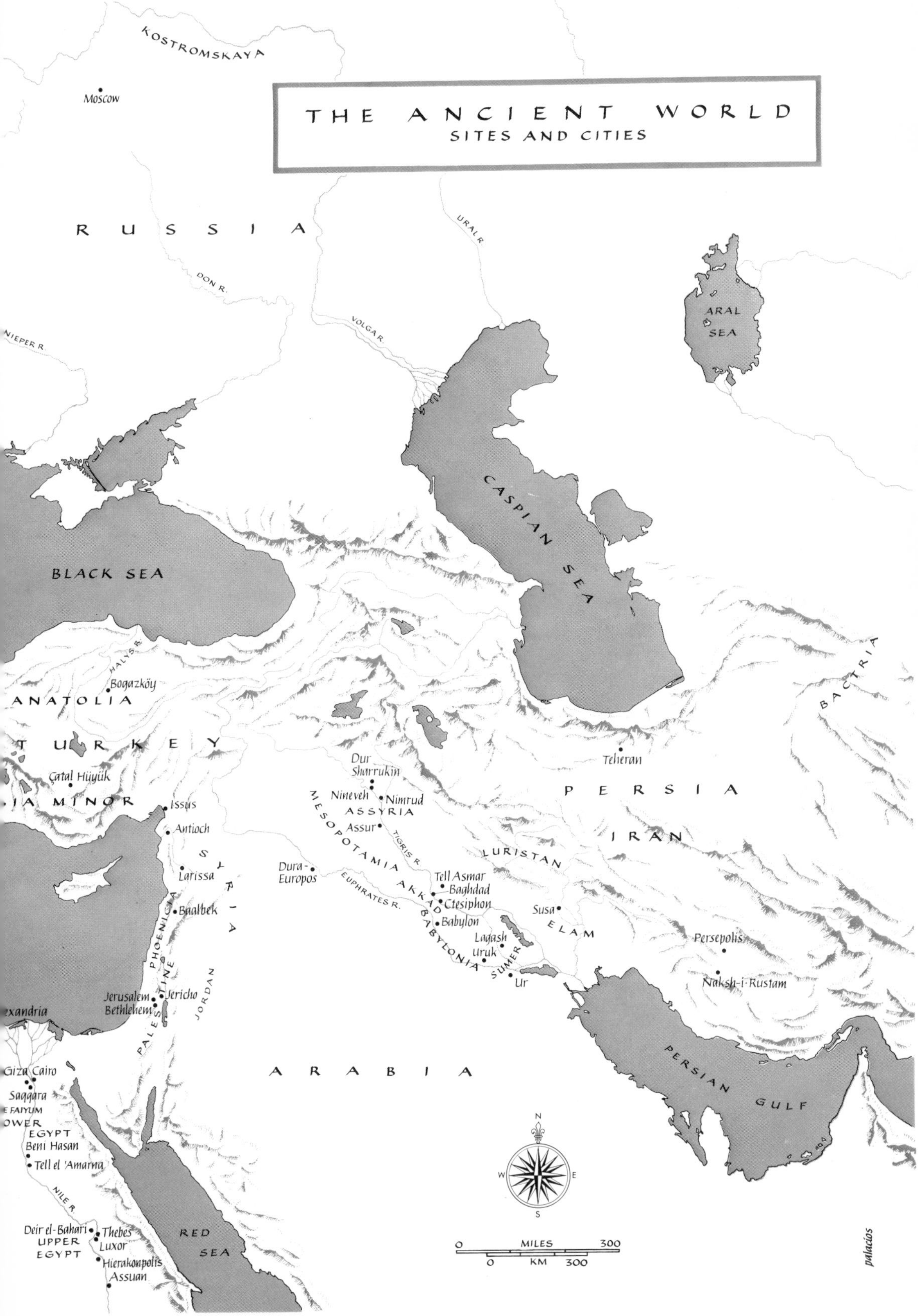

THE ANCIENT WORLD
SITES AND CITIES

KOSTROMSKAYA

Moscow

RUSSIA

URAL R.

DON R.

VOLGA R.

NIEPER R.

ARAL SEA

CASPIAN SEA

BLACK SEA

HALYS R.

Bogazköy

ANATOLIA

BACTRIA

TURKEY

Çatal Hüyük

IA MINOR

Issus

Antioch

Dur-Sharrukin

Nineveh Nimrud
ASSYRIA

Assur

MESOPOTAMIA

TIGRIS R.

Teheran

PERSIA

IRAN

LURISTAN

Larissa

Cyprus

Dura-Europos

EUPHRATES R.

AKKAD

Tell Asmar
Baghdad
Ctesiphon
Babylon

BABYLONIA

Susa

ELAM

Lagash
Uruk

SUMER

Ur

Persepolis

Naksh-i-Rustam

S Y R I A

Baalbek

PHOENICIA

PALESTINE

JORDAN

Jerusalem
Bethlehem

Jericho

exandria

PERSIAN GULF

A R A B I A

RED SEA

Giza Cairo

Saqqara

E FAIYUM

OWER
EGYPT

Beni Hasan

Tell el 'Amarna

NILE R.

Deir el-Bahari Thebes
UPPER   Luxor
EGYPT

Hierakonpolis

Assuan

MILES
0   300

0   KM   300

palacios

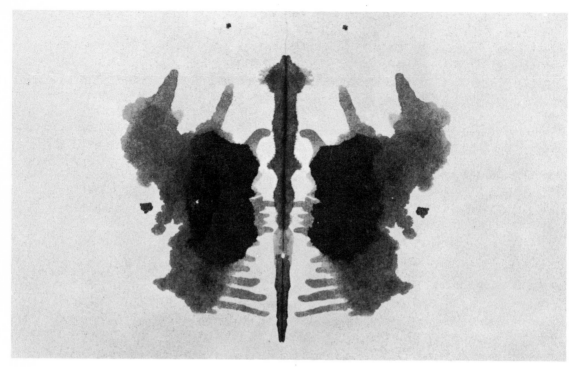

1. Ink blot on folded paper

Images and Imagination

Everyone dreams. Even animals dream. A cat's ears and tail may twitch as he sleeps, and a sleeping dog may whine and growl and paw the air, just as if he were having a fight. Even when awake, animals "see" things. For no apparent reason a cat's fur may rise on his back as he peers into a dark closet. And you or I may get goose pimples from phantoms we neither see nor hear.

That is imagination at work. Human beings are not the only creatures who have imagination, although they are the only creatures who can tell one another about it. If we tell in words what we imagine, we have made a story. If we take a pencil and draw it, we have made a picture. To imagine means "to make an image"—a picture—in our minds.

There are many different ways our imaginations can be triggered. When we are ill in bed and have nothing to do, a ceiling crack on which we have kept our eye may begin to look like an animal or a tree. Our imagination adds the lines that were not there

before. Again, an ink blot (see fig. 1) will remind us of other things, although it was made by accident. Psychologists know this and have made up ink-blot tests to find out what is in our minds, for each of us, depending on the sort of person he is, sees a different picture in the same blot.

The *Bull's Head* by Picasso (fig. 2) is a striking example of how an artist saw something new and exciting in two very ordinary objects. Look closely. The bull's head is the seat and handle bars of an old bicycle. To put them together was ridiculously simple. But there was nothing simple about the leap of imagination that recognized a powerful hidden image. *That* was a master stroke. Where an ordinary person's eyes and brain would find no connection, Picasso's did. His hands finished the job and translated the image that had been in his head into something that could be seen and touched.

The making of a work of art has little in common with what we ordinarily mean by "making." We all tend to think of "making" in terms of the craftsman or manufacturer who knows from the outset exactly what he wants to produce. The creative process, on the other hand, consists of a series of leaps of the imagination and the artist's attempts to give them form by shaping his materials. It is a strange and risky business in which the maker never quite knows what he is making until he has actually made it. To put it another way, it is a game of hide-and-seek in which the seeker is not sure what he is looking for until he has found it.

Here we have another paradox: the birth of a work of art is an intensely private experience, yet it must, as a final step, be shared by a public, in order for the birth to be successful. The audience whose approval looms so large in the artist's mind is a limited and special one, not the general public: the merits of the artist's work can never be determined by a popularity contest. Its members may be other artists, as well as patrons, friends, critics, and interested bystanders. The one qualification they all have in common is an informed love of works of art—an attitude at once discriminating and enthusiastic that lends particular weight to their judgments. They are, in a word, *experts*, people whose authority rests on experience rather than theoretical knowledge.

The active minority which we have termed the artist's primary audience draws its recruits from a much larger and more passive secondary audience, whose contact with works of art is less direct and continuous. This group, in turn, shades over into the vast numbers of those who believe they "don't know anything about art," the laymen pure-and-simple. When they say, "I know what I like," they really mean, "I like what I know (and I reject whatever fails to match the things I am familiar with)"; such likes are not in truth theirs at all, for they have been imposed upon them by habit and circumstance, without any personal choice. In reality, there is no sharp break, no difference in kind, between them and the experts, only a difference in degree. The road to expertness invites anyone with an open mind and a capacity to absorb new experiences. As we travel on it, and as our understanding grows, we shall be able to say, with some justice, that we know what we like.

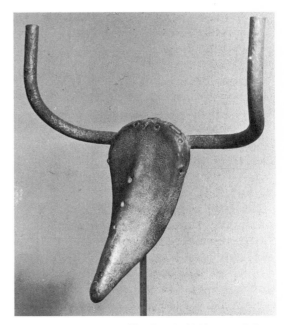

2. PABLO PICASSO. *Bull's Head.* 1943. Handlebars and seat of a bicycle, height 16 1/8". Galerie Louise Leiris, Paris

The Magic Art of Cavemen and Primitive Peoples

THE OLD STONE AGE

When did man start creating works of art? What did they look like? What prompted him to do so? Every history of art must begin with these questions—and with the admission that we cannot answer them. Our earliest ancestors began to walk on the earth with two feet more than a million years ago, but not until some six hundred thousand years later do we meet the earliest traces of man the toolmaker. He must have been *using* tools all along, for apes will pick up a stick to knock down a banana, or a stone to throw at an enemy. The *making* of tools is a more complex matter. It demands first of all the ability to think of sticks or stones as "fruit knockers" or "bone crackers" even at times when they are not needed for such purposes. Once man was able to do that, he discovered that some sticks and stones had a handier shape than others and put them aside for future use—he "appointed" them as tools because he had begun to link *form* and *function*. Some of these stones have survived; they are large pebbles or chunks of rock showing the marks of repeated use for the same operation, whatever that may have been. The next step was for man to try chipping away at these tools-by-appointment so as to improve their shape. This is the earliest craft of which we have evidence, and with it we enter a phase of human development known as the Old Stone Age.

CAVE ART

It is during the late stages of the Old Stone Age, some twenty thousand years ago, that we encounter the earliest works of art known to us. These, however, already show an assurance and refinement far removed from any humble beginnings; they must have been preceded by thousands of years of slow growth about which we know nothing at all. At that time, the last Ice Age was drawing to a close in Europe, and the climate between the Alps and Scandinavia resembled that of present-day Alaska. Reindeer and other large herbivores roamed the plains and valleys, preyed upon by the ancestors of today's lions and tigers—and by our own ancestors. These men lived in caves or in the shelter of overhanging rocks. Many such sites have been discovered, and scholars have divided up the "cavemen" into several groups, each named after a characteristic site. Among these it is the so-called Aurignacians and Magdalenians who stand out as especially gifted artists.

The most striking works of Old Stone Age art are the images of animals painted on the rock surfaces of caves, such as those in the cave of Lascaux, in the Dordogne region of France (fig. 3). Bison, deer, horses, and cattle race across walls and ceiling in wild profusion, some simply outlined in black, others filled in with bright earth colors, but all showing the same uncanny sense of life. Even more impressive is the *Wounded Bison* on the ceiling of the cave at Altamira in northern Spain (fig. 4): the dying animal has collapsed, yet even in this helpless state it has lowered its head in self-defense. We are amazed not only by the keen observation, the assured, vigor-

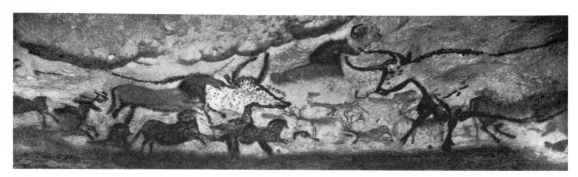

3. *Frieze of Animals* (wall painting). c. 15,000–10,000 B.C. Cave of Lascaux (Dordogne), France

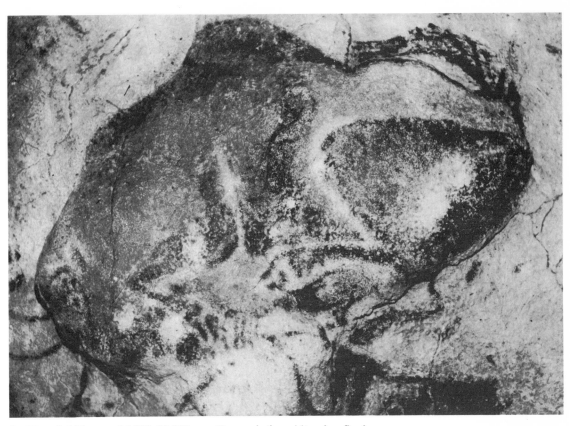

4. *Wounded Bison*. c. 15,000–10,000 B.C. Cave painting. Altamira, Spain

ous outlines, the subtly controlled shading that lends bulk and roundness to the forms, but even more perhaps by the power and dignity of this creature in its final agony.

How did this art develop? What purpose did it serve? And how did it happen to survive intact over so many thousands of years? The last question can be answered readily enough: the pictures rarely occur near the mouth of a cave, where they would be open to easy view (and destruction), but only in the darkest recesses, as far from the entrance as possible. Hidden away as they are in the bowels of the earth, these images must have served a purpose far more serious than mere decoration. There can be little doubt, in fact, that they were part of a magic ritual to ensure a successful hunt. We gather this not only from their secret location and from the lines representing spears or darts that are often found pointing at the animals, but also from the disorderly way the images are placed on top of each other (as in fig. 3). Apparently, for the men of the Old Stone Age there

was no clear distinction between image and reality; by making a picture of an animal they meant to bring the animal itself within their grasp, and in "killing" the image they thought they had killed the animal's vital spirit. Hence every image could serve only once—when the killing ritual had been performed, it was "dead" and could be disregarded. The magic worked, too, we may be sure. Hunters whose courage was thus fortified were bound to be more successful when slaying these formidable beasts with their primitive weapons. Nor has the emotional basis for this kind of magic been lost even today; people have been known to tear up the photograph of someone they have come to hate.

Still, there remains a good deal that puzzles us about the cave paintings. Why are they in such inaccessible places? And why are they so marvelously lifelike? Could not the "killing" magic have been practiced just as effectively on less realistic images? Perhaps the Magdalenian cave pictures are the final phase of a

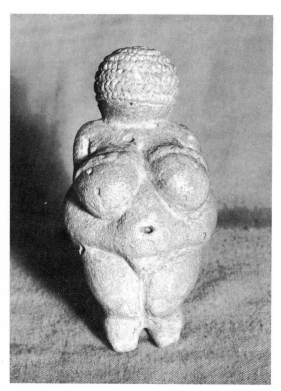

5. *Venus of Willendorf.* c. 15,000–10,000 B.C. Stone, height 4 3/8″. Museum of Natural History, Vienna

development that began as simple killing magic but shifted its meaning when the animals became scarce (apparently the big herds withdrew northward as the climate of Central Europe grew warmer). If so, the main purpose of the Lascaux and Altamira paintings may have been not to "kill" but to "make" animals—to increase their supply. Could it be that the Magdalenians had to practice their fertility magic in the bowels of the earth because they thought of the earth itself as a living thing from whose womb all other life springs? This would help to explain the admirable realism of these images, for an artist who believes he is actually "creating" an animal is more likely to strive for this quality than one who merely sets up an image for the kill. Some of the cave pictures even provide a clue to the origin of this fertility magic: the shape of the animal often seems to have been suggested by the natural formation of the rock, so that its body coincides with a bump or its contour follows a vein or crack. A Stone Age hunter, his mind filled with thoughts of the big game on which he depended for survival, would

have been quite likely to recognize such animals among the rock surfaces of his cave and to attribute deep significance to his discovery. It is tempting to think that those who were particularly good at finding such images gained a special status as artist-magicians and were permitted to perfect their image-hunting instead of having to face the dangers of the real hunt, until finally they learned to make images with little or no aid from chance formations.

OBJECTS

Apart from large-scale cave art, Old Stone Age men also produced small hand-size carvings in bone, horn, or stone, cut by means of flint tools. They, too, seem to have originated with chance resemblances. At an earlier stage, Stone Age men had been content to collect pebbles in whose natural shape they saw a "magic" representational quality; the more fully worked pieces of later times still reflect this attitude. Thus the so-called *Venus of Willendorf* in Austria (fig. 5), one of several such fertility figurines, has a bulbous roundness of form that may suggest an egg-shaped "sacred pebble."

THE NEW STONE AGE

The art of the Old Stone Age in Europe marks the highest achievement of a way of life that could not survive beyond the special conditions created by the receding ice of the Ice Age which was ending. Between c. 10,000 and 5,000 B.C. the Old Stone Age came to an end when men made their first successful attempts to domesticate animals and food grains—one of the truly revolutionary steps in human history, even though the revolution extended over several thousand years. Old Stone Age man had led the unsettled life of a hunter and food gatherer, reaping where nature sowed and thus at the mercy of forces he could neither understand nor control. Once men had learned how to assure their food supply by their own efforts, they settled down in permanent village communities; a new discipline and order entered their lives. There is, then, a basic difference between the

New Stone Age and the Old, even though men still depended on stone as the material of their main tools and weapons. The new mode of life brought forth a number of new crafts and inventions long before the earliest appearance of metals: pottery, weaving and spinning, basic methods of architectural construction. We know all this from New Stone Age settlements that have been uncovered by excavation. But these remains tell us very little, as a rule, of the spiritual condition of New Stone Age men; they include stone implements of ever greater technical refinement and a vast variety of clay vessels covered with abstract ornamental patterns, but hardly anything comparable to the art of the Old Stone Age. Yet the change-over from hunting to husbandry must have brought about profound changes in man's view of himself and the world, and it seems hard to believe that these did not find expression in art. There may be a vast chapter in the development of art here that is lost simply because New Stone Age artists worked in wood and other impermanent materials.

One exception to this general rule is the great stone circle at Stonehenge in southern England (figs. 6, 7), the best preserved of several such megalithic, or "large stone," monuments. Its purpose was religious; apparently the sustained effort required to build it could be compelled only by faith—a faith that almost literally demanded the moving of mountains. The entire structure is oriented toward the exact point where the sun rises on the longest day of the year, and therefore it must have served a sun-worshiping ritual. Even today, Stonehenge has an awe-inspiring, superhuman quality, as if it were the work of a forgotten race of giants. Whether a monument such as this should be termed architecture is a matter of definition: we tend to think of architecture in terms of enclosed interiors, yet we also have landscape archi-

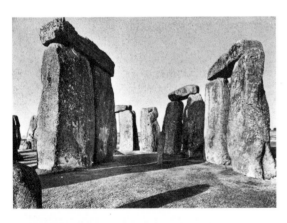

6. Stonehenge. c. 1800–1400 B.C. Diameter of circle 97′, height of stones above ground 13 1/2′. Salisbury Plain (Wiltshire), England

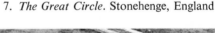

7. *The Great Circle*. Stonehenge, England

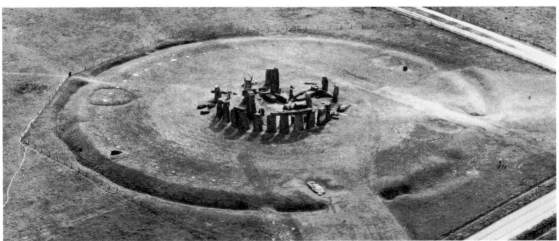

tects, the designers of parks and gardens; nor would we want to deny the status of architecture to open-air theaters or stadiums. Perhaps we ought to consult the ancient Greeks, who coined the word. To them, "archi-tecture" meant something higher than ordinary "tecture" (that is, "construction," or "building"), a structure set apart from the merely practical, everyday kind by its scale, order, permanence, or solemnity of purpose. A Greek would certainly have called Stonehenge architecture. And we, too, shall have no difficulty in doing so once we understand that it is not necessary to *enclose* space in order to define or articulate it. If architecture is "the art of shaping space to human needs and aspirations," then Stonehenge more than meets the test.

PRIMITIVE ART

There are only a few human groups for whom the Old Stone Age has lasted until the present day. Modern survivors of the New Stone Age are far easier to find. They include all of the so-called primitive societies of tropical Africa, the Americas, and the South Pacific. "Primitive" is an unfortunate word: it suggests— quite wrongly—that these societies represent

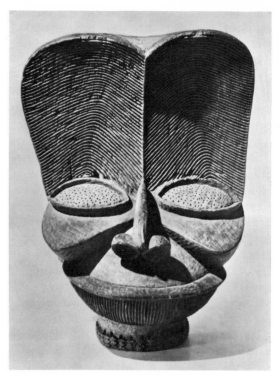

9. Mask, from the Bamenda area, Cameroons. 19th–20th century A.D. Wood, height 26 1/2". Rietberg Museum, Zurich (E. v.d. Heydt Collection)

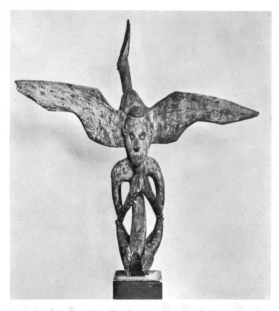

8. *Male Figure Surmounted by a Bird*, from the Sepik River, New Guinea. 19th–20th century A.D. Wood, height 48". Washington University Art Collection, St. Louis

the original condition of mankind and has thus come to be burdened with all sorts of emotional overtones. Still, no other single term will do better. Primitive art, despite its limitless variety, shares one dominant trait: the imaginative reshaping, rather than the careful observation, of the forms of nature. Its concern is not the visible world but the invisible, disquieting world of spirits. To the primitive mind, everything is alive with powerful spirits—men, animals, plants, the earth, rivers and lakes, the rain, the wind, sun and moon. All these spirits had to be appeased, and it was the task of art to provide suitable dwelling places for them and thus to "trap" them. Such a trap is the splendid ancestor figure from New Guinea (fig. 8). It belongs to a large class of similar objects, ancestor worship being perhaps the most persistent feature of primitive society. The entire design is centered on the head, with its intensely staring shell-eyes, while the body—as in primitive art generally—has been reduced to a mere support. The bird emerging from behind the head represents the ancestor's spirit or life force. Its soaring movement, contrasted with the rigidity of the human figure, forms a compelling image—and a strangely familiar one, for our own tradition, too, includes the "soul bird," from the dove of the Holy Spirit to the albatross of the Ancient Mariner, so that we find ourselves responding, almost against our will, to a work of art that at first glance might seem both puzzling and alien.

MASKS AND COSTUMES

In dealing with the spirit world, primitive man was not content with rituals or offerings before his spirit traps. He needed to act out his relations with the spirit world through dances and similar dramatic ceremonials in which he himself could temporarily assume the role of the spirit trap by disguising himself with elaborate masks and costumes. Nor has the fascination of the mask died out even today; we still feel the thrill of a real change of identity when we wear one at Halloween or carnival time. Masks form by far the richest chapter in primitive art, and one of the most puzzling. Their meaning is often impossible to ascertain, since the ceremonies they served usually had elements of secrecy that were jealously guarded from the uninitiated.

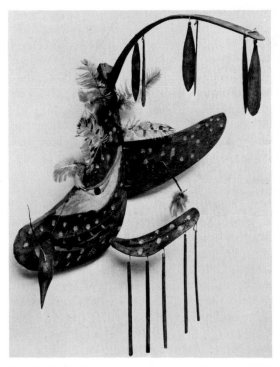

11. Mask (Eskimo), from southwest Alaska. Early 20th century. Wood, height 22″. Museum of the American Indian, Heye Foundation, New York

This emphasis on the mysterious and spectacular not only heightened the emotional impact of the ritual, it also encouraged the makers of masks to strive for imaginative new effects, so that masks in general are less bound by tradition than other kinds of primitive art. The example in figure 9 shows the symmetry of design and the precision and sharpness of carving characteristic of African sculpture. The features of the human face have not been rearranged but restructured, as it were, with the tremendous eyebrows arching above the rest like a protective canopy. The solidity of these shapes becomes strikingly evident as we turn to the fluid, ghostly features of a mask from the island of New Britain in the South Pacific (fig. 10). It is meant to represent an animal spirit, said to be a crocodile. Even stranger is the Eskimo mask from southwest Alaska (fig. 11). The single eye and the mouth full of teeth are the only recognizable details to the outsider, yet to those who know how to "read" this assembly of shapes it is the condensed representation of a tribal myth about a swan that drives white whales to the hunters.

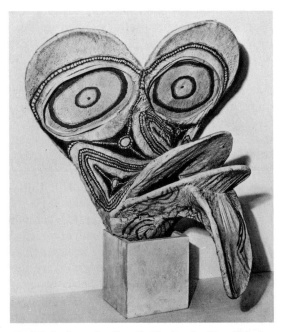

10. Mask, from the Gazelle Peninsula, New Britain. 19th–20th century. Bark cloth, height 18″. Museo Nacional de Antropología, Mexico

PAINTING

Compared to sculpture, painting plays a subordinate role in primitive society. Although widely used to color wood carvings or the human body, sometimes with intricate ornamental patterns, it could establish itself as an independent art only under exceptional conditions. Thus the Indian tribes inhabiting the arid Southwest of the United States developed the unique art of sand painting (fig. 12). The technique, which demands considerable skill, consists of pouring powdered rock or earth of various colors on a flat bed of sand. Despite (or perhaps because of) the fact that these pictures are impermanent and must be made fresh for each occasion, the designs are rigidly traditional; they are also rather abstract, like any fixed pattern that is endlessly repeated. The compositions may be likened to recipes, prescribed by the medicine man and "filled" under his supervision by the painter, for the main use of sand paintings is in ceremonies of healing. That these are sessions of great emotional intensity on the part of both doctor and patient is well attested by our illustration. Such a close union—or even, at times, identity—of priest, healer, and artist may be difficult to understand today. (Or could it be that all these qualities are present to some degree in the personality and work of Sigmund Freud?) But to primitive man, trying to bend nature to his needs by magic and ritual, the three functions must have appeared as different aspects of a single process. And the success or failure of that process was to him quite literally a matter of life and death.

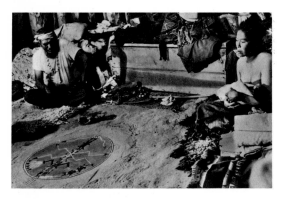

12. Sand Painting Ritual for a Sick Child (Navaho) Arizona

Art for the Dead–Egypt

THE OLD KINGDOM

History, we are often told, begins with the invention of writing, some five thousand years ago. This makes a convenient landmark, for the absence of written records is surely one of the key differences between prehistoric and historic societies. Obviously, prehistory was far from uneventful: the road from hunting to husbandry is a long and arduous one. The beginning of history, then, means a sudden increase in the speed of events, a shifting from low into high gear. And we shall see that it also means a change in the *kinds* of events.

Prehistory might be defined as that phase of human evolution during which man as a species learned how to survive in a hostile environment; his achievements were responses to threats of physical extinction. With the domestication of animals and food plants, he had won a decisive battle in this war. But the hunting-to-husbandry revolution placed him on a level at which he might well have remained indefinitely, and in many parts of the globe man was content to stay there. In a few places, however, the balance of primitive society was upset by a new threat, posed not by nature but by man himself: competition for grazing land among tribes of herdsmen or for arable soil among farming communities. Such a situation might be resolved in one of two ways: constant tribal warfare could reduce the population, or the people could unite in larger and more disciplined social units for the sake of group efforts (such as building fortifications, dams, or irrigation canals) that no loosely organized tribal society would have been able to achieve. Conflicts of this kind arose in the Nile valley and that of the Tigris and Euphrates some six thousand years ago and generated enough pressure to produce a new kind of society, very much more complex and efficient than had ever existed before. These societies quite literally *made* history; they not only brought forth "great men and great deeds" but also made them *memorable*. (To be memorable, an event has to be more than "worth remembering"; it must happen quickly enough to be grasped by man's memory. Prehistoric events were too slow-paced for that.) From then on, men were to live in a new, dynamic world where their capacity to survive was threatened not by the forces of nature but by conflicts arising either within society or through competition between societies. These efforts to cope with his human environment have proved a far greater challenge to man than his struggle with nature.

The invention of writing was an early and indispensable achievement of the historic civilizations of Egypt and Mesopotamia. We do not know the beginnings of its development, but it must have taken several centuries after the new societies were already past their first stage. History was well under way by the time writing could be used to record historic events. Egyptian civilization has long been regarded as the most rigidly conservative ever known. There is some truth in this belief, for the basic pattern of Egyptian institutions, beliefs, and artistic ideas was formed between 3000 and 2500 B.C. and kept reasserting itself for the next two thousand years, so that all Egyptian art, at first glance, tends to have a certain sameness. Actually, Egyptian art alternates between conservatism and innovation, but is never static. Some of its great achievements had a decisive influence on Greece and Rome. We can thus feel ourselves linked to the Egypt of five thousand years ago by a continuous, living tradition.

The history of Egypt is divided into dynasties of rulers, in accordance with ancient Egyptian practice, beginning with the First Dynasty, shortly before 3000 B.C. This method of counting historic time conveys at once the strong Egyptian sense of continuity and the overwhelming importance of the Pharaoh (king), who was not only the supreme ruler but a god. All kings claim to rule in the name or by the grace of some superhuman authority (that is what makes them superior to tribal chiefs); the Pharaoh transcended them all—his kingship was not delegated to him from above but was absolute, divine. We do not know exactly how the early Pharaohs established their claim to divinity, but we know that they molded the Nile valley into a single, effective state and increased its fertility by regulating the annual floods of the river waters through dams and canals.

Of these public works nothing remains today. Our knowledge of Egyptian civilization rests almost entirely on the tombs and their contents, since little has survived of ancient Egyptian palaces and cities. This is no accident, for these tombs were built to endure forever. Yet the Egyptians did not view life on this earth mainly as a road to the grave; their cult of the dead is a link with the New Stone Age, but the meaning they gave it was quite devoid of that dark fear of the spirits of the dead which dominates primitive ancestor cults. Their attitude was, rather, that man can provide for his own happy afterlife by equipping his tomb as a kind of shadowy replica of his daily environment for his spirit, the *ka*, to enjoy, and by making sure that the *ka* would have a body to dwell in (his own mummified corpse, or, as a substitute, a statue of himself).

EGYPTIAN STYLE AND
THE PALETTE OF KING NARMER

At the threshold of Egyptian history stands a work of art that is also a historic document: a carved slate palette (fig. 13) celebrating the victory of Narmer, king of Upper Egypt, over Lower Egypt, the oldest known image of a historic personage identified by name. It already shows most of the features characteristic of Egyptian art. But before we concern ourselves with these, let us first "read" the scene. That we are able to do so is another indication that we have left primitive art behind, for the meaning of the relief is made clear not only by means of the hieroglyphic labels, but also through the rational orderliness of the design. Narmer has seized an enemy by the hair and is about to slay him with his mace; two more fallen enemies are placed in the bottom compartment (the small rectangular shape next to the one on the left stands for a fortified town). In the upper right we see a complex bit of picture writing: a falcon above a clump of papyrus plants holds a tether attached to a human head that "grows" from the same soil as the plants. This image actually repeats the main scene on a symbolic level—the head and the papyrus plants stand for Lower Egypt, while the victorious falcon is Horus, the god of Upper Egypt. Clearly, Horus and Narmer are the same: a god triumphs over human foes.

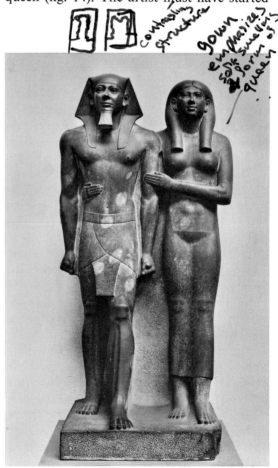

Combined views

Falcon-Horus-god of upper egypt

mace for ceremonial slayings

court official w/ sandals

taken off sandals bcd Holy ground

fortified town

upper egypt

may but not animal

1 head + papyrus (lower Egypt)

embarrasses him (note the oddly rubberlike figures of the fallen enemies). Moreover, he is faced with the fact that the standing human figure, unlike that of an animal, does not have a single main profile but two competing profiles, so that, for the sake of clarity, he must combine these views. How he does this is clearly shown in the figure of Narmer: eye and shoulders in frontal view, head and legs in profile. The method worked so well that it was to survive for twenty-five hundred years, in spite—or perhaps because—of the fact that it does not lend itself to representing movement or action. The frozen quality of the image would seem to be especially suited to the divine nature of the Pharaoh; ordinary mortals *act*, he simply *is*.

The "cubic" approach to the human form can be observed most strikingly in Egyptian sculpture in the round, such as the splendid group of the Pharaoh Mycerinus and his queen (fig. 14). The artist must have started

contrasting structure

gown emphasizes so form of queen. so sweling of queen

13. *Palette of King Narmer*, from Hierakonpolis. c. 3100 B.C. Slate, height 25″. Egyptian Museum, Cairo

Hence, Narmer's gesture must not be taken as representing a real fight. The enemy is helpless from the very start, and the slaying is a ritual, rather than a physical effort. We gather this from the fact that Narmer has taken off his sandals (the court official behind him carries them in his left hand), an indication that he is standing on holy ground. The same notion recurs in the Old Testament when the Lord commands Moses to remove his shoes before He appears to him in the burning bush.

The new inner logic of the Narmer palette is readily apparent, even though the modern notion of showing a scene as it would appear to a single observer at a single moment is as alien to the Egyptian artist as it had been to his Stone Age predecessors. He strives for clarity, not illusion, and therefore picks the most telling view in each case. But he imposes a strict rule on himself: when he changes his angle of vision, he must do so by 90 degrees, as if he were sighting along the edges of a cube. He thus acknowledges only three possible views: full face, strict profile, and vertically from above. Any intermediate position

face profile vertically above

14. *Mycerinus and His Queen*, from Giza. c. 2500 B.C. Slate, height 56″. Museum of Fine Arts, Boston

out by drawing the front and side views on the faces of a rectangular block and then worked inward until these views met. Only in this way could he have achieved figures of such overpowering three-dimensional firmness and immobility. What magnificent vessels for the *ka* to inhabit! Both have the left foot placed forward, yet there is no hint of a forward movement. The group also affords an interesting comparison of male and female beauty as interpreted by a fine sculptor, who knew not only how to contrast the structure of the two bodies but also how to emphasize the soft, swelling form of the queen through a thin, close-fitting gown.

Colorplate 1 shows us another type of statue made according to the strict rules of the Old Kingdom: the seated pair. This pair owes its strikingly lifelike appearance to the vividly painted surface. Rahotep is shown darker than his wife—in Egyptian art men are always darker than women. The eyes have been inlaid with glittering stones. The faces, in keeping with this emphasis upon surface detail, are more individual than the highly idealized faces of Mycerinus and his queen, and therefore are more clearly portraits.

THIRD DYNASTY

When we speak of the Egyptians' attitude toward death and afterlife, we must be careful to make it clear that we do not refer to the average man but only to the small aristocratic caste clustered around the royal court. There is still a great deal to be learned about the origin and significance of Egyptian tombs, but the concept of afterlife they reflect apparently applied only to the privileged few because of their association with the immortal Pharaohs. The standard form of these tombs was the *mastaba*, a squarish mound faced with brick or stone, above a burial chamber that was deep underground and linked with the mastaba by a shaft. Inside the mastaba there is a chapel for offerings to the *ka* and a secret cubicle for the statue of the deceased. Royal mastabas grew to conspicuous size and soon developed into pyramids. The earliest is probably that of King Zoser (fig. 15) at Saqqara, a step pyramid suggestive of a stack of mastabas as against the smooth-sided later examples at Giza.

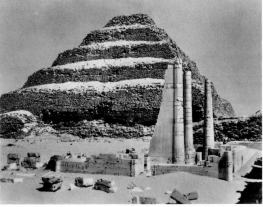

15. Step Pyramid, Funerary District of King Zoser. c. 2650 B.C. Saqqara

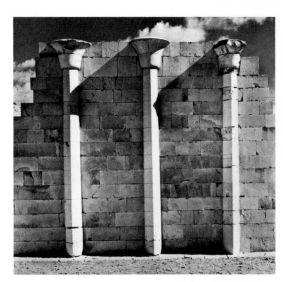

16. Papyrus Half-Columns, North Palace, Funerary District of King Zoser. c. 2650 B.C. Saqqara

Pyramids were not isolated structures but were linked with vast funerary districts, with temples and other buildings which were the scene of great religious celebrations during the Pharaoh's lifetime as well as after. The most elaborate of these is the funerary district around the pyramid of Zoser; its creator, Imhotep, is the first artist whose name has been recorded in history, and deservedly so, since his achievement—or what remains of it—is most impressive even today. Egyptian architecture had begun with structures made of mud bricks, wood, reeds, and other light materials. Imhotep used cut stone, but his repertory of architectural forms still reflects shapes and devices developed during that earlier phase. Thus we find columns—always "engaged" rather than freestanding—which echo the bundles of reeds or the wooden supports that used to be set into mud-brick walls to give them added strength. But the very fact that these members no longer had their original function made it possible for Imhotep and his fellow architects to redesign them so as to make them serve a new, *expressive* purpose (fig. 16).

FOURTH DYNASTY

The development of the pyramid reaches its climax during the Fourth Dynasty in the famous triad of great pyramids at Giza (fig. 17), all of them of the familiar, smooth-sided shape. They originally had an outer casing of carefully dressed stone, which has disappeared except near the top of the pyramid of Chefren. Clustered about the three great pyramids are several smaller ones and a large number of mastabas for members of the royal family and high officials, but the unified funerary district of Zoser has given way to a simpler arrangement; adjoining each of the great pyramids to the east is a funerary temple, from which a processional causeway leads to a second temple at a lower level, in the Nile valley, at a distance of about a third of a mile. Next to the valley temple of the second pyramid, that of Chefren, stands the Great Sphinx carved from the live rock (fig. 18), perhaps an even more impressive embodiment of divine kingship than the pyramids themselves. The royal head rising from the body of a lion towers to a height of 65 feet, and bore, in all probability, the features of Chefren (damage inflicted upon it during Islamic times has obscured the details of the face). Its awesome majesty is such that a thousand years later it could be regarded as an image of the sun-god.

Enterprises of this huge scale mark the high point of Pharaonic power. After the end of the Fourth Dynasty (less than two centuries after Zoser) they were never attempted again, although pyramids on a much more modest scale continued to be built. The world has always marveled at the sheer size of the great pyramids as well as at the technical accomplishment they represent; but they have also

come to be regarded as symbols of slave labor—thousands of men forced by cruel masters to serve the aggrandizement of absolute rulers. Such a picture may well be unjust: certain records have been preserved indicating that the labor was paid for, so that we might be nearer the truth in considering these monuments as vast "public work projects" providing a form of economic security for a good part of the population.

THE NEW KINGDOM

The Pharaohs of the Old Kingdom placed much power in the hands of great lords who ruled over the various provinces of Egypt. Eventually these lords became so powerful that they overthrew the Pharaoh, putting an end to central, unified government. Five unsettled centuries of political disturbance and changing fortunes followed, as provincial rulers struggled for supremacy over all Egypt.

The princes of Thebes, in the south, won out in this struggle. They became stronger than their competitors and established a flourishing local art and culture from about 2134 to 1785 B.C. This period of comparative stability and peace is called the Middle Kingdom. Egypt as a whole remained weak and divided, however, and was an easy prey to invasion by Asiatic tribesmen under the so-called Shepherd Kings.

The Shepherd Kings ruled Egypt harshly for 150 years. They made a genuine contribution to later Egyptian life, nevertheless, for they brought in the horse, the chariot, and new weapons of war. In particular, they did away with the local overlords, except for the princes of Thebes, whom they never managed to subdue completely. Thus they removed the greatest obstacle to the centralization of Egypt. Around 1570 B.C., the princes of Thebes expelled the invaders and restored single rule over all Egypt. They became the new Pharaohs, richer and more powerful than those of the Old Kingdom. Egypt became an empire, extending its rule far beyond its own borders. This renewal of Egypt's golden age is known as the New Kingdom, and it lasted for five centuries.

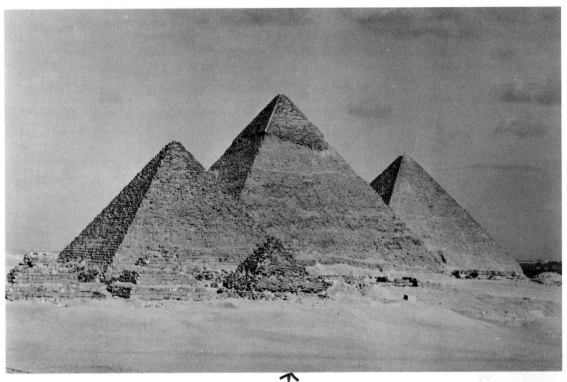

17. Pyramids of Mycerinus (about 2470 B.C.), Chefren (about 2500 B.C.), and Cheops (about 2530 B.C.), Giza

18. *The Great Sphinx*. Old Kingdom. About 2500 B.C. Giza. The colossal head rises to a height of sixty-five feet.

big one

features of chefren

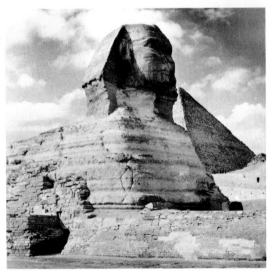

PAINTING

New Kingdom art was tremendously varied. Figure 19 shows you a painting still done, for the most part, according to the prescribed rules laid down just before the Old Kingdom. It is a tomb painting of a harvest scene. At the top, the dead man's servants are measuring a wheat field with a rope. At the bottom, they are cutting the wheat with sickles, while the deceased himself sits under an awning that protects him from the sun. In the center are his chariot and some servants measuring a pile of grain. The figures are still put together in the same way that we saw in the *Palette of King Narmer* (fig. 13). But whenever physical activity demanding any sort of effort must be depicted, the Egyptian artist does not hesitate to abandon the composite view of the body,

for such activities are always performed by underlings whose dignity does not have to be preserved.

In planning his "layout" the Egyptian artist realized that a lifelike painting, of the kind the caveman had done, was not what he wanted, because it would let him show the harvest only the way it looked at one particular moment, and not the whole story of the harvest. These scenes are part of a cycle of

(handwritten margin note, top) — lowlings — so artist does not worry about individuals composure

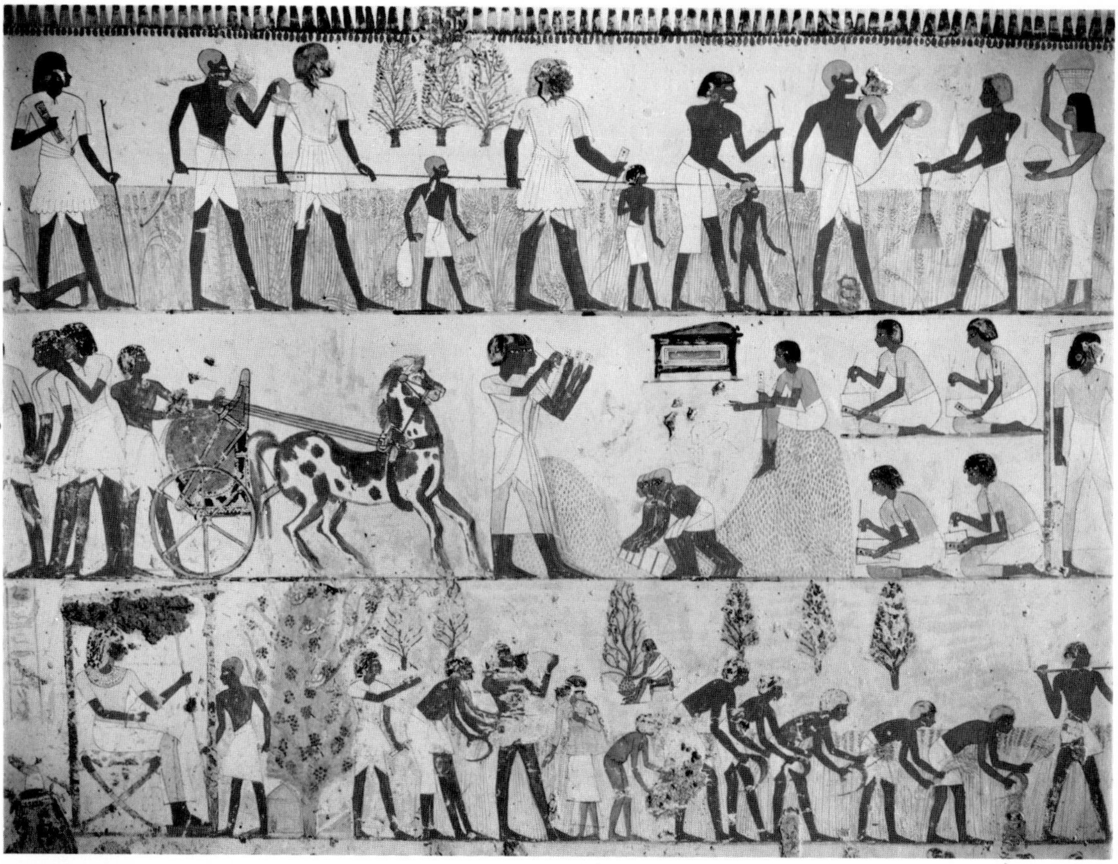

(handwritten margin notes, left) measuring wheat field w/ rope

chariots & servants measuring pile of grain

deceased

19. *Harvest Scenes*. New Kingdom. c. 1400 B.C. Thebes, southern Egypt

(handwritten) in a tomb

(handwritten notes below caption) greater size ≈ greater importance   far away → above figures   cutting wheat w/ sickles

seasons, a sort of perpetual calendar of re-curring events that the spirit could watch year in and year out. So our painter has made everything much clearer and more orderly than it ever is in real life. His figures are spread out on the wall, and they overlap only when several of them are doing the same thing; some are extra large, to show that they are more important than the others. And if he wants to tell us that something is far away, such as the three trees in the top strip, he puts it above, not behind, the figures in the fore-ground. Our painter, then, does not show us what he actually *sees*, but what he *knows*.

The tomb painting of flute players and dancing girls (fig. 20) is, by comparison, much freer. Not only do the dancers seem alive and moving, but they are shown com-pletely from the side; except for their eyes, they are not a combination of side and front views. The arms and faces of two of the flute players are shown from the front. Their eyes

actually meet ours! The arm of the musician at the right of the group is foreshortened—in using this device that shows depth we see a radical departure from the absolute flatness of the traditional Egyptian style.

(handwritten notes) not combination of side and front   depth

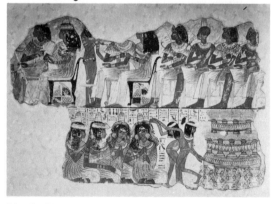

20. *Girl Dancers and Musicians*, from Thebes. New Kingdom. c. 1400 B.C. British Museum, London

ARCHITECTURE

The divine kingship of the Pharaoh was asserted in a new way during the New Kingdom: by association with the god Amen, whose identity had been fused with that of the sun-god Ra, and who became the supreme deity, towering above the lesser gods as the Pharaoh towered above the provincial nobility. Thus vast architectural energies were devoted to the building of huge temples of Amen under royal sponsorship, such as that at Luxor (fig. 21). Its plan is characteristic of the general pattern of later Egyptian temples. The façade (fig. 21, far left) consists of two massive walls, with sloping sides, that flank the entrance; this gateway, or pylon, leads to a court, a pillared hall, a second court, and another pillared hall, beyond which is the temple proper. The entire sequence of courts, halls, and temple was enclosed by high walls that shut off the outside world. Except for the monumental façade, such a structure is designed to be experienced from within; ordinary worshipers were confined to the courts and could but marvel at the forest of columns that screened the dark recesses of the sanctuary. The columns had to be closely spaced, for they supported the stone beams (lintels) of the ceiling, and these had to be short to keep them from breaking under their own weight. Yet the architect has consciously exploited this condition by making the columns far heavier than they need be. As a result, the beholder feels almost crushed by their sheer mass. The overawing effect is certainly impressive, but also rather vulgar when measured against the earlier masterpieces of Egyptian architecture. We need only compare the papyrus columns at Luxor with their ancestors at Saqqara (fig. 15) to realize how little of Imhotep's genius still survives here.

AKHENATEN; TUTANKHAMEN

The growth of the Amen cult produced an unexpected threat to royal authority: the priests of Amen grew into a caste of such wealth and power that the king could maintain his position only with their consent. One remarkable Pharaoh, Amenhotep IV, tried to defeat them by proclaiming his faith in a single god, the sun disk Aten. He changed his name to Akhenaten, closed the Amen temples, and moved the capital to a new site. His attempt to place himself at the head of a new monotheistic faith, however, did not outlast his reign (1372–1358 B.C.), and under his successors orthodoxy was speedily restored. During the long period of Egypt's decline, after 1000 B.C., the country became

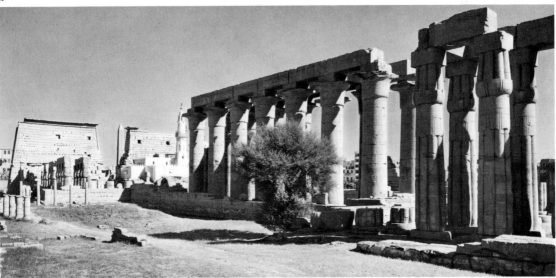

21. Court and Pylon of Ramesses II (c. 1260 B.C.) and Colonnade and Court of Amenhotep III (c. 1390 B.C.). Temple of Amen-Mut-Khonsu, Luxor

[handwritten annotation: Specific — tells sculptor tells & an individual instead of anyone with particular looks]

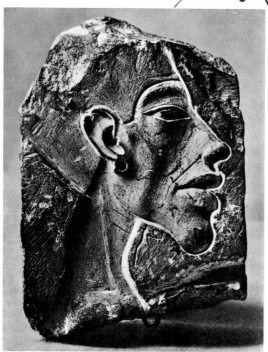

22. *Akhenaten (Amenhotep IV).* c. 1365 B.C. Stone, height 3 1/8″. State Museums, Berlin

she is a person, not a formula. What distinguishes the "Akhenaten style" is not greater realism so much as a new sense of form that seeks to unfreeze the immobility of Egyptian art—the contours as well as the plastic shapes are more pliable and relaxed, as if they had been suddenly released from the grip of geometry that underlies Egyptian art.

The Akhenaten style gradually faded after the Pharaoh's early death. The priests of Amen regained their authority, and the conservative style returned. But there is still a trace of the expressiveness of the Akhenaten style in the magnificent gold and jeweled coffin of Tutankhamen, the boy Pharaoh who succeeded Akhenaten and died only a few years later (see colorplate 2).

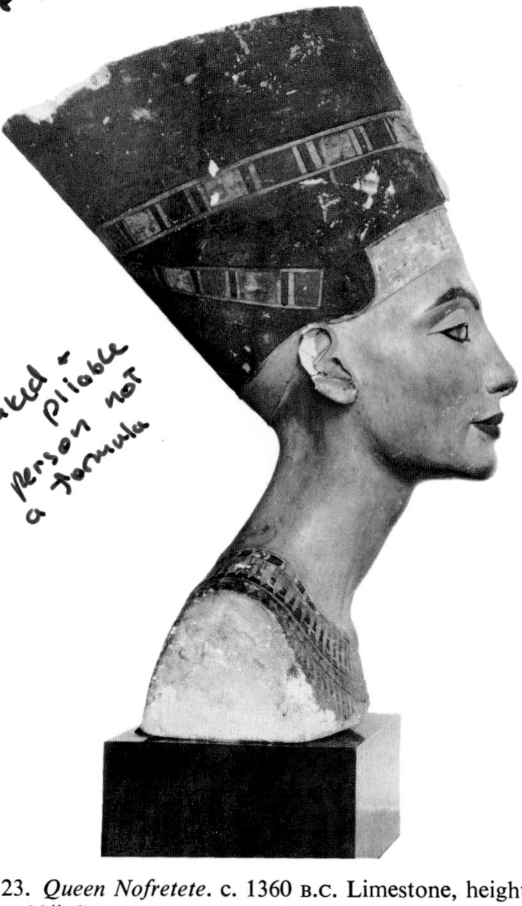

[handwritten annotation: tells about the individual subject "a psychological portrait"]

ever more priest-ridden, until, under Greek and Roman rule, Egyptian civilization came to an end in a welter of esoteric religious doctrines.

Akhenaten was a revolutionary not only in his faith but in his artistic tastes as well, consciously fostering a new style and a new ideal of beauty. The contrast with the past is strikingly evident in a low-relief portrait of Akhenaten (fig. 22); compared with works in the traditional style (see fig. 13), this head seems at first glance like a brutal caricature, with its oddly haggard features and over-emphatic, undulating lines. The sculptor tells us what kind of man Akhenaten was—sensitive, troubled, intellectual. This is a psychological portrait.

The masterpiece of the Akhenaten style is the famous colored bust of Akhenaten's queen, Nofretete (fig. 23). What makes this sculpture seem so real to us? Not its accuracy of detail, nor its subtlety and refinement—these qualities are found in the conservative, frozen style too. Nofretete seems to live and breathe; she is pliable and relaxed;

[handwritten annotation: relaxed & pliable — a person not a formula]

23. *Queen Nofretete.* c. 1360 B.C. Limestone, height c. 20″. State Museums, Berlin

Temples, Palaces, and Citadels– The Ancient Near East and the Aegean

MESOPOTAMIA

[handwritten annotation: founding fathers Sumerians]

It is astonishing that men should have emerged into the light of history at the same time in separate places. Between 3500 and 3000 B.C., when Egypt was being united under the rule of the Pharaohs, another great civilization arose in Mesopotamia, the "land between the two rivers."

Unlike the valley of the Nile, which is protected by desert and sea, the land between the Tigris and the Euphrates is exposed on all sides. It was hard to unite this area under a single monarch like the Pharaoh. Thus Mesopotamian history is a chronicle of rivalries between local city-states, of foreign invasions, of the sudden rise and equally sudden collapse of political and military power.

The founding fathers of Mesopotamian civilization were the Sumerians, a people of mysterious origin and a language unlike any other that we know. They established a number of communities in the southern part of Mesopotamia, where the Tigris and Euphrates now come together but in ancient times flowed separately into the Persian Gulf.

In theory, each Sumerian city-state was owned and governed by its god; his commands were made known by his human steward, who therefore ruled as priest as well as a sort of king. All the people were subjects of the god, and lived in a kind of planned society of which the priesthood was in charge. The priests kept the records, stored and distributed much of the food, and administered such community projects as the building of dikes and irrigation ditches, which were necessary to keep the land fertile.

ARCHITECTURE

The remains of Sumerian civilization are few because, having no stone, the Sumerians made their buildings of mud brick, which does not last. Almost nothing is left of their architecture but foundations.

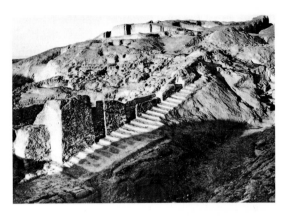

24. The "White Temple" on its Ziggurat, Uruk (Warka). c. 3500–3000 B.C.

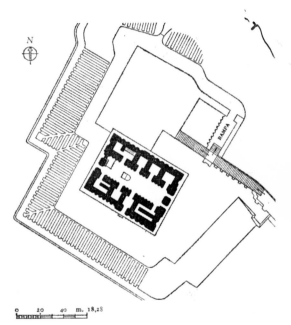

25. Plan of "White Temple" on its Ziggurat (after H. Frankfort)

The layout of Sumerian cities shows us that the temple of the city god was the center of existence, physical as well as spiritual. The houses clustered about a sacred area— a vast architectural array of workshops, storehouses, scribes' quarters, and shrines. In the midst of this area, on an immense, high platform, stood the temple. These sloping platforms soon became man-made mountains. They were like Egyptian pyramids, both in the effort that they required and in their effect as landmarks towering above the featureless plain. They are known as ziggurats.

[handwritten annotation: Ziggurats- man made mountains which were immense platforms for the temples]

The most famous ziggurat was the Biblical Tower of Babel—now destroyed. But an older ziggurat known as the White Temple, built before 3000 B.C. and thus earlier than the earliest of Egyptian pyramids, survives at Uruk (figs. 24, 25). Enough is left of the heavy walls, recessed at regular intervals, to suggest something of how it looked originally.

SCULPTURE

We are much better supplied with examples of Sumerian sculpture. Among these is a group of statuettes in stone, from the city now known as Tell Asmar (fig. 26). The tallest is Abu, god of vegetation, and the second tallest is a mother goddess. The others are priests and worshipers. The two gods are made different from the other figures, not only by their greater size but by the proportionately larger pupils of their inlaid eyes—although the eyes of all the figures are enormous. The whole group stood in the sanctuary of the temple of Abu. The priests and worshipers faced the two deities and communicated with them through their insistently staring eyes, praying to them or sending messages. Thus, the eyes here are truly "windows of the soul." In order to avoid drawing attention away from the all-important eyes, the sculptor simplified both bodies and faces, making them geometric rather than living forms. If the Egyptian sculptor's sense of form was based on the cube, the Sumerian sculptor's sense of form was based on the cylinder and the cone. Arms and legs are as round and smooth as pipes; the long conical skirts are smoothly curved. As a result, these statuettes look like stiff dolls.

Sumerian sculptors were softer and more flexible in handling forms and more realistic in describing things when they worked in wood and metal. An example is the sound box of a harp used in the temple at Ur

26. Statues, from the Temple of Abu, Tell Asmar. c. 2700–2500 B.C. Marble, height of tallest figure about 30″. The Iraq Museum, Baghdad, and the Oriental Institute, University of Chicago

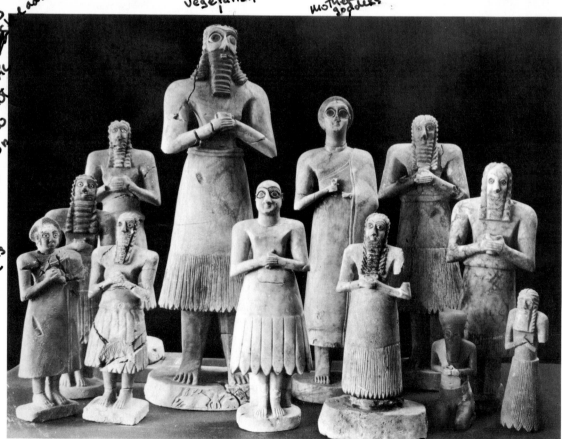

(fig. 27). The sound box is inlaid with fascinating scenes from sacred mythology. The top section shows a hero embracing two human-headed bulls. Below, a wolf and a lion carry food and wine to a banquet that we do not see. Then comes a scene in which an ass, a bear, and a deer provide musical entertainment—the harp shown is the same type as that from which the inlaid panel comes. At the bottom we see a scorpion-man and a goat carrying objects they have taken from a large vase. The skillful artist who did this work was far less bound by rules than were artists working in Egypt at the same time; although he, too, places his figures on ground lines, he is not afraid

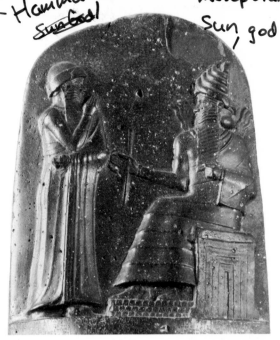

28. Top of stone slab inscribed with the law code of Hammurabi. c. 1760 B.C. Diorite, height of slab 7′, height of relief 28″. The Louvre, Paris

of overlapping forms or foreshortened shoulders. If we only knew the context in which these actors play their roles!

The same realism can be seen in a sculpture in the round, also from the temple at Ur. This is a little offering stand made of wood covered with gold and inlaid with blue stones called lapis lazuli (colorplate 3). It is in the shape of a billy goat, sacred to the god Tammuz, rearing up against a flowering tree. The goat is marvelously alive and full of energy; it stares at us with almost demonic power.

Sumerian civilization was adopted by the Akkadians, a Semitic-speaking people who drifted into Sumer from the north. The Akkadians produced the first Mesopotamian rulers who openly called themselves kings and proclaimed their ambition to conquer the whole earth.

BABYLON

After a few centuries of turmoil, the Babylonians became masters of all Mesopotamia around 1700 B.C. The founder of the Babylonian dynasty was Hammurabi. He was the greatest figure of the age, combining military ability with respect for Sumerian tradition: he saw himself as the "favorite shepherd" of the sun-god, with the mission to "cause justice to prevail in the land." His most

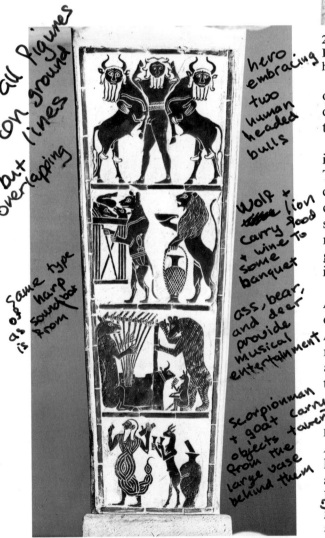

27. Soundbox of a Harp, from Ur. c. 2600 B.C. Bitumen with shell inlay, height 8 1/2″. The University Museum, Philadelphia

[handwritten note at top: Much as Assyrian Art is to Glorify the king through depictions of his military conquests or the king depicted as the killer of lions]

memorable achievement was his law code, the earliest uniform written body of law in the world. Hammurabi's code was amazingly reasonable and humane. Under Hammurabi, Babylon became the cultural center of Mesopotamia, and was to remain so for more than a thousand years after its power had declined.

Hammurabi had his code engraved on a tall slab of hard stone: at the top (fig. 28), in deeply carved relief against a flat background, he is shown standing before the enthroned sun-god, who holds a scepter in his right hand. The stone has been worked to a high finish, inviting a wonderful play of light on the two imposing figures. The relief is so high that the sculptor was able to carve the eyes to their full depth, and Hammurabi and the sun-god stare at each other with a force that reminds us of the early Sumerian statuettes from the temple of Abu, where the enormous eyes established a similar relation between gods and men.

ASSYRIANS *900 BC.*

Around 900 B.C., all Mesopotamia was taken over by the terrifying, powerful, and efficient Assyrians, who came from the northern part of the region. During the three centuries that followed, they created an empire that extended as far as Egypt. Then their subjects and neighbors, inflamed by the

Assyrians' merciless conquests and harsh rule, joined together and defeated them.

The Assyrians, it has been said, were to the Sumerians what the Romans were to the Greeks. The Assyrians took over the achievements of the south, changing them to fit their own needs. The palaces of Assyrian kings grew to unprecedented size and magnificence. A reconstruction of the eighth-century palace of King Sargon II at ancient Khorsabad shows that the palace was on a high platform where there also stood a Sumerian-style ziggurat. About it was a citadel, a commanding fortress wall set with scores of heavily garrisoned towers.

Much of Assyrian art is devoted to glorifying the power of the king, either by detailed depictions of his military conquests or by showing the sovereign as the killer of lions. These royal hunts were ceremonial combats (the animals were released from cages within a square formed by soldiers with shields) in which the king re-enacted his ancient role as supreme shepherd who kills the predators menacing the communal flock. Here Assyrian art rises to impressive heights. Figure 29 shows us King Ashurnasirpal II killing lions. How well the sculptor understood the anatomy of lions and horses, and how well he knew how to suggest weight and volume! He used very low relief, but skillfully created an effect of depth through minute differences in height of surface. The scene, charged with

[handwritten note: life drama + emotion not in earlier art]

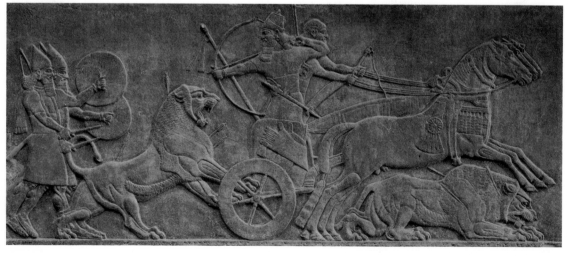

29. *Ashurnasirpal II Killing Lions*, relief from Palace at Nimrud. c. 850 B.C. Limestone, 3′ 3″ × 8′ 4″. British Museum, London

[handwritten note: The king is great if we can kill ferocious lions]

[handwritten annotations: "animals portrayed very accurately and physically correct. Bulls, Dragons + other animals"]

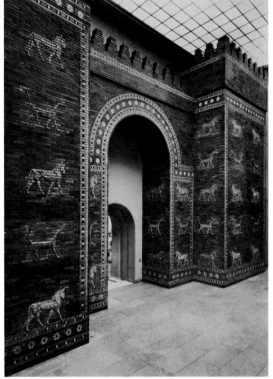

30. The Ishtar Gate (restored), from Babylon. c. 575 B.C. State Museums, Berlin *[handwritten: glazed bricks]*

energy, fills us with a sense of life, drama, and emotion that we experience from no art of earlier times. By endowing the lions with magnificent strength and courage, the sculptor exalts the king who is able to slay such formidable adversaries.

NEO-BABYLONIANS

The Assyrian Empire fell before an invasion from the east. At that time the commander of the Assyrian army in southern Mesopotamia made himself king of Babylon, which had a final brief flowering between 612 and 539 B.C. Unlike the Assyrians, the "Neo-Babylonians" used baked and glazed bricks for their buildings, because they were farther removed from the sources of stone slabs. This technique, too, had been developed in Assyria, but now it was used on a far larger scale, both for surface ornament and for architectural reliefs. Its distinctive effect is evident in the Ishtar Gate of Nebuchadnezzar's sacred precinct in Babylon (fig. 30). The stately procession of bulls, dragons, and other animals of molded brick within a framework of vividly colored ornamental bands has a grace and gaiety far removed from Assyrian art. Here, for the last time, we sense again that special genius of ancient Mesopotamian art in the portrayal of animals.

[handwritten: "Starting to get more graceful and refined"]

PERSIA *[handwritten: 539 BC   Egypt   Asia Minor   Macedonia]*

In 539 B.C., nomadic tribesmen from the mountain-fringed Iranian plateau east of Mesopotamia captured the city of Babylon and became the heirs of what had been the Assyrian Empire. These were the Persians. The Persians rapidly expanded their empire to include Egypt and Asia Minor. They even got a toehold in Europe by taking the coastline of Macedonia and a narrow strip to its north. The Greek mainland, on the south, escaped the same fate by the narrowest of margins. The vast Persian Empire endured for two centuries—it was toppled by Alexander the Great in 331 B.C.—during which it was ruled efficiently and humanely.

Drawing inspiration from all parts of their widespread territories, the Persians created a grand and imposing art of remarkable originality within a single generation. They were not builders of temples, for their religious practices centered on fire altars in the open air. Their beliefs came from Zoroaster's prophecies, which pictured the world as a struggle between the rival principles of Good and Evil. In this struggle, a redeemer would come to lead the eventual victory of Good, embodied in Ahuramazda (Light), over Evil, embodied in Ahriman (Darkness). If the Persians were not builders of temples, they were builders of huge and impressive palaces. The most ambitious of these palaces was at Persepolis (fig. 31) and was begun under Darius I in 518 B.C. It had a vast number of rooms, halls, and courts arranged on a raised platform. The Audience Hall of Darius, a room 250 feet square, was supported by 36 columns 40 feet tall—a massing of columns that clearly reminds us of Egyptian architecture (compare figure 21). The columns, however,

light, slender columns w/ grooves to make them seem more slender

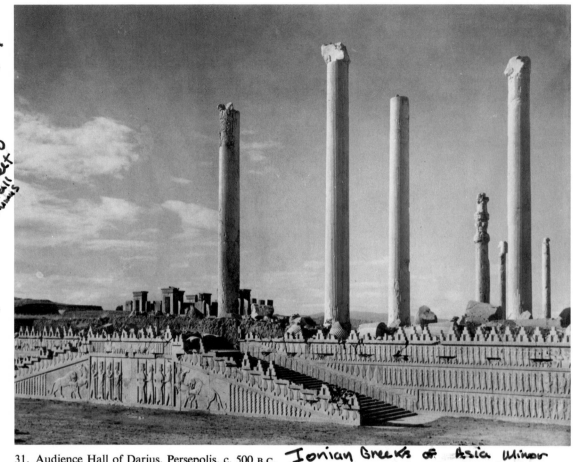

40 feet tall columns

31. Audience Hall of Darius, Persepolis. c. 500 B.C.

Ionian Greeks of Asia Minor furnished artists to the Persian court

nomadic tribesmen so had to have portable property

Winged lion

GOLD

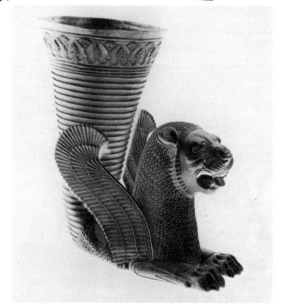

32. Gold Drinking Horn. 5th–3rd century B.C. Archaeological Museum, Teheran

are not squat and heavy, as in Egypt. They are slender, and their shafts have long vertical grooves that make them seem slenderer still. These characteristics are owed to the Ionian Greeks of Asia Minor, who, it is known, furnished artists to the Persian court. But all these separate elements are combined into one whole that is genuinely Persian.

Nomadic tribesmen have no use for architecture; their possessions must be easily portable, and they generally devote their artistic energies to the making of small, often precious ornamental objects. The Persians had a tradition of skills in such decorative art long before their conquests. Their remarkable goldsmith work can be seen in a drinking vessel in the shape of a winged lion (fig. 32). It shows a blend of Assyrian and Greek influences, but the emphasis on texture and all-over pattern stems from the native Persian artistic heritage.

Men always darker than women in Egyptian Art

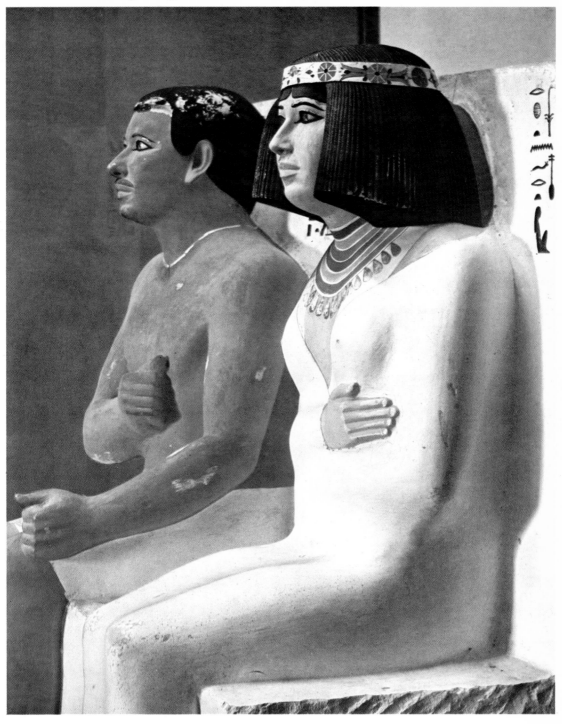

Colorplate 1. *Prince Rahotep and His Wife Nofret*. c. 2580 B.C. Painted limestone, height 47 1/4″. Egyptian Museum, Cairo

34

Eventhough the Akhenaten style gradually faded away after Akhenaten died in 1358 BC there is still a trace of his style in king Tut

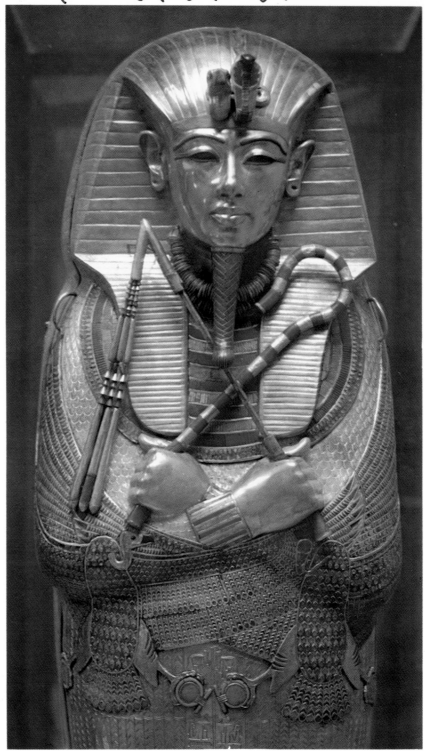

Colorplate 2. EGYPTIAN. Cover of the Coffin of Tutankhamen (portion). c. 1340 B.C. Gold (inlaid with enamel and semiprecious stones), height of whole 72 7/8″. Egyptian Museum, Cairo

billy goat – sacred to the God Tammuz

alive full of energy

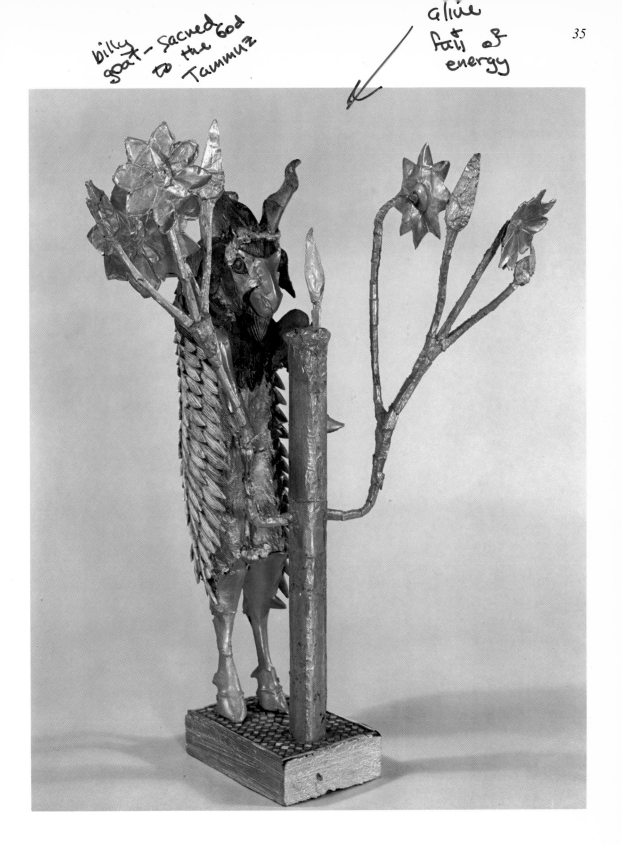

Colorplate 3. *Billy Goat and Tree,* offering stand from Ur. c. 2600 B.C. Wood, gold, and lapis lazuli, height 20″. The University Museum, Philadelphia

Artist stressed harmonious, playful, fluid, rhythemic, and effortless aspect

Grabbing horns of charging bull

somersaulting over his back

landing on the ground

girl ↓

youth ↓

girl ↓

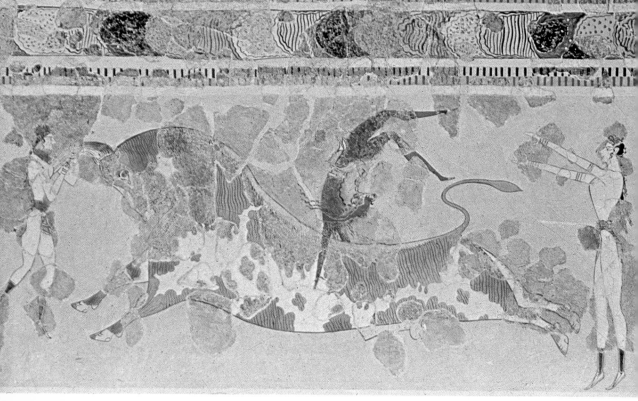

bull — very long to emphasize strength and dramatic power

Religious Ritual not sport

Colorplate 4. *"Toreador Fresco."* from the Palace of Minos, Knossos, Crete. c. 1500 B.C. Height about 24 1/2".
Archaeological Museum, Candia, Crete

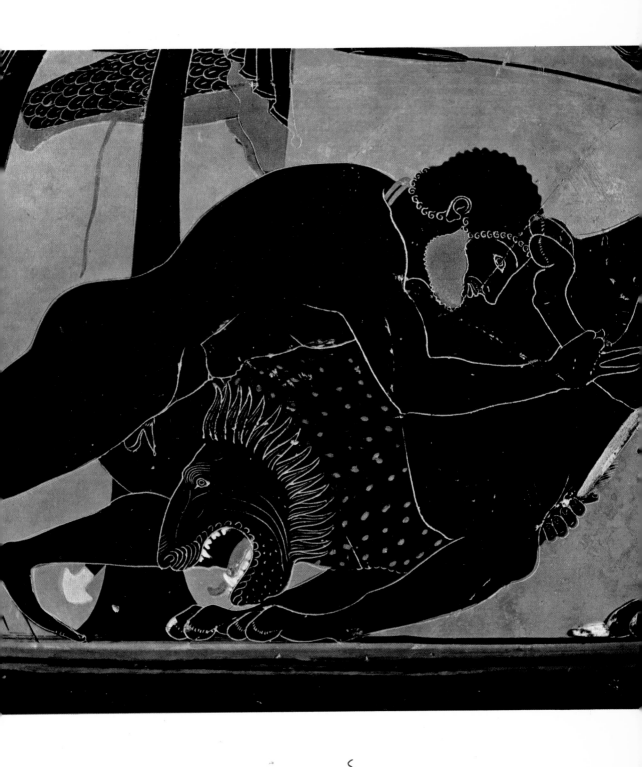

Colorplate 5. PSIAX. *Hercules Strangling the Nemean Lion* (detail of figure 38)

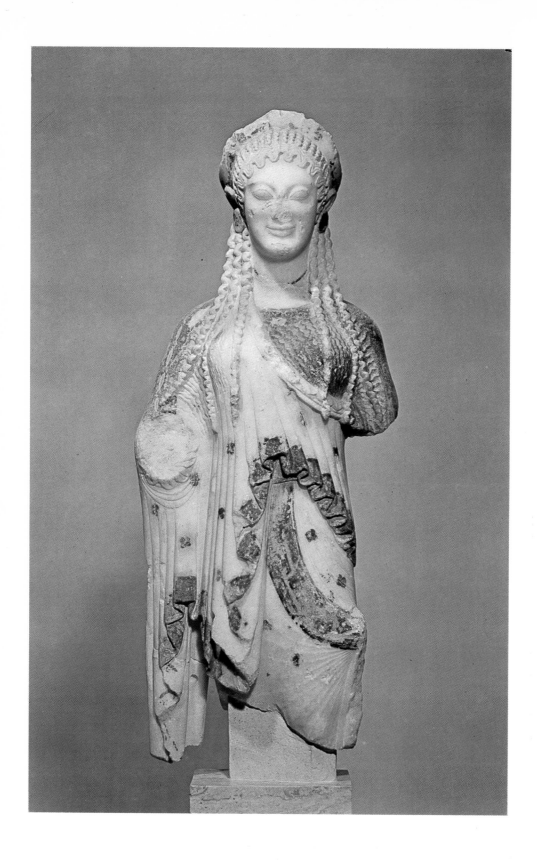

Colorplate 6. *Maiden*, from Chios (?) c. 520 B.C. Marble, height 21 7/8″. Acropolis Museum, Athens

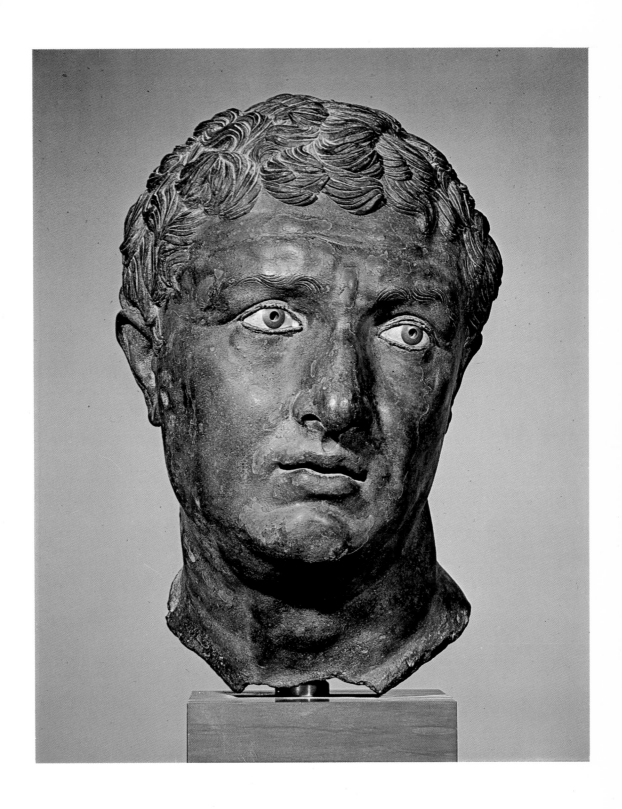

Colorplate 7. *Portrait Head,* from Delos. c. 80 B.C. Bronze, height 12 3/4″. National Museum, Athens

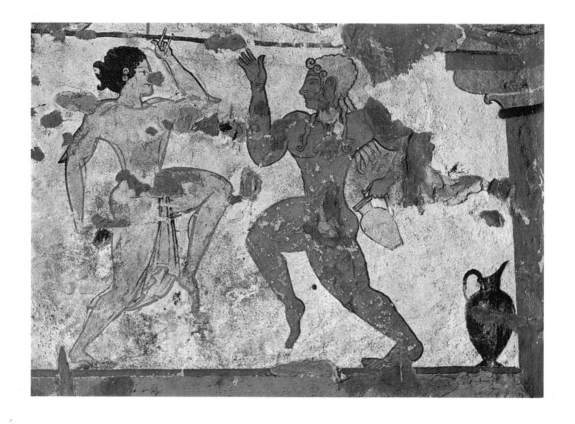

Colorplate 8. *Two Dancers* (detail of wall painting). c. 480–470 B.C. Tomb of the Lionesses, Tarquinia

AEGEAN ART

The Aegean Sea is an arm of the Mediterranean that stretches from the long, rocky island of Crete, about two hundred miles north of Egypt, to Asia Minor and the southern tip of mainland Greece. An astonishing nation of sailors, quite unlike the Egyptians or the peoples of Mesopotamia, developed a high civilization on Crete about 2000 B.C. and maintained it for a thousand years. We call this civilization Minoan, after the legendary Cretan king, Minos. The Minoans were bold traders and pirates who made up for the poor soil of their homeland by bringing in food and other important items from every country that they could reach with their ships.

[handwritten: + traders + pirates] *[handwritten: after Minos legendary king of Crete]*

MINOAN ART AND ARCHITECTURE

We have not yet learned to read the Minoan's writing very well, so that we do not know a great deal about them. But from the ruins of their palaces and from the pictures they made, we can see that they were the richest and the most adventurous of early Western nations. We can see that they were a luxurious and pleasure-loving people, too. Their palaces were comfortable and elegant, unlike Persian palaces (see fig. 31), which in contrast were grand and imposing. Minoan palaces were not fortified—naval power protected them.

The so-called Palace of Minos, at Knossos, was the most ambitious. It covered a wide area and was composed of so many rooms that it survived in Greek legend as the labyrinth of the Minotaur. It was richly decorated and built of masonry, but its columns were made of wood. None of these columns has survived, but we know, from paintings and sculptures depicting them, that they had bulging cushion-shaped capitals and smooth shafts that tapered downward. In figure 33 we see a reconstructed corner

[handwritten: Minoan Palaces— not fortified naval power protected them]
[handwritten: luxurious + pleasure loving people]
[handwritten: comfortable and elegant (unlike the grand, + imposing Persian palaces)]
[handwritten: life of settlements centered on palaces]

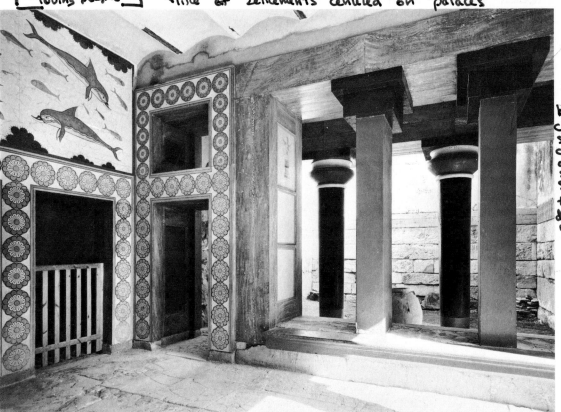

[handwritten: bulging cushion-shaped capitals and smooth shafts tapering downward]

33. Queen's Chamber, Palace of Minos, Knossos, Crete. c. 1500 B.C.

[handwritten: richly decorated and built of masonry w/ wood columns]

Minoans— Cretans
Mycenaeans— Greek tribesmen who had entered Greece about 1800 BC.

of the palace, with columns of this kind and with characteristic Minoan decoration.

Colorplate 4, the so-called *Toreador Fresco*, shows us a wall painting from the Palace of Minos. Here, a youth and two girls—all wasp-waisted, in the Cretan manner—play a dangerous game. They seize the horns of a charging bull and somersault over his back. Actually this is a religious ritual, not a sport —but the Minoan artist has stressed the harmonious, playful aspect of the ritual. Fluid, rhythmic, effortless movement was more important to him than accurate description—the bull is very long indeed for dramatic power.

1400 BC.— Mycenaeans were rulers of Crete

MYCENAEAN ART AND ARCHITECTURE

Minoan civilization touched the coastline of southeastern mainland Greece. The inhabitants of this shore were not the same people as the Minoans but early Greek tribesmen who had entered Greece about 1800 B.C. Their most important settlement was Mycenae. Crete and Mycenae had close relations which lasted a long time; by about 1400 B.C.

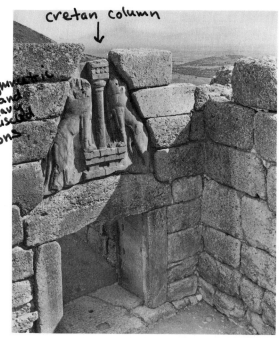

cretan column

Symmetric and heavy muscled lions

34. The Lion Gate, Mycenae. c. 1250 B.C.

35. *Boar Hunt,* from the Palace at Tiryns, Greece. c. 1200 B.C. Wall painting. National Museum, Athens

Mycenaean Palaces— hilltop fortresses w/ rough, massive walls of huge stone blocks
↳ like ⌖ settlements centered on palaces

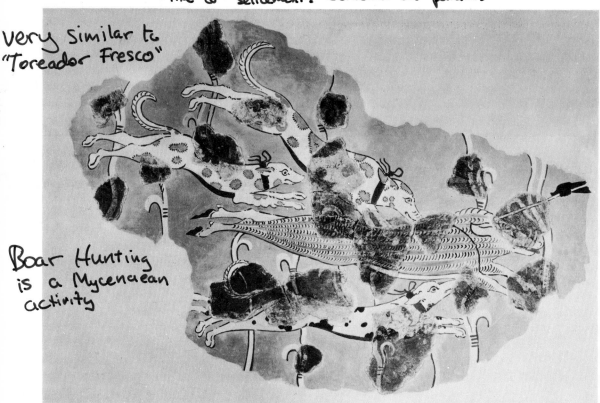

Very similar to "Toreador Fresco"

Boar Hunting is a Mycenaean activity

Handwritten margin notes (top): Men catching bulls w/ rope + net

Handwritten margin notes (top): same dress on these mycenaean men as on Minoan men — Wasp-waisted

Handwritten margin notes (top): Bull catching is a Mycenaean activity

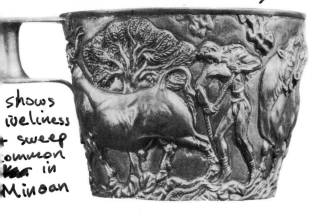

Handwritten margin notes (left): shows liveliness + sweep common ?er in Minoan

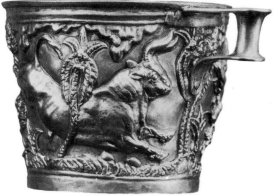

36. *The Vaphio Cups.* c. 1500 B.C. Gold, height 3–3 1/2″. National Museum, Athens

the Mycenaeans were the rulers of Crete, either by conquest or through dynastic marriage. In any event, the power of Mycenae rose as that of the Minoans fell, and Mycenaean civilization continued to flourish until about 1100 B.C.

As in Crete, the life of Mycenaean settlements centered on the palace. Basically, the palaces were very different from those of Crete, for they were hilltop fortresses with rough, massive walls of huge stone blocks, such as those framing the Lion Gate at Mycenae (fig. 34). So massive are these ramparts that the Greeks of a later time called them "Cyclopean," thinking that such stones could only have been moved by the Cyclopes, a race of giants. The column between the two lions, tapering from top to bottom, is of the same design as those used in Cretan palaces. But the artistic ancestry most evident in the two carved lions is Mesopotamian: we have seen symmetrically confronted animals in figure 27; and the lion in figure 29 is surely of the same heavy-muscled artistic species as the guardians of the gate.

Nevertheless, the wall paintings of the palaces and most other decorative features were like those of Crete. The beasts of the vigorous *Boar Hunt* wall painting from the Palace at Tiryns (fig. 35) are unmistakably similar in conception to the bull of the Minoan *"Toreador Fresco."* The two golden cups from Vaphio (fig. 36) show us men—wasp-waisted, as in Crete—catching bulls with rope and net. The netting scene is very Minoan in its liveliness and sweep. But as in the *Boar Hunt*, the activity is Mycenaean.

It would seem, then, that the painting and the cups are Mycenaean adaptations of Minoan forms, either by a mainland artist or by a Cretan working for Mycenaean patrons.

Handwritten margin note: Minoan

Greek Art

The works of art we have come to know so far are like fascinating strangers: we approach them fully aware of their alien background and of the "language difficulties" they present. As soon as we come to the sixth century B.C. in Greece, however, our attitude undergoes a change: these are not strangers but relatives, we feel—older members of our own family. It is just as well to remember, as we turn to these "ancestors" of ours, that the continuous tradition that links us to the ancient Greeks is a handicap as well as an advantage: we must be careful, in looking at Greek originals, not to let our memories of their countless later imitations get in the way.

The Mycenaeans and the other clans described by Homer were the first Greek-speaking tribes to wander into the peninsula, around 2000 B.C. Then, around 1100 B.C., others came, overwhelming and absorbing those who were already there. Some of the late arrivals, the Dorians, settled on the mainland; others, the Ionians, spread out to the Aegean islands and Asia Minor. A few centuries later they ventured into the waters of the western Mediterranean, founding colonies in Sicily and southern Italy. Though the Greeks were united by language and religious beliefs, old tribal loyalties continued to divide them into city-states. The intense rivalry among these for power, wealth, and status undoubtedly stimulated the growth of ideas and institutions; but in the end they paid dearly for their inability to compromise, at least sufficiently to broaden their concept of state government. The Peloponnesian War (431–404 B.C.), in which the Spartans and their allies defeated the Athenians, was a catastrophe from which Greece never recovered.

PAINTING

the oldest characteristically Greek style in the fine arts

GEOMETRIC STYLE

The formative phase of Greek civilization embraces about four hundred years, from c. 1100 to 700 B.C. Of the first three centuries of this period we know very little, but after about 800 B.C. the Greeks rapidly emerge into the full light of history. That period also saw the full development of the oldest characteristically Greek style in the fine arts, the so-called Geometric. We know it only from painted pottery and small-scale sculpture (monumental architecture and sculpture in stone did not appear until the seventh century). At first the pottery had been decorated only with abstract designs—triangles, checkers, concentric circles—but toward 800 B.C. human and animal figures began to appear within the geometric framework, and in the most mature examples these figures could form elaborate scenes. Our specimen (fig. 37), from the Dipylon cemetery in Athens, belongs to a group of very large vases that served as grave monuments; its bottom has holes through which liquid offerings could filter down to the dead below. On the body of the vessel we see the deceased lying in state, flanked by figures with their arms raised in a gesture of mourning, and a funeral procession of chariots and warriors on foot. The most remarkable thing about this scene is that it contains no reference to an afterlife; its purpose is purely commemorative. Here lies a worthy man, it tells us, who was mourned by many and had a splendid funeral. Did the Greeks, then, have no conception of a hereafter? They did, but the

Funeral procession of chariots and warriors on foot

no reference to an afterlife just a commemoration

It says: Here lies a worthy man, who was mourned by many and had a splendid funeral

realm of the dead to them was a colorless, ill-defined region where the souls, or "shades," led a feeble and passive existence without making any demands upon the living.

ARCHAIC STYLE

Toward 700 B.C. Greek art, stimulated by an increased trade with Egypt and the Near East, began to absorb powerful influences from these regions that put flesh on the bare bones of the Dorians' Geometric images. From the later seventh century to about 480 B.C., this amalgamation produced what we call the "Archaic" style; while it does not yet have the balance and perfection of the "Classic" style, which followed in the later part of the fifth century B.C., the Archaic style has an appealing freshness that makes many persons consider it the most vital phase of Greek art.

mourners w/ arms raised

deceased

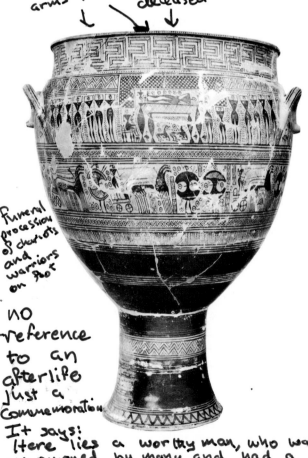

37. Dipylon Vase. 8th century B.C. Height 42 1/2". The Metropolitan Museum of Art, New York (Rogers Fund)

BLACK-FIGURE

By about the middle of the sixth century B.C., vase painters in particular were so highly esteemed that the best of them signed their works. The scene of Hercules strangling the Nemean lion on Psiax's amphora (fig. 38, colorplate 5) is a far cry from the conventionalized figures of the Geometric style. The two heavy bodies almost seem united forever in their grim struggle; incised line and touches of colored detail have been kept to a minimum so as not to break up the compact black mass, yet both figures show such a wealth of anatomical knowledge and skillful use of foreshortening that they give an amazing illusion of existing in the round.

Unlike most earlier art, Psiax's vase tells a story. Narrative painting tapped a nearly inexhaustible source of subjects from Greek myths and legends. These tales were the result of mixing local Doric and Ionic deities and heroes into the pantheon of Olympian gods and Homeric sagas. They also represent a comprehensive attempt to understand the world. The Greeks grasped the internal meaning of events in terms of fate and human character rather than the accidents of history, in which they had little interest before c. 500 B.C. The main focus was on explaining why the legendary heroes of the past seemed incomparably greater than men of the present. Some were historical figures, including Hercules, who was the king of Tiryns, but all were believed to have been descended from gods, themselves very human in quality, who had children with mortals. This lineage explained the hero's extraordinary powers. Such an outlook helps us to understand the strong appeal exerted on the Greek imagination by Oriental lions and monsters. Hercules in his struggle reminds us of the hero on the sounding board of the harp from Ur (fig. 27). Both show a hero facing the unknown forces of life embodied by terrifying mythical creatures. The Nemean lion in turn is derived ultimately from Ashurnasirpal's prey in the relief from the Palace at Nimrud (fig. 29) and likewise serves to underscore the hero's might and courage.

could think complexly

anatomical knowledge

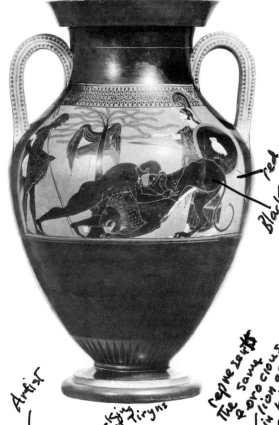

Black *red*

RED-FIGURE

Psiax must have felt that the silhouette-like black-figured technique made the study of foreshortening unduly difficult, for in some of his vases he tried the reverse procedure, leaving the figures red and filling in the background. This red-figured technique gradually replaced the older method toward 500 B.C. Its advantages are well shown in figure 39, a kylix of c. 490–480 B.C. by an unknown master nicknamed the "Foundry Painter." The details of the Lapith and Centaur are now freely drawn with the brush, rather than laboriously incised, so the artist depends far less on the profile view than before; instead, he exploits the internal lines of communication that permit him to show boldly foreshortened and overlapping limbs, precise details of costume (note the pleated skirt), and interesting facial expressions. He is so fascinated by all these new effects that he has made the figures as large as he possibly could.

38. PSIAX. *Hercules Strangling the Nemean Lion.* Attic black-figured amphora from Vulci. Archaic Period. c. 525 B.C. Height 19". Civic Museum, Brescia, Italy (see also colorplate 5)

Artist

King of Tiryns

The same ferocious lion in King Ashurnasirpal's relief

[handwritten: seems to burst from its circular frame] *[handwritten: black]* *[handwritten: "Red-figured"]* *[handwritten: red]*

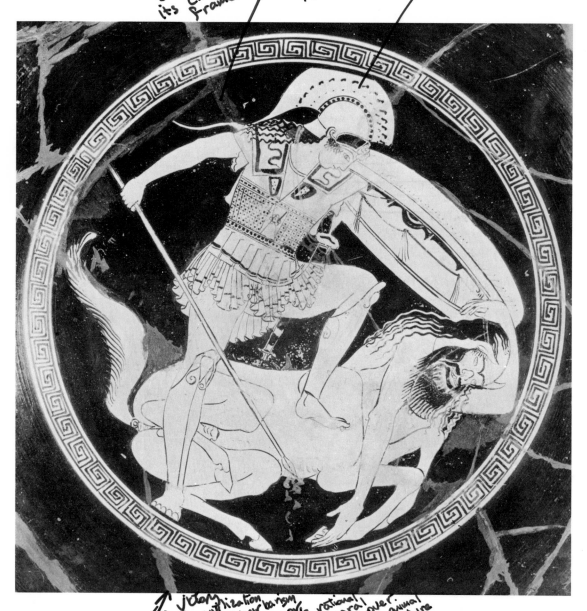

[handwritten: The victory of civilization over barbarism or man's rational and moral side over his animal nature]

39. THE FOUNDRY PAINTER. *Lapith and Centaur.* Attic red-figured ware. Archaic Period. c. 490–480 B.C. Diameter 15″. Staatliche Antikensammlungen, Munich

They almost seem to burst from their circular frame, and a piece of the Lapith's helmet has actually been cut off.

The Lapith and Centaur are counterparts to Hercules and the Nemean lion. But just as the style has changed, so has the meaning of this combat: the painting now stands for the victory of civilization over barbarianism and ultimately of man's rational and moral side over his animal nature.

CLASSICAL STYLE

According to literary sources, Greek artists of the Classical period, which began around 480 B.C., achieved great breakthroughs in painting, including the mastering of illusionistic space. Unhappily, we have no murals or panels to verify this claim; and vase painting by its very nature could echo the new concept of pictorial space only in rudimentary fashion. Still, there are vessels that form an exception to this general rule; we find them mostly in a special class of vases, the lekythoi (oil jugs) used as funerary offerings. These had a white coating on which the painter could draw as freely, and with the same spa-

[handwritten: lekythoi (oily jug) used as funerary offerings]
[handwritten: lekythoi]
[handwritten: white background treated as empty space]

tial effect, as his modern successor using pen and paper. The white ground, in both cases, is treated as empty space from which the sketched forms seem to emerge—if the draftsman knows how to achieve this. Not many lekythos painters were capable of bringing off the illusion. Foremost among them was the unknown artist, nicknamed the "Achilles Painter," who drew the woman in figure 40. Our chief interest is the masterly draftsmanship; with a few lines, sure, fresh, and fluid, the artist not only creates a three-dimensional figure but reveals the body beneath the drapery as well. How does he manage to persuade us that these shapes exist in depth rather than merely on the surface of the vase? First of all, by his command of foreshortening. But the "internal dynamics" of the lines are equally important, their swelling and fading, which make some contours stand out boldly while others merge with one another or disappear into the white ground.

Considering its artistic advantages, we might expect the white-ground technique to have been more generally adopted. Such, however, was not the case. Instead, from the mid-fifth century on, the impact of monumental painting gradually transformed vase painting as a whole into a satellite art that tried to reproduce large-scale compositions

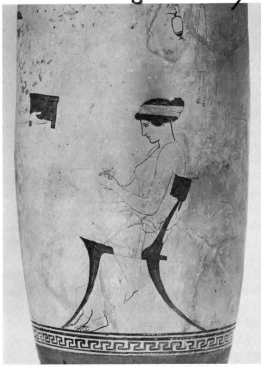

40. THE ACHILLES PAINTER. Attic white-ground vase (detail). Classic Period. c. 440–430 B.C. Private Collection

41. *The Battle of Issus*, from Pompeii. Mosaic copy (c. 100 B.C.) of a Hellenistic Greek painting. Width of this portion about 10 1/2′. National Museum, Naples, Italy

[handwritten: Persian King Darius defeated By Alexander The Great]
[handwritten: Something that actually Happened]

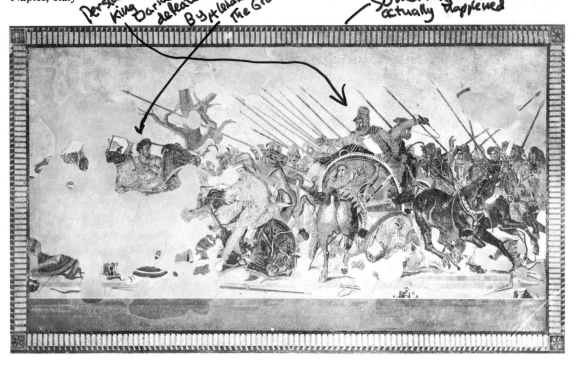

in a kind of shorthand dictated by its own limited technique. We can get some idea of what Greek wall painting looked like from later copies and imitations. For example, the mosaic from Pompeii showing *The Battle of Issus* (fig. 41) probably reflects a famous Greek painting of about 315 B.C. depicting the defeat of the Persian king Darius by Alexander the Great. The scene is far more complicated and dramatic than anything from earlier Greek art. And for the first time it shows something that actually happened, without the symbolic overtones of *Hercules and the Nemean Lion* or the *Lapith and Centaur*. In character and even in appearance, it is close to Assyrian reliefs commemorating specific historic events.

TEMPLES

The Greek achievement in architecture has been identified since ancient Roman times with the creation of the three Classical architectural orders: the Doric, Ionic, and Corinthian. Of these, the Doric may well claim to be the basic order, being older and more sharply defined than the Ionic; the Corinthian is a variant of the latter. What do we mean by "architectural order"? The term is used only for Greek architecture (and its descendants), and rightly so, for none of the other architectural systems known to us has produced anything like it. Perhaps the simplest way to make clear the unique character of the Greek orders is this: there is no such thing as "the Egyptian temple" or "the Gothic church"—the individual buildings, however much they may have in common, are so varied that we cannot distill a generalized type from them—while "the Doric temple" is a real entity that inevitably forms in our minds as we examine the monuments themselves. This abstraction is not, of course, an ideal against which we may measure the degree of perfection of any given Doric temple; it simply means that the elements of which a Doric temple is composed are extraordinarily constant in number, in kind, and in their relation to one another. Doric temples all belong to the same clearly recognizable family; they show an internal con-

sistency, a mutual adjustment of parts, that gives them a unique quality of wholeness and organic unity.

DORIC ORDER

The term Doric order refers to the standard parts, and their sequence, making up the exterior of any Doric temple. Let us note the three main divisions in figure 42: the stepped platform, the columns, and the entablature (which includes everything that rests on the columns). The column consists of the shaft, made of sections (drums) and marked with vertical grooves called flutes, and the capital, which supports the horizontal stone blocks of the architrave. Above the architrave is the frieze and the cornice. On the long sides of the temple, the cornice is horizontal; on the short sides (or façades) it is split open so as to enclose the pediment between its upper and lower parts.

The plans of Greek temples are not directly linked to the orders. The basic features of all of them are so much alike that it is useful to study them from a generalized "typical" plan (fig. 43). The nucleus is the cella or naos (the room where the image of the deity is placed), and the entrance porch (pronaos) with two columns flanked by pilasters. Often a second porch is added behind the cella, for symmetry. In large temples, this central unit is surrounded by a row of columns (the colonnade, also called the peristyle).

How did the Doric temple originate? Its essential features were already well established about 600 B.C., but how they developed, and why they congealed so rapidly into a system, as it seems they did, remains a puzzle to which we have few reliable clues. The notion that temples ought to be built of stone, with large numbers of columns, must have come from Egypt; the fluted half-columns at Saqqara (see fig. 16) strongly suggest the Doric column. Egyptian temples, it is true, are designed to be experienced from the inside, while the Greek temple is arranged so that the exterior matters most (religious ceremonies usually took place out of doors, in front of the temple façade). But might not a Doric temple be interpreted as the columned hall of an Egyptian sanctuary turned inside out? The Greeks also owed something to the Mycenaeans—we have seen an elementary

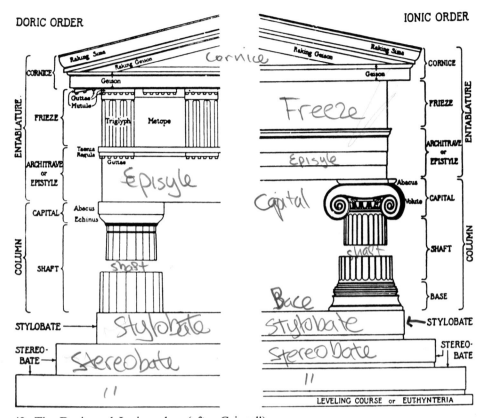

42. The Doric and Ionic orders (after Grinnell)

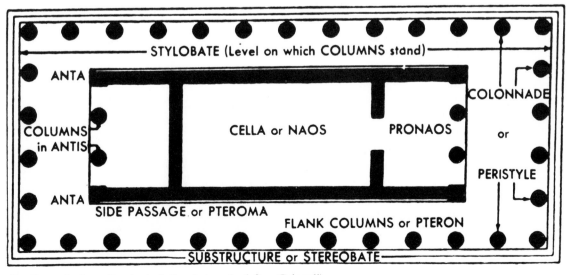

43. Ground plan of a typical Greek temple (after Grinnell)

kind of pediment in the Lion Gate, and the capital of a Mycenaean column is rather like a Doric capital (compare fig. 34). There is, however, a third factor: to what extent can the Doric order be understood as a reflection of wooden structures? Our answer to this thorny question will depend on whether we believe that architectural form follows function and technique, or whether we accept the striving for beauty as a motivating force. The truth may well lie in a combination of both these approaches. At the start, Doric architects certainly imitated in stone some features of wooden temples, if only because these features served to identify the building as a temple. But when they became enshrined in the Doric order, it was not from blind conservatism; by then, the wooden forms had been so thoroughly transformed that they were an organic part of the stone structure.

PAESTUM

Of the ancient Greek buildings here illustrated, the oldest is the "Basilica" in Paestum (fig. 44, background); near this south-Italian town a Greek colony flourished during the Archaic period. The Temple of Poseidon (fig. 44, foreground) was erected about a hundred years later. How do the two temples differ? The "Basilica" looks low and sprawling—and not only because its roof is lost— while the Temple of Poseidon, by comparison, appears tall and compact. The difference is partly psychological, produced by the outline of the columns which, in the "Basilica," are more strongly curved and are tapered to a relatively tiny top. This makes one feel that they bulge with the strain of supporting the superstructure, and that the slender tops, even though aided by the widely flaring cushionlike capitals, are just barely up to the job. This sense of strain has been explained on the grounds that Archaic architects were not fully familiar with their new materials and engineering procedures, but such a view judges the building by the standards of later temples—and overlooks the expressive vitality of the building, as of a living body, the vitality we also sense in the Archaic Kouros (fig. 47)

In the Temple of Poseidon the exaggerated curvatures have been modified; this, combined with a closer ranking of the columns,

literally as well as expressively brings the stresses between supports and weight into more harmonious balance. Perhaps because the architect took fewer risks, the building is better preserved than the "Basilica," and its air of self-contained repose parallels the *Hera* (fig. 48) in the field of sculpture.

ATHENS

As the most perfect embodiment of the Classic period of Greek architecture, the Parthenon (fig. 45) takes us a step further toward harmonious completeness. Although it is only a few years younger than the Temple of Poseidon, the fact that it was built in Athens, then at the peak of its glory and wealth, ensured it the best of design, material, and workmanship. In spite of its greater size it seems less massive than the earlier temple; rather, the dominant impression is one of festive, balanced grace. A general lightening and readjustment of the proportions accounts for this: the horizontal courses above the columns are not so wide in relation to their length; the framework of the gable projects less insistently; and the columns, in addition to being slenderer, are more widely spaced. The curvature of the columns and the flare of the capitals are also discreetly lessened, adding to the new sense of ease. Instead of resembling an Archaic Atlas, straining to hold up the weight of a world placed on his shoulders, the Parthenon performs with apparent facility. Unobtrusive refinements of proportion and line, measurable but not immediately apparent, add to the overall impression of springy vitality: horizontal elements, such as the steps, are not straight but

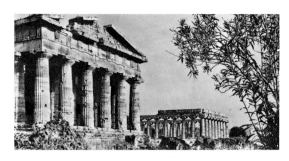

44. The Temple of Poseidon (foreground; c. 460 B.C.) and the "Basilica" (background; c. 550 B.C.). Paestum, Italy

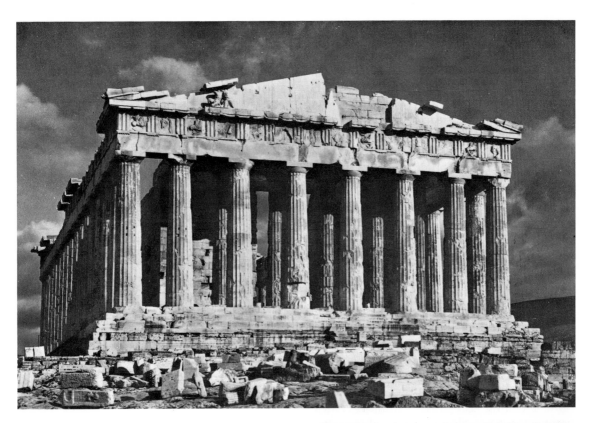

45. The Parthenon, by Iᴄᴛɪɴᴜs and Cᴀʟʟɪᴄʀᴀᴛᴇs (view from west). 448–432 B.C. Acropolis, Athens

46. The Propylaea, by Mɴᴇsɪᴄʟᴇs (view from west; 437–432 B.C.), and the Temple of Athena Nike (upper right; 427–424 B.C.). Acropolis, Athens

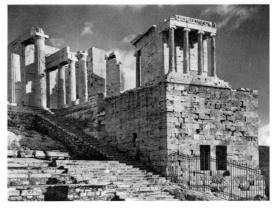

curve upward slightly toward the middle; the columns tilt inward; and the interval between each corner column and its neighbor is smaller than the standard interval used in the rest of the colonnade. Such intentional departures from strict geometric regularity are not made of necessity; they give us visual reassurance that the points of greatest stress are supported, and provided with a counter-stress as well.

Shortly afterward an impressive gateway, the Propylaea (fig. 46), was built upon the rough, irregular hill which one has to climb to reach the Parthenon. It is fascinating to see how the familiar elements of the Doric order are here adapted to a totally different purpose and a difficult terrain. The architect has ac-

quitted himself nobly: not only does the gateway fit the steep and craggy hillside, it transforms it from a rude passage among the rocks into a majestic overture to the sacred precinct above.

IONIC ORDER

Next to the Propylaea is the elegant little Temple of Athena Nike (fig. 46, right), displaying the slenderer proportions and the scroll capitals of the Ionic order. The previous development of the order is known only in very fragmentary fashion, and it did not really become an order in the strict sense until the Classical period. Even then it continued to be rather more flexible than the Doric order. In pre-Classical times, the only Ionic structures on the Greek mainland had been the small treasuries built by eastern Greek states at Delphi in their regional styles. Hence the Athenian architects who took up the Ionic order about 450 B.C. thought of it, at first, as suitable only for small temples of simple plan. Such a building is the Temple of Athena Nike, probably built 427–424 B.C. from a design prepared twenty years earlier by Callicrates. Its most striking feature is the Ionic column, which differs from the Doric not only in body but also in spirit (see fig. 42). The column rests on an ornately profiled base of its own; the shaft is more slender, and there is less tapering and swelling; the capital shows a large double scroll, or volute, between the echinus and abacus, which projects strongly beyond the width of the shaft. That these details add up to an entity very distinct from the Doric column becomes clear as soon as we turn from the diagram to an actual building. How shall we define it? The Ionic column is, of course, lighter and more graceful than its mainland cousin; it lacks the latter's muscular quality. Instead, it evokes the echo of a growing plant, of something like a formalized palm tree. And this vegetal analogy is not sheer fancy, for we have early ancestors, or relatives, of the Ionic capital that bear it out. If we were to pursue these plantlike columns all the way back to their point of origin, we would eventually find ourselves at Saqqara, where we not only encounter "proto-Doric" supports but the wonderfully graceful papyrus half-columns of figure 16, with their curved, flaring capitals. It may well be, then, that the Ionic column, too, had its ultimate source in Egypt, but instead of reaching Greece by sea, as we suppose the proto-Doric column did, it traveled a slow and tortuous path by land, through Syria and Asia Minor.

In the end, the greatest achievement of Greek architecture was much more than just beautiful buildings. Greek temples are governed by a structural logic which makes them look stable because of the precise arrangement of their parts. The Greeks tried to regulate their temples in accordance with nature's harmony by constructing them of measured units which were so proportioned that they would all be in perfect agreement. ("Perfect" was as significant an idea to the Greeks as "forever" was to the Egyptians.) Now men could create organic unities, not by copying nature, not by divine inspiration, but by design. Thus their temples seem to be almost alive. They achieved this triumph chiefly by expressing the structural forces active in buildings. In the Classical period, expressions of force and counterforce in both Doric and Ionic temples were proportioned so exactly that their opposition produced the effect of a perfect balancing of forces, and harmonizing of sizes and shapes. This, then, is the real reason why, for so many centuries, the orders have been considered the only true basis for beautiful architecture. They are so perfect that they could not be surpassed, only equaled.

SCULPTURE

While enough examples of metalwork and ivory carvings of Near Eastern and Egyptian origin have been found on Greek soil to account for their influence on Greek vase painting, the origins of monumental sculpture and architecture in Greece are a different matter. To see such things, the Greeks had to go to Egypt or Mesopotamia. There is no doubt that they did so (we know that there were small colonies of Greeks in Egypt at the time), but this does not explain why the Greeks should have developed a sudden desire during the seventh century B.C., and not before, to create such things for themselves. The mystery may never be cleared up, for the oldest existing examples of Greek stone sculpture and architecture show that Egyptian tradition had already been well assimilated, and that skill to match was not long in developing.

ARCHAIC STYLE

Let us begin by comparing a late seventh-century statue of a Greek youth, called a Kouros (fig. 47), with the statue of Mycerinus (fig. 14). The similarities are certainly

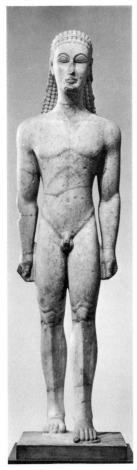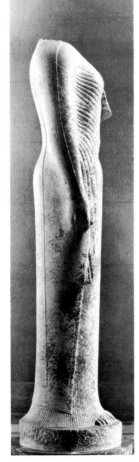

left: 47. *Standing Youth.* c. 600 B.C. Marble, height 6' 1 1/2". The Metropolitan Museum of Art, New York. (Fletcher Fund, 1932)

right: 48. "*Hera*," from Samos. c. 570–560 B.C. Marble, height 6' 4". The Louvre, Paris

entire history of art there are no earlier examples of a sculptor's being daring enough to liberate a lifesize figure completely from the surrounding block of stone. What had doubtless started as a timid precaution against breakage of arms, or the crumbling of the legs under the weight of the body, became a convention. Here, however, the artist has carved away every bit of "dead" stone except for the tiny bridges that connect the fists to the thighs. This is a matter not merely of technical daring but of a new intention: it was important to the Greek artist to dissociate his statue from inert matter, the better to approximate the living being that it represented. Unlike Mycerinus, who looks as though he could stand in the same pose till the end of time, the Kouros is tense with a vitality that seems to promise movement. The calm, distant gaze of the Egyptian prince has been replaced by larger-than-life, wide-open eyes that remind us of early Mesopotamian art (see fig. 26).

Statues of the Kouros type were produced in great quantity during the Archaic period, destined for temple offerings or graves. Like the decorated vases of the period, some of them were signed ("So-and-so made me"); but whether they represent gods, or donors, or victors in athletic games, nobody knows for sure. Since they vary but little in their essentials, we assume that they were meant to represent an ideal—a godlike man, or a manlike god.

The male figures show best the innovations that give Greek sculpture its particular character, but there is no dearth of female statues of the same period. Since these were invariably clothed, skirts and shawls fill in those empty spaces that make the contrast so clear between Greek sculpture and all that came before it. Nevertheless, the Kore, as the female statue type is called, shows more variations than the Kouros. In part these are due to local differences in dress, but the drapery itself posed a problem—how to relate it to the body—and artists solved it in various ways. The *Hera* (fig. 48), so called because of her impressive size and because she was found in the ruins of the Temple of Hera on the island of Samos, is slightly later than our Kouros (fig. 47). This smooth-skirted figure with the folds of her hem fan-

striking: in both we note the same cubic character, as though the sculptor were still conscious of the original block of stone; the broad-shouldered, slim silhouettes; the position of the arms with their clenched hands; the stance with the left leg forward; the emphatic rendering of the kneecaps; and the wiglike curls of the Greek boy that resemble the headdress worn by the Pharaoh. Judged by the Egyptian level of accomplishment the Archaic Greek example seems somewhat awkward—oversimplified, rigid, less close to nature. But the Greek statue has some virtues that cannot be measured in Egyptian terms. First of all, it is freestanding. In the

ning out over a circular base seems to have evolved from a column rather than from a rectangular block. But the majestic effect of the statue depends not so much on its closeness to an abstract shape as on the way the column has blossomed forth with the swelling softness of a living body. Following the unbroken upward sweep of the lower folds of drapery, the eye slows to the gently curving hips, torso, and breast. If we turn back to figure 14, we realize suddenly that Mycerinus' wife, with far more explicit anatomy, looks squat and lifeless by comparison.

Both types, youth and maiden, continued to be produced through the Archaic period and beyond. We find here the same thread of stylistic development that we have already traced in Greek vase painting. The maiden of colorplate 6, for example, is a stylistic counterpart of the late Archaic red-figured vase of figure 39, especially in the treatment of drapery. In many ways she seems akin to the *Hera* from Samos: in fact, she probably came from Chios, another island of Ionian Greece. The architectural grandeur of her ancestress has now given way to ornate, refined grace. The garments still loop around the body in spiraling curves, but the intricate play of folds and pleats has become almost an end in itself. The maiden's hair has been given a similar treatment, and her face wears a soft, almost natural expression—the so-called "Archaic smile." This statue still has much of its original color, and shows us how important color actually was in Greek sculpture.

ARCHITECTURAL SCULPTURE

When the Greeks began to build their temples in stone, they fell heir to age-old traditions of architectural sculpture as well. The Egyptians covered the walls and even the columns of their buildings with reliefs, but these carvings were so shallow that they had no weight or volume of their own. The guardian figures of the Lion Gate at Mycenae are of a different type: although they are carved in high relief on a huge slab, this slab is thin and light compared to the Cyclopean blocks around it. In building the gate, the architect had left an empty triangle above the lintel, for fear that the weight of the wall above

would crush it, and then filled the hole with the relief panel. This kind of architectural sculpture is a separate entity, not merely a modified wall surface. The Greeks followed the Mycenaean example—in their temples, stone sculpture is confined to the pediment (the "empty triangle" between the ceiling and the sloping sides of the roof) and to the zone immediately below it (the "frieze")—but they retained the narrative wealth of Egyptian reliefs. The *Battle of Gods and Giants* (fig. 49), part of a frieze, is executed in very high relief with deep undercutting (the hind leg of one of the lions has broken off because it was completely detached from the background). The sculptor has taken full advantage of the spatial possibilities of this bold technique; the projecting ledge at the bottom has become a stage on which to place the figures in depth. As they recede from us, the carving becomes shallower, yet even the furthest plane is not allowed to merge into the background. The result is a condensed but very convincing space that permits a dramatic interplay among the figures such as we have not seen before. Not only in the physical but in the expressive sense, a new dimension has here been conquered.

Meanwhile, in pedimental sculpture, relief has been abandoned altogether. Instead, we find separate statues placed side by side in complex dramatic sequences designed to fit the triangular frame. The most ambitious ensemble of this kind, that of the east pediment of the temple at Aegina, was created about 490 B.C., and thus brings us to the final stage in the evolution of Archaic sculpture. The figures were found in pieces on the ground and are now in the Glyptothek in Munich. Among the most impressive is the fallen warrior from the left-hand corner (fig. 50), whose lean, muscular body seems marvelously functional and organic. That in itself, however, does not explain his great beauty, much as we may admire the artist's command of the human form in action. What really moves us is his nobility of spirit, whether in the agony of dying or in the act of killing. This man, we sense, is suffering—or carrying out—what fate has decreed, with tremendous dignity and resolve. And this communicates itself to us in the very feel of the magnificently firm shapes of which he is composed.

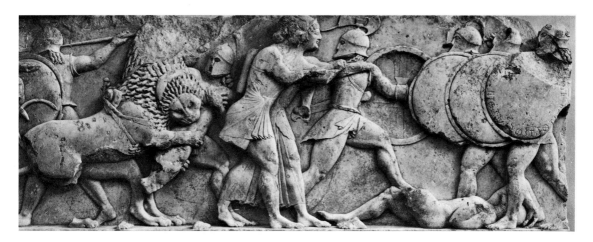

49. *Battle of Gods and Giants*, portion of north frieze, Treasury of the Siphnians, Delphi. c. 530 B.C. Marble, height 26″. Museum, Delphi

CLASSICAL STYLE

Sometimes things that seem simple are the hardest to achieve. Greek sculptors of the late Archaic period (see figs. 47, 49) were adept at representing battle scenes full of struggling, running figures, but their freestanding statues also have an unintentional military air, as of soldiers standing at attention. It took over a century after our Kouros was made before the Greeks discovered the secret of making a figure stand "at ease." *The Kritios Boy* (fig. 51), named after the Athenian sculptor to whom it has been attributed, is the first statue we know that "stands" in the full sense of the term. Just as in military drill, this is simply a matter of allowing the weight of the body to shift

from equal distribution on both legs (as is the case with the Kouros, even though one foot is in front of the other), to one leg. The resulting stance—called *contrapposto* (or counterpoise)—brings about all kinds of subtle curvatures: the bending of the "free" knee results in a slight swiveling of the pelvis, a compensating curvature of the spine, and an adjusting tilt of the shoulders. Like the refined details of the Parthenon, these variations have nothing to do with the statue's ability to maintain itself erect but greatly enhance its lifelike impression; in repose, it will still seem capable of movement; in motion, of maintaining its stability.

Life now suffuses the entire figure; hence the Archaic smile, the "sign of life," is no longer needed, and has given way to a serious, pensive expression. The forms, moreover, have a new naturalism and harmonious

50. *Dying Warrior*, from the east pediment of the Temple at Aegina. c. 490 B.C. Marble, length 72″. Glyptothek, Munich

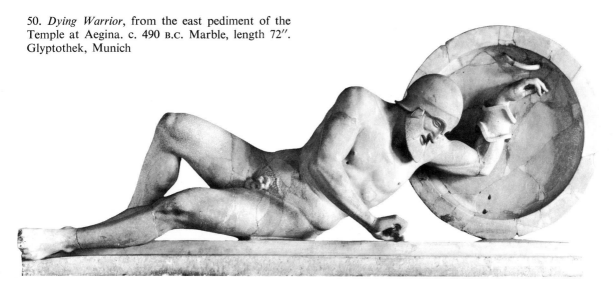

proportion which together provide the basis for the strong idealization characteristic of all subsequent Greek art.

Stability in the midst of action becomes outright grandeur in the bronze *Poseidon* or *Zeus* (fig. 52), an over-lifesize statue that was recovered from the sea near the coast of Greece over thirty years ago. The pose, to be sure, is that of an athlete, but it is not merely a moment in some continuing exercise; rather, it is an awe-inspiring gesture that reveals the power of the god. Here, the hurling of a weapon (originally, we may be sure, he held a thunderbolt or a trident in his right hand) is a divine attribute, not an act of war.

Battered though it is, the group of *Three Goddesses* (fig. 53) that originally belonged to the scene in the east pediment of the Parthenon, showing the birth of Athena from her father's head, is a good example of that other quality mentioned above: the possibility of action even in repose. Though all are seated, or even half-reclining, the turning of the bodies under the elaborate folds of their costumes makes them seem anything but static. In fact they seem so capable of arising that it is hard to imagine them "shelved" up under the gable. Perhaps the sculptors who achieved such lifelike figures also found this incongruous; at any rate, the sculptural decoration of later buildings tended to be placed in areas where they would seem less boxed in.

This Athenian style, so harmonious in both feeling and form, did not long survive the defeat of Athens by Sparta in the Peloponnesian War. Building and sculpture continued in the same tradition for another three centuries, but without the subtleties of the Classic age whose achievements we have just discussed. The post-Classical, or "Hellenistic," style spread far and wide around the Mediterranean shores, but in a sense it turned backward to the scenes of violent action so popular in the Archaic period. Scopas, who was very probably the sculptor of the frieze showing *Greeks Battling Amazons* (fig. 54), was familiar with the figure style of the Parthenon, but he has rejected its rhythmic harmony, its flow of action from one figure to the next. His sweeping, impulsive gestures require a lot of elbow room. Judged by Parthenon standards, the composition lacks

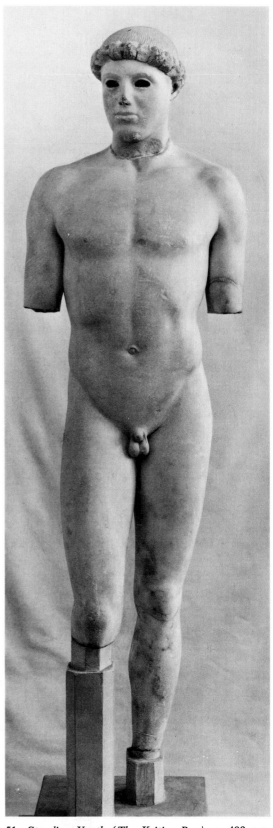

51. *Standing Youth (The Kritios Boy).* c. 480 B.C. Marble, height 34″. Acropolis Museum, Athens

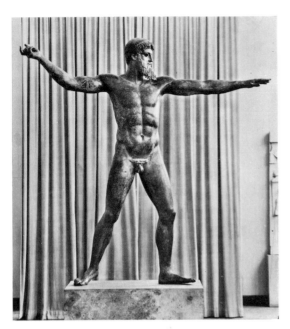

52. *Poseidon (Zeus?)*. c. 460–450 B.C. Bronze, height 6' 10". National Museum, Athens

continuity, but it makes up for this in bold innovation (note, for instance, the Amazon seated backward on her horse) as well as heightened expressiveness.

In many more instances than we would like, the most famous works of Greek sculptors of the fifth and fourth centuries B.C. have been lost and only copies are preserved. There is some doubt whether the famous *Hermes* by Praxiteles (fig. 55) is the original, or a copy made some three centuries later. If it is the latter, however, it is a very skillful copy, for it fits perfectly the qualities for which Praxiteles was admired in his own day. The lithe grace, the play of gentle curves, the feeling of complete relaxation (enhanced by an outside support for the figure to lean against) are quite the opposite of Scopas' energetic innovations. The Hermes' bland, lyrical charm is further enhanced by the caressing treatment of the surfaces: the meltingly soft, "veiled" features, and even the hair, which has been left comparatively rough

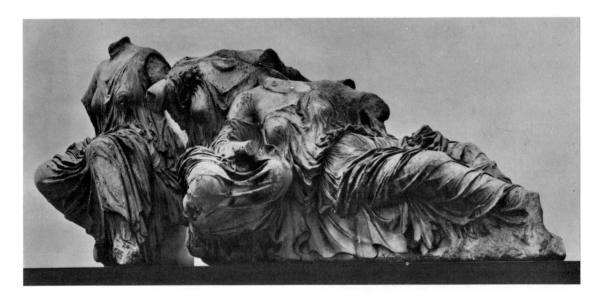

53. PHIDIAS (?). *Three Goddesses*, from east pediment of the Parthenon. c. 438–432 B.C. Marble, over life-size. British Museum, London

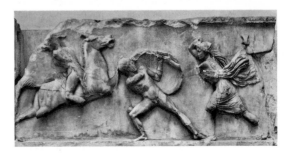

54. SCOPAS (?). *Greeks Battling Amazons*, portion of east frieze, Mausoleum, Halicarnassus. 359–351 B.C. Marble, height 35". British Museum, London

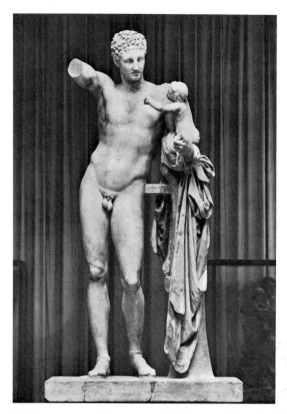

55. PRAXITELES. *Hermes.* c. 330–320 B.C. (or copy?). Marble, height 7′ 1″. Museum, Olympia

for contrast, all share a misty, silken quality. Here, for the first time, there is an attempt to modify the stony look of a statue by giving to it this illusion of an enveloping atmosphere.

HELLENISTIC STYLE

Compared to Classical statues, the sculpture of the Hellenistic age often shows a more pronounced realism and expressiveness, as well as a greater experimentation with drapery and pose, which often exhibits considerable torsion. These changes should be seen as a valid, even necessary, attempt to extend the subject matter and dynamic range of art in accordance with a new temperament and outlook. The difference in psychology is suggested by the *Portrait Head* in colorplate 7. The serenity of Praxiteles' *Hermes* is replaced by a troubled look. And for the first time, this is an individual portrait, something that was inconceivable in earlier Greek

art, which emphasized ideal, heroic types. The features have an unprecedented softness as well, and must have been modeled in wax, not clay, before being cast.

This more human conception is found again in the *Dying Gaul* (fig. 56), an ancient copy in marble of one of a number of bronze statues dedicated by Attalus I of Pergamum (a city in northwestern Asia Minor) shortly before 200 B.C. to commemorate his victory over invading Gauls. The sculptor who conceived the figure must have known the Gauls well, for he has carefully rendered the ethnic type in the facial structure and in the bristly shock of hair. The torque around the neck is another characteristically Celtic feature. Otherwise, however, the Gaul shares the heroic nudity of Greek warriors, such as those on the Aegina pediments (see fig. 50); and if his agony seems infinitely more realistic in comparison, it still has considerable dignity and *pathos*. Clearly, the Gauls were not considered unworthy foes. "They knew how to die, barbarians though they were," is the thought conveyed by the statue. Yet we also sense something else, an animal quality that had never before been part of the Greek image of man. Death, as we witness it here, is a very concrete physical process: no longer able to move his legs, the Gaul puts all his waning strength into his arms, as if to prevent some tremendous invisible weight from crushing him against the ground.

Even more dramatic is the *Nike of Samothrace* (fig. 57)—the goddess of victory who has just alighted on the prow of a warship; her great wings spread wide, she is still partially airborne by the powerful headwind against which she advances. The invisible force of onrushing air becomes a tangible reality that balances the forward thrust of the figure and shapes every fold of the wonderfully animated drapery. This is not merely a relationship between the statue and the space which the sculptor imagined it inhabiting, but an interdependence more active than we have seen before. Nor shall we see it again for a long time. The *Nike* deserves her fame as the greatest work of Hellenistic sculpture.

By the end of the second century B.C. much of Greek sculpture was made on commission for Rome, the rising power of the Mediter-

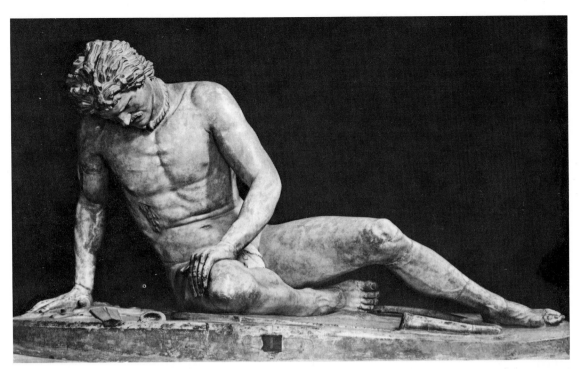

56. *Dying Gaul.* Roman copy after a bronze original of c. 230–220 B.C. from Pergamum. Marble, lifesize. Capitoline Museum, Rome

57. *Nike of Samothrace.* c. 200–190 B.C. Marble, height 8′. The Louvre, Paris

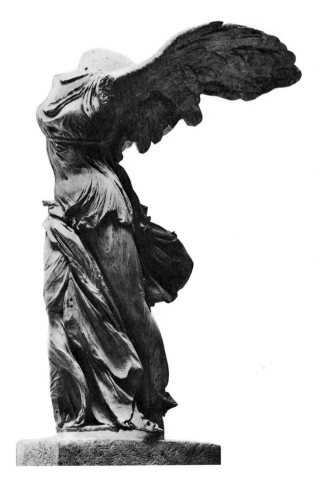

ranean region and a center of great admiration for Greek learning and art. The *Laocoön* group (fig. 58) was dug up in Rome in 1506, and it made a tremendous impression upon Italian sculptors of that time, notably Michelangelo. It is all violence and strain: the bodies writhe in the serpents' grip; the faces cannot hold back a show of agonizing pain; the muscles bulge; the elaborate detail and the high finish trumpet the sculptor's remarkable technical skill. As theater, the *Laocoön* could hardly be improved upon, but such a work was possible only when the prime impulse of Greek art was coming to an end. Today we tend to find the group (which had special significance for the founding of Rome) somewhat contrived and its pathos and dynamism self-conscious, even though the straining figures remind us of the dramatic style invented by Scopas.

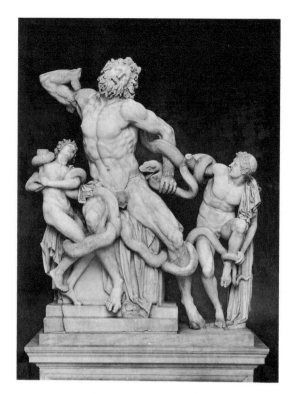

58. AGESANDER, ATHENODORUS and POLYDORUS of Rhodes. *The Laocoön Group*. c. 125 B.C. Marble, height 7'. Vatican Museums, Rome

Etruscan Art

Strange as it may seem, we know very little about the early Etruscans. According to the Classical Greek historian Herodotus, they left their homeland of Lydia in Asia Minor and settled in the area between Florence and Rome which is known to this day as Tuscany. But they may be a people whose presence on Italian soil goes back much further. If so, the sudden flowering of Etruscan civilization from about 700 B.C. onward could have resulted from a fusion of this prehistoric Italian stock with small but powerful groups of seafaring invaders from Lydia during the course of the eighth century. Interestingly enough, such a hypothesis comes very close to the legendary origin of Rome.

Be that as it may, the Italian peninsula did not emerge into the light of history until fairly late. The Bronze Age came to an end there only in the eighth century B.C., about the time the earliest Greeks began to settle along the southern shores of Italy and in Sicily. The seventh and sixth centuries B.C. saw the Etruscans at the height of their power, which extended over a large part of central Italy. But the Etruscans, like the Greeks, never formed a unified nation, and they were never more than a loose federation of city-states. By the end of the third century B.C., all of them lost their independence to Rome, which had once been ruled by Etruscan kings.

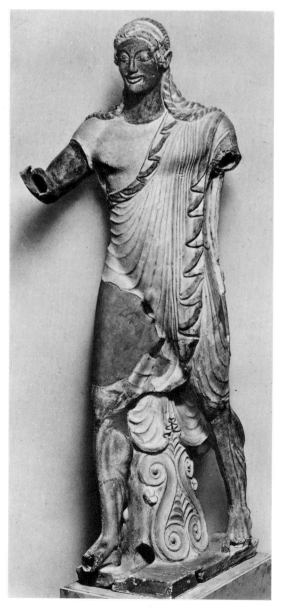

59. *Apollo*, from Veii. c. 510 B.C. Terra-cotta, height 69". Museo Nazionale di Villa Giulia, Rome

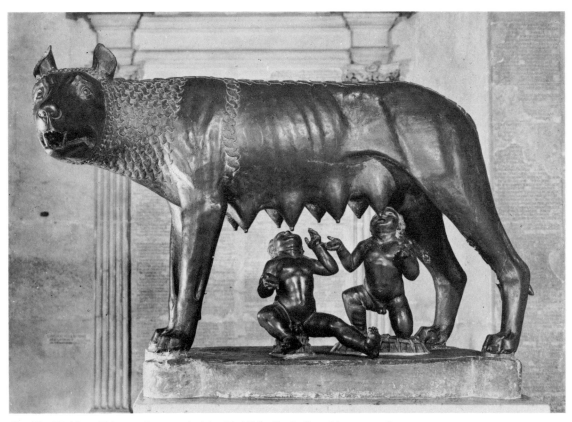

60. *She-Wolf.* c. 500 B.C. Bronze, height 33 1/2". Capitoline Museums, Rome

SCULPTURE

Etruscan civilization thus coincides largely with the Archaic age in Greece. It was during this period, especially toward the end of the sixth and in the early years of the fifth century, that Etruscan art showed its greatest vigor under the Greek Archaic influence. But Etruscan artists did not simply imitate their Hellenic models, as we can see from the *Apollo* in figure 59, which has long been acknowledged as the masterpiece of Etruscan Archaic sculpture. His massive body, completely revealed beneath the ornamental striations of the drapery; the sinewy, muscular legs; the hurried, purposeful stride—all these betray an expressive power that has no counterpart in freestanding Greek statues of the same date. Likewise, the famous bronze statue of a she-wolf (fig. 60; the two infants are Renaissance additions) has the same awesome quality in the wonderful ferocity of her expression and the latent physical power of the body and legs.

TOMBS

We would know practically nothing about the Etruscans at first hand were it not for their elaborate tombs, which the Romans did not molest when they destroyed or rebuilt Etruscan cities and which, therefore, have survived intact until modern times. Those of the late sixth and early fifth century B.C. are filled with a wonderfully rich array of murals. Since nothing of the sort has survived in Greek territory, they are uniquely important, not only as an Etruscan achievement, but also as a possible reflection of Greek wall painting. Colorplate 8 shows a pair of ecstatic dancers from a tomb in Tuscany; the passionate energy of their movements strikes us as characteristically Etruscan rather than Greek in spirit. Of particular interest is the transparent garment of the woman, which lets the body shine through. In Greece, this differentiation appears only a few years earlier, in the final phase of Archaic vase painting. The contrasting body color of the two figures continues a practice introduced by the Egyptians more than two thousand years before (colorplate 1). But how are we to understand the purpose of such murals? We do not know precisely what ideas the Archaic Etruscans held about man's afterlife. They may have regarded the tomb as an abode not only for the body but for the soul as well. Or perhaps they believed that by filling the tomb with dancing and similar pleasures they could induce the soul to remain in the city of the dead and, therefore, not haunt the realm of the living.

During the fifth century, the Etruscan view of the hereafter must have gradually become a good deal more complex and less festive. We notice the change immediately in a cinerary container carved soon after 400 B.C. (fig. 61). A woman sits at the foot of the couch, but she is not the wife of the young man. Her wings indicate that she is the demon of death, and the scroll in her left hand records the fate of the deceased. The young man is pointing to it as if to say, "Behold, my time has come." The thoughtful, melancholy air of the two figures may be due to some extent to the influence of Classical Greek art which pervades the style of our group. At the same time, however, a new mood of uncertainty and regret is reflected: man's destiny is in the hands of inexorable supernatural forces; death is the great divide rather than a continuation, albeit on a different plane, of life on earth. In later tombs, the demons of death gain an ever more fearful aspect; other, more terrifying demons enter the scene, often battling against benevolent spirits for possession of the soul of the deceased.

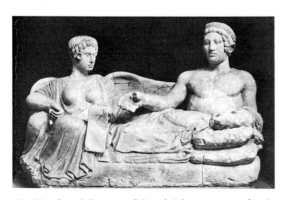

61. *Youth and Demon of Death* (cinerary container). Early 4th century B.C. Stone (pietra fetida), length 47″. Archaeological Museum, Florence

Roman Art

Among the civilizations of the ancient world, that of the Romans is far more accessible to us than any other, for they have left us a vast literary legacy which permits us to trace their history with a wealth of detail that never ceases to amaze us. Yet, paradoxically, few questions are more difficult to answer than "What is Roman art?" The Roman genius, so clearly recognizable in every other sphere of human activity, becomes oddly elusive when we ask whether there was a characteristic Roman style in the fine arts. Why is this so? The most obvious reason is the great admiration the Romans had for Greek art of every period and variety. Not only did they import Greek originals of earlier date by the thousands and have them copied in even greater numbers, their own productions were clearly based on Greek sources, and many of their artists were of Greek origin. But beyond the different subject matter, the fact is that, as a whole, the art produced under Roman auspices does look distinctly different from Greek art and has positive non-Greek qualities expressing different intentions. Thus we must not insist on evaluating Roman art by the standards of Greek art, next to which it might superficially appear to be a final decadent phase. The Roman Empire was an extraordinarily open, cosmopolitan society which absorbed national or regional traits into a common all-Roman pattern that was homogeneous and diverse at the same time. The "Roman-ness" of Roman art must be found in this complex pattern, rather than in a single and consistent quality of form.

ARCHITECTURE

If the autonomy of Roman sculpture and painting has been questioned, Roman architecture is a creative feat of such magnitude as to remove all such doubts. From the very start, moreover, its growth reflected a specifically Roman way of public and private life. The Romans learned a great deal about the art of building from the Etruscans. According to Roman writers the Etruscans were masters of architectural engineering, of town planning, and of surveying. Little remains above-ground of either Etruscan or early Roman architecture; but such works as we have, plus the information collected from recent excavations, show that the Etruscans were, in fact, highly skilled builders. This heritage was to be of particular importance as Rome expanded her rule around the shores of the Mediterranean and toward the less populous north of Europe, building new cities to serve as seats of colonial government. Perhaps the single most important feature of this Etruscan legacy was the true arch, made up of wedge-shaped sections that lock each other securely in place. Not that the Etruscans invented the arch: its use dates as far back as the Egyptians, but they, and the Greeks after them, seem to have considered it merely a useful "beast of burden," and not a form beautiful enough to be used for its own sake. In ancient Mesopotamia it occasionally appeared above-ground in city gates; but it remained for the Etruscans to make it fully "respectable."

The growth of the capital city of Rome is hardly thinkable without the arch and the vaulting systems derived from it: the barrel vault—a half-cylinder; the groin vault, which consists of two barrel vaults intersecting each other at right angles; and the dome.

Greek buildings, however beautiful, were seldom built with a view to accommodating a large crowd of people under one roof; even the temples were considered houses of the gods rather than gathering places for worshipers. Whether the Romans became "indoor people" because of the climate, which seems to have been colder in those days than it is now (forests populated with wolves and bears extended nearly the whole length of the peninsula), or whether the sheer numbers of the population necessitated large administrative buildings and gathering places, the fact remains that Greek models, although much admired, no longer sufficed. Small buildings, such as a votive chapel or a family mausoleum, might imitate a Greek example; but when it came to supplying the citizenry with everything it needed, from water to entertainment on a vast scale, radical new forms had to be invented, and cheaper materials and quicker methods had to be used.

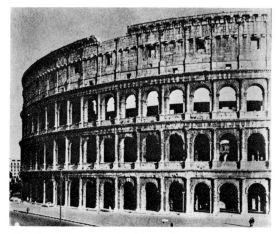

62. The Colosseum. 72–80 A.D. Rome

COLOSSEUM

The Colosseum (fig. 62), a huge amphitheater in the center of the old city which could seat 50,000 spectators, is still one of the largest buildings anywhere. Its core is made of a kind of concrete, and it is a masterpiece of engineering and efficient planning, with miles of vaulted corridors to ensure the smooth flow of traffic to and from the arena. It utilizes the arch, the barrel vault, and the groin vault. The exterior, dignified and monumental, reflects the subdivisions of the interior, but clothed and accentuated in cut stone. There is a fine balance between the vertical and horizontal members that frame the endless series of arches. Reverence for Greek architecture is still visible in the use of half-columns and pilasters reflecting the Greek orders; structurally these have become ghosts—the building would still stand if one stripped them off—but aesthetically they are important, for through them the enormous façade becomes related to the human scale.

PANTHEON

The same innovations in engineering and materials permitted the Romans to create vast covered spaces as well. The best preserved of these is the Pantheon (figs. 63, 64), a very large, round temple dedicated, as the name indicates, to all the gods. The portico, originally preceded by a colonnaded forecourt which blocked off the view we now have of the circular walls, looks like the standard en-

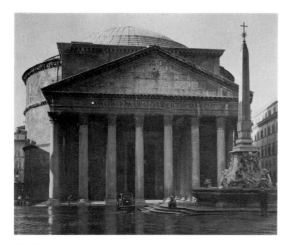

63. The Pantheon. 118–125 A.D. Rome

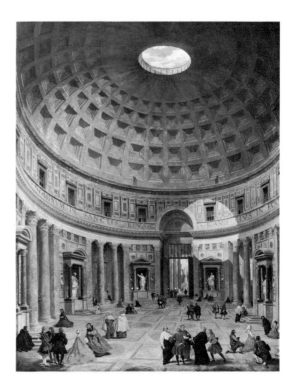

64. *The Interior of the Pantheon*, painting by G.P. PANNINI, c. 1750 A.D. National Gallery of Art, Washington, D.C. (Kress Collection)

trance to a typical Roman temple (derived from Greek temple façades, with columns in the Corinthian order). All the more breathtaking, then, is the sight as we step through the tall portals, and the great domed space opens before us with dramatic suddenness. That the architects did not have an easy time with the engineering problems of supporting the huge hemisphere of a dome may be deduced from the heavy plainness of the exterior wall. Nothing on the outside gives any hint of the airiness and elegance of the interior; photographs fail to capture it, and even the painting (fig. 64) that we use to illustrate it does not do it justice. The height from the floor to the opening of the dome (called the "oculus," or "eye") is exactly that of the diameter of the dome's base, thus giving the proportions perfect balance. The weight of the dome is concentrated on the eight solid sections of wall; between them, with graceful columns in front, niches are daringly hollowed out of the massive concrete, and these, while not connected with each other, give the effect of an open space behind the supports, making us feel that the walls are less thick and the dome much lighter than is actually the case. The multicolored

marble panels and paving stones are still essentially as they were, but originally the dome was gilded to resemble "the golden dome of heaven."

Though it is hard to believe, the essential features of this awesome temple were already described (although on a smaller scale) a century earlier, by the architect Vitruvius—for the construction of steam rooms in public baths. In these, the oculus could be covered by a bronze lid that opened and closed to regulate the temperature. Nor was the Pantheon the only huge building to be derived from similar designs for the popular bath establishments that were placed conveniently in various quarters of the city. The Basilica of Constantine (fig. 65), probably the largest roofed space in ancient Rome, is another example. Only one side, consisting of three enormous barrel vaults, still stands today; the center tract (or "nave") was covered by three groin vaults and rose a good deal higher. Since a groin vault is like a canopy, with all the weight concentrated at the four corners, the wall surfaces in between could be pierced by windows, called a "clerestory." Like the niches in the Pantheon, these helped break up the ponderous mass and made it seem less overpowering. We meet echoes of this vaulting system in many later buildings, from churches to railway stations.

PALACE OF DIOCLETIAN

In discussing the new forms based on arched, vaulted, and domed construction, we have noted the Roman architect's continued allegiance to the Classic Greek orders. While he no longer relied on them in the structural sense, he remained faithful to their spirit; column, architrave, and pediment might be merely superimposed on a vaulted brick-and-concrete core, but their shape, as well as their relationship to each other, still followed the original grammar of the orders. Only

when the Roman Empire was in decline did this reverential attitude give way to unorthodox ideas, as in the Palace of Diocletian (fig. 66) on the coast of present-day Yugoslavia. Here the architrave between the two center columns is curved, echoing the arch of the doorway below; on the left we see an even more revolutionary device—a series of arches resting directly on columns. Thus, on the eve of the victory of Christianity, the marriage of arch and column was finally legitimate. Their union, indispensable for the subsequent development of architecture, seems so natural that we wonder why it was ever opposed.

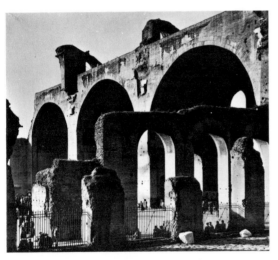

65. The Basilica of Constantine. c. 310–320 A.D. Rome

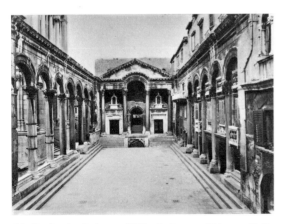

66. Peristyle, Palace of Diocletian. c. 300 A.D. Split, Yugoslavia

SCULPTURE

Although there is no doubt that the Romans created a bold new architecture, the question of whether they had anything original to give to the field of sculpture has been hotly disputed, and for quite understandable reasons. A taste for opulent decoration, both exterior and interior, led to wholesale importation of Greek statuary, when it could be obtained, or mass copying of Greek—sometimes even of Egyptian—models. There are entire categories of Roman sculpture which deserve to be called "deactivated echoes" of Greek creations, emptied of their former meaning and reduced to the status of refined works of craftsmanship. On the other hand, certain kinds of sculpture had serious and important functions in ancient Rome, and it is these that continue the living sculptural tradition. Portraiture and narrative reliefs are the two aspects of sculpture most conspicuously rooted in the real needs of Roman society.

PORTRAIT BUST

The portrait bust in figure 67, dating from the beginning of the Republican era, is probably one of the first permanent embodiments of a much older tradition that we know about from literary sources. When the head of a prominent family died, a wax image was made of his face, and these images were preserved by subsequent generations and carried in the funeral processions of the family. Start-

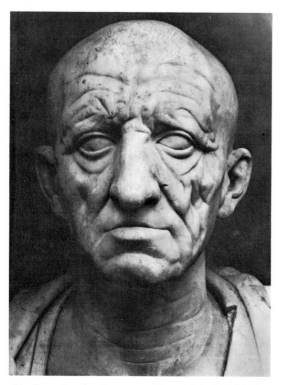

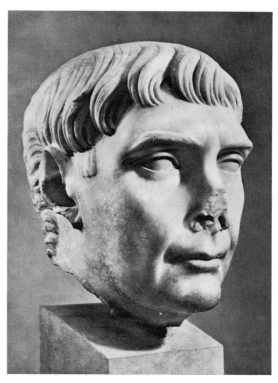

67. *Portrait of a Roman.* c. 80 B.C. Marble, lifesize. Palazzo Torlonia, Rome

68. *Trajan.* c. 100 A.D. Marble, lifesize. Museum, Ostia

ing as ancestor worship back in prehistoric times, this custom became a convenient way to demonstrate the importance and continuity of a family—a habit that continues practically unbroken to our own day in the displaying of family portraits. Wax, however, is a very impermanent material, and for some reason—perhaps a crisis of self-confidence—it became important to the patrician families of Rome in the first century B.C. to put these ancestor likenesses into a more enduring substance (fig. 67). What differentiates this head from a late, expressive example of Greek sculpture? Can we say that it has any new, specifically Roman qualities? At first it may strike us as nothing more than the detailed record of a facial topography, sparing neither wrinkle nor wart. Yet the sculptor has exercised a choice among which wrinkles to emphasize and which features (the jutting lower lip, for instance) to make a little larger-than-life. The face emerges as a specifically Roman personality—stern, rugged, iron-willed. It is a "father image" of frightening

authority; one that can be imagined to rule not merely a family, but a colony or even an empire. Perhaps this fierce expression is inherited from Etruscan sculpture (see fig. 60); by contrast, even the agonized face of Laocoön (fig. 58) seems lacking in forcefulness.

It may seem surprising that when the Republic, under Julius Caesar, gave way to the Empire (shortly after this head was made), portraiture lost something of its intense individuality. Depictions of the emperors such as Trajan (fig. 68), while not lacking in recognizable personality, set the fashion for more heroic and idealized likenesses. One suspects that as the Empire became larger, more complex, and more difficult to govern, the rulers were at great pains to give the impression that they were cool in the face of any and all crises. The Greeks had given the world unsurpassable forms in conjuring up gods in the guise of men; the Romans now went back to these forms to elevate the images of men to the level of gods.

A portrait which succeeds in being human, in the noblest sense of the word, is the equestrian statue of the Emperor Marcus Aurelius (fig. 69); as a learned man, his ideal was the ancient Greek "philosopher-king" who ruled by wisdom rather than by force and cunning. Astride his noble horse (which seems, like its master, to control itself rather than to be controlled) he gazes downward at the passerby with an expression of lofty calm tinged with compassion.

Alas, the turmoil of the overextended Empire had already begun. Soon the ruler's supernatural power, whether conferred by divinity or wisdom, no longer seemed plausible, especially (as was increasingly the case in the third century A.D.) if he had been merely a successful general who attained the throne by overthrowing his predecessor. Such a man was Philippus the Arab (fig. 70), who reigned for five brief years, 244 to 249 A.D. What a portrait it is! For realism, feature by feature, it is as stark as the Republican bust; but here the aim is expressive rather than documentary: all the dark passions of the human mind—fear, suspicion, cruelty—stand revealed with a directness that is almost unbelievable. The face of Philippus mirrors all the violence of the time, yet in a strange way it moves us to pity: there is a psychological nakedness about it that recalls a brute creature, cornered and doomed. Clearly, the agony of the Roman world was not only physical but spiritual.

So, too, were the glories of its dwindling years; or so they must have seemed to Constantine the Great (fig. 71), reorganizer of the Roman State and the first Christian emperor. No mere bust, this head is one of several remaining fragments of a colossal statue (the head alone is over eight feet tall) that once stood in Constantine's gigantic basilica (see fig. 65). In this head everything is so out of proportion to the scale of ordinary men that we feel crushed by its immensity. The impression of being in the presence of some unimaginable power was deliberate, we may be sure, for it is reinforced by the massive, immobile features out of which the huge, radiant eyes stare with hyp-

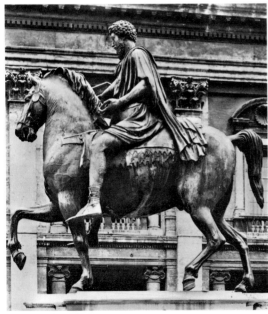

above: 69. *Equestrian Statue of Marcus Aurelius.* 161–180 A.D. Bronze, over lifesize. Piazza del Campidoglio, Rome

right: 70. *Philippus the Arab.* 244–249 A.D. Marble, lifesize. Vatican Museums, Rome

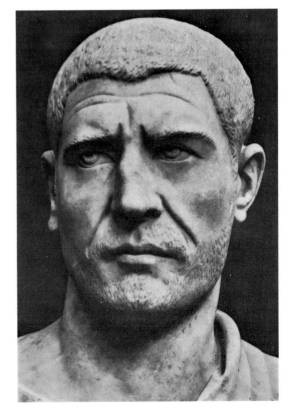

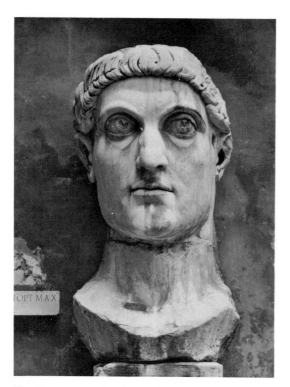

71. *Constantine the Great*. Early 4th century A.D. Marble, height 8'. Capitoline Museums, Rome

notic intensity. All in all, it tells us less about the way Constantine looked than about his view of himself and his exalted office.

NARRATIVE RELIEF

It is almost with the feeling of ridding ourselves of an insupportable weight that we turn back to the early years of the Empire to investigate another type of sculpture, the narrative relief. The *Ara Pacis* (or "peace altar"; fig. 72) was built for Augustus Caesar, nephew and successor to Julius Caesar, and the first to call himself "Emperor." For him, the present and the future looked bright and promising, and he could confidently celebrate Peace, by name and also in spirit. There is a self-assurance about this procession which does not depend upon superhuman intervention, and a kind of joyful dignity that puts us in mind of the Parthenon sculptures when Athens, too, serene in her leadership, could not foresee the bad times so soon to come. But there are also many things that differentiate the *Ara Pacis* from its Greek predecessor. The procession here is a specific occasion rather than a timeless and

impersonal event. The participants, at least so far as they belong to the imperial family, were meant to be identifiable portraits, including the children dressed in miniature togas, still too young to understand the solemnity of the occasion (note the little boy tugging at the mantle of the young man in front of him, while turning toward an older child who smilingly tells him to behave). In addition to taking delight in humanizing details, the sculptor has made advances in composition: there is a greater concern to give an illusion of spatial depth than in Greek reliefs, so that some of the faces farthest removed from us (such as the veiled young woman facing the youth whose cloak is being pulled) seem to be embedded in the stone of the background.

This illusion of depth given to a shallow space reached its most complete development in the large narrative panels that formed part of a triumphal arch erected in 81 A.D. to commemorate the victories of the Emperor Titus. One of them (fig. 73) shows the victory procession held after Rome conquered Jerusalem; the booty displayed includes the seven-branched candlestick from the Temple, and other sacred objects. The forward surge of the crowd is rendered with striking success: on the right, the procession turns away from us and disappears through an arch placed obliquely to the background plane so that only the nearer half actually emerges from it—a radical but effective device for conveying the depth of the scene.

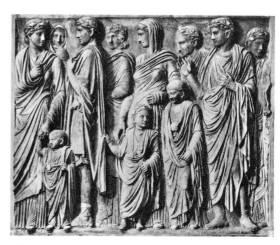

72. *Imperial Procession*, portion of frieze on the *Ara Pacis*. 13–9 B.C. Marble, height 63". Rome

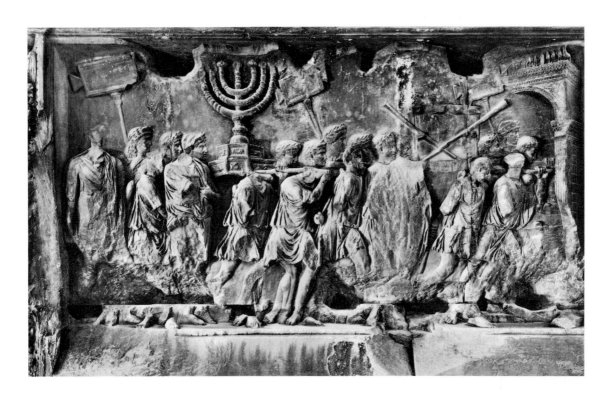

73. *Spoils from the Temple in Jerusalem*, relief in passageway, Arch of Titus. 81 A.D. Marble, height 7' 10". Rome

PAINTING

Because so little of either Greek or Roman painting has been preserved (and that little is largely thanks to the eruption of Mount Vesuvius in 79 A.D., which buried buildings erected during a relatively short time span—leaving us to wonder what sort of painting came before and after this catastrophe), what does remain is apt to strike the beholder as the most exciting, as well as the most baffling, aspect of art under Roman rule. That famous Greek designs were copied and even Greek painters imported, nobody will dispute; but the number of cases where a direct link can be surely established with the older art is small indeed. We have already seen one example, *The Battle of Issus* mosaic (fig. 41).

FRESCOES

Movable pictures on panels, such as we think of nowadays when we speak of "paintings," were not frequent in Roman times; or if they were, they have all disappeared like the wax ancestor images. Rather, pictures were in-

cluded in the fresco decorations (on more permanent surfaces of hard plaster) of interiors, such as the Ixion Room (fig. 74) from the House of the Vettii in Pompeii. While these scenes hardly ever give the impression of straightforward copies after Hellenistic originals, they often have the somewhat disjointed character of compilations of motifs from various sources. The panels are set into an elaborate ensemble combining imitation (painted) marble paneling and fantastic architectural vistas seen through make-believe windows. The illusion of surface textures and distant views has an extraordinary degree of three-dimensional reality; but as soon as we try to analyze the relationship of the various parts to each other, we find ourselves confused, and we quickly realize that the Roman painters had no systematic grasp of spatial depth.

When landscapes take the place of architectural features, however, the virtues of the Roman painter's approach outweigh its limitations. This is strikingly demonstrated by the *Odyssey Landscapes*, a continuous stretch of panorama subdivided into eight large panels, each illustrating an episode from the adventures of Odysseus (Ulysses). One of them has been recently cleaned, and is

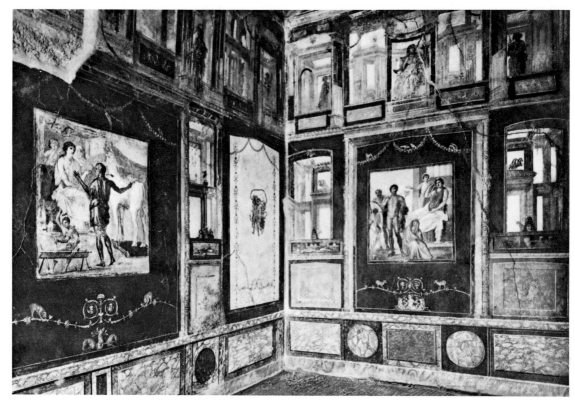

74. The Ixion Room, House of the Vettii, Pompeii. 63–79 A.D.

reproduced here in colorplate 9 to show the original brilliance of the tones. The airy, bluish atmosphere creates a wonderful impression of light-filled space that envelops and binds together all the forms within this warm Mediterranean fairyland, where the human figures seem to play no more than an incidental role. Only upon further reflection do we realize how frail the illusion of coherence is: if we were to try mapping this landscape, we would find it as ambiguous as the architectural decorations discussed above.

VILLA OF THE MYSTERIES

There exists one monument whose sweeping grandeur of design and coherence of style are unique in Roman painting: the great frieze in one of the rooms in the Villa of the Mysteries just outside Pompeii (fig. 75). The artist who created the frieze in the Villa of the Mysteries has placed his figures on a narrow ledge of green against a regular pattern of red panels separated by strips of black, a kind of running stage on which they

enact their strange and solemn ritual. Who are they, and what is the meaning of the cycle? Many details remain puzzling, but the program as a whole represents various aspects of the Dionysiac Mysteries, a semisecret cult of very ancient origin that had been brought to Italy from Greece. Many of the poses and gestures are taken from the repertory of Classical Greek art, yet they lack the studied and self-conscious quality we call Classicism. An artist of exceptional greatness of vision has filled these forms with new life. Whatever his relation to the famous masters of Greek painting whose works are lost to us forever, he was their legitimate heir.

PORTRAITS

It would be strange indeed if portraiture, which forms such an outstanding part of Rome's particular contribution to the history of sculpture, had not also existed in painting. Pliny, the Roman historian, mentions it as an established custom in Republican Rome. A few miniatures, painted on glass, have survived from the third century

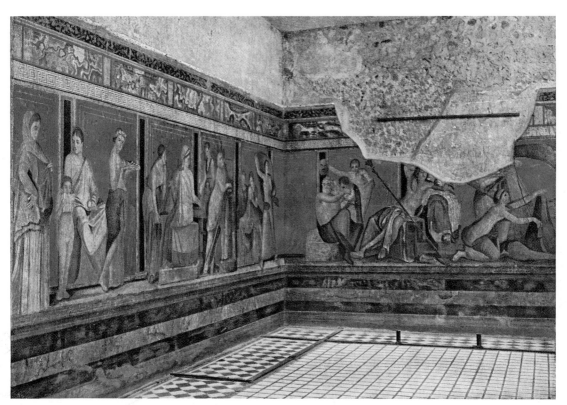

75. ROMAN. *Scenes of a Dionysiac Mystery Cult.* Wall painting. c. 50 B.C. Villa of the Mysteries, Pompeii

A.D., or later; however, if we want to get some idea of what Roman painted portraits looked like we must turn, strangely enough, to Egypt. There, in the region of Faiyum, a strange Romanized version of the traditional Egyptian mummy-case has been found. Before Egypt came under Roman dominion, the heads of mummy-cases were provided with conventionalized masks, modeled in stone, wood, or plaster; now these were replaced by painted portraits of the dead, executed in lifelike colors on wooden panels. The very fine portrait of a boy (colorplate 10) is as sparkling and natural as anyone might wish, exhibiting a sureness of touch on the part of the artist that has rarely been surpassed. As in the sculptured busts, the artist has magnified and stressed certain features: the eyes, for example, are exaggeratedly large. But in this happy instance the stylization has not been made with the intention of overawing us (as in the case of Constantine's hypnotic stare, fig. 71), but only to recall the attractive personality of a beloved child.

SYNOPTIC TABLE I

	POLITICAL HISTORY	RELIGION, LITERATURE	SCIENCE, TECHNOLOGY
B.C. 4000	Sumerians settle in lower Mesopotamia	Pictographic writing Sumer, c. 3500	Wheeled carts, Sumer, c. 3500–3000 Sailboats in Egypt after c. 3500 Use of potter's wheel, Sumer, c. 3250
3000	Old Kingdom, Egypt (Dynasties I–VI), c. 3100–2155 Early dynastic period, Sumer, c. 3000–2340; Akkadian kings 2340–2180	Hieroglyphic writing, Egypt, c. 3000 Divine kingship of the Pharaoh	First bronze tools and weapons, Sumer
2000	Middle Kingdom, Egypt, 2134–1785 Hammurabi founds Babylonian dynasty c. 1760 Flowering of Minoan civilization c. 1700–1500 New Kingdom, Egypt, c. 1500–1162	Code of Hammurabi c. 1760 Monotheism of Akhenaten (r. 1372–1358)	Bronze tools and weapons in Egypt Canal from Nile to Red Sea Mathematics and astronomy flourish in Babylon under Hammurabi Hyksos bring horses and wheeled vehicles to Egypt c. 1725
1000	Jerusalem capital of Palestine; rule of David; of Solomon (died 926) Assyrian Empire c. 1000–612 Persians conquer Babylon 539; Egypt 525 Romans revolt against Etruscans, set up republic 509	Hebrews accept monotheism Phoenicians develop alphabetic writing c. 1000; Greeks adopt it c. 800 First Olympic games 776 Homer (fl. c. 750–700) Zoroaster (born c. 660)	Coinage invented in Lydia (Asia Minor) c. 700–650; soon adopted by Greeks Pythagoras (fl. c. 520)
500	Persian Wars 499–478 Periclean Age in Athens c. 460–429 Peloponnesian War 431–404 Alexander the Great (356–323) occupies Egypt 333; defeats Persia 331; conquers Near East	Sophocles (496–406) Socrates (died 399) Plato (427–347); founds Academy 386 Aristotle (384–322)	Travels of Herodotus c. 460–440 Hippocrates (born 469) Euclid (fl. c. 300–280) Archimedes (287–212)
200	Rome dominates Asia Minor and Egypt 147		Invention of paper, China
100	Julius Caesar dictator of Rome 49–44 Emperor Augustus (r. 27 B.C.–A.D. 14)	Golden Age of Roman literature: Cicero, Catullus, Vergil, Horace, Ovid	Vitruvius' *De architectura*
A.D. 1	Jewish rebellion against Rome 66–70; destruction of Jerusalem	Crucifixion of Jesus c. 30 Paul (died c. 65) spreads Christianity to Asia Minor and Greece	Pliny the Elder, *Natural History*
100	Emperor Marcus Aurelius (r. 161–180)		Ptolemy, astronomer (died 160)
200	Shapur I (r. 242–272), Sassanian king of Persia Emperor Diocletian stops decline of Rome	Persecution of Christians in Roman Empire 250–302	

NOTE:

Figure numbers of black-and-white illustrations are in (italics). Colorplate numbers are in **(bold face)**.
Duration of papacy or reign is indicated by the abbreviation r.

ARCHITECTURE	SCULPTURE	PAINTING	
"White Temple" and ziggurat, Uruk (*24*)			B.C. 4000
Step pyramid and funerary district of Zoser, Saqqara by Imhotep (*15*) Pyramids at Giza (*17*)	Statues from Abu temple, Tell Asmar (*26*) *Rahotep and Nofret* (**1**) Harp and offering stand from Ur (*27*, **3**)		3000
Stonehenge (*6, 7*) Palace of Minos, Knossos, Crete (*33*) Temple of Amen, Luxor (*21*)	Stele of Hammurabi (*28*) Vaphio Cups (*36*) Heads of Akhenaten and Nofretete (*22, 23*) Coffin of Tutankhamen (**2**) Lion Gate, Mycenae (*34*)	"*Toreador Fresco*" (**4**) Girl Dancers and Musicians, Thebes (*20*)	2000
Ishtar Gate, Babylon (*30*) "Basilica," Paestum (*44*)	Reliefs from Nimrud (*29*) *Kouros* (*47*) "*Hera*" from Samos (*48*) *Kore* from Chios (**6**)	Dipylon vase (*37*) Black-figured amphora by Psiax (*38*, **5**)	1000
Palace, Persepolis (*31*) "Temple of Poseidon," Paestum (*44*) Parthenon, Acropolis, Athens (*45*) Temple of Athena Nike, Acropolis, Athens (*46*)	East pediment from Aegina (*50*) *The Kritios Boy* (*51*) Sculpture from the Parthenon (*53*) *Hermes* by Praxiteles (*55*) *Dying Gaul* (*56*)	*Lapith and Centaur*, red-figured ware (*39*) Tomb of Lionesses, Tarquinia (**8**) White-ground ware (*40*) *The Battle of Issus* (*41*)	500
	Nike of Samothrace (*57*) Laocoön Group (*58*)		200
	Portrait head from Delos (**7**)		100
Colosseum, Rome (*62*)	Arch of Titus (*73*)		A.D. 1
Pantheon, Rome (*63*)	Equestrian statue of Marcus Aurelius (*69*)	*Portrait of a Boy*, Faiyum (**10**)	100
			200

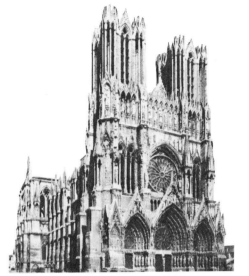

The Middle
Ages

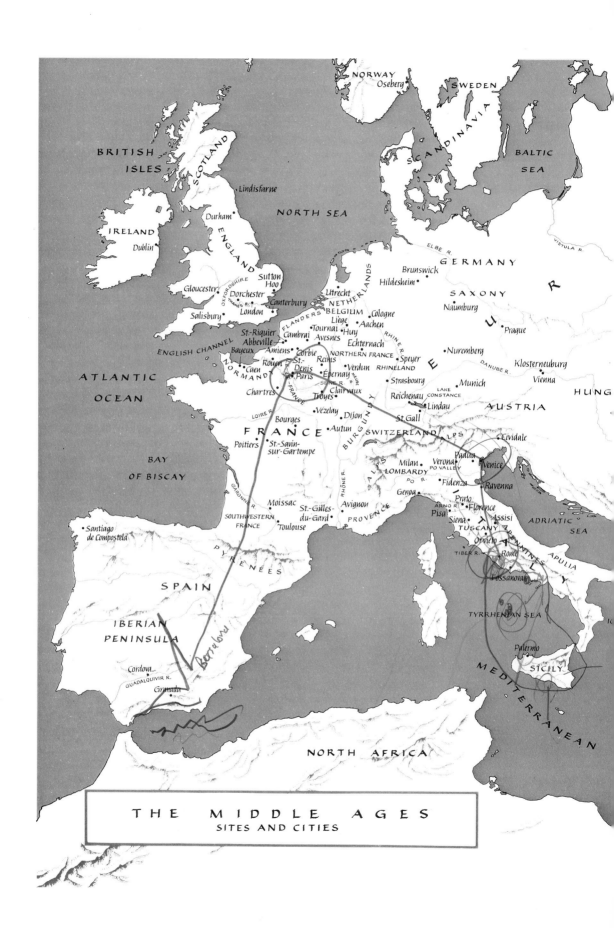

NORWAY
Oseberg
SWEDEN

SCANDINAVIA

BALTIC SEA

BRITISH ISLES

SCOTLAND

Lindisfarne

NORTH SEA

GERMANY

IRELAND
Dublin

ENGLAND

Durham

Brunswick
Hildesheim

SAXONY
Naumburg

E
U
R

VISTULA R.

Gloucester
OXFORDSHIRE
Dorchester
Salisbury
THAMES R.
London

Sutton Hoo

Canterbury

Utrecht

NETHERLANDS

BELGIUM
Liège

Cologne
Aachen

Prague

ELBE R.

St-Riquier
Abbeville
Bayeux
Caen

NORMANDY

Amiens
Cambrai
Corbie

FLANDERS
Tournai
Huy

Echternach

Nuremberg

RHINE R.

Klosterneuburg

DANUBE R.

Vienna

ATLANTIC OCEAN

ENGLISH CHANNEL

Rouen
St.-Denis
Paris

Reims

NORTHERN FRANCE

Speyer

Verdun
RHINELAND

Épernay

Strasbourg

Munich

LAKE CONSTANCE

HUNG

Chartres

SEINE R.

Troyes

Clairvaux

Reichenau

Lindau

AUSTRIA

FRANCE

LOIRE R.

Vézelay

Dijon

St Gall

SWITZERLAND

ALPS

Cividale

BAY OF BISCAY

Poitiers

Bourges

St-Savin-sur-Gartempe

Autun

BURGUNDY

ALPS

Padua
Verona
Venice

Milan
PO VALLEY

GARONNE R.

Moissac

SOUTHWESTERN FRANCE

St-Gilles-du-Gard

Toulouse

Avignon

PROVENCE

RHÔNE R.

LOMBARDY

Genoa

PO R.

Fidenza

Ravenna

Santiago de Compostela

Prato

ARNO R.

Florence

Pisa

Siena

Assisi

TUSCANY

APENNINES

ADRIATIC SEA

PYRENEES

Orvieto

TIBER R.

Rome

ITALY

APULIA

SPAIN

IBERIAN PENINSULA

Barcelona

Fossanova

Cordova
GUADALQUIVIR R.
Granada

MEDITERRANEAN

TYRRHENIAN SEA

Palermo

SICILY

NORTH AFRICA

THE MIDDLE AGES
SITES AND CITIES

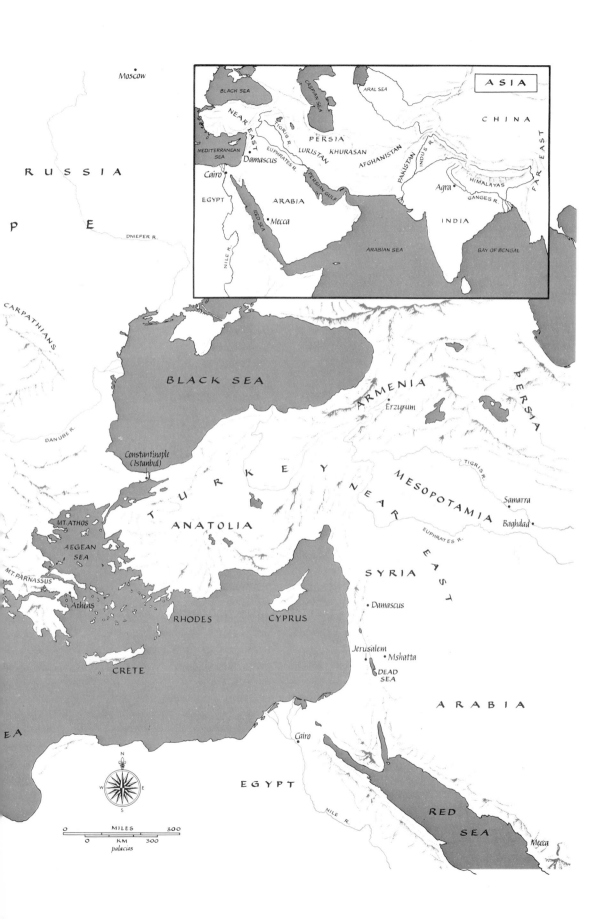

ASIA

BLACK SEA
CASPIAN SEA
ARAL SEA
CHINA
NEAR EAST
PERSIA
TIGRIS R.
MEDITERRANEAN SEA
Damascus
EUPHRATES R.
LURISTAN
KHURASAN
AFGHANISTAN
PAKISTAN
INDUS R.
HIMALAYAS
FAR EAST
Cairo
PERSIAN GULF
Agra
GANGES R.
EGYPT
ARABIA
RED SEA
Mecca
NILE R.
INDIA
ARABIAN SEA
BAY OF BENGAL

Moscow

RUSSIA

CARPATHIANS

P

E

DNIEPER R.

BLACK SEA

DANUBE R.

Constantinople
(Istanbul)

ARMENIA

Erzurum

PERSIA

TIGRIS R.

MESOPOTAMIA

Samarra

Baghdad

EUPHRATES R.

T   U   R   K   E   Y

N E A R   E A S T

MT. ATHOS

AEGEAN
SEA

ANATOLIA

SYRIA

MT. PARNASSUS

Athens

RHODES

CYPRUS

Damascus

Jerusalem

Mshatta

DEAD
SEA

EA

CRETE

ARABIA

Cairo

EGYPT

N
W   E
S

NILE R.

RED
SEA

Mecca

MILES
0   300
0   KM   300
palacias

Early Christian and Byzantine Art

In 323 A.D. Constantine the Great made a fateful decision, the consequences of which are still felt today: he resolved to move the capital of the Roman Empire to the Greek town of Byzantium, which henceforth was to be known as Constantinople. In taking this step, the Emperor acknowledged the growing strategic and economic importance of the eastern provinces (a development that had been going on for some time). The new capital also symbolized the new Christian basis of the Roman State, since it was in the heart of the most thoroughly Christianized region of the Empire. Constantine could hardly foresee that shifting the seat of imperial power would result in splitting the realm, yet within a hundred years the division had become an accomplished fact, even though the emperors at Constantinople did not relinquish their claim to the western provinces. The latter, ruled by western Roman emperors, soon fell prey to invading Germanic tribes—Visigoths, Vandals, Ostrogoths, Lombards. By the end of the sixth century the last trace of centralized authority had disappeared. The Eastern, or Byzantine, Empire, in contrast, survived these onslaughts, and under Justinian (527–565 A.D.) reached new power and stability. With the rise of Islam a hundred years later, the African and Near Eastern parts of the Empire were overrun by conquering Arab armies; in the eleventh century, the Turks occupied a large part of Asia Minor, while the last Byzantine possessions in the West (in southern Italy) fell to the Normans. Yet the Empire, with its domain reduced to the Balkans and Greece, held on till 1453, when the Turks finally conquered Constantinople itself.

The division of the Roman Empire soon led to a religious split as well. At the time of Constantine, the bishop of Rome, deriving his authority from St. Peter, was the acknowledged head—the Pope—of the Christian Church. His claim, however, soon came to be disputed; differences in doctrine began to develop, and eventually the division of Christendom into a Western, or Catholic, Church and an Eastern, or Orthodox, Church became all but final. The differences between them went very deep: Roman Catholicism maintained its independence from imperial or any other state authority, and became an international institution reflecting its character as the Universal Church. The Orthodox Church, in contrast, was based on the union of spiritual and secular authority in the person of the emperor. It was thus dependent on the State, exacting a double allegiance from the faithful but sharing the vicissitudes of political power. We will recognize this pattern as the Christian adaptation of a very ancient heritage, the divine kingship of Egypt and Mesopotamia; if the Byzantine emperors, unlike their pagan predecessors, could no longer claim the status of gods, they kept a unique and equally exalted role by placing themselves at the head of the Church as well as the State. Nor did the tradition die with the fall of Constantinople. The tsars of Russia claimed the mantle of the Byzantine emperors, and Moscow became "the third Rome"; thus the Russian Orthodox Church was closely tied to the State, as was its Byzantine parent body.

It is the religious even more than the political separation of East and West that makes it impossible to discuss the development of Christian art in the Roman Empire under a single heading. "Early Christian" does not, strictly speaking, define a style; it refers, rather, to any work of art produced by or for Christians during the time prior to the splitting off of the Orthodox Church—roughly, the first five centuries of our era. "Byzantine art," on the other hand, designates not only the art of the Eastern Roman Empire, but a specific quality of style as well. Since this style grew out of certain tendencies that can be traced back to the time of Constantine, or even earlier, there is no sharp dividing line between the two until after the reign of Justinian, who was not only conversant with artistic currents in both parts of the Empire, but almost succeeded in reuniting them politically as well. Soon after him, however, Celtic and Germanic peoples fell heir to the civilization of late Roman antiquity, of which Early Christian art had been a part, and transformed it into that of the Middle Ages. The East experienced no such break; there, late antiquity lived on, although the Greek and Oriental elements came increasingly to the fore at the expense of the Roman heritage. As a consequence Byzantine civilization never experienced the flux and fusion that created medieval art: "The Byzantines may have been senile," as one historian has observed, "but they remained Greeks to the end."

EARLY CHRISTIAN ART

Before Constantine, Rome was not yet the official center of the faith; older and larger Christian communities existed in the great cities of North Africa and the Near East, such as Alexandria and Antioch, and they probably had artistic traditions of their own of which we seem to catch glimpses in the mainstream of art at a much later date. Actually, our knowledge of them is scanty in the extreme; for the first three centuries of the Christian Era we have little to go on when trying to trace the evolution of art in the service of the new religion. The only exception is the painting found on the walls of catacombs, the underground passages in which the Roman Christians buried their dead.

PAINTING

If the dearth of material from the more flourishing Eastern Christian colonies makes it difficult to judge these pictures in a larger context, they nevertheless tell us a good deal about the spirit of the communities that sponsored them. The burial rite and safeguarding of the tomb were of vital concern to the early Christians, whose faith rested on the hope of eternal life in paradise. The imagery of the catacombs, as can be seen in the painted ceiling in figure 76, clearly expresses this otherworldly outlook, although the forms are in essence still those of pre-Christian Roman painting. Thus we recognize the compartmental divisions as a late and highly simplified echo of the illusionistic architectural schemes in Pompeian painting; and the modeling of the figures, too, though debased in the hands of an artist of very modest ability, also betrays its descent from the same Roman idiom. But the catacomb painter has used this traditional vocabulary to convey a new, symbolic content, so that

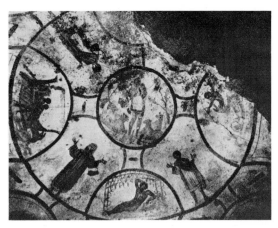

76. Painted Ceiling, Catacomb of SS. Pietro e Marcellino. Early 4th century A.D. Rome

to him the original meaning of the forms was a matter of small interest. Even the geometric framework shares in the new task: the great circle suggests the Dome of Heaven, much as the ceiling of the Pantheon was meant to (see p. 64), but here the oculus in the center has been connected to the outer ring by four pairs of brackets, a simple device that forms the cross, the main symbol of the faith. In the central medallion we see a youthful shepherd with a sheep on his shoulders. It is true that this form, too, can be traced as far back as the Archaic Greeks, but here it has become an emblem of Christ the Saviour—the Good Shepherd. The semicircular compartments contain episodes from the legend of Jonah: on the left he is cast from the ship; on the right he emerges from the whale; and at the bottom, safe again on dry land, he meditates upon the mercy of the Lord. This Old Testament miracle enjoyed immense favor in Early Christian art, as proof of the Lord's power to rescue the faithful from the jaws of death. The standing figures, their hands raised in a traditional gesture of prayer, represent members of the Church pleading for divine help.

ARCHITECTURE

With the triumph of Christianity as the State religion under Constantine, an almost overnight blossoming of church architecture began in both halves of the Empire. Before that, congregations had not been able to meet in public, and services were held inconspicuously in the houses of the wealthier members; now impressive new buildings were wanted, for all to see. Early Christian basilicas cannot be wholly explained in terms of their pagan Roman predecessors, although the latter served well as a point of departure, combining the spacious interior necessary for the performing of Christian ritual before a congregation, with imperial associations that proclaimed the exalted status of the new State religion. But, in addition, the Christian basilica had to serve as the Sacred House of God; for this reason the entrances, which in Roman secular basilicas had been along the flanks so as to provide many doorways for people bent on a variety of errands, were concentrated at one end in Christian basilicas, usually facing west. At the opposite end of the long nave was the altar, the focus of the ritual. This emphasis on the longitudinal axis is easily seen in the exterior view of Sant' Apollinare in Classe (fig. 77), a church built on Italian soil during the reign of Justinian. If we except the round bell tower (campanile) on the left, we will find many features to remind us of pagan buildings that have already been discussed: the transverse porch (narthex) which welcomes the visitor to the sacred building, while at the same time obscuring the view of what is to come, is a small-scale, simplified reminder of the portico of the Pantheon (see p. 64). The row of arches, echoed by a matching arcade in the interior, is a form of architecture pioneered under the Emperor Diocletian (p. 65); the clerestory too had appeared earlier in Roman basilicas (p. 64); and turning to the interior view (colorplate 11), we may note that the eastern end, where the altar was placed, is set off from the rest by a frame reminiscent of a Roman triumphal arch (see the one in fig. 73). What is new here, in addition to the more expert use of the column-plus-arch construction, is the astonishing contrast between the plain brick exterior which (unlike Classical temples) is merely an envelope for the interior, and the explosion of vivid colors and rich materials within. Having left the workaday world outside, we find ourselves in a shimmering realm of light, where precious marble and glittering mosaics evoke the unearthly splendor of the Kingdom of God.

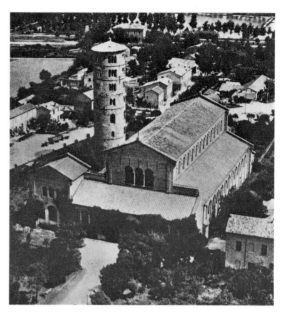

77. Sant' Apollinare in Classe, Ravenna; aerial view. 533–549 A.D. (for interior, see colorplate 11)

MOSAICS

Although the Romans, too, produced mosaics (see fig. 41), they had used marble tesserae having a limited range of colors; these mosaics were more suitable for floor decoration than for walls. The vast and intricate wall mosaics in Early Christian churches really have no precedent, either for expanse or for technique. Instead of stone, the tesserae are made of glass; they are brilliant in color but not rich in tonal gradations, so that they do not lend themselves readily to the copying of painted pictures. Instead, with each tiny square of glass also acting as a reflector, a glittering, screenlike effect is produced, as intangible as it is dazzling. If the exterior of Sant' Apollinare strikes us as unassuming— even antimonumental in comparison with previous building styles—the interior is its perfect complement. Here the dematerialization of the construction is turned to positive account, for the purpose of achieving an "illusion of unreality."

To transport the spectator into realms of glory was not, of course, the only purpose of these mosaics. Like the modest beginnings of Christian art (see fig. 76) they contain symbols of the faith (in Sant' Apollinare the Cross is plainly visible in the oculus that opens onto the starry skies, where Christ presides in the highest realm of heaven, flanked by the symbols of the four Evangelists). Sometimes they also illustrate scenes from both Old and New Testaments, thus serving the unlettered as picture-Bibles. *The Parting of Lot and Abraham* (fig. 78) is one frame of a long series that decorates the nave of Santa Maria Maggiore in Rome. The idea of making such a series, as well as some of the pictorial devices that the mosaicist has used (such as the "grape clusters" of heads arising behind the relatively few bodies that occupy the foreground), may well have been derived from Roman narrative reliefs. But the Early Christian artist was not constrained by the need to make a specific event look real; these Biblical scenes, whose stories were known already to most of the faithful, were not so much illustrations as symbolic events with a didactic purpose. Here, for instance, Abraham and his clan (the left-hand group) are about to go one way—the way of righteousness; while Lot and his family, about to exit right, are departing for Sodom, toward depravity and ruin.

ILLUSTRATED MANUSCRIPTS

For church use and the devotions of the learned there were also illustrated Bibles. The development of the book format itself is not entirely clear: we know that the Egyptians made a paperlike substance, only more brittle, out of papyrus reeds. Their "books," however, were scrolls to be unrolled as one read. This was not an ideal surface for painted illustration, for the repeated bending and unbending of each section would tend to make the paint flake off. The Torah, the sacred scriptures that are read at each service in synagogues, still preserves this ancient format. Not until late Hellenistic times did a better substance become available: parchment, or vellum (thin, bleached animal hide). It was strong enough to be creased without breaking, and thus made possible the kind of bound book (technically known as a codex) that we still have today. Between the first and the fourth centuries A.D. this gradually replaced the scroll, greatly enhancing the range of painted illustration (or, as it is called, illumination) so that it became the small-scale counterpart of murals, mosaics,

or panel pictures. One of the oldest illustrated manuscripts preserved, the *Vatican Vergil*, probably executed in Italy about the time of the Sta. Maria Maggiore mosaics, reflects this tradition, although the quality of the miniatures is far from inspired (fig. 79); the picture, separated from the rest of the page by a heavy frame, has the effect of a window,

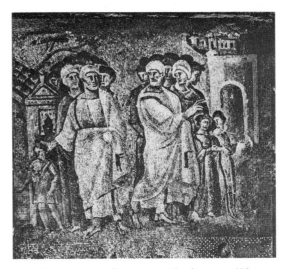

78. *The Parting of Lot and Abraham.* c. 430 A.D. Mosaic. Sta. Maria Maggiore, Rome

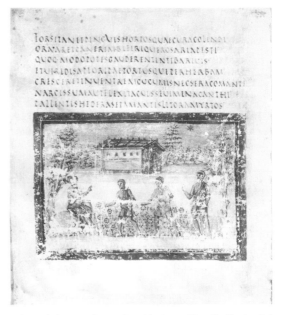

79. Miniature from the *Vatican Vergil.* Early 5th century A.D. Vatican Library, Rome

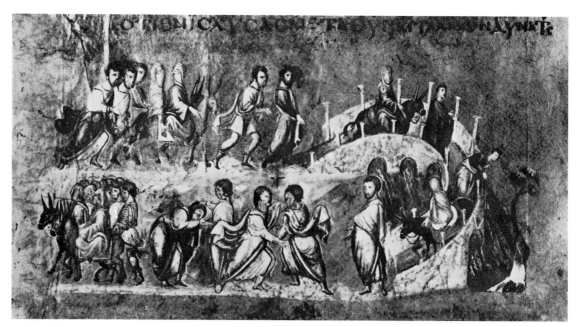

above: 80. *Jacob Wrestling with the Angel*, from the
Vienna Genesis. Early 6th century A.D. Manuscript
illumination. National Library, Vienna

below: 81. Sarcophagus of Junius Bassus. c. 359 A.D.
Marble, 3′ 10 1/2″ × 8′. Vatican Grottoes, Rome

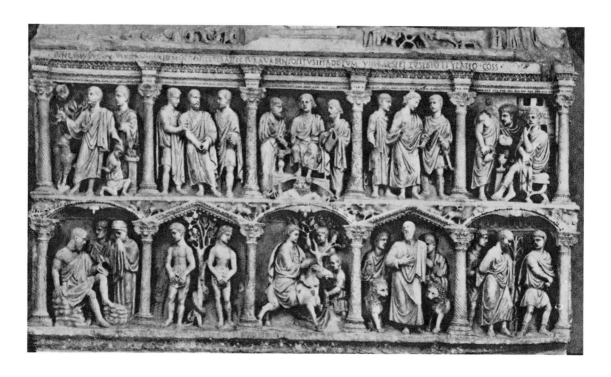

and in the landscape we find remnants of
deep space, perspective, and the play of light
and shade.

Jacob Wrestling with the Angel (fig. 80)
comes from one of the oldest extant examples
of an Old Testament book, though it must

have been preceded by others which have
been lost. This codex, called the *Vienna
Genesis*, was written in silver (now turned
black) on purple-tinted vellum, and adorned
with brilliantly colored miniatures; the effect
is not unlike that produced by the mosaics

which we have discussed. The scene itself does not show a single event, but a whole sequence strung out along a U-shaped path, so that progression in space also becomes progression in time. This method, known as continuous narration, has a long ancestry going back to sculptured relief, and possibly to scroll books. Here it permits the painter to pack a maximum of content into the area of the page at his disposal, and the continuous episodes were probably meant to be "read," like the letters themselves, rather than taken in all at once as a composition.

SCULPTURE

Compared to painting and architecture, sculpture played a secondary role in Early Christian times. The Old Testament prohibition of "graven images" was thought to apply with particular force to large cult statues—the idols worshiped in pagan temples. To avoid the taint of idolatry, religious sculpture had to develop from the very start in an antimonumental direction. Shallow carving, small-scale forms, and lacelike surface decoration came to be its characteristics. The earliest works of sculpture that can be called "Christian" are sarcophagi made for the wealthier members of the congregation; beginning about the middle of the third century, they differ from pagan sarcophagi not so much in form as in the subject matter of the decoration. At first this consisted of a somewhat limited repertory, such as we have seen in the catacomb painting: the Good Shepherd, Jonah, etc. (fig. 76). The sarcophagus of Junius Bassus (fig. 81) of a century later, however, shows a richly expanded repertory of subjects, taken from both the Old and the New Testaments, reflecting the new, out-in-the-open position of Christianity now that it was the established State religion and no longer had to allude to the faith in cryptic, symbolic terms. Junius Bassus himself was a Roman prefect.

To those of us who are familiar with only the later formulation of Christ's image, as a bearded and often suffering man, it may at first be difficult to recognize Him at all in these scenes. Youthful and serene, He sits enthroned in heaven (a bearded figure, personifying the sky, holds up His throne) between Saints Peter and Paul (center panel,

upper row); nor does He seem troubled in the scene of Christ before Pontius Pilate, which occupies the two panels directly to the right, where He stands, scroll in hand, like some young philosopher expounding his views. This aspect of Christ is in keeping with the Christian thought of the period that stressed His divinity and His power to redeem us from death, rather than the torments that He took on when He became flesh. This dignified conception lent itself well to a revival of some Classical features of composition and figures. Such revivals occurred quite frequently during the two centuries after Christianity had become the official religion: paganism still had many adherents (Junius Bassus himself was converted only shortly before his death) who may have fostered such revivals; there were important leaders of the Church who favored a reconciliation of Christianity with the Classical heritage; and the imperial courts, both East and West, always remained aware of their institutional links with pre-Christian times. Whatever the reasons, we must be glad that the Roman Empire in transition preserved, and thus helped transmit, a treasury of forms and an ideal of beauty that might have been irretrievably lost.

PANELS AND RELIEFS

All this holds true particularly for a class of objects whose artistic importance far exceeds their physical size: the ivory panels and other small-scale reliefs in precious materials. Designed for private ownership and meant to be enjoyed at close range, they often mirror a collector's taste, a refined aesthetic sensibility not found among the large, official enterprises sponsored by Church or State. Such a piece is an ivory leaf (fig. 82) done soon after 500 in the Eastern Roman Empire. It shows a Classicism that has become an eloquent vehicle of Christian content. The majestic archangel is clearly a descendant of the winged Victories of Graeco-Roman art, down to the richly articulated drapery. Yet the power he heralds is not of this world; nor does he inhabit an earthly space. The architectural niche against which he appears has lost all three-dimensional reality; its relationship to him is purely symbolic and ornamental, so that he seems

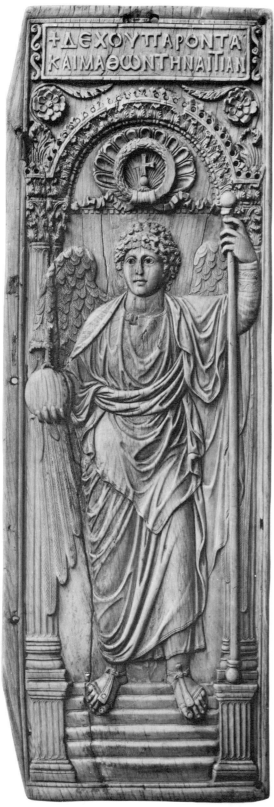

82. *The Archangel Michael* (leaf of a diptych). Early 6th century A.D. Ivory, 17 × 5 1/2". British Museum, London

to hover rather than to stand (notice the position of the feet on the steps). It is this disembodied quality, conveyed through Classically harmonious forms, that gives him so compelling a presence.

BYZANTINE ART

The reign of Emperor Justinian marks the point at which the ascendancy of the Eastern Roman Empire over the Western became complete and final. Justinian himself was an art patron on a scale unmatched since Constantine's day; the works he sponsored or promoted have an imperial grandeur that fully justifies the acclaim of those who have termed his era a Golden Age. They also display an inner coherence of style which links them more strongly with the future of Byzantine art than with the art of the preceding centuries.

ARCHITECTURE

Ironically enough, the richest array of the monuments of this period survives today not in Constantinople, but in the city of Ravenna, in Italy. We have already seen one of them, Sant' Apollinare in Classe, which—better than examples of Early Christian buildings in Rome itself—preserves unaltered the appearance, structural features, and decoration of the earliest churches. But there was another type of structure that had entered the tradition of Christian architecture in Constantinian times: round or polygonal buildings crowned with a dome. They had been developed, we will recall, as part of the elaborate Roman baths; the design of the Pantheon was derived from that source (see page 64). Similar structures had been built to serve as monumental tombs, or mausoleums, by the pagan emperors. In the fourth century, this type of building is given a Christian meaning in the baptisteries (where the bath becomes a sacred rite) and funerary chapels linked with basilican churches. San Vitale, the most important church built in Ravenna under Justinian, has an octagonal plan with a domed central core (fig. 83). In this central-plan church we find only the merest remnants of the longitudinal axis of the Early Christian basilica. The complexity of the exterior is matched by the spatial richness of the interior (fig. 84), with its lavish decoration. Remembering Sant' Apollinare in Classe, built at the same time on a straightforward basilican plan, we are particularly struck by the alien character of San Vitale, which is derived mainly from Constantinople, where domed churches were preferred. How did it happen that the East favored a type of church building (as distinct from baptisteries and mausoleums) so radically different from the basilica and—from the Western point of view—so ill-adapted to Christian ritual? After all, had not the design of the basilica been backed by the authority of Constantine himself? Many different reasons have been suggested—practical, religious, political. All of them may be relevant, yet, if the truth be told, they fall short of a really persuasive explanation. In any event, from the time of Justinian domed, central-plan churches were to dominate the world of Orthodox Christianity as thoroughly as the basilican plan dominated the architecture of the medieval West.

Among the surviving buildings of Justinian's reign, by far the greatest is Hagia Sophia (The Church of the Holy Wisdom) in Constantinople (figs. 85, 86). Built in 532–537, it was so famous in its day that even the names of the architects, Anthemius of Tralles and Isidorus of Miletus, have come down to us. The design of Hagia Sophia presents a unique combination of elements; it has the longitudinal axis of an Early Christian basilica, but the central feature of the nave is a square compartment crowned by a huge dome abutted at either end by half-domes, so that the effect is that of a huge oval. The weight of the dome is carried on four enormous arches; the walls below the arches have no supporting function at all. The transition from the square formed by the four arches to the circular rim of the dome is made by spherical triangles, called pendentives. This device permits the construction of taller, lighter, and more economical domes than the older method (as seen in the Pantheon). We do not know the ancestry of this useful scheme, but Hagia Sophia is the first example of its use on a monumental scale, and it was epoch-making; henceforth it was to be a basic feature of Byzantine architecture and, somewhat later, of Western architecture as well. The plan and size will recall the Basilica of Constantine (fig. 65), the greatest monument associated with the ruler for whom Justinian had a particular admiration. Hagia Sophia thus unites East and West, past and future, in a single overpowering synthesis. Once we are within, all sense of weight dis-

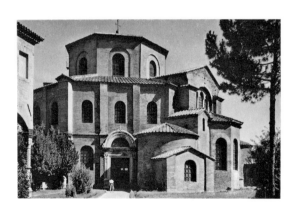

above: 83. San Vitale, Ravenna. 526–547 A.D.

right: 84. Interior (view from the apse), San Vitale, Ravenna

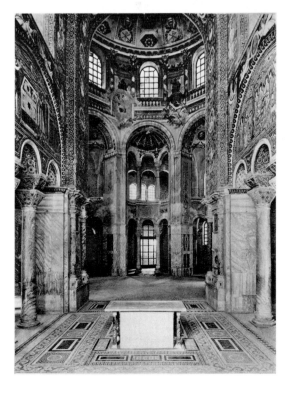

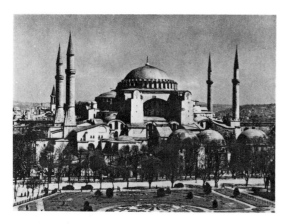

above: 85. ANTHEMIUS OF TRALLES and ISIDORUS OF
MILETUS. Hagia Sophia. 532–537 A.D. Istanbul

right: 86. Interior, Hagia Sophia. Istanbul

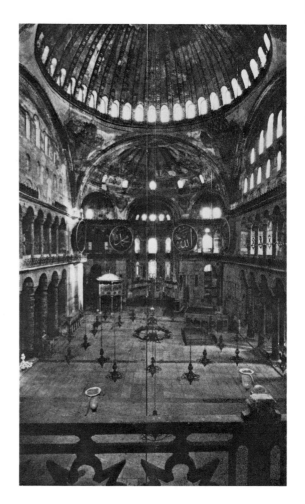

appears, as if the material, solid aspects of
the structure had been banished to the outside; nothing remains but an expanding space
that inflates, like so many sails, the apsidal
recesses, the pendentives, and the dome itself.
The golden glitter of the mosaics (covered
over when the Muslims captured the city,
and now only partially restored) must have
completed the "illusion of unreality."

MOSAICS

It is only fitting that we use, as an example
of the mosaics of Justinian's reign, the portrait of the Emperor himself, surrounded by
his courtiers, which has survived in good condition in the church of San Vitale in Ravenna (fig. 87). The design, and perhaps the
workmen, must have come directly from the
imperial workshop. Here we find a new ideal
of human beauty: extraordinarily tall, slim
figures, with tiny feet, small, almond-shaped
faces dominated by large eyes, and bodies
that seem capable only of ceremonial gestures
and the display of magnificent costumes.
Every hint of movement or change is carefully excluded—the dimensions of time and
of earthly space have given way to an eternal
present amid the golden translucency of
heaven, and the solemn frontal images seem
to present a celestial rather than a secular
court. This union of spiritual and political
authority accurately reflects the "divine
kingship" of Byzantine emperors.

PAINTING AND SCULPTURE

The development of Byzantine painting and
sculpture after the age of Justinian was dis-
rupted by the Iconoclastic Controversy,
which began with an imperial edict of 726
prohibiting religious images and raged for
more than a hundred years. The roots of the
conflict went very deep: on the plane of
theology they involved the basic issue of the
relationship of the human and divine in the
person of Christ, while socially and politically
they reflected a power struggle between State
and Church. The edict did succeed in reducing the production of sacred images greatly,
but failed to wipe it out altogether, so that
there was a fairly rapid recovery after the
victory of the iconophiles in 843. Iconoclasm
seems to have brought about a renewed interest in secular art, which was not affected by
the ban. This may help to explain the astonishing reappearance of Late Classical motifs
in the art of the Second Golden Age.

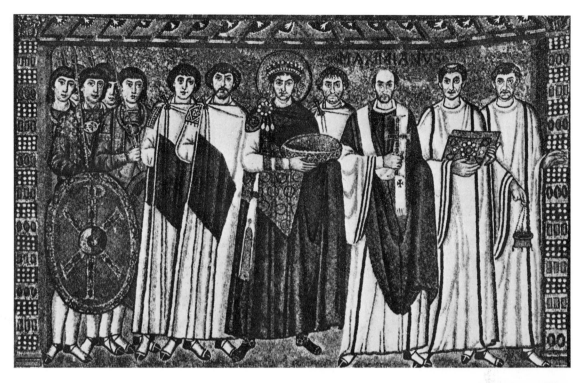

87. *Justinian and Attendants*. c. 547 A.D. Mosaic. San Vitale, Ravenna

88. *The Crucifixion*. 11th century. Mosaic. Monastery Church, Daphnē, Greece

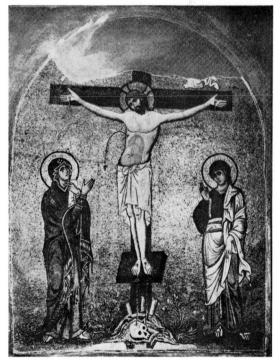

The finest works of the Second Golden Age show a Classicism that has been harmoniously merged with the spiritualized ideal of human beauty we encountered in the art of Justinian's reign. Among these, the *Crucifixion* mosaic at Daphnē (fig. 88) enjoys special fame. The statuesque, dignified figures seem extraordinarily organic and graceful compared to those of the Justinian mosaic at San Vitale (fig. 87). The most important aspect of their Classical heritage, however, is emotional rather than physical; it is the gentle *pathos* conveyed by their gestures and facial expressions, a restrained and noble suffering of the kind we first met in Greek art of the fifth century B.C. (see pages 54–55). Early Christian art had been devoid of this quality. Its view of Christ stressed the Saviour's divine wisdom and power, rather than His sacrificial death. In the *Crucifixion* we no longer find the youthful, heroic Christ that we saw in the Junius Bassus reliefs; the tilt of the head, the sagging lines of the body, the expression of suffering make a powerful appeal to the beholder's emotions. This compassionate quality was perhaps the greatest achievement of later Byzantine art, even though its full possibilities were to be explored not in Byzantium, but in the medieval West.

Not that it disappeared completely from Byzantine art, but after centuries of repetition, exquisiteness of craftsmanship rather than expressive impact came to dominate such images. The *Madonna Enthroned* (colorplate 12) is a work of this kind. The graceful drapery folds, the tender expression are still there; but they have become strangely abstract. The throne (which looks rather like a miniature Colosseum) has lost any semblance of solid three-dimensionality, as have the bodies—although some modeling is still to be found in the faces. With gold as a background, and gold used to pick out all the highlights of the forms, the effect cannot be called either flat or spatial; rather, it is transparent, for everywhere the golden background shines through, as though the picture were lit from behind. Panels such as ours, called icons (sacred images), should be viewed as the aesthetic offspring of mosaics, rather than as the descendants of the Classical panel painting tradition from which they spring (see fig. 74).

The Earlier Middle Ages in the West

When we think of the great civilizations of our past, we tend to do so in terms of visible monuments that have come to symbolize the distinctive character of each: the pyramids of Egypt, for example; or the Parthenon of Athens; the Colosseum of Rome—all were made famous (or infamous) by the part that they played in the history of their times. In such a review, the Middle Ages would undoubtedly be represented by a Gothic cathedral; we have many to choose from, but whichever one we pick, it will be well north of the Alps, although in territory that formerly belonged to the Roman Empire. And if we were to spill a bucket of water in front of that cathedral, the water would eventually make its way to the English Channel, rather than to the Mediterranean. This is the most important single fact about the Middle Ages: the center of gravity of European civilization had shifted to what had been the northern boundaries of the Roman world. The Mediterranean, for so many centuries the great highway of commercial and cultural exchange for all the lands along its shores, had become a barrier, a border zone.

In the preceding chapter we became familiar with some of the events that paved the way for the shift: the removal of the imperial capital to Constantinople; the growing split between the Catholic and Orthodox faiths; and the decay of the Western half of the Roman Empire under the impact of invasions by Germanic tribes. Yet these tribes, once they had settled-down in their new land, accepted the framework of late Roman, Christian civilization: the new states they founded, on the northern coast of Africa, and in Spain, Gaul, and northern Italy, were Mediterranean-oriented, provincial states along the borders of the Byzantine Empire, subject to the pull of its greater military, commercial, and cultural power. The reconquest of the lost Western provinces remained a serious political goal of Byzantine emperors until the middle of the seventh century. This possibility ceased to exist when a completely unforeseen new force made itself felt in the East: the Arabs, under the banner of Islam, were overrunning the Near Eastern and African provinces of Byzantium. By 732, within a century after the death of Muhammad, they had occupied North Africa as well as most of Spain, and threatened to add southwestern France to their conquests.

It would be difficult to exaggerate the impact upon the Christian world of the lightninglike advance of Islam. With more than enough to do to keep this new force at bay in its own backyard, the Byzantine Empire lost its bases in the western Mediterranean. Left exposed and unprotected, Western Europe was forced to develop its own resources, political, economic, and spiritual. The Church of Rome broke its last ties with the East and turned for support to the Germanic North, where the Frankish kingdom, under the leadership of the energetic Carolingian dynasty, aspired to the status of imperial power in the eighth century. When the pope, in the year 800, bestowed the title of emperor upon Charlemagne, he solemnized the new order of things by placing himself and all of Western Christendom under the protection of the king of the Franks and Lombards. He

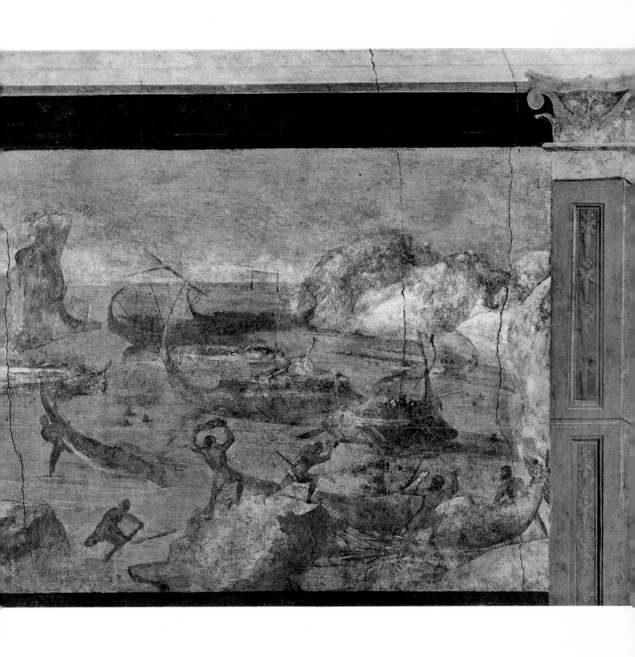

Colorplate 9. *The Laestrygonians Hurling Rocks at the Fleet of Odysseus*, panel of *Odyssey Landscapes*, wall painting in a house on the Esquiline Hill. Late 1st century B.C. Vatican Museums, Rome

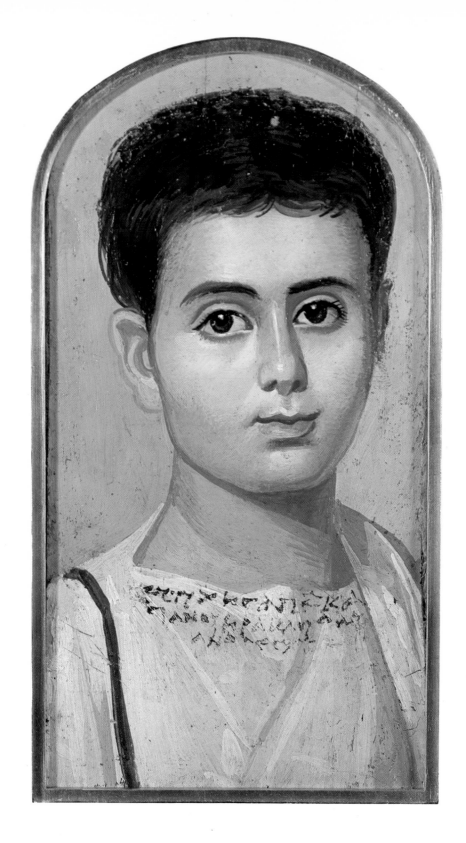

Colorplate 10. *Portrait of a Boy*, from the Faiyum, Egypt. 2nd century A.D. Encaustic on panel. 13 × 7 1/4″. The Metropolitan Museum of Art, New York (Gift of Edward S. Harkness, 1918)

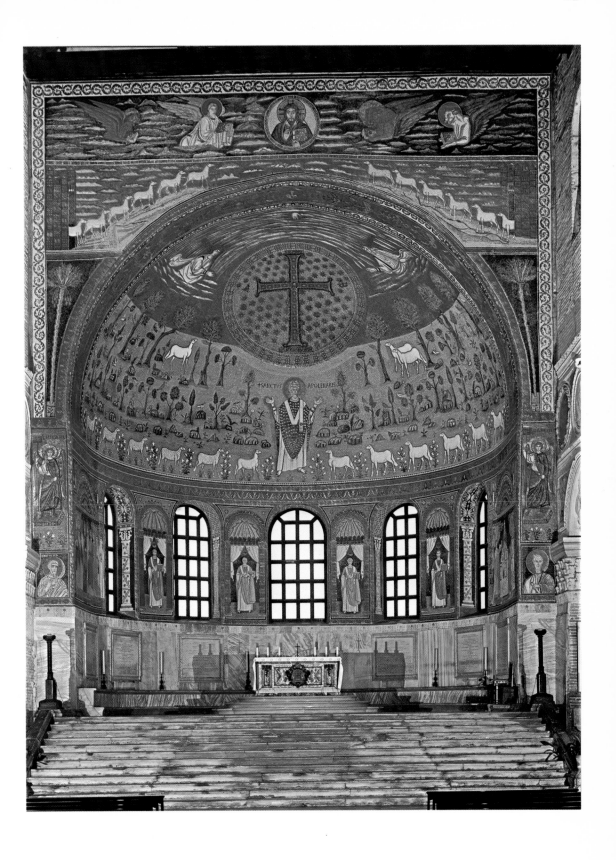

Colorplate 11. Interior (view toward the apse). Sant' Apollinare in Classe. Ravenna. 533–49 A.D.

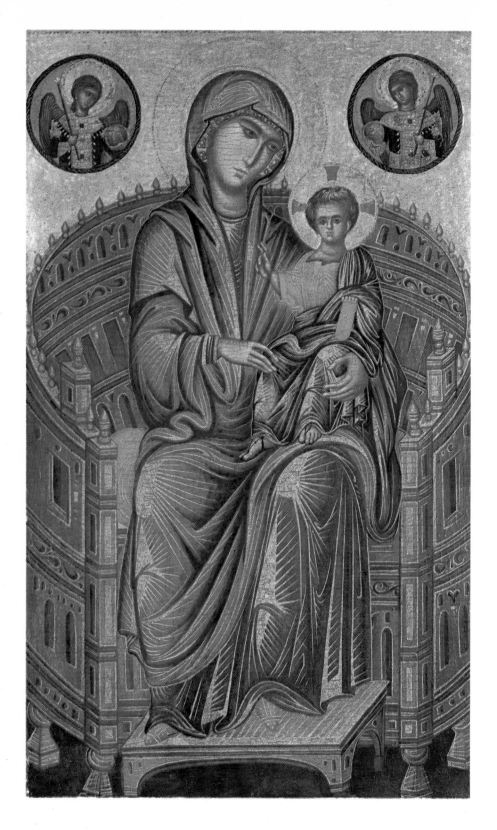

Colorplate 12. *Madonna Enthroned*. Late 13th century. Tempera on panel, 32 × 19 1/2″. National Gallery of Art, Washington, D.C. (Mellon Collection)

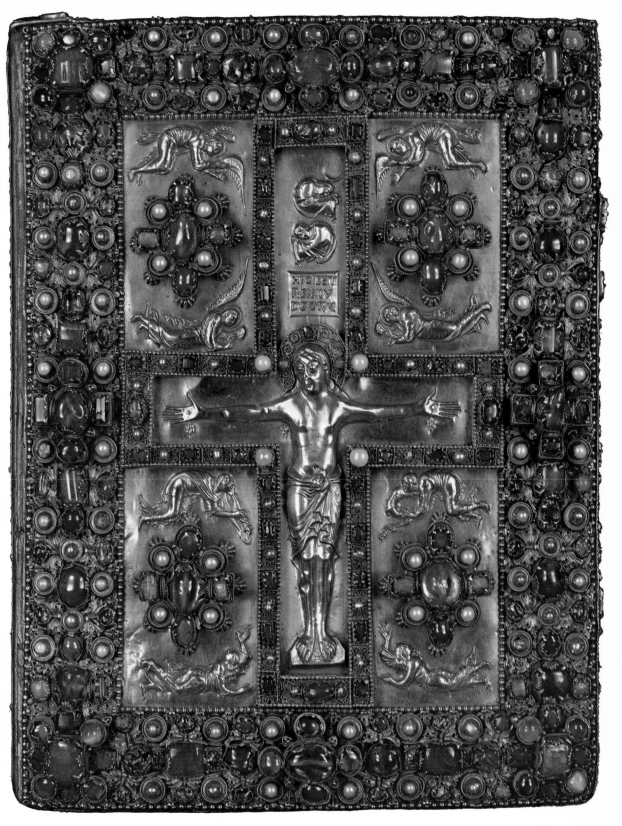

Colorplate 13. Upper Cover of binding, the *Lindau Gospels*. c. 870 A.D. Gold with jewels, 13 3/4 × 10 1/2".
The Pierpont Morgan Library, New York

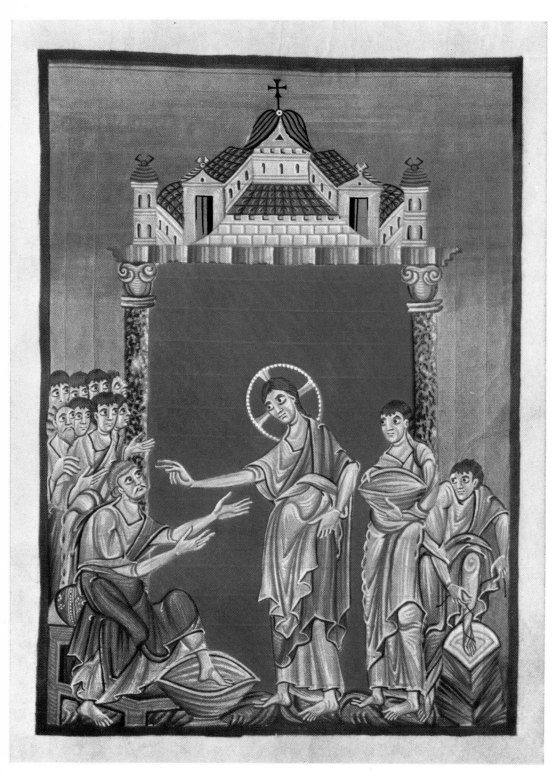

above: Colorplate 14. *Christ Washing the Feet of Peter,* from the *Gospel Book of Otto III.* c. 1000 A.D. Manuscript illumination. Bavarian State Library, Munich

opposite: Colorplate 15. *St. John the Evangelist,* from the *Gospel Book of Abbot Wedricus.* Shortly before 1147. Manuscript illumination. Société Archéologique, Avesnes, France

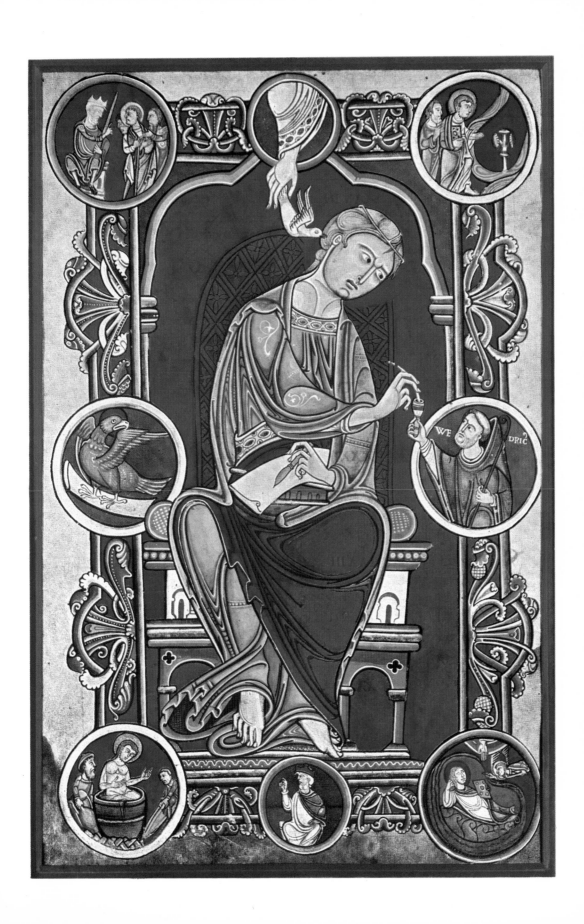

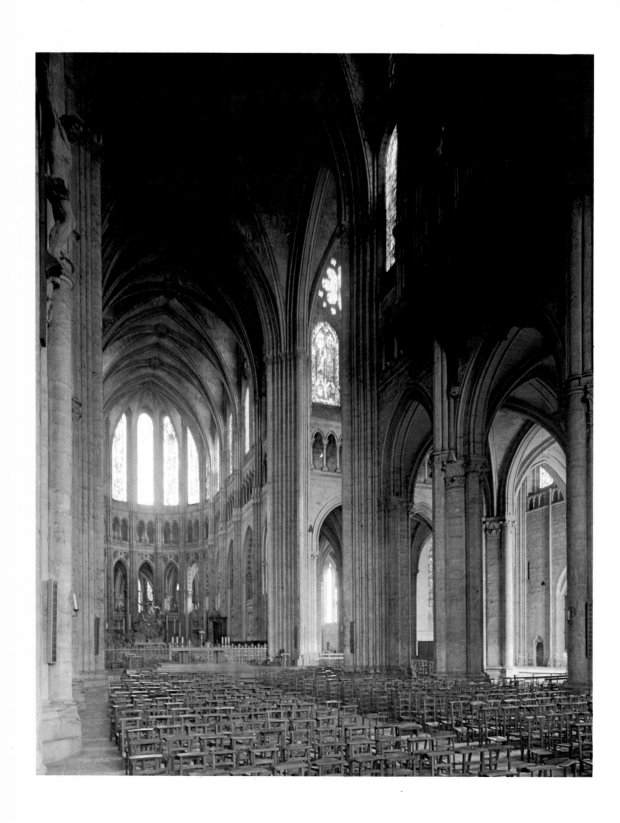

Colorplate 16. View of the Nave, Chartres Cathedral. 1194–1220

did not, however, subordinate himself to the newly created Catholic emperor; the legitimacy of the latter depended on the pope, whereas hitherto it had been the other way around (the emperor in Constantinople had always ratified the newly elected popes). This interdependent dualism of spiritual and political authority, of Church and State, was to distinguish the West from both the Orthodox East and the Islamic South. Outwardly it was symbolized by the fact that, although the emperor had to be crowned by the pope in Rome, he did not live there; Charlemagne built his capital at the center of his effective power, in Aachen, where Belgium, Germany, and the Netherlands meet today.

THE DARK AGES

The labels we use for historical periods tend to be like the nicknames of people: once established, they are almost impossible to change, even though they may no longer be suitable. Those who coined the term "Middle Ages" thought of the entire thousand years that came between the fifth and fifteenth centuries as an age of darkness, an empty interval between Classical antiquity and its revival, the Renaissance in Italy. Since then, our view of the Middle Ages has completely changed: we no longer think of the period as "benighted," but as the "Age of Faith." With the spread of this new, positive conception, the idea of darkness has become confined more and more to the early part of the Middle Ages, roughly between the death of Justinian and the reign of Charlemagne. Perhaps we ought to pare down the Dark Ages even further: there was a great deal of activity in that darkness while the economic, political, and spiritual framework of Western Europe was being established; and as we shall now see, the same period also gave rise to some important artistic achievements.

GERMANIC

The Germanic tribes that had entered Western Europe from the east during the declining years of the Roman Empire carried with them, in the form of nomads' gear, an ancient and widespread artistic tradition, the so-called animal style. Examples of it have been found in the form of bronzes in Iran, and gold in southern Russia. A combination of abstract and organic shapes, formal discipline and imaginative freedom, it became an important element in the Celto-Germanic art of the Dark Ages, such as the gold-and-enamel purse cover (fig. 89) from the grave of an East Anglian king who died in 654. Four pairs of motifs are symmetrically arranged on its surface; each has its own distinctive character, an indication that the motifs have been assembled from different sources. One of them, the standing man between two confronted animals, has a very long history indeed: we first saw it in figure 27—a panel more than three thousand years older. The eagles pouncing on ducks also date back a long way, to carnivore-and-victim motifs. The design just above them, however, is of more recent origin. It consists of fighting animals whose tails, legs, and jaws are elongated into bands forming a complex interlacing pattern. Interlacing bands, as an ornamental device, had existed in Roman and even Mesopotamian art (see fig. 27, bottom row), but their combination with the animal style, as shown here, seems to have been an invention of the Dark Ages.

Metalwork, in a variety of materials and techniques and often of exquisitely refined craftsmanship, had been the principal medium of the animal style. Such objects, small, durable, and eagerly sought after, account for the rapid diffusion of its repertory of forms. They "migrated" not only in the geographic sense, but also technically and artistically into other materials—wood, stone, even manuscript illumination. Wooden specimens, as we might expect, have not survived in large quantities; most of them come

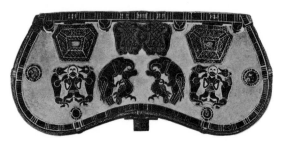

89. Purse Cover, from the Sutton Hoo Ship-Burial. Before 655 A.D. Gold and enamel. British Museum, London

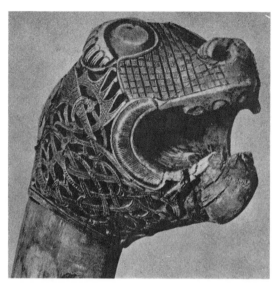

90. *Animal Head,* from the Oseberg Ship-Burial. c. 825 A.D. Wood, height c. 5″. University Museum of Antiquities, Oslo

from Scandinavia, where the animal style flourished longer than anywhere else. The splendid animal head of the early ninth century (fig. 90) is a terminal post that was found, along with much other equipment, in a buried Viking ship at Oseberg in southern Norway. Like the motifs on the purse cover, it shows a peculiar composite quality: the basic shape of the head is surprisingly realistic, as are certain details (teeth, gums, nostrils), but the surface has been spun over with interlacing and geometric patterns that betray their derivation from metalwork.

IRISH

This pagan Germanic version of the animal style is reflected in the earliest Christian works of art north of the Alps as well. In order to understand how they came to be produced, however, we must first acquaint ourselves with the important role played by the Irish, who, during the Dark Ages, assumed the spiritual and cultural leadership of Western Europe. The period 600–800 A.D. deserves, in fact, to be called the Golden Age of Ireland. Unlike their English neighbors, the Irish had never been part of the Roman Empire; thus the missionaries who carried the Gospel to them from the south in the fifth century found a Celtic society, entirely barbarian by Roman standards. The Irish readily accepted Christianity, which

brought them into contact with Mediterranean civilization, but without becoming Rome-oriented. Rather, they adapted what they had received in a spirit of vigorous local independence. The institutional framework of the Roman Church, being essentially urban, was ill suited to the rural character of Irish life. Irish Christians preferred to follow the example of the desert saints of North Africa and the Near East who had left the temptations of the city in order to seek spiritual perfection in the solitude of the wilderness. Groups of such hermits, sharing a common ideal of ascetic discipline, had founded the earliest monasteries. By the fifth century, monasteries had spread as far north as western Britain, but only in Ireland did monasticism take over the leadership of the Church from the bishops. Irish monasteries, unlike their desert prototypes, soon became seats of learning and the arts; they also developed a missionary fervor that sent Irish monks preaching to the heathen and founding monasteries in northern Britain as well as on the European mainland. These Irishmen not only speeded the conversion to Chris-

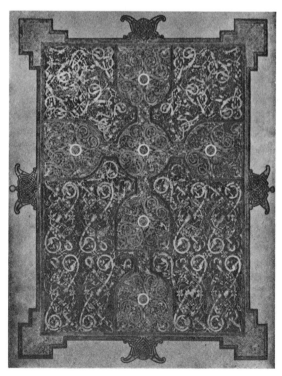

91. Cross Page, from *Lindisfarne Gospels.* c. 700 A.D. Manuscript illumination. British Museum, London

tianity of Scotland, northern France, the Netherlands, and Germany; they also established the monastery as a cultural center thoughout the European countryside. Although their Continental foundations were taken over before long by the monks of the Benedictine order, who were advancing north from Italy during the seventh and eighth centuries, Irish influence was to be felt within medieval civilization for several hundred years to come.

In order to spread the Gospel, the Irish monasteries had to produce copies of the Bible and other Christian books in large numbers. Their writing workshops (scriptoria) also became centers of artistic endeavor, for a manuscript containing the Word of God was looked upon as a sacred object whose visual beauty should reflect the importance of its contents. Irish monks must have known Early Christian illuminated manuscripts, but here again, as in so many other respects, they developed an independent tradition instead of simply copying their models. While pictures illustrating Biblical events held little interest for them, they did devote much effort to decorative embellishment. The finest of these manuscripts belong to the Hiberno-Saxon style, combining Celtic and Germanic elements, which flourished in those monasteries founded by Irishmen in Saxon England. The Cross Page in the *Lindisfarne Gospels* (fig. 91) is an imaginative creation of breathtaking complexity; the miniaturist, working with a jeweler's precision, has poured into the compartments of his geometric frame an animal interlace so dense and so full of controlled movement that the fighting beasts on the Sutton Hoo purse cover seem childishly simple in comparison. It is as if the world of paganism, embodied in biting, clawing monsters, had here suddenly been subdued by the superior authority of the Cross. In order to achieve this effect our artist has had to impose an extremely severe discipline upon himself. His "rules of the game," for example, demand that organic and geometric shapes must be kept separate; that within the animal compartments every line must turn out to be part of the animal's body, if we take the trouble to trace it back to its point of origin. There are also rules, too complex to

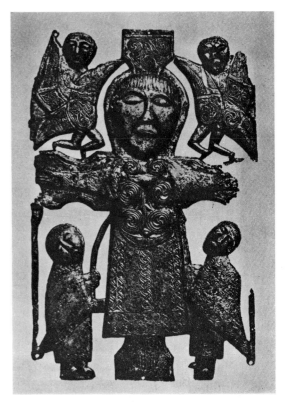

92. *The Crucifixion* (from a book cover?). 8th century A.D. Bronze. National Museum of Ireland, Dublin

go into here, governing symmetry, mirror-image effects, and repetitions of shape and color. Only by working these out for ourselves can we hope to enter into the spirit of this strange, mazelike world.

Of the representational images they found in Early Christian manuscripts, the Hiberno-Saxon illuminators generally retained only the symbols of the four Evangelists, since these could be translated into their ornamental idiom without difficulty. The bronze plaque (fig. 92), probably made for a book cover, shows how helpless they were when given the image of man to copy. In his attempt to reproduce an Early Christian composition, our artist suffered from an utter inability to conceive of the human frame as an organic unit, so that the figure of Christ becomes disembodied in the most elementary sense; head, arms, and feet are separate elements, attached to a central pattern of whorls, zigzags, and interlacing bands. Clearly, there is a wide gulf between the Celto-Germanic and the Mediterranean traditions,

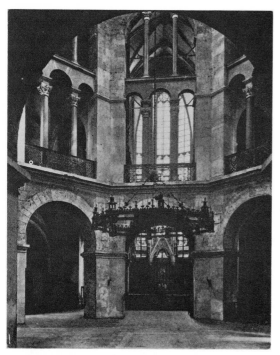

93. Interior, Palace Chapel of Charlemagne. 792–805 A.D. Aachen

a gulf that this Irish artist did not know how to bridge. Much the same situation prevailed elsewhere during the Dark Ages; even the Lombards, on Italian soil, did not know what to do with human images.

CAROLINGIAN ART

The empire built by Charlemagne did not endure for long. His grandsons divided it into three parts, and proved incapable of effective rule even in these, so that political power reverted to the local nobility. The cultural achievements of his reign, in contrast, have proved far more lasting; this very page would look different without them, for it is printed in letters whose shapes derive from the script in Carolingian manuscripts. The fact that these letters are known today as Roman rather than Carolingian recalls another aspect of the cultural reforms sponsored by Charlemagne: the collecting and copying of ancient Roman literature. The oldest surviving texts of a great many Classical Latin authors are to be found in Carolingian manuscripts which, until not long ago, were mistakenly regarded as Roman: hence their lettering, too, was called Roman. This interest

in preserving the Classics was part of an ambitious attempt to restore ancient Roman civilization (see also p. 102), along with the imperial title. Charlemagne himself took an active hand in this revival, through which he expected to implant the traditions of a glorious past in the minds of the semibarbarian people of his realm. To an astonishing extent, he succeeded. Thus the "Carolingian revival" may be termed the first—and in some ways the most important—phase of a genuine fusion of the Celto-Germanic spirit with that of the Mediterranean world.

ARCHITECTURE

The fine arts played an important role in Charlemagne's cultural program from the very start. On his visits to Italy, he had become familiar with the architectural monuments of the Constantinian era in Rome, and with those of the reign of Justinian in Ravenna; his own capital at Aachen, he felt, must convey the majesty of empire through buildings of an equally impressive kind. His famous Palace Chapel (fig. 93) is, in fact, directly inspired by the church of San Vitale in Ravenna (fig. 84). To erect such a structure on Northern soil was a difficult undertaking: columns and bronze gratings had to be imported from Italy, and expert stonemasons must have been hard to find. The design, by Odo of Metz (probably the earliest architect north of the Alps known to us by name), is by no means a mere echo of its model but a vigorous reinterpretation, with bold structural parts that outline and balance the clear, forthright divisions of the interior space.

The importance of the monasteries, which were encouraged by Charlemagne, is vividly suggested by a unique document of the period: the large drawing of a plan for a monastery, preserved in the Chapter Library of St. Gall in Switzerland (fig. 94). Its basic features seem to have been decided upon at a council held near Aachen in 816–817, and then this copy was sent to the abbot of St. Gall for his guidance in rebuilding the monastery. We may regard it, therefore, as a standard plan, to be modified according to local needs. (Our reproduction renders the exact lines of the original, but omits the explanatory inscriptions.) The monastery is

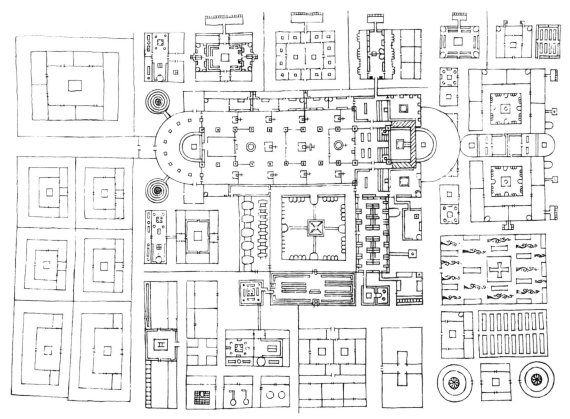

94. *Plan of a Monastery*. 819–830 A.D. Ink on parchment. Chapter Library, St. Gall, Switzerland

a complex, self-contained unit, occupying a rectangle about 500 by 700 feet. The main entry, from the west (left), passes between stables and a hostelry toward a gate which admits the visitor to a colonnaded semicircular portico, flanked by two round towers which must have loomed impressively above the lower outbuildings. It emphasizes the church as the center of the monastic community. The church is a basilica with a semicircular apse and an altar at either end, though the eastern end is given emphasis by a raised choir (with steps leading up to it) preceded by a space, partially screened off from the nave and organized transversally to it, which can be called a transept—a term that we shall meet again in later church plans. The nave and aisles, containing numerous other altars, do not form a single, continuous space but are subdivided into compartments by screens. There are several entrances: two beside the western apse, others on the north and south flanks. This entire arrangement reflects the functions of a monastery church, designed for the devotional needs of the

monks, rather than for a congregation of laymen. Adjoining the church to the south, there is an arcaded cloister with a well in the middle; around this are grouped the monks' dormitories (east side), a dining hall and kitchen (south side), and a cellar. The three large buildings to the north of the church are a guest-house, a school, and the abbot's house. To the east are the infirmary, novices' quarters and chapel, the cemetery (marked by a large cross), a garden, and coops for chickens and geese. The south side is occupied by workshops, barns, and other service buildings. There is, needless to say, no monastery exactly like this anywhere—even in St. Gall the plan was not carried out as drawn—yet its layout conveys an excellent notion of the character of such establishments throughout the Middle Ages.

MANUSCRIPTS AND BOOK COVERS
We know from literary sources that Carolingian churches contained murals, mosaics, and relief sculpture, but these have disappeared almost entirely. Smaller, portable works of

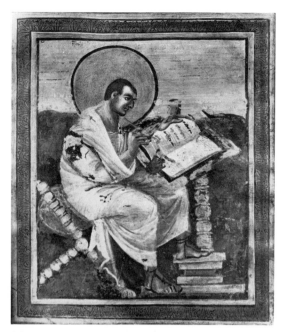

95. *St. Matthew,* from the *Gospel Book of Charlemagne.* About 800 A.D.

Junius Bassus (fig. 81) made some five hundred years earlier: the seated "stance," with one foot advanced; the diagonal drape of the upper part of the toga; the square outline of the face; even the hands, one holding a scroll or codex, the other with a quill pen that is added to what must once have been an expository gesture; and the throne on which Christ is seated in the earlier sculpture has exactly the same kind of animal legs as St. Mark's seat. But now the figure is filled with electrifying energy that sets everything in motion; the drapery swirls, the hills heave upward in the background, the vegetation seems tossed about by a whirlwind, and even the acanthus-leaf pattern on the frame assumes a strange, flamelike character. The Evangelist himself has been transformed from a Roman philosopher into a man seized with the frenzy of divine inspiration, an instrument for the recording of the Word of God. This dependence on the Will of the Lord, so powerfully expressed here, marks the contrast between the Classical and the medieval image of what Man is. But the

art, including books, have, however, survived in considerable numbers. The scriptoria of the various monasteries tended to produce book illuminations which can be grouped into distinct styles, though all of them went back to Late Classical models. Those that were produced in Aachen itself, under Charlemagne's watchful eye, are very close to the originals. As we look at the picture of St. Matthew from a manuscript (fig. 95) said to have been found in the tomb of Charlemagne and, in any event, closely linked with his court at Aachen, we find it hard to believe that such a work could have been executed in northern Europe about the year 800. Whoever the artist was—Byzantine, Italian, or Frank— he shows himself fully conversant with the Roman tradition of painting, down to the acanthus ornament on the wide frame, which emphasizes the "window" aspect of the picture. The *St. Matthew* represents the most orthodox phase of the Carolingian revival; it is the visual counterpart of copying the text of a Classical work of literature. But perhaps more interesting, if somewhat later, is the *Gospel Book of Archbishop Ebbo of Reims* (fig. 96). The St. Mark from this book has many features that will remind us of the Enthroned Christ from the sarcophagus of

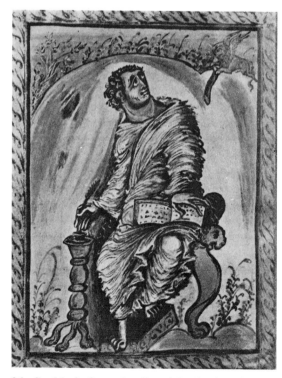

96. *St. Mark,* from the *Gospel Book of Archbishop Ebbo of Reims.* 816–835 A.D. Manuscript illumination. Municipal Library, Epernay, France

means of expression—the dynamism of line that distinguishes our miniature from its Classical predecessors—recalls the passionate movement we found in the ornamentation of Irish manuscripts of the Dark Ages.

The influence of the Reims school can still be felt in the reliefs of the bejeweled front cover of the *Lindau Gospels* (colorplate 13), a work of the third quarter of the ninth century. This masterpiece of the goldsmith's art shows how splendidly the Celto-Germanic metalwork tradition of the Dark Ages adapted itself to the Carolingian revival. The main clusters of semiprecious stones are not set directly on the gold ground, but raised on claw feet or arcaded turrets so that light can penetrate beneath them and make them glow. Interestingly enough, the crucified Christ betrays no hint of pain or death, and this, along with His youthful, beardless face, again takes us back to the spirit of the earliest Christian images of the Saviour, as yet untouched by human agony. He seems to stand, rather than hang, His arms spread wide in what one might almost call a welcoming gesture. To endow Him with human suffering was not yet conceivable, even though the expressive means were at hand, as we can see in the lamenting figures that surround Him.

OTTONIAN ART

In 870, about the time that the *Lindau Gospels* cover was made, the remains of Charlemagne's empire were ruled by his two surviving grandsons: Charles the Bald, the West Frankish king, and Louis the German, the East Frankish king, whose domains corresponded roughly to the France and Germany of today. Their power was so weak, however, that continental Europe once again lay exposed to attack. In the south, the Muslims resumed their depredations; Slavs and Magyars advanced from the east; and Vikings from Scandinavia ravaged the north and west. These Norsemen (the ancestors of today's Danes and Norwegians) had been raiding Ireland and Britain by sea from the late eighth century on; now they invaded northwestern France as well, occupying the area that has, ever since, been called Nor-

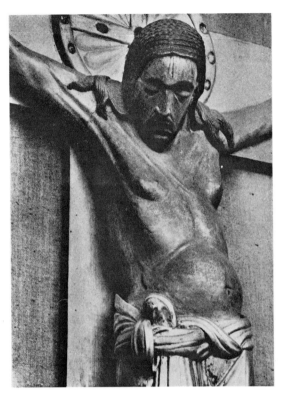

97. *The Gero Crucifix.* c. 975–1000 A.D. Wood, height 6′ 2″. Cologne Cathedral

mandy. Once established there, they soon adopted Christianity and Carolingian civilization, and, from 911 on, their leaders were recognized as dukes, nominally subject to the authority of the king of France. During the eleventh century, the Normans assumed a role of great importance in shaping the political and cultural destiny of Europe, with William the Conqueror being crowned king in England, while other Norman nobles expelled the Arabs from Sicily and the Byzantines from south Italy. In Germany, meanwhile, after the death of the last Carolingian monarch in 911, the center of political power had shifted north to Saxony. The Saxon kings (919–1024) then re-established an effective central government; the greatest of them, Otto I, also revived the imperial ambitions of Charlemagne. After marrying the widow of a Lombard king, he extended his rule over most of Italy and had himself crowned emperor by the pope in 962. From then on, the Holy Roman Empire was to be a German institution. Or perhaps we ought to call it a German dream, for Otto's successors never managed to consolidate their claim to sovereignty south of the Alps. Yet this claim had momentous consequences, since it led the German emperors into centuries of conflict with the papacy and local Italian rulers, linking North and South in a love-hate relationship whose echoes can be felt to the present day.

SCULPTURE

During the Ottonian period, from the mid-tenth century to the beginning of the eleventh, Germany was the leading nation of Europe, politically as well as artistically. German achievement in both areas began as a revival of Carolingian traditions but soon developed new and original traits. These are impressively brought home to us if we compare the Christ on the *Lindau Gospels* cover (colorplate 13) with the *Gero Crucifix* (fig. 97) in the Cathedral of Cologne. The two works are separated by little more than a hundred years' interval, but the contrast between them suggests a far greater span. In the *Gero Crucifix* we meet an image of the Saviour new to Western art, although a restrained beginning toward this interpretation (see fig. 88) was already in the making some-

what earlier in Byzantine art. We do not belittle the genius of the Ottonian sculptor by pointing this out, nor need we be surprised that Eastern influence should have been strong in Germany at this time, for Otto II had married a Byzantine princess, establishing a direct link between the two imperial courts. It remained for the German sculptor to transform the Byzantine image with its gentle pathos into large-scale sculptural terms, imbued with an expressive realism that has been the main strength of German art ever since. How did he arrive at this startling conception? Particularly bold is the forward bulge of the heavy body, which makes the physical strain on arms and shoulders seem almost unbearably real. The deeply incised, angular features of the face are a mask of agony from which all life has fled. The pervasive presence of Spirit, so new and striking in the St. Mark of the *Ebbo Gospels* (fig. 96), acquires added meaning if paired with this graphic visualization of its departure.

ARCHITECTURE

The tutor of Otto II's son and heir, Otto III, was a cleric named Bernward, who later became bishop of Hildesheim, where he ordered built the Benedictine abbey church of St. Michael (whose interior is shown in figure 98). Its system of nave supports did not consist of uniform columns, as in Early Christian basilicas, but of square piers alternating with pairs of columns. This arrangement was more like that of the Palace Chapel at Aachen, and went back to Byzantine antecedents. The heavy piers were the basic supports; the columns, with their richly carved capitals, were accented beats in the rhythm of the arcade. The nave, with its high expanse of wall between arcade and clerestory, was majestic and spacious. Columns, arches, piers, clerestory windows, horizontal bands, and vertical strips divided the nave walls into compartments and subcompartments. St. Michael's, then, compared with the Early Christian basilicas from which it ultimately derived, was both more complex and more unified—in other words, more organic in design.

The two sculptured bronze doors ordered for St. Michael's by Bishop Bernward represent an extraordinary technical achieve-

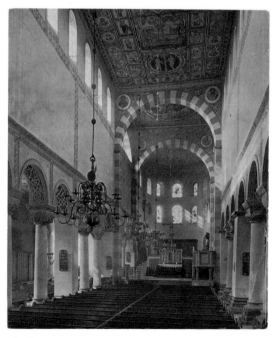

98. Interior (view toward the west, before World War II). St. Michael's, Hildesheim. 1001–33

ment, for they were cast whole. The idea of commissioning a pair of large bronze doors for the church may have come to him as the result of a visit to Rome, where ancient examples, perhaps Byzantine ones too, existed. The Bernward doors, however, differ from these; they are divided into broad, horizontal fields, rather than vertical panels, and each field contains a Biblical scene in high relief. Our detail (fig. 99) shows Adam and Eve after the Fall. Below it, in inlaid letters remarkable for their Classical Roman character, is part of the dedicatory inscription, with the date and Bernward's name. In these figures we find nothing of the monumental spirit of the *Gero Crucifix*; they seem far smaller than they actually are, so that one might easily mistake them for a piece of goldsmith's work such as the *Lindau Gospels* cover. The entire composition must have been derived from an illuminated manuscript; the oddly stylized bits of vegetation have a good deal of the twisting, turning movement we recall from Irish miniatures. Yet the story is conveyed with splendid directness and expressive force. The accusing finger of the Lord, seen against a great void of blank surface, is the focal point of the drama; it points to a cringing Adam, who passes the blame to his mate, while she, in turn, passes it to the dragonlike serpent at her feet.

MANUSCRIPTS

The same intensity of glance and gesture characterizes Ottonian manuscript painting, which blends Carolingian and Byzantine elements into a new style of extraordinary power and scope. Perhaps its finest achievement— and one of the great masterpieces of medieval art—is the *Gospel Book of Otto III,* from which we reproduce the scene of Christ washing the feet of the Disciples (colorplate 14). It contains echoes of ancient painting, filtered through Byzantine art; the soft pastel hues of the background recall the illusionism of Roman landscapes (see colorplate 9), and the architectural frame around Christ is a late descendant of the sort of painted architectural perspectives that decorated Pompeian houses (fig. 74). That these elements have been misunderstood by the Ottonian artist is obvious enough; but he has also put them to a new use: what was once an archi-

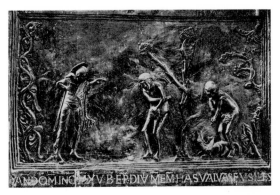

99. *Adam and Eve Reproached by the Lord,* from Doors of Bishop Bernward for Abbey Church of St. Michael. 1015. Bronze, c. 23 × 43″. Hildesheim Cathedral

tectural vista now becomes the Heavenly City—the House of the Lord, filled with golden celestial space, as against the atmospheric earthly space without. The figures have undergone a similar transformation: in Classical art this composition had been used to represent a doctor treating his patient. Now, St. Peter takes the place of the sufferer, and Christ—still beardless and young here—that of the doctor. A shift of emphasis from physical to spiritual action is conveyed not only through glances and gestures, but also by nonrealistic scale relationships: Christ and St. Peter are larger than the other figures; Christ's "active" arm is longer than the "passive" one; and the eight disciples who merely watch have been compressed into a space so small that we are conscious of them only as so many eyes and hands. Even the Early Christian crowd-cluster from which this derives (see fig. 78) is not quite so literally disembodied.

Romanesque Art

Looking back over the ground we have covered in this book so far, a thoughtful reader will be struck by the fact that many of the labels used to designate the art of a given place and period might serve equally well for a general history of civilization. They have been borrowed from technology (e.g., the

Stone Age, or the Bronze Age), or from geography, ethnology, or religion, although in our context they also designate artistic styles. There are two notable exceptions to this rule: Archaic and Classical are both primarily terms of style; they refer to qualities of form rather than to the setting in which these forms were created. Why don't we have more terms of this sort? We do—but only for the art of the last nine hundred years. The men who first conceived the history of art as an evolution of styles started out with the conviction that art had already developed to a single climax: Greek art from the age of Pericles to that of Alexander the Great. This style they called Classic (that is, perfect). Everything that came before was termed Archaic— still old-fashioned and tradition-bound, but striving in the right direction. The style that followed the peak did not deserve a special term since it had no positive qualities of its own, being merely an echo or a decadence of Classic art. The early historians of medieval art followed a similar pattern; to them the great climax was the Gothic style (the term itself, however, was invented by lovers of the Classical, and was meant to indicate that medieval art was the work of Goths, or barbarians). This flourished from the thirteenth to the fifteenth century. For whatever was not-yet-Gothic they invented the term "Romanesque"; in doing so they were thinking mainly of architecture: pre-Gothic churches, they noted, were round-arched, solid, and heavy, rather like the ancient Roman style of building, as against the pointed arches and the soaring lightness of Gothic structures.

In this sense, all of medieval art before 1200 could be called Romanesque if it showed any link at all with the Mediterranean tradition. But this usually happened only when an ambitious ruler, like Charlemagne, had dreams of reconstituting the Roman Empire and becoming emperor himself, with all the glorious trappings of old. Such Classical revivals rose and fell with the political fortunes of the dynasties that sponsored them. However, the style that is given the name "Romanesque" had a much broader base: it sprang up throughout Western Europe at about the same time, embracing a host of regional styles, distinct yet closely related in many ways, and without a single central source. In this it resembled the art of the Dark Ages which, as we have indicated, wandered with the nomadic tribes that came from Asia, all the way across northern and central Europe, picking up local modifications or putting old forms to new uses.

The welding of all these components into a coherent style during the second half of the eleventh century was not done by any single force, but by a variety of factors that made for a new burst of vitality throughout the West. Christianity had at last triumphed everywhere in Europe; the threat of hostile invading cultures around its outer edges had been stilled, either because their momentum gave out or because they were conquered or assimilated. There was a growing spirit of religious enthusiasm, reflected in the greatly increased pilgrimage traffic to sacred sites, and culminating, from 1095 on, in the crusades to liberate the Holy Land. Equally important was the reopening of Mediterranean trade routes by the navies of Venice, Genoa, and Pisa, and the revival of trade and manufacturing, with the consequent growth of city life. During the turmoil of the early Middle Ages, the towns of the Western Roman Empire had shrunk greatly (the population of Rome, about one million in 300 A.D., fell to less than 50,000 at one time); some were deserted altogether. From the eleventh century on, they began to regain their importance; new towns sprang up everywhere, and an urban middle class of craftsmen and merchants established itself between the peasantry and the landed nobility. In many respects, then, Western Europe between 1050 and 1200 A.D. did indeed become a great deal more "Roman-esque" than it had been since the sixth century, recapturing some of the trade patterns, the urban quality, and the military strength of ancient imperial times. The central political authority was lacking, to be sure (even the empire of Otto I did not extend much farther west than modern Germany does), but the central spiritual authority of the pope took its place, to some extent, as a unifying force. The international army that responded to Pope Urban II's call to the First Crusade was more powerful than anything a secular ruler could have raised for that purpose.

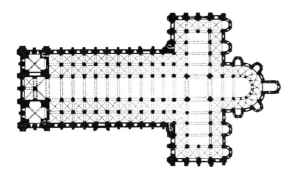

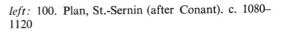

left: 100. Plan, St.-Sernin (after Conant). c. 1080–1120

below left: 101. St.-Sernin, aerial view. Toulouse

below right: 102. Nave and Choir, St.-Sernin. Toulouse

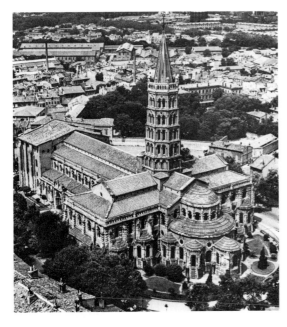

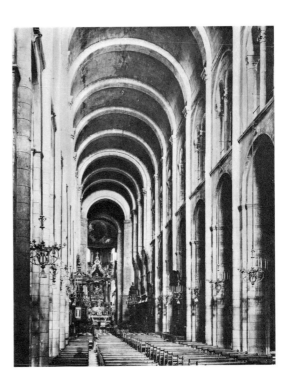

ARCHITECTURE

The quickening of energy in both spiritual and secular enterprise is responsible for the greatest single change that we discern in Romanesque architecture: the amazing number of new buildings which were begun all over Europe at about the same period. An eleventh-century monk, Raoul Glaber, summed it up well when he triumphantly exclaimed that the world was "putting on a white mantle of churches." These churches were not only more numerous than those of the early Middle Ages, they were also generally larger, more richly articulated, and more "Roman looking," for their naves now had vaulted roofs instead of wooden ones, and their exteriors, unlike those of Early Christian, Byzantine, Carolingian, and Ottonian churches, were decorated with both architectural ornament and sculpture. Romanesque monu-

ments of the first importance are distributed over an area that might well have represented the world—the Catholic world, that is—to Raoul Glaber: from northern Spain to the Rhineland, from the Scottish-English border to central Italy. The richest crop, the greatest variety of regional types, and the most adventurous ideas are to be found in France. If we add to this group those destroyed or disfigured buildings whose original design is known to us through archaeological research, we have a wealth of architectural invention unparalleled by any previous era.

SOUTHWESTERN FRANCE

Let us begin our sampling—it cannot be more than that—with St.-Sernin in the southern French town of Toulouse (figs. 100–102). The plan immediately strikes us as much more complex and more fully inte-grated than the plans of earlier structures, with the possible exception of Hagia Sophia. Its outline is an emphatic Latin cross, of the kind that appears in the mosaic half-dome in Sant' Apollinare (colorplate 11), with the stem longer than the three other projecting parts (the Greek cross, used as a symbol in the Eastern Orthodox Church, has all arms of the same length, rather like the cross inscribed in a circle that we saw in our earliest Christian paintings; see fig. 76). The nave is the largest space compartment, but it is extended by the transverse arms (called the transept) where more pilgrims could be ac-commodated to witness the sacred ritual which was concentrated in the smallest com-partment of all, the apse at the east end. Un-like the plan of the monastery church in St. Gall (fig. 94), where altars and chapels for special devotions are scattered fairly evenly throughout the enclosure, and where the tran-sept, though identifiable, tends to merge with the altar space at the east end, this church was plainly meant to accommodate large crowds of lay worshipers. The nave is flanked by two aisles on either side, the inner aisle continuing around the arms of the transept and the apse, thus forming a com-plete ambulatory (which means "for walk-ing") circuit, anchored to the two towers on either side of the main entrance (these can clearly be seen in the plan, but not in the superstructure). Chapels extrude from the ambulatory along the eastern edge of the transept arms, and all around the apse; the longest one at the eastern tip was usually dedicated to the Virgin Mary, and is thus of-ten referred to as the Lady Chapel. This type of apse with its elaborations of chapels and ambulatory is called a "pilgrimage choir"; pilgrims could "make the rounds" of the chapels even when there was no Mass being celebrated at the main altar.

The plan shows that the aisles of St.-Sernin were groin-vaulted throughout, and that the measurements of these compart-ments logically form the basic unit, or mod-ule, for all the other dimensions: the width of the central space of the nave, for example, equals twice the width of one compartment in the aisle. On the exterior this rich artic-ulation is further enhanced by the different roof levels of the aisles, set off against the higher gables of nave and transept, and the cluster of semicircular roofs, large and small and at every level, that cover the complex eastern end. Even necessary structural fea-tures, such as the thick pier buttresses be-tween the windows, which serve to stabilize the outward thrust of the ceiling vaults, be-come decorative assets, as is the tower over the crossing (although this was completed in Gothic style, and is taller than originally in-tended). The two façade towers unfortu-nately were never completed.

As we enter the nave (fig. 102), we are im-pressed by its tall proportions, the architec-tural elaboration of the walls, and the dim in-direct lighting, which is filtered through the aisles and the gallery above them, before reaching the nave. The contrast between St.-Sernin and a typical Early Christian basilica, such as Sant' Apollinare (colorplate 11), with its simple "blocks" of space and un-obtrusive masonry, does indeed point up the kinship between St.-Sernin and Roman build-ings, such as the Colosseum (fig. 62), that have vaults, arches, engaged columns, and pilasters all firmly knit within a coherent or-der. Yet the forces whose interaction is ex-pressed in the nave of St.-Sernin are no long-er the physical, "muscular" forces of Grae-co-Roman architecture, but spiritual forces—spiritual forces of the kind that we have seen governing the human body in Carolingian miniatures or Ottonian sculpture. The half-columns running the entire height of the nave wall would appear just as unnaturally drawn-out to an ancient Roman beholder as the arm of Christ in colorplate 14. They seem to be driven upward by some tremendous, unseen pressure, hastening to meet the transverse arches that subdivide the barrel vault of the nave. Their insistent rhythm propels us for-ward toward the eastern end of the church, with its light-filled apse and ambulatory (now partially obscured by a large altar of later date).

In thus describing our experience we do not, of course, mean to suggest that the ar-chitect consciously set out to achieve these ef-fects. For him, beauty and engineering were inseparable; if vaulting the nave so as to elim-inate the fire hazards of a wooden roof was a practical aim, it was also a challenge to

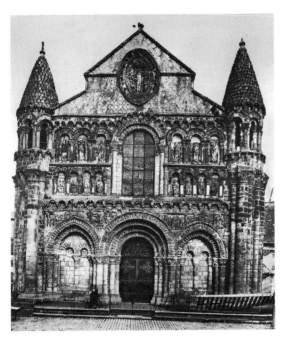

103. West Façade, Notre-Dame-la-Grande. Early 12th century. Poitiers

columns, is the main entrance. A wide band of relief extends from the center arch all across the façade until it is finally terminated by the two towers with their taller bundles of columns and open arcades, looking rather like fantastic chessmen. Their conical helmets match the height of the center gable (which rises above the height of the actual roof behind it). No doubt the columns, with their Classical foliage capitals, and the arches are every bit as "Roman" as those used in St.-Sernin. Yet we feel that the whole is neither rational nor organic, even though it provides a visual feast. Perhaps the designer had never studied actual Roman buildings, but had received their repertory of forms through Roman sarcophagi (which were abundant

see how high he could build it (a vault gets more difficult to sustain, the higher it is from the ground) in honor of the Lord, to make His house grander and more impressive. The ambitious height required the galleries over the aisles to carry the thrust of the central barrel vault and ensure its stability. Thus, the "mysterious" semi-gloom of the interior was not a calculated effect, but merely the result of the windows having to be at some distance from the center of the nave. St.-Sernin serves to remind us that architecture, like politics, is "the art of the possible," and that the designer here, as elsewhere, is successful to the extent that he explores the limits of what was possible for him under those particular circumstances, structurally and aesthetically.

WESTERN FRANCE

Since the west end of St.-Sernin with its towers was never completed, we shall examine Notre-Dame-la-Grande in Poitiers, a town in the west of France, for a lavish example of the Romanesque church façade (fig. 103). Low and wide, it has elaborately bordered arcades housing large seated or standing figures; below these, deeply recessed within a framework of arches resting on stumpy

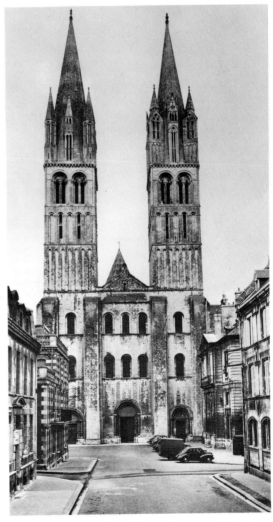

104. West Façade, St.-Etienne. Begun c. 1068. Caen

throughout the south of France); examples such as that of Junius Bassus (fig. 81) are decorated with a kind of two-story "doll's house" that serves to frame the various Biblical figures.

NORMANDY AND ENGLAND

Further north, in Normandy, the west façade evolved in an entirely different direction. That of the abbey church of St.-Etienne at Caen (fig. 104), founded by William the Conqueror soon after his successful invasion of England, offers a complete contrast to Notre-Dame-la-Grande. Decoration is at a minimum and even contrasts of the lesser architectural members are played down; four huge buttresses divide the front of the church into three vertical sections, and the vertical impetus continues triumphantly in the two splendid towers whose height would be impressive enough even without the tall Early Gothic spires on top. Where St.-Sernin strikes us as full-bodied and "muscular," St.-Etienne is cool and composed: a structure to be appreciated, in all its refinement of proportions, by the mind rather than the visual or tactile faculties. And, in fact, the thinking that went into Anglo-Norman architecture (for William started to build in England, too) is responsible for the next great breakthrough in structural engineering that made possible the soaring churches of the Gothic period.

For an example of Romanesque on English soil, we turn to the interior of Durham Cathedral, begun in 1093 (fig. 105), just south of the Scottish border. The nave that we see here is actually one-third wider than St.-Sernin, and it has a greater overall length: 400 feet, which places it among the largest churches of medieval Europe. Despite its width, the nave may have been designed from the start to be vaulted; and this vault is of great interest, for it represents the earliest systematic use (the east end vaulting was completed in 1107) of the ribbed groin vault over a three-story nave. The aisles, which we can glimpse through the arcade, consist of the same sort of nearly square groin-vaulted compartments that are familiar to us from St.-Sernin; but the bays of the nave, separated by strong transverse arches, are decidedly oblong. They are groin-vaulted in such

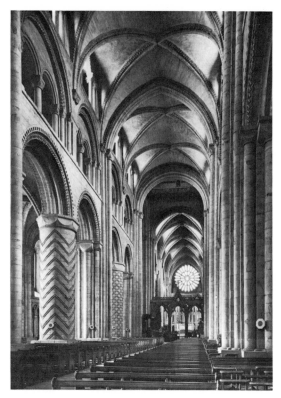

105. Nave (view toward east), Durham Cathedral. 1093–1130

a way that the ribs, used at the junctures of the intersections, form a double-X design, dividing the vault into seven sections, rather than the conventional four. Since the nave bays are twice as long as the aisle bays, the heavy transverse arches occur only at the odd-numbered piers of the nave arcade; thus the piers alternate in size, the larger ones, where the thrust of the vaulting is greatest, being of compound shape (that is, bundles of column shafts and pilaster shafts attached to a square or oblong core), the others cylindrical. But how did the architect come upon this peculiar solution? Let us assume that he was familiar with earlier churches on the order of St.-Sernin, and started out by designing a barrel-vaulted nave with galleries over the aisles, and no windows to light the nave directly. While he was doing so, it suddenly occurred to him that by putting groin vaults over the nave as well as the aisles, he would gain a semicircular area at the ends of each transverse vault; this area, since it had no essential supporting function, could be broken through to make windows. The result would be a pair of Siamese-twin groin vaults, divided into seven compartments, in each bay of the nave. The weight and thrust would be concentrated at six securely anchored points at the gallery level, and thence led down to the piers and columns below. The ribs, of course, were necessary to provide a skeleton, so that the various curved surfaces between them could be filled in with masonry of minimum thickness, thus reducing both weight and thrust.

We do not know whether this ingenious scheme was actually invented in Durham, but it could not have been created much earlier, for it is still in the experimental stage here; while the transverse arches at the crossing are round, those farther along toward the west end of the nave are slightly pointed, indicating a continuous search for improvements. Aesthetically, the nave of Durham is one of the finest in all Romanesque architecture; the sturdiness of the alternating piers makes a wonderful contrast with the dramatically lighted, sail-like surfaces of the vaults.

ITALY

Turning to central Italy, which had been part of the heartland of the original Roman Empire, we might expect it to have produced the noblest Romanesque of them all, since surviving Classical originals were close at hand to study. It comes as a slight shock, therefore, to realize that such was not the case: all of the rulers having ambitions to revive "the grandeur that was Rome," with themselves in the role of emperor, were in the north of Europe. The spiritual authority of the pope, reinforced by considerable territorial holdings, made imperial ambitions in Italy difficult. New centers of prosperity, whether arising from sea-borne commerce or local industries, tended rather to consolidate a number of small principalities, which competed among themselves or aligned themselves from time to time, if it seemed politically profitable, with the pope or the German emperor. Lacking the urge to re-create the old Empire, and furthermore having Early Christian church buildings as readily accessible as Classical Roman architecture, the Tuscans were content to continue what are basically Early Christian forms, but enlivened them with decorative features inspired

by pagan Roman architecture. If we take one of the best preserved Tuscan Romanesque examples, the Cathedral complex of Pisa (fig. 106), and compare it on the one hand with the view of Sant' Apollinare in Ravenna (fig. 77), and on the other with the view of St.-Sernin in Toulouse (fig. 101), we are left in little doubt as to which is its closer relation. True, it has grown taller than its ancestor, and a large transept has altered the plan to form a Latin cross, with the consequent addition of a tall lantern rising above the intersection. But the essential features of the earlier basilica type, with its files of flat arcades and even the detached bell tower (the famous "Leaning Tower of Pisa," which was not planned that way but began to tilt because of weak foundations), still continue, much as we see them in Sant' Apollinare.

The only deliberate revival of the antique Roman style was in the use of a multicolored marble "skin" on the exteriors of churches (Early Christian examples, we recall, tended to leave the outsides plain). Little of this is left in Rome, a great deal of it having literally been "lifted" for the embellishment of later structures; but the interior of the Pantheon (fig. 64) still gives us some idea of it, and we can recognize the desire to emulate such marble inlay in the Baptistery in Florence

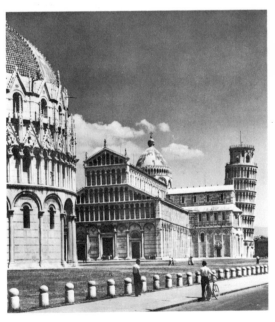

106. Cathedral, Baptistery, and Campanile. 1053–1272. Pisa

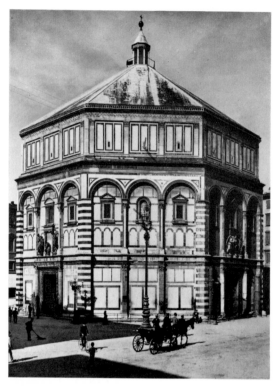

107. Baptistery. c. 1060–1150. Florence

(fig. 107). The green and white marble paneling follows severely geometric lines. The
blind arcades are eminently Classical in proportion and detail; the entire building in
fact, exudes such an air of Classicism that the
Florentines themselves came to believe, a few
hundred years later, that it had originally
been a temple of Mars, the Roman god of
war. We shall have to return to this Baptistery again, since it was destined to play an
important part in the Renaissance.

SCULPTURE

The revival of monumental stone sculpture
is even more astonishing than the architectural achievements of the Romanesque era,
since neither Carolingian nor Ottonian art
had shown any tendencies in this direction.
Freestanding statues, we will recall, all but
disappeared from Western art after the fifth
century; stone relief survived only in the form
of architectural ornament or surface decoration, with the depth of the carving reduced
to a minimum. Thus the only continuous
sculptural tradition in early medieval art was
of sculptures-in-miniature: small reliefs and

occasional statuettes, made of metal or ivory.
Ottonian art, in works such as the bronze
doors of Bishop Bernward, had enlarged the
scale of this tradition but not its spirit; and
truly large-scale sculpture, represented by the
impressive *Gero Crucifix* (fig. 97), was limited
almost entirely to wood.

SOUTHWESTERN FRANCE

Just when and where the revival of stone
sculpture began we cannot say with assurance, but if any one area has a claim to
priority it is southwestern France and northern Spain, along the pilgrimage roads leading to Santiago de Compostela. The link
with the pilgrimage traffic seems logical
enough, for architectural sculpture, especially
when applied to the exterior of a church, is
meant to appeal to the lay worshiper rather
than to the members of a closed monastic
community. Like Romanesque architecture,
the rapid development of stone sculpture between 1050 and 1100 reflects the growth of
religious fervor among the lay population
in the decades before the First Crusade. Of
course a carved image in stone, being three-
dimensional and tangible, is more "real"
than a painted one, and to a cleric steeped
in the abstractions of theology and edgy
about any signs of a revival of idolatry, this
might have seemed a frivolous, even dangerous novelty. St. Bernard of Clairvaux,
writing in 1127, denounced the sculptured
decoration of churches as a vain folly and
diversion that tempts us "to read in the marble rather than in our books." His warning
was not much heeded, however; to the un-
sophisticated, any large piece of sculpture
inevitably did have something of the quality
of an idol, but that very fact is what gave it
such great appeal: praying before a statue
of a saint made the worshiper feel that his
prayers were going in the right direction, not
wafting into the thin air that might or might
not transmit them to heaven.
    The *Apostle* of figure 108 is an early exam-
ple, having been carved around 1090. A
little over half lifesize, it was not intended for
close-range viewing only, for it has bulk and
weight enough to be read easily from a considerable distance. Where have we seen its
like before? Its Classical solidity of form suggests that the artist has taken a good look at

late Roman sculpture, of which a great quantity remained in southern France. The design as a whole, however—its frontality, its placement within an architectural frame—indicates a Byzantine source, perhaps a small ivory panel descended from the *Archangel Michael* of figure 82. In enlarging such a miniature form, our artist made sculpture spatial once again: the Apostle's body is blocklike; his hair is a round, close-fitting cap; the niche that surrounds him is a real cavity. And the whole work has much the same dignity and directness as the sculpture of Archaic Greece.

Some distance north of Toulouse stands the abbey church of Moissac; its south portal displays a richness of invention that would

have made St. Bernard wince. In figure 109 we see the magnificent trumeau (the center post supporting the lintel of the doorway) and the western jamb. Both have a scalloped profile—apparently a bit of Moorish influence—and within these outlines human and animal forms are treated with the same incredible flexibility, so that the spidery Prophet on the side of the trumeau seems perfectly adapted to his precarious perch. He even remains free to cross his legs in a dance-like movement, and to turn his head toward the interior of the church as he unfurls his scroll. But what of the crossed lions that form a symmetrical zigzag on the face of the trumeau—do they have a meaning? So far

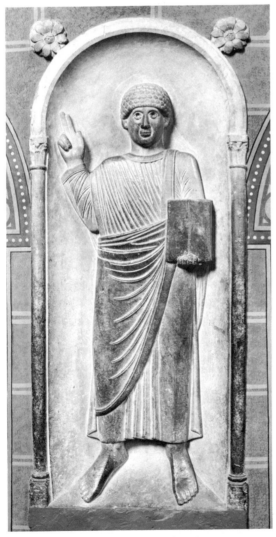

108. *Apostle.* c. 1090. St.-Sernin, Toulouse

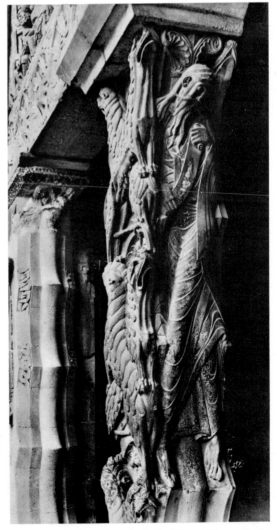

109. South Portal (portion), St.-Pierre. Stone. Early 12th century. Moissac

as we know, they simply "animate" the shaft, as the interlacing beasts of Irish miniatures (whose descendants they are) animated the compartments assigned them. In manuscript illumination, this tradition had never died out; our sculptor has undoubtedly been influenced by it, just as the agitated movement of the Prophet has its ultimate origin in miniature painting. Yet we cannot fully account for the presence of the lions in terms of their effectiveness as ornament. They belong to a vast family of savage or monstrous creatures in Romanesque art that retain their demoniacal vitality even though they are compelled—like our lions—to perform supporting functions. Their purpose, therefore, is also expressive; they embody dark forces that have been domesticated into guardian figures, or banished to a position that holds them fixed for all eternity, however much they may snarl in protest.

BURGUNDY

In Romanesque churches the tympanum (the lunette inside the arch above the lintel) of the main portal is usually given over to a composition centered on the Enthroned Christ, most often the Apocalyptic Vision of the Last Judgment—the most awesome scene of Christian art. At Autun Cathedral this subject has been visualized with singular expressive force. Our figure 110 shows part of the right half of the tympanum, with the weighing of the souls. At the bottom, the dead rise from their graves in fear and trembling; some are already beset by snakes or gripped by huge, clawlike hands. Above, their fate quite literally hangs in the balance, with devils yanking at one end of the scales and angels at the other. The saved souls cling, like children, to the hem of the angelic garments, while the condemned are seized by grinning demons and cast into the mouth of Hell. These devils betray the same nightmarish imagination we observed in the pre-Romanesque animal style; but their cruelty, unlike that of the animal monsters, goes unbridled; they enjoy themselves to the full in their grim occupation. No visitor, having "read in the marble" (to speak with St. Bernard), could fail to enter the church in a chastened spirit.

THE MEUSE VALLEY

The emergence of distinct artistic personalities in the twelfth century is rarely acknowledged, perhaps because it contravenes the widespread assumption that all medieval art is anonymous. It does not happen very often, of course, but it is no less significant for all that. In the valley of the Meuse River, which runs from northeastern France into Belgium and Holland, there had been a particularly strong awareness of Classical sources since Carolingian times (the *Ebbo Gospels*, fig. 96, and the *Lindau Gospels* cover, colorplate 13, originated in this region); it continued to be felt during the Romanesque period. Interestingly enough, the revival of individualism and personality may often be linked with a revival of ancient art, even if the Classical influence did not always produce monumental works. "Mosan" Romanesque sculpture excelled in metalwork, such as the splendid bronze baptismal font (fig. 111) of 1107–18 in Liège, which is the masterpiece of the earliest artist of the region whose name we know: Renier of Huy. The vessel rests on twelve oxen (symbolizing the Apostles), like

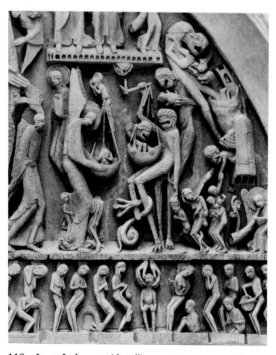

110. *Last Judgment* (detail), west tympanum, Autun Cathedral. Stone. c. 1130–35

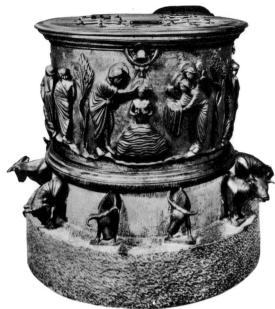

111. RENIER OF HUY. Baptismal Font. 1107–18. Bronze, height 25″. St. Barthélemy, Liège

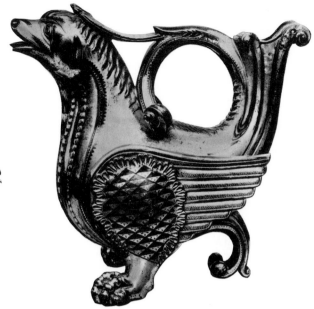

112. Ewer, from Meuse Valley. c. 1130. Gilt bronze, height 7 1/4″. Victoria & Albert Museum, London (Crown Copyright Reserved)

Solomon's basin in the Temple at Jerusalem as described in the Bible. The reliefs make an instructive contrast with those of Bernward's doors (see fig. 99) since they are about the same height. Instead of the rough, expressive power of the Ottonian panel, we find here a harmonious balance of design, a subtle control of the sculptured surfaces, and an understanding of organic structure that, in medieval terms, are amazingly Classical. The figure seen from the back (beyond the tree on the left in our picture), with its graceful turning movement and Greek-looking drapery, might almost be mistaken for an ancient work.

Of freestanding bronze sculpture, only one example of the period has survived; but related to it are the countless bronze water ewers, in the shapes of lions, dragons, and various monsters, that came into use during the twelfth century for the ritual washing of the priest's hands during Mass. These vessels—another instance of monsters doing menial service for the Lord (see p. 114)—were of Near Eastern inspiration. The beguiling specimen reproduced in figure 112 still betrays its descent from the winged beasts of Persian art (fig. 32), transmitted to the West through trade with the Islamic world.

PAINTING

Unlike architecture and sculpture, Romanesque painting shows no sudden revolutionary developments that set it apart immediately from Carolingian or Ottonian. Nor does it look any more "Roman." This does not mean that painting was less important than it had been before: it merely emphasizes the greater continuity of the pictorial tradition, especially in manuscript illumination. Nevertheless, soon after the year 1000 we find the beginnings of a painting style which corresponds to—and often anticipates—the monumental qualities of Romanesque sculpture. As in the case of architecture and sculpture, Romanesque painting developed a wide variety of regional styles; its greatest achievements emerged from the monastic scriptoria of northern France, Belgium, and southern England. The works produced in this area are so closely related in style that at times it is impossible to be sure on which side of the English Channel a given manuscript belongs. Thus, the style of the wonderful miniature of St. John (colorplate 15) has been linked with both Cambrai and Canterbury. The prevalent tendency of Romanesque painting toward uncompromising linearity has here been soft-

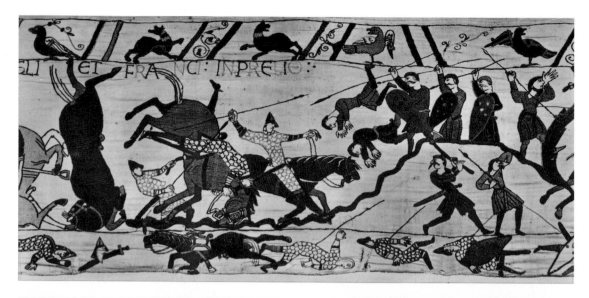

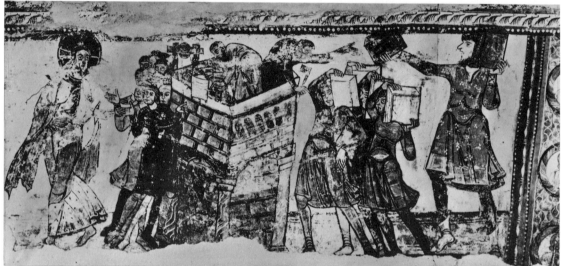

above top: 113. *The Battle of Hastings,* portion of the *Bayeux Tapestry.* c. 1073–83. Wool embroidery on linen, height 20″. Town Hall, Bayeux

above: 114. *The Building of the Tower of Babel,* portion of painted nave vault. Early 12th century. St.-Savin-sur-Gartempe

ened by Byzantine influence, without losing any of the energetic rhythm that it inherited from the Reims school of illumination. But ultimately the style of such a page as this goes back to the Celto-Germanic tradition (see fig. 91), to the precisely controlled dynamics of every contour, in both the main figure and the frame, that unite the varied elements of the composition into a coherent whole, even though in this instance human and floral forms may be copied from Carolingian or Byzantine models. The unity of the page is conveyed not only by style, but by content as well. The Evangelist "inhabits" the frame in such a way that we could not remove him from it without cutting off his ink supply (proffered by the donor of the manuscript, Abbot Wedricus), his source of inspiration (the dove of the Holy Spirit, in the hand of God), or his identifying symbol, the eagle.

The linearity and the simple, closed contours of a painting style such as this lend themselves very well to other mediums and to changes in scale (murals, tapestries, stained-glass windows, sculptured reliefs). The so-called Bayeux Tapestry is an embroidered strip of cloth 230 feet long illustrating William the Conqueror's invasion of England; in our detail (fig. 113), which shows the Battle of Hastings, the main scene is enclosed by two border strips performing a function not unlike the frame around the St. John (see above). Partly it is purely decorative (the upper tier with birds and animals), but partly it is integral to the central action (the lower strip is full of dead warriors and horses and thus forms part of the story). Devoid of nearly all the pictorial refinements of Classical painting (see fig. 41), it nevertheless manages to give us an astonishingly vivid and detailed account of warfare in the eleventh century; the massed discipline of the Graeco-Roman scene is gone, and this is not due to the artist's ineptitude at foreshortening and overlapping, but to a new kind of individualism that makes of each combatant a potential hero, whether by dint of force or cunning (observe how the soldier who has just fallen from the horse that is somersaulting with its hind legs in the air is, in turn, toppling his adversary by yanking at the saddle girth of his mount).

Firm outlines and a strong sense of pattern are equally characteristic of Romanesque wall painting. *The Building of the Tower of Babel* (fig. 114) is taken from the most impressive surviving cycle, on the nave vault of the church at St.-Savin-sur-Gartempe. It is an intensely dramatic design; the Lord Himself, on the far left, participates directly in the narrative as He addresses the builders of the growing structure. He is counterbalanced, on the right, by the giant Nimrod, the leader of the enterprise, who frantically passes blocks of stone to the masons atop the tower, so that the entire scene becomes a great test of strength between God and Man, somewhat reminiscent of the hand-to-hand combat in the Bayeux Tapestry.

Soon after the middle of the twelfth century, an important change in style begins to make itself felt in Romanesque painting on either side of the English Channel. *The Crossing of the Red Sea* (fig. 115), one of many enamel plaques that make up a large altarpiece at Klosterneuburg by Nicholas of Verdun, shows that lines have suddenly regained their ability to describe three-dimensional shapes. The drapery folds no longer lead an

ornamental life of their own but suggest the rounded volume of the body underneath. Here, at last, we meet the pictorial counterpart of that Classicism which we saw earlier in the Baptismal Font of Renier of Huy at Liège (see fig. 111). That the new style should have had its origin in metalwork (which includes not only casting, but also engraving, enameling, and goldsmithing) is not as strange as it might seem, for its essential qualities are sculptural rather than pictorial. In these "pictures on metal," Nicholas straddles the division between sculpture and painting, as well as that between Romanesque and Gothic art. Although the *Klosterneuburg Altar* was completed well before the end of the twelfth century, there is an understandable inclination to rank it as a harbinger of the style to come, rather than the culmination of a style that had been. Indeed, the altarpiece was to have a profound impact upon the painting and sculpture of the next fifty years, when the astonishing humanity of Nicholas' art found a ready response in a Europe that was generally reawakening to a new interest in man and the natural world.

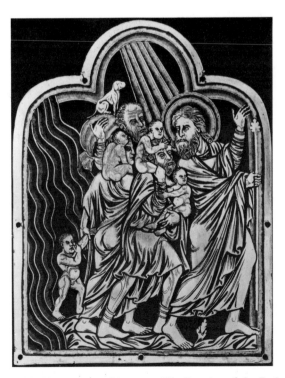

115. NICHOLAS OF VERDUN. *The Crossing of the Red Sea,* from *Klosterneuburg Altar*. 1181. Enamel plaque, height 5 1/2". Klosterneuburg Abbey, Austria

Towns, Cathedrals, and Gothic Art

ARCHITECTURE

Time and space, we have been taught, are interdependent. Yet we tend to think of history as the unfolding of events in time without sufficient awareness of their unfolding in space—we visualize it as a stack of chronological layers, or periods, each layer having a specific depth that corresponds to its duration. For the remote past, where our sources of information are scanty, this simple image works reasonably well. It becomes less and less adequate as we draw closer to the present and our knowledge grows more precise. Thus we cannot define the Gothic era in terms of time alone; we must consider the changing surface area of the layer as well as its depth.

At the start, about 1150, this area was small indeed. It embraced only the province known as the Ile-de-France (that is, Paris and vicinity), the royal domain of the French kings. A hundred years later, most of Europe from Sicily to Iceland, had "gone Gothic" with only a few Romanesque pockets left here and there; through the Crusaders, the new style had even been introduced in the Near East. About 1450 the Gothic area had begun to shrink—it no longer included Italy —and about 1550 it had disappeared almost entirely. The Gothic layer, then, has a rather complicated shape, its depth including nearly four hundred years in some places and a hundred and fifty at the least in others. This shape, moreover, does not emerge with equal clarity in all the visual arts. The term Gothic was coined for architecture, and it is in architecture that the characteristics of the style are most easily recognized. Only during the past hundred years have we become accustomed to speak of Gothic sculpture and painting. There is, as we shall see, some uncertainty even today about the exact limits of the Gothic style in these fields. The evolution of our concept of Gothic art suggests

the way the new style actually grew: it began with architecture, and for about a century—from c. 1150 to 1250, during the Age of the Great Cathedrals—architecture retained its dominant role. Gothic sculpture, at first severely architectural in spirit, tended to become less and less so after 1200; its greatest achievements are between the years 1220 and 1420. Painting, in turn, reached a climax of creative endeavor between 1300 and 1350 in central Italy. North of the Alps, it became the leading art after about 1400. We thus find, in surveying the Gothic era as a whole, a gradual shift of emphasis from architecture to painting, or, better perhaps, from architectural to pictorial qualities (characteristically enough, Early Gothic sculpture and painting both reflect the discipline of their monumental setting, while Late Gothic architecture and sculpture strive for "picturesque" effects rather than clarity and firmness). Overlying this broad pattern there is another one: international diffusion as against regional independence. Starting as a local development in the Ile-de-France, Gothic art radiates from there to the rest of France and to all Europe, where it comes to be known as *opus modernum* or *francigenum* ("modern" or "French work"). In the course of the thirteenth century, the new style gradually loses its "imported" flavor; regional variety begins to reassert itself. Toward the middle of the fourteenth century, we notice a growing tendency for these regional achievements to influence each other until, about 1400, a surprisingly homogeneous "International Gothic" style prevails almost everywhere. Shortly thereafter, this unity breaks apart: Italy, with Florence in the lead, creates a radically new art, that of the Early Renaissance, while north of the Alps, Flanders assumes an equally commanding position in the development of Late Gothic painting and sculpture. A century later, finally, the Italian Renaissance becomes the basis of another international style. With this skeleton outline to guide us, we can now explore the unfolding of Gothic art in greater detail.

FRANCE: ST.-DENIS

The origin of no previous architectural style can be pinpointed as exactly as that of

Gothic. It was born between 1137 and 1144 in the rebuilding, by Abbot Suger, of the royal Abbey Church of St.-Denis just outside the city of Paris. If we are to understand how it came to be just there, and just then, we must acquaint ourselves with the special relationship among St.-Denis, Suger, and the French monarchy. The kings of France claimed their authority from the Carolingian dynastic tradition. But their power was eclipsed by that of the nobles who, in theory, were their vassals; the only area they ruled directly was the Ile-de-France, and they often found their authority challenged even there. Not until the early twelfth century did the royal power begin to expand; and Suger, as chief adviser to Louis VI, played a key role in the process. He forged the alliance between the monarchy and the Church, which brought the bishops of France (and the cities under their authority) to the king's side, while the king, in turn, supported the papacy in its struggles against the German emperors. Suger, however, championed the monarchy not only on the plane of practical politics but on that of "spiritual politics"; by investing the royal office with religious significance, by glorifying it as the strong arm of justice, he sought to rally the nation behind the king. His architectural plans for St.-Denis must be understood in this context, for the church, founded in the late eighth century, enjoyed a dual prestige that made it ideally suitable for Suger's purpose: it was the shrine of the Apostle of France, the sacred protector of the realm, as well as the chief memorial of the Carolingian dynasty (Charlemagne as well as his father, Pepin, had been consecrated there as kings). Suger wanted to make the Abbey the spiritual center of France, a pilgrimage church to outshine the splendor of all the others, the focal point of religious as well as patriotic emotion. But in order to become the visible embodiment of such a goal, the old edifice would have to be enlarged and rebuilt. The great Abbot himself described the campaign in such eloquent detail that we know more about what he desired to achieve than we do about the final result, for the west façade and its sculpture are sadly mutilated today, and the east end (the choir), which Suger regarded as the most important part of the

church, has been much altered. Because of the disappointing visual remains of Suger's church today, we must be content here to take note of its importance—and important it was: every visitor, it seems, was overwhelmed by its extraordinary impact, and within a few decades the new style had spread far beyond the confines of the Ile-de-France.

NOTRE-DAME

Although St.-Denis was an abbey, the future of Gothic architecture lay in the towns rather than in rural monastic communities. There had been a vigorous revival of urban life, we will recall, since the early eleventh century; this movement continued at an accelerated pace, and the growing weight of the cities made itself felt not only economically and politically, but in countless other ways as well: bishops and the city clergy rose to new importance; cathedral schools and universities took the place of the monasteries as centers of learning (see p. 122), while the artistic efforts of the age culminated in the great cathedrals. That of Notre-Dame ("Our Lady") at Paris, begun in 1163, reflects the salient features of Suger's St.-Denis more directly than any other. Let us begin by comparing the plan (fig. 116) with that of a Romanesque church (fig. 100): it is very much more compact and unified, with the double ambulatory of the choir continuing directly into the aisles, the stubby transept barely exceeding the width of the façade. In preparation for what we shall find in the view of the interior, we may also take note of the vaulting system: each bay (except for the crossing and the apse) along the central axis has an oblong shape, divided by a rib system that we have not met heretofore; outlined by transverse ribs, each compartment is then not only subdivided by two crossed ribs (the groin vault familiar to us from the aisles of St.-Sernin and other churches), but also bisected by a third rib, the ends of each rib corresponding to a column on the floor of the nave. This is known as a sexpartite vault. Although not identical with the vaulting system that we found in Durham Cathedral (fig. 105—the "Siamese-twin" groin vault), it continues the kind of experimentation that was begun in the Norman Romanesque to find ways of lightening the load of masonry between the supports. In the interior (fig. 118) we find other echoes of Norman Romanesque in the galleries above the inner aisles, and the columns used in the nave arcade. Here, also, the use of pointed arches, which was pioneered in the western bays of the nave at Durham, has become systematic throughout the building. The two halves of a pointed arch, by eliminating the part of the round arch that responds the most to the pull of gravity, brace each other; the pointed arch thus exerts less outward pressure than the semicircular arch, and, depending on the angle at which the two sections meet, it can be made as steep as one wishes. The potentialities of the engineering advances that grew out of this discovery are already evident in Notre-Dame: the large clerestory windows, the lightness and slenderness of the forms, which reflect that of the ribs of the vault, create the "weightless" effect that we associate with Gothic interiors. In contrast to the heavily emphasized moldings of St.-Sernin, the walls here are left plain, which makes them seem thinner. Gothic, too, is the "verticalism" of the nave's interior. This depends less on the actual proportions—some Romanesque churches are equally tall, relative to their width—than on the constant accenting of the verticals and on the sense of ease with which the height has been attained.

In Notre-Dame the buttresses (the "heavy bones" of the structure that ultimately take the weight and thrust of the vaulting) are not visible from the inside. The plan shows them as massive blocks of masonry that stick out from the building like a row of teeth. From the outside (fig. 117) we can see that above the level of the aisle compartments, each of these buttresses turns into a diagonally pitched arch that reaches upward to meet the critical spot between the clerestory windows where the outward thrust of the nave vault is concentrated. These arches, called "flying buttresses," will remain one of the characteristic features of Gothic architecture. Although they certainly owed their origin to functional considerations, they soon became aesthetically important as well, and apart from supplying actual support, an architect could make them "express" it in a variety of ways.

The most monumental aspect of the exterior of Notre-Dame is the west façade (fig. 119). Except for its sculpture, which suffered heavily during the French Revolution and is for the most part the product of the restorer's art, it retains its original appearance. The design reflects the façade of St.-Denis, which, in turn, had been derived from Norman Romanesque façades such as that of St.-Etienne at Caen (fig. 104), where we find the same basic features: the pier buttresses that reinforce the corners of the towers and divide the façade into three parts; the placing of the portals; the three-story arrangement. The rich sculptural decoration, however, recalls the façades of the west of France (see fig. 103). Much more important than these resemblances are the qualities that distinguish the façade of Notre-Dame from its Romanesque ancestors. Foremost among these is the way all the details have been integrated into a harmonious whole, a formal discipline that also embraces the sculpture, which is no longer permitted the spontaneous (and often uncontrolled) growth that we found on some Romanesque churches. At the same time, the cubic severity of the unadorned front of St.-Etienne has been transformed into its very opposite; lacelike arcades, vast portals and windows dissolve the continuity of the wall surfaces, making a huge, openwork screen of the whole. How rapidly this tendency advanced during the first half of the thirteenth century can be seen by comparing the west façade with the somewhat later portal of the south transept (visible in fig. 117): in the former, the rose window (as the round windows in Gothic churches are called) is deeply recessed, and the stone tracery that makes the pattern is clearly set off from the masonry in which it is imbedded; in the latter, by contrast, we cannot distinguish the tracery of the window apart from its frame: a continuous web covers the whole area.

Though we may trace this or that feature of Gothic architecture back to some Romanesque source, the how and why of its success are a good deal more difficult to explain. Here we encounter an ever-present controversy: to the advocates of the functionalist approach, Gothic architecture has seemed the result of advances in engineering that made it possible to build more efficient vaults, to

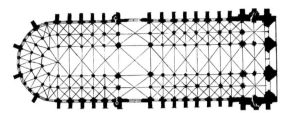

above: 116. Plan, Notre-Dame. 1163–c. 1250. Paris

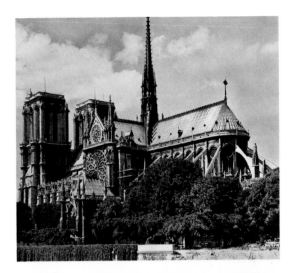

right: 117. Notre-Dame, view from southeast. 1163–c. 1250. Paris

below right: 118. Interior, Notre-Dame. 1163–c. 1200. Paris

below left: 119. West Façade, Notre-Dame. c. 1200–c.1250. Paris

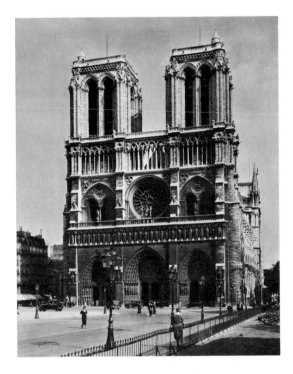

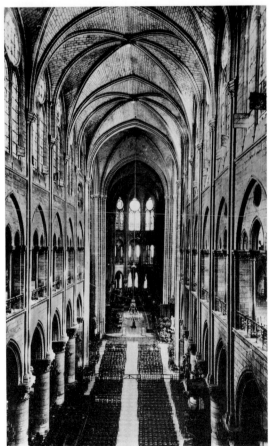

concentrate their thrust at a few critical points, and thus eliminate the solid walls of the Romanesque. But is that all there is to it? We must return briefly to Abbot Suger, who tells us himself that he was hard put to it

to bring together artisans from many different regions for his project. This would lend substance to the idea that all he needed was good technicians; yet, if that had been all, he would have found himself with nothing but a conglomeration of different regional styles in the end. Suger's account, however, stresses insistently that "harmony," the perfect relationship among parts, is the source of beauty, since it exemplifies the laws according to which divine reason has constructed the universe; the "miraculous" light flooding through the "most sacred" windows becomes the Light Divine, a mystic revelation of the spirit of God. Whether or not he was the architect of St.-Denis, his was the guiding spirit which made Gothic churches more than just the sum of their parts.

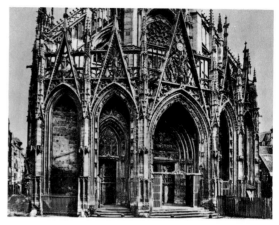

120. West Façade, St.-Maclou. Begun 1434. Rouen

CHARTRES; ROUEN

To suggest the fusion of material and spiritual beauty that impressed the visitors to St.-Denis, and which still overwhelms us when we step into the finest Gothic cathedrals, is not easy to do on a printed page. The view inside Chartres Cathedral (colorplate 16) will perhaps supply the dimension that is missing from black-and-white reproductions. Chartres alone, among the major Gothic cathedrals, still retains most of its original stained-glass windows; these act mainly as huge multicolored diffusing filters that change the quality of ordinary daylight, endowing it with the poetic and symbolic values so highly praised by Abbot Suger.

After the basic plan of the Gothic church, as exemplified in the Cathedral of Notre-Dame (fig. 116), had been found satisfactory and the heretofore unimagined flexibility of the groin vault based on the pointed arch had been grasped, the further evolution of Gothic architecture in France became ever more daring in testing the limits to which this kind of construction could be carried. Naves became ever loftier, buttresses lacier, until in a few cases they did collapse. Perhaps the purpose of glorifying the divine order, as Abbot Suger had set out to do, imperceptibly turned into a kind of Tower of Babel contest, which as we recall ended disastrously. Still, it is amazing to find that so much Flamboyant ("flame-like") Gothic, as the last phase is called, has stood up. The undulating patterns of curve and counter-curve of the pierced-stone ornament in St.-Maclou in Rouen (fig. 120) are so luxuriant that it almost becomes a game of hide-and-

seek to locate the "bones" of the building. The architect has turned into a virtuoso who overlays the structural skeleton with a web of decoration so dense and fanciful that structure becomes almost completely obscured.

One of the truly astonishing things about Gothic architecture is the enthusiastic adoption that this "royal French style" found abroad. Even more remarkable was its ability to acclimate itself to a variety of local conditions—so much so, in fact, that the Gothic monuments of England, Germany, and other countries have become objects of intense national pride in modern times. A number of reasons, singly or in combination, might be brought forward to explain this rapid spread: the superior skill of French architects and stone carvers; the vast prestige of French centers of learning, such as the Cathedral School of Chartres or the University of Paris; the vigor of the Cistercian order (founded in France) that built Gothic churches wherever it founded new abbeys. Ultimately, however, the international victory of Gothic art seems to have been due to the extraordinary persuasive power of the style itself, which kindled the imagination and aroused religious feelings even among people who were far removed from the cultural climate of the Ile-de-France.

ENGLAND

That England should have proved particularly receptive to the new style is hardly surprising. Yet English Gothic did not grow directly out of the Anglo-Norman Romanesque which had contributed so much of the technical experimentation that went into the realization of St.-Denis. Early English Gothic, although given its start by imported French architects, soon developed its own style, best exemplified in Salisbury Cathedral (fig. 121). We realize at once how different it is from the French example—and also how futile it would be to judge it by French Gothic standards, for its setting, in the middle of the open countryside, does not require it to rise high in order to dominate the clustered core of a city like Paris; nor had it the same mission as St.-Denis, to give spiritual sanction to a royal dynasty. By accepting certain French features, such as the emphasis placed on the main portal by the tall windows above it, it proclaims the new era in architecture—even if these features sometimes look like afterthoughts (note the flying buttresses, which seem structurally unnecessary). With its two strongly projecting transepts and its sprawling façade terminating in stumpy turrets, Salisbury has also retained important features from the Romanesque style. It gives us the impression of spaciousness and ease, as though it were comfortable not only in its setting, but in its links to the Anglo-Norman past.

The spire that rises above the crossing is about a hundred years later than the rest of the building, and it indicates the rapid de-

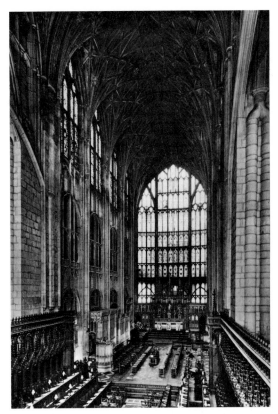

122. Choir, Gloucester Cathedral. 1332–57

velopment of English Gothic toward a more pronounced verticality. The choir of Gloucester Cathedral (fig. 122), in the English Late Gothic ("Perpendicular") style, is more akin to French church interiors, despite the repetition of small, identical tracery forms in the great window which recalls the repetition of carved motifs on the Salisbury façade. The vaulting displays an innovation which, although later adopted on the Continent, is truly English: the blossoming of the ribs into a multiple-strand ornamental network, obscuring the boundaries between the bays and their subdivisions, and giving the interior a greater visual unity. Even though the English style developed independent of French Flamboyant ornament, there is obviously an artistic kinship between these two varieties of intricately worked architectural decoration.

ITALY

Italian Gothic architecture stands apart from that of the rest of Europe. Judged by the style of the Ile-de-France, most of it hardly

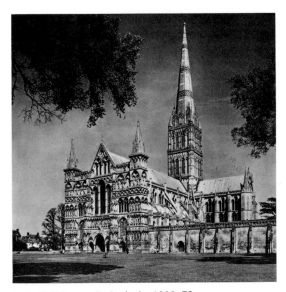

121. Salisbury Cathedral. 1220–70

can be called Gothic at all. Yet it produced structures of singular beauty and impressiveness. We must be careful to avoid too rigid or technical a standard in approaching these monuments, lest we fail to do justice to their unique blend of Gothic qualities and Mediterranean tradition. The Franciscan church of Santa Croce in Florence (fig. 123) is a masterpiece of Gothic, even though it has wooden ceilings instead of groin vaults. This surely was a matter of deliberate choice rather than of technical or economic necessity, evoking the simplicity of Early Christian basilicas and thereby linking Franciscan poverty with the traditions of the early Church. There is no trace of the Gothic structural system, except for the groin-vaulted choir; the walls remain intact as continuous surfaces (Santa Croce owes part of its fame to its wonderful murals); and there are no flying buttresses, since the wooden ceilings do not require them. Why, then, speak of Santa Croce as Gothic? Surely the use of the pointed arch is not enough to justify the term. Yet we sense immediately that this interior space creates an effect fundamentally different from either Early Christian or Romanesque architecture. The nave walls have the weightless, "transparent" qualities we saw in northern Gothic churches, and the dramatic massing of windows at the eastern end forcefully conveys the dominant role of light. Judged in terms of its emotional impact, Santa Croce is Gothic beyond doubt; it is also profoundly Franciscan—and Florentine—in the monumental simplicity of the means by which this impact is achieved.

If in Santa Croce the architect's main concern was an impressive interior, Florence Cathedral (fig. 124) was planned as a great landmark towering above the entire city. Its most striking feature is the huge octagonal dome (compare Pisa Cathedral, fig. 106), covering a central pool of space that makes the nave look like an afterthought. The actual building of the dome, and the details of its design, belong to the early fifteenth century. Apart from the windows and doorways, there is nothing Gothic about the exterior of Florence Cathedral. The solid walls, encrusted with geometric marble inlays, are a perfect match for the Romanesque Baptistery across the way (see fig. 107); and a separate bell

tower, in accordance with Italian tradition (see figs. 77, 106), takes the place of the façade towers familiar to us from French Gothic churches. The west façade, so dramatic a feature in French cathedrals, never achieved the same importance in Italy. It is remarkable how few Italian Gothic façades were ever carried near completion (those of Santa Croce and Florence Cathedral are both modern). Among those that were, the finest is Orvieto Cathedral (fig. 125); it makes an instructive comparison with Tuscan Romanesque façades (see fig. 106) on the one hand, and French Gothic façades on the other (see fig. 119). Many of its ingredients clearly derive from the latter source, and its screen-like lightness, too, is unmistakably Gothic. Yet these features have been superimposed on what is essentially a basilican façade like that of Pisa Cathedral; the towers have been reduced to turrets so as not to compete with the central gable, and the entire design has a strangely small-scale quality that has nothing to do with its actual size. The Orvieto façade, unlike that of Notre-Dame in Paris,

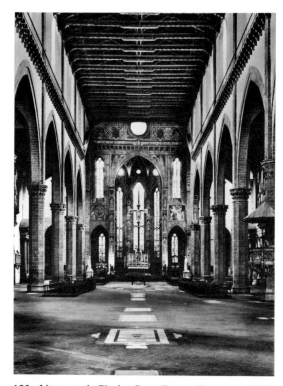

123. Nave and Choir, Sta. Croce. Begun c. 1295. Florence

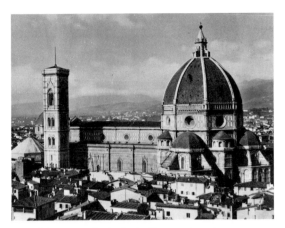

124. Florence Cathedral. Begun by Arnolfo di Cambio, 1296; dome by Filippo Brunelleschi, 1420–36

lacks a dominant motif, so that its elements seem "assembled" rather than merged into a single whole. Except for the modest-sized rose window and the doorways, the Orvieto façade has no real openings, and large parts of it consist of framed sections of wall area. Yet we experience these not as solid, material surfaces but as translucent, since they

are filled with brilliantly colored mosaics—an effect equivalent to Gothic stained glass in the North.

The secular buildings of Gothic Italy convey as distinct a flavor as the churches. There is nothing in the cities of northern Europe to match the impressive grimness of the Palazzo Vecchio (fig. 126), the town hall of Florence. Fortresslike structures such as this reflect the factional strife—among political parties, social classes, and prominent families—so characteristic of life within the Italian city-states. The wealthy man's home (or *palazzo*, a term denoting any large urban house) was quite literally his castle, planned both to withstand armed assault and to proclaim the owner's importance. The Palazzo Vecchio, while larger, follows the same pattern. Behind its battlemented walls, the city government could feel well protected from the wrath of angry crowds. The tall tower not only symbolizes civic pride but has an eminently practical purpose: dominating the city as well as the surrounding countryside, it served as a lookout against enemies from within or without.

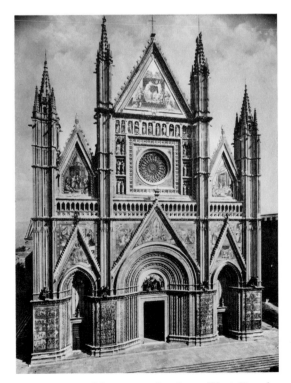

125. Lorenzo Maitani and others. West Façade, Orvieto Cathedral. Begun c. 1310

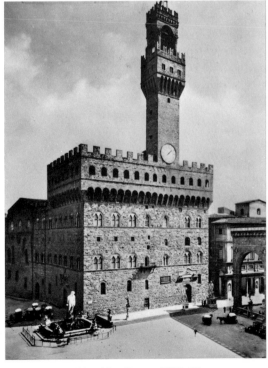

126. Palazzo Vecchio. Begun 1298. Florence

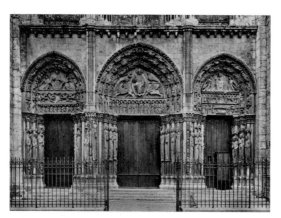

127. West Portals, Chartres Cathedral. c. 1145–70 (for view of interior, see colorplate 16)

SCULPTURE 1150–1420

FRANCE

The portals of the west façade of St.-Denis were far larger and even more richly decorated than those of Romanesque churches. They paved the way for the admirable west portals of Chartres Cathedral (fig. 127), begun about 1145 under the influence of St.-Denis, but even more ambitious in conception. These probably represent the oldest full-fledged examples of Gothic sculpture. Comparing them with a Romanesque portal such as Moissac (fig. 109), we are impressed first by a new sense of order, as if all the figures had suddenly come to attention, conscious of their responsibility to the architectural framework. Symmetry and clarity have taken the place of crowding and frantic movement; figures are no longer entangled with each other, but stand out separately, so that the whole carries much better over a long distance. Particularly striking is the treatment of the door jambs, lined with long figures attached to columns (fig. 128). Instead of being treated essentially as reliefs carved into (or protruding from) the masonry, these are statues, each with its own axis; in theory, at least, they could be detached from their supports. Apparently this first step since the end of Classical times toward recapturing monumental stone sculpture in the round could be taken only by "borrowing" the cylindrical shape of the column for the figures. This method traps them into a certain air of immobility, yet the heads already show a gentle, human quality that evinces the search for more realism. It is as though Gothic sculptors had to relive the same experiences as Archaic sculptors in Greece (see fig. 48). Realism is, of course, a relative term whose meaning varies greatly according to circumstances; on the Chartres west portals it appears to spring from a reaction against the demoniacal aspects of Romanesque art, a reaction that may be seen

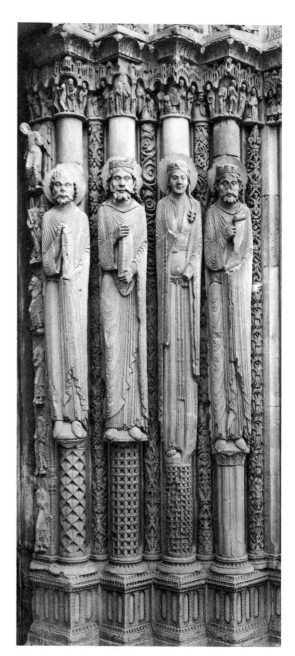

128. Jamb Statues, from west portals, Chartres Cathedral. Begun 1145.

not only in the calm, solemn spirit of the figures, but also in the rational discipline of the underlying symbolic scheme. The subtler aspects of this symbolic program can only be understood by minds well versed in theology; but its main elements are simple enough to be grasped by anyone imbued with the fundamentals of the Bible. The jamb statues, a continuous sequence linking all three portals, represent the prophets, kings, and queens of the Old Testament; their purpose is to acclaim the rulers of France as the spiritual descendants of Biblical rulers, and also—an idea insistently stressed by Abbot Suger—the harmony of secular and spiritual rule. Christ Himself appears enthroned above the main doorway as Judge and Ruler of the Universe, flanked by the symbols of the four Evangelists, with the Apostles assembled below, and the twenty-four Elders of the Apocalypse in the archivolts above. The right-hand tympanum shows His incarnation with scenes from His life below, and personifications of the liberal arts (human wisdom paying homage to divine wisdom) above. In the left-hand tympanum, finally, we see the timeless Heavenly Christ, the Christ of the Ascension, framed by the signs of the zodiac, and their earthly counterparts, the labors of the months—an ever-repeating cycle of the year.

Instructive programs of this type remained a constant feature of Gothic cathedrals; but styles of sculpture developed rapidly, and varied from region to region. The vast sculptural program for Reims Cathedral had made it necessary to bring together masters and entire workshops from various other building sites, and so we have there a compact sampling of several styles. On the right side of figure 129 we see the encounter between the Virgin Mary and St. Elizabeth (the *Visitation*); so expert is the Classicism of these figures that, at first glance, they seem almost to have stepped out of the *Ara Pacis* relief (see fig. 72). No longer governed, as the Chartres figures were, by the strictly vertical columns, they turn toward each other with the same human warmth that links the two older children in the *Ara Pacis*.

In the *Annunciation* group (fig. 129, left) the Virgin is in a severe style, with a rigidly vertical body axis and straight, tubular folds

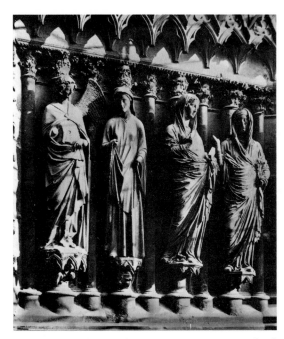

129. *Annunciation* and *Visitation*, center portal of west façade. Stone, over lifesize. c. 1225–45. Reims Cathedral

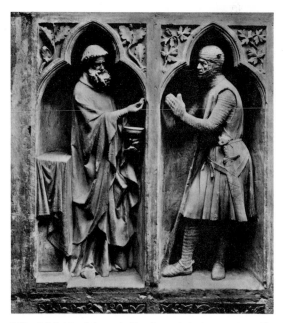

130. *Melchizedek and Abraham*, interior west wall. Stone. After 1251. Reims Cathedral

meeting at sharp angles. The angel, in contrast, is conspicuously graceful: we note the tiny, round face framed by a cap of curls, the emphatic smile, the strong S-curve of the slender body, the ample, richly accented drapery. This "elegant style," created about

1240 by Parisian masters working for the royal court (see also p. 127), was such a success that it soon became the standard formula for High Gothic sculpture all over Europe.

A slightly later group (fig. 130) in the interior of Reims Cathedral offers a new pictorialism: light and shade now give the deeply recessed figures an atmospheric setting which we have not seen before. Again there is a contrast of styles: Abraham, clad in contemporary armor, is quite bluntly realistic, whereas the priest Melchizedek exhibits a further elaboration of the "courtly" style of the angel in the previous picture. So rich is the intricate drapery that the body almost disappears beneath it—a characteristic that was to become more and more pronounced as Gothic progressed toward its final stage.

GERMANY

Though artists from all over Europe came to be trained in the great cathedral workshops of France, the style that they took home with them rapidly acquired some of the character of older native traditions. Thus, the relief showing the *Kiss of Judas* (fig. 131), part of the choir screen of Naumburg Cathedral in Germany, makes us recall the dramatic emotionalism of the much earlier *Gero Crucifix* (see fig. 97), here brought to a theatrical pitch by the contrast of Christ's meekness and the passionate wrath of the sword-wielding St. Peter.

Gothic art, as we have come to know it so far, reflects a desire to endow the traditional themes of Christianity with an ever-greater emotional appeal. It is not surprising, therefore, that Germany played a particular role, near the end of the thirteenth century, in developing a new kind of religious imagery, designed to serve private devotions. The most characteristic and widespread of these images is the so-called *Pietà* (an Italian word derived from the Latin *pietas*, the root word for both "piety" and "pity"), a representation of the Virgin grieving over the dead Christ. No such scene occurs in the Scriptures; it was invented as a counterpart to the familiar Madonna and Child. Our example (fig. 132), like most such groups, is carved of wood and vividly painted. Realism here has

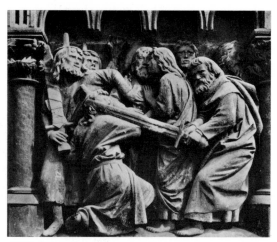

131. *The Kiss of Judas*, on choir screen. c. 1250–60. Stone. Naumburg Cathedral

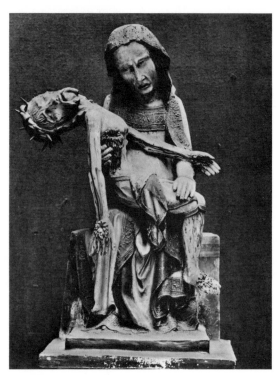

132. *Pietà*. Early 14th century. Wood, height 34 1/2". Provinzialmuseum, Bonn

become purely a vehicle of expression—the agonized faces and Christ's blood-encrusted wounds are enlarged to an almost grotesque degree, so as to arouse an overwhelming sense of horror and pity.

The *Pietà*, with its emaciated, puppetlike bodies, reaches an extreme in the negation of the physical aspects of the human figure.

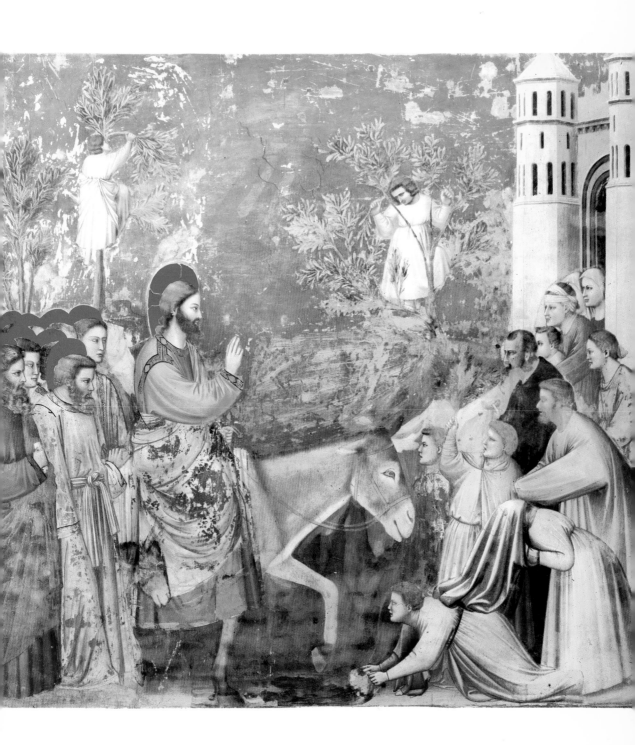

Colorplate 17. GIOTTO. *Christ's Entry into Jerusalem.* 1305–06. Fresco. Arena Chapel, Padua

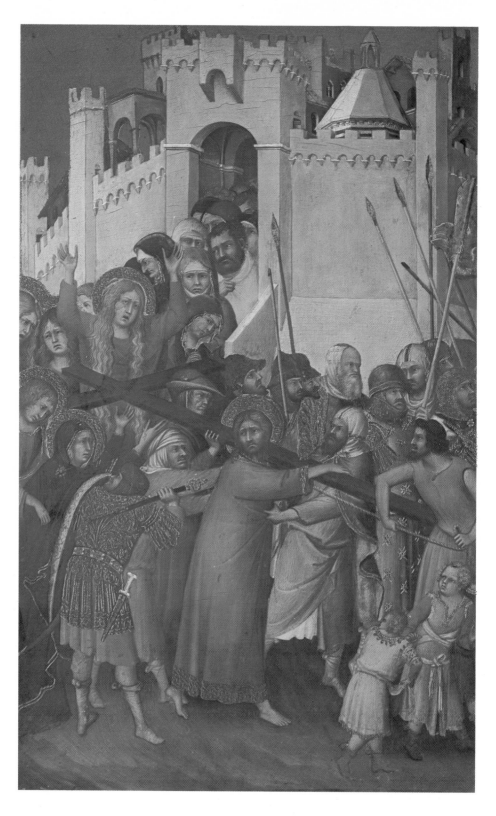

Colorplate 18. SIMONE MARTINI. *The Road to Calvary*. About 1340. Tempera on panel, 9 7/8 × 6 1/8″. The Louvre, Paris

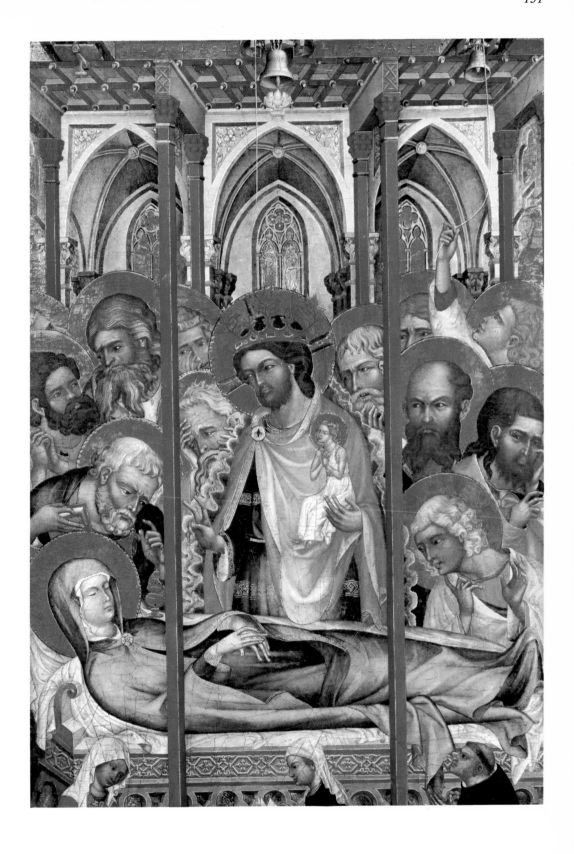

Colorplate 19. BOHEMIAN MASTER. *Death of the Virgin.* c. 1350–60. Panel, 39 × 27 3/4″. Museum of Fine Arts, Boston

132

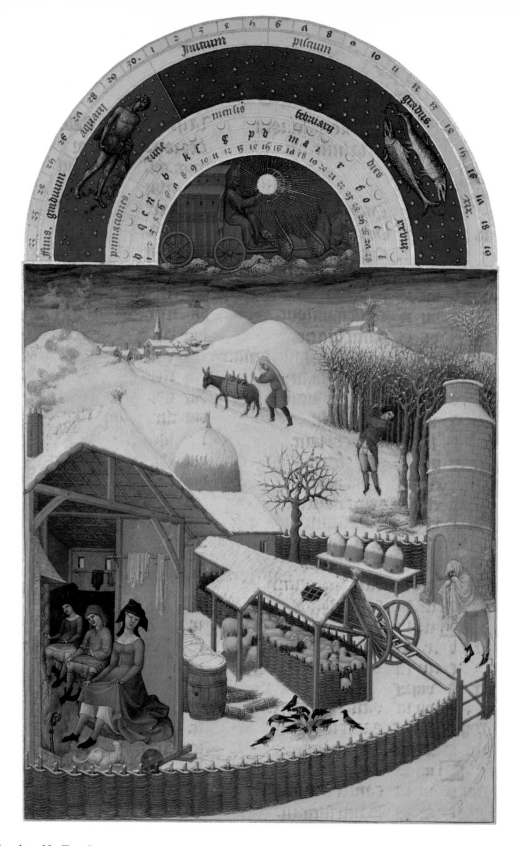

Colorplate 20. THE LIMBOURG BROTHERS. *February*. Manuscript illumination from the *Very Rich Book of Hours of the Duke of Berry*. c. 1415. Condé Museum, Chantilly

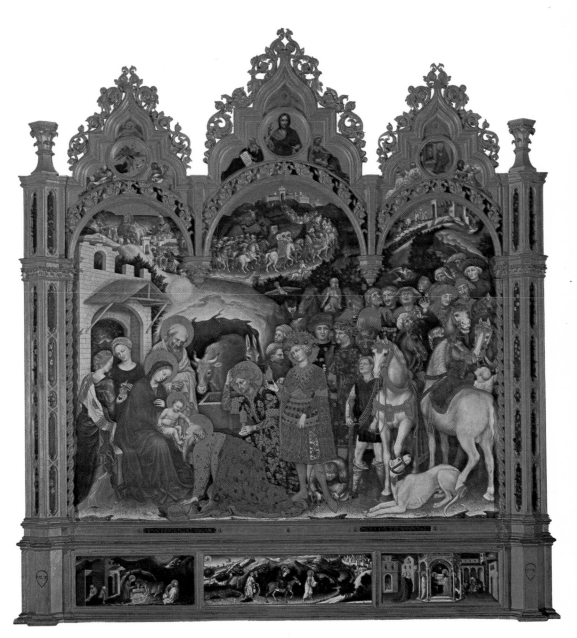

Colorplate 21. GENTILE DA FABRIANO. *The Adoration of the Magi.* 1423. Panel, 9′ 10 1/8″ × 9′ 3″. Uffizi Gallery, Florence

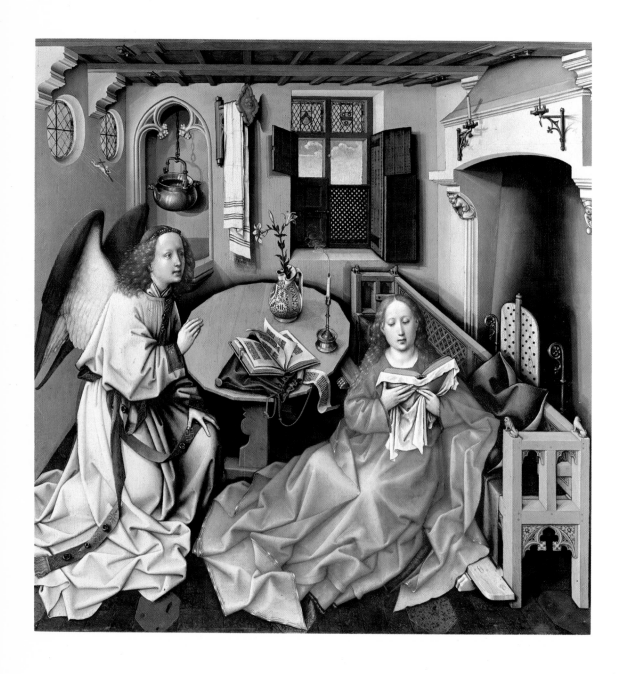

Colorplate 22. THE MASTER OF FLÉMALLE. *Annunciation*, center panel of the *Merode Altarpiece*. c. 1425–28. Oil on panel, 25 1/4 × 24 7/8″. The Metropolitan Museum of Art, New York (Purchase. The Cloisters Collection)

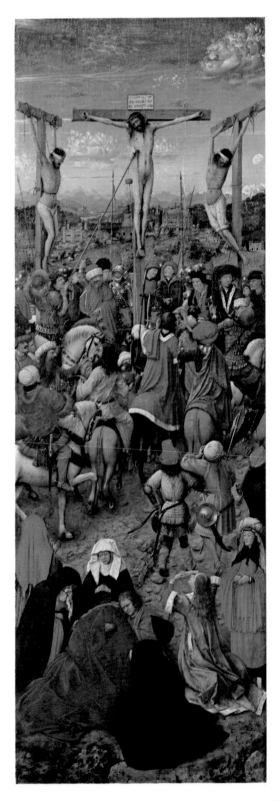 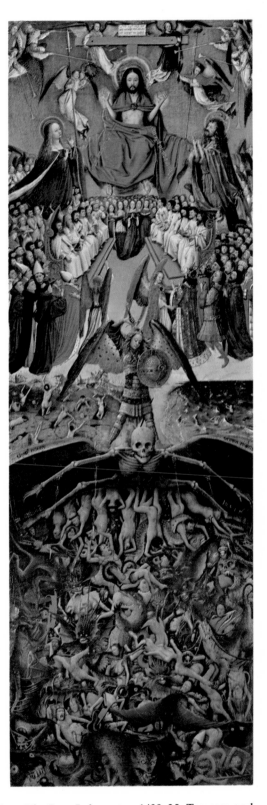

Colorplate 23. HUBERT AND JAN VAN EYCK. *Crucifixion: The Last Judgment.* c. 1420–25. Tempera and oil on canvas transferred from panel, each panel 22 1/4 × 7 3/4″. The Metropolitan Museum of Art, New York (Fletcher Fund, 1933)

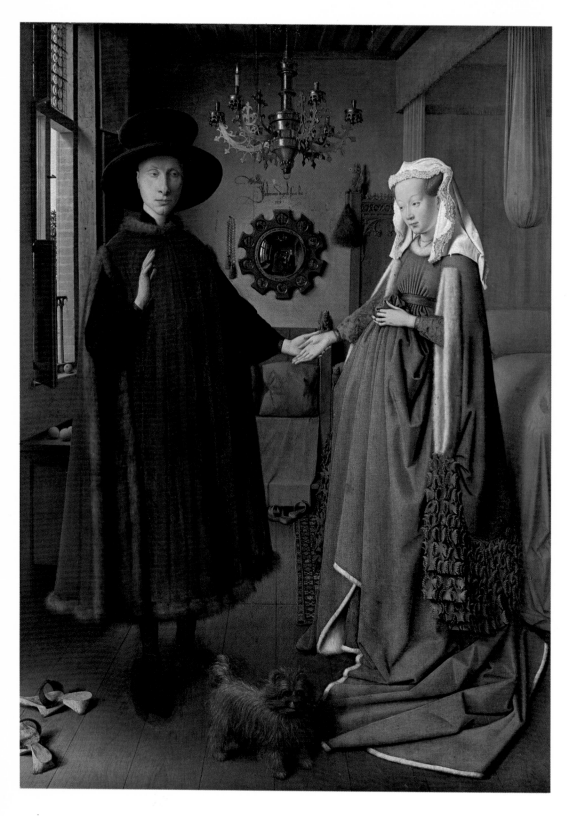

Colorplate 24. JAN VAN EYCK. *Giovanni Arnolfini and His Bride.* 1434. Oil on panel, 33 × 22 1/2″. The National Gallery, London (see also figure 148)

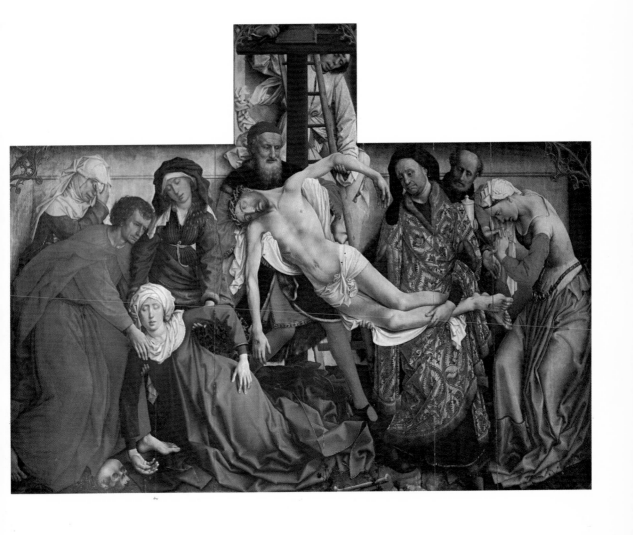

Colorplate 25. ROGIER VAN DER WEYDEN. *The Descent from the Cross*. c. 1435. Oil on panel, 7′ 2 5/8″ × 8′ 7 1/8″. The Prado, Madrid

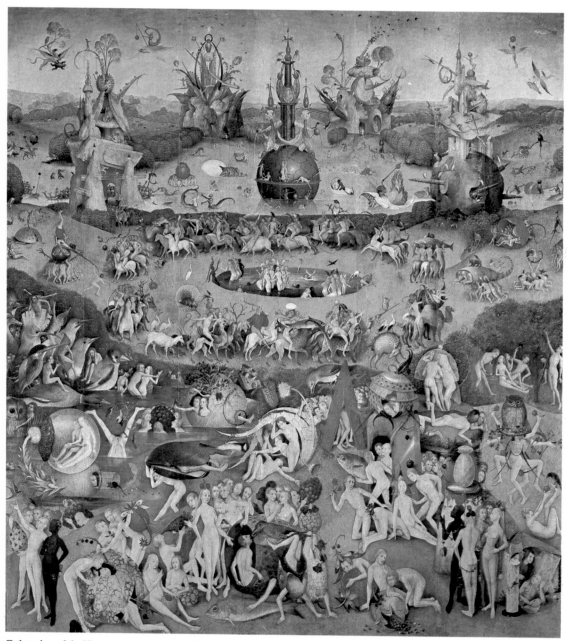

Colorplate 26. HIERONYMUS BOSCH. Center panel of *The Garden of Delights* (see figure 155)

opposite: Colorplate 27. MASACCIO. *The Holy Trinity*. 1425. Fresco. Sta. Maria Novella, Florence

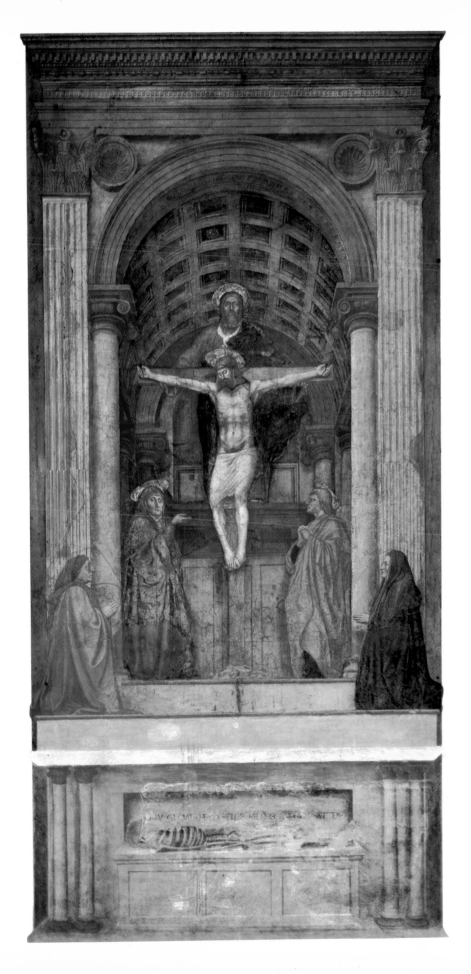

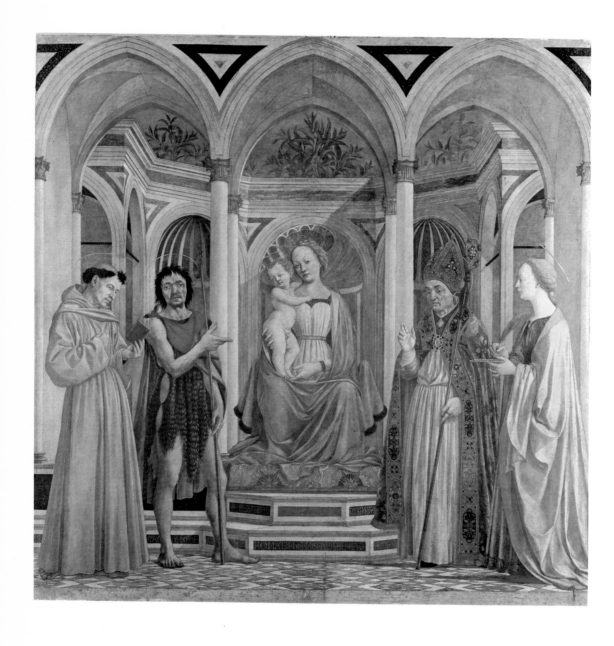

Colorplate 28. DOMENICO VENEZIANO. *Madonna and Child with Saints.* c. 1445. Tempera on panel, 6′ 7 1/2″ × 6′ 11 7/8″. Uffizi Gallery, Florence

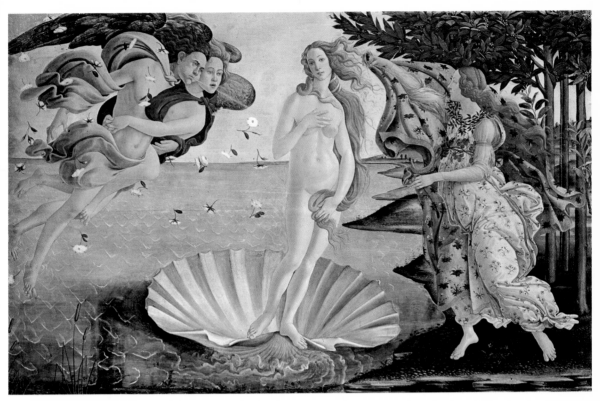

Colorplate 29. SANDRO BOTTICELLI. *The Birth of Venus*. c. 1480. Tempera on canvas, 5′ 8 7/8″ × 9′ 1 7/8″ Uffizi Gallery, Florence

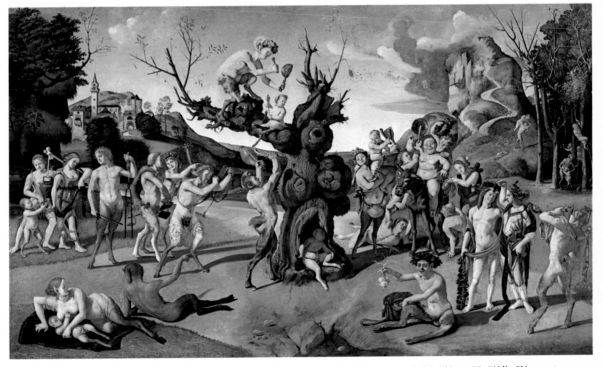

Colorplate 30. PIERO DI COSIMO. *The Discovery of Honey*. c. 1498. Oil on panel, 31 1/4 × 50 5/8″. Worcester Art Museum, Massachusetts

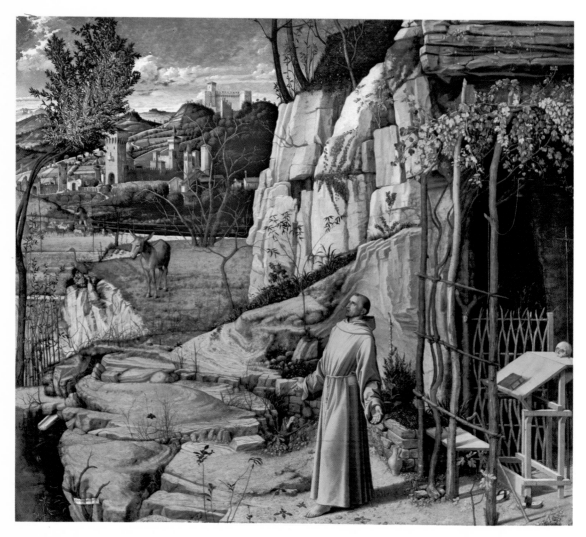

Colorplate 31. GIOVANNI BELLINI. *St. Francis in Ecstasy*. c. 1485. Oil on panel, 48 1/2 × 55″. The Frick Collection, New York (Copyright)

opposite: Colorplate 32. LEONARDO DA VINCI. *Mona Lisa*. 1503–05. Panel. 30 × 21″. The Louvre, Paris

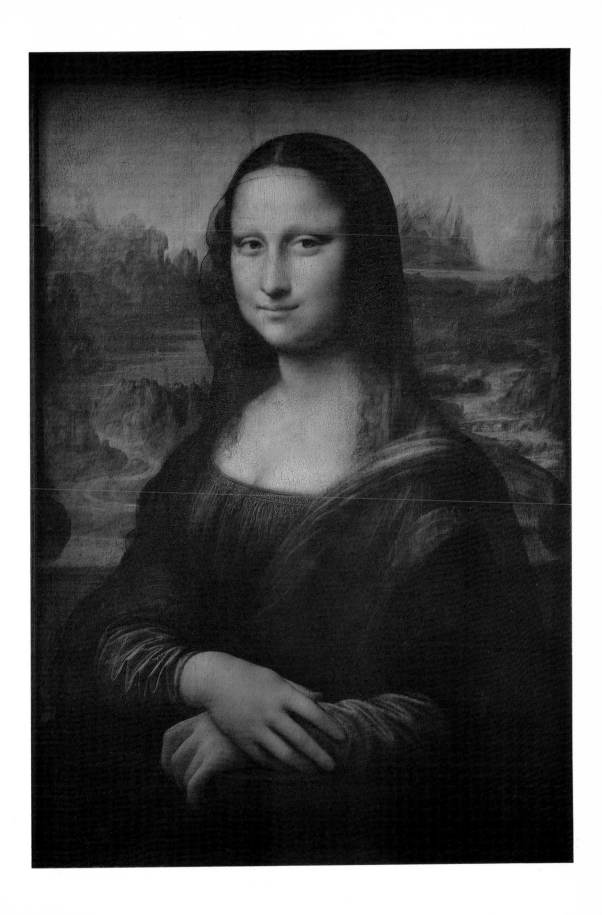

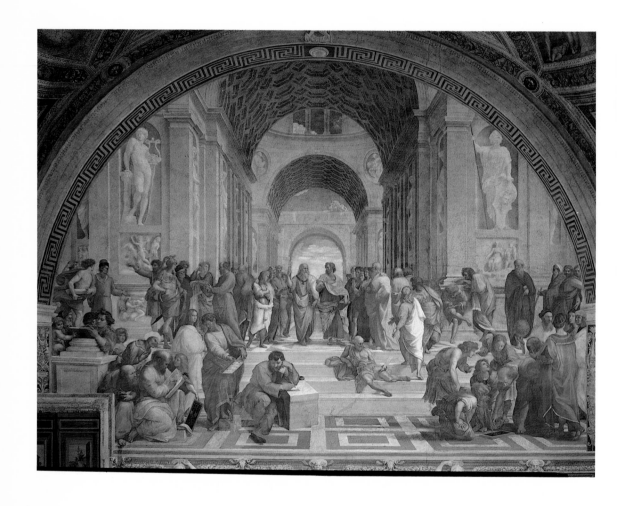

Colorplate 33. RAPHAEL. *The School of Athens*. 1510–11. Fresco. Stanza della Segnatura, Vatican Palace, Rome

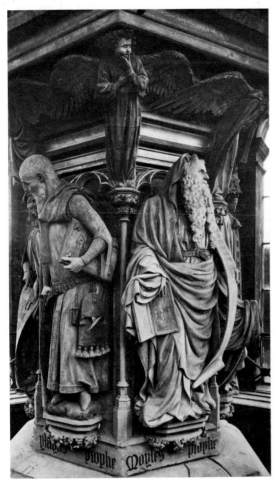

133. CLAUS SLUTER. *The Moses Well.* 1395–1406. Stone, height of figures c. 6'. Chartreuse de Champmol, Dijon

ITALY

Italian Gothic sculpture, like Italian Gothic architecture, stands apart from that of the rest of Europe. It probably began in the extreme south, in Apulia and Sicily, which were part of the domain of the German Emperor, Frederick II. The works made for him have fared badly, but he seems to have favored the Classical style of the "Visitation Master" (fig. 129, right) of Reims Cathedral, which fitted well with the imperial image of himself.

Such was the background of Nicola Pisano, who came to Tuscany from southern Italy about 1250 (the year of Frederick II's death). In 1260 he finished a marble pulpit for the Baptistery of Pisa Cathedral (see fig. 106, foreground), from which we illustrate the *Nativity* (fig. 134); turning back briefly to the Ixion Room decorations (fig. 74) we can spot certain types—the semi-reclining figure, or the crouching one—that have here been revived twelve hundred years later. But the treatment of space in our relief is certainly different: instead of the ample, if imprecise, atmosphere that envelops the Roman scenes, this is a kind of shallow box filled to bursting with solid forms that tell not only the story of the Nativity itself, but all the episodes (Annunciation to Mary, Annunciation to the Shepherds) associated with it. There is no precise counterpart of this in Northern Gothic sculpture, and Nicola must have got it from the late Roman style which is also reflected in figure 78, with its crowded space.

After 1350 a reaction set in, and we again find an interest in weight and volume, coupled with a new impulse to explore tangible reality. The climax was reached about 1400, in the works of Claus Sluter, a Netherlandish sculptor working at the court of Burgundy. His *Moses Well* (fig. 133), so called for the group of Old Testament prophets around the base, including Moses (right) and Isaiah (left), explores sculptural style in two new directions: the Isaiah shows a realism that ranges from the most minute details of the costume to the surprisingly individualized head; the Moses, a new sense of weight and volume. Note that the soft, swinging lines seem to reach out, determined to capture as much of the surrounding space as possible.

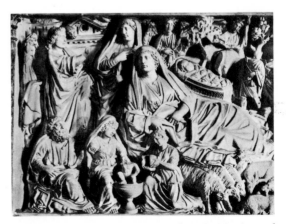

above: 134. NICOLA PISANO. *The Nativity,* panel on pulpit. 1259–60. Marble, 33 1/2 × 43". Baptistery, Pisa

Half a century after the Baptistery pulpit, Nicola's son, Giovanni Pisano, made sculpture that was much more in tune with the mainstream of Gothic style. His *Madonna* (fig. 135) still has the rather squat proportions and the Roman facial type that we saw in his father's work, but these have been combined with such up-to-date Gothic traits as the S-curved stance. The weightiness of the classical top half of the figure would make us fear that the Gothic bottom half might collapse under the burden, had Gio-

vanni not used the drapery lines to buttress the top-heavy composition.

By about 1400, at the time of the International Style (see pp. 118, 154), French influence had been thoroughly assimilated in Italy. Its foremost representative was a Florentine, Lorenzo Ghiberti, who, in 1401–2, won a competition for a pair of richly decorated bronze doors for the Baptistery in Florence. We reproduce the trial relief that he submitted, showing the *Sacrifice of Isaac* (fig. 136); the perfection of craftsmanship, which reflects his training as a goldsmith, makes it easy to understand why he won the prize. If the composition seems somewhat lacking in dramatic force, that was in line with the taste of the period, for the realism of the International Style, which developed out of the same courtly art in France that had earlier produced the smiling angel of Reims (see figure at left, fig. 129), did not extend to the realm of the emotions. This also seems to have suited Ghiberti's own lyrical temperament; but however much he may have owed to French influence, Ghiberti remained thoroughly Italian in one respect—his admiration for ancient sculpture, as evidenced by the beautiful nude body of Isaac.

Spatial depth, so notably absent in figure 134, has been greatly advanced by Ghiberti; for the first time since Classical antiquity, we experience the flat background not as a limiting "wall" but as empty space from which the figures emerge toward the beholder (note especially the angel in the upper right-hand corner). While Ghiberti was no revolutionary himself, he prepares for the great revolution in the arts that we call the Florentine Renaissance, in the second quarter of the fifteenth century.

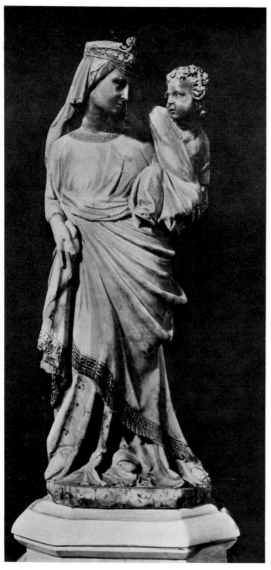

135. GIOVANNI PISANO. *Madonna.* c. 1315. Marble, height 27″. Prato Cathedral

PAINTING 1200–1400

FRANCE: STAINED GLASS; MANUSCRIPTS
Though Abbot Suger's St.-Denis had an immediate effect in changing the course of architecture and sculpture, it did not demand any radical change of style in painting.

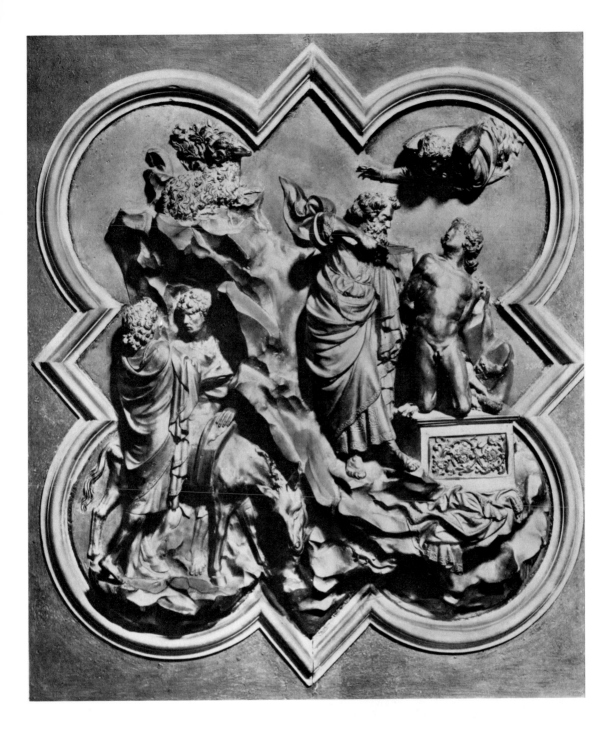

136. LORENZO GHIBERTI. *The Sacrifice of Isaac.* 1401–02. Gilt bronze, 21 × 17″. National Museum, Florence

Suger himself places a great deal of emphasis on the miraculous effect of stained glass, which was used in ever-increasing quantities as the new architecture made room for more and larger windows. Yet the technique of stained-glass painting had already been perfected in Romanesque times, and the style of the designs did not change quickly, even though the amount of stained glass required in the new cathedrals caused it to displace manuscript illumination as the leading form of painting. Working in the cathedral workshops, the window designers came to be influenced more and more by the style of the

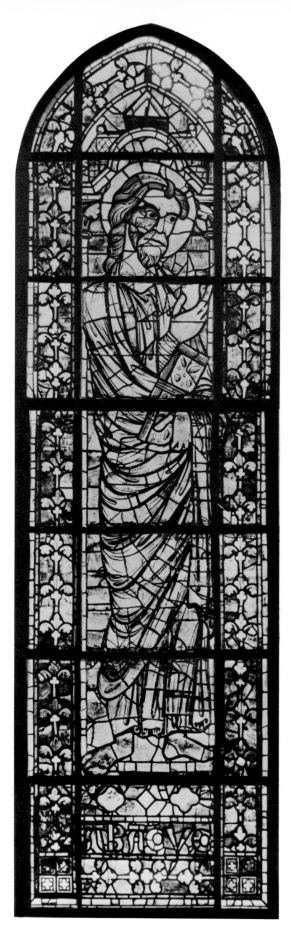

137. *Habakkuk*. c. 1220. Stained-glass window, height c. 14′. Bourges Cathedral

138. MASTER HONORÉ. *David and Goliath*, from the *Prayer Book of Philip the Fair*. 1295. Manuscript illumination. Bibliothèque Nationale, Paris

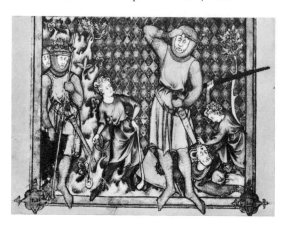

sculptors. The majestic *Habakkuk* (fig. 137), one of a series of windows representing Old Testament prophets, is the direct kin of statues like the *Visitation* group at Reims (fig. 129), and the descendant of Nicholas of Verdun's revival of Classicism a generation before. To create a figure of true monumentality in this medium is something of a miracle in itself: the primitive methods of medieval glass manufacture made it impossible to produce large panes, so that these works are not painting on glass, but "painting with glass," except for linear details that were added in black or brown. More laborious than the mosaicist's technique, that of the window-maker involved the fitting together, by means of lead strips, of odd-shaped fragments that followed the contours of his design. Well suited to abstract ornamental pattern, stained glass tends to resist any attempt at three-dimensional effects. Yet in the compositions of a great master the maze of leaded puzzle pieces could resolve itself into figures that have a looming monumentality, such as the *Habakkuk*.

opposite: 139. DUCCIO. *Christ Entering Jerusalem*, from the back of the *Maestà Altar*. 1308–11. Panel. Cathedral Museum, Siena

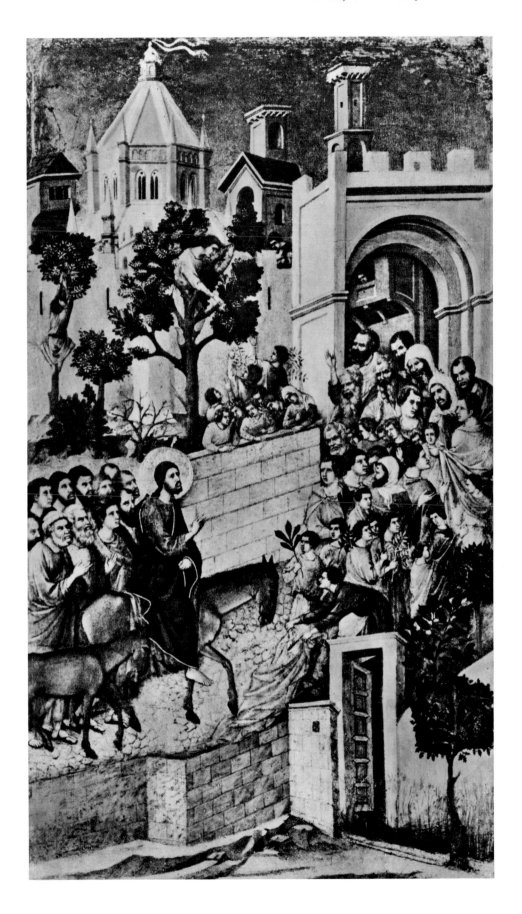

After 1250 architectural activity declined and the demand for stained glass began to slacken. By then, however, miniature painting had caught up with the new style pioneered in stone and glass. However, the centers of production now shifted from monastic scriptoria to urban workshops run by laymen—the ancestors of our modern publishing houses. Some names in this secular breed of illuminators now become known to us; an instance is Master Honoré of Paris who did the miniatures in the *Prayer Book of Philip the Fair*. In the scene of *David and Goliath* (fig. 138) the figures do not seem very firmly anchored to the ground, but the attention given to modeling indicates that stone sculpture, such as in figure 130, has been carefully studied. Here, too, a still-timid wish seems to be at work to give the figures a real space of their own to move in. Against the patterned background, Master Honoré has placed a stage-prop landscape; and since the figures obviously cannot step very far to the rear, they assert their mobility by stepping forward onto the frame.

ITALY: FRESCOES; ALTAR PANELS

We must now turn our attention to Italian painting, which at the end of the thirteenth century produced an explosion of creative energy as spectacular and far-reaching in its effects as the rise of the Gothic cathedral in France. A single glance at Giotto's mural, *Christ's Entry into Jerusalem* (colorplate 17), will convince us that we are faced with a truly revolutionary development here. How, we wonder, could a work of such monumental power have been produced by a contemporary of Master Honoré? Oddly enough, when we delve into the background of Giotto's art, we find it arose from the same "old-fashioned" attitude that we met in Italian Gothic architecture and sculpture; as a result, panel painting, mosaics, and murals—techniques that had never taken firm root north of the Alps—were kept alive in Italy. At the very same time when stained glass became the dominant pictorial art in the north of Europe, a new wave of Byzantine influence overwhelmed the lingering Romanesque elements in Italian painting. There is

a certain irony in the fact that this neo-Byzantine style (or "Greek manner," as the Italians called it) appeared soon after the conquest of Constantinople in 1204 by the armies of the Fourth Crusade—one thinks of the way Greek art had captured the taste of the victorious Romans of old. The Greek manner prevailed until almost the end of the thirteenth century, so that Italian painters were able to absorb the Byzantine tradition far more thoroughly than ever before. In the same years, as we recall, architects and sculptors were assimilating the Gothic style, and toward 1300 this spilled over into painting. It was the interaction of these two currents that produced the new style, of which Giotto is the greatest exponent.

The historical process outlined above will, perhaps, make more sense to us if we consider a fine example of "Greek manner" Italian painting, in conjunction with Giotto's *Entry into Jerusalem*. For this purpose, a panel that shows the same subject and was painted about the same time by the Sienese master, Duccio di Buoninsegna, is especially instructive (fig. 139).

DUCCIO

In contrast to what we have seen of Northern Gothic painting, here the struggle to create pictorial space seems to have been won. Duccio had mastered enough of the devices of Hellenistic-Roman illusionism to know how to create space in depth by the placement of various architectural features which lead the viewer from the foreground and up the path, through the city gate. Whatever the faults of Duccio's perspective, his architecture demonstrates a capacity to contain and define space in a manner vastly more intelligible than anything medieval art had produced, and superior to most Classical settings and their Byzantine derivatives. Gothic elements are present, too, in the soft modeling of human forms, and the unmistakable desire on the part of the artist to give his scene lively, even contemporary, touches in order to make us feel that "we are there" (thus, the contemporary costumes and the woebegone expressions in Master Honoré's *David and Goliath*, and the up-to-date Gothic tower, pennant aflutter, in the Duccio panel).

GIOTTO

In Giotto, we meet an artist of far bolder and more dramatic temper. Giotto was less close to the Greek manner from the start, and he was a wall painter by instinct, rather than a panel painter. His *Entry into Jerusalem* ultimately derives from the same sort of Byzantine composition as Duccio's, although the figure style is another matter entirely, and develops out of the sculpture of Nicola and Giovanni Pisano (see figs. 134, 135). But where Duccio had enriched the traditional scheme, spatially as well as in narrative detail, Giotto subjects it to a radical simplification. The action proceeds parallel to the picture plane; landscape, architecture, and figures have been reduced to the essential minimum; and the limited range and intensity of tones in fresco painting (watercolors applied to the freshly plastered wall) further emphasizes the austere quality of Giotto's art, as against the jewel-like brilliance of Duccio's panel (colorplate 18, though done slightly later by Simone Martini, gives some idea of its brightness).

Yet it is Giotto who succeeds in overwhelming us with the reality of the event. How does this come about? First of all, the action takes place in the foreground, much as is the case in the tiny French miniature where we noted that some figures were almost advancing toward us out of the frame (fig. 138). On Giotto's much larger scale, however, and placed so that the beholder's eye-level is at the same height as the heads of the figures, the picture space seems to be a continuation of the space we are standing in. Nor does Giotto have to make his characters step in our direction in order to have them "jump out at us": their forcefully modeled three-dimensionality is so convincing that they seem almost as solid as sculpture in the round. With Giotto, the figures create their own space, and architecture is kept to the minimum required by the narrative. Its depth, consequently, is produced by the combined volumes of the overlapping bodies in the picture, but within these limits it is very persuasive. To those who first saw painting of this sort, the effect must have been as sensational as the first Cinerama films in our own day; and his contemporaries praised him as equal, or even superior, to the greatest of the ancient painters because his forms seemed so lifelike that they could be mistaken for reality itself. His boast was that painting is superior to sculpture—not an idle boast, for Giotto does indeed mark the start of what might be called "the era of painting" in Western art. Yet his aim was not merely to rival statuary; rather, he wanted the total impact of the whole scene to hit the spectator all at once. If we look at earlier pictures, we find our glance traveling at a leisurely pace from detail to detail, until we have surveyed the entire area. But Giotto does not invite us to linger over small things, nor to wander back into the picture space, and even the groups of figures are to be taken as blocks, rather than agglomerations of individuals. Christ stands out alone, in the center, and at the same time bridges the gap between the advancing Apostles on the left, and the bowing townspeople on the right. The more we study the picture, the more we realize that its majestic firmness and clarity harbor great depths of expressiveness.

There are few men in the entire history of art to equal the stature of Giotto as a radical innovator. His very greatness, however, tended to dwarf the next generation of Florentine painters. Siena was more fortunate in this respect, for Duccio had never had the same overpowering impact; so it is there, rather than in Florence, that the next step is taken in the development of Italian Gothic painting.

SIMONE MARTINI

Simone Martini, who painted the tiny but intense *Road to Calvary* (colorplate 18) about 1340, may have been the most distinguished of Duccio's disciples. He spent the last years of his life in Avignon, the town in southern France that served as the residence-in-exile of the popes during most of the fourteenth century. Our panel, originally part of a small altar, was probably done there. In its sparkling colors, and especially in the architectural background, it still echoes the art of Duccio (fig. 139). The vigorous modeling of the figures, on the other hand, as well as their dramatic gestures and expressions, betray the influence of Giotto. While Simone Martini is not much concerned with spatial clarity, he proves to be an extraordinarily acute observer; the sheer variety of costumes and physical types, the wealth of human incident, create a sense of down-to-earth reality very different from both the lyricism of Duccio and the grandeur of Giotto.

THE LORENZETTI BROTHERS

This closeness to everyday life also appears in the work of the brothers Pietro and Ambrogio Lorenzetti, but on a more monumental scale and coupled with a keen

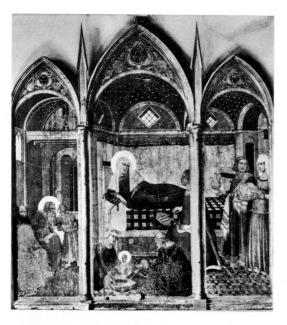

interest in problems of space. The boldest spatial experiment is Pietro's triptych of 1342, *The Birth of the Virgin* (fig. 140), where the painted architecture has been correlated with the real architecture of the frame in such a way that the two are seen as a single system. Moreover, the vaulted chamber where the birth takes place occupies two panels—it continues unbroken behind the column that divides the center from the right wing. The left wing represents an anteroom which leads to a vast and only partially glimpsed hall, suggesting the interior of a Gothic church. Here the picture surface begins to assume the quality of a transparent window, which shows the same kind of space that we know from daily experience. The same procedure enabled Ambrogio Lorenzetti, in his fresco *Good Government* in the Siena City Hall, to unfold a comprehensive view of the town before our eyes (fig. 141). In order to show the life of a well-run city-state, he had to fill the streets and houses with teeming activity; his plausible

140. PIETRO LORENZETTI. *The Birth of the Virgin.* 1342. Panel, 6′ 1 1/2″ × 5′ 11 1/2″. Cathedral Museum, Siena

141. AMBROGIO LORENZETTI. *Good Government* (portion). 1338–40. Fresco. Palazzo Pubblico, Siena

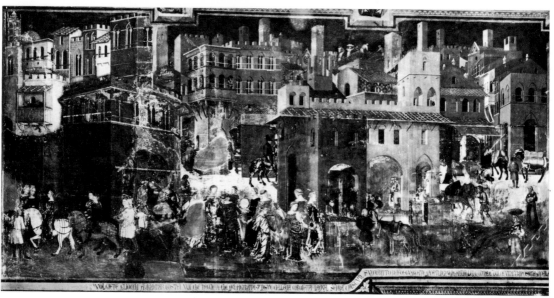

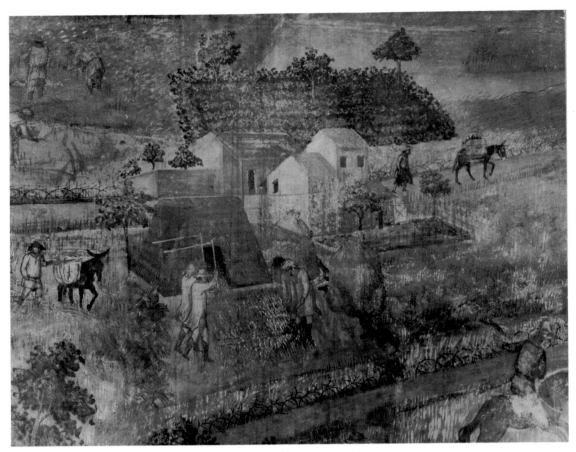

142. AMBROGIO LORENZETTI. *Good Government* (detail)

organization of the many people and buildings comes from a combination of Duccio's panoramic picture space with the immediacy of Giotto's sculptural picture space. The Sienese countryside and mountains beyond were portrayed also. Figure 142 is a detail of that part of the fresco. Here is a true landscape, the first since ancient Rome. And it is not only a landscape but an authentic human environment. That characteristic scene of vineyards, valleys, fields, pastures, farm buildings, and peasants at their labors can still be seen in Italy today.

NORTHERN GOTHIC

We are now in a position to return to Gothic painting north of the Alps; for what happened there in the latter half of the fourteenth century was determined in large measure by the influence of the great Italians. One of the chief gateways of Italian influence was the city of Prague, which in 1347 became the residence of Emperor Charles IV and rapidly developed into an international center second only to Paris. The *Death of the Virgin* (colorplate 19) was painted by a Bohemian, about 1360. Although he probably knew the work of the Sienese masters only at second or third hand, the architectural interior betrays its descent from works such as Pietro Lorenzetti's *Birth of the Virgin*. Italian, too, is the vigorous modeling of the heads and the overlapping of the figures that enhance the three-dimensional quality of the composition. Still, the Bohemian master's picture is no mere echo of Italian painting: the gestures and facial expressions convey an intensity of emotion that represents the finest heritage of Northern Gothic art.

The merging of Northern and Italian traditions in an International Gothic style, around the year 1400, has already been mentioned in connection with sculpture; but painters clearly played the major role in this development. The "realism of particulars" that we first encountered in Gothic sculpture, and later in miniatures, was continued by Northern painters. The panel in figure 143 was painted in the 1390s by Melchior Broederlam for the Duke of Burgundy. It is one of the two shutters of an altar shrine—hence its odd shape. On the left we see the Christ Child being presented to the High Priest in the Temple. Broederlam's picture space is not Pietro and Ambrogio Lorenzetti's—his architecture is rather like a doll's house—but no previous Northern painting ever gave us such a sense of depth. And the softly rounded shapes and dark, velvety shadows evoke a sense of light and air that more than compensates for any shortcomings in perspective or scale. The loose, ample, flowing garments remind us of the sculptured drapery of Sluter and Ghiberti (see figs. 133 and 136). On the right we see the Holy Family—Mary, Joseph, and the Infant Christ—on its flight to Egypt. The softly shaded rocky slopes and lovingly detailed trees and flowers tell us that landscape has now become important in the North. For Broederlam, every detail of the natural world was worth looking at—its plants, animals, and people. His charming donkey was certainly painted from life; and his Joseph makes us think of a rough, simple farmer.

THE INTERNATIONAL STYLE

Although panels were taking on importance in the North around 1400, book illumination remained the leading form of painting. The International Style reached its peak in the workshop of the Limbourg brothers soon after the turn of the fifteenth century. They were Flemings who, like Claus Sluter, the sculptor, had settled in France; but they must have visited Italy as well, for their work includes a great number of motifs, and some entire compositions, borrowed from the great masters of Florence and Siena. The *Very Rich Book of Hours* that they made for the King of France's brother, the Duke of

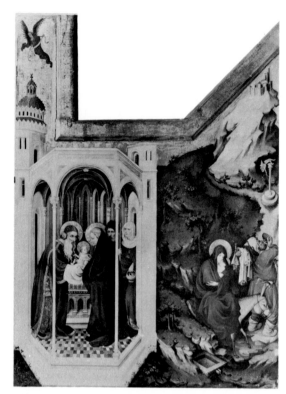

143. MELCHIOR BROEDERLAM. *Presentation in the Temple and Flight into Egypt*. 1394–99. Tempera on panel, 64 × 51″. Museum of Fine Arts, Dijon

Berry, contains a group of remarkable calendar pages. Calendar cycles depicting the labors of each month had long been an established part of medieval art (see p. 127). The Limbourg brothers, however, enlarged such examples into panoramas of man's life in nature. Thus the February miniature (colorplate 20), the earliest snow landscape in the history of Western art, gives an enchantingly lyrical account of village life in the dead of winter. Here the promise of the Broederlam panel has been fulfilled, as it were: landscape, architectural interiors and exteriors are harmoniously united in deep, atmospheric space. Even such intangible, evanescent things as the frozen breath of the maid, the smoke curling from the chimney, and the clouds in the sky have become "paintable." Some of the calendar pages, such as April (fig. 144), are devoted to the life of the nobility. Once more we marvel at the wealth of realistic detail. Yet the figures display an odd lack of individuality. They are all of the same type, in face as well as stature: aristocratic mannequins of superhuman slenderness who are differentiated only by the luxuriance and variety of their clothing. Surely the gulf between them and the peasants of the February miniature could not have been greater in real life than it appears in these pictures!

From the courtly throng of the April page it is but a step to the three Magi and their train in the altarpiece by Gentile da Fabriano, the greatest Italian painter of the International Style (colorplate 21). The costumes here are as colorful, the draperies as ample and softly rounded, as in the North. The Holy Family on the left almost seems in danger of being overwhelmed by the gay and festive pageant pouring down upon it from the hills in the distance. Again we admire the marvelously well-observed animals, which now include not only the familiar ones but hunting leopards, camels, and monkeys. (Such creatures were eagerly collected by the princes of the period, many of whom kept private zoos.) The Oriental background of the Magi is further emphasized by the Mongolian facial cast of some of their companions. It is not these exotic touches, however, that mark our picture as the work of an Italian master but something else, a greater sense of weight, of physical substance, than we could hope to find among the Northern representatives of the International Style. Gentile, despite his love of fine detail, is obviously a painter used to working on a monumental scale, rather than a manuscript illuminator at heart.

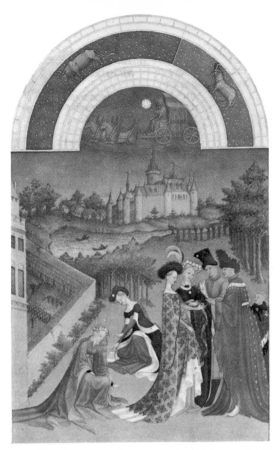

144. THE LIMBOURG BROTHERS. *April*. Manuscript illumination from the *Very Rich Book of Hours of the Duke of Berry*. c. 1415. Condé Museum, Chantilly

SYNOPTIC TABLE II

	POLITICAL HISTORY	RELIGION, LITERATURE	SCIENCE, TECHNOLOGY
300	Emperor Constantine the Great (r. 324–337) Roman Empire split into Eastern and Western branches 395	Christianity legalized by Edict of Milan 313; state religion 395 St. Augustine, St. Jerome	
400	Rome sacked by Visigoths 410 Fall of Western Roman Empire 476 "Golden Age" of Justinian 527–565	Split between Eastern and Western Churches begins 451 St. Patrick (died c. 461) founds Celtic Church in Ireland	Silk cultivation brought to eastern Mediterranean from China
600	Muhammad (570–632) Byzantium loses Near Eastern and African provinces to Muslims 632–732; to Seljuk Turks 1071 Muslims invade Spain 711–718; defeated by Franks, battle of Tours, 732 Independent Muslim state established in Spain 756	Isidore of Seville (died 636) *Beowulf* epic Iconoclastic controversy 726–843	Paper-making introduced into Near East from China Stirrup introduced into Western Europe
800	Charlemagne (r. 768–814) crowned Emperor of Romans by Pope 800 Alfred the Great (r. 871–899?), Anglo-Saxon King of England	Carolingian revival of Latin Classics	Earliest documented church organ, Aachen, 822 Horse collar adopted in Western Europe, makes horses efficient draft animals
900	Otto I (the Great) crowned Emperor by Pope 962 Otto II (r. 973–983) defeated by Muslims in southern Italy	Monastic Order of Cluny founded 910 Conversion of Russia to Orthodox Church c. 990	Earliest application of water power to industry
1000	Normans arrive in Italy 1016 Reconquest of Spain from Muslims begins William the Conqueror defeats Harold at Battle of Hastings 1066 First Crusade 1095–96	College of Cardinals formed to elect pope 1059 Cistercian Order founded 1098	Leif Ericson sails to North America 1002
1100	Frederick Barbarossa (r. 1155–90) titles his realm "Holy Roman Empire," tries to assert his authority in Italy King Henry II founds Plantagenet line in England	Rise of universities (Bologna, Paris, Oxford) based on faculties of law, medicine, theology Peter Abelard (1079–1142) First flowering of vernacular literature; age of the troubadours	Earliest manufacture of paper in Europe, by Muslims in Spain Earliest use of magnetic compass for navigation
1200	Fourth Crusade (1202–4) conquers Constantinople Latin Empire in Constantinople 1204–61 Magna Carta limits power of English kings 1215 Louis IX (St. Louis, r. 1226–70), King of France Philip IV (the Fair, r. 1285–1314), King of France, humiliates Pope Boniface VIII 1303	St. Dominic (1170–1221) founds Dominican Order; Inquisition established to combat heresy St. Francis of Assisi (died 1226) St. Thomas Aquinas (died 1274) Dante Alighieri (1265–1321)	Marco Polo travels to China and India c. 1275–93
1300	Exile of papacy at Avignon 1309–76 Hundred Years' War between England and France begins 1337	*Canterbury Tales* by Chaucer c. 1387	First large-scale production of paper in Italy and Germany First large-scale production of gunpowder; earliest known use of cannon 1326 Earliest cast iron in Europe
1400	Great Papal Schism (since 1378) settled 1417; Pope returns to Rome	Jan Hus burned at stake for heresy 1415	Gutenberg invents printing with movable type 1446–50

NOTE:
Figure numbers of black-and-white illustrations are in (italics). Colorplate numbers are in **(bold face)**.
Duration of papacy or reign is indicated by the abbreviation r.

ARCHITECTURE	SCULPTURE	PAINTING	
Basilica of Constantine (65)	Sarcophagus of Junius Bassus (81)	Catacomb of SS. Peter and Marcellinus, Rome (76)	300
Hagia Sophia, Istanbul (86) S. Apollinare in Classe, Ravenna (77)	*Archangel Michael*, diptych (82)	*Vatican Vergil* (79) Mosaics, Sta. Maria Maggiore, Rome (78) *Vienna Genesis* (80) Mosaics, S. Apollinare in Classe and S. Vitale, Ravenna (**11**, 87)	400
	Sutton Hoo ship-burial treasure (89)	*Lindisfarne Gospels* (91)	600
Palace Chapel of Charlemagne, Aachen (93)	Oseberg ship-burial (90)	*Gospel Book of Charlemagne* (95)	800
		Gospel Book of Ebbo of Reims (96)	900
St. Michael's, Hildesheim (98) Pisa Cathedral (106) Baptistery, Florence (107) St.-Étienne, Caen (104) St.-Sernin, Toulouse (100–102) Durham Cathedral (105)	Bronze doors of Bernward, Hildesheim (99) Apostle, St.-Sernin, Toulouse (108)	*Gospel Book of Otto III* (**14**) Mosaics, Daphnē (88)	1000
Notre-Dame, Paris (116–119)	South portal, Moissac (109) *Last Judgment* tympanum, Autun (110) West portals, Chartres Cathedral (128)	Nave vault murals, St.-Savin-sur-Gartempe (114) *Gospel Book of Wedricus* (**15**)	1100
Salisbury Cathedral (121) Florence Cathedral (124)	West portals, Reims Cathedral (129) Choir screen, Naumburg Cathedral (131)	Nave, Chartres Cathedral (**16**) Stained glass, nave clerestory, Bourges Cathedral (137) *Madonna Enthroned*, icon (**12**) *Prayer Book of Philip the Fair*, by Master Honoré (138)	1200
Choir, Gloucester Cathedral (122)	*Pietà*, Bonn (132) *Moses Well*, by Claus Sluter (133)	Arena Chapel frescoes, Padua, by Giotto (**17**) *Maestà* altar, Siena, by Duccio (139) *Good and Bad Government* frescoes, Siena, by Ambrogio Lorenzetti (141, 142) Altar wings, Dijon, by Melchior Broederlam (143)	1300
	Trial relief for Baptistery doors, Florence by Ghiberti (136)	*Very Rich Book of Hours of the Duke of Berry*, by Limbourg Brothers (144, **20**)	1400

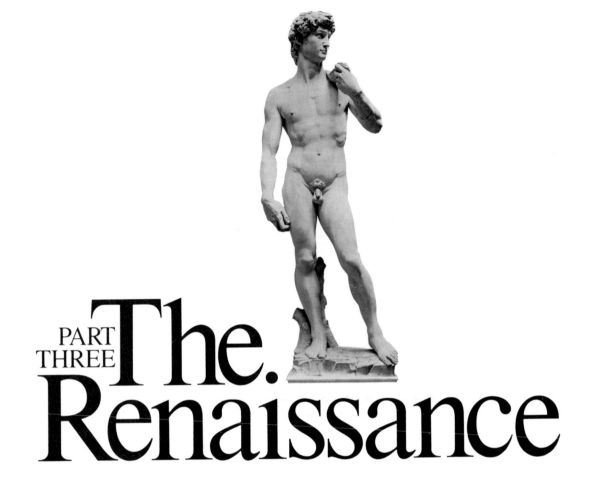

PART
THREE The.
Renaissance

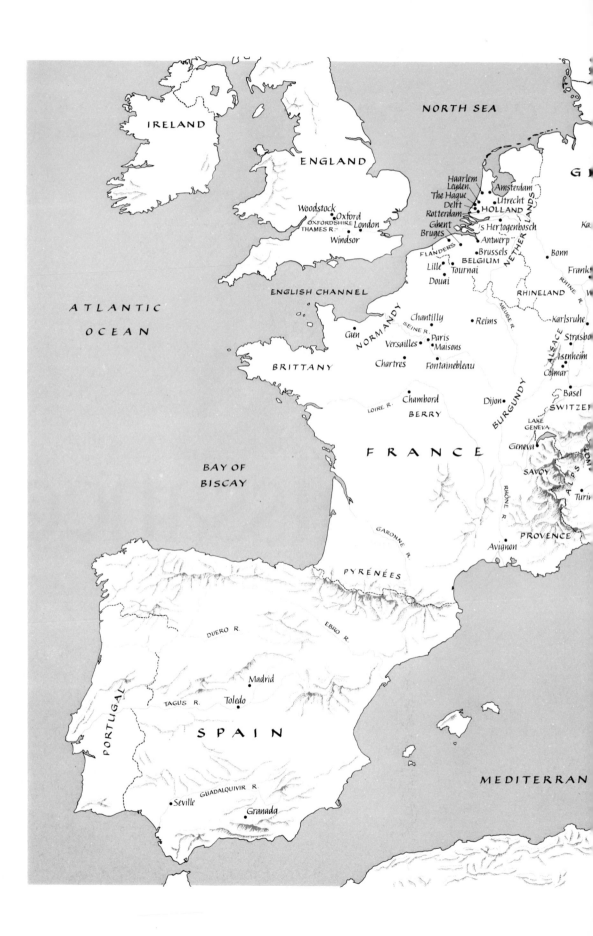

NORTH SEA

IRELAND

ENGLAND

Woodstock
Oxford
OXFORDSHIRE London
THAMES R.
Windsor

Haarlem
Leyden
The Hague   Amsterdam
Delft   Utrecht
Rotterdam   HOLLAND
Ghent   's Hertogenbosch
Bruges
             Antwerp
             Brussels
FLANDERS
Lille   BELGIUM
    Tournai
Douai

G

Ka.

Bonn

Frank

NETHERLANDS

RHINELAND

RHINE R.

W

ATLANTIC

OCEAN

ENGLISH CHANNEL

Chantilly
Caen   Reims
        SEINE R.
NORMANDY   Paris
Versailles   Maisons
Chartres   Fontainebleau

Karlsruhe

ALSACE
Strasbo
Isenheim
Colmar

Basel

BRITTANY

Chambord
BERRY

Dijon

SWITZER

BURGUNDY

LAKE
GENEVA

BAY OF
BISCAY

FRANCE

Geneva

SAVOY

ALPS

Turi

GARONNE R.

RHONE R.

PROVENCE
Avignon

PYRÉNÉES

DUERO R.

EBRO R.

PORTUGAL

Madrid

Toledo

TAGUS R.

SPAIN

MEDITERRAN

GUADALQUIVIR R.

Seville

Granada

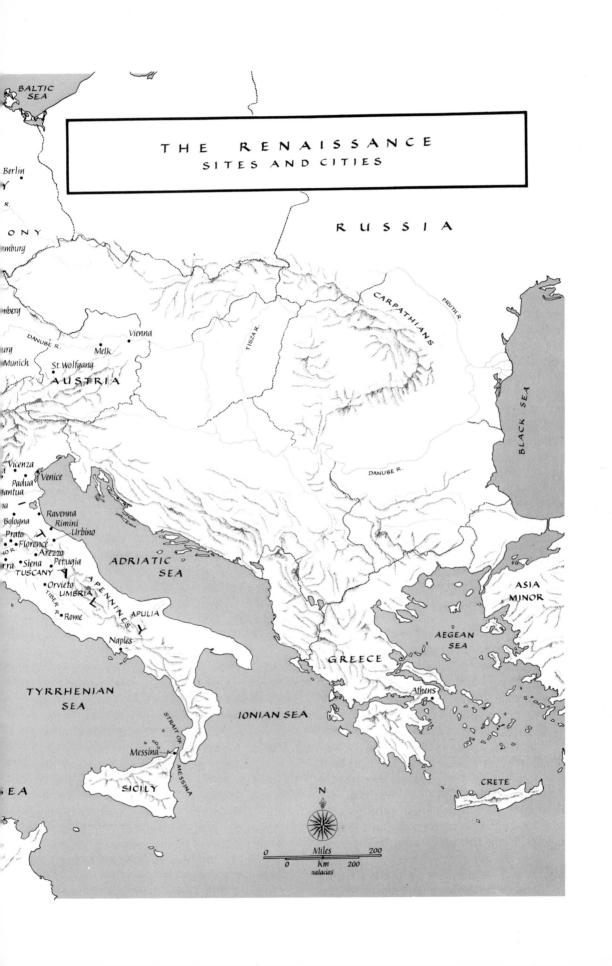

BALTIC
SEA

Berlin

ONY

mburg

urg
Munich

RUSSIA

DANUBE R.

Vienna

Melk

St.Wolfgang

AUSTRIA

CARPATHIANS

PRUTH R.

TISZA R.

DANUBE R.

BLACK
SEA

THE RENAISSANCE
SITES AND CITIES

Vicenza

Padua
Mantua

Venice

Bologna
Prato
Florence

Siena

TUSCANY

Ravenna
Rimini
Urbino

Arezzo

Perugia

Orvieto

UMBRIA

TIBER R.

Rome

APENNINES

ADRIATIC
SEA

APULIA

ASIA
MINOR

AEGEAN
SEA

Naples

GREECE

TYRRHENIAN
SEA

IONIAN SEA

Athens

STRAIT OF MESSINA

Messina

SEA

SICILY

N

CRETE

0   Miles   200

0   Km   200
nalacias

The "New Age"

In discussing the transition from Classical antiquity to the Middle Ages, we were able to point to a great crisis—the rise of Islam—separating the two eras. No comparable event divides the Middle Ages from the Renaissance. The fifteenth and sixteenth centuries did witness far-reaching developments: the fall of Constantinople and the Turkish conquest of southeastern Europe; the journeys of exploration that led to the founding of overseas empires in the New World, in Africa, and in Asia, with the subsequent rivalry of Spain and England as the foremost colonial powers; the deep spiritual crises of Reformation and Counter Reformation. But none of these can be said to have produced the new era. By the time they occurred, the Renaissance was well under way. Thus it is no surprise that scholars debating the causes of the Renaissance disagree, like the proverbial blind men trying to describe an elephant. Even if we disregard those few who would deny the existence of the animal altogether, we are left with a wide range of views. Every branch of historic study has developed its own image of the period. While these images overlap, they do not coincide, so that our concept of the Renaissance may vary as we focus on its fine arts, music, literature, philosophy, politics, economics, or science. Perhaps the one point on which most experts agree is that the Renaissance had begun when people realized they were no longer living in the Middle Ages.

This statement is not as simple-minded as it sounds, for the Renaissance was the first period in history to be aware of its own existence and to coin a label for itself. Medieval man did not think he belonged to an age distinct from Classical antiquity; the past, to him, consisted simply of "B.C." and "A.D."; history, from this point of view, is made in Heaven rather than on earth. The Renaissance, by contrast, divided the past not according to the Divine plan of salvation, but on the basis of human actions. It saw Classical antiquity as the era when man had reached the peak of his creative powers, an era brought to a sudden end by the barbarians who destroyed the Roman Empire. In the

thousand-year interval of "darkness" which then followed, little was accomplished, but now at last this "time in-between" or "Middle Ages" had given way to a revival of all those arts and sciences that flourished in ancient times. The present could thus be fittingly labeled a "rebirth"—*renaissance* in French and, by adoption, in English. The origin of this revolutionary view of history can be traced back to the 1330s in the writings of the Italian poet Petrarch, the first of the great men who initiated the Renaissance. That it should have begun in the mind of one man is itself a telling comment on the new era, for Petrarch embodies two salient features of the Renaissance: individualism and humanism. Individualism—a new self-awareness and self-assurance—enabled him to claim, against all established authority, that the "age of faith" was actually an era of darkness, and that the "benighted pagans" of antiquity represented the most enlightened stage of history. Humanism, to Petrarch, meant a belief in the importance of what we still call "the humanities" or "humane letters" (as against Divine letters, the study of Scripture): the pursuit of learning in languages, literature, history, and philosophy for its own end, in a secular rather than religious framework. Again he set a pattern because the humanists, the new breed of scholar following him, became the intellectual leaders of the Renaissance.

Yet Petrarch and his successors did not want to revive Classical antiquity lock, stock, and barrel. By interposing the concept of "a thousand years of darkness" between themselves and the ancients, they acknowledged—unlike medieval Classicists—that the Graeco-Roman world was now irretrievably dead. Its glories could be revived only in the mind, across the barrier of the "dark ages," by rediscovering the full greatness of ancient achievements in art and thought and by trying to compete with them on an ideal plane. The aim of the Renaissance was not to duplicate the works of antiquity but to equal and perhaps to surpass them. In practice, this meant that the authority granted to the ancient models was far from unlimited. The humanists did not become neo-pagans but went to great lengths seeking to reconcile Classical philosophy with Christianity; and architects continued to build churches, not pagan temples, but in doing so they used an architectural vocabulary based on the study of Classical structures. Renaissance physicians admired the anatomical handbooks of the ancients, but they discovered errors when they matched the books against the direct experience of the dissection table, and learned to rely on the evidence of their own eyes. It is a fundamental paradox that the desire to return to the Classics, based on a rejection of the Middle Ages, brought to the new era not the rebirth of antiquity but the birth of Modern Man.

Late Gothic Painting North of the Alps

RENAISSANCE VS. "LATE GOTHIC"

As we narrow our focus from the Renaissance as a whole to the Renaissance in the fine arts, we are faced with some questions that are still being debated: Did it, like Gothic art, originate in a specific center, or in several places at the same time? Should we think of it as one new, coherent style, or as a new attitude that might be embodied in more than one style? So far as architecture and sculpture are concerned, there is general agreement that the Renaissance began in Florence soon after 1400. In painting, the situation is less clear-cut. Some scholars believe that the first Renaissance painter was Giotto—an understandable claim, since his achievement (and that of his contemporaries in Siena) had revolutionized painting throughout Europe (see p. 150). Nevertheless, it took a second revolution, a century after Giotto, for Renaissance painting to be born, and this revolution began independently both in Florence and in the Netherlands. The twin revolutions were linked by a common aim— the conquest of the visible world beyond the limits of the International Gothic style—yet they were sharply separated in almost every other respect. While the new realism of Florentine painting after about 1420 is clearly part of the Early Renaissance movement, we have no satisfactory name for its counterpart in the North. The label "Late Gothic," often

applied to it, hardly does justice to its special character, although the term has some justification. It indicates, for instance, that the creators of the new style in Flanders, unlike their Italian contemporaries, did not reject the International Style; rather, they took it as their point of departure, so that the break with the past was less abrupt in the North than in the South. It also reminds us that fifteenth-century architecture in the North remained firmly rooted in the Gothic tradition. Whatever we choose to call the style of Northern painters at this time, their environment was clearly Late Gothic. How could they create a genuinely post-medieval style in such a setting? Would it not be more reasonable to regard their work, despite its great importance, as the final phase of Gothic painting? If we treat them here as the Northern counterpart of the Early Renaissance, we do so for several reasons. The great Flemish masters whose work we are about to examine were as much admired in Italy as they were at home, and their intense realism had a conspicuous influence on Early Renaissance painting. Moreover, they have a close parallel in the field of music: from about 1420 on, the Netherlands produced a school of composers so revolutionary as to dominate the development of music throughout Europe for the next hundred years. A contemporary said of them that nothing worth listening to had been composed before their time. An analogous claim might well have been made for the new school of Flemish painters.

THE MASTER OF FLÉMALLE
The first phase of the pictorial revolution in Flanders is represented by an artist known as the Master of Flémalle. He was probably Robert Campin, the foremost painter of Tournai, who is recorded there from 1406 until his death in 1444. Among his finest works is the *Annunciation*, the center panel of the *Merode Altarpiece*, done soon after 1425 (colorplate 22). Comparing it with the Franco-Flemish pictures of the International Style (see fig. 143), we recognize that it belongs within that tradition; yet we also find in it a new pictorial experience. For the first time, we have the sensation of actually looking *through* the surface of the panel into a spatial world with all the essential qualities

of everyday reality: unlimited depth, stability, continuity, and completeness. The painters of the International Style had never aimed at such consistency; their pictures have the enchanting quality of fairy tales where the scale and relationship of things can be shifted at will, where fact and fancy mingle without conflict. Campin, in contrast, has undertaken to tell the truth, the whole truth, and nothing but the truth. He does not yet do it with ease—his objects, overly foreshortened, tend to jostle each other in space. But, with obsessive determination, he defines every aspect of every last object: its individual shape and size, its color, material, texture, and its way of responding to light (note the surface reflections and sharply defined shadows). The *Merode Annunciation*, in short, transports us quite abruptly from the aristocratic world of the International Style to the household of a Flemish burgher. This is the earliest Annunciation in panel painting that occurs in a fully equipped domestic interior. Campin has here faced a problem no one had met before: how to transfer a supernatural event (the angel announcing to Mary that she will bear the Son of God) from a symbolic setting to an everyday environment, without making it look either trivial or incongruous. He has solved the problem by a method known as "disguised symbolism," which means that any detail within the picture, however casual, may carry a symbolic message. Thus the lilies denote the Virgin's chastity, and the shiny water basin and the towel on its rack are not merely household equipment but further tributes to Mary as the "vessel most clean" and the "well of living waters." Perhaps the most intriguing symbol is the candle next to the lilies. It was extinguished only moments ago; but why, in broad daylight, had it been lit, and what made the flame go out? Has the Divine radiance of the Lord's presence overcome the material light? Or did the flame itself represent the Divine light, now extinguished to show that God has become man, that in Christ "the Word was made flesh"? Clearly, the entire wealth of medieval symbolism survives in our picture, but it is so immersed in the world of everyday appearances that we are often left to doubt whether a given detail demands symbolic interpretation. How, we wonder, could Campin pursue simultaneously what we tend to regard as opposite goals, realism and symbolism? To him, apparently, the two were interdependent, rather than in conflict. He must have felt that he had to "sanctify" everyday reality with the maximum of spiritual significance in order to make it worth painting. This deeply reverential attitude toward the physical universe as a mirror of Divine truth helps us to understand why in our panel even the least conspicuous details are rendered with the same concentrated attention as the sacred figures; potentially, at least, everything is a symbol, and thus merits an equally exacting scrutiny.

If we compare our colorplate of the *Merode Annunciation* with that of an earlier panel painting (colorplate 19), we become aware of another revolutionary quality of Campin's work. The jewel-like brightness of the older picture, its pattern of brilliant hues and lavish use of gold, have given way to a color scheme far less decorative but much more flexible and differentiated. The subdued tints—muted greens, bluish or brownish grays—show a new subtlety, and the scale of intermediate shades is smoother and has a wider range. All these effects are essential to the realistic style of Campin; they were made possible by the use of oil, the medium he was among the first to exploit. The basic technique of medieval painting had been tempera, in which the powdered pigments were mixed ("tempered") with diluted egg yolk. It produced a thin, tough, quick-drying coat admirably suited to the medieval taste for high-keyed, flat color surfaces. Oil, in contrast, was a viscous, slow-drying medium. It could yield a vast range of effects, from thin, translucent films (called "glazes") to the thickest impasto (a dense layer of creamy, heavy-bodied paint). It also permitted the blending of colors right on the panel, which produced a continuous scale of hues that included rich, velvety dark shades unknown before. Without oil, the Flemish masters' conquest of visible reality would have been much more limited. Thus, from the technical point of view, too, they were the "fathers of modern painting," for oil was to become the painter's basic medium everywhere.

VAN EYCK

Needless to say, the full range of effects made possible by oil was not discovered all at once, nor by any one man. Campin contributed less than Jan van Eyck, a somewhat younger and much more famous artist, who was long credited with the actual "invention" of oil painting. About Jan's life and career we know a good deal, while his older brother Hubert, apparently also a painter, remains a disputed figure. There are several works that may have been painted by either of the two, including the pair of panels showing the Crucifixion and the Last Judgment (colorplate 23). Scholars agree that their date is between 1420 and 1425, if not on whether Jan or Hubert was the author. The style of these panels has much in common with that of the *Merode Annunciation*—the all-embracing devotion to the visible world, the deep space, the angular drapery folds, less graceful but far more realistic than the unbroken loops of the International Style. Yet the individual forms are not so tangible, they seem less isolated, less "sculptural"; and the sweeping sense of space comes not so much from violent foreshortening as from subtle changes of light and color. If we inspect the *Crucifixion* slowly, from the foreground figures to the distant city of Jerusalem and the snow-capped peaks beyond, we see a gradual decrease in the intensity of local colors and in the contrast of light and dark. Everything tends toward a uniform tint of light bluish gray, so that the furthest mountain range merges with the color of the sky. This optical phenomenon is known as "atmospheric perspective," since it results from the fact that the atmosphere is never wholly transparent. Even on the clearest day, the air between us and the things we are looking at acts as a hazy screen that interferes with our ability to see distant shapes and colors clearly; as we approach the limit of visibility, it swallows them altogether. Atmospheric perspective is more fundamental to our perception of deep space than linear perspective, which records the diminution in the apparent size of objects as their distance from the observer increases. It is effective not only in faraway vistas; in the *Crucifixion*, even the foreground seems enveloped in a delicate haze that softens contours, shadows, and colors. The entire scene

has a continuity and harmony quite beyond Campin's pictorial range. Clearly, the Van Eycks used the oil medium with extraordinary refinement.

Viewed as a whole, the *Crucifixion* seems singularly devoid of drama, as if the scene had been becalmed by some magic spell. Only when we concentrate on the details do we become aware of the violent emotions in the faces of the crowd beneath the Cross, and the restrained but profoundly touching grief of the Virgin and her companions in the foreground. In the *Last Judgment*, this dual aspect of the Eyckian style takes the form of two extremes: above the horizon, all is order and calm, while below it—on earth and in the realm of Satan—the opposite condition prevails. The two states thus correspond to Heaven and Hell, contemplative bliss as against physical and emotional turbulence. The lower half, clearly, was the greater challenge to the artist's imaginative powers. The dead rising from their graves with frantic gestures of fear and hope, the damned being torn apart by devilish monsters more frightful than any we have seen before, all have the awesome reality of a nightmare—a nightmare "observed" with the same infinite care as the natural world of the *Crucifixion*.

The *Ghent Altarpiece* (figs. 145, 146), the greatest monument of early Flemish painting, presents problems so complex that our discussion must be limited to bare essentials. The inscription informs us that the work, begun by Hubert, was completed by Jan in 1432. Since Hubert died in 1426, the altarpiece was presumably made in the seven-year span between 1425 and 1432. We may expect it, therefore, to introduce to us the next phase of the new style, following that of the pictures we have discussed so far. Although its basic form is a triptych—a central body with two hinged wings—each of the three units consists of four separate panels, and since, in addition, the wings are painted on both sides, the altarpiece has a total of twenty component parts of assorted shapes and sizes. The ensemble makes what has rightly been called a "super-altar," overwhelming but far from harmonious, which could not have been planned this way from the start. Apparently Jan took over a number of panels left unfinished by Hubert, com-

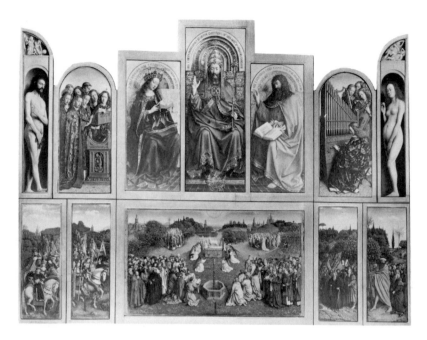

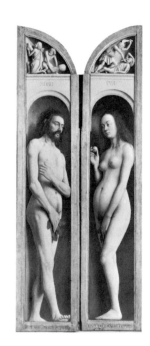

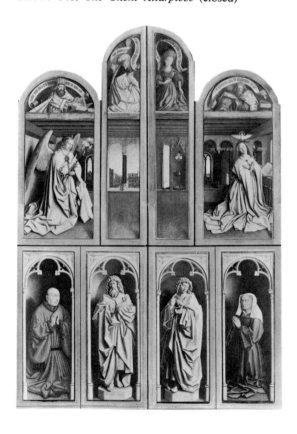

above left: 145. HUBERT AND JAN VAN EYCK. *The Ghent Altarpiece* (open). Completed 1432. Oil on panel, 11′ 3″ × 14′ 15″. St. Bavo, Ghent

above right: 145. *Adam* and *Eve* (detail of *The Ghent Altarpiece*)

below: 146. *The Ghent Altarpiece* (closed)

pleted them, added some of his own, and assembled them at the behest of the wealthy donor whose portrait we see on the outside of the altar. To reconstruct this train of events, and to determine each brother's share, is a fascinating but treacherous game. Suffice it to say that Hubert remains a somewhat shadowy figure; his style, overlaid with re-touches by Jan, can probably be found in the four central panels, although these did not belong together originally. The upper three, whose huge figures in the final arrangement crush the multitude of small ones below, were intended, it seems, to form a self-con-tained triptych: the Lord between the Virgin Mary and St. John the Baptist. The lower panel and the four flanking it probably formed a separate altarpiece, the Adoration of the Lamb, symbolizing Christ's sacrificial death. The two panels with music-making angels may have been planned by Hubert as a pair of organ shutters. If this set of conjectures is correct, the two tall, narrow panels showing Adam and Eve (fig. 145) are the only ones added by Jan to Hubert's stock. They cer-tainly are the most daring of all: the earliest monumental nudes of Northern panel paint-ing (hardly less than lifesize), magnificently observed, and caressed by the most delicate play of light and shade. Their quiet dignity—

and their prominent place in the altar—suggests that they should remind us not so much of Original Sin, as of man's creation in God's own image. Actual evil, by contrast, is represented in the small, violently expressive scenes above, which show the story of Cain and Abel. Still more extraordinary, however, is the fact that the Adam and Eve were designed specifically for their present positions in the ensemble. Acknowledging that they would really appear this way to the spectator whose eye-level is below the bottom of the panels, Jan van Eyck has depicted them in accordance with this abnormal viewpoint and thereby established a new, direct relationship between picture space and real space.

The outer surfaces of the two wings (fig. 146) were evidently planned by Jan as one coherent unit. Here, as we would normally expect, the largest figures are not above. but in the lower tier. The two St. Johns (painted in grays to simulate sculpture, like the scenes of Cain and Abel), the donor, and his wife, each in his separate niche, are the immediate kin of the Adam and Eve panels. The upper tier has two pairs of panels of different width; the artist has made a virtue of this awkward necessity by combining all four into one interior. Such an effect, we recall, had first been created almost a century earlier (compare fig. 140), but Jan, not content with perspective devices alone, heightens the illusion by painting the shadows cast by the frames of the panels on the floor of the Virgin's chamber. Interestingly enough, this *Annunciation* resembles, in its homely detail, the *Merode Altarpiece*, thus providing a valuable link between the two great pioneers of Flemish realism.

Donors' portraits of splendid individuality occupy conspicuous positions in both the Merode and the Ghent altarpieces. A renewed interest in realistic portraiture had developed in the mid-fourteenth century, but not until the Master of Flémalle did the portrait play a major role in Northern painting. In addition to donors' portraits, we now begin to encounter in growing numbers small, independent likenesses whose peculiar intimacy suggests that they were treasured keepsakes. One of the most fascinating is Jan van Eyck's *Man in a Red Turban* of 1433 (fig. 147), which may well be a self-portrait—the slight strain

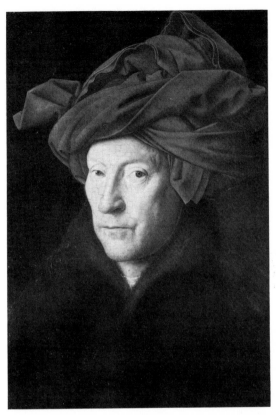

147. JAN VAN EYCK. *Man in a Red Turban* (*Self-Portrait?*). 1433. Oil on panel, 10 1/4 × 7 1/8″. The National Gallery, London (Reproduced by courtesy of the Trustees)

about the eyes seems to come from gazing into a mirror. Every detail of shape and texture has been recorded with almost microscopic precision. Jan does not suppress the sitter's personality, yet this face, like all of Jan's portraits, remains a psychological puzzle. The stoic calm of his portraits surely reflects his conscious ideal of human character rather than his indifference or lack of insight.

Jan van Eyck's most remarkable portrait, and a major masterpiece of the period, was his *Giovanni Arnolfini and His Bride* (colorplate 24). The Flemish cities where the new style of painting flourished—Tournai, Ghent, Bruges—rivaled Florence as centers of international banking and trade. Their foreign residents included many Italian businessmen, such as Giovanni Arnolfini. In the picture, he and his bride are solemnly exchanging marriage vows in the privacy of the bridal chamber. They seem to be quite alone, but as we look at the mirror behind them, we discover in the reflection that two other persons have entered the room. One must be the artist, since the words above the mirror (fig. 148), in florid legal lettering, tell us that "Johannes de eyck fuit hic" (Jan van Eyck was here) and the date, 1434. Jan's role, then, is that of a witness; the panel purports to show exactly what he saw and has the function of a pictorial marriage certificate. Yet the setting, however realistic, is replete with disguised symbolism of the most subtle kind, conveying the sacramental nature of marriage. The single candle in the chandelier, burning in broad daylight, stands for the all-seeing Christ; the shoes which the couple have taken off remind us that this is "holy ground" (see p. 20); even the little dog is an emblem of marital fidelity. Here, as in the *Merode Annunciation*, the natural world is made to contain the world of the spirit in such a way that the two actually become one.

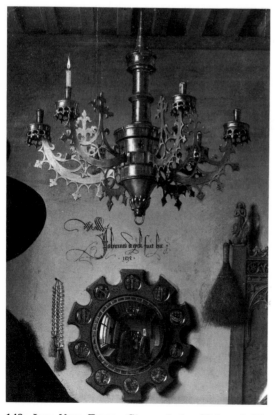

148. JAN VAN EYCK. *Giovanni Arnolfini and His Bride* (detail of colorplate 24)

ROGIER VAN DER WEYDEN

In the work of Jan van Eyck, the exploration of the reality made visible by light and color had reached a limit that was not to be surpassed for another two centuries. Rogier van der Weyden, the third great master of early Flemish painting, set himself a different though equally important task: to recapture, within the framework of the new style created by his predecessors, the emotional drama, the pathos, of the Gothic past. We can see this immediately in his early masterpiece, *The Descent from the Cross* (colorplate 25), painted about the same time as the Arnolfini double portrait. The modeling here is sculpturally precise, with brittle drapery folds like those of Campin, while the soft half-shadows show the influence of Jan van Eyck. Yet Rogier is far more than a mere follower of the two older men; what he owes to them he uses for ends that are not theirs but his. The outward event (the lowering of Christ's body from the Cross) concerns him less than the world of human feeling: the artistic ancestry of these grief-stricken gestures and faces lies in Gothic sculpture such as the Bonn *Pietà* (see fig. 132) and the lamenting angels of Sluter's *Moses Well* (see fig. 133). Indeed, Rogier has staged the scene in a shallow architectural shrine, as if his figures were colored statues, thus focusing our entire attention on the foreground. No wonder that Rogier's art, which has been well described as "at once physically barer and spiritually richer than Jan van Eyck's," set an example for countless other artists. So great was the authority of his style that between 1450 and 1500 it had supreme influence not only in European painting north of the Alps, but in sculpture as well.

HUGO VAN DER GOES; GEERTGEN

Among the artists who followed Rogier van der Weyden, few succeeded in escaping from the great master's shadow. The most dynamic of these was Hugo van der Goes, an unhappy genius whose tragic end suggests an unstable personality peculiarly interesting to us today. After a spectacular rise to fame in the cosmopolitan atmosphere of Bruges, he decided in 1478, when he was about forty years of age, to enter a monastery as a lay

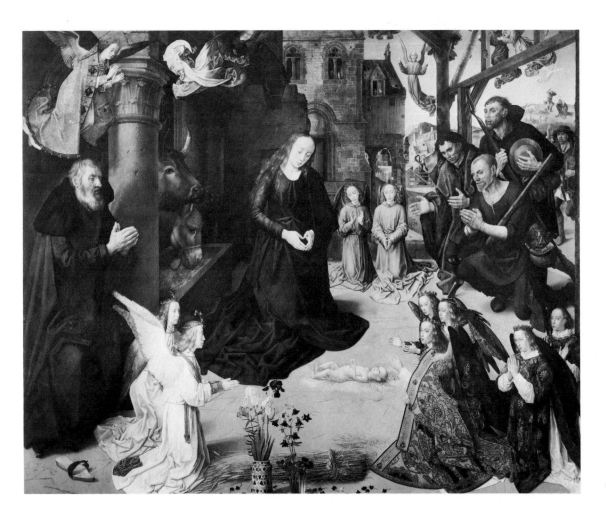

149. Hugo Van Der Goes. *The Portinari Altarpiece* (center). c. 1476. Oil on panel, 8′ 3 1/2″ × 10′. Uffizi Gallery, Florence

brother; for some time he continued to paint, but increasing fits of depression drove him to the verge of suicide, and four years later he was dead. His most ambitious work, the huge altarpiece he completed about 1476 for Tommaso Portinari, is an awesome achievement (fig. 149). While we need not search it for hints of Hugo's future mental illness, it nonetheless evokes a tense, explosive personality. In the wings, for instance, the kneeling members of the Portinari family are dwarfed by their patron saints, whose gigantic size characterizes them as beings of a higher order, like Joseph and the Virgin Mary, and by the shepherds of the *Nativity* in the center panel, who share the same huge scale. There is striking contrast between the frantic excite-

ment of the shepherds and the ritual solemnity of all the other figures. These field hands, gazing in breathless wonder at the newborn Child, react to the dramatic miracle of the Nativity with a wide-eyed directness never attempted before.

During the last quarter of the fifteenth century there were no painters in Flanders comparable to Hugo van der Goes, and the most original artists appeared further north, in Holland. To one of these, Geertgen tot Sint Jans of Haarlem, we owe the enchanting *Nativity* reproduced in figure 150, a picture as daring, in its quiet way, as the center panel of the *Portinari Altarpiece*. The idea of a nocturnal Nativity, illuminated mainly by radiance from the Christ Child, goes back to the International Style (see colorplate 21), but Geertgen, applying the pictorial discoveries of Jan van Eyck, gives new, intense reality to the theme. The magic effect of his little panel is greatly enhanced by the smooth,

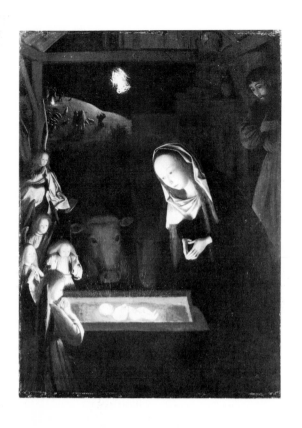

simplified shapes that record the impact of light with striking clarity: the manger is a rectangular trough; the heads of the angels, the Infant, and the Virgin are as round as objects turned on a lathe.

Among the artists from neighboring countries who felt Rogier's influence was a Frenchman whose name has been forgotten. He left us a large work, one of the most famous in all Late Gothic painting (fig. 151). We call it *The Avignon Pietà*, since it was found near Avignon, in the south of France. The figure types and tragic mood could come from no source other than Rogier. The design, however, is much simpler, and has a bigness about it that makes us think of Giotto. This

150. GEERTGEN TOT SINT JANS. *The Nativity.* c. 1490. Oil on panel, 13 1/2 × 10″. The National Gallery, London (Reproduced by courtesy of the Trustees)

151. SOUTHERN FRENCH MASTER. *The Avignon Pietà.* c. 1470. Oil on panel, 64 × 86″. The Louvre, Paris

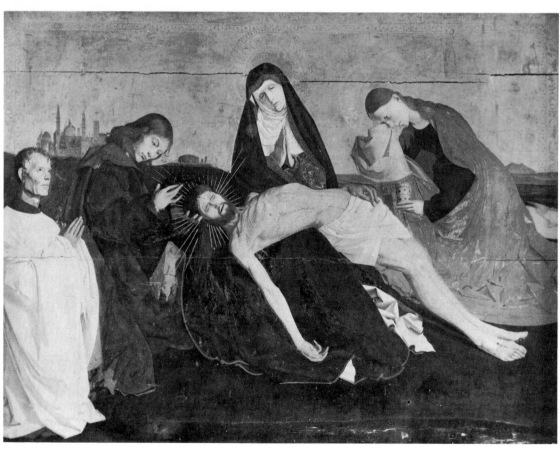

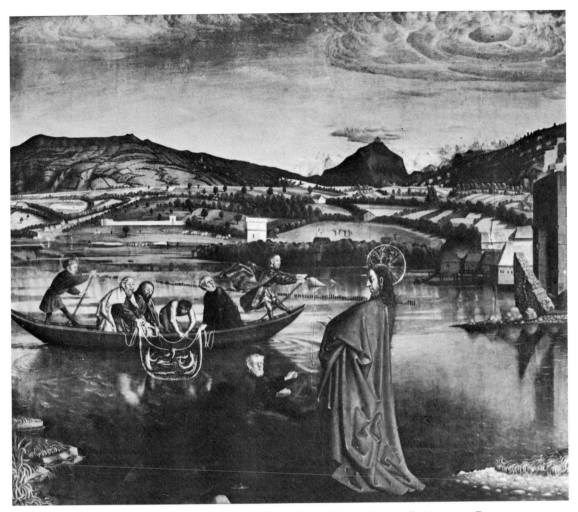

152. CONRAD WITZ. *The Miraculous Draught of Fishes*. 1444. Panel, 51 × 61″. Museum, Geneva

master must have been touched by Italian art, no matter how Late Gothic his figure style and depth of feeling.

WITZ

Countless artists from Spain to the Baltic turned out provincial adaptations of the new Flemish style. One of the earliest and most original was Conrad Witz of Basel, whose altarpiece for the Geneva Cathedral, painted in 1444, includes the remarkable panel shown in figure 152. To judge from the drapery, he must have had close contact with Campin. But it is the setting more than the figures that attracts our interest, and here the influence of the Van Eycks seems dominant. Nevertheless, Witz was an explorer in his own right, who knew more about the optical properties

of water than any painter of that time (note especially the bottom of the lakeshore in the foreground). The landscape, too, is an original venture, representing a specific part of the shore of the Lake of Geneva—the earliest "portrait" landscape that we know.

PRINTING

Germany's chief contribution to fifteenth-century art, however, was the development of printing, for pictures as well as books. The earliest typeset printed books were produced in the Rhineland soon after 1450. The new technique spread all over Europe and grew into an industry that had the most profound effect on Western civilization. Printed pictures, however, had hardly less importance; without them, the printed book

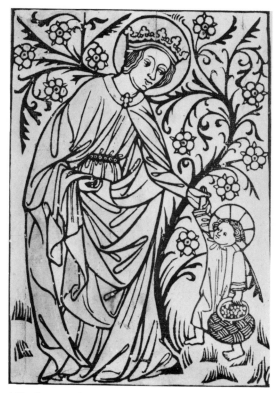

153. *St. Dorothy*. c. 1420. Woodcut. Staatliche Graphische Sammlung, Munich

the start. Unlike woodcuts, engravings are printed not from a raised design but from V-shaped grooves cut into a copper plate with a steel tool known as a burin, so that fine lines are very much easier to achieve. The oldest examples we know, dating from around 1430, already show the influence of the great Flemish painters. Nor do engravings share the anonymity of early woodcuts: individual hands can be distinguished almost from the beginning; dates and initials appear soon after; and the most important engravers of the later fifteenth century are known to us by name. The greatest of them, Martin Schongauer, might be called the Rogier van der Weyden of engraving, since his prints are full of Rogierian motifs and expressive devices. Yet Schongauer had his own powers of invention; his finest prints have a complexity of design, spatial depth, and richness of texture that are fully equivalent to panel paintings. *The Temptation of St. Anthony* (fig. 154) masterfully combines sav-

could not have replaced the work of the medieval scribe and illuminator so quickly and completely. The oldest pictorial printing technique is the woodcut, printed from wooden blocks carved in relief (the areas meant to remain white being hollowed out). The earliest examples all show the familiar qualities of the International Style (fig. 153), but they have a flat, ornamental pattern; forms are defined by simple, heavy contours. Since the outlines were meant to be filled in with color, these prints often recall stained glass (see fig. 137) more than the miniatures which they replaced. They were a popular art, on a level that did not attract masters of high ability until shortly before 1500. A single wood block yielded thousands of copies, to be sold for a few pennies apiece, bringing the individual ownership of pictures within everyone's reach for the first time in our history.

ENGRAVING: SCHONGAUER

Engraving, somewhat younger than woodcuts, was a more sophisticated medium from

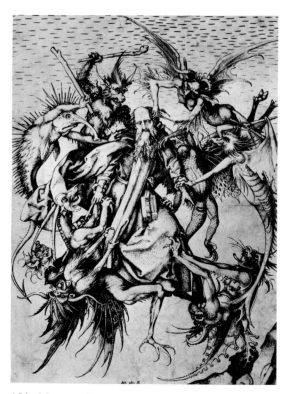

154. MARTIN SCHONGAUER. *The Temptation of St. Anthony*. c. 1480–90. Engraving. The Metropolitan Museum of Art, New York (Rogers Fund, 1920)

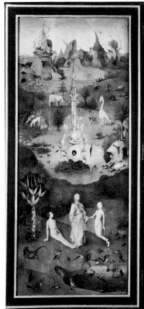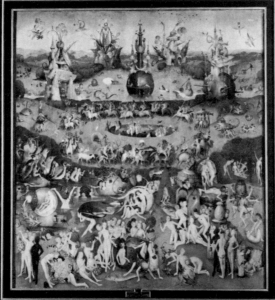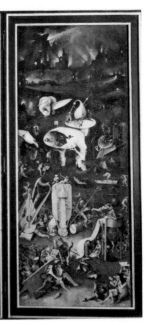

155. HIERONYMUS BOSCH. *The Garden of Delights.* c. 1500. Oil on panel, center 86 1/2 × 76 3/4″; wings 86 1/2 × 38″ each. The Prado, Madrid (see also colorplate 26)

age expressiveness and formal precision, violent movement and ornamental stability. The longer we look at it, the more we marvel at its range of tonal values, the rhythmic beauty of the engraved line, and the artist's ability to render every conceivable surface texture merely by varying his burin's attack upon the plate. He was not to be surpassed by any later engraver in this respect.

BOSCH

Schongauer's engraving of the tormented *St. Anthony* reflects a taste for the gruesome and fantastic that can be found more than once in Northern European art toward the end of the fifteenth century. We encounter its extreme form in the strange works of a Dutch painter, Hieronymus Bosch, who spent his life in the provincial town of s'Hertogenbosch. His pictures, full of weird and seemingly irrational imagery, have proved so difficult to interpret that many of them still remain a puzzle. We can readily believe this if we study the triptych known as *The Garden of Delights* (colorplate 26, fig. 155). Of the three panels, only the left one has a clearly recognizable subject: the Lord introducing the newly created Eve to Adam in the Garden of Eden. The landscape, almost Eyckian in its airy vastness, is filled with animals and with hybrid monsters of odd and sinister kinds. The right wing, a nightmarish scene of burning ruins and fantastic instruments of torture, surely represents Hell. But what of the center? Here is a landscape much like that of the Garden of Eden, filled with countless nude men and women performing a variety of peculiar actions: in the middle ground, they parade around a circular basin on the backs of all sorts of beasts; many disport themselves in pools of water; most of them are closely linked with enormous birds, fruit, flowers, or marine animals (colorplate 26). Only a few are openly engaged in making love, yet there can be no doubt that the delights in this "garden" are those of carnal desire, however oddly disguised. The birds, fruit, etc., are symbols or metaphors that Bosch uses to depict man's life on earth as an unending repetition of the Original Sin of Adam and Eve, whereby we are all doomed to be the prisoners of our appetites. Nowhere does he so much as hint at the possibility of Salvation; corruption, on the animal level at least, had already asserted itself in the Garden of Eden (witness the monsters in the left wing), and we are all destined for Hell, the Garden of Satan (fig. 155, right). Despite Bosch's deep pessimism, there is an innocence, even a haunting poetic beauty, in this panorama of sinful mankind. Consciously, he was a stern moralist painting a visual sermon, every detail packed with didactic meaning. Unconsciously, however, he must have been so enraptured by the sensuous appeal of the world of the flesh that the images he coined tend to celebrate what they are meant to condemn. That, surely, is why *The Garden of Delights* still evokes so strong a response today, even though we no longer understand every word of the sermon.

The Early Renaissance in Italy

When we discussed the new style of painting that arose in Flanders about 1420, we did not try to explain why this revolution took place where and when it did. This does not mean, however, that no explanation is possible. It is simply that we do not yet fully understand the link between the great Flemish painters and the social, political, and cultural setting in which they worked. Regarding the origins of Early Renaissance art in Florence, we are in a better position. In the years around 1400, Florence faced an acute threat to its independence from the powerful Duke of Milan, who was trying to bring all of Italy under his rule. Florence remained the only serious obstacle to his ambition. The successful resistance of the city gave rise to a new, civic-patriotic kind of humanism, which hailed Florence as the "new Athens," the champion of freedom as well as the home of arts and letters. So, in the midst of the crisis, the Florentines embarked upon a vast campaign to embellish their city with monuments worthy of the "new Athens." The huge investment was itself no guarantee of artistic quality, but it provided a splendid opportunity for creative talent of every kind. From the start, the visual arts were considered essential to the resurgence of the Florentine spirit. They had been classed with the crafts, or "mechanical arts," throughout antiquity and the Middle Ages; now, for the first time, they were given the rank of liberal arts. A century later, this

claim was to win general acceptance in the Western world. What does it imply? The liberal arts, by a tradition going back to Plato, comprised the intellectual disciplines necessary for a gentleman's education—mathematics (geometry, arithmetic, musical theory), dialectic, grammar, rhetoric, and philosophy; the fine arts were excluded because they were "handiwork" having no basis in theory. Thus, when the artist gained admission to this select group, the nature of his work had to be redefined: he came to be looked upon as a man of ideas, not a mere manipulator of materials, and the work of art was viewed as the visible record of his creative mind. This meant that works of art ought not to be judged by fixed standards of craftsmanship. Soon everything that bore a great master's imprint—drawings, sketches, fragments, unfinished pieces—was eagerly collected. The artist's own outlook, too, underwent a change; now in the company of scholars and poets, he often became a man of learning and literary culture, who might write poems, an autobiography, or treatises on art theory (until then, there had been only "pattern books" for artists). As another consequence of their new social status, artists tended to develop into one of two contrasting personality types: the man of the world, at ease in aristocratic society, or the solitary genius, likely to be in conflict with his patrons. It is remarkable how soon this modern view of art and artists became a living reality in Early Renaissance Florence.

SCULPTURE

DONATELLO

Donatello, the greatest sculptor of the fifteenth century, was a founding father of the Renaissance. We have clearly entered a new epoch when we look at his *St. George* (fig. 156), carved in marble for a niche of the church of Or San Michele around 1415. Here is the first statue we have seen since ancient times that can stand by itself, or, put another way, the first to recapture the full meaning of Classic counterpoise (for a discussion of counterpoise turn to page 55). The artist has mastered at one stroke the central

be taken away from his architectural setting and lose none of his immense authority. His stance, with his weight placed on the forward leg, conveys the idea of readiness for combat (the right hand originally held a weapon). The controlled energy of his body is echoed in his eyes, which seem to scan the horizon for the approaching enemy. For this St. George, slayer of dragons, is a proud and heroic defender of the "new Athens."

The unidentified prophet (fig. 157) nicknamed *Zuccone* ("Pumpkinhead"), for a reason that should be obvious, was carved some eight years later for the bell tower of the Cathedral. Unquestionably, it is more realistic, more like a real person, than any other statue we have seen so far. But what kind of realism do we have here? The artist has not given us a bearded old man holding a scroll— the traditional Christian image of a prophet. Nor has he given us a fellow townsman in the

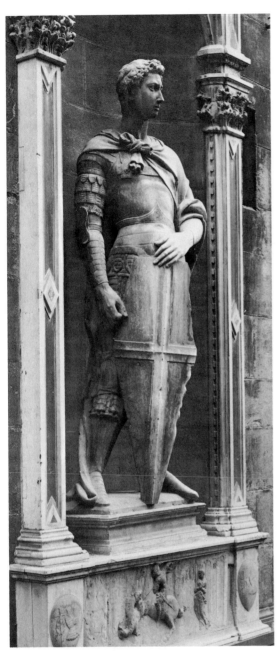

156. DONATELLO. *St. George.* c. 1415–17. Marble, height 6′ 10″. Or San Michele, Florence (statue now in the National Museum, replaced here by a bronze copy).

achievement of ancient sculpture: he has treated the human body as an articulated *structure* capable of movement. Its armor and its drapery are a secondary structure shaped by the body underneath; unlike any Gothic statue, St. George can take off his clothes. And, also unlike any Gothic statue, he can

below left: 157. DONATELLO. *Prophet (Zuccone),* on the campanile of Florence Cathedral. 1423–25. Marble, height 6′ 5″. The original is now in the Cathedral Museum, Florence

below right: 158. DONATELLO. *David.* c. 1430–32. Bronze, height 62 1/4″. National Museum, Florence

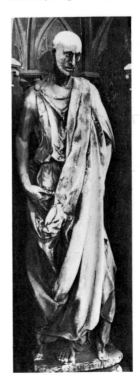

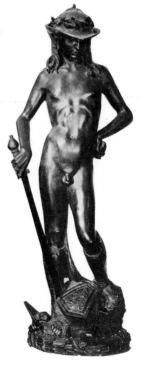

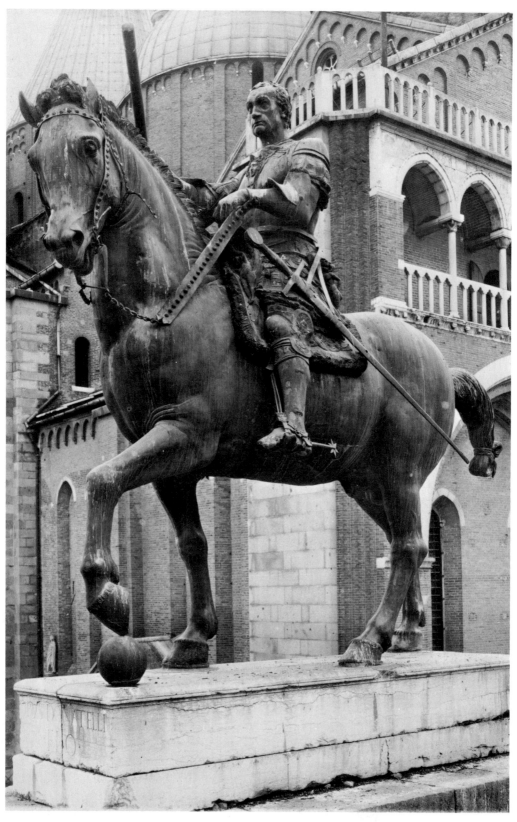

159. DONATELLO. *Equestrian Monument of Gattamelata*. 1445–50. Bronze, over lifesize.
Piazza del Santo, Padua

costume of the day. Why not? Why was it not enough for Donatello to be like Sluter and reinterpret the traditional type from a contemporary realistic point of view?

Donatello, the first solitary genius of the Renaissance, was compelled from within to create a new type on the basis of his own thinking and feeling. From his reading of the Old Testament he had formed a mental picture of the Biblical prophets, an impression of divinely inspired orators haranguing the multitude; and this, in turn, he had connected with the Roman orators he had seen in ancient sculpture. Hence the Classical costume of the *Zuccone*, whose mantle falls from one shoulder and whose head is lined and ugly, yet noble (compare the toga-clad patricians of fig. 74). To shape these elements into a coherent image was a revolutionary feat and required an almost visible struggle. Donatello looked upon this achievement as particularly hard-won; and the *Zuccone* is his earliest known work to carry his signature. He swore "by the Zuccone," it is said, when he wished to speak emphatically; and he shouted at it as he worked, "Speak! speak! or the plague take you!"

Medieval nudes lacked sensuous appeal— a quality we take for granted in every nude of Classical antiquity. Such appeal was avoided purposely, for to the medieval mind the physical beauty of ancient "idols" was paganism at its most insidious. The rediscovery of the beauty of the unclothed human body in the fifteenth century took different paths in Flanders and Italy; the two paths were to come together in the Venetian painting of the following century. Jan van Eyck's *Adam and Eve* (fig. 145) and Bosch's unclothed figures in *The Garden of Delights* (colorplate 26, fig. 155) were unlike the nudes of ancient or, indeed, medieval art. Rather than "nude," they were "naked"—people who, normally, were fully dressed but who, for some particular reason, had their clothes off. Italian artists, however, created "nudes" in the full Classical sense. Donatello's bronze *David* (fig. 158) of around 1430 was such a nude—the first life-size, freestanding nude statue since ancient times, and a truly revolutionary achievement. Donatello's contemporaries must have felt uneasy about it, for it remained the only work of its kind for many years. David is,

in a sense, partly dressed, for he wears rather ornate military boots and a hat; but we tend to wonder why he wears these, rather than what has happened to the rest of his clothes. Nudity is his natural state. Otherwise, he resembles a Classical statue mainly in his marvelous counterpoise. Donatello shows us a wiry stripling rather than a full-grown athlete with crisply articulated body masses and swelling muscles, like the gods and heroes of Classic Greece. The spirit of the David is profoundly Classical, nevertheless, for, as in ancient statues, the body speaks to us more eloquently than the face, which is impassive by Donatello's standards.

Donatello was called to Padua in 1443 to create a monument to Gattamelata, the commander of the Venetian armies, who had just died. This equestrian statue (fig. 159) was Donatello's largest freestanding work. We have already seen its major source, the equestrian statue of the Roman emperor Marcus Aurelius (fig. 69). The *Gattamelata*, without imitating the *Marcus Aurelius* directly, shares its bronze material, its impressive scale, and its great balance and dignity. The horse is a tremendous animal, fit to carry a man in full armor. Yet the man dominates him completely, not by physical strength but by force of character. In the new Renaissance fashion, the statue's purpose was to pay official honor to a great soldier who had served the Venetian Republic well. To this purpose, Donatello created an image that fuses the real and the ideal in a perfect union. The general's armor combines fifteenth-century construction with Classical detail. His head is powerfully individual, yet truly Roman in its expression of nobility.

GHIBERTI; DELLA ROBBIA

Two important sculptors were left in Florence after Donatello's departure: Lorenzo Ghiberti and Luca della Robbia. Ghiberti, in his middle and late years, was a convert to the new style, although his figures continued to hark back to the International Style in their flow of drapery and their gentle grace (see page 146 and fig. 136). *The Story of Jacob and Esau* relief (fig. 160) from his second pair of bronze doors for the Baptistery—the "Gates of Paradise," as the Florentines named them because of their great beauty—belongs to the Early Renaissance. The hint of spatial depth we saw in *The Sacrifice of Isaac* has now grown in *The Story of Jacob and Esau* into a complete setting for the figures that goes back as far as the eye can reach. We can imagine the figures leaving the scene—the deep, continuous space of this "pictorial relief" in no way depends on their presence. How did Ghiberti achieve this effect? In part by varying the degree of relief, with the forms closest to the beholder being modeled almost in the round—a method fa-

160. LORENZO GHIBERTI. *The Story of Jacob and Esau,* panel of the "Gates of Paradise." c. 1435. Gilt bronze, 31 1/4" square. Baptistery, Florence

miliar to us from ancient art (see figs. 49, 72, 73). Far more important, however, is the carefully controlled recession of figures and architecture, causing their apparent size to diminish systematically (rather than haphazardly, as before) as their distance from the beholder increases. This system, which we call scientific perspective, was one of the fundamental innovations that distinguish Early Renaissance art from everything that had gone before, as well as from the great Flemish masters of realism, who had achieved the effect of unlimited depth in their pictures by empirical means, through subtle gradations of light and color. Scientific perspective was not discovered by Ghiberti, nor

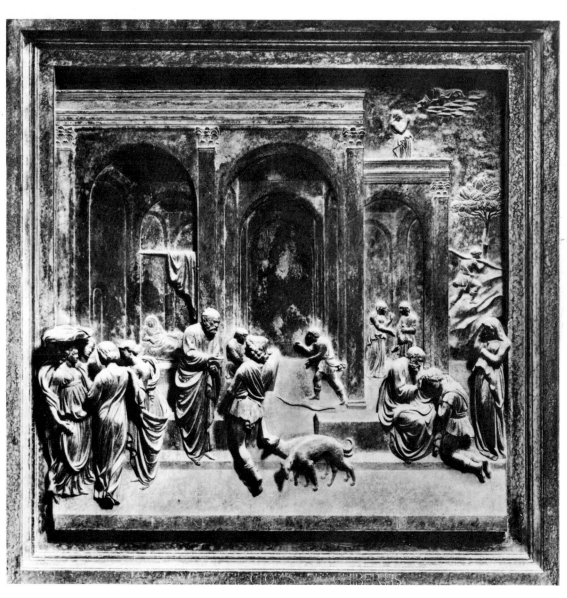

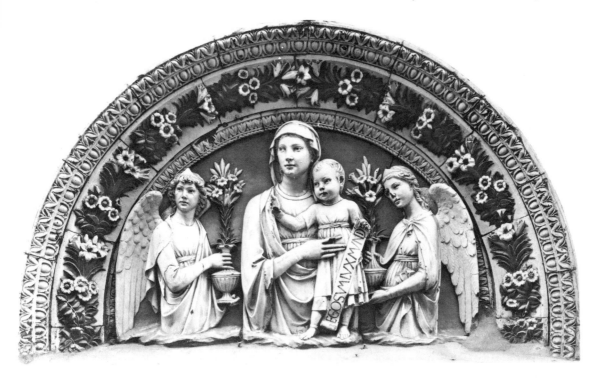

161. Luca Della Robbia. *Madonna and Angels.* c. 1460. Glazed terra-cotta, 63 × 87 1/2″. National Museum, Florence

by a painter, but by Filippo Brunelleschi, the creator of Early Renaissance architecture (the building in Ghiberti's relief, figure 160, is designed in this new style). His purpose, apparently, was to find a method of making visual records of architecture on a flat surface in such a way that the depth of the foreshortened flanks of buildings could be measured as precisely as the height or width of the façade. The details of the system need not concern us here, beyond saying that it is a geometric procedure analogous to the way the camera lens projects a perspective image on the film. Its central feature is the vanishing point, toward which any set of parallel lines will seem to converge. If these lines are perpendicular to the picture plane, their vanishing point will be on the horizon, corresponding exactly to the position of the beholder's eye. Brunelleschi's discovery in itself was scientific rather than artistic, but sculptors and painters took it up enthusiastically. Here at last was a theoretical basis for representing the visible world, proving that the fine arts were now indeed "liberal" rather than "mechanical"!

Luca della Robbia, a gifted sculptor who did not share Donatello's passion for experimentation and growth, never made a free-standing statue and, in the 1440s, gave up carving in marble—at which he was a master —for the cheaper and less demanding medium of glazed terra cotta (baked clay). His semicircular *Madonna and Angels* in this medium (fig. 161) shows us the appealing combination of sweetness and solemnity that has made Luca so popular a sculptor. The color combination here is characteristic of Luca. Except in the border wreath of flowers, where several colors are used, it is restricted to blue and white—a deep blue for the background, a smooth, lustrous white for the figures.

Luca's withdrawal into terra-cotta gave younger Florentine marble carvers freedom to develop into artists of importance. These men produced Florence's marble tombs, church furniture, and Madonna reliefs during the later fifteenth century, and, besides, originated a new form of large-scale sculpture: the Renaissance portrait bust. One of the earliest and best is Antonio Rossellino's bust of Giovanni Chellini (fig. 162), carved around 1455. The sitter's personality, at once ironical and kindly, has been observed with great penetration. Although it is as documentary as a Roman head (fig. 67)—not one wrinkle has been ignored—Antonio has not

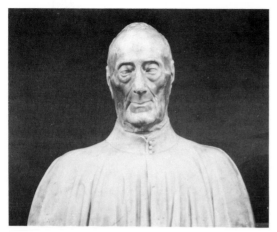

162. ANTONIO ROSSELLINO. *Giovanni Chellini.* 1456. Marble, height 20″. Victoria and Albert Museum, London

permitted detailed realism to obscure the sitter's qualities as a human being.

The popularity of portrait busts after 1450 can be explained by the growing demand for works of art to be placed in private homes rather than in churches and civic buildings. Decades earlier, artists and humanists had begun to collect ancient Roman busts and small bronzes. The vogue for collecting spread, and soon sculptors were being called upon for busts and bronzes "in the manner of the ancients."

POLLAIUOLO

Antonio del Pollaiuolo's *Hercules and Antaeus* (fig. 163) is a particularly fine bronze "in the manner of the ancients." The way the limbs are flung out in every direction is even more extraordinary than we see it in our illustration, for the complexity of the action is fully revealed only when we look at the bronze from every angle. No matter how we shift our viewpoint, the statuette remains in balance all around the point where Antonio has attached the two adversaries to each other.

If this kind of design had no predecessors in sculpture, it did have them in painting, for example, Castagno's *David* (fig. 171). Antonio del Pollaiuolo took a composition from drawing and painting and put it in the round; he was a painter and engraver as well as a sculptor (see fig. 172). Of all the masters of his time, he contributed most

to the solution of the difficult problem of anatomy in action. He was as passionately devoted to the scientific study of anatomy as Piero della Francesca (see pages 186, 187 and fig. 170) was to the scientific study of perspective, and it is said that he was the first artist to dissect the human body in order to learn its structure and workings at firsthand. He must have developed deep understanding, for he shows us living anatomy, the anatomy of bones and muscles in use and under strain, not the anatomy of lifeless forms on a dissecting table. His study of anatomy in action extended to the facial expressions that went with the strained and struggling nude bodies that he described. Artists before him had described contorted features, but none had so united the show of motion and emotion to create a single, fused expression.

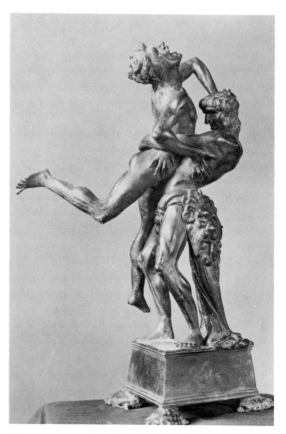

163. ANTONIO DEL POLLAIUOLO. *Hercules and Antaeus.* c. 1475. Bronze, height 18″. National Museum, Florence

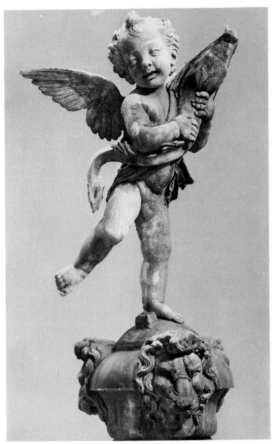

164. ANDREA DEL VERROCCHIO. *Putto with Dolphin.* c. 1470. Bronze, height 27″ without base. Palazzo Vecchio, Florence

VERROCCHIO

Pollaiuolo, although he did large-scale tombs in bronze, never had the opportunity to create a lifesize freestanding statue. For such works we turn to his younger contemporary Andrea del Verrocchio, the greatest sculptor of his day. Verrocchio's most popular work in Florence is his *Putto with Dolphin* (fig. 164). The Early Renaissance reintroduced the putto—which in Roman art was a winged child as the embodiment of a spirit—both in its original sense and as a child angel. Our putto is the centerpiece of a fountain—the dolphin spouts because the putto hugs. In spite of his larger scale, ampler volume, and more playful spirit, this putto is close to Pollaiuolo's *Hercules and Antaeus*. Again the limbs swing out in all directions from a

central axis. But here the movement is graceful and continuous, not jagged and broken. The outstretched leg, dolphin, arms, and wings describe an ascending spiral; the statue seems to revolve before our eyes.

ARCHITECTURE

BRUNELLESCHI

The towering genius of Filippo Brunelleschi ushered the new architecture into history. Goldsmith and sculptor as well as architect, skilled in mechanics and military engineering, builder of clocks and scientific apparatus, the correspondent of mathematicians, and the inventor of mathematical perspective, he was the first great representative of the "universal man" for whom the Early Renaissance is famous.

Brunelleschi was twenty-five years old when he lost out to Ghiberti in the 1401–2 competition for the bronze doors of the Florence Baptistery. Shortly thereafter, he went to Rome. He was the first, it seems, to take careful measurements of ancient Roman buildings. He was back in Florence between 1417 and 1419, and competing with Ghiberti again. The competition was for the job of building the Cathedral dome. This time he won.

The vastness of the projected dome presented a construction problem of frightening dimensions. Built solid in the traditional way, it would have had an outward push so great as to defy bracing. Its cost, assuming it could be put up at all, threatened to bankrupt the Republic. But Brunelleschi had a solution. He envisioned a dome that would be light in weight and almost thrustless: a tall double shell. He proposed to build it without the mountain-high web of scaffolding required by the older construction method. Both the man and his ideas so impressed the authorities that they awarded him the job. Construction began in 1420 and was completed sixteen years later (see fig. 124).

There was nothing new about the basic shape of the dome: an older, Gothic design was being carried out. As an achievement of a different kind, however, it had enormous significance, for it marked the transformation of architecture from craft to learned profession. Brunelleschi's dome freed his successors from the tyranny of traditions and gave them a new foundation for their work: the scientific point of view. Thereafter, when faced with technical challenges, they would submit their problems to scientific analysis in order to come up with workable solutions. Brunelleschi's questing spirit brought architecture, which is a marriage of engineering and art, squarely into a new era.

Brunelleschi's ideas were equally bold and new in architectural design. In 1419, while working on the final plans for the Cathedral dome, he received his first opportunity to carry out a design of his own. The Medici commissioned him to build an addition to the Romanesque church of San Lorenzo. The new part of the church was to be both a sacristy and a burial chapel for the Medici family. The interior of the church of San Lorenzo (fig. 165) strikes us first of all as a conscious return to the vocabulary of the Greeks and Romans: round arches instead of pointed arches, columns instead of piers, barrel vaults and domes in preference to groin vaults. But Brunelleschi did not revive these forms out of mere antiquarian enthusiasm. What attracted him to them was what, from the medieval point of view, must have seemed their chief drawback: their inflexibility. A Classical column, unlike a medieval column or pier, is strictly defined and self-sufficient, and its shape can be varied only within narrow limits (the ancients, we recall, thought of it as comparable to the human body); the Classical round arch has only one possible shape, a semicircle; and the Classical architrave and all its details are subject to the strict rules of the "orders" of ancient architecture. Brunelleschi's aim was to rationalize architectural design, and for this he needed the standardized and regular vocabulary of the ancients, based on the circle and the square. The secret of their buildings, he thought, was harmonious proportion—the same ratios of simple whole numbers that determine musical harmony, for they recur throughout the universe and must thus be of Divine origin. The theory of proportions provided him with the syntax, as it were, that ruled the use of his architectural vocabulary. Looking at the interior of San

Lorenzo, we immediately sense its cool, controlled quality; unlike a Gothic church interior, which invites us to move forward and explore what seems an architectural miracle, San Lorenzo reveals itself to us completely as soon as we set foot inside it.

San Lorenzo, with its wooden ceiling over the nave, recalls the interior of Santa Croce (see fig. 123) translated into Early Renaissance terms. A similar process of rationalization reshaped another traditional building type, the *palazzo*. When the Medici, the most powerful family in Florence, had a new palace built for them in the 1440s (fig. 166), their architect, Michelozzo, produced a design recalling the fortresslike older structures (see fig. 126; the windows on the ground floor of the Medici Palace were added a century later). But the three stories are in a graded sequence, each complete in itself: the lowest is built of rough-hewn, "rustic"

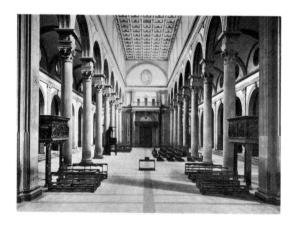

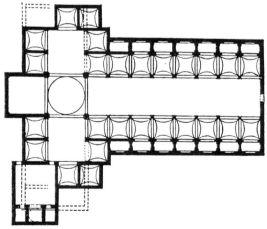

165. FILIPPO BRUNELLESCHI. Interior and Plan, S. Lorenzo. 1421–69. Florence

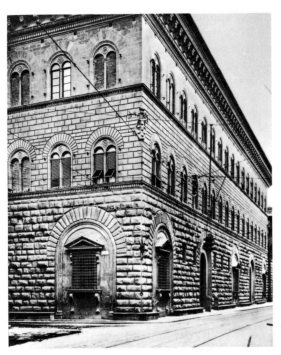

166. MICHELOZZO. Palazzo Medici-Riccardi. Begun 1444. Florence

the continuity of the wall surface. They are of two sizes: the smaller ones sustain the arch over the huge center niche, while the larger ones form what is known as a "colossal" order including all three stories of the façade. So intent was Alberti on harmonious proportions that he inscribed the entire design within a square.

The church behind the façade of Sant' Andrea was not the ideal shape that Alberti had glorified in his treatise on architecture. The plan of a sacred building, he had written, ought to be a circle or a shape derived from a circle—a square, a hexagon, an octagon, and so forth—for the circle is the perfect as well as the most natural figure, and therefore a direct image of Divine Reason. The structure should stand alone, raised above its everyday surroundings. Openings to the outside should be placed high, for only God's sky should be seen through them.

Alberti never received an opportunity to make his dream of the ideal church come true. But after his death, his treatise began to be widely known, and the central-plan church gained acceptance. It reigned su-

masonry like the Palazzo Vecchio; the second of smooth-faced blocks with "rusticated" (that is, indented) joints; the surface of the third is unbroken. On top of the structure rests, like a heavy lid, a strongly projecting cornice inspired by those of Roman temples, emphasizing the finality of the three stories.

ALBERTI

Brunelleschi's death in 1446 brought another "universal man" into the forefront. Leone Battista Alberti was a scholar, poet, playwright, musician, mathematician, philosopher, painter, architect, and man of the world. As a theoretician, he wrote treatises on painting, sculpture, and architecture. At first an amateur artist, later a practicing architect of outstanding ability, he went beyond Brunelleschi in reviving Classical antiquity. In his majestic façade for the church of Sant' Andrea, Mantua (fig. 167), we see an extremely imaginative combination of a Classical pedimented temple front and an arch of triumph (see figs. 106, 125).

To harmonize this "marriage," he used pilasters instead of columns, thus stressing

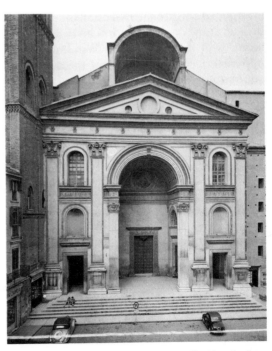

167. LEONE BATTISTA ALBERTI. Sant' Andrea, Mantua. Designed 1470

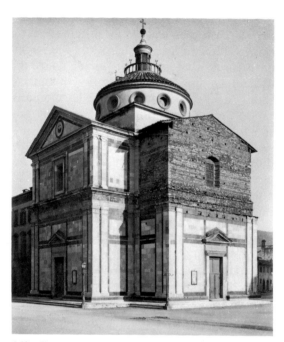

168. GIULIANO DA SANGALLO. Santa Maria delle Carceri. 1485. Prato

preme in the first quarter of the sixteenth century. Giuliano da Sangallo's church of Santa Maria delle Carceri (fig. 168) in the town of Prato is an early and distinguished example of this trend. Essentially it is a cube, broken at the corners to form an equal-armed cross, with a dome above. Windows in the upper stories and the drum of the dome give an outlook on the sky. In all probability, it was no accident that the foundation of this church was laid in 1485, the year in which Alberti's treatise was first printed.

PAINTING

MASACCIO

In the early 1420s, a decade later than in sculpture, the new style sprang up in painting. A twenty-one-year-old genius, Masaccio, created it singlehanded. Only twenty-seven when he died, he left us a mere handful of pictures.

The fresco of *The Holy Trinity with the Virgin and St. John* (colorplate 27) shows us that Masaccio was a bolder explorer even than Jan van Eyck. He was trained in the

International Style, but we could never tell it from this painting. The new style was by that time well established in sculpture and architecture, making his task easier, but his achievement remains stupendous, nevertheless. Here, as in the case of the *Merode Annunciation* (see colorplate 22), we seem to plunge into a new environment, a realm of monumental grandeur rather than the concrete, everyday reality of Robert Campin. What the *Trinity* fresco brings to mind is not the immediate past (see colorplate 21) but Giotto's art, with its sense of large scale, its compositional severity and sculptural volume. Yet the differences are as striking as the similarities: for Giotto, body and drapery form a single unit, as if both had the same substance, while Masaccio's figures, like Donatello's (see fig. 157), are "clothed nudes," their drapery falling like real fabric. The setting, equally up-to-date, reveals a thorough command of both scientific perspective and Brunelleschi's new architecture. This barrel-vaulted chamber is no mere niche, but a deep space in which the figures could move freely if they wished. And—for the first time in history—we are given all the needed data to measure the depth of this painted interior, to draw its plan, and to duplicate the structure in three dimensions. It is, in a word, the earliest example of a *rational* picture space. For Masaccio, it must also have been a symbol of the universe ruled by Divine Reason.

In Masaccio's *Trinity*, as well as in Ghiberti's later relief panel, the new rational picture space is independent of the figures; they inhabit it but do not create it; take away the architecture and you take away the figures' space. We could go even further and say that scientific perspective depends not just on architecture, but on this particular *kind* of architecture, so different from Gothic.

VENEZIANO

Masaccio had died too young to found a "school," and his style was too bold to be taken up immediately by his contemporaries. Their work, for the most part, combines his influence with lingering elements of the International Style. Then, in 1439, Domenico Veneziano—which is to say, Domenico the Venetian—came to Florence. He became a

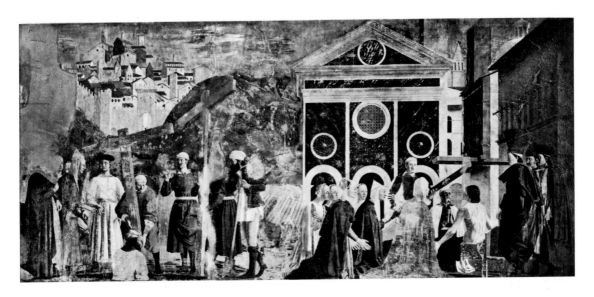

169. PIERO DELLA FRANCESCA. *The Discovery and Proving of the True Cross.* c. 1460. Fresco. S. Francesco, Arezzo

thoroughgoing Florentine and a very important master of the Early Renaissance. His *Madonna and Child with Saints* (colorplate 28) shows us that he studied Masaccio's *Trinity* very carefully, for his St. John the Baptist looks at us while pointing to the Madonna and Child, repeating the glance and gesture of Masaccio's Virgin. The saints also turn toward one another, as though in conversation. The figures thus are linked with us and with one another by a thoroughly human awareness. But, even though admitted to their presence, we do not join them; like theatergoers, we are not allowed on stage. For the world to which St. John the Baptist calls our attention, despite its utter clarity of architecture and of the space the architecture defines, is not our earthly world but a place far more elevated and solemn.

Domenico's figures are less massive than Masaccio's; their slim bodies and expressive faces remind us more of Donatello (see fig. 157). But in the use of color, he was his own man; this altar is quite as remarkable for its color scheme as for the skill with which the artist has grouped the figures and placed them within their setting. The blond tonality, with its harmonious combination of pink, light green, and white set off by carefully placed spots of red, blue, and yellow, combines the decorative brightness of Gothic panels with the new qualities given by perspective space and natural-looking light. The scene is set in an outdoor loggia flooded with sunlight streaming from the upper right (notice the cast shadow behind the Madonna). The architectural surfaces reflect light so strongly that even the shadowed areas glow with color. The influence of Domenico's remarkable color sense was to be felt in Florentine painting for the next half-century.

PIERO DELLA FRANCESCA; CASTAGNO
Domenico's pupil Piero della Francesca became one of the truly great artists of the Early Renaissance. His major work was a series of frescoes telling the legendary history of the True Cross—the cross used for Christ's crucifixion. The section seen in figure 169 shows the discovery of the True Cross by St. Helena, mother of Emperor Constantine the Great. On the left, three crosses are dug out of the ground, the True Cross and the crosses of the thieves who died beside Christ. On the right, the True Cross is distinguished from the other two by its power to bring a dead youth back to life. The early-morning light enters the scene at a low angle, defining every solid shape finely and clearly. Piero's link with Domenico Veneziano is apparent in this dramatic light. But the figures have a harsh grandeur that reminds us much more of Masaccio. These men and women seem to belong to a lost heroic race, beautiful, strong, and silent. What goes on inside them is con-

veyed by glances and gestures, not by facial expression; in their gravity and poise, they seem the kin of Greek sculptures of the Archaic style (see pages 52–54). How did Piero come to these memorable images?

More than any other artist of his day, Piero believed in scientific perspective as the basis of great painting. He wrote a famous book that demonstrated how the rules of perspective apply to shapes of solid geometry, architectural shapes, and the human form. Figure 170 shows us some illustrations from this book: at the top is a cube with foreshortened surfaces; aligned below are three views of a man's head—from the side, from above, and from below. The last two of these drawings show the odd contours that would be produced if the head were sliced through at various levels; corresponding points in the three views are connected by an array of parallel lines. Piero's geometrical outlook pervaded all his work. When he drew a head, an arm, or a fold of drapery, he saw it as a combination of sphere, cylinder, cone, cube, and pyramid. He saw the world as a great realm of geometric form; and to explore that realm and reveal its clarity and permanence was a gripping adventure. Piero was the spiritual ancestor of the abstract artists of our time; they, too, systematically simplify natural forms.

The Florentines must have regarded Piero's style as somewhat outmoded, for in the 1450s a new trend made its appearance in Florentine painting. We see it in the remarkable *David* by Andrea del Castagno (fig. 171), a work contemporary with Piero's Arezzo frescoes. This picture is on a leather shield —a shield used for display, not combat—and tells us that the owner will be as brave as the Biblical hero when he does confront an enemy in battle. David is a slim young athlete, tense and energetic as a coiled spring. As he bestrides the head of the fallen giant, his hair and drapery are blown by the wind, and he flings up his arm in a proud gesture of challenge. Outline, not solid volume, de-

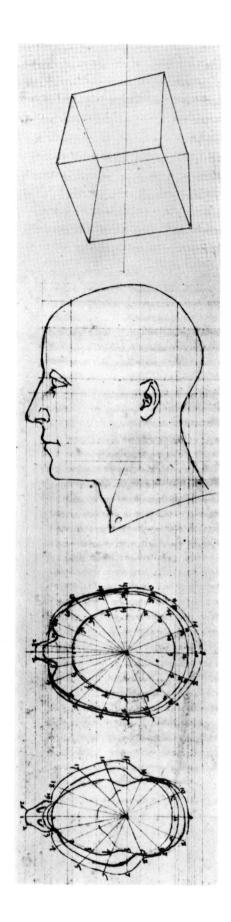

right: 170. PIERO DELLA FRANCESCA. Illustrations from the treatise *De Prospectiva Pingendi (Of Perspective in Painting).* c. 1480. Biblioteca Palatina, Parma

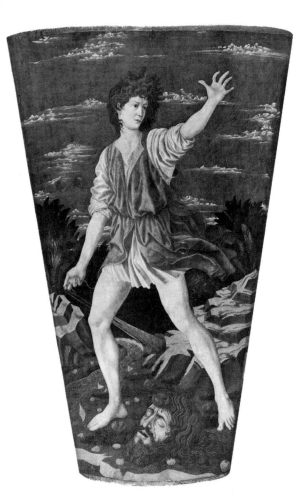

fines the forms of which he is made; and the outlines are nervous and agitated, not smooth and harmonious. The modeling is flatter than Masaccio's or Piero della Francesca's, so that Castagno's forms look as if they were in relief, rather than in the round.

This dynamic linear style was to dominate the second half of the century in Florentine art. We now see it in Pollaiuolo's one surviving engraving, the *Battle of Ten Naked Men* (fig. 172), which shows an indebtedness to both Castagno and ancient art. The subject—undoubtedly a Classical one—has not yet been convincingly identified, but it does not matter a great deal; the primary purpose of the engraving obviously was to display Pollaiuolo's mastery of the human body in action. His devotion to the scientific study of anatomy is even plainer here, for the

171. ANDREA DEL CASTAGNO. *David.* c. 1450–57. Leather, height 45 1/2″. National Gallery of Art, Washington, D. C. (Widener Collection)

172. ANTONIO DEL POLLAIUOLO. *Battle of Ten Naked Men.* c. 1465–70. Engraving. The Metropolitan Museum of Art, New York (Joseph Pulitzer Bequest, 1917)

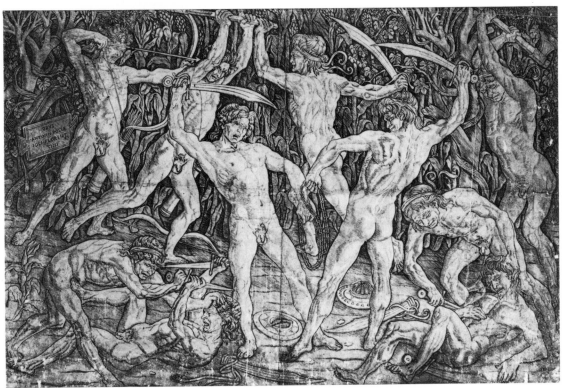

ten naked men do indeed have an oddly "flayed" look, as if their skin has been stripped away to reveal the play of muscles underneath. As in the statue of *Hercules and Antaeus* (fig. 163), the integration of motion and emotion seems to have been his particular concern.

BOTTICELLI

Pollaiuolo's style strongly influenced the last great Early Renaissance painter of Florence, Sandro Botticelli, whose best-known pictures were done for the so-called Medici circle. This consisted of the patricians, literati, and scholars surrounding Lorenzo the Magnificent, the head of the Medici family and, for all practical purposes, the ruler of the city. It was for one member of this group that Botticelli did his *Birth of Venus* (colorplate 29). The kinship with Pollaiuolo's *Ten Naked Men* is unmistakable: in both, the shallow modeling and the emphasis on outline produce an effect of low relief rather than of solid, three-dimensional shapes; in both we note an unconcern with deep space—the thicket behind the *Ten Naked Men* forms an ornamental screen much like the grove on the right-hand side of the *Venus*. Yet the differences are equally striking. Botticelli evidently does not share Pollaiuolo's passion for anatomy. His bodies are more attenuated, and drained of all weight and muscular power; they appear to float even when they touch the ground. All this seems to deny the basic values of the founding fathers of Renaissance art. Still, the picture does not look medieval; the bodies, ethereal though they be, retain their voluptuousness, and they enjoy full freedom of movement. To understand this paradox, we must consider the general use of Classical subjects in Early Renaissance art. During the Middle Ages, the forms used in Classical art had become divorced from Classical subject matter; pictures of the pagan gods were based on literary descriptions rather than Classical images. Only toward 1450 did Classical form begin to rejoin Classical content. Botticelli's *Venus* is the first monumental image, since Roman times, of the nude goddess derived from Classical statues of Venus. Moreover, the sub-

ject is clearly meant to be serious, even solemn. How could such images be justified in a Christian civilization? In the Middle Ages, Classical myths had at times been interpreted didactically as allegories of Christian ideas. Europa abducted by the bull, for instance, could be declared to signify the soul redeemed by Christ. But to fuse the Christian faith with ancient mythology required a more sophisticated argument than such forced interpretations. This was provided by the Neo-Platonic philosophers, who enjoyed tremendous prestige in the late fifteenth century and subsequently. They believed that the life of the universe, including that of man, was linked to God by a spiritual circuit continuously ascending and descending, so that all revelation—from the Bible, Plato, or Classical myths—was one. Similarly, they proclaimed that beauty, love, and beatitude, being phases of this circuit, were one. Thus the Neo-Platonists could invoke the "celestial Venus" (the nude Venus born of the sea) interchangeably with the Virgin Mary as the source of "divine love." This celestial Venus, it was said, dwells purely in the sphere of mind, while her twin, the ordinary Venus, engenders "human love." Botticelli's picture, then, has a quasi-religious meaning. As baptism is a "rebirth in God," so the birth of Venus evokes the hope for "rebirth" from which the Renaissance takes its name (see p. 162). Thanks to the fluidity of Neo-Platonic doctrine, the possible associations to be linked with our picture are almost limitless. All of them, however, "dwell in the sphere of mind," and Botticelli's Venus would hardly be a fit vessel for them if she were less ethereal.

PIERO DI COSIMO; GHIRLANDAIO

A slightly later painting by Piero di Cosimo, *The Discovery of Honey* (colorplate 30), approaches Classical mythology from a very different point of view. Instead of "spiritualizing" the pagan gods, it brings them down to earth as beings of flesh and blood. In this alternate theory, man had slowly risen from a barbaric state through the discoveries and inventions of a few exceptionally gifted individuals; gratefully remembered by posterity, these men were finally accorded the status of gods. *The Discovery of Honey* refers to the central episode, a group of satyrs busying themselves about an old willow tree. They have discovered a swarm of bees, and are trying to collect the honey, from which they will produce mead. Behind them, to the right, some of their companions are about to discover the source of another fermented beverage; they are climbing trees to collect wild grapes. Beyond is a barren rock, while on the left there are gentle hills and a town. This contrast does not imply that the satyrs are city dwellers; it merely juxtaposes civilization, the goal of the future, with untamed nature. Here the "culture hero" is, of course, Bacchus, who appears in the lower right-hand corner, a tipsy grin on his face, next to his lady-love, Ariadne. Despite their Classical appearance, Bacchus and his companions do not in the least resemble the frenzied revelers of ancient mythology. They have an oddly domestic air, suggesting a fun-loving family clan on a picnic. The brilliant sunlight, the rich colors, and the far-ranging landscape make the scene a still more plausible extension of everyday reality. We can well believe that Piero di Cosimo, in contrast to Botticelli, admired the great Flemish realists, and this landscape would be inconceivable without the strong influence of the Portinari Altarpiece (compare fig. 149).

Not only Piero was receptive to the realism of the Flemings; Domenico Ghirlandaio, another contemporary of Botticelli, shared this attitude. His panel of an old man with his grandson (fig. 173), while lacking the pictorial delicacy of Flemish portraits, nevertheless reflects their precise attention to surface texture and facial detail. But no Northern painter could have rendered as well as Ghirlandaio the tender human relationship between the little boy and his grandfather. Psychologically, our panel plainly bespeaks its Italian origin.

MANTEGNA

So far, we have looked only at Florentine developments in examining Early Renaissance style. There has been justice in this, for Florence was not only the birthplace of the new style, but, throughout the fifteenth century, its greatest center of architecture and

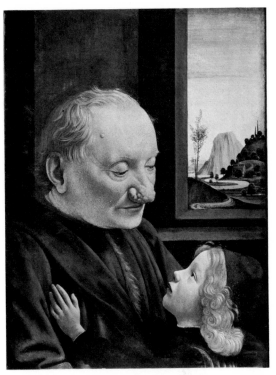

173. DOMENICO GHIRLANDAIO. *An Old Man and His Grandson*. c. 1480. Tempera on panel, 24 1/2 × 18″. The Louvre, Paris

sculpture. The first impulse of the Florentine Renaissance, however, had an impact on the cities of central and northern Italy. Florentine masters had been carrying the new style to Venice and the neighboring city of Padua since the 1420s, but they evoked only rather timid local responses until, shortly before 1450, the young Andrea Mantegna emerged as an independent master. Next to Masaccio, Mantegna was the most important painter of the Early Renaissance; and he, too, was a precocious genius, fully capable at seventeen of carrying out commissions on his own, such as the frescoes in the Eremitani Church in Padua. They were almost entirely destroyed in 1944—perhaps the most serious artistic loss during World War II. The scene shown in figure 174, *St. James Led to His Execution*, is the most dramatic of the cycle because of its daring "worm's-eye" perspective, which is based on the beholder's actual eye-level (the horizon is below the bottom of the picture). The architectural setting looms large, as in Masaccio's *Trinity*

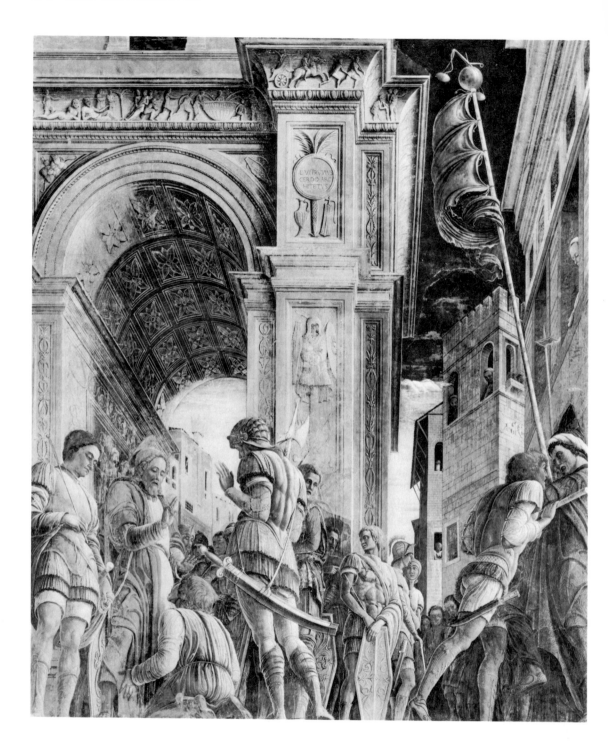

174. ANDREA MANTEGNA. *St. James Led to His Execution.* c. 1455. Fresco. Ovetari Chapel, Church of the Eremitani, Padua (destroyed 1944)

(colorplate 27). Its main feature, a triumphal arch, although not a direct copy of any Roman monument, looks so authentic that it might as well be. Mantegna's devotion to the visible remains of antiquity, his desire for almost archaeological authenticity, can also be seen in the costumes of the Roman soldiers. But these figures, lean and firmly constructed, are clearly of Florentine ancestry; Mantegna owed most to Donatello, who had spent ten years in Padua. The large crowd of bystanders generates an extraordinary emotional tension, which erupts in real physical violence on the far right; and the great spiral curl of the banner echoes the turbulence below.

BELLINI

If Mantegna's style impresses us with its dramatic force, his brother-in-law in Venice, Giovanni Bellini, was a poet of light and color. Bellini was slow to mature; his finest pictures, such as *St. Francis in Ecstasy* (colorplate 31), date from the last decades of the century or later. The saint has been made so small a detail that he seems incidental—or would seem incidental if his rapture at the view spread out before him did not key our own response to it. Like Giovanni Arnolfini (see colorplate 24), St. Francis has taken off his shoes (we see them in the right-hand corner) because he is standing on holy ground—that is, the ordinary visible world in all its beauty. The wonderfully atmospheric landscape, bathed in the radiance of late-afternoon sunlight, has sweeping breadth and close intimacy at the same time. Above it is a deep blue sky dotted with the softest of white clouds. This scene shows strong influence from the style of the Van Eycks (compare colorplate 23, left). Bellini surely knew and admired the work of the great Flemish painters (Venice had strong trade links with the North). Bellini's contours are less crisp than Mantegna's, his colors softer, his light more glowing. He shares the tender regard of the great Flemings for every detail of nature. Unlike the Flemings, however, he locates every form in a clear, mathematically defined space, organizing the rock formations in the foreground according to the rules of scientific perspective.

PERUGINO

Rome, long neglected during the papal exile in Avignon, became once more, in the later fifteenth century, an important center of art patronage. The most ambitious pictorial project of those years was the decoration of the walls of the Sistine Chapel about 1482. Among the artists who carried out this large cycle of Old and New Testament scenes we encounter most of the important painters of

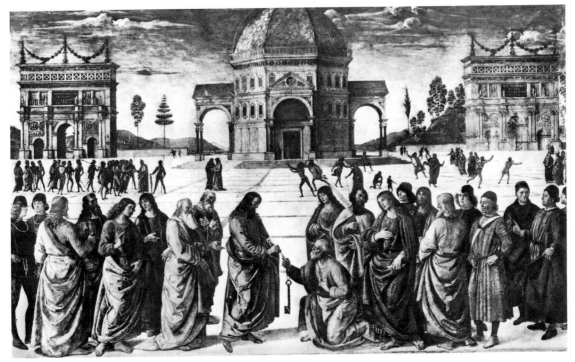

175. PIETRO PERUGINO. *The Delivery of the Keys.* 1482. Fresco. Sistine Chapel, The Vatican, Rome

central Italy, including not only Botticelli and Ghirlandaio, but also Pietro Perugino, who painted *The Delivery of the Keys* (fig. 175). Born near Perugia in Umbria (the region southeast of Tuscany), Perugino maintained close ties with Florence. His early development had been decisively influenced by Verrocchio, as the statuesque balance and solidity of the figures in *The Delivery of the Keys* still suggest. The gravely symmetrical design conveys the special importance of the subject in this particular setting (the authority of St. Peter as the first pope—and that of all his successors—rests on his having received the keys to the Kingdom of Heaven from Christ Himself). A number of contemporaries, with powerfully individualized features, witness the solemn event. Equally striking is the vast expanse of the background, its two Roman triumphal arches (both modeled on the Arch of Constantine) flanking a domed structure in which we recognize the ideal church of Alberti's *Treatise on Architecture.* The spatial clarity, the mathematically exact perspective of this view, are the heritage of Piero della Francesca, who spent much of his later life working for Umbrian clients, notably the Duke of Urbino. And also from Urbino, shortly before 1500, Perugino received a pupil whose fame soon obscured his own—Raphael, the most classic master of the High Renaissance.

The High Renaissance in Italy

It used to be taken for granted that the High Renaissance followed upon the Early Renaissance as naturally as noon follows morning. The great masters of the sixteenth century—Leonardo, Bramante, Michelangelo, Raphael, Titian—were thought to have shared the ideals of their predecessors, but to have expressed them so completely that their names became synonyms of perfection. They represented the climax, the Classic phase, of

Renaissance art, just as the architects and sculptors of Athens had brought Greek art to its highest point in the later fifth century B.C. This view also explained why these two Classic phases were so brief: if art develops along the pattern of a ballistic curve, its highest point cannot be expected to last more than a moment, and must be followed by a decadent phase, "Hellenistic" in the one case, "Late Renaissance" in the other.

Today we have a less assured, but also a less arbitrary, estimate of what, for lack of a better term, we still call the High Renaissance. In some respects, it was indeed the culmination of the Early Renaissance, while in others it represented a departure. Certainly the tendency to view the artist as a sovereign genius was never stronger. Men of genius were thought to be set apart from ordinary mortals by the divine inspiration guiding their efforts, and were called "divine," "immortal," and "creative" (before 1500, *creating*, as distinct from *making*, had been the privilege of God alone). This cult of genius had a profound effect on the artists themselves: it spurred them on to vast and ambitious goals, often unattainable, and their faith in the divine origin of inspiration led them to rely on subjective standards of truth and beauty, rather than on the universally valid rules acknowledged by the Early Renaissance (such as scientific perspective and the ratios of musical harmony). That may be the reason why the great artists of the High Renaissance did not set the pace for a broadly based "period style" that could be practiced on every level of quality. The High Renaissance produced very few minor masters; it died with the men who created it, or even before. Of the great personalities mentioned above, only Michelangelo and Titian lived beyond 1520. In pointing out the limited and precarious nature of the High Renaissance, however, we do not mean to deny its tremendous impact upon later art. For most of the next three hundred years, the great personalities of the early sixteenth century loomed so large that their predecessors seemed to belong to a forgotten era. When they were finally rediscovered, people still acknowledged the High Renaissance as the turning point by referring to all painters before Raphael as "the Primitives."

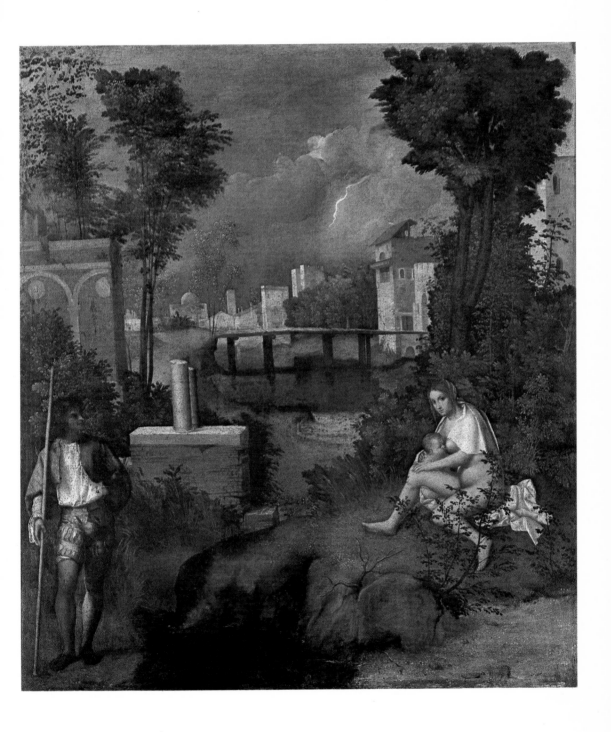

Colorplate 34. GIORGIONE. *The Tempest*. c. 1505. Oil on canvas, 31 1/4 × 28 3/4″. Academy, Venice

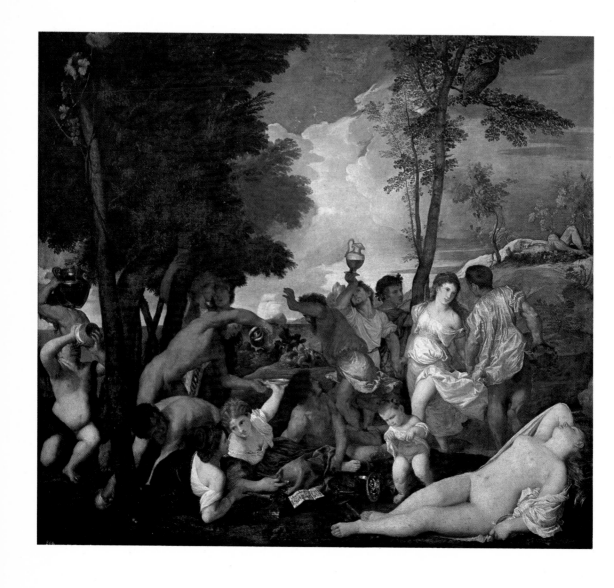

Colorplate 35. TITIAN. *Bacchanal.* c. 1518. Oil on canvas, 5′ 8 7/8″ × 6′ 4″. The Prado, Madrid

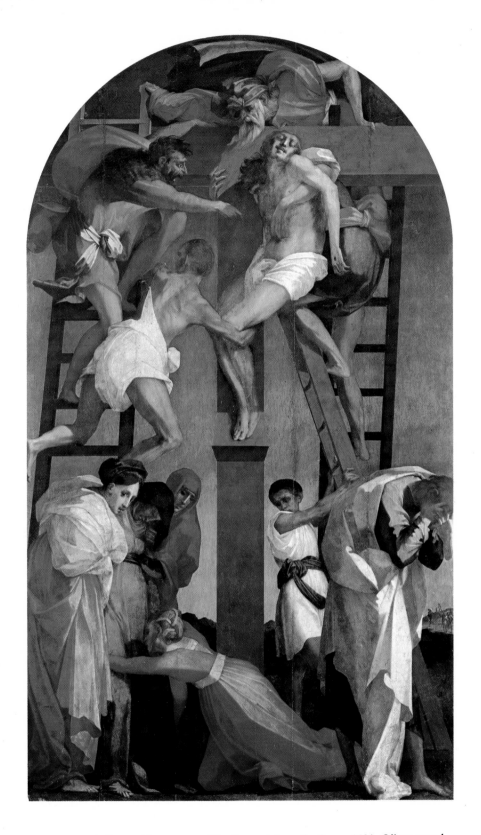

Colorplate 36. Rosso Fiorentino. *The Descent from the Cross*. 1521. Oil on panel, 11′ × 6′ 5″. Pinacoteca, Volterra, Italy

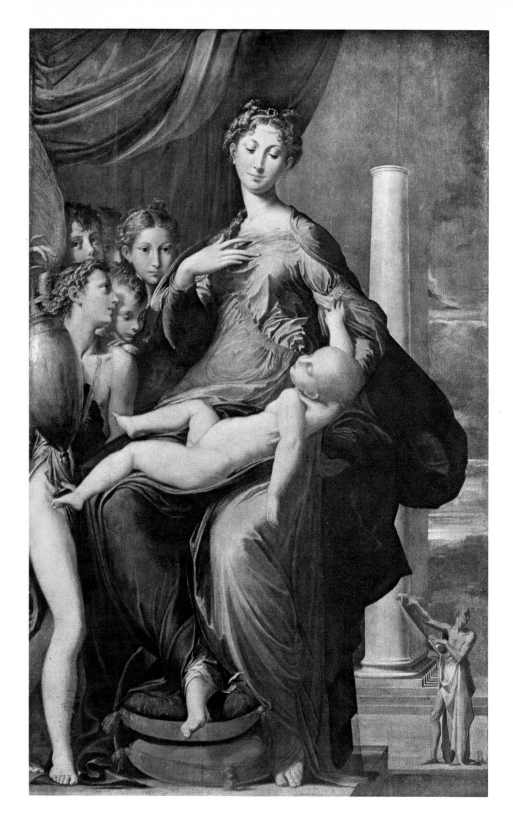

Colorplate 37. PARMIGIANINO. *The Madonna with the Long Neck*. c. 1535. Oil on panel, 7′ 1″ × 4′ 4″. Uffizi Gallery, Florence

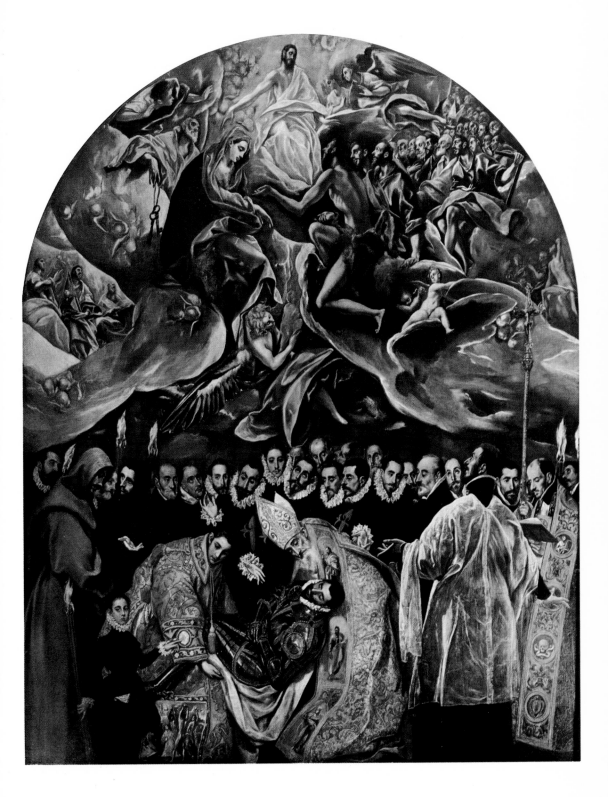

Colorplate 38. EL GRECO. *The Burial of Count Orgaz*. 1586. Oil on canvas, 16′ × 11′ 10″. Santo Tomé, Toledo, Spain

198

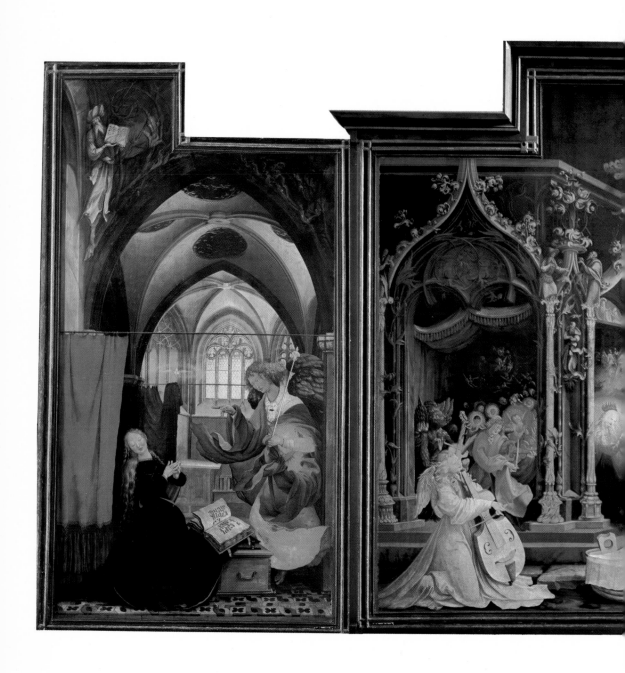

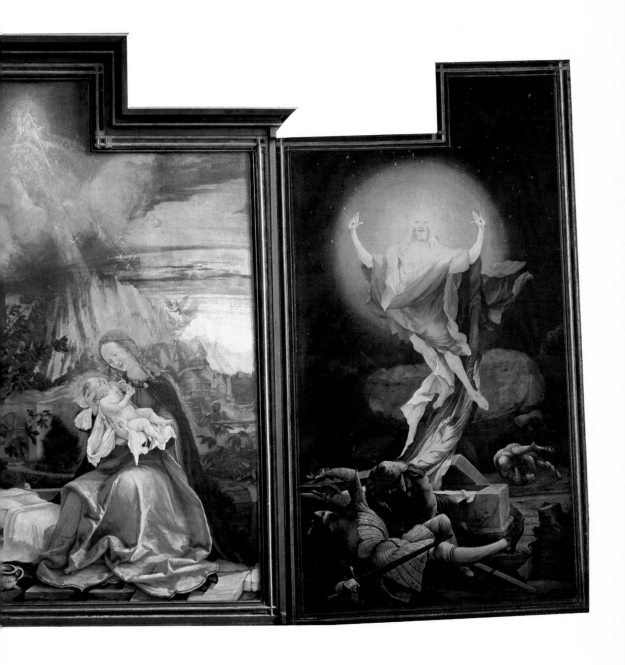

Colorplate 39. MATTHIAS GRÜNEWALD. *The Annunciation; Virgin and Child with Angels; The Resurrection.*
The Isenheim Altarpiece. (open) c. 1510–15. Panel, each wing 8′ 10″ × 4′ 8″, central scene 8′ 10″ × 11′ 2 1/2″.
Musée Unterlinden, Colmar

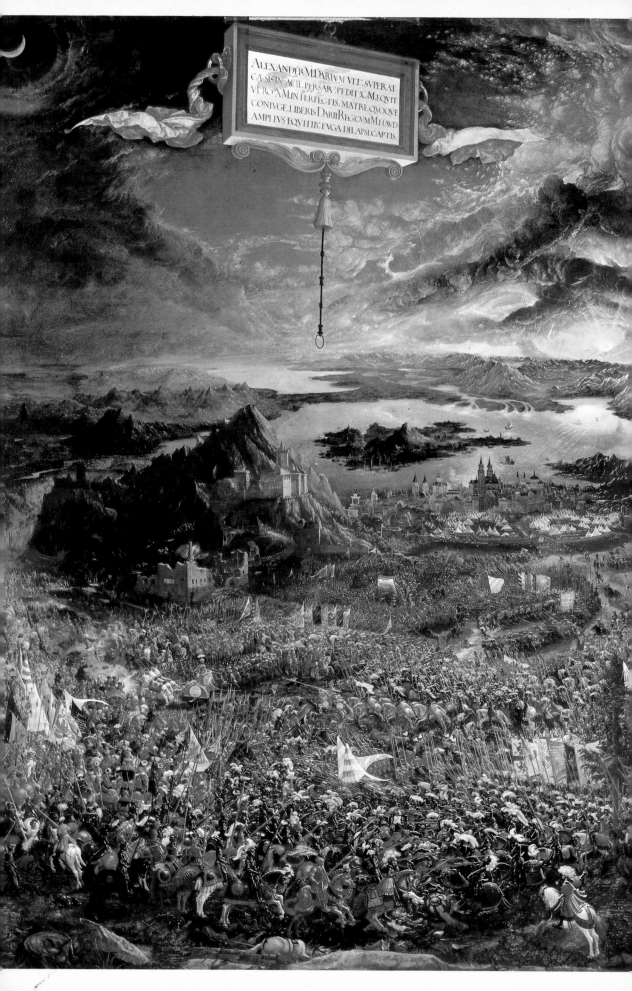

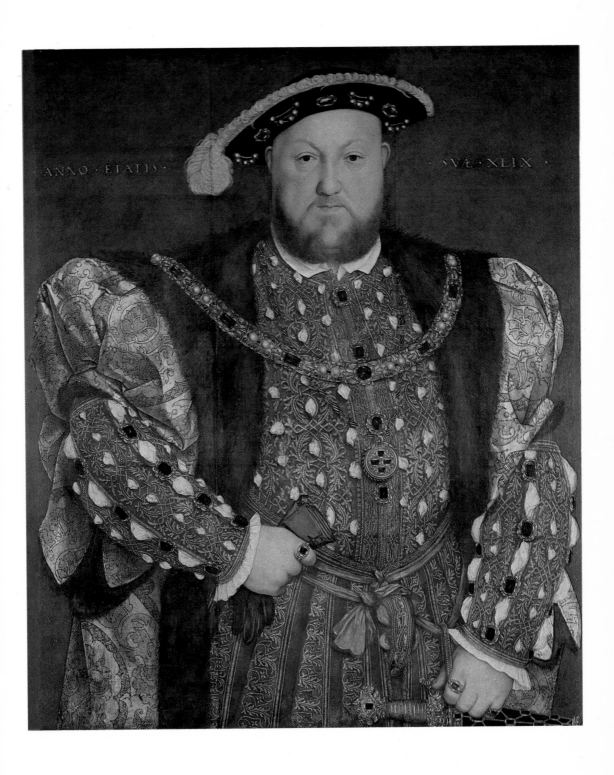

opposite: Colorplate 40. ALBRECHT ALTDORFER. *The Battle of Issus.* 1529. Panel, 62 × 47″. Pinakothek, Munich

above: Colorplate 41. HANS HOLBEIN THE YOUNGER. *Henry VIII.* 1540. Oil and tempera on panel, 32 1/2 × 29″. National Gallery, Rome

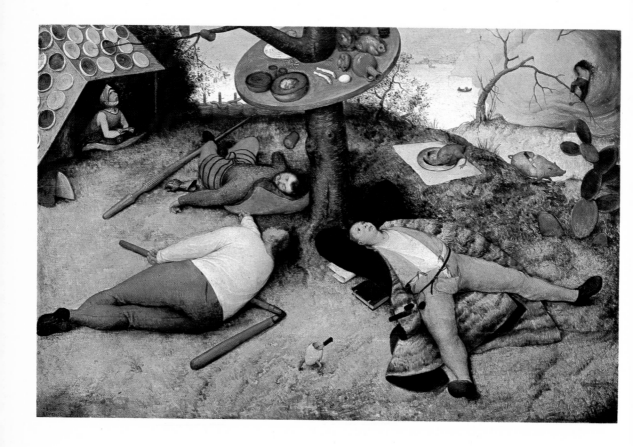

Colorplate 42. PIETER BRUEGEL THE ELDER. *The Land of Cockayne.* 1567. Oil and tempera on panel, 20 1/2 ×
30 3/4″. Pinakothek, Munich

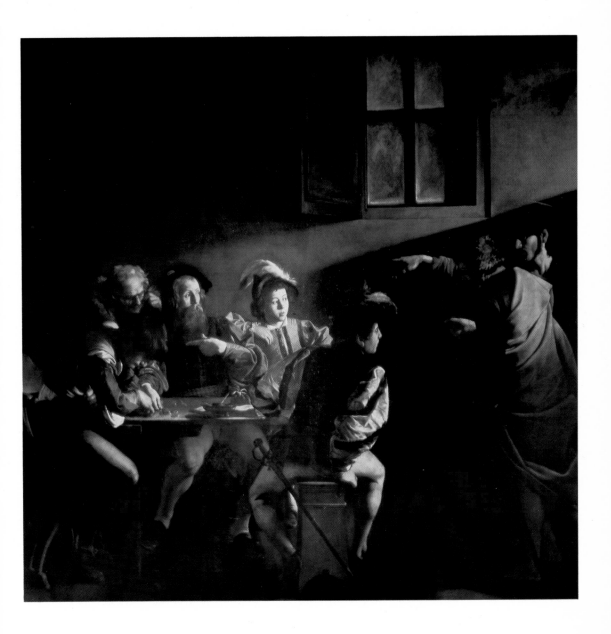

Colorplate 43. CARAVAGGIO. *The Calling of St. Matthew.* c. 1596–98. Oil on canvas, 11′ 1″ × 11′ 5″. Contarelli Chapel, San Luigi dei Francesi, Rome

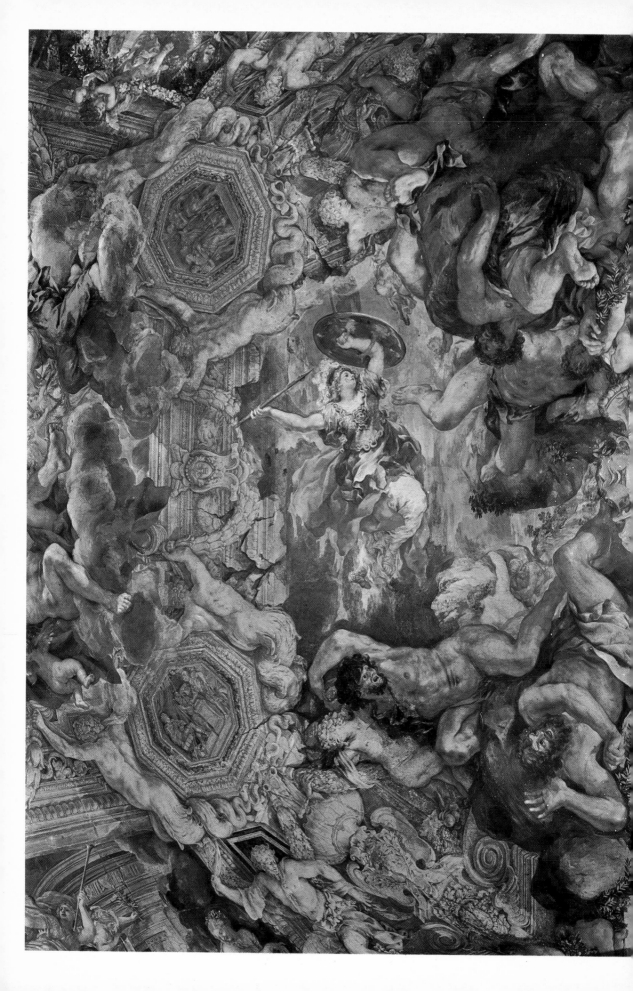

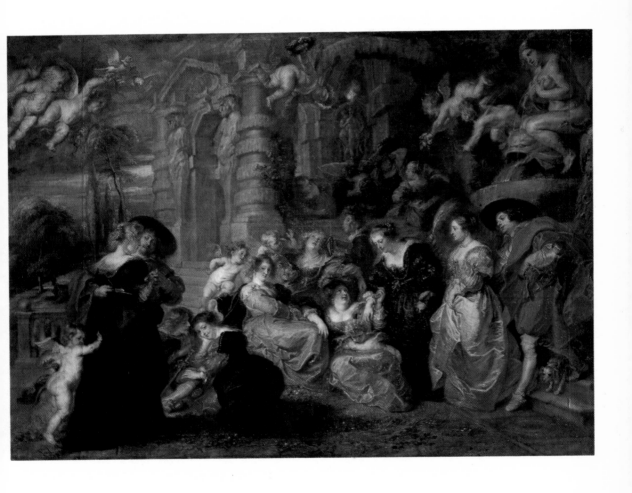

opposite: Colorplate 44. PIETRO DA CORTONA. *Glorification of the Reign of Urban VIII* (portion). Ceiling Fresco. 1633–39. Palazzo Barberini, Rome

above: Colorplate 45. PETER PAUL RUBENS. *The Garden of Love.* c. 1632–34. Oil on canvas, 6′ 6″ × 9′ 3 1/2″. The Prado, Madrid

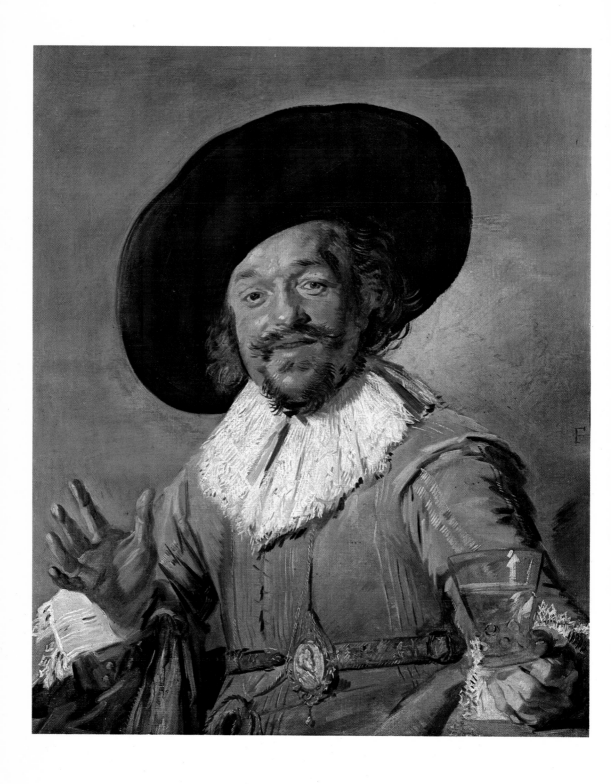

Colorplate 46. FRANS HALS. *The Jolly Toper*. 1627. Oil on canvas. 31 7/8 × 26 1/4″. Rijksmuseum, Amsterdam

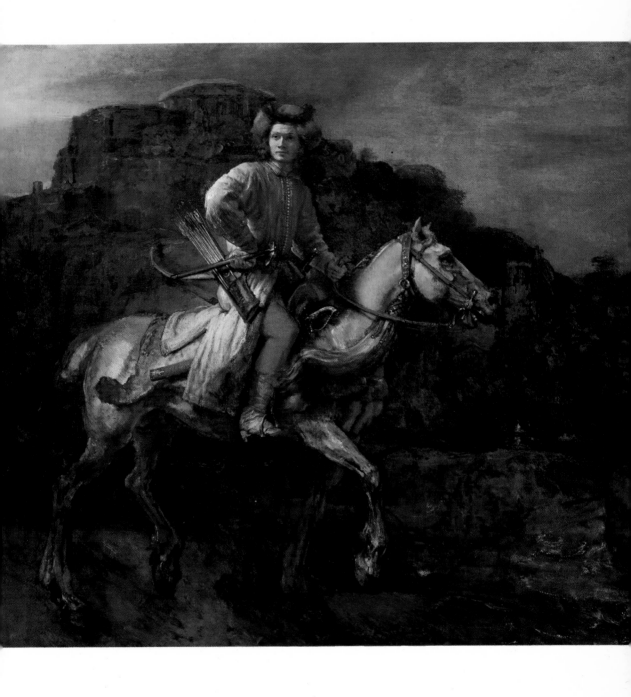

Colorplate 47. REMBRANDT. *The Polish Rider*. c. 1655. Canvas, 46 × 53″. The Frick Collection, New York

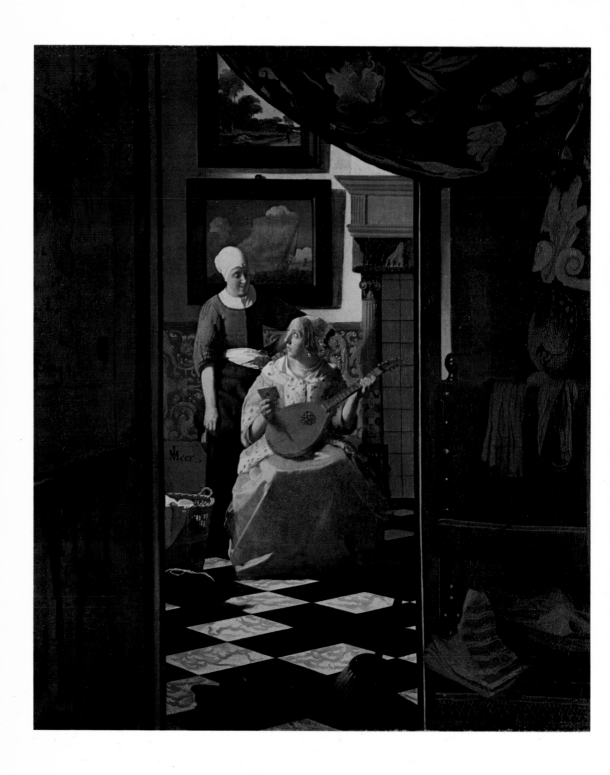

Colorplate 48. JAN VERMEER VAN DELFT. *The Letter*. 1666. Oil on canvas, 17 1/4 × 15 1/4″. Rijksmuseum, Amsterdam

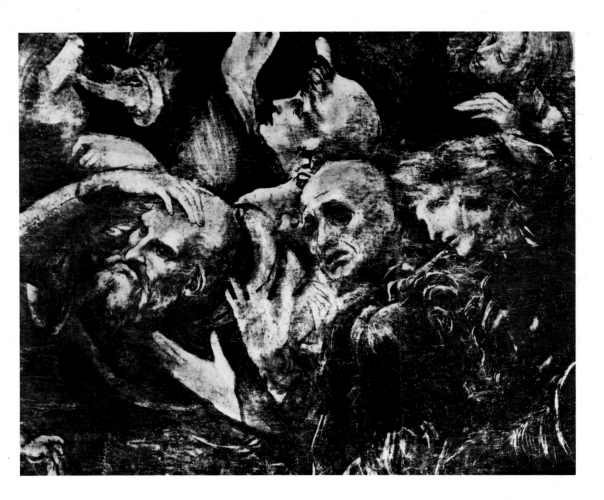

176. LEONARDO DA VINCI. *Adoration of the Magi* (detail). 1481–82. Panel, size of area shown c. 24 × 30″. Uffizi Gallery, Florence

FLORENCE AND MILAN: LEONARDO DA VINCI

One of the strange and compelling aspects of the High Renaissance is the fact that its key monuments were all produced between 1495 and 1520, despite the differences in age of the men who created them (Bramante was born in 1444, Titian about 1490). Leonardo, though not the oldest of the group, is the earliest of the High Renaissance masters. Conditions in Florence did not favor him after he had completed his training under Verrocchio; at the age of thirty he went to work for the Duke of Milan—as military engineer, architect, sculptor, and painter— leaving behind unfinished a large *Adoration of the Magi*. The panel's remarkable—and indeed, revolutionary—feature is the way it is painted. Our detail (fig. 176) shows the area to the right of center, which is more

nearly finished than the rest; the forms seem to materialize softly and gradually, never quite detaching themselves from a dusky realm. Leonardo, unlike Castagno or Botticelli, thinks not of outlines, but of three-dimensional bodies made visible in varying degrees by light. In the shadows, these shapes remain incomplete, their contours merely implied. In this method of modeling (called *chiaroscuro*, "light-and-dark") the forms no longer stand abruptly side by side. And there is a comparable emotional continuity as well: the gestures and faces of the crowd convey with touching eloquence the reality of the miracle—the newborn Christ—they have come to behold.

Toward the end of his stay in Milan, Leonardo tried to apply this method of painting to a fresco of the *Last Supper* (fig. 177). Unhappily, the mural began to deteriorate within a few years, since the artist had experimented with an oil-tempera medium that did not adhere well to the wall. Yet what re-

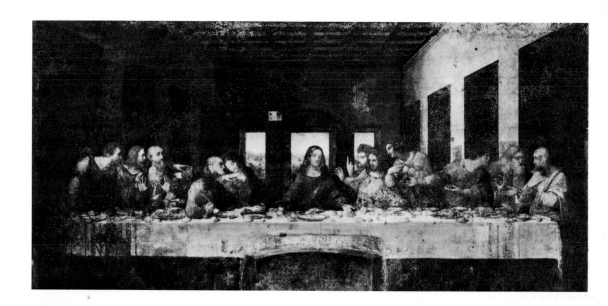

177. LEONARDO DA VINCI. *The Last Supper*. c. 1495–98. Mural. Sta. Maria delle Grazie, Milan

mains is more than enough to explain why the *Last Supper* became famous as the first Classic statement of the ideals of the High Renaissance. Viewing the composition as a whole, we see at once its balanced stability; only afterward do we discover that this balance has been achieved by the reconciliation of competing, even conflicting claims. In Early Renaissance art, the architecture often threatens to overpower the figures (see figs. 160, 174). Leonardo, in contrast, began with the figure composition, and the architecture had merely a supporting role from the start, even though it obeys all the rules of scientific perspective. The central vanishing point is behind the head of Christ in the exact middle of the picture, thus becoming charged with symbolic significance. Equally plain is the symbolic function of the main opening in the rear wall; its pediment acts as the architectural equivalent of a halo. We thus tend to see the setting almost entirely in relation to the figures, rather than as a pre-existing entity. We can test this by covering the upper third of the picture: the composition then looks like a frieze, the grouping of the Apostles is less clear, and the calm triangular shape of Christ becomes merely passive, instead of acting as a physical and spiritual focus. The Saviour, presumably, has just spoken the fateful words, "One of you shall

betray me," and the disciples are asking, "Lord, is it I?" But to view the scene as one particular moment in a psychological drama hardly does justice to Leonardo's intentions. The gesture of Christ is one of submission to the Divine will, and of offering. It hints at Christ's main act at the Last Supper, the institution of the Eucharist ("Jesus took bread . . . and said, Take, eat; this is my body. And he took the cup . . . saying, Drink ye all of it; for this is my blood . . ."). And the Apostles are not merely responding; each reveals his own personality, his own relationship to the Saviour. (Note the dark, defiant profile of Judas, that sets him apart from the rest.) They exemplify what the artist wrote in one of his notebooks, that the highest aim of painting is to depict "the intention of man's soul" through gestures and the movements of limbs—a dictum that refers not to momentary emotional states but to man's inner life as a whole.

In 1499, the duchy of Milan fell to the French, and Leonardo returned to a Florence very different from the city he remembered. The Medici had been expelled, and Florence was briefly a republic again. There Leonardo painted his most famous portrait, the *Mona Lisa* (colorplate 32). The chiaroscuro we noted in the *Adoration* is now so perfected that it seemed miraculous to his contemporaries. The forms are built from layers of glazes so gossamer-thin that the entire panel seems to glow with a gentle light from within. But the fame of the *Mona Lisa* comes not from this pictorial subtlety alone; even more intriguing is her psychological fascination. Why, among all the smiling faces ever painted, has this one been singled out as "mysterious"? Perhaps because, as a portrait, the picture does not fit our expectations. The features are too individual for an ideal type, yet the element of idealization is so strong that it blurs the sitter's character. Once again the artist has brought two opposites into harmonious balance. The smile, too, may be read in two ways: as the echo of a mood, and as a timeless, symbolic expression. Clearly, the *Mona Lisa* embodies a quality of maternal tenderness which was to Leonardo the essence of womanhood. Even the landscape, composed mainly of rocks and water, suggests elemental generative forces.

In the later years of his life, Leonardo devoted himself more and more to his scientific interests. Art and science had first been united in Brunelleschi's discovery of perspective; Leonardo's work is the climax of this trend. The artist, he believed, must know all the laws of nature, and the eye was to him the perfect instrument for gaining such knowledge. The extraordinary scope of his own inquiries is attested by the hundreds of drawings and notes which he hoped to incorporate into an encyclopedic set of treatises. How original he was as a scientist is still a matter of debate, but in one field his importance is undisputed: he created the modern scientific illustration, an essential tool for anatomists and biologists. A drawing such as the *Embryo in the Womb* (fig. 178) combines vivid observation with the clarity of a diagram, or—to paraphrase Leonardo's own words—sight and insight.

FLORENCE AND ROME: MICHELANGELO

The concept of genius as divine inspiration, a superhuman power granted to a few rare individuals and acting through them, is nowhere exemplified more fully than in Michelangelo. Not only his admirers viewed him in this light; he himself, steeped in Neo-Platonism, accepted the idea of his genius as a living reality, although it seemed to him at times a curse rather than a blessing. Conventions, standards, and traditions might be observed by lesser spirits; he could acknowledge no authority higher than the dictates of his genius. Unlike Leonardo, for whom painting was the noblest of the arts because it embraced every visible aspect of the world, Michelangelo was a sculptor—more specifically, a carver of marble statues—to the core. Art, for him, was not a science but "the making of men," analogous to divine creation. Only the "liberation" of real, three-dimensional bodies from recalcitrant matter could satisfy the urge within him. Painting, he believed, should imitate the roundness of sculptured forms, and architecture, too, must partake of the organic qualities of the human figure. Michelangelo's faith in the image of man as the supreme vehicle of expression gave him a sense of kinship with Classical sculpture closer than that of any other Renaissance artist, although he admired Giotto, Masaccio, and Donatello. Yet, as a Neo-Platonist, he looked upon the body as the earthly prison of the soul—noble, surely, but a prison nevertheless. This dualism endows

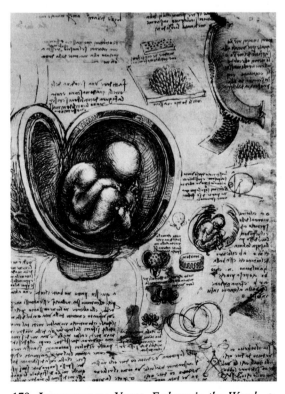

178. LEONARDO DA VINCI. *Embryo in the Womb.* c. 1510. Ink. Royal Library, Windsor Castle (Crown Copyright)

his figures with their extraordinary pathos; outwardly calm, they seem stirred by an overwhelming psychic energy that can find no true release in physical action.

The unique qualities of Michelangelo's art are fully present in the *David* (fig. 179), the earliest monumental statue of the High Renaissance, commissioned in 1501, when the artist was twenty-six. The huge figure was put at the left of the entrance to the Palazzo Vecchio as the civic-patriotic symbol of the Florentine Republic (see fig. 126; a modern copy has now replaced the original). This role was a suitable one for the *David*. Without the head of Goliath, he looks challenging— not a victorious hero but the champion of a just cause. Nude, like Donatello's bronze *David* (see fig. 158), he boldly faces the world, vibrant with pent-up energy. But the style of the figure proclaims an ideal very different from Donatello's. Michelangelo had just spent several years in Rome, and had been strongly impressed with the emotion-filled, muscular bodies of Hellenistic sculpture. Their heroic scale, their superhuman beauty and power, and the swelling volume of their forms became part of Michelangelo's style, and through him part of Renaissance art in general. Still, the *David* could never be taken for an ancient statue. In the *Laocoön* (see fig. 58) and similar works, the body "acts out" the spirit's agony, while the *David*, characteristically, is both calm and tense.

THE SISTINE CHAPEL

Soon after, Michelangelo was called to Rome by Pope Julius II, the greatest and most ambitious of Renaissance popes, for whom he designed an enormous tomb. After a few years, however, the Pope changed his mind and set the reluctant artist to work on the ceiling fresco of the Sistine Chapel (fig. 180). Driven by his desire to resume the tomb project, Michelangelo finished the entire ceiling in four years (1508–12). He produced a masterpiece of truly epochal importance. The ceiling is a huge organism with hundreds of figures rhythmically distributed within the painted architectural framework, dwarfing the earlier murals below by its size, and still more by its compelling inner unity. In the central area, subdivided by five pairs of

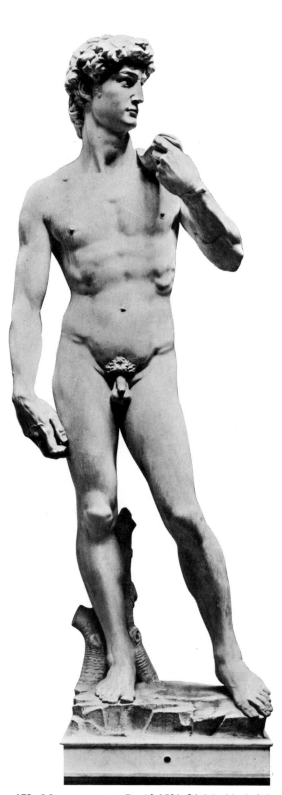

179. MICHELANGELO. *David.* 1501–04. Marble, height 13′ 5″. Academy, Florence

girder arches, are nine scenes from Genesis, from the Creation of the World (at the far end of the Chapel) to the Drunkenness of Noah. The theological scheme behind the choice of these scenes and the rich program surrounding them—the nude youths, the medallions, the prophets and sibyls, the scenes in the spandrels—has not been fully explained, but we know that it links the early history of man and the coming of Christ, the

beginning of time and its end (the *Last Judgment* on the wall above the altar). How much responsibility did Michelangelo have for the program? He was not a man to submit to dictation, and the subject matter as a whole fits his cast of mind so perfectly that his own desires cannot have conflicted strongly with those of his patron. What greater theme could he wish than the Creation, Man's Fall, and Man's ultimate reconciliation with the Lord? A detailed survey of the Sistine Ceiling would fill a book; we shall have to be content with the *Creation of Adam* (fig. 181), the most famous of the major scenes. It

180. Interior, Sistine Chapel (showing Michelangelo's Ceiling Fresco and *Last Judgment*). The Vatican, Rome

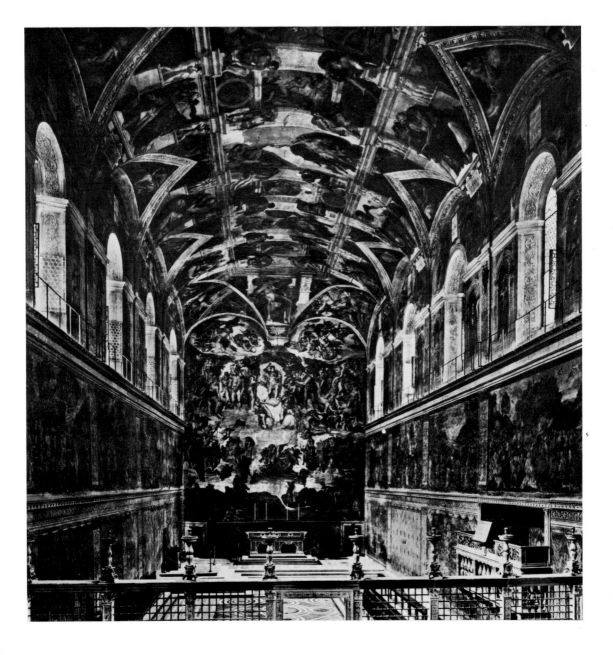

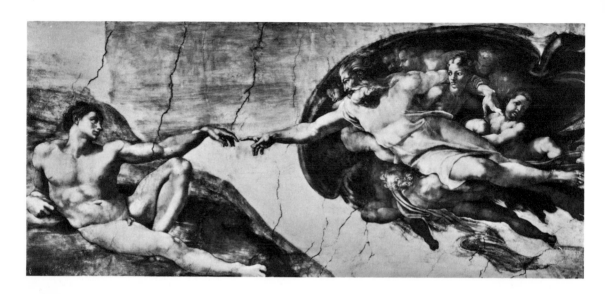

181. MICHELANGELO. *The Creation of Adam,* detail of Sistine Ceiling. 1508–12. Fresco. The Vatican, Rome

shows not the physical molding of Adam's body but the passage of the divine spark—the soul—and thus achieves a dramatic juxtaposition of Man and God unrivaled by any other artist. The relationship between the earth-bound Adam and the figure of God rushing through the sky becomes even more meaningful when we realize that Adam strains not only toward his Creator but toward Eve, whom he sees, yet unborn, in the shelter of the Lord's left arm. Our illustration also shows the garland-bearing nude youths that accompany the main sections. These wonderfully animated figures play an important role in Michelangelo's design; they form a kind of chain linking the Genesis scenes, yet their significance remains uncertain. Are they images of human souls? Do they represent the world of pagan antiquity? Whatever their symbolic intent, it is overpowered by the wealth of expression Michelangelo has poured into these figures.

When Michelangelo returned to the Sistine Chapel over twenty years later, the Western world was gripped by the spiritual and political crisis of the Reformation (see p. 234). We observe with shocking directness how the mood has changed as we turn from the radiant vitality of the ceiling fresco to the somber vision of the *Last Judgment.* Mankind, Blessed and Damned alike, huddles together in tight clumps, pleading for mercy before a wrathful God (figs. 180, 182). Seated on a cloud below the Lord is the Apostle Bartholomew, holding a human skin to represent his martyrdom (he had been flayed). The face on that skin is not the saint's, however; it is Michelangelo's own. In this grimly sardonic self-portrait the artist has left his personal confession of guilt and unworthiness.

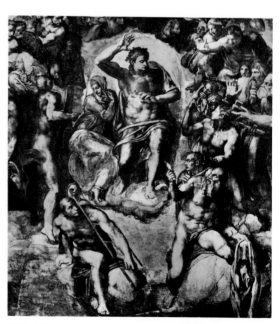

182. MICHELANGELO. *The Last Judgment* (detail, with self-portrait). 1534–41. Fresco. Sistine Chapel, The Vatican, Rome

THE MEDICI CHAPEL

The interval between the Sistine Ceiling and the *Last Judgment* coincided with the papacies of Leo X and Clement VII; both were members of the Medici family and preferred to employ Michelangelo in Florence. His activities centered on San Lorenzo, the Medici church, where Leo X had decided to build a chapel containing four monumental tombs for members of the family. Michelangelo worked on the project for fourteen years, completing the chapel and two tombs. It is the artist's only work where his statues remain in the setting planned specifically for them (figure 183 shows the tomb of Giuliano). The design of the monument is strangely impersonal: there is no inscription, two allegorical figures (*Day* on the right, *Night* on the left) recline on the sarcophagus, and the statue of Giuliano, in Classical military garb, bears no resemblance to the deceased. ("A thousand years from now, nobody will want to know what he really looked like" Michelangelo is said to have remarked.) What is the meaning of the monument? The question, put countless times, has never found a definitive answer. Michelangelo's plans for the Medici tombs underwent so many changes while the work was under way that the present state of the monuments can hardly be the final solution; rather, the dynamic process of design was arbitrarily halted by the artist's departure for Rome in 1534. *Day* and *Night* were certainly planned for horizontal surfaces, not for the curved lid of the present sarcophagus. Perhaps they were not even intended for this particular tomb. Giuliano's niche is too narrow and shallow to hold him comfortably. Other figures and reliefs were planned, but never executed. Yet the tomb of Giuliano remains a compelling visual unit. The great triangle of the statues is held in place by a network of verticals and horizontals whose slender, sharp-edged forms heighten the roundness and weight of the sculpture. In the brooding menace of *Day* and the disturbed slumber of *Night*, the dualism of body and soul is expressed with unforgettable grandeur.

ROME: BRAMANTE

During the last thirty years of his long career, architecture became Michelangelo's main pre-

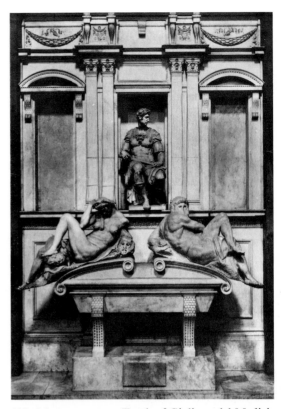

183. MICHELANGELO. Tomb of Giuliano de' Medici. 1524–34. Marble, height of central figure 71″. New Sacristy, S. Lorenzo, Florence

occupation. In order to understand his achievement in that field, we must discuss briefly his most important predecessor, Donato Bramante. Bramante had been working for the Duke of Milan in the 1490s, together with Leonardo. After Milan fell, he went to Rome, and there he became the creator of High Renaissance architecture. The new style is fully evident in his Tempietto at San Pietro in Montorio (fig. 184), designed soon after 1500. Its nickname, "little temple," seems well deserved: in the three-step platform, and the severe Doric order of the colonnade, Classical temple architecture is more directly recalled than in any fifteenth-century structure. Equally striking is the "sculptural" treatment of the walls: deeply recessed niches "excavated" from heavy masses of masonry. These cavities are counterbalanced by the convex shape of the dome and by strongly projecting moldings and cornices. As a result, the Tempietto has a monumental weight that belies its modest size.

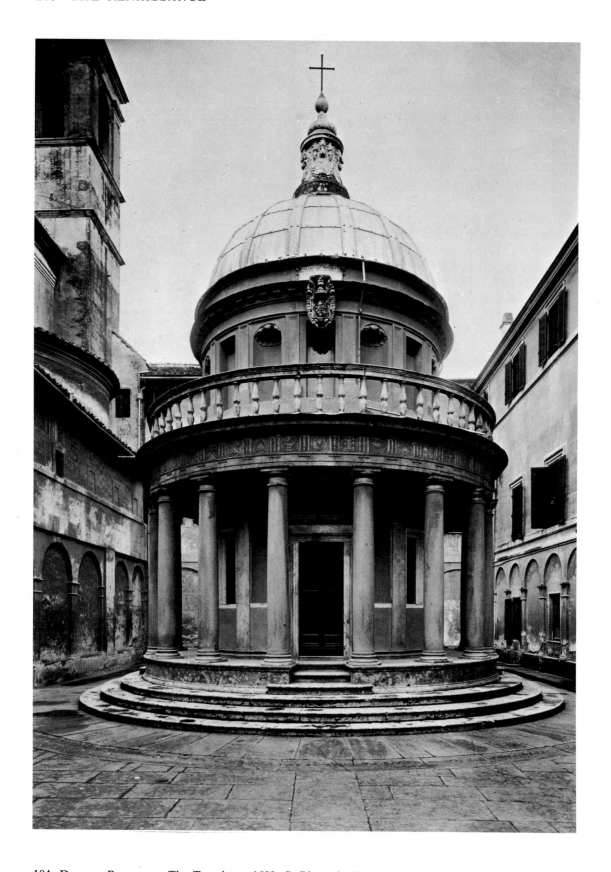

184. Donato Bramante. The Tempietto. 1502. S. Pietro in Montorio, Rome

The Tempietto is the earliest of the great achievements that made Rome the center of Italian art during the first quarter of the sixteenth century. Most of them belong to the decade 1503–13, the papacy of Julius II. It was he who decided to replace the Early Christian basilica of St. Peter's with a church so magnificent as to overshadow all the monuments of ancient imperial Rome. The task naturally fell to Bramante. His design, of 1506, is known to us mainly from a plan (fig. 185), which bears out the words Bramante reportedly used to define his aim: "I shall place the Pantheon on top of the Basilica of Constantine." (See figs. 63–65.) Bramante's design is indeed of truly imperial magnificence: a huge dome crowns the crossing of the barrel-vaulted arms of a Greek cross, with four lesser domes and tall corner towers filling the angles. This plan fulfills all the demands laid down by Alberti for sacred architecture (see p. 183); based entirely on the circle and the square, it is so rigidly symmetrical that we cannot tell which apse was to hold the high altar. Bramante envisioned four identical façades like that on the medal of 1506 (fig. 186), dominated by the same repertory of severely Classical forms we saw in the Tempietto: domes, half-domes, colonnades, pediments. These simple geometric shapes, however, do not prevail inside the church. Here the "sculptured wall" reigns supreme: the plan shows no continuous surfaces, only great, oddly shaped "islands" of masonry that have been well described by one critic as giant pieces of toast half-eaten by a voracious space. Their actual size can be visualized only if we compare the measurements of Bramante's church with those of earlier buildings. San Lorenzo in Florence, for instance, is 268 feet long, less than half the length of the new St. Peter's (550 feet). Each arm of Bramante's Greek cross has about the dimensions of the Basilica of Constantine. No wonder the construction of St. Peter's progressed at a snail's pace. At Bramante's death, in 1514, only the four crossing piers had actually been built.

For the next three decades the campaign was carried out hesitantly by architects trained under Bramante. A new and decisive phase began only in 1546, when Michelangelo took charge; the present appearance of the church (fig. 187) is largely shaped by his ideas. Michelangelo simplified Bramante's overly complex plan without changing its basic character; he also redesigned the exterior, using a colossal order to emphasize the compact body of the structure, thus setting off the dome more dramatically. Although largely built after his death, the dome reflects Michelangelo's ideas in every im-

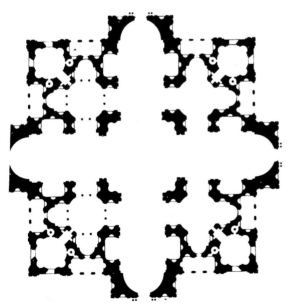

185. DONATO BRAMANTE. Original Plan for St. Peter's, Rome (after Geymüller). 1506

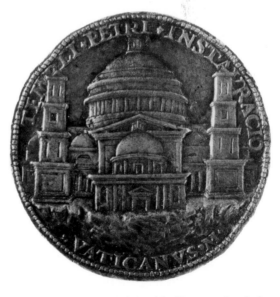

186. CARADOSSO. Medal with Bramante's design for St. Peter's. 1506. British Museum, London

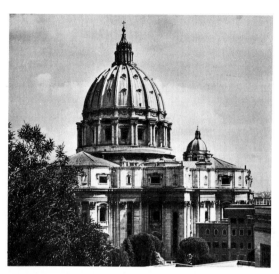

187. MICHELANGELO. St. Peter's, view from west. 1546–64 (dome completed by Giacomo della Porta, 1590). Rome

portant respect. Bramante had planned a stepped hemisphere, somewhat like the dome of the Pantheon, which would have seemed to press down on the church below; Michelangelo's dome conveys the opposite sensation, a powerful thrust that draws energy upward from the main body of the structure. The high drum, the strongly projecting buttresses accented by double columns, the ribs, the raised curve of the cupola, the tall lantern—all contribute verticality at the expense of the horizontals. We may recall Brunelleschi's Florence Cathedral dome (see fig. 124), from which Michelangelo clearly borrowed a great deal. Yet the effect is immensely different: the Florence dome gives no hint of the internal stresses, while Michelangelo finds a sculptured shape for these contending forces and relates them to those in the rest of the building (the impulse of the paired colossal pilasters below is taken up by the double columns of the drum, continues in the ribs, and culminates in the lantern). The logic of this design is so persuasive that few domes built between 1600 and 1900 fail to acknowledge it.

ROME: RAPHAEL

If Michelangelo exemplifies the solitary genius, Raphael belongs to the opposite type: the artist as a man of the world. Although each had his partisans, both enjoyed equal

fame. Today our sympathies are less evenly divided—

In the room the women come and go
Talking of Michelangelo.

(T. S. Eliot)

So do many of us, including the authors of historical novels and fictionalized biographies, whereas Raphael is usually discussed only by historians of art. His career is too much of a success story, his work too replete with seemingly effortless grace, to match the tragic heroism of Michelangelo. As an innovator, Raphael contributed less than either Leonardo or Michelangelo, yet he is the central painter of the High Renaissance; our conception of the entire style rests on his work more than on any other master's. His genius was a unique power of synthesis that enabled him to merge the qualities of Leonardo and Michelangelo, creating an art at once lyric and dramatic, pictorially rich and sculpturally solid. At the time Michelangelo began to paint the Sistine Ceiling, Julius II summoned Raphael from Florence to decorate a series of rooms in the Vatican Palace. In the first, the Stanza della Segnatura, Raphael's frescoes refer to the four domains of learning—theology, philosophy, law, and the arts. Of these frescoes, *The School of Athens* (colorplate 33) has long been acknowledged as the perfect embodiment of the Classic spirit of the High Renaissance. Its subject is "the Athenian school of thought"; a group of famous Greek philosophers is gathered around Plato and Aristotle, each in a characteristic pose or activity. Raphael must have already seen the Sistine Ceiling, then nearing completion, for he evidently owes to Michelangelo the expressive energy, the physical power, and the dramatic grouping of his figures. Yet Raphael has not simply borrowed the older master's repertory of gestures and poses; he has absorbed it into his own style, and thereby given it different meaning. Body and spirit, action and feeling, are now balanced harmoniously, and every member of this great assembly plays his role with magnificent, purposeful clarity. *The School of Athens* suggests the spirit of Leonardo's *Last Supper* (fig. 177) rather than that of the Sistine Ceiling (fig. 180). This holds true of the way each philosopher reveals "the intention of his soul," of the formal rhythm linking

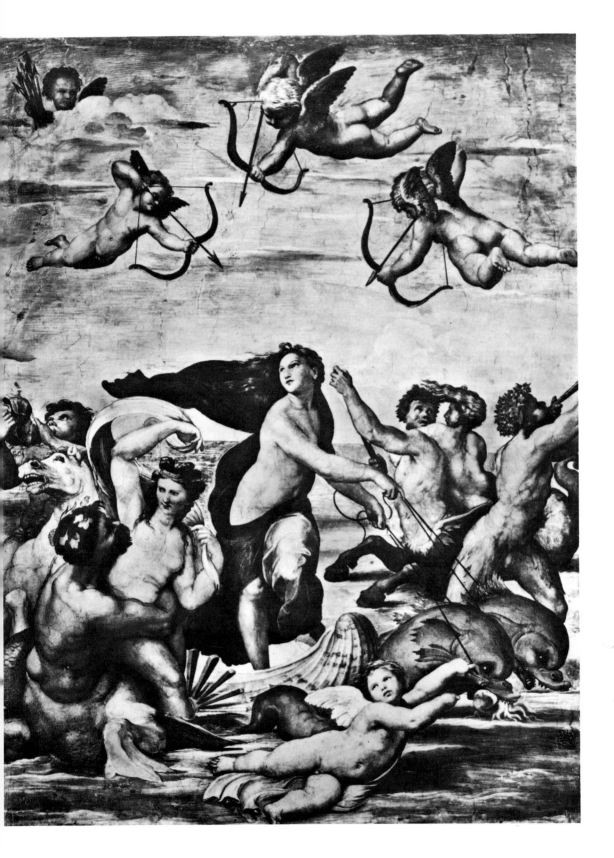

188. RAPHAEL. *Galatea.* 1513. Fresco. Villa Farnesina, Rome

individuals and groups, of the centralized, symmetrical design, and of the interdependence of the figures and their architectural setting. But compared with the hall of the *Last Supper*, Raphael's Classical edifice shares far more of the compositional burden. Inspired by Bramante, it seems like an advance view of the new St. Peter's (fig. 185). Its geometric precision and spatial grandeur bring to a climax the tradition we have seen begun by Masaccio (see colorplate 27) and continued by Domenico Veneziano and Mantegna.

Raphael never again set so splendid an architectural stage. To create pictorial space, he relied increasingly on the movement of human figures, rather than on perspective vistas. In his *Galatea* (fig. 188), the subject is again Classical—the nymph Galatea, vainly pursued by Polyphemus, belongs to Greek mythology—but here the gay and sensuous aspect of antiquity is celebrated, in contrast to the austere idealism of *The School of Athens*. Its composition recalls *The Birth of Venus* (see colorplate 29), which Raphael knew from his Florence days, yet their very resemblance emphasizes their profound dissimilarity. Raphael's full-bodied, dynamic figures take on their expansive spiral movement from the vigorously twisting pose of Galatea; in Botticelli's picture, the movement is not generated by the figures but imposed upon them from without, so that it never detaches itself from the surface of the canvas.

VENICE: GIORGIONE; TITIAN

The distinction between Early and High Renaissance art, so marked in Florence and Rome, is far less sharp in Venice. Giorgione (1478–1510), the first Venetian painter to belong to the new, sixteenth century, left the orbit of Giovanni Bellini only during the final years of his short career. Among his very few mature works, *The Tempest* (colorplate 34) is both the most individual and the most enigmatic. Our first glance may show us little more than a particularly charming reflection of Bellinesque qualities, familiar from the *St. Francis in Ecstasy* (colorplate 31). The difference is one of mood—and this mood, in *The Tempest*, is subtly, pervasively pagan. Bellini's landscape is meant to be seen through the eyes of St. Francis, as a piece of

God's creation. Giorgione's figures, by contrast, do not interpret the scene for us; belonging themselves to nature, they are passive witnesses—victims, almost—of the thunderstorm about to engulf them. Who are they? So far, the young soldier and the nude mother with her babe have refused to disclose their identity, and the subject of the picture remains unknown. The present title is a confession of embarrassment, yet it is not inappropriate, for the only "action" is that of the tempest. Whatever its intended meaning, the scene is like an enchanted idyll, a dream of pastoral beauty soon to be swept away. Only poets had hitherto captured this air of nostalgic reverie; now, it entered the repertory of the painter. *The Tempest* initiates what was to become an important new tradition.

Giorgione died before he could explore in full the sensuous, lyrical world he had created in *The Tempest*. He bequeathed this task to Titian, an artist of comparable gifts who was decisively influenced by Giorgione, and who dominated Venetian painting for the next half-century. Titian's *Bacchanal* of about 1518 (colorplate 35) is frankly pagan, inspired by an ancient author's description of such a revel. The landscape, rich in contrasts of cool and warm tones, has all the poetry of Giorgione, but the figures are of another breed: active and muscular, they move with a joyous freedom that recalls Raphael's *Galatea*. By this time, many of Raphael's compositions had been engraved, and from these reproductions Titian became familiar with the Roman High Renaissance. A number of the celebrants in his *Bacchanal* also reflect the influence of Classical art. Titian's approach to antiquity, however, is very different from Raphael's; he visualizes the realm of Classical myths as part of the natural world, inhabited not by animated statues but by beings of flesh and blood. The figures of the *Bacchanal* are idealized beyond everyday reality just enough to persuade us that they belong to a long-lost Golden Age. They invite us to share their blissful state in a way that makes Raphael's *Galatea* seem cold and remote by comparison.

Aside from all his other achievements, Titian also was the greatest portraitist of the century. His *Man with the Glove* (fig. 189),

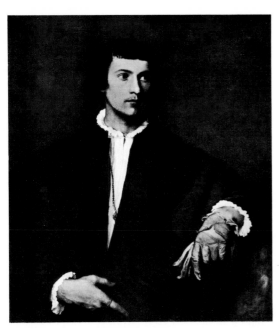

189. TITIAN. *Man with the Glove.* c. 1520. Canvas, 39 1/2 × 35″. The Louvre, Paris

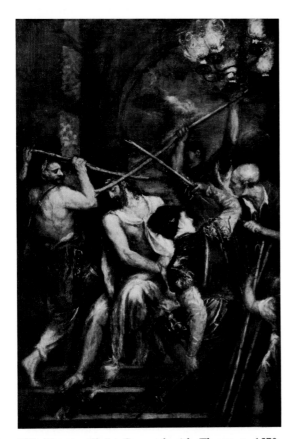

190. TITIAN. *Christ Crowned with Thorns.* c. 1570. Oil on canvas, 9′ 2″ × 6′. Pinakothek, Munich

unlike the *Mona Lisa* (see colorplate 32), offers no disquieting mysteries but a profound sense of the sitter's individuality. Casually posed and lost in thought, the young man seems quite unaware of us. The dreamy intimacy of this portrait, the hint of melancholy in its mood, the soft outlines and deep shadows, give it a haunting poetic appeal reminiscent of Giorgione's *Tempest*. In Titian's hands, the possibilities of oil technique—rich, creamy highlights, dark tones that are yet transparent and delicately modulated—are now fully realized; the separate brushstrokes, hardly visible before, become increasingly free, so that the personal rhythms of the artist's "handwriting" are an essential element of the finished work. In this respect, Titian seems infinitely more "modern" than Leonardo, Michelangelo, or Raphael.

The new broad manner of the *Man with the Glove* is pushed to its limits in the *Christ Crowned with Thorns* (fig. 190), a masterpiece of Titian's old age. The shapes emerging from the semi-darkness now consist wholly of light and color; despite the heavy impasto, the shimmering surfaces have lost every trace of material solidity and seem translucent, aglow from within. In consequence, the violent physical action has been miraculously suspended. What lingers in our minds is not the drama but the strange mood of serenity—engendered by deep religious feeling.

Mannerism and Other Trends

What happened after the High Renaissance? About fifty years ago the answer would have been: the Late Renaissance, which was dominated by shallow imitators of the great masters of the previous generation and lasted until the Baroque style emerged at the end of the century. Today we take a far more positive view of the artists who reached maturity after 1520, but we have yet to agree on a name for the seventy-five years separating the High Renaissance from the Baroque. Any one label implies that the period had one style, and nobody has succeeded in defining such a style. But if there was no single style, why should the span 1525–1600 be regarded as a period at all? Perhaps the difficulty can be resolved by thinking of it as a time of crisis that gave rise to several competing tendencies rather than one dominant ideal—or as a time full of inner contradictions, not unlike the present and thus peculiarly fascinating to us. Among these trends, that of Mannerism is the most discussed today. The scope and significance of the term remain problematic: its original meaning was narrow and derogatory, designating a group of painters in Rome and Florence whose self-consciously "artificial" style was derived from certain aspects of Raphael and Michelangelo. More recently, the cold formalism of their work has been recognized as part of a wider movement that placed "inner vi-

sion," however subjective and fantastic, above the twin authority of nature and the ancients. Its first signs appear shortly before 1520 in the work of some young painters in Florence. By 1521, Rosso Fiorentino, the most eccentric member of this group, expressed the new attitude with full conviction in *The Descent from the Cross* (colorplate 36). Nothing has prepared us for the shocking impact of this latticework of spidery forms spread out against the dark sky. The figures are agitated yet rigid, as if congealed by a sudden, icy blast; even the draperies have brittle, sharp-edged planes; the acid colors and the brilliant but unreal light reinforce the nightmarish effect of the scene. Here is what amounts to a revolt against the Classical balance of High Renaissance art—a profoundly disquieting, willful, visionary style that indicates a deep-seated anxiety.

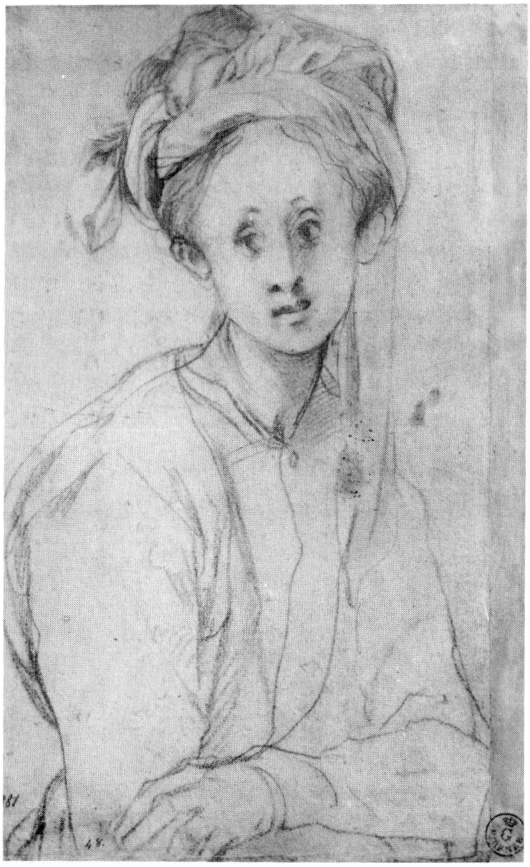

191. PONTORMO. *Study of a Young Girl.* c. 1526. Red chalk drawing. Uffizi Gallery, Florence

PONTORMO; PARMIGIANINO

Pontormo, a friend of Rosso, had an equally strange personality. Introspective and shy, he shut himself up in his quarters for weeks on end, inaccessible even to his friends. His wonderfully sensitive drawings, such as the *Study of a Young Girl* (fig. 191), well reflect these facets of his character; the sitter, moodily gazing into space, seems to shrink from the outer world, as if scarred by the trauma of some half-remembered experience.

This "anticlassical" style of Rosso and Pontormo, the first phase of Mannerism, was soon replaced by another aspect of the movement. This was less overtly anticlassical, less laden with subjective emotion, but equally far removed from the confident, stable world of the High Renaissance. Parmigianino's *Self-Portrait* (fig. 192) suggests no psychological turmoil; the artist's appearance is bland and well groomed, veiled by a delicate Leonardesque haze. The distortions, too, are objective, not arbitrary, for the picture records what Parmigianino saw as he gazed at his reflection in a convex mirror. Yet why was he so fascinated by this view "through the looking glass"? Earlier painters, such as Jan van Eyck, who used the same device as an aid to observation had "filtered out" the distortions (as in figure 147), except when the mirror image was contrasted with a

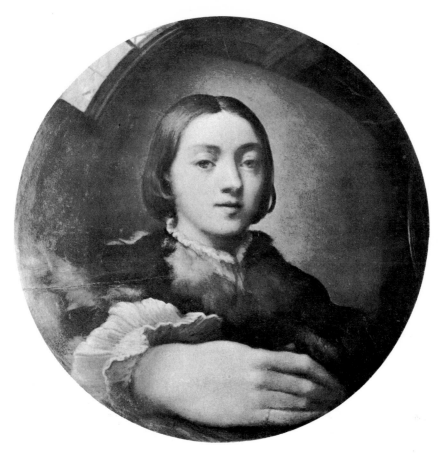

192. PARMIGIANINO. *Self-Portrait*. 1524. Oil on panel, diameter 9 5/8″. Kunsthistorisches Museum, Vienna

direct view of the same scene (colorplate 24, fig. 148). But Parmigianino substitutes his painting for the mirror itself, even employing a specially prepared convex panel. Did he perhaps want to demonstrate that there is no single, "correct" reality, that distortion is as natural as the normal appearance of things? Characteristically, his scientific detachment soon changed into its very opposite. Vasari tells us that Parmigianino, toward the end of his brief career (he died in 1540 at thirty-seven), was obsessed with alchemy and became "a bearded, long-haired, neglected, and almost savage or wild man." Certainly his strange imagination is evident in his most famous work, *The Madonna with the Long Neck* (colorplate 37), painted after he had returned to his native Parma from several years' sojourn in Rome. He had been deeply impressed with the rhythmic grace of Raphael's art (compare colorplate 33), but he has transformed the older master's figures into a remarkable new breed: their limbs, elongated and ivory-smooth, move with effortless lan-

guor, embodying an ideal of beauty as remote from nature as any Byzantine figure. Their setting is equally arbitrary, with a gigantic—and apparently purposeless—row of columns looming behind the tiny figure of a prophet; Parmigianino seems determined to prevent us from measuring anything in this picture by the standards of ordinary experience. Here we have approached that "artificial" style for which the term Mannerism was originally coined. *The Madonna with the Long Neck* is a vision of unearthly perfection, its cold elegance no less compelling than the violence in Rosso's *Descent*.

Keyed to a sophisticated, even rarefied taste, the elegant phase of Italian Mannerism appealed particularly to such aristocratic patrons as the Grand Duke of Tuscany and King Francis I of France, and soon became international (see fig. 208). The style produced splendid portraits, like that of Eleanora of Toledo, the wife of Cosimo I de' Medici, by Cosimo's court painter Agnolo Bronzino (fig. 193). The sitter here appears as the

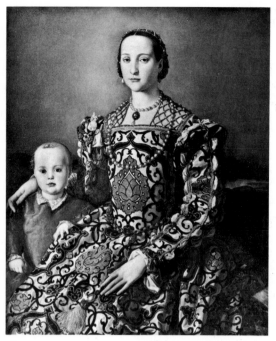

193. AGNOLO BRONZINO. *Eleanora of Toledo and Her Son Giovanni de' Medici.* c. 1550. Oil on canvas, 45 1/4 × 37 3/4″. Uffizi Gallery, Florence

below: 194. TINTORETTO. *The Last Supper.* 1592–94. Canvas, 12′ × 18′ 8″. S. Giorgio Maggiore, Venice

member of an exalted social caste, not as an individual personality; congealed into immobility behind the barrier of her lavishly ornate costume, Eleanora seems more akin to Parmigianino's *Madonna*—compare the hands—than to ordinary flesh and blood.

TINTORETTO

In Venice, Mannerism appeared only toward the middle of the century. Its leading exponent, Tintoretto, was an artist of prodigious energy and inventiveness, combining elements of both "anticlassical" and "elegant" Mannerism in his work. He reportedly wanted "to paint like Titian and to design like Michelangelo," but his relationship to these two masters, though real enough, was as peculiar as Parmigianino's was to Raphael. Tintoretto's last major work, *The Last Supper* (fig. 194), is also his most spectacular; it denies in every possible way the Classic values of Leonardo's version of the subject (see fig. 177), painted a century before. Christ, to be sure, still occupies the center of the composition, but now the table is placed at right angles to the picture plane, so that

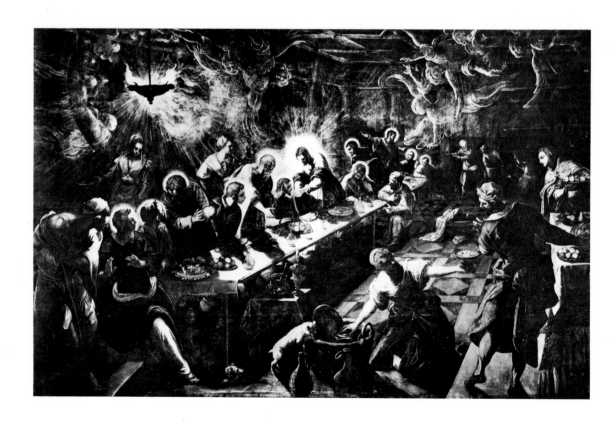

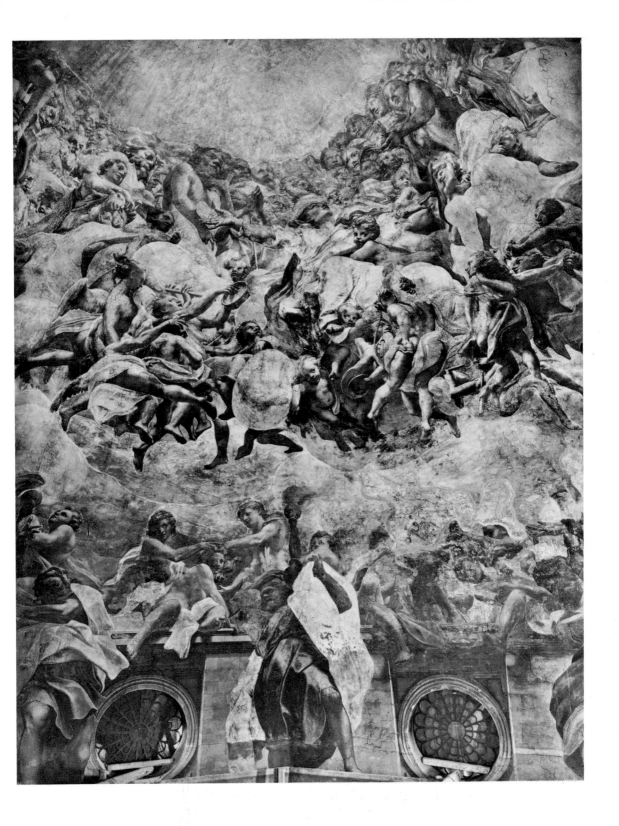

195. CORREGGIO. *The Assumption of the Virgin* (detail). c. 1525. Fresco. Dome, Parma Cathedral

His small figure in the middle distance is distinguishable only by the brilliant halo. Tintoretto has given the scene an everyday setting, cluttering it with attendants, containers of food and drink, and domestic animals. But this serves only to dramatically contrast the natural with the supernatural, for there are also celestial attendants—the smoke from the blazing oil lamp miraculously turns into clouds of angels that converge upon Christ just as He offers His body and blood, in the form of bread and wine, to His disciples. Tintoretto's main concern has been to make visible the institution of the Eucharist, the transubstantiation of earthly into Divine food; he barely hints at the human drama of Judas' betrayal (Judas is the tiny figure to the rear on the near side of the table).

EL GRECO

The last—and perhaps greatest—Mannerist painter was also trained in Venice. Domenicos Theotocopoulos, nicknamed El Greco, came from Crete. His earliest training must have been under a local master still working in the Byzantine tradition, but in Venice he quickly absorbed the lessons of Titian, Tintoretto, and other Venetian painters. Later, in Rome, he came to know the art of Michelangelo, Raphael, and the central Italian Mannerists. In 1576–77 he went to Spain, settling in Toledo for the rest of his life. Yet he remained an alien in his new homeland; although the spiritual climate of the Counter Reformation, which was especially intense in Spain, may account for the exalted emotionalism of his mature work, his style had already been formed before he arrived in Toledo. Nor did he ever forget his Byzantine background—until the end of his career, he signed his pictures in Greek. The largest and most resplendent of El Greco's commissions is The Burial of Count Orgaz (colorplate 38); the huge canvas honors a medieval benefactor of the Church who was so pious that St. Stephen and St. Augustine miraculously appeared at his funeral to lower the body into its grave. El Greco represents the burial as a contemporary event, portraying among the attendants many of the local nobility and clergy; the dazzling display of

color and texture in the armor and vestments could hardly be surpassed by Titian himself. Directly above, the count's soul (a small, cloudlike figure, like the angels in Tintoretto's Last Supper) is carried to Heaven by an angel. The celestial assembly filling the upper half of the picture is painted very differently from the lower half: every form—clouds, limbs, draperies—takes part in the sweeping, flame-like movement toward the distant figure of Christ. Here, even more than in Tintoretto's art, the various aspects of Mannerism fuse into a single ecstatic vision. Like an enormous window, the canvas fills one entire wall of its chapel, so that we must look sharply upward to see the upper half of the picture. El Greco's violent foreshortening is calculated to achieve an illusion of boundless space above, while the foreground figures appear as on a stage (note that their feet are cut off by the frame). El Greco's task may be compared to Masaccio's in his Trinity mural (see colorplate 27). The contrast measures the dynamic evolution of Western art since the beginning of the Early Renaissance.

PROTO-BAROQUE: CORREGGIO

If Mannerism produced the personalities that today seem most "modern"—El Greco's fame is greater now than it ever was before— its dominance was not uncontested in the sixteenth century. Another trend that also emerged about 1520 anticipated so many features of the Baroque style that it might be labeled Proto-Baroque. Its most important representative, Correggio, was a phenomenally gifted painter who spent most of his brief career in Parma. He absorbed the influence of Leonardo and the Venetians, then of Michelangelo and Raphael, but their ideal of Classical balance did not attract him. His art is filled with movement that sweeps through the composition, carrying the figures along with it. His largest work, the fresco of the Assumption of the Virgin in the dome of Parma Cathedral (fig. 195), is a masterpiece of illusionistic perspective, a vast, luminous space filled with soaring figures. Although they move with such exhilarating ease that the force of gravity seems not to exist for them, they are healthy, energetic beings of flesh and blood, not disembodied

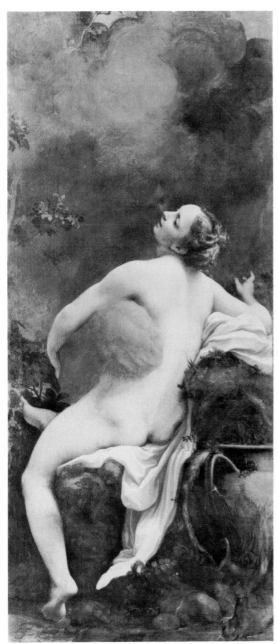

196. CORREGGIO. *Jupiter and Io*. c. 1532. Oil on canvas, 64 1/2 × 27 3/4″. Kunsthistorisches Museum, Vienna

spirits, and they frankly delight in their weightless condition. For Correggio there was little difference between spiritual and physical ecstasy, as we see by comparing the *Assumption of the Virgin* with his *Jupiter and Io* (fig. 196), one canvas in a series illustrating the Loves of the Classical Gods. The nymph, swooning in the embrace of a

cloudlike Jupiter, is the direct kin of the jubilant angels in the fresco. Leonardesque atmosphere, combined with a Venetian sense of color and texture, produces an effect of exquisite voluptuousness that far exceeds Titian's in his *Bacchanal* (see colorplate 35). Correggio had no immediate successors nor any lasting influence on the art of his century, but toward 1600 his work began to be widely appreciated. For the next century and a half he was admired as the equal of Raphael and Michelangelo—while the Mannerists, so important before, were largely forgotten.

REALISM: SAVOLDO; VERONESE

A third trend in sixteenth-century painting in Italy is to be associated with the towns along the northern edge of the Lombard plain, such as Brescia and Verona. A number of artists in that region worked in a style based on Giorgione and Titian, but with a stronger interest in everyday reality. One of the earliest and most attractive of these North Italian Realists was Girolamo Savoldo, from Brescia, whose *St. Matthew* (fig. 197) must be contemporary with Parmigianino's *Madonna with the Long Neck*. The broad, fluid manner of painting reflects the dominant influence of Titian, yet the great Venetian master would never have placed the Evangelist in so thoroughly domestic an environment. The humble scene in the background shows the saint's milieu to be lowly indeed, and makes

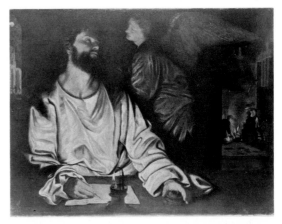

197. GIROLAMO SAVOLDO. *St. Matthew*. c. 1535. Oil on canvas, 36 3/4 × 49″. The Metropolitan Museum of Art, New York. (Marquand Fund, 1912)

the presence of the angel doubly miraculous. This tendency to visualize sacred events among ramshackle buildings and simple people had been characteristic of "Late Gothic" painting; Savoldo must have acquired it from that source. The nocturnal lighting, too, recalls such Northern pictures as the *Nativity* by Geertgen tot Sint Jans (fig. 150). But the main source of illumination in Geertgen's panel is the divine radiance of the Christ Child, and Savoldo uses an ordinary oil lamp for his similarly magic and intimate effect.

In the work of Paolo Veronese, North Italian Realism takes on the splendor of a pageant. Born and trained in Verona, Veronese became, after Tintoretto, the most important painter in Venice; although utterly unlike each other in style, both found favor with the public. The contrast is strikingly evident if we compare Tintoretto's *Last Supper* (see fig. 194) with Veronese's *Christ in the House of Levi* (fig. 198), which deals with a similar subject. Veronese avoids all reference to the supernatural; at first glance, the picture looks like a High Renaissance work born fifty years too late. Yet we miss one essential—the elevated, ideal conception of man that underlies the work of the High Renaissance masters. Veronese paints a sumptuous banquet, a true feast for the eyes, but not "the intention of man's soul." We are not even sure which event from the life

of Christ he originally meant to depict, for he gave the canvas its present title only after he had been summoned by a religious tribunal on the charge of filling his picture with "buffoons . . . and similar vulgarities" unsuited to its sacred character. Veronese's dogged refusal to admit the justice of the charge, his insistence on his right to introduce directly observed details, however "improper," and his indifference to the subject of the picture spring from an attitude so startlingly "extroverted" that it was not generally accepted until the nineteenth century. The painter's domain, Veronese seems to say, is the entire visible world, and in it he acknowledges no authority other than his senses.

SCULPTURE: CELLINI; DA BOLOGNA

The later sixteenth century was far less an age of sculpture than of painting. The anticlassical Mannerist painting of Rosso and Pontormo had no sculptural counterpart, but the second, elegant phase appeared in countless sculptures both in Italy and abroad. The best-known representative of the style is Benvenuto Cellini, the Florentine goldsmith and sculptor famous for his colorful autobiography. The gold saltcellar for King Francis I of France (fig. 199) is his only major work in precious metal to have escaped destruction. Holding condiments is the least important function of this luxurious conversation piece, which reflects Cellini's admiration for Michelangelo's *Tomb of Giuliano de' Medici* (fig. 183). Cellini's major concern

198. PAOLO VERONESE. *Christ in the House of Levi.* 1573. Canvas, 18' 2" × 42'. Academy, Venice

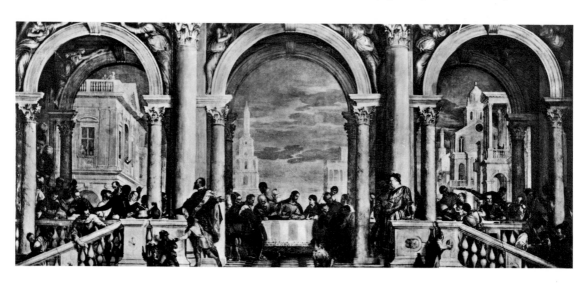

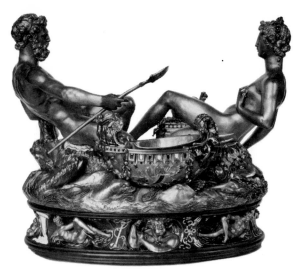

199. BENVENUTO CELLINI. *The Saltcellar of Francis I.* 1539–43. Gold and enamel, 10 1/4 × 13 1/8″. Kunsthistorisches Museum, Vienna

was to amaze his royal patron with a dazzling display of ingenuity and skill, and to charm him with the grace of his figures, which are as elegant, smooth, and elongated as Parmigianino's (see colorplate 37).

Mannerism became the dominant style in sixteenth-century France, and its influence penetrated far beyond the royal court. It reached a gifted young French sculptor, Jean de Boulogne, who went to Italy and, as Giovanni da Bologna, became the most important sculptor in Florence during the last few decades of the century. Like Cellini's saltcellar, his *Abduction of the Sabine Woman* (fig. 200) is a demonstration of skill, for it was carved in order to silence critics who had cast doubts on his ability to create monumental sculpture in marble. He selected what seemed to him the most difficult feat, three figures of contrasting character united in a common action. Their identities were disputed among the learned connoisseurs of the day, who finally settled on the Abduction of the Sabine Woman as the most suitable title. Here, then, is another artist who is noncommittal about subject matter, although his unconcern had a different motive from Veronese's. Giovanni da Bologna's self-imposed task was to carve in marble, on a massive scale, a sculptural composition that was to be seen not from one but from all sides; this had hitherto been attempted only in bronze and on a much smaller scale (see fig. 163). He has solved this purely formal problem, but only

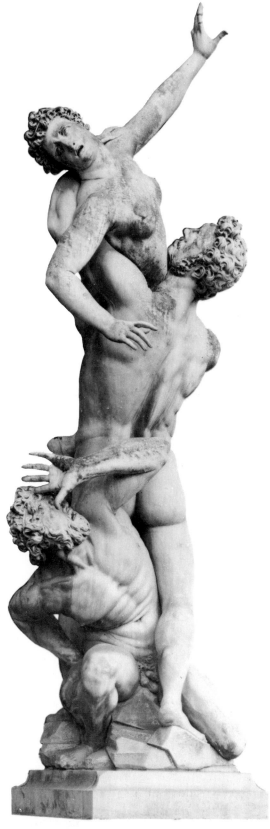

200. GIOVANNI DA BOLOGNA. *The Abduction of the Sabine Woman.* Completed 1583. Marble, height 13′ 6″. Loggia dei Lanzi, Florence

by insulating his group from the world of human experience. These figures, spiraling upward as if confined inside a tall, narrow cylinder, perform a well-rehearsed choreographic exercise the emotional meaning of which remains obscure. We admire their discipline, but we find no trace of genuine *pathos*.

ARCHITECTURE: PALLADIO

Although some late-sixteenth-century architecture is plainly Mannerist, the work of Andrea Palladio—next to Michelangelo the most important architect of the period— stands in the tradition of the humanist and theoretician Leone Battista Alberti (see p. 183). Although his career centered on his native town of Vicenza, not far from Venice, his buildings and theoretical writings soon brought him international renown. Architecture, according to Palladio, must be governed both by reason and by certain universal rules that were perfectly exemplified by the buildings of the ancients. He thus

shared Alberti's basic outlook and his firm faith in the cosmic significance of numerical proportions. They differed in how each man related theory and practice. With Alberti, this relationship had been loose and flexible, whereas Palladio believed quite literally in practicing what he preached. His architectural treatise is consequently more practical than Alberti's—this helps to explain its huge success—while his buildings are linked more directly with his theories. It has even been said that Palladio designed only what was, in his view, sanctioned by ancient precedent. If the results are not necessarily Classic in style, we may call them "Classicistic" (to denote a conscious striving for Classic qualities); this is indeed the usual term for both Palladio's work and his theoretical attitude. The Villa Rotonda (fig. 201), one of his most famous buildings, perfectly illustrates the meaning of Classicism. An aristocratic country residence near Vicenza, it consists of a square block surmounted by a dome and is faced on all four sides with identical porches having the shape of temple fronts. Alberti defined the ideal church as a completely symmetrical, centralized design; Palladio evidently found

201. ANDREA PALLADIO. Villa Rotonda. 1567–70. Vicenza

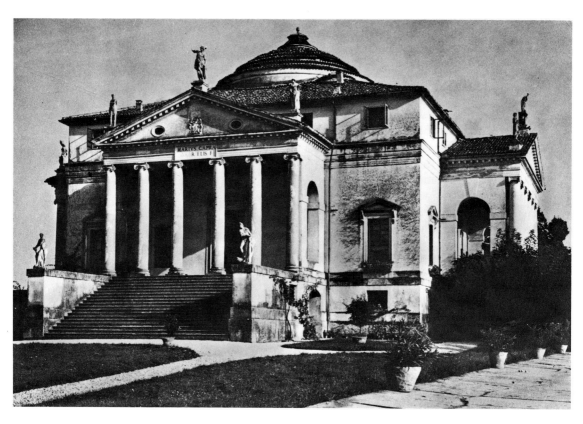

in the same principles the ideal country house. But how could he justify the use of so solemn a motif as the temple front in this context? Surprisingly enough, he was convinced that Roman private houses had porticoes such as these (excavations have since proved him wrong). Yet Palladio's use of the temple front here was not mere antiquarianism; he probably persuaded himself that it was legitimate because he regarded it as desirable for both beauty and utility. In any case, the porches of the Villa Rotonda, perfectly correlated with the walls behind, are an organic part of his design. They lend the structure an air of serene dignity and festive grace that still appeals to us today.

The Renaissance in the North

North of the Alps, the majority of fifteenth-century artists had remained indifferent to Italian forms and ideas. Since the time of Robert Campin and the Van Eycks, they had looked to Flanders, not Tuscany, for leadership. This isolation ends suddenly, toward the year 1500. As if a dam had burst, Italian influence flows northward in an ever-widening stream, and Northern Renaissance art begins to replace Late Gothic. That term, however, is much less well defined than Late Gothic, which refers to a single, clearly recognizable stylistic tradition. The diversity of trends north of the Alps is even greater than in Italy during the sixteenth century. Nor does Italian influence provide a common denominator, for this influence is itself diverse: Early Renaissance, High Renaissance, and Mannerist, each in some regional variant from Lombardy, Venice, Florence, or Rome. And its effects may be superficial or profound, direct or indirect, specific or general. Moreover, the Late Gothic tradition remained very much alive, if no longer dominant, and its encounter with Italian art resulted in a kind of Hundred Years' War of styles which ended only when, about 1600, the Baroque emerged as an international movement. The course of this "war" was decisively affected by the

Reformation, which had a far more immediate impact on art north of the Alps than in Italy. Our account, then, must be oversimplified, emphasizing the heroic phases of the struggle at the expense of the lesser engagements.

GERMANY: GRÜNEWALD

Let us begin with Germany, the home of the Reformation, where the main battles of the "war of styles" took place during the first quarter of the century. Between 1475 and 1500, it had produced such important masters as Schongauer (see p. 172), but these hardly prepare us for the astonishing burst of creative energy that was to follow. The achievements of this period—comparable in its brevity and brilliance to the Italian High Renaissance—are measured by the contrasting personalities of its greatest artists, Matthias Grünewald and Albrecht Dürer. Both died in 1528, probably at about the same age. Dürer quickly became internationally famous, while Grünewald remained so obscure that his real name, Mathis Gothart Nithart, was discovered only recently. His fame, like El Greco's, is almost entirely of our own century. In Northern art of his time, he alone overwhelms us in his main work, the *Isenheim Altarpiece* (colorplate 39, fig. 202), with something like the power of the Sistine Ceiling. Painted in 1509–15 for the monastery church of the Order of St. Anthony at Isenheim, in Alsace, it is now in the museum of the nearby town of Colmar. The altarpiece has three stages, or "views." The first, when all the wings are closed, shows *The Crucifixion* (fig. 202)—probably the most impressive ever painted. In one respect it is very medieval: Christ's unbearable agony, and the desperate grief of the Virgin, St. John, and Mary Magdalen, recall older devotional images such as the Bonn *Pietà* (see fig. 132). But the body on the cross, with its twisted limbs, countless lacerations, and rivulets of blood, is on a heroic scale that raises it beyond the merely human: thus the two natures of Christ are revealed. The same message is conveyed by the flanking figures: the three historic witnesses on the left mourn Christ's death as a man, while John the Baptist, on the right, points with calm emphasis to Him as the Saviour. Even the background

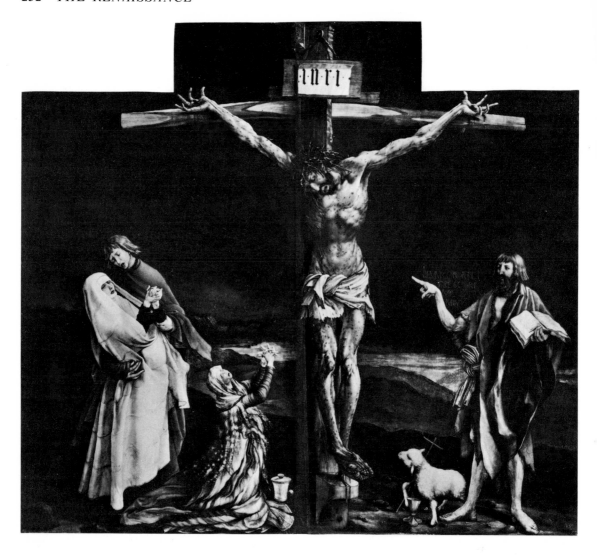

202. MATTHIAS GRÜNEWALD. *The Crucifixion,* from
The Isenheim Altarpiece (closed). c. 1510–15. Panel,
8′ 10″ × 10′ 1″. Musée Unterlinden, Colmar (for the
second view of altarpiece, see colorplate 39)

suggests this duality: this Golgotha is not a
hill outside Jerusalem, but a mountain towering above lesser peaks. The Crucifixion becomes a lonely event silhouetted against a
deserted, ghostly landscape and a blue-black
sky. Darkness is over the land, in accordance
with the Gospels, yet brilliant light bathes the
foreground with the force of sudden revelation. This union of time and eternity, of
reality and symbolism, gives Grünewald's
Crucifixion its awesome grandeur.

When the outer wings are opened, the
mood of the *Isenheim Altarpiece* changes dramatically (colorplate 39). All three scenes in

this second "view"—the *Annunciation,* the
Virgin and Child with Angels, and the
Resurrection—celebrate events as jubilant in
spirit as the *Crucifixion* is austere. Most
striking is the sense of movement pervading
these panels—everything twists and turns
as though it had a life of its own. This
vibrant energy has thoroughly reshaped the
brittle, spiky contours and angular drapery
patterns of Late Gothic art; Grünewald's
forms are soft, elastic, fleshy. His light and
color show a corresponding change: commanding all the resources of the great Flemish masters, he employs them with un-
exampled boldness and flexibility. His color
scale is richly iridescent, its range matched
only by the Venetians'. And his exploitation
of colored light is altogether without parallel at that time. In the luminescent angels of
the *Virgin and Child* and, most spectacularly,

in the rainbow-hued radiance of the Risen Christ, Grünewald's genius has achieved miracles-through-light that are unsurpassed to this day.

How much did Grünewald owe to Italian art? Nothing at all, we are tempted to reply. Yet he must have learned from the Renaissance in more ways than one: his knowledge of perspective (note the low horizons) and the physical vigor of some of his figures cannot be explained by the Late Gothic tradition. Perhaps the most important effect of the Renaissance on him, however, was psychological. We know little about his career, but apparently he did not lead the settled life of a craftsman-painter controlled by the rules of his guild; he was also an architect, engineer, and entrepreneur who worked for many different patrons without staying anywhere for long. He was in sympathy with Martin Luther (who frowned upon religious images as "idolatrous") even though, as a painter, he depended on Catholic patronage. In a word, Grünewald seems to have shared the free, individualist spirit of Italian Renaissance artists. The daring of his pictorial vision likewise suggests a reliance on his own resources. The Renaissance, then, had a liberating effect on him but did not change the basic cast of his imagination. Instead, it helped him to epitomize the expressive aspects of the Late Gothic in a style of unique intensity and individuality.

DÜRER

For Albrecht Dürer, the Renaissance held a different and richer meaning. He visited Venice as a young journeyman and returned to his native Nuremberg with a new conception of the world and the artist's place in it. The unbridled fantasy of Grünewald's art was to him "a wild, unpruned tree" which needed the discipline of the objective, rational standards of the Renaissance. Taking the Italian view that the fine arts belong among the liberal arts, he also adopted the ideal of the artist as a gentleman and humanistic scholar. By steadily cultivating his mind he came to encompass a vast variety of techniques and subjects. And since he was the greatest printmaker of the time, he had a wide influence on sixteenth-century art through his wood-

cuts and engravings, which circulated throughout the Western world. The first artist to be fascinated by his own image, Dürer was in this respect more of a Renaissance personality than any Italian. His earliest known work, a drawing made at thirteen, is a self-portrait, and he continued to produce them throughout his career. Most impressive, and peculiarly revealing, is the panel he painted in 1500 (fig. 203): pictorially, it belongs to the Flemish tradition (compare fig. 147), but the solemn, frontal pose and the Christ-like idealization of the features assert an authority quite beyond the range of ordinary portraits. The picture looks, in fact, like a secularized icon, reflecting not so much Dürer's vanity as the seriousness with which he regarded his mission as an artistic reformer.

The didactic aspect of Dürer's art is evident in many of his greatest prints. The gruesome vision of the *Four Horsemen* (fig. 204) seems at first to return completely to the Late Gothic world of Martin Schongauer (compare fig. 154). Yet the physical energy and solid, full-bodied volume of these figures would

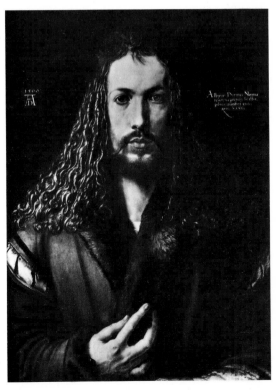

203. ALBRECHT DÜRER. *Self-Portrait*. 1500. Panel, 26 1/4 × 19 1/4″. Pinakothek, Munich

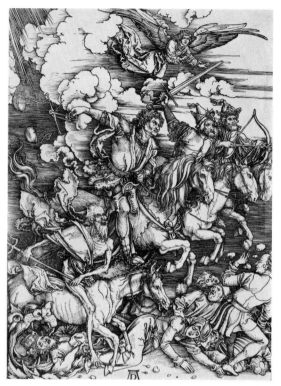

204. ALBRECHT DÜRER. *The Four Horsemen of the Apocalypse*. c. 1497–98. Woodcut

and skulls in his path. Italian Renaissance form, united with the heritage of Late Gothic symbolism (whether open or disguised), here takes on a new, characteristically Northern significance. The subject of *Knight, Death, and Devil* seems to have been derived from a book called the *Manual of the Christian Soldier* by Erasmus of Rotterdam, the greatest of Northern humanists. Dürer's own convictions were essentially those of Christian humanism; they made him an early and enthusiastic follower of Martin Luther, although, like Grünewald, he continued to work for Catholic patrons. In the 1520s he tried to create a monumental art embodying the Protestant faith, but his efforts were doomed by the spiritual leaders of the Reformation, who looked upon them with indifference, or, more often, outright hostility. Dürer thus turned to the theory of art, devoting a good part of his final years to this. His work includes a treatise on geometry based on a thorough study of Piero della Francesca's discourse on perspective.

have been impossible without Dürer's earlier experience in Italy. At this stage, Dürer's style has much in common with Grünewald's. The comparison with Schongauer's *Temptation of St. Anthony*, however, is instructive from another point of view; it shows how thoroughly Dürer has redefined his medium —the woodcut—by enriching it with the linear subtleties of engraving. In his hands, woodcuts lose their former charm as popular art, but gain the precise articulation of a fully matured graphic style. He set a standard that soon transformed the technique of woodcuts all over Europe.

Knight, Death, and Devil (fig. 205) is one of Dürer's most beautiful engravings. The knight on his mount, poised and confident like an equestrian statue, embodies an ideal both aesthetic and moral: he is the Christian Soldier, steadfast on the road of faith toward the Heavenly Jerusalem and undeterred by the hideous horseman threatening to cut him off, or by the grotesque devil behind him. The dog, another symbol of virtue, loyally follows his master despite the lizards

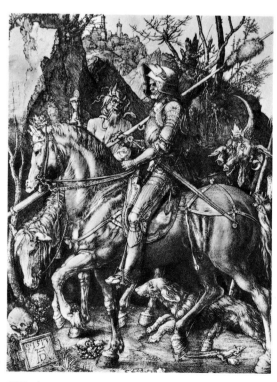

205. ALBRECHT DÜRER. *Knight, Death, and Devil*. 1513. Engraving. Museum of Fine Arts, Boston

CRANACH; ALTDORFER

Dürer's hope for a monumental art embodying the Protestant faith remained unfulfilled. Other German painters, notably Lucas Cranach the Elder, also tried to cast Luther's doctrines into visual form, but created no viable tradition. Lucas Cranach is best remembered today for his portraits and his delightfully incongruous mythological scenes. In his *Judgment of Paris* (fig. 206) nothing could be less Classical than the wriggly nakedness of these three coquettish damsels. Paris is a German knight clad in fashionable armor, indistinguishable from the nobles at the court of Saxony who were the artist's patrons. The playful eroticism, small size, and precise, miniature-like detail of the picture make it plainly a collector's item, attuned to the tastes of a provincial aristocracy.

As remote from the Classic ideal, but far more impressive, is *The Battle of Issus* by Albrecht Altdorfer, a Bavarian painter somewhat younger than Cranach (colorplate 40). Unless we read the text on the tablet suspended in the sky, we cannot possibly identify the subject, Alexander's victory over Darius. Altdorfer has tried to follow ancient descriptions of the actual number and kind of combatants, but this required him to adopt a bird's-eye view whereby the two protagonists are lost in the antlike mass of their own armies (in contrast, see the Hellenistic representation of the same subject, fig. 41). Moreover, the soldiers' armor and the town in the distance are unmistakably of the sixteenth century. The picture might well show some contemporary battle, except for one feature: the spectacular sky, with the sun triumphantly breaking through the clouds and "defeating" the moon. The celestial drama above a vast Alpine landscape, obviously correlated with the human contest below, raises the scene to the cosmic level. Altdorfer may be viewed as a later, and lesser, Grünewald; although he, too, was an architect, well acquainted with perspective and the Italian stylistic vocabulary, his paintings show the unruly imagination already familiar from the work of the older master. But, unlike Grünewald, Altdorfer makes the human figure incidental to its spatial setting. The tiny soldiers of *The*

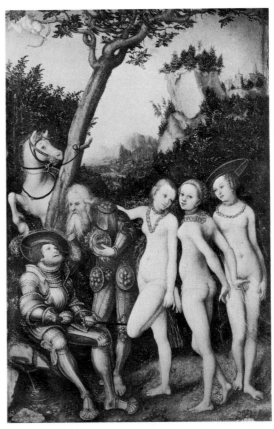

206. LUCAS CRANACH THE ELDER. *The Judgment of Paris*. 1530. Oil on panel, 13 1/2 × 8 3/4″. Staatliche Kunsthalle, Karlsruhe, Germany

Battle of Issus have their counterparts in his other pictures, and he painted at least one landscape with no figures at all—the earliest example of "pure" landscape.

HOLBEIN AND PORTRAITURE

Although greatly gifted, Altdorfer and his German contemporaries evaded the main challenge of the Renaissance that was so bravely faced—if not always mastered—by Dürer: the image of man. Their style, antimonumental and miniature-like, set the pace for dozens of lesser masters; perhaps the rapid decline of German art after Dürer's death was due to a failure of ambition among artists and patrons alike. The career of Hans Holbein the Younger—the one painter of whom this is not true—confirms the general rule. Younger than Dürer by twenty-six years, Holbein grew up in Augsburg, a city

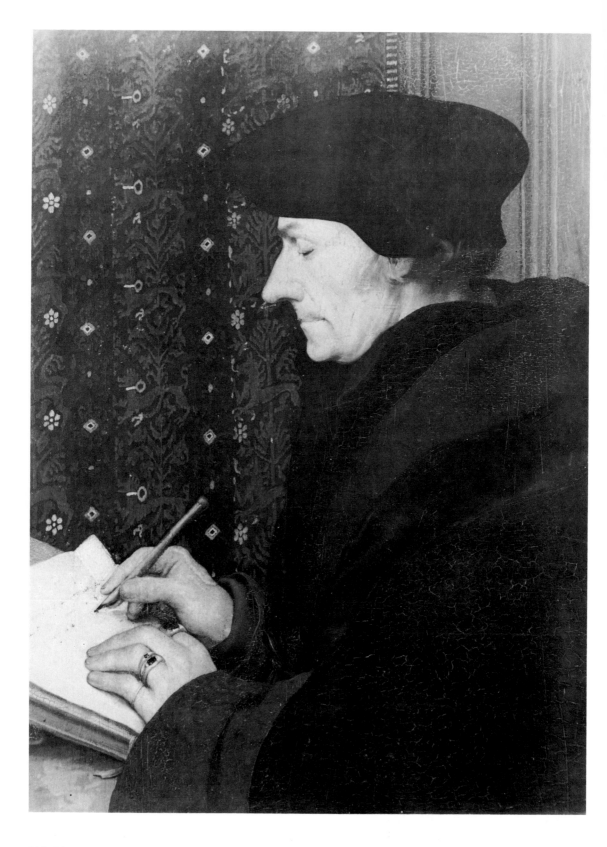

207. Hans Holbein the Younger. *Erasmus of Rotterdam.* c. 1523. Oil on panel, 16 1/2 × 12 1/2″. The Louvre, Paris

in Southern Germany particularly open to Renaissance ideas, and then became the leading artist of Basel, in Switzerland. His likeness of Erasmus of Rotterdam (fig. 207), painted soon after the famous author had settled in Basel, gives us a truly memorable image of Renaissance man: intimate yet monumental, this doctor of humane letters has an intellectual authority formerly reserved for the doctors of the Church. Yet Holbein must have felt confined in Basel, for in 1523–24 he traveled to France, apparently intending to offer his services to Francis I. In 1526, when Basel was in the throes of the Reformation crisis, he went to England, hoping for commissions at the court of Henry VIII. On his return to Basel two years later, he saw fanatical mobs destroying religious images as "idols," and in 1532 he settled permanently in London as court painter to Henry VIII. His portrait of the king (colorplate 41) shares the rigid frontality of Dürer's self-portrait (see fig. 203), but its purpose is to convey the almost divine authority of the absolute ruler: the immobile pose, the air of unapproachability, the display of precisely rendered jewels and gold embroidery—all create an overpowering sensation of the monarch's ruthless, commanding presence. Both Holbein's portrait of Henry VIII and Bronzino's *Eleanora of Toledo* (see fig. 193) belong to the same world of court portraiture. The link between Bronzino's picture and Holbein's may be such French works as Clouet's *Francis I* (fig. 208), which Holbein could have seen on his travels. (See page 228 for Francis I as a patron of Italian Mannerists.) This type of portrait seems to have been invented in France and to have spread beyond French borders after 1525.

THE NETHERLANDS; BRUEGEL

The Netherlands in the sixteenth century had the most turbulent and painful history of any country north of the Alps. They were then part of the far-flung empire of the Hapsburgs under Charles V, who was also king of Spain. The Reformation quickly became powerful in the Netherlands, and the attempts of the Crown to suppress it led to open revolt against foreign rule. After a bloody struggle, the northern provinces (today's Holland) gained their independence, while the southern ones (now called Belgium) remained in Spanish hands. The religious and political strife might have had catastrophic effects on the arts, yet this, astonishingly, did not happen. While the Netherlands had no pioneers of the Northern Renaissance comparable to Dürer, they absorbed Italian elements more steadily than did Germany. Between 1550 and 1600, their most troubled time, the Netherlands produced the major painters of Northern Europe, who paved the way for the great Dutch and Flemish masters of the next century. Apart from the assimilation of Italian art, Netherlandish sixteenth-century painters had one main concern: to develop a repertory of subjects to supplement, and eventually replace, the traditional religious themes. The process was gradual, shaped less by individual achievement than by the need to cater to popular taste as Church commissions became steadily scarcer. Pieter Bruegel the Elder, the only genius among these painters, explored landscape,

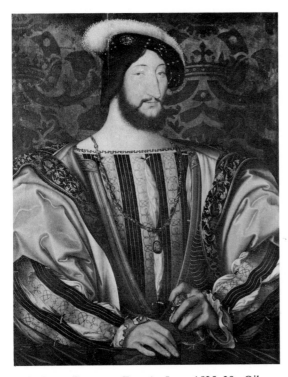

208. JEAN CLOUET. *Francis I.* c. 1525–30. Oil on panel, 37 3/4 × 29″. The Louvre, Paris

peasant life, and moral allegory, such as *The Land of Cockayne* (colorplate 42). It shows a fool's paradise where tables are always laden with tasty dishes, houses have roofs made of pies, and pigs and chickens run about roasted to a turn. The lesson Bruegel teaches us here is philosophical rather than religious: the men under the tree are not sinners in the grip of evil, like those in Bosch's *Garden of Delights* (see colorplate 26), they are simply not wise enough to know what is best for them. By becoming slaves to their stomachs, they have given up all ambition, all self-respect, for the sake of a kind of animal happiness—the knight has dropped his lance, the farmer his flail, and the scholar his books. "Beware of the fool's paradise," Bruegel seems to say, "it's more dangerous than hell because people *like* going there." And the monumental design of the painting, in the shape of a great wheel turned on its side, proves that he must have

thought his subject serious and important.

The sweeping landscape of *The Return of the Hunters* (fig. 209) belongs to a set of paintings depicting the months of the year. Series of this kind, we recall, began with medieval calendar illustrations, and this winter scene shows its descent from the February page in the *Very Rich Book of Hours of the Duke of Berry* (see colorplate 20). In Bruegel's painting, however, the natural world is more than a setting for human activities; it is the main subject. The seasonal occupations of men are incidental to nature's majestic cycle of death and rebirth.

FRANCE: ARCHITECTURE AND SCULPTURE

In architecture and sculpture, it took the Northern countries longer to assimilate Italian forms than in painting. France, more closely linked with Italy than the rest (we recall the French conquest of Milan), was the first to achieve an integrated Renaissance style. In 1546 King Francis I, who had

209. PIETER BRUEGEL THE ELDER. *The Return of the Hunters*. 1565. Tempera on panel, 46 × 63 3/4″. Kunsthistorisches Museum, Vienna

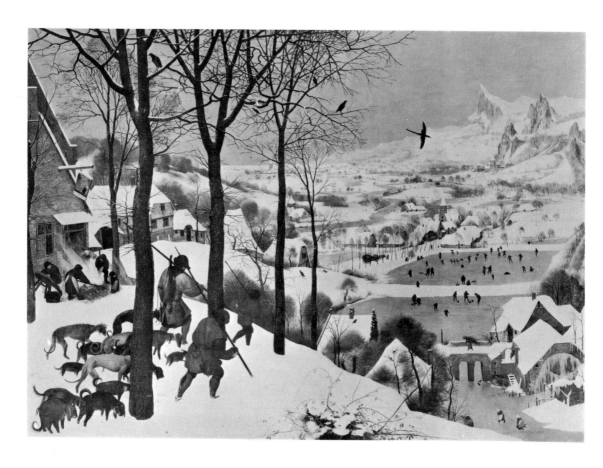

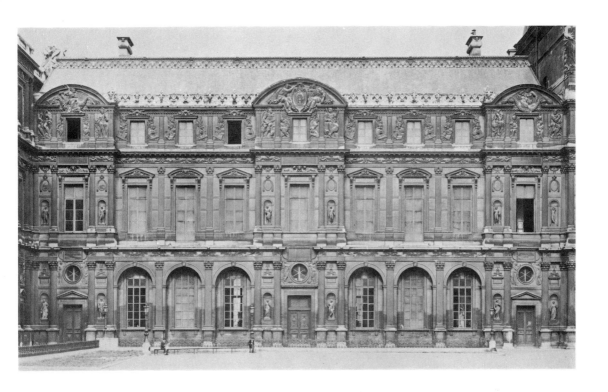

210. PIERRE LESCOT. Square Court of the Louvre, Paris. Begun 1546

shown his admiration for Italian art earlier by inviting Leonardo to France, decided to replace the old Gothic royal castle, the Louvre, with a new and much larger structure on the same site. The project, barely begun at the time of his death, was not completed until more than a century later; but its oldest portion, by Pierre Lescot (fig. 210), is the finest surviving example of Northern Renaissance architecture. The details of Lescot's façade are derived from Bramante and his successors and have an astonishing Classical purity, yet we would not mistake it for an Italian structure. Its distinctive quality comes not from Italian forms superficially applied, but from a genuine synthesis of the traditional Gothic castle with the Renaissance palace. Italian, of course, are the superimposed Classical orders, the pedimented window frames, and the arcade on the ground floor. But the continuity of the façade is interrupted by three projecting pavilions which take the place of the castle turrets, and the steep roof is also traditionally Northern. The vertical accents thus overcome the horizontal ones (note the broken

architraves), their effect reinforced by the tall, narrow windows. Equally un-Italian is the rich sculptural decoration covering almost the entire wall surface of the third story. These reliefs, admirably adapted to the architecture, are by Jean Goujon, the finest French sculptor of the mid-sixteenth century. Unfortunately, they have been much restored. To get a more precise idea of Goujon's style we must turn to the relief panels from the *Fountain of the Innocents* (two are shown in fig. 211), which have survived intact, although their architectural framework is lost. These graceful figures recall the Mannerism of Cellini (see fig. 199). Like Lescot's architecture, Goujon's figures combine Classical details with a delicate slenderness that gives them a uniquely French elegance.

The Baroque in Italy, Flanders, and Spain

Baroque has been the term used by art historians for almost a century to designate the style of the period 1600–1750. Its original meaning—"irregular, contorted, grotesque"

—is now largely forgotten. There is also general agreement that the new style was born in Rome around 1600. What remains under dispute is the impulse behind it. Thus it has been claimed that the Baroque style expresses the spirit of the Counter Reformation; yet the Counter Reformation, a dynamic movement of self-renewal within the Catholic Church, had already done its work by 1600; Protestantism was on the defensive, and neither side any longer had the power to upset the new balance. The princes of the Church who supported the growth of Baroque art were known for worldly splendor rather than piety. Besides, the new style penetrated the Protestant North so quickly that we must be careful not to overstress its Counter Reformation aspect. Equally questionable is the claim that Baroque is "the style of absolutism," reflecting the centralized state ruled by an autocrat of unlimited powers. Although absolutism reached its climax in France in the later seventeenth century, during the reign of Louis XIV, it had been in the making since the 1520s. Moreover, Baroque art flourished in bourgeois Holland no less than in the absolutist monarchies; and the style officially sponsored under Louis XIV was a notably subdued, Classicistic kind of Baroque. There are similar difficulties if we try to relate Baroque art to the science and philosophy of the period. Such a link did exist in the Early and High Renaissance: an artist then could also be a humanist and scientist. But now scientific and philosophical thought became too complex, abstract, and systematic for him to share; gravitation, calculus, and *Cogito, ergo sum* could not stir his imagination. Baroque art, then, was not simply the result of religious, political, or intellectual developments. Interconnections surely existed, but we do not yet understand them fully. Until we do, let us think of the Baroque style as one among other basic features—the newly fortified Catholic faith, the absolutist state, and the new role of science—that distinguish the period 1600–1750 from what had gone before.

ROME: CARAVAGGIO

Rome became the fountainhead of the Baroque, as it had of the High Renaissance a century earlier, by gathering artists from other regions to perform challenging tasks. The papacy once again patronized art on a large scale, aiming to turn Rome into the most beautiful city of the entire Christian world. At first, the artists on hand were late Mannerists of feeble distinction, but the campaign soon attracted ambitious younger masters. They were the ones who created the new style. Foremost was a painter of genius, called Caravaggio after his birthplace near Milan, who did several monumental canvases for the church of San Luigi dei Francesi, including *The Calling of St. Matthew* (colorplate 43). The style shown in this extraordinary picture is remote from both Mannerism and the High Renaissance; its realism is so uncompromising that a new term, "naturalism," is needed to distinguish it from the earlier kind. Never have we seen a sacred

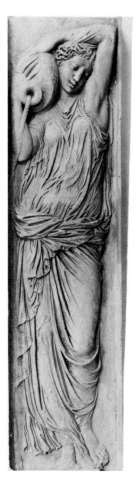 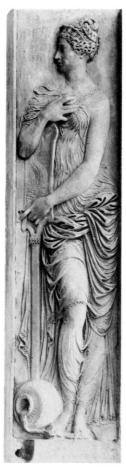

211. JEAN GOUJON. Reliefs from the *Fountain of the Innocents*. 1548–49. Paris

subject depicted so entirely in terms of con-temporary low life. Matthew the tax gatherer sits with some armed men—evidently his agents—in what appears to be a common Roman tavern; he points questioningly at himself as two figures approach from the right. They are poor people, whose bare feet and simple garments contrast strongly with the colorful costumes of Matthew and his companions. Why do we sense a religious quality in this scene? What identifies one of the figures as Christ? Surely it is not the Saviour's halo, an inconspicuous gold band that we might well overlook. Our eyes fasten instead on His commanding gesture, bor-rowed from Michelangelo's *Creation of Adam* (see fig. 181), which bridges the gap between the two groups. Most important of all, however, is the strong beam of sunlight above Christ that illuminates His face and hand in the gloomy interior, thus carrying His call across to Matthew. Without this light—so natural yet so charged with sym-bolic meaning—the picture would lose its magic, its power to make us aware of the Divine presence. Caravaggio here gives moving, direct form to an attitude shared by some of the great saints of the Counter Reformation: that the mysteries of faith are revealed not by intellectual speculation but spontaneously, through an inward experi-ence open to all men. His paintings have a "lay Christianity," untouched by theological dogma, that appealed to Protestants no less than to Catholics. Hence his profound—though indirect—influence on Rembrandt, who was the greatest religious artist of the Protestant North.

CARRACCI AND HIS FOLLOWERS

In Italy, Caravaggio fared less well. His work was acclaimed by artists and connoisseurs, but to the man in the street, for whom it was intended, it lacked propriety and reverence. The simple people resented meeting their likes in his paintings; they preferred religious imagery of a more idealized and rhetorical sort. Their wishes were met by artists less radical—and less talented—than Caravaggio, who took their lead from another newcomer among Roman painters, Annibale Carracci. Annibale came from Bologna, where he and

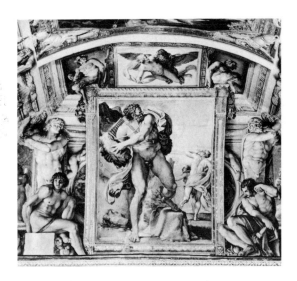

212. ANNIBALE CARRACCI. Ceiling Fresco (detail). 1597–1601. Gallery, Palazzo Farnese, Rome

two other members of his family had evolved an anti-Mannerist style since the 1580s. In 1597–1604 he produced his most ambitious work, the ceiling fresco in the gallery of the Farnese Palace, which soon became so fa-mous that it was thought second only to the murals of Michelangelo and Raphael. The historical significance of the Farnese Gallery is indeed great, though our enthusiasm for it as a work of art may no longer be undivided. Our detail (fig. 212) shows Annibale's rich and intricate design: the narrative scenes, like those of the Sistine Ceiling, are surrounded by painted architecture, simulated sculpture, and nude, garland-holding youths. Yet the Farnese Gallery does not merely imitate Michelangelo's masterpiece. The style of the main subjects, the Loves of the Classical Gods, is reminiscent of Raphael's *Galatea* (see fig. 188), and the whole is held together by an illusionistic scheme that reflects An-nibale's knowledge of Correggio and the great Venetians. Carefully foreshortened and illuminated from below (note the shadows), the nude youths and the simulated sculpture and architecture appear real; against this background the mythologies are presented as simulated easel pictures. Each of these levels of reality is handled with consummate skill, and the entire ceiling has an exuberance that sets it apart from both Mannerism and High Renaissance art. Annibale Carracci was a reformer rather than a revolutionary; like Caravaggio, with whom he was on the best of terms, he felt that art must return to nature, but his approach was less single-minded, balancing studies from life with a revival of the Classics (which to him meant the art of antiquity, and of Raphael, Michelangelo, Titian, and Correggio). At his best, he succeeded in fusing these diverse elements, although their union always remained somewhat precarious. To his disciples, the Farnese Gallery seemed to offer two alternatives: pursuing the Raphaelesque style of the mythological panels, they could arrive at a deliberate, "official" Classicism; or they could take their cue from the sensuous illusionism present in the framework. The first choice is best exemplified by Nicolas Poussin (see page 274), the second by Pietro da Cortona. Colorplate 44 shows a detail of Pietro's ceiling fresco in the great hall of the Barberini Palace in Rome glorifying the reign of the Barberini pope, Urban VIII. As in the Farnese Gallery, the ceiling area is subdivided by a painted framework simulating architecture and sculpture, but beyond it we now see the unbounded space of the sky. Clusters of figures, perched on clouds or soaring freely, swirl above as well as below this framework, creating a dual illusion: some figures appear to hover well inside the hall, perilously close to our heads, while others recede into a light-filled, infinite distance. Their dynamism almost literally sweeps us off our feet. Here the Baroque style reaches a thunderous climax.

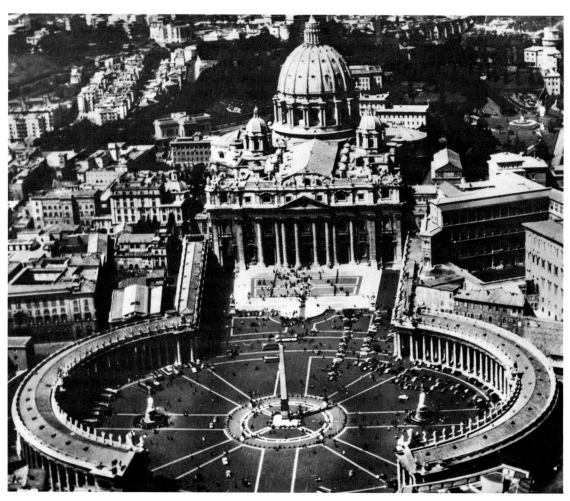

213. St. Peter's, aerial view. Nave and façade by CARLO MADERNO, 1607–15; colonnade by GIANLORENZO BERNINI, designed 1657. Rome

ST. PETER'S: MADERNO; BERNINI

In architecture, the beginnings of the Baroque style cannot be defined as precisely as in painting. In the vast church-building program that got under way in Rome toward 1600, the most talented young architect was Carlo Maderno; in 1603 he was given the task of completing, at long last, the church of St. Peter's, after the pope had decided to add a nave, converting Bramante's and Michelangelo's central-plan building into a basilica (fig. 213). Maderno's design for the façade follows the pattern established by Michelangelo for the exterior (compare fig. 187), but with a dramatic emphasis on the portals. There is what can only be called a crescendo effect from the corners toward the center: the spacing of the colossal order

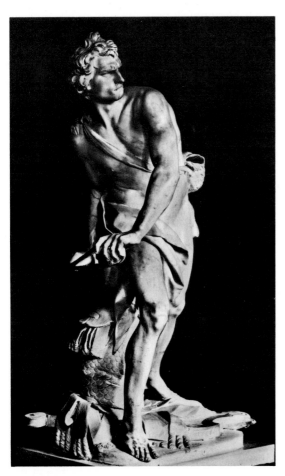

214. GIANLORENZO BERNINI. *David*. 1623. Marble, lifesize. Borghese Gallery, Rome

becomes closer, pilasters turn into columns, and the façade wall projects step by step. This quickened rhythm became the dominant principle of Maderno's façade designs, not only for St. Peter's but for smaller churches as well; it replaced the traditional notion of the church façade as one continuous wall surface with the "façade-in-depth" dynamically related to the open space before it. The possibilities implicit in this new concept were not to be exhausted for a hundred and fifty years. Maderno's work on the St. Peter's façade was completed by Gianlorenzo Bernini, the greatest sculptor-architect of the century. It was he who molded the open space in front of the façade into a magnificent oval "forecourt" framed by colonnades which Bernini himself likened to the motherly, all-embracing arms of the Church.

Such a charging of space with active energy is a key feature of Baroque art. Caravaggio had achieved it, with the aid of a sharply focused beam of light, in his *St. Matthew*; Bernini was a master of it, not only in architecture but in sculpture as well. If we compare his *David* (fig. 214) with Michelangelo's (see fig. 179), and ask what makes Bernini's Baroque, the simplest answer would be: the implied presence of Goliath. Bernini's *David* is conceived not as a self-contained figure but as "half of a pair," his entire action focused on his adversary. Did the artist, we wonder, plan a statue of Goliath to complete the group? He never did, for his David tells us clearly enough where *he* sees the enemy. Thus the space between David and his invisible opponent is charged with energy: it "belongs" to the statue. If we stand directly in front of this formidable fighter, our first impulse is to get out of the line of fire. Baroque sculpture, then, eschews the self-sufficiency of Early and High Renaissance sculpture for an illusion—the illusion of presences or forces that are implied by the behavior of the sculptured figure. Because of this "invisible complement," Baroque sculpture has been denounced as a tour de force, attempting illusionistic effects that are outside its province. The accusation is pointless, for illusion is the basis of every artistic experience, and we cannot very well regard some kinds or degrees of illusion as less legitimate than others. It is true, however, that Baroque

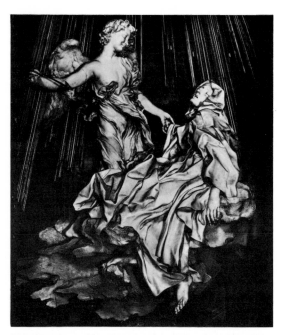

215. BERNINI. *The Ecstasy of St. Theresa*. 1645–1652. Marble, lifesize. Sta. Maria della Vittoria, Rome

art acknowledges no sharp distinction between sculpture and painting. The two may enter into a symbiosis previously unknown, or, more precisely, both may be combined with architecture to form a compound illusion, like that of the stage. Bernini was at his best when he could merge all three arts in this fashion. His masterpiece is the Cornaro Chapel, containing the famous group called *The Ecstasy of St. Theresa* (fig. 215), in the church of Santa Maria della Vittoria. Theresa of Avila, one of the saints of the Counter Reformation, had described how an angel once pierced her heart with a flaming golden arrow: "The pain was so great that I screamed aloud; but at the same time I felt such infinite sweetness that I wished the pain to last forever." Bernini has made this visionary experience as sensuously real as Correggio's *Jupiter and Io* (see fig. 196); the angel, in a different context, would be indistinguishable from Cupid, and the saint's ecstasy is palpably physical. Yet the two figures, on their floating cloud, are lit (from a hidden window above) in such a way as to seem almost dematerialized in their gleaming whiteness. The beholder experiences them as visionary. The "invisible complement" here, less specific than David's but equally impor-

tant, is the force that carries the figures heavenward, causing the turbulence of their drapery. Its nature is suggested by the golden rays, which come from a source high above the altar: in an illusionistic fresco on the vault of the chapel, the glory of heaven is revealed as a dazzling burst of light from which tumble clouds of jubilant angels. It is this celestial "explosion" that gives force to the thrusts of the angel's arrow and makes the ecstasy of the saint believable. Such displays, designed to overwhelm the beholder emotionally, may well be termed "theatrical," both in spirit and in some of the devices employed. Bernini himself had a passionate interest in the theater. Looking at a typical Baroque stage with all its illusionistic devices, such as the one in figure 216 by Lodovico Burnacini, we sense its kinship with the Cornaro Chapel.

BORROMINI

As a personality type, Bernini represents the self-assured, expansive man of the world. His great rival in architecture, Francesco Borromini, was the opposite: a secretive and emotionally unstable genius, he died by suicide. The temperamental contrast between the two would be evident from their works alone, even without the testimony of their contemporaries. Both exemplify the climax of Baroque architecture in Rome, yet Bernini's design for the colonnade of St. Peter's is dramatically simple and unified, while Bor-

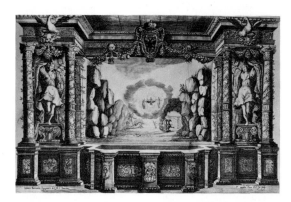

216. LODOVICO BURNACINI. Stage Design for *"La Zenobia di Radamisto,"* Opera by G.A. Boretti, Vienna, Hoftheater, 1662 (engraving by F. van den Steen). Theater Collection, Houghton Library, Harvard University, Cambridge, Massachusetts

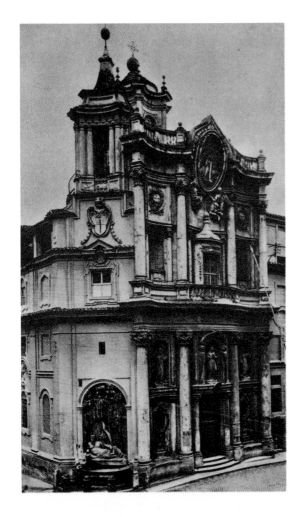

romini's structures are extravagantly complex. Bernini himself agreed with those who denounced Borromini for disregarding the Classical tradition, enshrined in Renaissance theory and practice, that architecture must reflect the proportions of the human body. We understand this accusation when we look at Borromini's first project, the church of San Carlo alle Quattro Fontane (fig. 217). The vocabulary is not unfamiliar, but the syntax is new and disquieting; the ceaseless play of concave and convex surfaces makes the entire structure seem elastic, "pulled out of shape" by pressures that no previous building could have withstood. The plan is a pinched oval suggesting a distended and half-melted Greek cross, as if it had been drawn on rubber. In the façade, designed almost thirty years later, these pressures and counterpressures reach their maximum intensity. Characteristically, it incorporates sculpture and even a painting, borne aloft by flying angels. San Carlo alle Quattro Fontane established Borromini's local and international fame. "Nothing similar," wrote the head of the religious order for which the church was built, "can be found anywhere in the world."

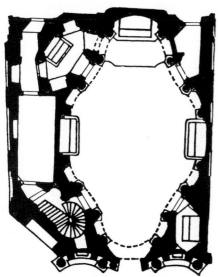

217. FRANCESCO BORROMINI. Façade and Plan, S. Carlo alle Quattro Fontane. 1638–67. Rome

218. GUARINO GUARINI. Palazzo Carignano. Begun 1679. Turin

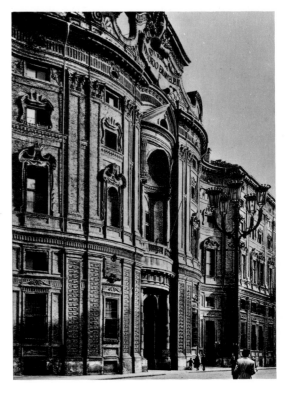

The wealth of new ideas introduced by Borromini was exploited not in Rome but in Turin, the capital of Savoy, which became the creative center of Baroque architecture in Italy toward the end of the seventeenth century. In 1666, that city attracted Borromini's most brilliant successor, Guarino Guarini, a monk whose architectural genius was deeply grounded in philosophy and mathematics. His design for the façade of the Palazzo Carignano (fig. 218) repeats on a larger scale the undulating movement of San Carlo alle Quattro Fontane, using a highly individual vocabulary. Incredibly, the exterior of the building is entirely of brick, down to the last ornamental detail.

RUBENS

Although Rome was its birthplace, the Baroque style soon became international. Among the artists who helped bring this about, the great Flemish painter Peter Paul Rubens holds a place of special importance. It might be said that he finished what Dürer had started—the breaking down of artistic barriers between North and South. Rubens grew up in Antwerp, the capital of the "Spanish Netherlands" (see p. 237), and remained a devout Catholic all his life. Trained by local painters, he became a master in 1598, but developed a personal style only when, two years later, he went to Italy. During his eight years' stay he eagerly studied ancient sculpture, the masterpieces of the High Renaissance, and the work of Caravaggio, absorbing the Italian tradition far more thoroughly than had any Northerner before him. He competed, in fact, with the best Italians of his day on even terms, and could well have made his career in Italy. He chose instead to settle down in Antwerp as court painter to the Spanish regent, a special appointment that exempted him and his workshop from local taxes and guild rules. Rubens thus had the best of both worlds: at court, he was valued not only as an artist but as a diplomat, so that he had entree to the royal households of the major powers, while he was also free to carry out a vast volume of work for the city of Antwerp, for the Church, and for private patrons. The *Raising of the Cross*

(fig. 219), the first big altarpiece Rubens produced after his return, reveals a strong debt to the Italians. Here we find the powerfully modeled, muscular bodies of Michelangelo, the glowing color and confident brushwork of Titian, and the dramatic lighting of Caravaggio. The painting is heroic both in scale and in conception beyond any previous Northern work. Rubens is a Northerner, however, in his conception of the subject, which reminds us of Rogier van der Weyden's *Descent from the Cross* (colorplate 25). He is a genuine Flemish realist, too, in such details as the foliage, the soldier's armor, and the curly-haired dog. The elements of the picture are widely scattered in origin, but Rubens has brought them into unity in so masterly a fashion that the only style of which we are conscious is his. The composition—a swaying pyramid of bodies that seem to travel on and out without even pausing at the frame—has tremendous force. For this master, nothing stands still. Energy leaps from form to form and builds up in a swirl of movement that sweeps through the picture like a high wind.

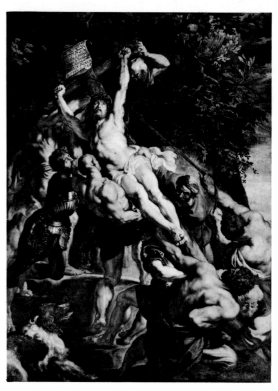

219. PETER PAUL RUBENS. *The Raising of the Cross.* 1609–10. Panel, 15′ 2″ × 11′ 2″. Antwerp Cathedral

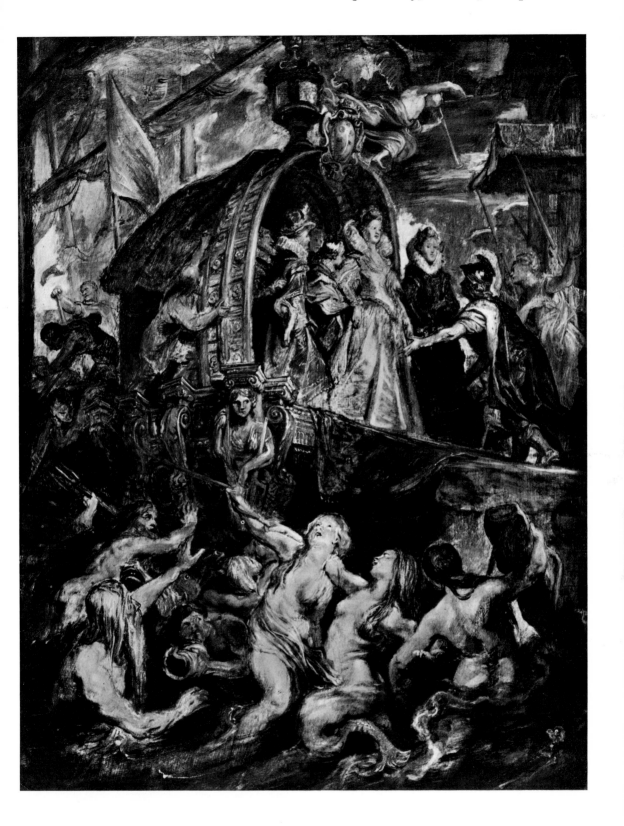

220. PETER PAUL RUBENS. *Marie de' Medici, Queen of France, Landing in Marseilles.* 1622–23. Panel, 25 × 19 3/4". Pinakothek, Munich

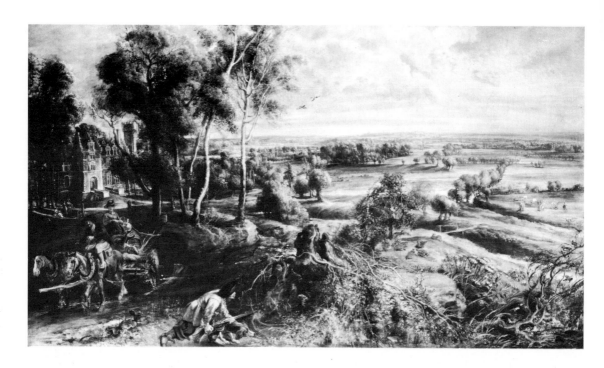

In the 1620s, Rubens' dynamic style reached a climax in his huge decorative schemes for churches and palaces. The most famous, probably, is the cycle for the Luxembourg Palace in Paris, glorifying Marie de' Medici, the widow of Henri IV and the mother of Louis XIII. Figure 220 shows the artist's oil sketch for one episode, the young queen landing in Marseilles. Hardly an exciting subject—yet Rubens has turned it into a spectacle of unprecedented splendor. As Marie de' Medici walks down the gangplank, Fame flies overhead sounding a triumphant blast on two trumpets, and Neptune rises from the sea with his fishtailed crew; having guarded the queen's journey, they rejoice at her arrival. Everything flows together here in swirling movement: heaven and earth, history and allegory—even drawing and painting, for Rubens used oil sketches like this one to prepare his compositions. Unlike earlier artists, he preferred to design his pictures in terms of light and color from the very start. This unified vision, approached but never fully achieved by the great Venetians of the previous century, was Rubens' most precious legacy to subsequent painters.

Around 1630, the turbulent drama of Rubens' preceding work changes to a late style of lyrical tenderness inspired by Titian, whom Rubens rediscovered, as it were, in

221. PETER PAUL RUBENS. *Landscape with the Château of Steen.* 1636. Panel, 53 × 93″. The National Gallery, London

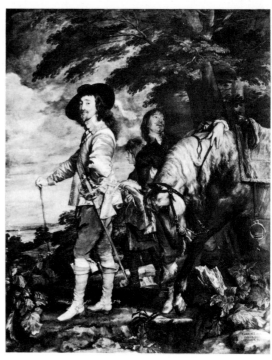

222. ANTHONY VAN DYCK. *Portrait of Charles I Hunting.* c. 1635. 107 × 83 1/2″. The Louvre, Paris

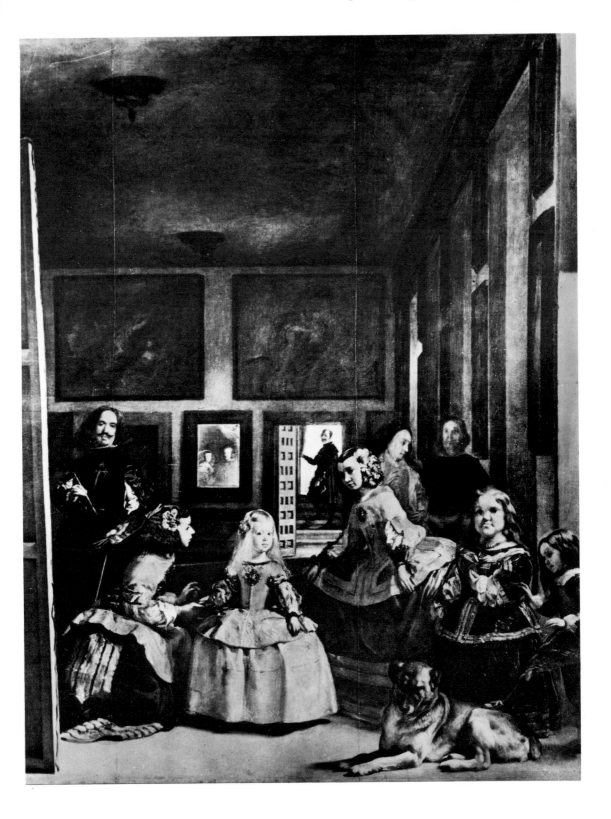

223. Diego Velázquez. *The Maids of Honor.* 1656. Canvas, 10′ 5″ × 9′. The Prado, Madrid

the royal palace while he visited Madrid. *The Garden of Love* (colorplate 45) combines a traditional Northern subject with Titian's Classical mythologies, to create an enchanted realm where myth and reality become one. The picture must have had special meaning for him, since he had just married a beautiful girl of sixteen (his first wife died in 1626). He also bought a country house, the Château of Steen, and led the leisurely life of a squire. This change induced a renewed interest in landscape painting, which he had practiced only intermittently before. Here, too, the power of his genius is undiminished. In the *Landscape with the Château of Steen* (fig. 221), a magnificent open space sweeps from the hunter and his prey in the foreground to the mist-veiled hills along the horizon. As a landscapist, Rubens is the heir of both Pieter Bruegel and the Venetians (compare fig. 209, colorplate 34), again creating a synthesis from his Northern and Southern sources.

VAN DYCK

The only other Flemish Baroque artist to win international stature was Anthony van Dyck, Rubens' most valued assistant. His fame is based mainly on his portraits—for example, *Charles I Hunting* (fig. 222), done while the artist was court painter in England during 1632–41. It might be called a "dismounted equestrian portrait"—less rigid than a formal state portrait, but hardly less grand. Van Dyck has brought the Mannerist court portrait up-to-date, rephrasing it in the language of Rubens and Titian. He created a new aristocratic portrait tradition that continued in England until the late eighteenth century, and had considerable influence on the Continent as well.

VELÁZQUEZ

In Madrid, Rubens befriended the recently appointed court painter, Diego Velázquez. The superbly gifted young artist had been deeply impressed with the style of Caravaggio; Rubens helped him to discover the beauty of Titian and develop a new fluency and richness. No picture displays Velázquez' mature style more fully than *The Maids of Honor* (fig. 223), which is both a group portrait and an everyday scene. It might be subtitled "the artist in his studio," for Velázquez shows

himself at work on a huge canvas; in the center is the little Princess Margarita, who has just posed for him, among her playmates and maids of honor. The faces of her parents, the king and queen, appear in the mirror on the back wall. Have they just stepped into the room, to see the scene exactly as we do, or does the mirror reflect part of the canvas—presumably a full-length portrait of the royal family—on which the artist has been working? This ambiguity is characteristic of Velázquez' fascination with light. The varieties of direct and reflected light in *The Maids of Honor* are almost limitless, and the artist challenges us to find them: we are expected to match the mirror image against the paintings on that wall, and against the "picture" of the man in the open doorway. The side lighting (from the right) and the strong contrasts of light and dark still suggest the influence of Caravaggio, but Velázquez' technique is far more varied and subtle, with delicate glazes setting off the impasto of the highlights, and brushwork even freer and more sketchy than that of Titian or Rubens. The colors, too, have a Venetian warmth and brilliance. Yet Velázquez does not seem interested in catching time on the wing; his aim is to show not figures in motion but the movement of light itself and the infinite range of its effects on form and color. For Velázquez, light *creates* the visible world. Not until two centuries later shall we meet painters capable of realizing the implications of this discovery.

The Golden Age of Dutch Painting

In contrast to Flanders, where painting was overshadowed by the majestic personality of Rubens, Holland produced a bewildering variety of masters and styles. The new nation was proud of its hard-won freedom. Though the cultural links with Flanders remained strong, several factors encouraged the rapid growth of Dutch artistic traditions. Unlike Flanders, where all artistic activity radiated from Antwerp, Holland had many flourishing local schools: besides Amsterdam, the commercial center, we find important groups of painters in Haarlem, Utrecht, Leyden, Delft, and other towns. Holland was a nation of merchants, farmers, and seafarers, and the Reformed faith was its official religion; thus Dutch artists lacked the large-scale public commissions sponsored by State and Church that were available throughout the Catholic world. As a consequence, the private collector now became the painter's chief source of support. There was no shrinkage of output; on the contrary, the Dutch public developed so insatiable an appetite for pictures that the whole country became gripped by a kind of collector's mania. Everyone invested in paintings, just as millions of Americans played the stock market in the 1920s. The comparison is not far-fetched, for pictures became an important commodity in Holland, and their trade followed the law of supply and demand. Many artists produced "for the market" instead of relying on commissions from individual patrons. The mechanism of the art market has been said to raise a barrier between artist and public, and to falsify the "true worth" of the work of art. Such charges, however, are unrealistic: the true worth of a work of art is always unstable, and depends on time and circumstance; even those who believe in timeless values in art will concede that these values cannot be expressed in money. Because the art market reflects the dominant, rather than the most discerning, taste of the moment, works by artists now regarded as mediocre may once have been overpriced; others, highly valued today, seem once to have sold too cheaply. Yet the system that prevailed in antiquity and the Middle Ages, when artists were paid on standards of craftsmanship, was hardly fairer in rewarding aesthetic merit. The market does form a barrier between artist and public, but there are advantages in this as well as drawbacks. To subject the artist to the pressure of supply and demand is not necessarily worse than to make him depend on the favor of princes. The lesser men will tend to become specialists, steadily producing their marketable pictures, while artists of independent spirit, perhaps braving economic hardship, will paint as they please and rely for support on the discerning minority. From the collector's mania in seventeenth-century Holland came an outpouring of artistic talent comparable only to Early Renaissance Florence, although many Dutchmen were lured into becoming painters by hopes of success that failed to come true. Even the greatest masters were sometimes hard-pressed (it was not unusual for an artist to keep an inn, or run a small business on the side). Yet they survived—less secure, but freer.

HALS

The Baroque style came to Holland from Antwerp, through the work of Rubens, and from Rome, through direct contact with Caravaggio and his followers, some of whom were Dutchmen. One of the first to profit from this experience was Frans Hals, the great portrait painter of Haarlem. He was born in Antwerp, and what little is known of his early work suggests the influence of Rubens. His mature style, however, seen in such pictures as *The Jolly Toper* (colorplate 46), combines Rubens' robustness and breadth with a concentration on the "dramatic moment" that was derived from the followers of Caravaggio who had settled in Utrecht. Everything here conveys complete spontaneity: the twinkling eyes and the half-open mouth, the raised hand, the teetering wineglass, and—most important of all—the quick way of setting down the forms. Hals works in dashing brushstrokes, each so clearly visible as a separate entity that we can almost count the total number of "touches." With this open, split-second technique, the completed picture has the immediacy of a sketch. The impression of a race against time is, of course, deceptive; Hals spent hours, not minutes, on this lifesize canvas, but he maintains the illusion of having done it in the wink of an eye. In the artist's last canvases these pictorial fireworks are transmuted into an austere style of great emotional depth. His group portrait, *The Woman Regents of the Old People's Home at Haarlem* (fig. 224), the institution where he spent his final years, has an insight into human character matched only in Rembrandt's late style (compare fig. 226). The daily experience of suffering and death has so etched the faces of these women that they seem themselves to have become images of death—gentle, inexorable, and timeless.

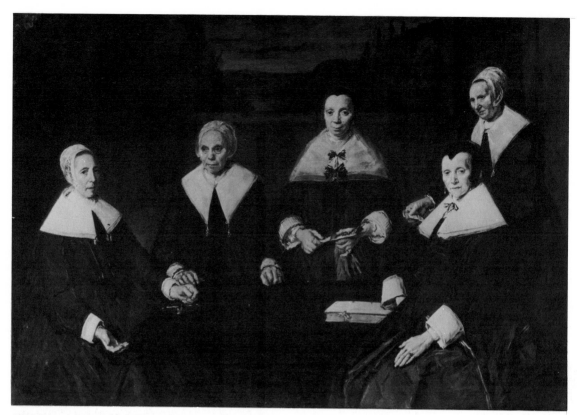

224. FRANS HALS. *The Women Regents of the Old People's Home at Haarlem*. 1664. Oil on canvas, 67 × 98″
Frans Hals Museum, Haarlem

REMBRANDT

Rembrandt, the greatest genius of Dutch art, was also stimulated at the beginning of his career by indirect contact with Caravaggio; his earliest pictures are small, sharply lit, and intensely realistic. From these he developed, in the 1630s, a full-blown High Baroque style. *The Blinding of Samson* (fig. 225) shows us the Old Testament world in oriental splendor and violence, cruel yet seductive. The sudden flood of brilliant light pouring into the dark tent is unabashedly theatrical, heightening the drama to the pitch of Rubens' *Raising of the Cross* (fig. 219).

Rembrandt was at this time an avid collector of Near Eastern paraphernalia, which serve as props in these pictures. He was now Amsterdam's most sought-after portrait painter and a man of considerable wealth. This prosperity petered out in the 1640s, although the artist's fall from public favor was less sudden and catastrophic than his roman-

tic admirers would have us believe. Still, the 1640s were a period of crisis, of inner uncertainty and external troubles. Rembrandt's outlook changed profoundly: after about 1650, his style eschews the rhetoric of the High Baroque for lyric subtlety and pictorial breadth. We sense the difference in his late *Self-Portrait* (fig. 226). While partially indebted to Titian's sumptuous portraits (compare fig. 189), Rembrandt scrutinizes himself with the same typically Northern frankness found in Jan van Eyck's *Man in a Red Turban* (fig. 147). This self-analytical approach accounts for the simple dignity we see in the artist toward the end of his life.

In his later years, Rembrandt often adapted, in a very personal way, pictorial ideas from the Northern Renaissance, as in *The Polish Rider* (colorplate 47). We cannot be sure that the rider is Polish—the title was given to him later—although his costume is of the kind worn by the local troops then

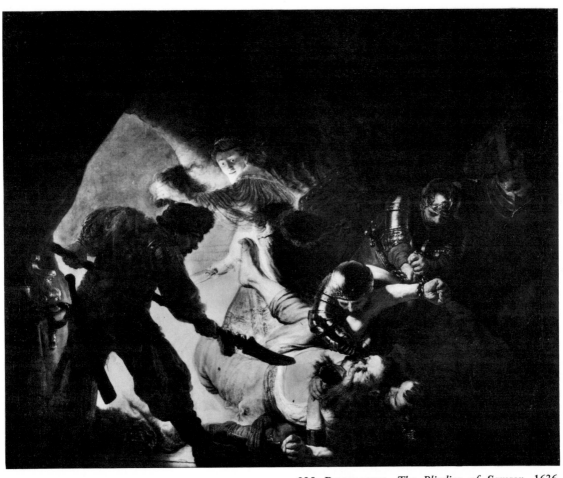

225. REMBRANDT. *The Blinding of Samson*. 1636. Canvas, 93 × 119″. Städel Institute, Frankfurt

226. REMBRANDT. *Self-Portrait*. About 1660. Oil on canvas, 45 × 38″. The Iveagh Bequest, Kenwood, London

227. REMBRANDT. *Christ Preaching*. c. 1652. Etching. The Metropolitan Museum of Art, New York (Bequest of Mrs. H. O. Havemeyer, 1929)

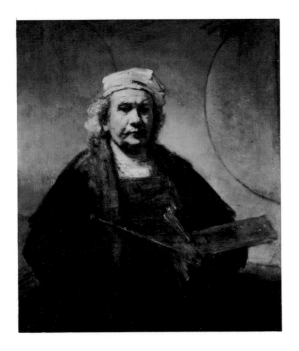

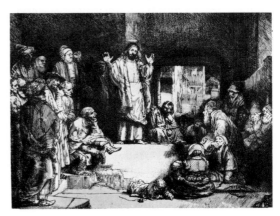

fighting the Turks in eastern Europe; nor is Rembrandt's exact purpose clear. But Dürer's famous engraving, *Knight, Death, and Devil* (see fig. 205), which Rembrandt surely admired, may be the key to the picture. Is not the Polish Rider another Christian Soldier bravely making his way through a perilous world? The dangers in this case are ours to imagine in the gloomy landscape, but the rider's serious, alert glance suggests unseen threats. With such a relationship of form and content, the differences between the painting and the print make a rewarding study. Dürer's horseman, boxed into the composition, is balanced and stationary like an equestrian statue; Rembrandt's, slightly foreshortened and off center, is in motion—urged on, as it were, by the light from the left. The curving path he follows will soon lead him beyond the frame. This subtle imbalance implies a space far vaster than the compass of the picture and stamps Rembrandt's work as Baroque, despite the absence of the more obvious hallmarks of the style. Much the same may be said of the religious scenes that play so large a part in Rembrandt's later work, such as the etching, *Christ Preaching* (fig. 227). It is a quiet scene, full of the artist's deep feeling of compassion for the poor and outcast who make up Christ's audience. Rembrandt had a special sympathy for the Jews, as the heirs of the Biblical past and as the patient victims of persecution; they were often his models. This print strongly suggests some corner in the Amsterdam ghetto. As in *The Polish Rider*, it is the magic of Rembrandt's light that endows *Christ Preaching* with spiritual significance.

Rembrandt's importance as a graphic artist is second only to Dürer's, although we get no more than a hint from this single example. But we must add a word about his medium. By the seventeenth century, the techniques of woodcut and engraving were employed mainly to reproduce other works. The creative printmakers, including Rembrandt, preferred etching. An etching is made by coating a copper plate with resin to make an acid-resistant "ground," through which the design is scratched with a needle, laying bare the metal surface underneath. The plate is then bathed in an acid that etches ("bites") the lines into the copper. To scratch a design into the resinous ground is, of course, an easier task than cutting it into the copper plate directly, hence an etched line is freer and more individual than an engraved line. The chief virtue of etching is its wide tonal range, including velvety dark shades not possible in engravings or woodcuts. No etcher ever exploited this quality more subtly than Rembrandt.

VAN RUISDAEL; HEDA

Rembrandt's religious pictures demand an insight that was beyond the capacity of all but a few collectors. Most art buyers in Holland preferred subjects within their own experience—landscapes, still lifes, scenes of everyday life. These were produced in ever greater volume and variety by specialists, so that we can here illustrate only a small sampling. Perhaps the richest of the newly developed "specialties" was landscape, both as a portrayal of familiar views and as an imaginative vision of nature. Of the latter kind is *The Cemetery* (fig. 228) by Jacob van Ruisdael: the thunderclouds passing over a wild, deserted mountain valley, the medieval ruin, the torrent that has forced its way between ancient graves, all create a mood of deep melancholy. Nothing endures on this earth, the artist tells us—time, wind, and water grind all to dust, the feeble works of man as well as the trees and rocks. This view of man's impotence in the face of natural forces has an awe-inspiring quality on which the Romantics, a century later, were to base their concept of the Sublime. Even still life can be tinged with a melancholy sense of the passing of all earthly pleasures, sometimes through such established symbols as death's-heads and extinguished candles, or by more subtle means. Our example by Willem Heda (fig. 229) belongs to a widespread type, the "breakfast piece," showing the remnants of a meal. Food and drink are less emphasized than luxury objects—crystal goblets and silver dishes—carefully juxtaposed for their contrasting shape, color, and texture. But virtuosity was not the artist's only aim: his "story," the human context of these grouped objects, is suggested by the broken glass, the half-peeled lemon, the overturned silver dish; whoever sat at this table has suddenly been

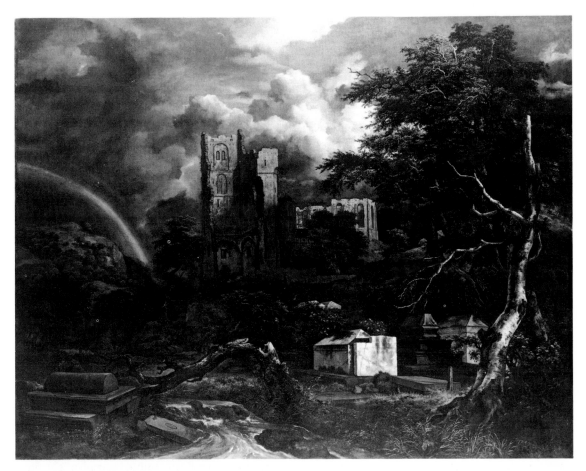

228. JACOB VAN RUISDAEL. *The Cemetery.* c. 1655. Canvas, 56 × 74 1/2″. Courtesy of The Detroit Institute of Arts

229. WILLEM HEDA. *Still Life.* 1634. Panel, 17 × 22 1/2″. Boymans-van Beuningen Museum, Rotterdam

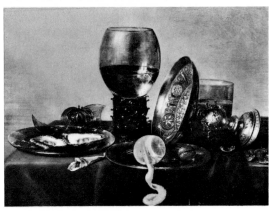

forced to abandon his meal. The curtain that time has lowered on the scene, as it were, invests the objects with a strange pathos. Here the disguised symbolism of Late Gothic painting (see p. 164) lives on in a new form.

STEEN; VERMEER

The pictures of everyday life (also known as "genre" pictures) range from tavern brawls to refined domestic interiors. *The Eve of St.*

Nicholas (fig. 230) by Jan Steen is midway between these extremes. St. Nicholas has just paid his pre-Christmas visit to the household, leaving toys, candy, and cake for the children; everyone is jolly except the bad boy on the left, who has received only a birch rod. Steen tells this story with relish, embroidering it with many delightful details. Of all the Dutch painters of daily life, he was the sharpest, and most good-humored, observer. To supplement his earnings he kept an inn, which perhaps explains his keen insight into human behavior. His sense of timing often reminds us of Frans Hals (compare colorplate 46), while his storytelling stems from the tradition of Pieter Bruegel (compare colorplate 42).

In the genre scenes of Jan Vermeer, by contrast, there is hardly any narrative. Single figures, usually women, engage in simple, everyday tasks; when two are present, as in *The Letter* (colorplate 48), they no more than exchange glances. They exist in a timeless "still-life" world, seemingly calmed by some magic spell. The cool, clear light that filters in from the left is the only active element, working its miracles upon all the objects in its path. As we look at *The Letter*, we feel as if a veil had been pulled from our eyes; the everyday world shines with jewellike freshness, beautiful as we have never seen it before. No painter since Jan van Eyck *saw* as intensely as this. But Vermeer, unlike his predecessors, perceives reality as a mosaic of colored surfaces—or, perhaps more accurately, he translates reality into a

mosaic as he puts it on canvas. We see *The Letter* as a perspective "window," but also as a plane, a "field" composed of smaller fields. Rectangles predominate, carefully aligned with the picture surface, and there are no "holes," no undefined empty spaces. These interlocking shapes give to Vermeer's work a uniquely modern quality. How did he acquire it? We know little about him except that he was born in Delft in 1632 and lived and worked there until his death at forty-three. The Dutch followers of Caravaggio had influenced him but this is hardly enough to explain the genesis of his style, so daringly original that his genius was not recognized until a century ago.

The Age of Versailles

FRANCE

Our discussion of Baroque art in Flanders, Spain, and Holland has been limited to painting; architecture and sculpture in these countries have no basic importance for the history of art. In France, however, the situation is different. Under Louis XIV France became the most powerful nation of Europe, militarily and culturally; by the late seventeenth century, Paris had replaced Rome as the world capital of the visual arts. How did this astonishing change come about? Because of the Palace of Versailles and other vast projects glorifying the king, we are tempted to think of French art in the age of Louis XIV as the expression of absolutism. This is true of the climactic phase of Louis' reign, 1660–85, but by that time French seventeenth-century art had already formed its distinctive style. Frenchmen are reluctant to call this style Baroque; to them it is the Style of Louis XIV; often they also describe the art and literature of the period as "Classic." The term, so used, has three meanings: as a synonym for "highest achievement," it implies that the style of Louis XIV corresponds to the High Renaissance in Italy, or the age of Pericles in Greece; the term also refers to the emulation of the form and subject matter of ancient art;

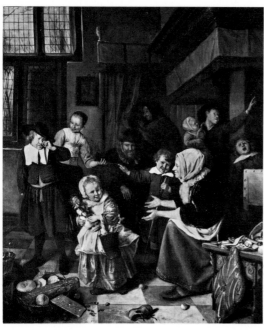

230. JAN STEEN. *The Eve of St. Nicholas.* c. 1660–65. Canvas, 32 1/4 × 27 3/4". Rijksmuseum, Amsterdam

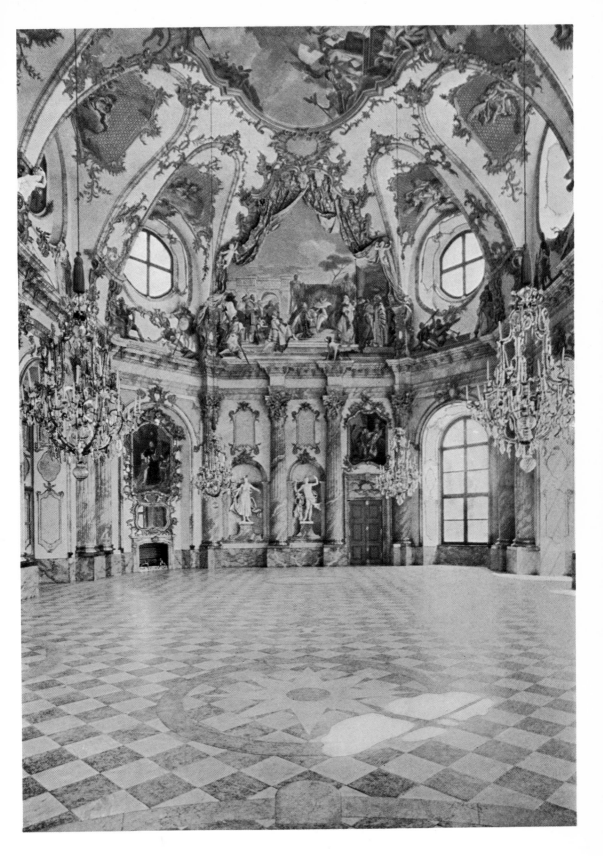

Colorplate 49. BALTHASAR NEUMANN. The Kaisersaal, Episcopal Palace, Würzburg. 1719–44

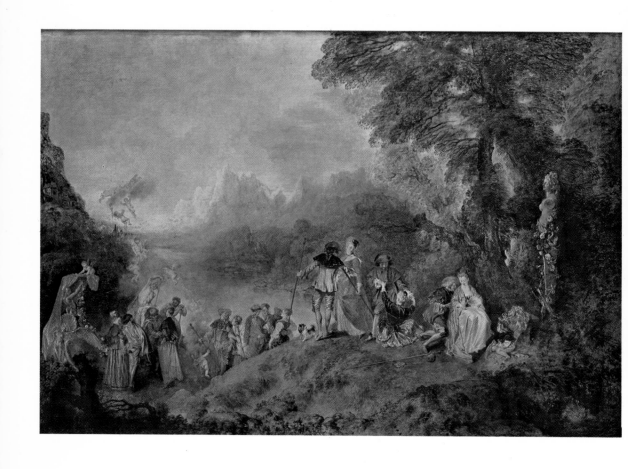

Colorplate 50. ANTOINE WATTEAU. *A Pilgrimage to Cythera.* 1717. Oil on canvas, 4′ 3″ × 6′ 4 1/2″. The Louve, Paris

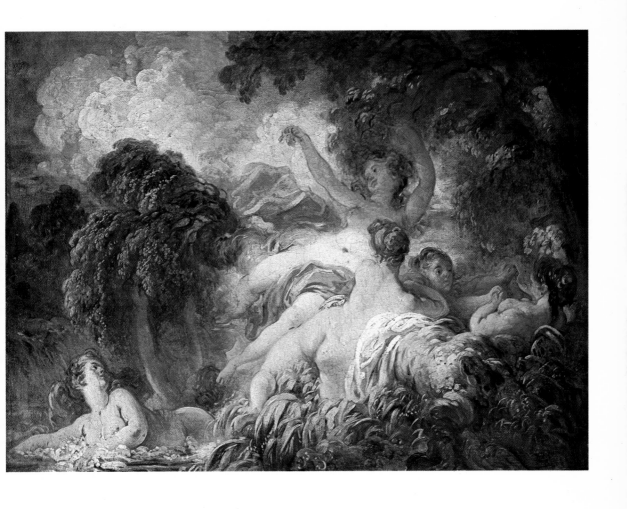

Colorplate 51. JEAN-HONORÉ FRAGONARD. *Bathers*. c. 1765. Oil on canvas, 25 1/4 × 31 /12″. The Louvre, Paris.

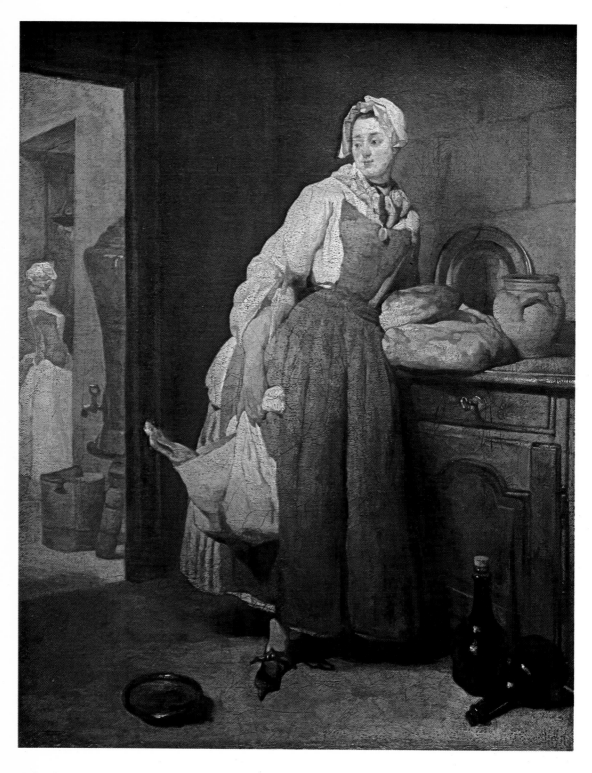

Colorplate 52. JEAN-BAPTISTE SIMÉON CHARDIN. *Back from the Market*. 1739. Oil on canvas, 18 1/2 × 14 3/4″. The Louvre, Paris

261

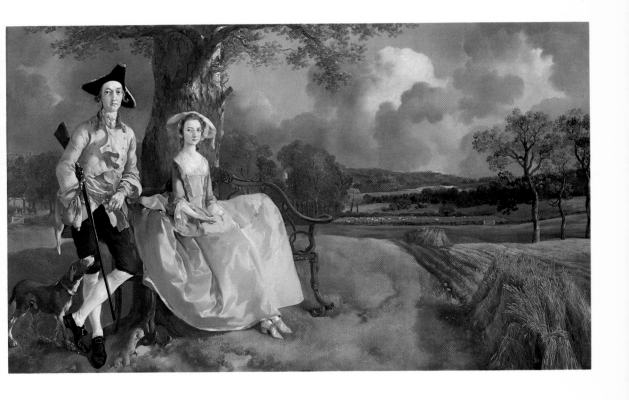

Colorplate 53. THOMAS GAINSBOROUGH. *Robert Andrews and His Wife*. c. 1748–50. Oil on canvas, 27 1/2 × 47″.
The National Gallery, London (Reproduced by courtesy of the Trustees)

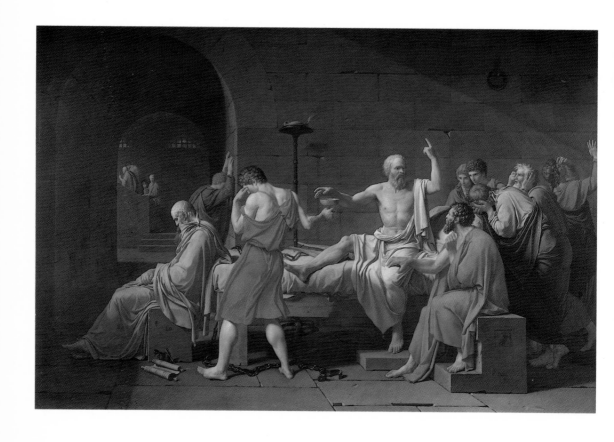

Colorplate 54. JACQUES LOUIS DAVID. *The Death of Socrates*. 1787. The Metropolitan Museum of Art, New York

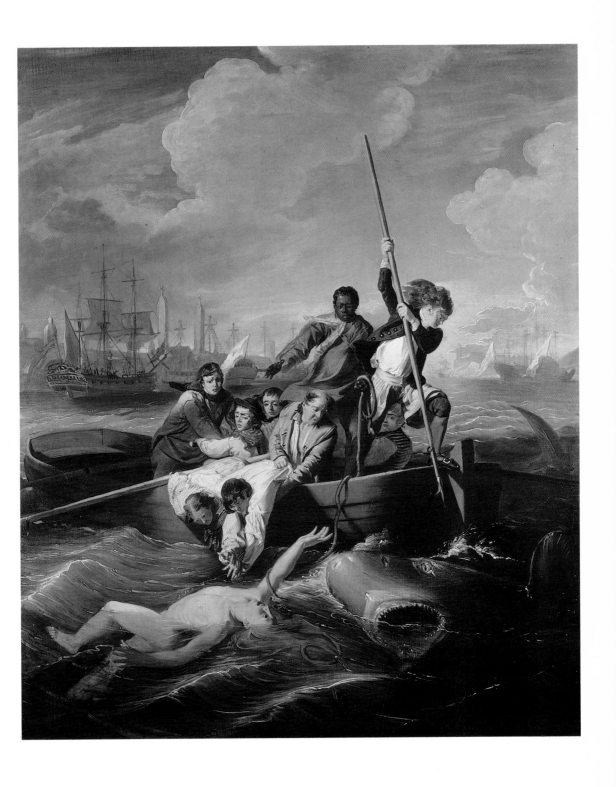

Colorplate 55. JOHN SINGLETON COPLEY. *Waston and the Shark*. 1782. Oil on canvas, 36 × 30 1/2″. The Detroit Institute of Arts (Purchase, The Dexter M. Ferry, Jr. Fund)

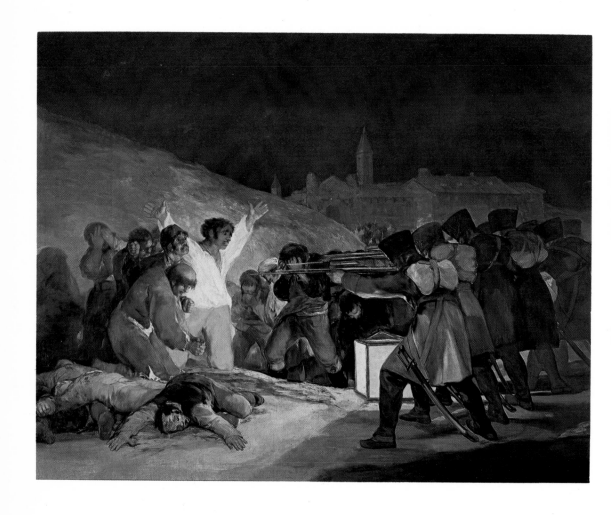

Colorplate 56. FRANCISCO GOYA. *The Third of May, 1808*. 1814–15. Oil on canvas, 8′ 9″ × 13′ 4″. The Prado, Madrid

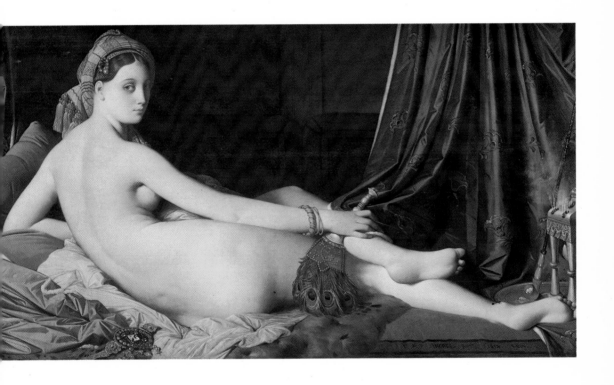

Colorplate 57. JEAN-AUGUSTE DOMINIQUE INGRES. *Odalisque*. 1814. Oil on canvas, 35 1/4 × 63 3/4″. The Louvre, Paris

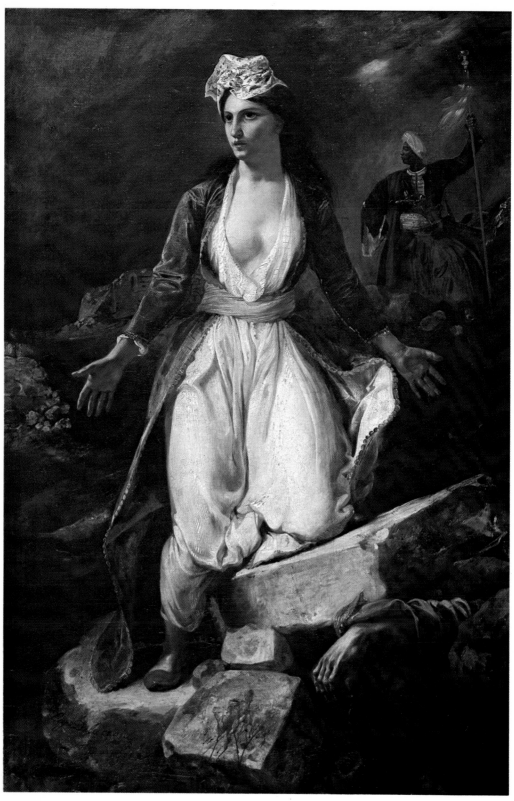

Colorplate 58. Eugéne Delacroix. *Greece Expiring on the Ruins of Missolonghi.* 1827. Oil on canvas, 6′ 11 1/2″ × 4′ 8 1/4″. Museum of Fine Arts, Bordeaux, France

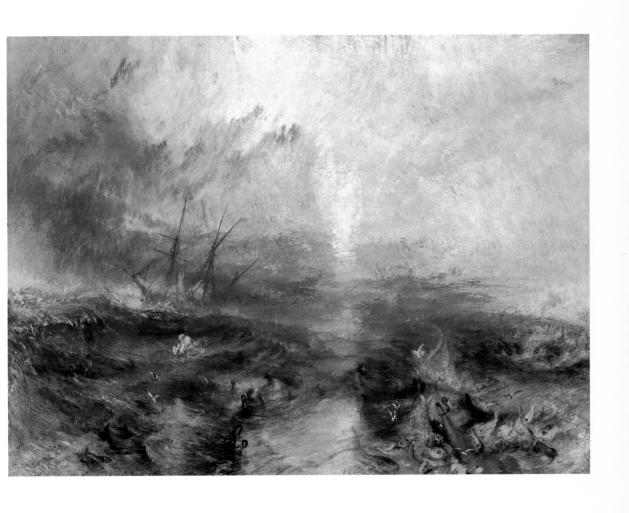

Colorplate 59. JOSEPH M. W. TURNER. *The Slave Ship*. 1839. Canvas, 35 3/4 × 48″. Museum of Fine Arts, Boston

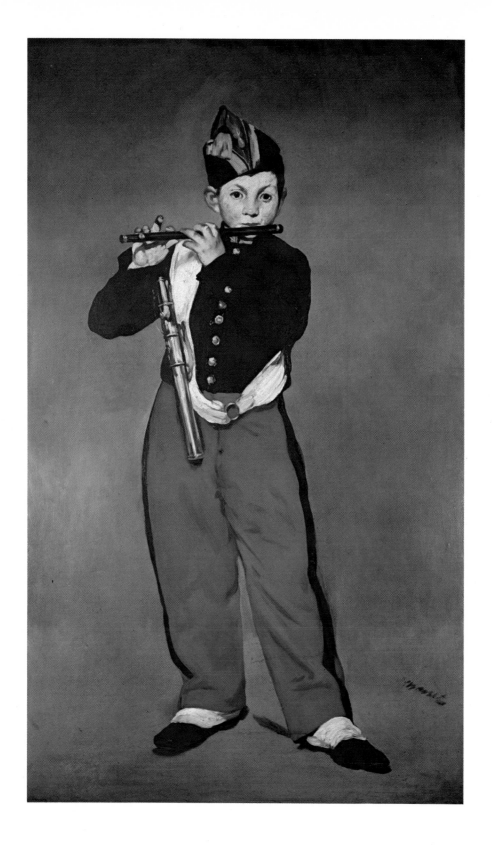

Colorplate 60. EDOUARD MANET. *The Fifer*. 1866. Oil on canvas, 63 × 38 1/4″. The Louvre, Paris

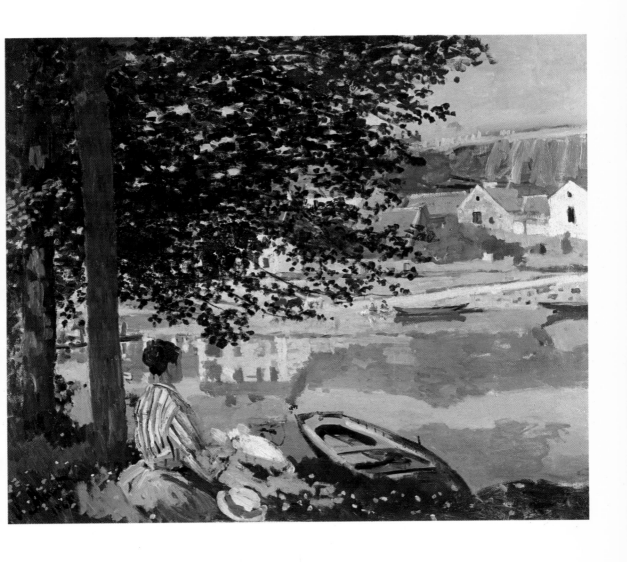

Colorplate 61. CLAUDE MONET. *The River*. 1868. Canvas, 32 × 39 1/2." The Art Institute of Chicago (Potter Palmer Collection)

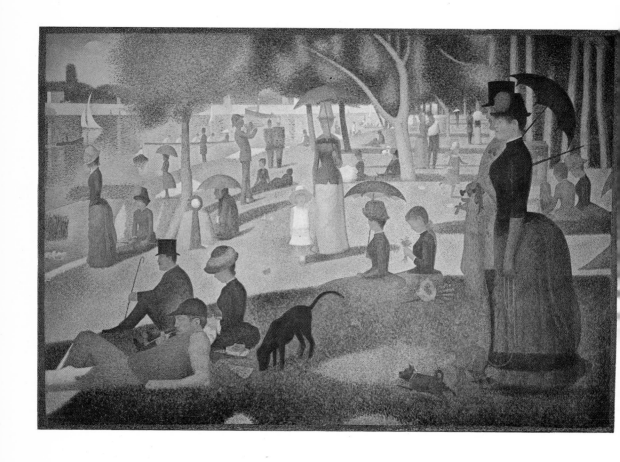

Colorplate 62. GEORGES SEURAT. *A Sunday Afternoon on the Grande Jatte.* 1884–86. Oil on canvas, 6′ 9 1/4″ × 10′. The Art Institute of Chicago (Helen Birch Bartlett Memorial Collection)

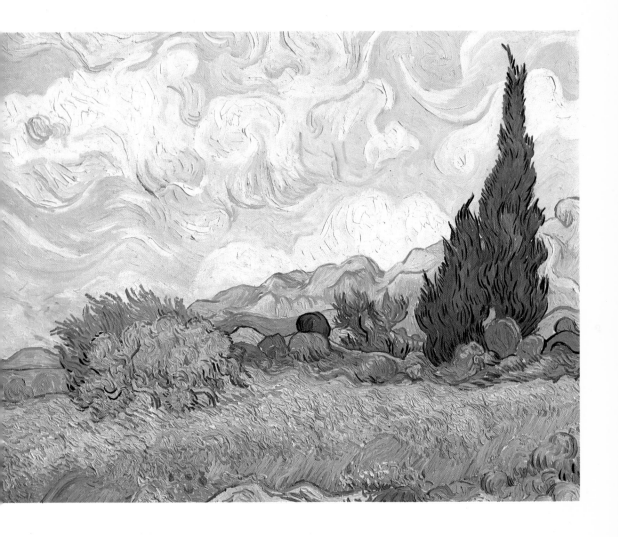

Colorplate 63. VINCENT VAN GOGH. *Wheat Field and Cypress Trees*. 1889. Oil on canvas, 28 1/2 × 36″. The National Gallery, London (Reproduced by courtesy of the Trustees)

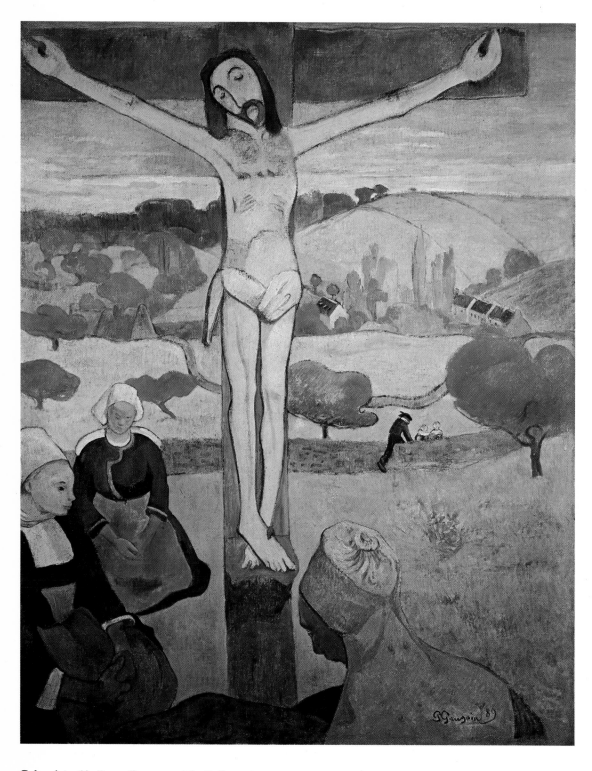

Colorplate 64. PAUL GAUGUIN. *The Yellow Christ.* 1889. Oil on canvas, 36 3/8 × 28 3/4." Albright-Knox Art Gallery, Buffalo

finally, "Classic" suggests qualities of balance and restraint, like those of the Classic styles of the High Renaissance and of ancient Greece. The second and third of these meanings describe what could be called, more accurately, "Classicism." And since the Style of Louis XIV reflects Italian Baroque art, however modified, we must label it either "Classicistic Baroque" or "Baroque Classicism."

PAINTING

This Classicism was the official court style by 1660–85, but its origin was not political. It sprang, rather, from the persistent tradition of sixteenth-century art, which in France was more intimately linked with the Italian Renaissance than in any other Northern country (see p. 237). Classicism was also nourished by French humanism, with its intellectual heritage of reason and Stoic virtue. These factors retarded the spread of the Baroque in France and modified its interpretation. Rubens' Medici cycle, for example, had no effect on French art until the very end of the century; in the 1620s, the young painters in France were still assimilating Caravaggio. Some developed astonishingly original styles. Louis Le Nain's *Peasant Family* (fig. 231) has a human dignity and a compassion for the poor that seem akin to Rembrandt. The candle held by Jesus in *Joseph the Carpenter* (fig. 232) by Georges de La Tour gives the scene the intimacy and tenderness of Geertgen's *Nativity* (fig. 150), in which light also reduces forms to geometric simplicity. Yet both Le Nain and De La Tour, like Vermeer, had to be rediscovered in modern times. In their day both were soon forgotten because from about 1650 on Classicism was supreme in France, and neither was a Classicist.

POUSSIN; LORRAIN

The artist who did most to bring about this change of taste was Nicolas Poussin. The greatest French painter of the century, and the earliest French painter to win international fame, Poussin nevertheless spent almost his entire career in Rome. There, under the inspiration of Raphael (colorplate 33, fig. 188), he formulated the style that was to become the ideal model for French painters of the second half of the century. Its quali-

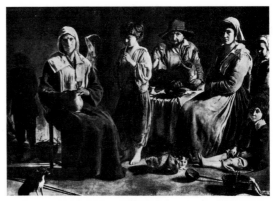

231. LOUIS LE NAIN. *Peasant Family.* c. 1640. Canvas, 44 1/2 × 62 1/2″. The Louvre, Paris

ties are well displayed in *The Rape of the Sabine Women* (fig. 233): the strongly modeled figures are "frozen in action," like statues, and many are in fact derived from Hellenistic sculpture (compare fig. 58). Behind them, Poussin has placed reconstructions of Roman architecture that he believed to be archaeo-

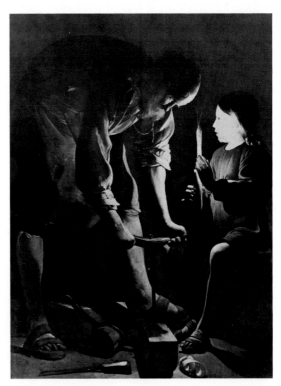

232. GEORGES DE LA TOUR. *Joseph the Carpenter.* c. 1645. Oil on canvas, 38 1/2 × 25 1/2″. The Louvre, Paris

logically correct. As in Giovanni da Bologna's statue of the same subject (fig. 200), emotion is abundantly in evidence, yet it so lacks spontaneity that it fails to touch us. All sensuous appeal has been consciously suppressed from the severe discipline of an intellectual style. Poussin strikes us as a man who knew his own mind only too well, an impression confirmed by the numerous letters in which he expounded his views. The highest aim of painting, he believed, is to represent noble and serious human actions. These must be shown in a logical and orderly way—not as they really happened, but as they would have happened if nature were perfect. To this end, the artist must strive for the general and typical; appealing to the mind rather than the senses, he suppresses such trivialities as glowing color, and stresses form and composition. In a good painting, the beholder should be able to "read" the exact emotions of each figure, and relate them to the event depicted. These ideas were not new—we recall Leonardo's statement that the highest aim of painting is to portray "the intention of man's soul"—but before Poussin no one

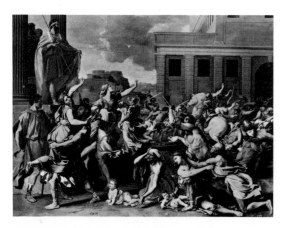

233. NICOLAS POUSSIN. *The Rape of the Sabine Women*. c. 1636–37. Canvas, 61 × 82 1/2″. The Metropolitan Museum of Art, New York (Dick Fund, 1946)

234. NICOLAS POUSSIN. *Landscape with the Burial of Phocion*. 1648. Oil on canvas, 44 7/8 × 68 7/8″. The Louvre, Paris

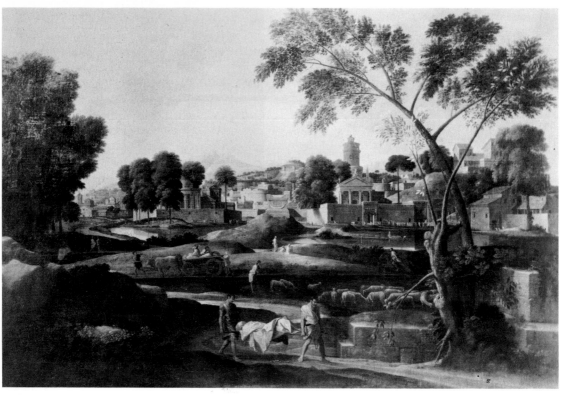

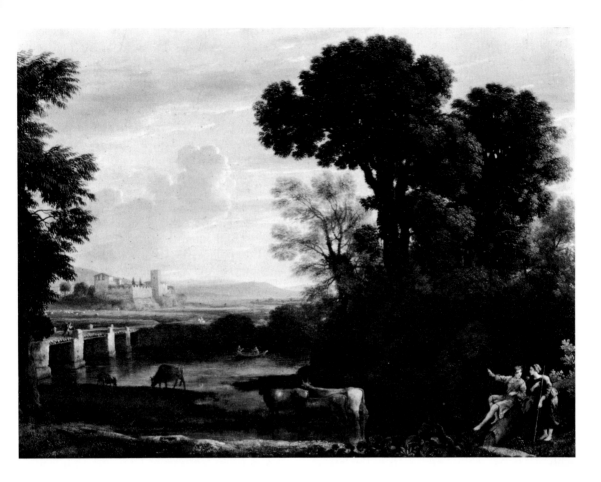

235. CLAUDE LORRAIN. *A Pastoral*. c. 1650. 15 7/8
× 21 5/8″. Yale University Art Gallery, New Haven,
Connecticut

had made the analogy between painting and
literature so closely nor put it into practice
so single-mindedly.

Poussin's genius speaks to us with full
voice in the marvelously organized *Landscape
with the Burial of Phocion* (fig. 234), where
structural clarity and mathematical discipline
are sustained through every square inch of
canvas. The theme is the burial of a Greek
hero who died because he would not conceal
the truth. The austerely beautiful landscape
of this picture is in keeping with the theme,
a memorial to Stoic virtue.

If Poussin celebrated the heroic aspects
of antiquity, the great French landscapist
Claude Lorrain brought out its idyllic aspects. He, too, spent almost his entire career
in Rome, and explored the countryside
nearby—the Campagna—more thoroughly
and affectionately than any Italian. Countless

drawings, each made on the spot, bear
witness to his extraordinary powers of observation. These sketches, however, were only
the raw material for his paintings, which do
not aim at topographic exactitude but evoke
the poetic essence of a countryside filled with
echoes of antiquity. Often, as in *A Pastoral*
(fig. 235), the compositions are suffused with
the hazy, luminous atmosphere of early
morning or late afternoon; the space expands
serenely, rather than receding step-by-step
as in Poussin's landscapes. An air of nostalgia
hangs over such vistas, of past experience
gilded by memory; hence they appealed especially to Northerners who had seen Italy
only briefly—or, perhaps, not at all.

ARCHITECTURE

In France itself, meanwhile, Baroque Classicism in architecture became the official
"royal style" when young Louis XIV took
over the reins of government in 1661. Colbert, the king's chief adviser, built the administrative apparatus supporting the power

of the absolute monarch. In this system, aimed at subjecting the thoughts and actions of the entire nation to strict control from above, the visual arts had the task of glorifying the king. The painter Charles Lebrun became supervisor of all the king's artistic projects. As chief dispenser of royal art patronage, he commanded so much power that for all practical purposes he was the dictator of the arts in France. Centralized control over the visual arts was exerted by Lebrun not only through the power of the purse; it also included a new system of educating artists in the officially approved style. In antiquity and the Middle Ages, artists had been trained by apprenticeship, and this time-honored practice still prevailed in the Renaissance. But as artists gained a liberal-arts status (see p. 179), they wished to supplement their "mechanical" training with theoretical knowledge. For this purpose, they founded "art academies," patterned after the academies of the humanists (the name is derived from the grove of Academe where Plato met with his disciples). Art academies first appeared in Italy; they seem to have been private associations of artists who met periodically to draw from the model and discuss questions of art theory. Later, these academies took over some functions from the guilds, but their teaching was limited and far from systematic. Such was the Royal Academy of Painting and Sculpture in Paris, founded in 1648; when Lebrun became its director, in 1663, he established a rigid curriculum of compulsory instruction in practice and theory, based on a system of "rules"; this set the pattern for all later academies, including their modern successors, the art schools of today. Much of this body of doctrine was derived from Poussin's views but carried to rationalistic extremes. The Academy even devised a method of tabulating, in numerical grades, the merits of artists past and present in such categories as drawing, expression, and proportion. The ancients received the highest marks, needless to say, then came Raphael and Poussin; the Venetians, who overemphasized color, ranked low, and the Flemish and Dutch lower still. Subjects were similarly classified, from history (Classical or Biblical) at the top to still life at the bottom.

That Louis XIV's choice of Classicism was deliberate we know from the first great project of his reign, the completion of the Louvre. Work on the palace had proceeded intermittently for over a century, along the lines of Lescot's design (see fig. 210); what remained to be done was to close the court on the east side with an impressive façade. Colbert invited Bernini to Paris, hoping the famous master of the Roman Baroque would do for the French king what he had already done so magnificently for the Church. Bernini submitted three designs, all on a scale that would have dwarfed the existing parts of the palace. After much argument and intrigue, Louis XIV rejected these plans, and turned over the problem to a committee of three: Louis Le Vau, his court architect, who had worked on the project before; Charles Lebrun, his court painter; and Claude Perrault, who was a student of ancient architecture, not a professional architect. All three were responsible for the structure that was actually built (fig. 236), although Perrault is usually credited with the major share. The design in some ways suggests the mind of an archaeologist, but one who knew how to select those features of Classical architecture that would link Louis XIV with the glory of the Caesars and yet be compatible with the older parts of the palace. The center pavilion is a Roman temple front, and the wings look like the flanks of that temple folded outward to form one plane. The temple theme demanded a single order of freestanding columns, yet the Louvre had three stories—a difficulty skillfully resolved by treating the ground story as the base of the temple, and recessing the upper two behind the screen of the colonnade. The entire design combines grandeur and elegance in a way that fully justifies its fame.

Ironically, this great exemplar of Classicism proved too pure. Perrault soon faded from the architectural scene, and Baroque features reappeared in the king's vastest enterprise, the Palace of Versailles. Louis XIV himself was less interested in architectural theory and monumental exteriors than in the lavish interiors that would make appropriate settings for himself and his court. The man to whom he really listened was not an architect, but the painter Lebrun. Lebrun had

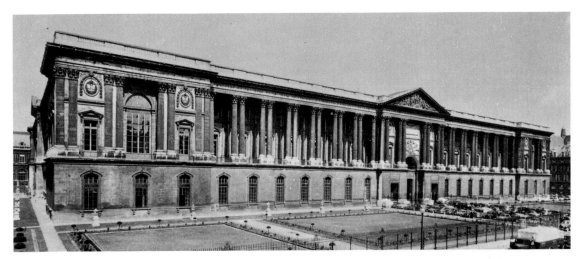

236. CLAUDE PERRAULT. East Front, the Louvre. 1667–70. Paris

studied under Poussin in Rome, but the great decorative schemes of the Roman Baroque must also have impressed him. He became a superb decorator, utilizing the combined labors of architects, sculptors, painters, and craftsmen for ensembles of unheard-of splendor, such as the Salon de la Guerre at Versailles (fig. 237). To subordinate all the arts to a single goal—here, the glorification of Louis XIV—was in itself Baroque; if

Lebrun went less far than Bernini, he nevertheless drew freely on his memories of Rome. The Salon de la Guerre seems in many ways closer to Burnacini's stage design (see fig. 216) than to Perrault's Louvre façade. And, as in so many Italian Baroque interiors, the separate ingredients are less impressive than the effect of the whole.

The Palace of Versailles, just over eleven miles from the center of Paris, was begun by Le Vau. After his death, the entire project, under Jules Hardouin-Mansart, was vastly expanded to accommodate the ever-growing royal household. The Garden Front, in-

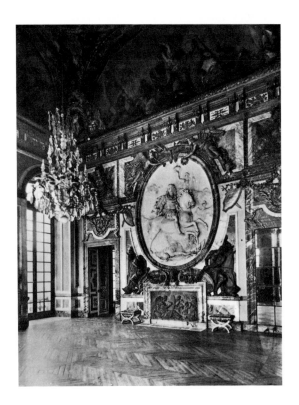

237. JULES HARDOUIN-MANSART, CHARLES LEBRUN, and ANTOINE COYSEVOX. Salon de la Guerre, Palace of Versailles. Begun 1678

238. LOUIS LE VAU and JULES HARDOUIN-MANSART. Palace of Versailles, aerial view from west. 1669–85. (Gardens by ANDRE LE NOTRE, 1664–72)

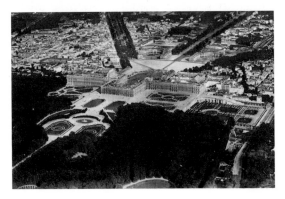

tended as the principal view of the palace, was stretched to enormous length (fig. 238), so that the façade design, a less severe variant of Perrault's Louvre colonnade, looks repetitious and out of scale. The whole center block contains a single room, the famous Hall of Mirrors, with the Salon de la Guerre

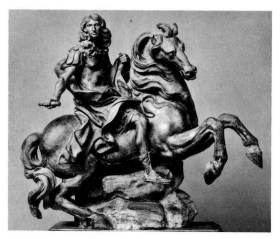

239. GIANLORENZO BERNINI. *Model for Equestrian Statue of Louis XIV.* 1670. Terra-cotta, height 30″. Borghese Gallery, Rome

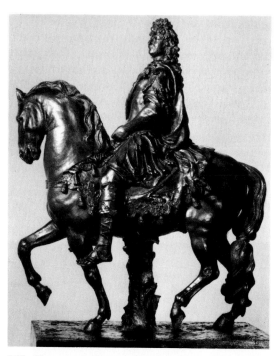

240. FRANÇOIS GIRARDON. *Model for Equestrian Statue of Louis XIV.* 1687? Wax, height 30 1/4″. Yale University Art Gallery, New Haven, Connecticut (Gift of Mr. and Mrs. James W. Fosburgh, 1933)

and its counterpart, the Salon de la Paix, at either end. Apart from its magnificent interior, the most impressive aspect of Versailles is the park extending west of the Garden Front for several miles (the aerial view in figure 238 shows only a small portion). Its design, by André Le Nôtre, is so strictly correlated with the plan of the palace that it becomes a continuation of the architectural space. Like the interior of Versailles, these formal gardens, with their terraces, basins, clipped hedges, and statuary, were meant to provide an appropriate setting for the king's appearances in public. The spirit of absolutism is even more striking in this geometric regularity imposed upon an entire countryside than it is in the palace itself.

SCULPTURE

The official "royal style" was attained in sculpture by a process much like that in architecture. Bernini, while in Paris, had carved a marble bust of Louis XIV, and had also been commissioned to do an equestrian statue of the king. This project, for which he made a splendid terra-cotta model (fig. 239), shared the fate of his Louvre designs. Although he portrayed the king in Classical military garb, the statue was rejected; apparently it was too dynamic to safeguard the dignity of Louis XIV. This decision was farreaching, for equestrian statues of the king were later erected throughout France as symbols of royal authority, and Bernini's design, had it succeeded, might have set the pattern for these monuments. They were all destroyed in the French Revolution; we know them only from engravings, reproductions, and such models as that by François Girardon (fig. 240), who also did much garden sculpture at Versailles. Characteristically, this is an adaptation of the equestrian Marcus Aurelius on the Capitoline Hill (see fig. 69). While it may look static—lame, in fact—next to Bernini's design, its Baroque qualities show up clearly in comparison with its ancient prototype: the fluid modeling, the windblown movement of the king's cloak. There is even a hint at an "invisible complement"— instead of looking at us, the king raises his head and leans back as if communicating with some celestial power.

Rococo

ARCHITECTURE: GERMANY AND FRANCE

The ultimate development of the style invented by Borromini took place north of the Alps, in Austria and southern Germany. In these countries, ravaged by the Thirty Years' War, there was little building activity until near the end of the seventeenth century; Baroque was an imported style, practiced mainly by visiting Italians. Not until the 1690s did native designers come to the fore. There followed a fifty-year period of intense activity that gave rise to some of the most imaginative creations in the history of architecture. We must be content with a small sampling of these monuments, erected for the glorification of princes and prelates who, generally speaking, deserve to be remembered only as lavish patrons of the arts. Johann Fischer von Erlach, the first great architect of the Late Baroque in Central Europe, is linked most directly to the Italian tradition. His design for the Church of St.

Charles Borromaeus in Vienna (fig. 241) combines reminiscences of the exterior of St. Peter's and the portico of the Pantheon with a pair of huge columns which here substitute for façade towers. With these inflexible elements of Roman imperial art embedded in the elastic curvatures of his church, Fischer von Erlach expresses, more boldly than any Italian Baroque architect, the power of the Christian faith to absorb and transfigure the splendors of antiquity.

The architects of the next generation, among whom Balthasar Neumann was the most prominent, favored a tendency toward lightness and elegance. Neumann's largest project, the Episcopal Palace in Würzburg, includes the breath-taking Kaisersaal (colorplate 49), a great oval hall decorated in white, gold, and pastel shades—the favorite color scheme of the mid-eighteenth century. The structural members, such as columns, pilasters, and architraves, are minimized; windows and vault segments are framed with continuous, ribbonlike moldings, and the white surfaces are spun over with irregular

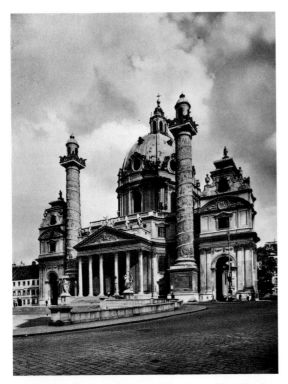

241. JOHANN FISCHER VON ERLACH. St. Charles Borromaeus. 1716–37. Vienna

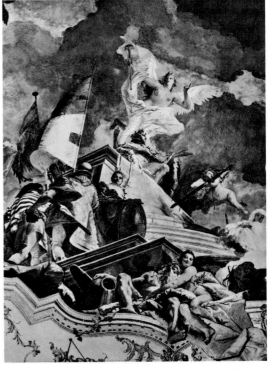

242. GIOVANNI BATTISTA TIEPOLO. Ceiling Fresco, Kaisersaal (detail). 1751. Episcopal Palace, Würzburg (see colorplate 49)

ornamental designs. This repertory of lacy, curling motifs, invented in France about 1700, is the hallmark of the Rococo style (see p. 279), which is here happily combined with German Late Baroque architecture. The membranelike ceiling so often gives way to illusionistic openings of every sort that we no longer feel it to be a spatial boundary. These openings do not, however, reveal avalanches of figures amid dramatic bursts of light, like those of Roman ceilings (compare colorplate 44), but blue sky and sunlit clouds, and an occasional winged creature soaring in this limitless expanse. Only along the edges are there solid clusters of figures (fig. 242). Here the last, and most refined, stage of illusionistic ceiling decoration is represented by its greatest master, Giovanni Battista Tiepolo. Venetian by birth and training, Tiepolo blended the tradition of High Baroque illusionism with the pageantry of Veronese. His mastery of light and color, the grace and felicity of his touch, made him famous far beyond his home territory. In the Würzburg frescoes his powers are at their height. He was afterward invited to decorate the Royal Palace in Madrid, where he spent his final years.

In France after the death of Louis XIV, the centralized administrative machine that Colbert had created ground to a stop. The nobility, hitherto attached to the court at Versailles, were now freer of royal surveillance. Many of them chose not to return to their ancestral homes in the provinces, but to live in Paris, where they built themselves elegant town houses, known as *hôtels*. Because these city sites were usually cramped and irregular, they offered scant opportunity for impressive exteriors; the layout and décor of the rooms became the architects' main concern. As the state-sponsored buildings became fewer, the field of "design for private living" took on new importance. The *hôtels* demanded a style of decoration less grandiloquent than Lebrun's—an intimate, flexible style that would give greater scope to individual fancy uninhibited by Classicistic dogma. French designers created the Rococo style in response to this need. Rococo was a refinement in miniature of the curvilinear, "elastic" Baroque of Borromini and Guarini, and thus could be happily united with Austrian and German

Late Baroque architecture. In France, most examples of the style, such as the Salon de la Princesse in the Hôtel de Soubise, by Germain Boffrand (fig. 243), are smaller in scale and less exuberant than those in Central Europe; the ceiling frescoes and the decorative sculpture in palaces and churches are unsuited to domestic interiors, however lavish. We must therefore remember that in France, Rococo painting and sculpture were less closely linked with their architectural settings than in Italy, Austria, and Germany, although they reflect the same taste that produced the Hôtel de Soubise. Characteristic of Rococo sculpture are small, coquettishly erotic groups designed to be viewed at close range, playful echoes of the ecstasies of Bernini. Monumental commissions were few, but the equestrian statue of Peter the Great, made for Catherine of Russia by Etienne Maurice Falconet (fig. 244), recaptures the essence of Baroque movement and grandeur. Bernini, we will recall, had proposed such a monument to Louis XIV (fig. 239), who turned him down because he found the rearing horse incompatible with royal dignity.

PAINTING: FRANCE

It is hardly surprising that the straitjacket of the French academic system produced no significant artists. Its absurd rigidity gener-

243. GERMAIN BOFFRAND. Salon de la Princesse, Hôtel de Soubise. Begun 1732. Paris

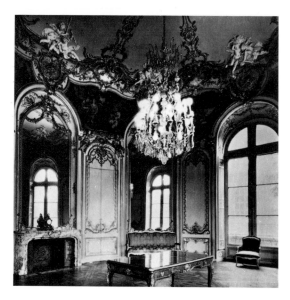

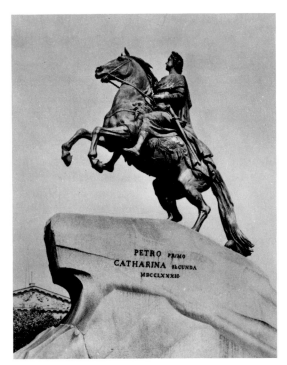

244. Etienne Maurice Falconet. *Equestrian Monument of Peter the Great*. 1766–82. Bronze, over lifesize. Leningrad

Academy, now very accommodating, invented for Watteau the new category of *fêtes galantes* (elegant fetes or entertainments). The term refers less to this one canvas than to the artist's work in general, which mainly shows scenes of elegant society, or comedy actors, in park-like settings. He characteristically interweaves theater and real life so that no clear distinction can be made between the two. The *Pilgrimage* includes yet another element, Classical mythology: these young couples have come to Cythera, the island of love, to pay homage to Venus (whose garlanded image appears on the far right). As the enchanted day draws to a close, they are about to go aboard the boat, accompanied by swarms of cupids, and be transported back to the everyday world. The style at once recalls Rubens' *Garden of Love* (see colorplate 45), but Watteau adds a poignant touch, a poetic subtlety of his own. His figures have not the robust vitality of Rubens'; slim and graceful, they move with the studied assurance of actors who play their roles so superbly that they touch us more than reality ever could.

Watteau signals the shift in French art and French society. Most subsequent French Rococo painting follows the "Rubéniste" style of Watteau, intimate in scale and deliciously sensual in style and subject, although without the emotional depth that distinguishes Watteau's art. The finest painter in this vein was Jean-Honoré Fragonard; his *Bathers* (colorplate 51) must here suffice to represent its class. A franker "Rubéniste" than Watteau, Fragonard paints with a fluid breadth and spontaneity reminiscent of Rubens' oil sketches (see fig. 220). His figures move with a floating grace that also links him with Tiepolo, whose work he had admired in Italy (compare fig. 242).

Yet there were other painters whose style can be termed Rococo only with reservations, such as Jean-Baptiste Siméon Chardin. The "Rubénistes" had cleared the way for a new interest in the Dutch masters as well, and Chardin was the finest painter of still life and genre representing this trend. His genre scenes, such as *Back from the Market* (colorplate 52), show life in a Parisian middle-class household with such feeling for the beauty hidden in the commonplace, and so

ated a counterpressure that vented itself as soon as Lebrun's authority began to decline. Toward 1700, the members of the Academy formed two warring factions over the issue of drawing versus color: the conservatives (or "Poussinistes") against the "Rubénistes." The former defended Poussin's view that drawing, which appealed to the mind, was superior to color, while the latter advocated color as being more true to nature. They also pointed out that drawing, admittedly based on reason, appeals only to the expert few, whereas color appeals to everyone. This argument had revolutionary implications, for it proclaimed the layman to be the ultimate judge of artistic values, and challenged the Renaissance view that painting, as a liberal art, could be appreciated only by the educated mind. In 1717, soon after Lous XIV's death, the "Rubénistes" scored a final triumph when Antoine Watteau was admitted to the Academy on the basis of *A Pilgrimage to Cythera* (colorplate 50). This picture violated all academic canons, and its subject did not conform to any established category. But the

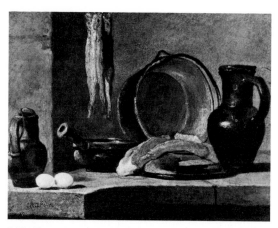

245. JEAN-BAPTISTE SIMEON CHARDIN. *Kitchen Still Life.* c. 1730–35. Canvas, 12 1/2 × 15 1/4″. Ashmolean Museum, Oxford

clear a sense of spatial order, that we can compare him only to Vermeer. But his remarkable technique is quite unlike any Dutch artist's. Devoid of bravura, his brushwork renders the light on colored surfaces with a creamy touch that is both analytical and subtly poetic. His still lifes usually reflect the same modest environment, eschewing the "object appeal" of their Dutch predecessors. In the example shown in figure 245, we see only the common objects that belong in any kitchen: earthenware jugs, a casserole, a copper pot, a piece of raw meat, smoked herring, two eggs. But how important they seem, each so firmly placed in relation to the rest, each so worthy of the artist's—and our —scrutiny! Despite his concern with formal problems, evident in the beautifully balanced design, Chardin treats these objects with a respect close to reverence. More than shapes, colors, and textures, they are to him symbols of the life of the common man. In spirit, if not in subject matter, Chardin is more akin to Louis Le Nain than to any Dutch painter.

It is from portraits that we perhaps gain the clearest understanding of the French Rococo, for the transformation of the image of man lies at the heart of the entire era. In portraits of the aristocracy, men were endowed with the illusion of character as a natural attribute of their station in life stemming from their noble birth. But the finest achievements of Rococo portraiture were reserved for women, hardly a surprising fact in a

society that idolized the cult of love and feminine beauty One of the finest practitioners in this vein was herself a beautiful woman: Marie-Louise-Elizabeth Vigée-Lebrun. Although Pliny's *Natural History* (Book XXXV) mentions the names and describes the work of women artists in Greece and Rome, and there are records of their accomplishments during the Middle Ages, women artists began to play a significantly noted role only in the seventeenth century. However, with few exceptions (notably Italians who were members of artistic families), seventeenth-century women artists were restricted to painting portraits and still lifes, which were deemed appropriately genteel, rather than more demanding narrative subjects. Within these more modest realms, however, many were able to carve out successful careers, often emerging as the equals or superiors of the men whose styles they emulated. Madame Vigée enjoyed great fame, which took her to every corner of Europe,

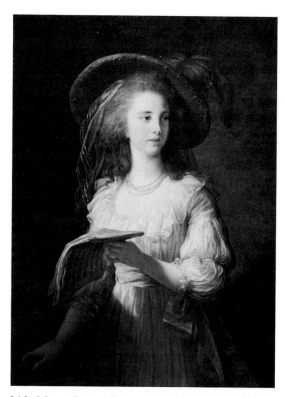

246. MARIE-LOUISE-ELIZABETH VIGÉE-LEBRUN. *Princesse de Polignac.* 1783. Canvas, 38 3/4 × 28″. National Trust, Waddesdon Manor. Photo: Courtesy Courtauld Institute of Art, London

including Russia, during the course of her long life. *Princesse de Polignac* (fig. 246) was painted a few years after Vigée began working for Marie Antoinette and amply demonstrates her ability. The princess has the eternally youthful loveliness of Fragonard's *Bathers* (colorplate 51), made all the more persuasive by the ravishing treatment of her clothing. At the same time, there is a sense of transience in the engaging mood which exemplifies the Rococo's whimsical theatricality. Interrupted in her singing, the lyrical princess becomes a real-life counterpart to the poetic creatures in Watteau's *Pilgrimage to Cythera* (colorplate 50) through the delicate sentiment she shares with the girl in Chardin's *Back from the Market* (colorplate 52).

ARCHITECTURE: ENGLAND

We have not considered English architecture since our discussion of the Perpendicular style (see p. 123). This insular form of Late Gothic proved extraordinarily persistent; it absorbed the stylistic vocabulary of the Italian Renaissance during the sixteenth century, but as late as 1600 English buildings still retained a "Perpendicular syntax." It was the influence of Palladio that finally brought this lingering Gothic tradition to an end, replacing it with an equally strong allegiance to Classicism. We can see this Classicism in some parts of St. Paul's Cathedral (fig. 247) by Sir Christopher Wren, the great English architect of the late seventeenth century: the dome looks like a vastly enlarged version of Bramante's Tempietto (see fig. 184). St. Paul's is otherwise an up-to-date Baroque design reflecting a thorough acquaintance with contemporary architecture in Italy and France. Sir Christopher came close to being a Baroque counterpart of the Renaissance artist-scientists. An intellectual prodigy, he studied anatomy first, then physics, mathematics, and astronomy, and was highly esteemed by Sir Isaac Newton. His serious interest in architecture did not begin until he was about thirty. There is, however, apparently no direct link between his scientific and artistic ideas. Had not the great London fire of 1666 destroyed the Gothic Cathedral of St. Paul, and many lesser churches, Sir Christopher might have remained an amateur

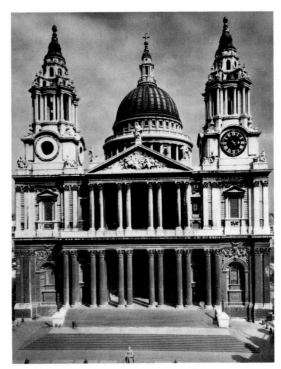

247. CHRISTOPHER WREN. Façade, St. Paul's Cathedral. 1675–1710. London

architect. But after that catastrophe he was named to the royal commission for rebuilding the city, and a few years later he began his designs for St. Paul's. On his only trip abroad, he had visited Paris at the time of the dispute over the completion of the Louvre, and he must have sided with Perrault, whose design for the East Front is clearly reflected in the façade of St. Paul's. Yet, despite his belief that Paris provided "the best school of architecture in Europe," Sir Christopher was not indifferent to the achievements of the Roman Baroque. He must have wanted the new St. Paul's to be the St. Peter's of the Church of England, soberer and less large, but equally impressive.

PAINTING: ENGLAND

England never accepted the Rococo style in architecture. French Rococo painting, on the other hand, had a decisive—though unacknowledged—effect across the Channel and helped to bring about the first school of English painting since the Middle Ages that had more than local importance. The earliest

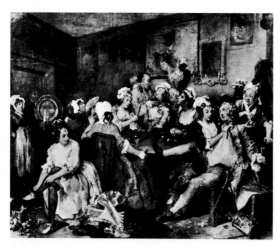

248. WILLIAM HOGARTH. *The Orgy,* Scene III from *The Rake's Progress.* c. 1734. Canvas, 24 1/2 × 29 1/2″. Sir John Soane's Museum, London

Portraiture remained the only constant source of income for English painters. Here, too, the eighteenth century produced a style that differed from the Continental traditions that had dominated this field ever since the days of Holbein. Its greatest master, Thomas Gainsborough, began by painting landscapes, but ended as the favorite portraitist of British high society. His early portraits, such as *Robert Andrews and His Wife* (colorplate 53), have a lyrical charm that is not always found in his later pictures. Compared to Van Dyck's artifice in *Charles I Hunting* (see fig. 222), these two people, members of the landed gentry, are naturally, and unpretentiously, at home in their setting. The landscape, although derived from Ruisdael and his school, has a sunlit, hospitable air never achieved (or desired) by the Dutch masters; and the casual grace of the figures indirectly recalls Watteau's style. Later portraits by Gainsborough, such as the very fine one of the great actress, Mrs. Siddons (fig. 249), have other virtues: a cool elegance that translates Van Dyck's aristocratic poses into late-

of these painters, William Hogarth, made his mark in the 1730s with a new kind of picture, which he described as "modern moral subjects . . . similar to representations on the stage." He wished to be judged as a dramatist, he said, even though his "actors" could only "exhibit a dumb show." These paintings, and the engravings he made from them for popular sale, came in sets, with details recurring in each scene to unify the sequence. Hogarth's "morality plays" teach, by horrid example, the solid middle-class virtues: they show a country girl who succumbs to the temptations of fashionable London; the evils of corrupt elections; aristocratic rakes who live only for ruinous pleasure, marrying wealthy women of lower status for their fortunes (which they promptly dissipate). In *The Orgy* (fig. 248), from *The Rake's Progress,* the young wastrel is overindulging in wine and women. The scene is so full of visual clues that a full account would take pages, plus constant references to the adjoining episodes. Yet, however literal-minded, the picture has great appeal. Hogarth combines some of Watteau's sparkle with Jan Steen's narrative gusto, and so entertains us that we enjoy his sermon without being overwhelmed by its message. He is probably the first artist in history to become also a social critic in his own right.

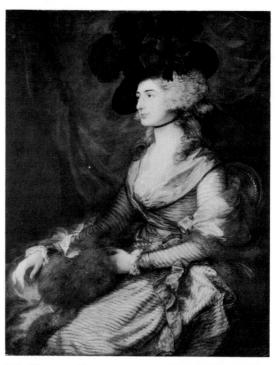

249. THOMAS GAINSBOROUGH. *Mrs. Siddons.* 1785. Oil on canvas, 49 1/2 × 39″. The National Gallery, London

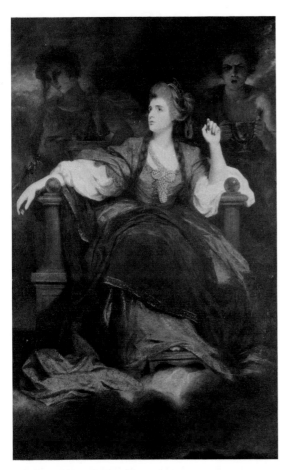

250. SIR JOSHUA REYNOLDS. *Mrs. Siddons as the Tragic Muse.* 1784. Oil on canvas, 93 × 57 1/2″. Henry E. Huntington Library and Art Gallery, San Marino, California

eighteenth-century terms, and a fluid, translucent technique reminiscent of Rubens. Gainsborough painted *Mrs. Siddons* in conscious opposition to his great rival on the London scene, Sir Joshua Reynolds, who a year before had portrayed the same sitter as the Tragic Muse (fig. 250). Reynolds, the President of the Royal Academy since its founding in 1768, was the protagonist of the academic approach to art, which he had acquired during two years in Rome. Like his French predecessors, he formulated in his famous *Discourses* what he felt were necessary rules and theories. His views were essentially those of Lebrun, tempered by British common sense. Again like Lebrun, he found it difficult to live up to his theories in actual practice. Although he preferred history painting in the grand style, the vast majority of his works are portraits "ennobled," whenever possible, by allegorical additions or disguises like those in his picture of Mrs. Siddons. His style owed a good deal more to the Venetians, the Flemish Baroque, and even to Rembrandt (note the lighting in *Mrs. Siddons*) than he would concede in theory. While both portraits of Mrs. Siddons are distinctly English in character, their relationship to the Rococo style of France is unmistakable—note their resemblance to Vigée's *Princesse de Polignac* (fig. 246) of almost the same period.

SYNOPTIC TABLE III

	POLITICAL HISTORY	RELIGION, LITERATURE	SCIENCE, TECHNOLOGY
1300		Petrarch, first humanist (1304–74) Boccaccio (1313–75)	
1400		Leonardo Bruni (c. 1374–44) Leone Battista Alberti (1404–72) Council of Florence attempts to reunite Catholic and Orthodox faiths 1439	Prince Henry the Navigator of Portugal (1394–1460) promotes geographic exploration
1450	End of Hundred Years' War 1453; Joan of Arc Ferdinand and Isabella unite Spain 1469 Spain and Portugal divide New World 1493–94 Charles VIII of France invades Italy 1494–99	Marsilio Ficino (1433–99) Sebastian Brant's *Ship of Fools* 1494 Savonarola burned at the stake for heresy in Florence 1498	Bartholomeu Diaz rounds Cape of Good Hope 1486 Christopher Columbus discovers America 1492 Vasco da Gama reaches India, returns to Lisbon 1497–99
1500	Charles V elected Holy Roman Emperor 1519 Hernando Cortés wins Aztec Empire in Mexico for Spain 1519 Henry VIII of England (r. 1509–47) founds Anglican Church 1534 Wars of Lutheran vs. Catholic princes in Germany; Peace of Augsburg (1555) lets each sovereign decide religion of his subjects	Erasmus of Rotterdam's *Praise of Folly* 1511 Thomas More's *Utopia* 1516 Martin Luther (1483–1546) posts theses 1517; excommunicated and outlawed 1521 Castiglione's *The Courtier* 1528 Ignatius of Loyola founds Jesuit Order 1534	Vasco de Balboa sights Pacific Ocean 1513 First circumnavigation of the globe by Ferdinand Magellan and crew 1520–22

NOTE:

Figure numbers of black-and-white illustrations are in (italics). Colorplate numbers are in (bold face).
Duration of papacy or reign is indicated by the abbreviation r.

ARCHITECTURE	SCULPTURE	PAINTING	
			1300
Brunelleschi begins career as architect 1419; Florence Cathedral dome (*124*); S. Lorenzo (*165*) Michelozzo, Palazzo Medici-Ricardi (*166*)	Donatello, *St. George* (*156*) Donatello, *"Zuccone"* (*157*) Donatello, *David* (*158*) Ghiberti, "*Gates of Paradise*" (*160*) Donatello, *Gattamelata* (*159*)	Masaccio, *Trinity* fresco (**27**) Master of Flémalle, *Merode Altarpiece* (**22**) Jan van Eyck, *Ghent Altarpiece* (*145, 146*); *Arnolfini and Bride* (*148*, **24**) Rogier van der Weyden, *Descent from the Cross* (**25**) Witz, Geneva altarpiece (*152*) Domenico Veneziano, *Madonna and Child with Saints* (**28**)	1400
Alberti, S. Andrea, Mantua (*167*) Giuliano da Sangallo, Sta. Maria delle Carceri, Prato (*168*)	Antonio Rossellino, *Giovanni Chellini* (*162*) Luca della Robbia, *Madonna and Angels* (*161*) Verrocchio, *Putto* (*164*) Pollaiuolo, *Hercules and Antaeus* (*163*)	Mantegna, Ovetari Chapel frescoes (*174*) Piero della Francesca, Arezzo frescoes (*169*) Pollaiuolo, *Battle of Ten Naked Men*, engraving (*172*) Hugo van der Goes, *Portinari Altarpiece* (*149*) Schongauer, *Temptation of Anthony*, engraving (*154*) Botticelli, *Birth of Venus* (**29**) Leonardo, *Adoration of the Magi* (*176*) Giovanni Bellini, *St. Francis* (**31**) Leonardo, *Last Supper* (*177*) Dürer, *Four Horsemen of the Apocalypse*, woodcut (*204*)	1450
Bramante, Tempietto, Rome (*184*) Michelangelo becomes architect of St. Peter's, 1546 (*187*) Lescot, Louvre court (*210*)	Michelangelo, *David* (*179*) Cellini, Saltcellar of Francis I (*199*) Goujon, *Fountain of the Innocents* (*211*)	Bosch, *Garden of Delights* (*155*, **26**) Leonardo, *Mona Lisa* (**32**) Giorgione, *Tempest* (**34**) Michelangelo, Sistine Ceiling (*181*) Raphael, *School of Athens* (**33**) Grünewald, *Isenheim Altarpiece* (*202*, **39**) Titian, *Bacchanal* (**35**) Rosso, *Descent from the Cross* (**36**) Dürer, *Self-Portrait* (*203*) Correggio, *Assumption of the Virgin* (*195*) Altdorfer, *Battle of Issus* (**40**) Parmigianino, *Madonna with Long Neck* (**37**) Michelangelo, *Last Judgment* (*180, 182*) Holbein, *Henry VIII* (**41**)	1500

	POLITICAL HISTORY	RELIGION, LITERATURE	SCIENCE, TECHNOLOGY
1550	Elizabeth I of England (r. 1558–1603) Netherlands revolt against Spain 1568 Spanish Armada defeated by English 1588 Lutheranism becomes state religion in Denmark 1560, in Sweden 1593	Council of Trent 1545–63 St. Theresa of Avila (1515–82) Miguel de Cervantes (1547–1616) William Shakespeare (1564–1616)	
1600	Jamestown, Virginia, founded 1607; Plymouth, Mass., 1620 Cardinal Mazarin governs France during minority of Louis XIV 1643–61 (civil war 1648–53) Charles I of England beheaded 1649; Commonwealth under Cromwell 1649–53	King James Bible 1611 René Descartes (1596–1650)	Harvey describes circulation of blood 1628 Galileo (1564–1642)
1650	Parliament passes Habeas Corpus Act 1679 Louis XIV absolute ruler of France (r. 1661–1715)	Molière (1622–73) Pascal (1623–62) Racine (1639–99) Milton's *Paradise Lost* 1667 Bunyan's *Pilgrim's Progress* 1678	Isaac Newton (1642–1727)
1700	Peter the Great (r. 1682–1725) westernizes Russia, defeats Sweden	Defoe's *Robinson Crusoe* 1719 Swift's *Gulliver's Travels* 1726 Wesley brothers found Methodism 1738 Voltaire (1694–1778)	
1750	Seven Years' War (1756–63); called French and Indian War in U.S.		

ARCHITECTURE	SCULPTURE	PAINTING	
Palladio, Villa Rotonda, Vicenza (*201*)	Giovanni da Bologna, *The Abduction of the Sabine Woman* (*200*)	Bruegel, *Land of Cockayne* (**42**) Veronese, *Christ in the House of Levi* (*198*) El Greco, *Burial of Count Orgaz* (**38**) Caravaggio, *Calling of St. Matthew* (**43**) Annibale Carracci, Farnese Gallery Ceiling (*212*)	1550
Maderno, nave and façade of St. Peter's; Bernini's colonnade (*213*) Borromini, S. Carlo alle Quattro Fontane, Rome, plan (*217*)	Bernini, *David* (*214*) Bernini, Cornaro Chapel (*215*)	Rubens, *Raising of the Cross* (*219*) Hals, *Jolly Toper* (**46**) Rembrandt, *Blinding of Samson* (*225*) Poussin, *Burial of Phocion* (*234*)	1600
Borromini, S. Carlo alle Quattro Fontane, Rome, façade (*217*) Perrault, east front of Louvre (*236*) Le Vau and Hardouin-Mansart, Versailles (*238*) Wren, St. Paul's, London (*247*)	Bernini, Model for Equestrian Statue of Louis XIV (*239*) Girardon, Model for Equestrian Statue of Louis XIV (*240*)	Ruisdael, *The Cemetery* (*228*) Rembrandt, *The Polish Rider* (**47**) Velázquez, *Maids of Honor* (*223*) Vermeer, *The Letter* (**48**)	1650
Neumann, Episcopal Palace, Würzburg (**49**) Boffrand, Hôtel de Soubise (*243*)		Watteau, *A Pilgrimage to Cythera* (**50**) Hogarth, *Rake's Progress* (*248*) Chardin, *Back from the Market* (**52**) Gainsborough, *Robert Andrews and His Wife* (**53**)	1700
	Falconet, Equestrian monument of Peter the Great (*244*)	Tiepolo, Würzburg ceiling fresco (*242*) Fragonard, *Bathers* (**51**)	1750

The
Modern
World

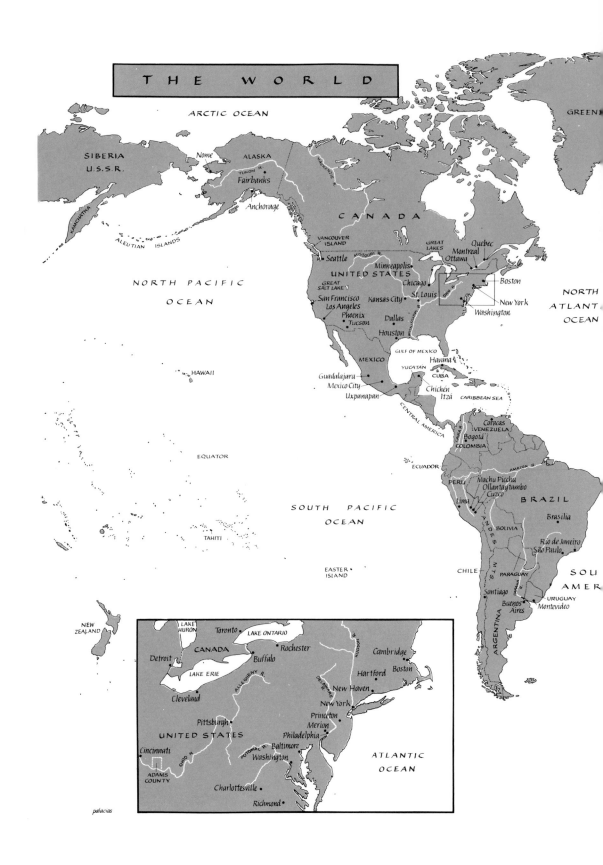

THE WORLD

ARCTIC OCEAN

GREEN

SIBERIA
U.S.S.R.

Nome

ALASKA

Fairbanks

Anchorage

CANADA

KAMCHATKA

ALEUTIAN ISLANDS

VANCOUVER
ISLAND

GREAT
LAKES

Quebec
Montreal
Ottawa

NORTH PACIFIC

OCEAN

Seattle

UNITED STATES

GREAT
SALT LAKE

San Francisco
Los Angeles
Phoenix
Tucson

Chicago

Kansas City

St. Louis

Boston

New York
Washington

NORTH
ATLANT
OCEAN

Minneapolis

Dallas

Houston

GULF OF MEXICO

MEXICO

YUCATAN

Havana

CUBA

HAWAII

Guadalajara
Mexico City
Uxpanapan

Chichén
Itzá

CARIBBEAN SEA

CENTRAL AMERICA

Caracas
VENEZUELA
Bogotá
COLOMBIA

EQUATOR

ECUADOR

PERU

Machu Picchu
Ollantaytambo
Cuzco

BRAZIL

SOUTH   PACIFIC

OCEAN

TAHITI

Lima

BOLIVIA

Brasília

Rio de Janeiro
São Paulo

EASTER
ISLAND

CHILE

PARAGUAY

ANDES MTS.

SOU
AMER

NEW
ZEALAND

Santiago

ARGENTINA

Buenos
Aires

URUGUAY
Montevideo

LAKE
HURON

Toronto

LAKE ONTARIO

Rochester

CANADA

Detroit

Buffalo

Cambridge

Boston

LAKE ERIE

Hartford

Cleveland

Pittsburgh

ALLEGHENY R.

DELAWARE R.

New Haven

New York

Princeton
Merion
Philadelphia

UNITED STATES

Cincinnati

OHIO R.

POTOMAC R.

Baltimore
Washington

ATLANTIC

OCEAN

ADAMS
COUNTY

Charlottesville

Richmond

palacios

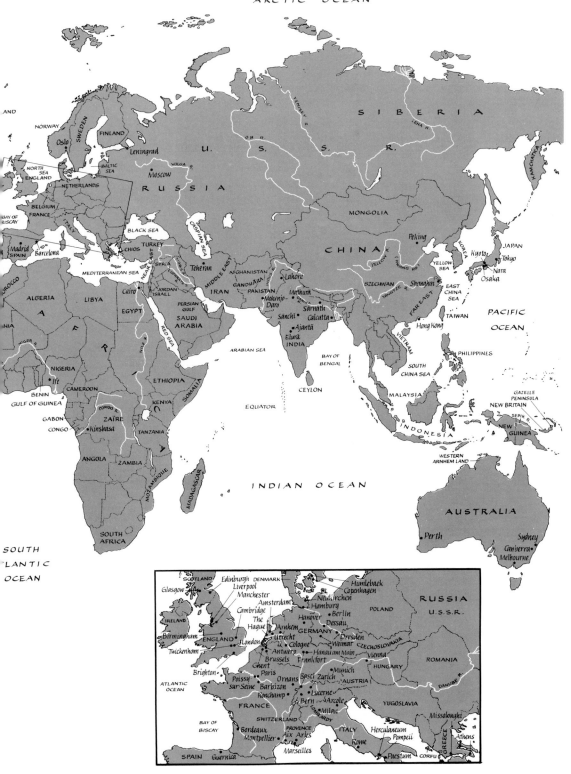

ARCTIC OCEAN

NORWAY
Oslo
SWEDEN
FINLAND
Leningrad
Moscow
NORTH SEA
ENGLAND
BALTIC SEA
NETHERLANDS
BELGIUM
FRANCE
BAY OF BISCAY
ITALY
Madrid
SPAIN
Barcelona
MOROCCO
ALGERIA
LIBYA
Cairo
EGYPT
BLACK SEA
CHIOS
TURKEY
SYRIA
Tcheran
JORDAN
ISRAEL
MEDITERRANEAN SEA
NEAR EAST
MIDDLE EAST
CASPIAN SEA
VOLGA R.
RUSSIA
OB R.
U. S. S. R.
YENISEI R.
SIBERIA
LENA R.
KAMCHATKA

IRAN
PERSIAN GULF
SAUDI ARABIA
RED SEA
NILE R.
AFGHANISTAN
GANDHĀRA
PAKISTAN
Lahore
Mohenjo-Daro
Mathurā
Sānchi
Ajantā
Elurā
Sārnath
Calcutta
INDIA
MONGOLIA
CHINA
Peking
SZECHWAN
HWANG HO
YELLOW R.
YANGTZE R.
Shanghai
KOREA
Kyoto
Nara
Osaka
Tokyo
JAPAN
YELLOW SEA
EAST CHINA SEA
FAR EAST
TAIWAN
Hong Kong
PACIFIC OCEAN

NIGER R.
NIGERIA
Ife
BENIN
CAMEROON
GULF OF GUINEA
GABON
CONGO
CONGO R.
ZAÏRE
Kinshasa
KENYA
ETHIOPIA
SOMALIA
TANZANIA
ZAMBIA
ANGOLA
MOZAMBIQUE
MADAGASCAR
SOUTH AFRICA

ARABIAN SEA
EQUATOR
CEYLON
BAY OF BENGAL
VIETNAM
SOUTH CHINA SEA
MALAYSIA
PHILIPPINES
INDONESIA
GAZELLE PENINSULA
NEW BRITAIN
SEPIK R.
NEW GUINEA
WESTERN ARNHEM LAND

INDIAN OCEAN

SOUTH ATLANTIC OCEAN

AUSTRALIA
Perth
Sydney
Canberra
Melbourne

SCOTLAND
Glasgow
Edinburgh
Liverpool
Manchester
Cambridge
IRELAND
Birmingham
ENGLAND
London
Twickenham
Brighton
DENMARK
Humlebaek
Copenhagen
Neukirchen
Hamburg
Amsterdam
Hanover
Dessau
Berlin
POLAND
RUSSIA
U.S.S.R.
The Hague
Utrecht
Arnhem
Cologne
Antwerp
Hanau am Main
GERMANY
Dresden
Weimar
CZECHOSLOVAKIA
Ghent
Brussels
Frankfort
Vienna
HUNGARY
ROMANIA
Paris
Poissy-sur-Seine
Ornans
Barbizon
Ronchamp
FRANCE
Basel Zurich
Lucerne
Bern
Arcole
AUSTRIA
Munich
Milan
LOMBARDY
YUGOSLAVIA
DANUBE R.
Missolonghi
SWITZERLAND
PROVENCE
Aix Arles
Marseilles
Bordeaux
Montpellier
BAY OF BISCAY
ATLANTIC OCEAN
SPAIN
Guernica
ITALY
Rome
Herculaneum
Pompeii
Paestum
GREECE
CORFU
Athens

Introduction

The era to which we belong has not yet acquired a name of its own. Perhaps this does not strike us as peculiar at first, but considering how promptly the Renaissance coined a name for itself, we may well wonder why no such key idea has emerged in the two centuries since our era began. Perhaps "revolution" is a suitable concept, since rapid and violent change has indeed characterized the development of the modern world. Our era began with revolutions of two kinds: the industrial revolution, symbolized by the steam engine, and the political revolution, under the banner of democracy, in America and France. Both revolutions are still continuing—industrialization and democracy are world-wide goals. Western science and Western political ideology (and in their wake the various other products of modern Western civilization, from food and dress to art and literature) will soon belong to all mankind. We tend to think of these two movements as different aspects of one process—with effects more far-reaching than any since the New Stone Age revolution (see p. 14)—yet the twin revolutions of modern times are not identical. The more we try to define their relationship, the more paradoxical it seems. Both are founded on the idea of progress, and both command an emotional allegiance that was once reserved for religion; but while progress in science and industry during the past two centuries has been continuous and palpable, we can hardly make this claim for man's pursuit of happiness, however we choose to define it.

Here, then, is the conflict fundamental to our era. Man today, having cast off the framework of traditional authority which confined and sustained him before, can act with a latitude both frightening and exhilarating. In a world where all values may be questioned, man searches constantly for his own identity, and for the meaning of human existence, both individual and collective. His knowledge about himself is now vastly greater, but this has not reassured him as he had hoped. Modern civilization thus lacks the cohesiveness of the past; it no longer proceeds by readily identifiable periods, nor are

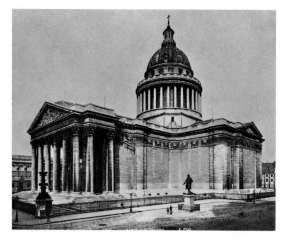

251. JACQUES GERMAIN SOUFFLOT. The Panthéon (Ste.-Geneviève). 1755–92. Paris

there clear period styles in art or in any other form of endeavor. Instead, we find another kind of continuity, that of movements and countermovements. Spreading like waves, these "isms" defy national, ethnic, and chronological boundaries; never dominant anywhere for long, they compete or merge with each other in endlessly shifting patterns. Hence our account of modern art must be by movements rather than by countries; for, all regional differences notwithstanding, modern art is as international as modern science.

Neoclassicism

ARCHITECTURE

If the modern era was born during the American Revolution of 1776 and the French Revolution of 1789, these cataclysmic events were preceded by a revolution of the mind that had begun half a century earlier. Its standard-bearers were those thinkers of the Enlightenment in England and France—Hume, Voltaire, Rousseau, and others—who proclaimed that all human affairs ought to be ruled by reason and the common good, rather than by tradition and established authority. In the arts, as in economics, politics, and religion, this rationalist movement turned against the prevailing practice: the ornate and aristocratic Baroque-Rococo. In the mid-eighteenth century the call for a return to reason, nature, and morality in art, meant a return to the ancients—after all, had not the

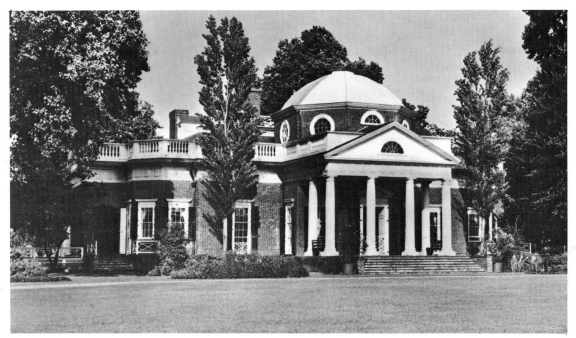

252. Thomas Jefferson. Garden Façade, Monticello. 1770–84; 1796–1806. Charlottesville, Virginia

Classic philosophers been the original "apostles of reason"? In 1755, when the German art historian and critic Johann Winckelmann published a famous tract urging the imitation of the "noble simplicity and calm grandeur" of the Greeks, the first great monument of the new style was begun in Paris: the Panthéon (fig. 251) by Jacques Germain Soufflot, built as a church but secularized during the Revolution. The smooth, sparsely decorated surfaces are abstractly severe, while the huge portico is modeled directly on ancient Ro-

man temples. What distinguishes this cool, precise Neoclassicism from earlier Classicisms is less its external appearance than its motivation; instead of merely reasserting the superior authority of the ancients, it claimed to be more rational, and hence more "natural," than the Baroque. In England and America, the same trend produced the architectural style known as "Georgian." A fine example is Monticello, the home Thomas Jefferson designed for himself in Virginia (fig. 252). Executed in brick with wooden

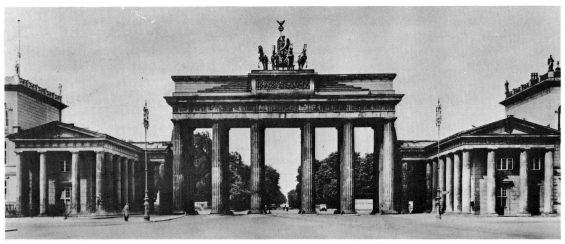

253. Karl Langhans. The Brandenburg Gate. 1788–91. Berlin

trim, it is less austere than the Panthéon, except for the use of the Doric order. Jefferson still preferred the Roman Doric, but late eighteenth-century taste began to favor the heavier and more "authentic" Greek Doric, in what is known as the Greek Revival phase of Neoclassicism. Greek Doric, however, was also the least flexible order, and so was particularly difficult to adapt to modern requirements even when combined with Roman or Renaissance elements. Only rarely could it furnish a direct model for Neoclassic structures, as in the Brandenburg Gate in Berlin (fig. 253), derived from the Propylaea (see fig. 46).

PAINTING: GREUZE; DAVID

In painting, the anti-Rococo trend was initially a matter of content rather than style. This accounts for the sudden popularity, about 1760, of Jean-Baptiste Greuze: *The Village Bride* (fig. 254), like the other pictures he painted during those years, is a scene of lower-class family life. In contrast to earlier genre paintings (compare fig. 230) it has a contrived, stage-like character, borrowed from the "dumb-show" narratives of Hogarth (see fig. 248). But Greuze has neither wit nor satire. His pictorial sermon illustrates the social gospel of the Enlightenment—that the poor, unlike the immoral aristocracy, are full of "natural" virtue and honest sentiment. Everything is calculated to remind us of this, from the declamatory gestures and expressions of the actors to the hen with her chicks in the foreground: one chick has left the brood and sits alone on a saucer, like the bride who is about to leave *her* "brood." *The Village Bride* was acclaimed as a masterpiece. Here at last was a painter who appealed to the beholder's moral sense instead of merely giving him pleasure like the frivolous artists of the Rococo! The highest praise came from

254. JEAN-BAPTISTE GREUZE. *The Village Bride.* 1761. Canvas, 36 × 46 1/2″. The Louvre, Paris

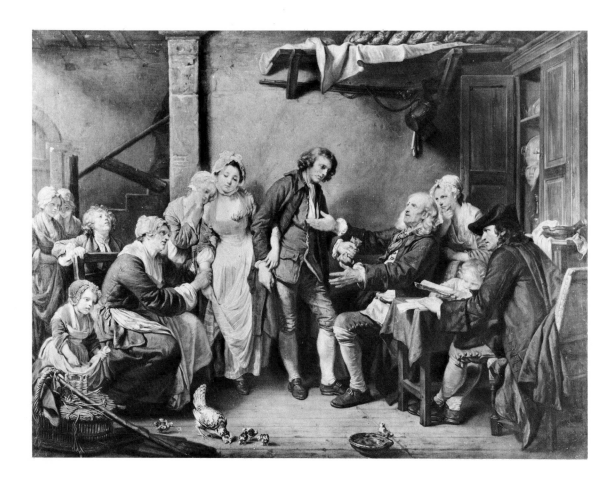

Diderot, that apostle of Reason and Nature, who accepted such narratives as "noble and serious human action" in Poussin's sense (see p. 274). Later, he modified his views when a far more gifted and rigorous "Neo-Poussinist" appeared on the scene—Jacques Louis David. In *The Death of Socrates* (colorplate 54), David seems more "Poussiniste" than Poussin himself (compare fig. 233); the composition unfolds like a relief, parallel to the picture plane, and the figures are as solid—and as immobile —as statues. Yet there is one unexpected element: the lighting, with its precisely cast shadows, is derived from Caravaggio (see colorplate 43), and so is the firmly realistic detail. Consequently, the picture has a quality of life rather astonishing in so doctrinaire a statement of the new ideal style. The very harshness of the design suggests that its creator was passionately engaged in the issues of his time, artistic as well as political. Socrates, about to drain the poison cup, is shown here not only as an example of Ancient Virtue but as a Christ-like figure (there are twelve disciples in the scene).

David took an active part in the French Revolution, and for some years he practically controlled the artistic affairs of the nation. During this time he painted his greatest picture, *The Death of Marat* (fig. 255). David's deep emotion has created a masterpiece from a subject that would have embarrassed any lesser artist: for Marat, one of the political leaders of the Revolution, had been murdered in his bathtub. A painful skin condition caused him to do his paperwork there, with a wooden board for a desk. One day a young woman named Charlotte Corday burst in with a personal petition and plunged a knife into him while he read it. David has composed the scene with a stark directness that is truly awe-inspiring. In this canvas, a public memorial to the martyred hero, devotional image and historical account coincide. Because Classical art could offer little guidance here, the artist has again drawn upon the Caravaggesque tradition of religious art.

WEST; COPLEY

The martyrdom of another hero was immortalized by Benjamin West in *The Death of General Wolfe* (fig. 256). West came to

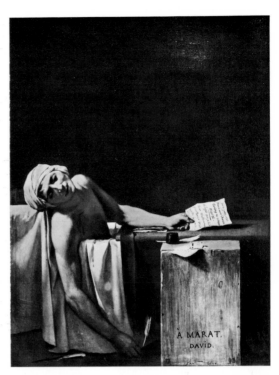

255. JACQUES LOUIS DAVID. *The Death of Marat.* 1793. Canvas, 65 × 50 1/2″. Museums of Fine Arts, Brussels

Rome in 1760 from Pennsylvania and caused something of a sensation, since no American painter had appeared in Europe before. He relished his role of frontiersman and always took pride in his New World background, even after he had settled in London, where he succeeded Reynolds as president of the Royal Academy. We can sense this in *The Death of General Wolfe*, his most famous work. Wolfe's death in the siege of Quebec, during the French and Indian War, had aroused considerable feeling in London. When West decided to paint it, two approaches were open to him: he could give a factual account with the maximum of historical accuracy, or he could idealize it in the manner of the "Neo-Poussinist" painters, with the figures in "timeless" Classical costume. Although he had absorbed the influence of the Neo-Poussinists in Rome, he did not follow them in this painting; he knew the American locale of the subject too well for that. Instead, he merged the two approaches: his figures wear modern dress, and the conspicuous Indian

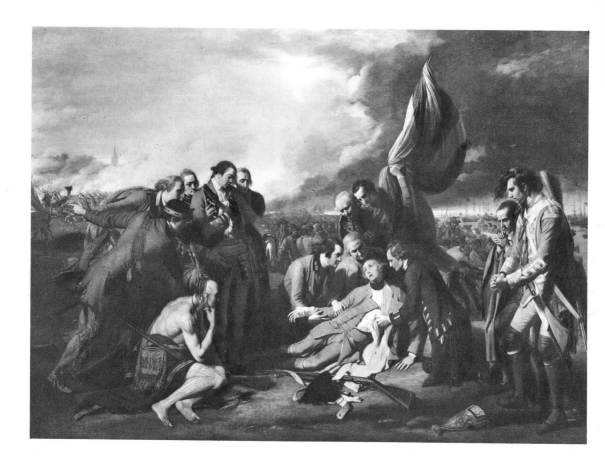

256. BENJAMIN WEST. *The Death of General Wolfe.*
1770. Canvas, 59 1/2 × 84″. National Gallery of
Canada, Ottawa

places the event in the New World, yet all of
the attitudes and expressions are "heroic."
The composition indeed recalls an old and
hallowed theme, the lamentation over the
dead Christ (see colorplate 25), dramatized
by Baroque lighting. West thus endowed the
death of a modern hero both with the rhetorical pathos of "noble and serious human
action" as defined by Poussin, and with the
trappings of a real event. He created an
image that expresses a phenomenon basic to
modern times, the shift of emotional allegiance from religion to nationalism. No
wonder his picture had countless successors
during the nineteenth century.

John Singleton Copley of Boston moved to
London just two years before the American
Revolution. Already an accomplished por-
traitist, he now turned to history painting in

the manner of West. His first work in that
field was *Watson and the Shark* (colorplate
55). Watson, a young Englishman attacked
by a shark while swimming in Havana
harbor, had been dramatically rescued; many
years later he commissioned Copley to depict
his gruesome experience. Perhaps he thought
that only a painter from America could do
full justice to the exotic nature of the subject.
Copley, following West's example, has made
every detail as authentic as possible (note the
Negro, who serves the same purpose as the
Indian in West's picture), while making use
of all the resources of Baroque painting to
invite the emotional participation of the
beholder. The shark becomes a monstrous
embodiment of evil, the man with the boat
hook resembles an Archangel Michael fighting Satan, and the nude youth flounders help-
lessly between the forces of doom and salvation. This kind of moral allegory is typical of
Neoclassicism as a whole, and despite its
charged emotion, the picture has the same
logic and clarity found in David's *Death of
Socrates.*

SCULPTURE

The development of Neoclassic sculpture follows the pattern of architecture and painting but is less venturesome than either. Sculptors were overwhelmed by the authority accorded (since Winckelmann) to ancient statues; how could a modern artist compete with these works, which everyone acclaimed as the acme of sculptural achievement? At the same time, the new standard of uncompromising realistic "truth" embarrassed the sculptor. When a painter renders anatomical detail, clothing, or furniture with photographic precision he produces not a duplicate of reality but a representation of it, while to do so in sculpture comes dangerously close to mechanical reproduction—a handmade equivalent of the plaster cast. Thus, as we might deduce, portraiture proved the most viable field for Neo-

classic sculpture. Its most distinguished practitioner, Jean Antoine Houdon, has an acute sense of individual character. His fine statue of Voltaire (fig. 257) does full justice to the sitter's skeptical wit and wisdom, and the Classical drapery enveloping the famous sage —to stress his equivalence to ancient philosophers—is not incongruous, for he wears it as casually as a dressing gown. The more doctrinaire Neoclassic sculptors often adopted a less happy solution by portraying their sitters in Classic nudity.

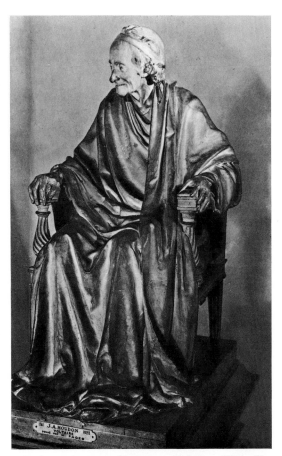

257. JEAN ANTOINE HOUDON. *Voltaire.* 1781. Terra-cotta model for marble, height 47″. Fabre Museum, Montpellier, France

The Romantic Movement

The Enlightenment, paradoxically, liberated not only reason but also its opposite: it helped to create a new wave of emotionalism that was to last for the better part of a century, and came to be known as Romanticism. Those who, in the mid-eighteenth century, shared a revulsion against the established social order and religion—against established values of any sort—could either try to found a new order based upon their faith in the power of reason, or they could seek release in a craving for emotional experience. Their common denominator was a desire to "return to Nature." The rationalist acclaimed Nature as the ultimate source of reason, while the Romantic worshiped her as unbounded, wild and ever-changing, sublime and picturesque. If man were only to behave "naturally," the Romantic believed, giving his impulses free rein, evil would disappear. In the name of nature, he exalted liberty, power, love, violence, the Greeks, the Middle Ages, or anything else that aroused him, although actually he exalted emotion as an end in itself. In its most extreme form, this attitude could be expressed only through direct action, not through works of art. (It has motivated some of the noblest—and vilest—acts of our era.) No artist, then, can be a wholehearted Romantic, for the creation of a work of art demands some detachment, self-awareness, and discipline. What Wordsworth, the great Romantic poet, said of poetry—that it is "emotion recollected in tranquillity"—applies also to the visual arts. To cast his experience into permanent form, the Romantic artist needs a style. But since he is in revolt against the old order, this cannot be the established style of his time; he must search for some phase of the past to which he can feel linked by "elective affinity" (another Romantic concept). Romanticism thus favors the revival, not of one style, but of a potentially unlimited number of styles. In fact, revivals—the rediscovery and utilization of forms hitherto neglected or disliked—became a stylistic principle: the "style" of Romanticism in art (also, to a degree, in literature and music). It can be argued that, seen in this context, Neoclassicism was no more than an aspect of Romanticism—at least during the nineteenth century.

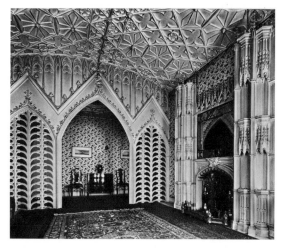

258. HORACE WALPOLE, with WILLIAM ROBINSON and others. Strawberry Hill. 1749–77. Twickenham, England

ARCHITECTURE

Given the individualistic nature of Romanticism, we might expect the range of revival styles to be widest in painting, the most personal and private of the visual arts, and narrowest in architecture, the most communal and public form of expression. Yet the opposite is true. Painters and sculptors were unable to abandon Renaissance habits of representation, and they never really revived medieval art, or pre-Classic ancient art. Architects were not subject to this limitation, however, and the revival styles persisted longer in their work than in the other arts.

259. CHARLES BARRY and A. WELBY PUGIN. The Houses of Parliament. Begun 1836. London

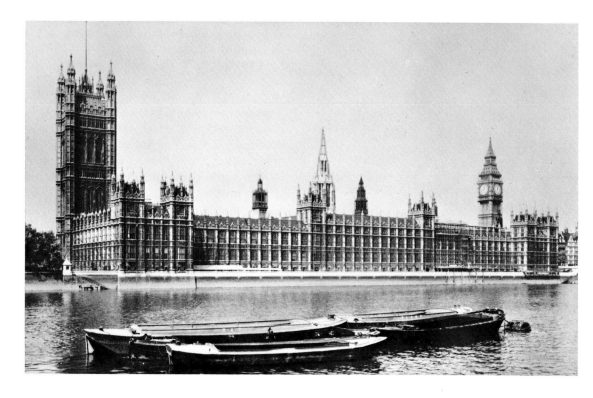

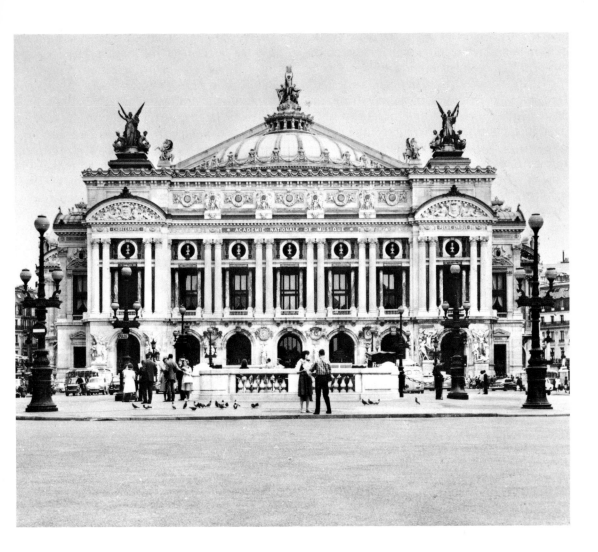

260. CHARLES GARNIER. The Opéra. 1861–74. Paris

Characteristically, at the time they launched the Classic revival, they also started a Gothic revival in architecture. England was far in advance here, as it was in the development of Romantic literature and painting. Horace Walpole, influential both as a man of letters and as an amateur of the arts, set the example for the others when, in 1749, he began to "gothicize" his country house, Strawberry Hill; its dainty, playful interiors (fig. 258) look almost as if decorated with lace-paper doilies. Gothic here is still an "exotic" style. It appeals because it is strange, like the Oriental tales of the *Thousand and One Nights*, or the medieval romances (such as the legends of King Arthur) that were being revived in the "Gothick" novels of the time.

After 1800, the choice between the Classic and Gothic modes was more often resolved in favor of Gothic. Nationalist sentiment, strengthened in the Napoleonic wars, favored the "native" style, for England, France, and Germany each tended to think that Gothic expressed its particular national genius. Thus, when a spectacular fire gutted the Houses of Parliament in London in 1834, the rebuilding had to be done in Gothic style (fig. 259). As the seat of a vast government apparatus, but at the same time a focus of patriotic feeling, it presents a curious mixture—repetitious symmetry governs the main body of the structure, and "picturesque" irregularity its silhouette. Meanwhile, the stylistic alternatives were continually increased for architects by other revivals. By the middle of the nineteenth century, the Renaissance and then the Baroque returned to favor, bringing the revival movement full circle. This last phase of Romantic architecture, which lingered on past 1900, is summed up in the Paris Opéra (fig. 260), designed by Charles Garnier. Its Neo-Baroque quality stems more from the profusion of sculpture and ornament than from its architectural vocabulary: the paired columns of the façade, "quoted" from the Louvre (see fig. 236), are combined with a smaller order, in Italian Renaissance fashion (compare fig. 198). The whole building looks "overdressed," its luxurious vulgarity so naïve as to be ultimately disarming. It reflects the taste of the beneficiaries of the industrial revolution, newly rich and powerful, who saw themselves as the heirs of the old aristocracy and thus found prerevolutionary styles more appealing than Classic or Gothic. This "architecture of conscious display" was divorced from the practical demands of the industrial age—the factories, warehouses, stores, and city apartments that formed the bulk of building construction. There, in the world of commercial architecture, we find soon after 1800 the gradual introduction of new materials and techniques that were to have a profound effect on architectural style by the end of the century. The most important was iron, never before used as an actual building material. Within a few decades of its first appearance, iron columns and arches

had become the standard means of supporting the roofs over the large spaces required by railroad stations, exhibition halls, and public libraries. A noted early example is the Bibliothèque Ste.-Geneviève in Paris, built by Henri Labrouste (fig. 261); in the reading room a row of cast-iron columns supports two barrel roofs resting on cast-iron arches. Labrouste chose to leave this iron skeleton uncovered, and to face the difficulty of relating it to the massive Renaissance revival style of his building. If his solution does not fully integrate the two systems, it at least allows them to coexist. The iron columns are as slender as the new material permits; their collective effect is that of a space-dividing screen, belying their structural importance, even though Labrouste has tried to make them weightier by putting them on tall pedestals of solid masonry. With the arches, Labrouste has gone to the other extreme: since there was no way to make them look as powerful as their masonry ancestors, he has perforated them with lacy scrolls as if they were pure ornament. This aesthetic use of exposed iron members has a fanciful and delicate air that links it, indirectly, to the Gothic revival.

SCULPTURE

In sculpture, as we suggested earlier, there was no Gothic revival, despite some isolated essays in that direction. Instead, we find at first an adaptation of the Neoclassical style to new ends by sculptors, especially older ones. The most famous of them, Antonio Canova, produced a colossal nude statue of Napoleon, inspired by portraits of ancient rulers whose nudity indicates their status as divinities. The elevation of the emperor to a god marks a shift away from the noble ideals of the Enlightenment that had given rise to Neoclassicism. The glorification of the hero as a noble example is abandoned in favor of the Romantic cult of the individual. Not to be outdone, Napoleon's sister Pauline Borghese permitted Canova to sculpt her as a reclining Venus (fig. 262). The statue is so obviously idealized as to still any gossip; we recognize it as a precursor, more Classically proportioned, of Ingres' *Odalisque* (see colorplate 57). She is equally typical of early Ro-

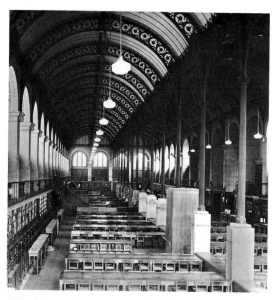

261. HENRI LABROUSTE. Reading Room, Bibliothèque Ste.-Geneviève. 1843–50. Paris

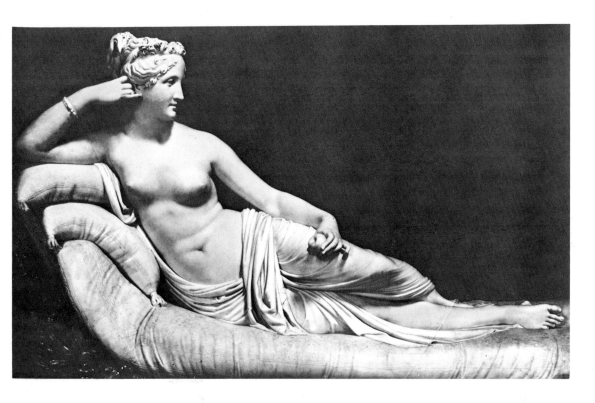

262. ANTONIO CANOVA. *Pauline Borghese as Venus.*
1808. Marble, lifesize. Borghese Gallery, Rome

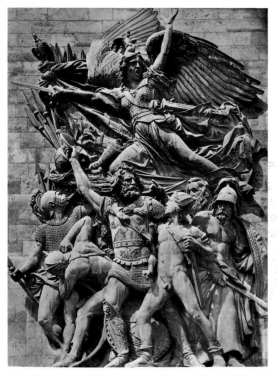

263. FRANÇOIS RUDE. *La Marseillaise.* 1833–36.
Stone, c. 42 × 26′. Arc de Triomphe, Paris

manticism, which incorporated Rococo eroticism but in a less sensuous form. Strangely
enough, *Pauline Borghese* seems less three-
dimensional than the painting. She is designed like a "relief in the round," for front
and back view only, and her very considerable charm radiates almost entirely from the
fluid grace of her contours. Here we again
encounter the problem of representation
versus duplication (see page 299), not in the
figure itself but in the pillows, mattress, and
couch.

Neoclassicism in sculpture was followed by
a return to the emotionalism and theatricality
of the Baroque, long before the Baroque
revival in architecture. By the 1830s, Neo-
Baroque sculpture had produced a masterpiece in the splendidly rhetorical *Marseillaise*
by François Rude (fig. 263) on the Arc de
Triomphe in Paris. The soldiers, volunteers
of 1792 rallying to defend the Republic, are
still in Classical guise, but the Genius of
Liberty above them imparts her great for-
ward-rushing movement to the entire group.
She would not be unworthy of Bernini (see
figs. 214, 215).

Rude's successor in architectural sculpture
was Jean-Baptiste Carpeaux, whose famous
Dance for the Paris Opéra may be seen in the

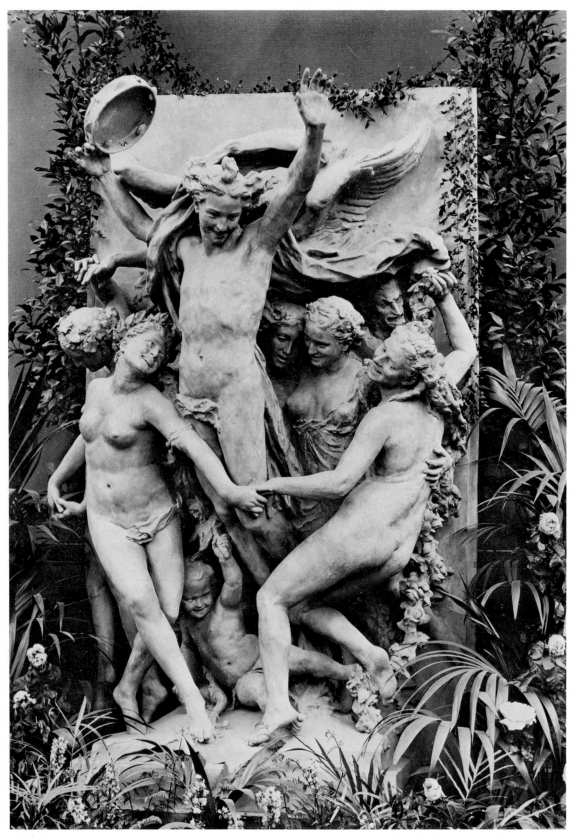

264. JEAN-BAPTISTE CARPEAUX. *The Dance*. 1867–69. Plaster model, about 15′ × 8′ 6″. Musée de l'Opéra, Paris

bottom right of figure 260. Figure 264 shows us the plaster model for the group. It is both livelier and more precise than the final version. A perfect match for Garnier's architecture, it is very Rococo in feeling, being both gay and coquettish. Yet the figures look undressed rather than nude, so photographically realistic in detail that they seem more like real people acting out a Rococo scene than fanciful beings sprung from the realm of myth.

Romanticism produced few memorable works in sculpture. The unique virtue of sculpture, its solid, space-filling reality, was no more congenial to the Romantic temperament than the laborious process of translating a sketch into a permanent, finished work. Painting, in contrast, remains the greatest creative achievement of Romanticism in the visual arts, on a par with poetry and second only to music. Literature, both past and present, now became a more important source of inspiration for painters than ever

before, and provided them with a new range of subjects, emotions, and attitudes. Romantic poets, in turn, often saw nature with a painter's eye. Many had a strong interest in art criticism and theory; some were capable draftsmen; and William Blake cast his visions in pictorial as well as literary form. Within the Romantic movement, painting and literature had a complex, subtle, and by no means one-sided relationship.

PAINTING: GOYA

Before we pursue Romantic painting in France, however, we must consider the great Spanish painter Francisco Goya, David's contemporary and the only artist of the age who may be called, unreservedly, a genius. His early works, in a delightful late-Rococo vein, reflect the influence of Tiepolo and the

265. FRANCISCO GOYA. *The Family of Charles IV*. 1800. 9′ 2″ × 11′. The Prado, Madrid

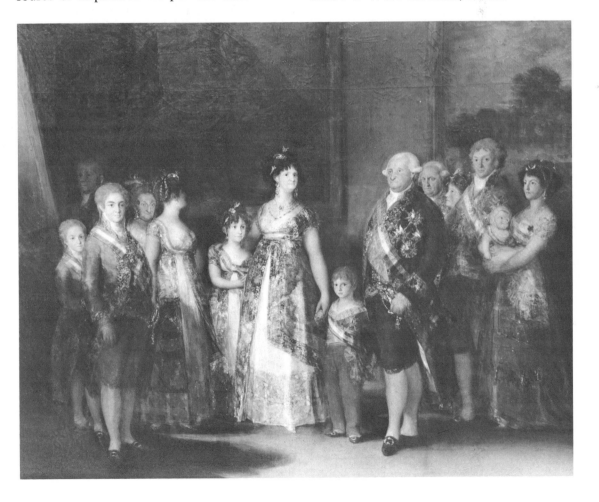

French masters (Spain had produced no important painters for a century). During the 1780s, however, Goya absorbed the libertarian ideas of the Enlightenment; even though he was a court painter, he surely sympathized with the Revolution, and not with the king of Spain, who had joined other monarchs in war against the young French Republic. Yet Goya was much esteemed at court, especially as a portrait painter. He now abandoned the Rococo for a Neo-Baroque style based on Velázquez and Rembrandt, the masters he had come to admire most. *The Family of Charles IV* (fig. 265), his largest royal portrait, deliberately echoes *The Maids of Honor* (see fig. 223): the entire clan has come to visit the artist, who is painting in one of the picture galleries of the palace. As in the earlier work, shadowy canvases hang behind the group and the light pours in from the side, although its

subtle gradations owe as much to Rembrandt as to Velázquez. The brushwork, too, has an incandescent sparkle rivaling that of *The Maids of Honor*. Measured against the Caravaggesque Neoclassicism of David, Goya's performance may seem thoroughly "pre-revolutionary," not to say anachronistic. Yet Goya has more in common with David than we might think: he, too, practices a revival style and, in his way, is equally devoted to the unvarnished truth. Psychologically, *The Family of Charles IV* is almost shockingly modern. No longer shielded by the polite conventions of Baroque court portraiture, the inner beings of these individuals have been laid bare with pitiless candor. They are like a collection of ghosts: the frightened children, the bloated vulture of a king, and—in a master stroke of sardonic humor—the grotesquely vulgar queen, posed like Velázquez' Princess Margarita (note the left arm, and the turn of the head). How, we wonder today, could the royal family tolerate this? Were they so dazzled by the splendid painting of their costumes that they failed to realize what Goya had done to them?

266. FRANCISCO GOYA. *Bobabilicon* (*Los Proverbios*, No. 4). c. 1818. Etching. The Metropolitan Museum of Art, New York (Dick Fund, 1931)

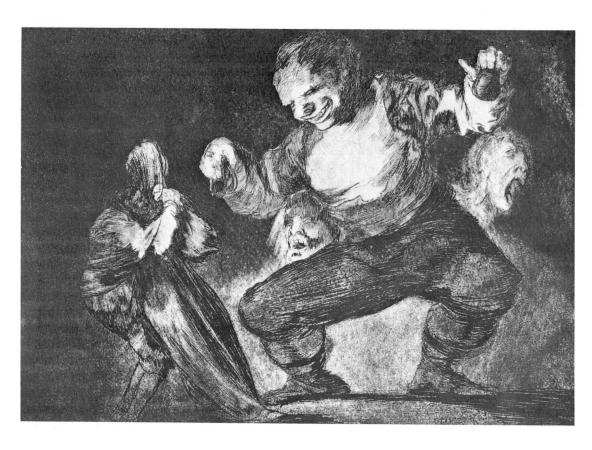

When Napoleon's armies occupied Spain in 1808, Goya and many of his countrymen hoped that the conquerors would bring the liberal reforms so badly needed. The savage behavior of the French troops crushed these hopes and generated a popular resistance of equal savagery. Many of Goya's works from 1810–15 reflect this bitter experience. The greatest is *The Third of May, 1808* (colorplate 56), commemorating the execution of a group of Madrid citizens. Here the blazing color, broad fluid brushwork, and dramatic nocturnal light are more emphatically Neo-Baroque than ever. The picture has all the emotional intensity of religious art, but these martyrs are dying for Liberty, not the Kingdom of Heaven; and their executioners are not the agents of Satan but of political tyranny—a formation of faceless automatons, impervious to their victims' despair and defiance. The same scene was to be re-enacted countless times in modern history. With the vision of genius, Goya created an image that has become a terrifying symbol of our era.

After the defeat of Napoleon, the restored Spanish monarchy brought a new wave of repression, and Goya withdrew more and more into a private world of nightmarish visions such as *Bobabilicon* (Big Booby), an etching from the series *Los Proverbios* (fig. 266). Although suggested by proverbs and popular superstitions, many of these scenes defy exact analysis. They belong to a realm of subjectively experienced horror even more terrifying than *The Third of May, 1808*. Finally, in 1824, he went into exile in France, where he died. Although Goya's influence made itself felt in France only after his death, his importance for the French Romantic painters was recognized by the greatest of them, Eugène Delacroix, who said that the ideal style would be a combination of Michelangelo's art with Goya's.

DAVID; INGRES

French Romantic painting emerged from the studio of Jacques Louis David, who became an ardent admirer of Napoleon and executed several large pictures glorifying the emperor —although as a portrayer of the Napoleonic myth he was partially eclipsed by younger men who had been his students. After Na-

poleon's downfall, however, David spent his last years in exile in Brussels, where his major works were playfully amorous subjects drawn from ancient myths or legends and painted in a coolly sensuous style he had initiated in Paris. His mantle eventually descended upon his pupil, Jean-Auguste Ingres, who had been an artistic rebel as a youth. Never an enthusiastic Bonapartist, Ingres went to Italy in 1806 where he remained for eighteen years. Only after his return did he become the high priest of the Davidian tradition. What had been a revolutionary style only half a century before, now congealed into rigid dogma, endorsed by the government and backed by the weight of conservative opinion. Fortunately, Ingres' pictures were far less doctrinaire than his theories. He always held that drawing was superior to painting, yet in a canvas such as his *Odalisque* (colorplate 57) he sets off the petal-smooth limbs of this Oriental Venus ("odalisque" is a Turkish word for a harem slave girl) with a dazzling array of rich tones and textures. The subject itself, redolent with the enchantment of the *Thousand and One Nights*, is characteristic of Romanticism, which Ingres professed to despise. Nor does this nude embody a Classical ideal of beauty. Her proportions, her strange mixture of coolness and voluptuousness, remind us, rather, of Parmigianino (see colorplate 37).

History painting as defined by Poussin and David remained Ingres' lifelong ambition, but he had great difficulties with it, while portraiture, which he pretended to dislike, was his strongest gift. He was, in fact, the last great professional in a field soon to be monopolized by the camera. Although photography became a practical process only about 1840, its experimental background can be traced back to the late eighteenth century. The impulse behind these experiments was not so much scientific curiosity as a quest for the True and Natural. The harsh realism of David's *Marat* proclaims this standard of unvarnished truth; so does Ingres' *Louis Bertin* (fig. 267), which at first glance looks like a kind of "super-photograph." But this impression is deceptive. Upon closer inspection, we realize how much interpretation the portrait contains. The painting, through subtle shifts of emphasis and proportion,

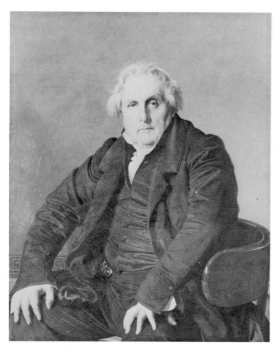

267. JEAN-AUGUSTE DOMINIQUE INGRES. *Louis Bertin.* 1832. Oil on canvas, 46 × 37 1/2″. The Louvre, Paris

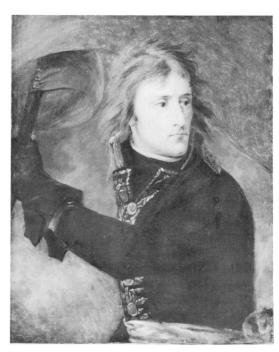

268. ANTOINE-JEAN GROS. *Napoleon at Arcole.* 1796. Oil on canvas, 29 1/2 × 23″. The Louvre, Paris

endows the sitter with a massive force of personality that has a truly frightening intensity. Only Ingres could so unify psychological depth and physical accuracy. His followers, on the other hand, concentrated on physical accuracy alone, competing vainly with the camera.

GROS; GÉRICAULT

Meanwhile, the reign of Napoleon, with its glamour, its adventurous conquests in remote parts of the world, had given rise to a Baroque revival among the younger painters, who felt the style of David too confining for the excitement of the age. David's favorite pupil, Antoine-Jean Gros, shows us Napoleon as a twenty-seven-year-old general leading his troops at the Battle of Arcole in northern Italy (fig. 268). Painted in Milan, soon after the series of victories that gave the French the Lombard plain, it conveys Napoleon's magic as an irresistible "man of destiny." with a Romantic enthusiasm David could never match. Much as Gros respected his teacher's doctrines, his

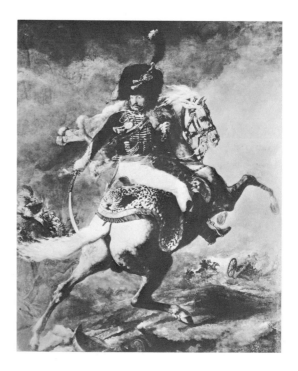

269. THÉODORE GÉRICAULT. *Mounted Officer of the Imperial Guard.* 1812. Canvas, 9′ 7″ × 6′ 4 1/2″. The Louvre, Paris

emotional nature impelled him toward the color and drama of the Baroque. What he accomplished in this case seems especially remarkable if we consider the circumstances, recounted by an eyewitness: Napoleon, too impatient to pose, was made to sit still by his wife, who held him firmly on her lap. The *Mounted Officer of the Imperial Guard* (fig. 269), painted by Théodore Géricault at the astonishing age of twenty-one, renders a vision of the Romantic hero with Rubens-like energy (see fig. 219). For Géricault, politics no longer had the force of a faith. All he saw in Napoleon's campaigns was the thrill—irresistible to the Romantic—of violent action.

DELACROIX

The year 1824 was crucial for French painting. Géricault died (in consequence of a riding accident); Goya arrived from Spain; Ingres returned home and had his first public success; the first showing in Paris of works by Constable was a revelation to many French artists; and Eugène Delacroix established his reputation as the foremost Neo-Baroque Romantic painter. Like West's *Death of General Wolfe* (fig. 256), Delacroix's painting of *Greece Expiring on the Ruins of Missolonghi* (colorplate 58) was inspired by a contemporary event: the Greek war of independence against the Turks, which stirred a sympathetic response throughout Western Europe. Delacroix, however, aimed at "poetic truth" rather than at recapturing a specific, actual event. He shows us an intoxicating mixture of sensuousness and cruelty: a dead Greek fighter lies crushed amidst marble blocks in the foreground; a Moor triumphs; and the defenseless maiden symbolizing Greece is fully as appealing as any martyred saint. Contemporary beholders, remembering that Lord Byron, the quintessential Romantic poet, had died at Missolonghi, must surely have found in the picture a special pathos. The painting has a great deal in common with the *Mounted Officer of the Imperial Guard* by Géricault, whom Delacroix admired. Sonorous color and the energetically fluid brushwork shows Delacroix to be a "Rubéniste" of the first order. In his *Odalisque* (colorplate 57), Ingres had also celebrated the exotic world of

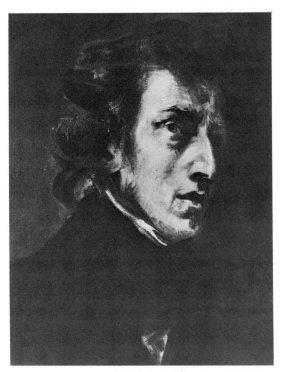

270. EUGENE DELACROIX. *Frédéric Chopin*. 1838. Canvas, 18 × 15″. The Louvre, Paris

the Near East—alien, seductive, and violent—but how different the result! No wonder that for the next quarter-century, he and Delacroix were acknowledged rivals, and their polarity, fostered by partisan critics, dominated the artistic scene in Paris. The same contrast is found in the portraiture of these perennial antagonists. Delacroix rarely painted portraits on commission; he felt at ease only when portraying his personal friends and fellow victims of the "Romantic agony," such as the Polish composer Frédéric Chopin (fig. 270). Here is the Romantic hero at his purest, consumed by the fire of his genius, like Gros' *Napoleon at Arcole*.

DAUMIER

Delacroix reflects the attitude that eventually doomed the Romantic movement: its growing detachment from contemporary life. It is ironic that Honoré Daumier, the one great Romantic artist who did not shrink from reality, remained practically unknown in his day as a painter. A biting political cartoonist, Daumier contributed masterful satirical drawings to various Paris weeklies for most of his life. He turned to painting in the 1840s, but found no public for his work. Only a few friends encouraged him, and, a year before his death, arranged his first one-man show. Daumier's mature paintings have the full pictorial range of the Neo-Baroque, but the subjects of many of them are scenes of daily life like those he treated in his cartoons. *The Third-Class Carriage* (fig. 271) is such a work. Painted very freely, it must have seemed raw and "unfinished" even by Delacroix's standards. Yet its power is derived from this very freedom, and for that reason Daumier cannot be labeled a realist; his concern is not for the tangible surface of reality but for the emotional meaning behind it. In this picture, he captures a peculiarly modern human condition, "the lonely crowd" composed of people who have nothing in common apart from

271. HONORÉ DAUMIER. *The Third-Class Carriage.* c. 1862. Canvas, 26 × 35 1/2″. The Metropolitan Museum of Art, New York (Bequest of Mrs. H.O. Havemeyer, 1929. The H.O. Havemeyer Collection)

the fact that they are traveling together in the same railway car. Though physically crowded, they take no notice of one another—each is alone with his own thoughts. Daumier explores this state with an insight into character and a breadth of human sympathy worthy of Rembrandt, whose work he revered. His feeling for the dignity of the poor also suggests Louis Le Nain (see fig. 231), who had recently been rediscovered by French critics.

Other paintings by Daumier have subjects more typical of Romanticism. Many of his drawings and paintings of the adventures of Don Quixote show how fascinated he was by Cervantes' sixteenth-century novel. The lanky knight-errant, vainly trying to live out his dreams of noble deeds, and Sancho Panza, the dumpy materialist, seemed to Daumier to embody a tragic conflict within human nature, the war between soul and body, between ideal aspiration and harsh reality. In *Don Quixote and Sancho Panza* (fig. 272), the mock hero dashes off toward his unrealistic goal while Sancho wrings his

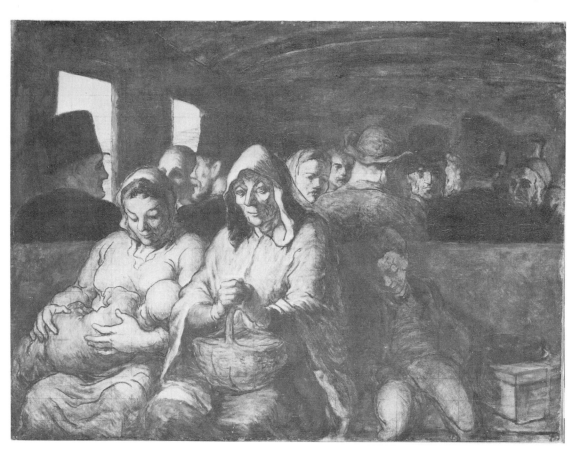

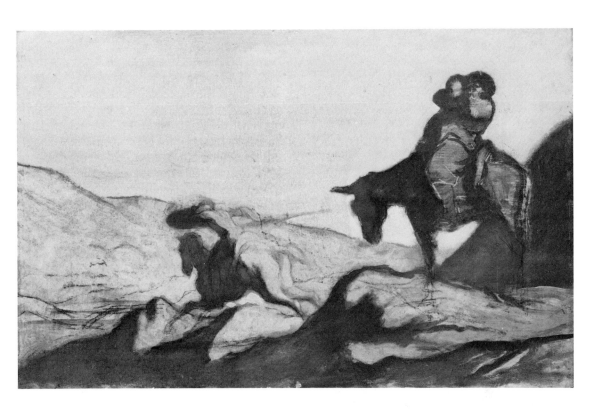

272. HONORÉ DAUMIER. *Don Quixote and Sancho Panza.* c. 1866. Oil sketch, 15 7/8 × 25 1/4″. The National Gallery, London

hands in helpless despair. We marvel at the strength, the sculptured simplicity, of Daumier's shapes and the expressive power of his brushwork.

It was, however, in landscape rather than in narrative painting that Romanticism reached its fullest expression, above all in England.

CONSTABLE

During the eighteenth century, landscape paintings were, for the most part, imaginative exercises conforming to Northern and Italian examples, as in Gainsborough's *Robert Andrews and His Wife* (colorplate 53). John Constable admired both Ruisdael and Claude, yet he strenuously opposed all flights of fancy. Landscape painting, he believed, must be based on observable facts; it should aim at "embodying a pure apprehension of natural effect." All his pictures show familiar views of the English countryside. And although he painted the final versions in his studio, he prepared them by making countless oil sketches out of doors. In these he was less concerned with concrete detail than with the qualities of light and atmosphere, so that the land often serves as a mere foil for the everchanging drama of wind, sunlight, and clouds. The sky, to Constable, was "the key note, the standard scale, and the chief organ of sentiment"; he studied it with a meteorologist's precision, the better to grasp its infinite variety as a mirror of those sweeping forces so dear to the Romantic view of nature. Trying to record these effects, he developed an increasingly broad, free technique, which explains why the large pictures of Constable's final years retained more and more of the quality of his oil sketches; in *Stoke-by-Nayland* (fig. 273) both the earth and the sky seem to have become "organs of sentiment" that pulsate with the artist's poetic sensibility.

TURNER

Meanwhile, William Turner had arrived at a style which Constable, deprecatingly but acutely, called "airy visions, painted with tinted steam." Turner, too, made copious studies from nature (although in watercolor, not oils), but he chose scenery that satisfied the Romantic taste for the Picturesque and

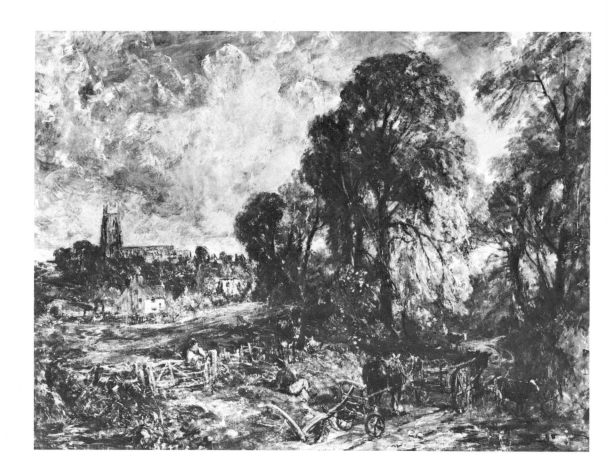

273. John Constable. *Stoke-by-Nayland.* 1836. Canvas, 49 1/2 × 66 1/2″. The Art Institute of Chicago

the Sublime—mountains, the sea, or the sites of historic events; in his large pictures he often changed these views so freely that they became quite unrecognizable. Many of his landscapes are linked with literary themes. When exhibiting them, Turner would add appropriate quotations from ancient or modern authors to the catalogue, or he would make up some lines himself and claim to be citing his own unpublished poem, "Fallacies of Hope." Yet these canvases are the opposite of history paintings as defined by Poussin: the titles indeed indicate "noble and serious human actions," but the tiny figures, lost in the seething violence of nature, suggest the ultimate defeat of all endeavor—"the fallacies of hope." *The Slave Ship* (colorplate 59), one of Turner's most spectacular visions, shows how he transmuted his literary sources into "tinted steam." Originally entitled *Slavers*

Throwing Overboard the Dead and Dying— Typhoon Coming On, the painting compounds several levels of meaning. In part, it has to do with a specific incident Turner had read about: when an epidemic broke out on a slave ship, the captain jettisoned his human cargo because he was insured against the loss of slaves at sea, but not by disease. Turner also thought of a passage from James Thomson's *The Seasons,* which describes how sharks follow a slave ship during a typhoon, "lured by the scent of steaming crowds, or rank disease, and death." But what is the relation between the slaver's action and the typhoon in the painting? Are the slaves being cast into the sea against the threat of the storm (perhaps to lighten the ship)? Is the typhoon Nature's retribution for the captain's greed and cruelty? Of the many storms at sea that Turner painted, none has quite this apocalyptic quality. A cosmic catastrophe seems about to engulf everything, not merely the slaver but the sea itself with its crowds of fantastic and oddly harmless-

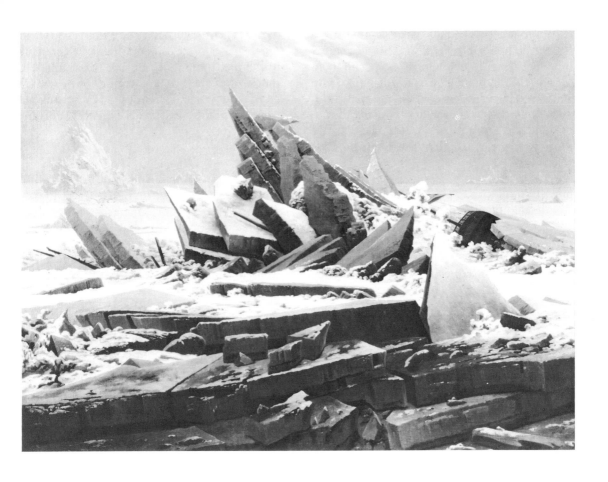

274. CASPAR DAVID FRIEDRICH. *The Polar Sea.*
1824. 38 1/2 × 50 1/2″. Kunsthalle, Hamburg

looking fish. While we still feel the force of
Turner's imagination, most of us today, perhaps with a twinge of guilt, enjoy the "tinted
steam" for its own sake, rather than as a
vehicle of the awesome emotions the artist
meant to evoke. Perhaps Turner himself
sometimes wondered if his "tinted steam"
had its intended effect on all beholders. In
Goethe's *Color Theory*, then recently translated into English, he could have read that
yellow has a "gay, softly exciting character,"
while orange-red suggests "warmth and glad-
ness." Would *The Slave Ship* arouse the
intended emotions in a viewer who did not
know the title?

FRIEDRICH

In Germany, as in England, landscape was
the finest achievement of Romantic painting,
and the underlying ideas, too, were often

strikingly similar. When Caspar David Friedrich, the most important German Romantic
artist, painted *The Polar Sea* (fig. 274), he
may have known of Turner's "Fallacies of
Hope," for in an earlier picture on the same
theme, now lost, he had inscribed the name
"Hope" on the crushed vessel. In any case,
he shared Turner's attitude toward human
fate. The painting, as so often before, was
inspired by a specific event which the artist
endowed with symbolic significance: a dangerous moment in William Parry's Arctic
expedition of 1819–20. One wonders how
Turner might have depicted this scene—
perhaps it would have been too static for him.
But Friedrich was attracted by this immobility; he has visualized the piled-up slabs of
ice as a kind of megalithic monument to
man's defeat built by Nature herself. Infinitely
lonely, it is a haunting reflection of the
artist's own melancholy. There is no hint of
"tinted steam"—the very air seems frozen—
nor any subjective handwriting; we look right
through the pigment-covered surface at a

reality that seems to have been created without the painter's intervention. This technique, impersonal and meticulous, is peculiar to German Romantic painting. It stems from the early Neoclassicists—Mengs, Hamilton, and Vien—but the Germans, whose tradition of Baroque painting was weak, adopted it more wholeheartedly than the English or the French.

BINGHAM

The Romantic view of nature as embodied in English painting and poetry soon spread to the Continent and across the Atlantic. A charming American example, although less daring than either Constable or Turner, is George Caleb Bingham's *Fur Traders on the Missouri*

275. GEORGE CALEB BINGHAM. *Fur Traders on the Missouri*. 1845. Canvas, 29 × 36". The Metropolitan Museum of Art, New York (Morris K. Jesup Fund, 1933)

(fig. 275). In the silence of these vast, wide-open spaces, two trappers glide downstream in the misty sunlight, a black fox chained to the prow of their dugout canoe. They remind us of how much Romantic adventurousness went into the westward expansion of the United States.

COROT

Landscape in French Romantic art was of far less importance than in English art. France did, however, produce one great landscapist, Camille Corot, whose early work has an important place in the development of modern landscape painting. In 1825, Corot went to Italy and explored the countryside around Rome, like a latter-day Claude Lorrain (see fig. 235). But he did not transform his sketches into pastoral visions; what Claude recorded only in his drawings—the quality of a particular place at a particular

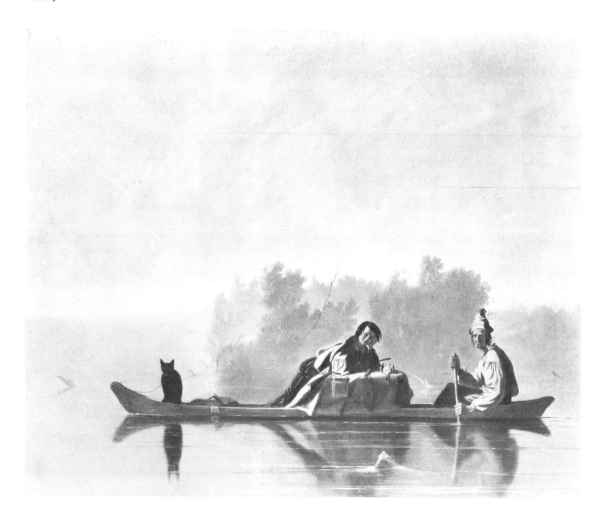

time—Corot captured in small canvases done on the spot in an hour or two, which are paintings in their own right. Such a work is his view of Papigno, an obscure little hill town (fig. 276). In size and immediacy, these pictures are analogous to Constable's oil sketches, yet they stem from a different tradition. If Constable's view of nature, which emphasizes the sky as "the chief organ of sentiment," derives from Dutch seventeenth-century landscapes, Corot's instinct for architectural clarity and stability recalls Poussin and Claude. Yet he, too, insists on "the truth of the moment"—his exactness of observation, and his readiness to seize any view that attracted him during his excursions, show the same commitment to direct visual experience that we find in Constable.

Realism and Impressionism

COURBET

"Can Jupiter survive the lightning rod?" asked Karl Marx, not long after the middle of the century. The French poet and art critic Charles Baudelaire was addressing himself to the same problem when, in 1846, he called for paintings that expressed "the heroism of modern life." At that time, only one painter was willing to make an artistic creed of this demand: Baudelaire's friend Gustave Courbet. Proud of his rural background and a socialist in politics, Courbet had begun as a Neo-Baroque Romantic, but by 1848, under the impact of the revolutionary upheavals then sweeping Europe, he had come to believe that the Romantic emphasis on feeling and imagination was merely an escape from the realities of the time. The modern artist must rely on his own direct experience ("I

276. CAMILLE COROT. *Papigno.* 1826. Canvas, 13 × 15 3/4″. Collection Dr. Fritz Nathan, Zurich

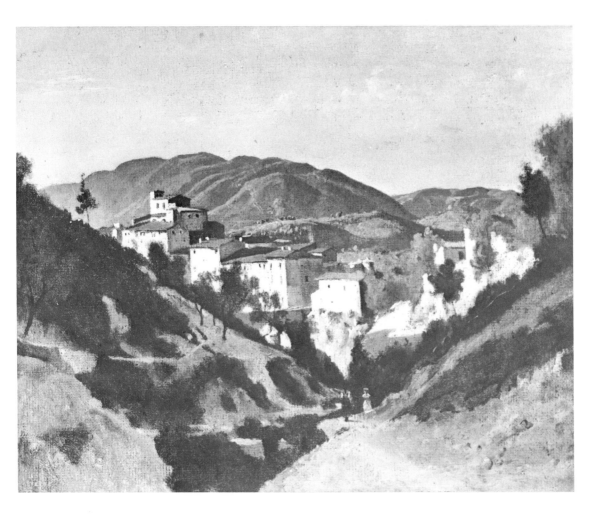

cannot paint an angel because I have never seen one," he said); he must be a Realist. As a descriptive term, "realism" is not very precise. For Courbet, it meant something akin to the "naturalism" of Caravaggio (see page 240). As an admirer of Louis Le Nain and Rembrandt he had, in fact, strong links with the Caravaggesque tradition, and his work, like Caravaggio's, was denounced for its supposed vulgarity and lack of spiritual content. The storm broke in 1849 over *The Stone Breakers* (fig. 277), the first canvas fully embodying Courbet's programmatic Realism. He had seen two men working on a road, and had asked them to pose for him in his studio, where he painted them lifesize, solidly and matter-of-factly, without pathos or sentiment; the young man's face is averted, the old one's half hidden by a hat. Yet he cannot have picked them casually: their contrast in age is significant—one is too old for such heavy work, the other too young. Endowed with the dignity of their symbolic status, they do not turn to us for sympathy.

277. GUSTAVE COURBET. *The Stone Breakers*. 1849. Canvas, 63 × 102″. Formerly State Gallery, Dresden (destroyed 1945)

Courbet's friend, the socialist Proudhon, likened them to a parable from the Gospels. Courbet's Realism, then, was a revolution of subject matter more than of style. Yet the conservatives' rage at him as a dangerous radical is understandable; his sweeping condemnation of *all* traditional subjects drawn from religion, mythology, allegory, and history only spelled out what many others had begun to feel, but had not dared to put into words.

MANET; MONET

Courbet's art helps us to understand a picture that shocked the public even more than any of his: Edouard Manet's *Luncheon on the Grass* (fig. 278), which shows a nude model accompanied by two gentlemen in frock coats. Manet was the first to grasp Courbet's full importance—the *Luncheon* is, among other things, a tribute to the older artist. Renaissance masters had often juxtaposed nude and clothed figures in outdoor settings, but when Manet did so, he caused a scandal, since his painting gives no hint of a "higher" significance. Yet the group has so formal a pose that he could not possibly have intended to depict an actual event. In fact, the main

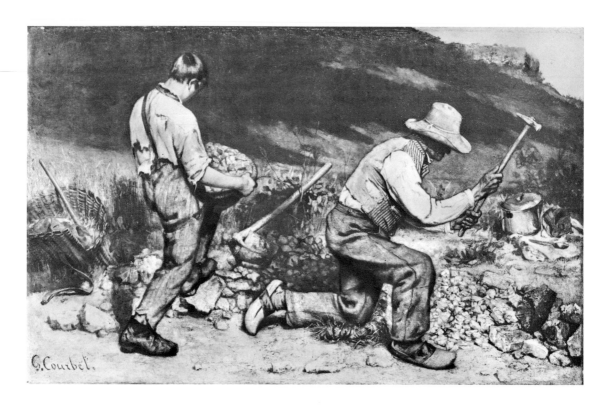

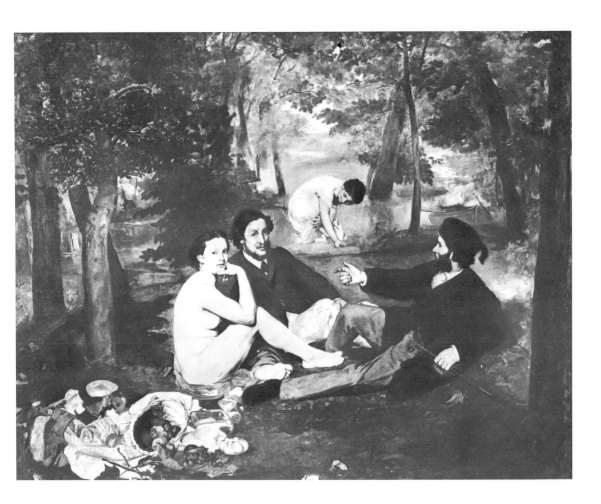

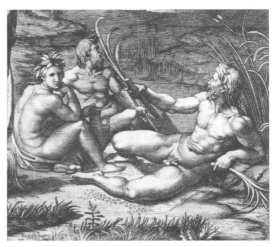

figures were borrowed from a print after Raphael (fig. 279). Perhaps the meaning of the canvas lies in this denial of plausibility, for the scene fits neither the plane of everyday experience nor that of allegory. The *Luncheon* is a manifesto of artistic freedom, asserting the painter's privilege to combine whatever elements he pleases for aesthetic effect alone. The nudity of the model is "explained" by the contrast between her warm, creamy flesh tones and the cool black-and-gray of the men's attire. Or, to put it another way, the *Luncheon* tells us that the world of painting has an internal logic distinct from the logic of familiar reality, and that the painter's first loyalty is to his canvas, not to the outside world. Here begins an attitude that was to become a bone of contention later under the slogan "art for art's sake" (see p. 320). Manet himself disdained controversy, but his work attests his lifelong devotion to "pure painting"—to the belief that brushstrokes and color patches, rather than the things they

278. EDOUARD MANET. *Luncheon on the Grass (Le Déjeuner sur l'Herbe)*. 1863. Canvas, 7' × 8' 10". The Louvre, Paris

279. MARCANTONIO RAIMONDI, after RAPHAEL. *The Judgment of Paris* (detail). c. 1520. Engraving. The Metropolitan Museum of Art, New York

stand for, are the artist's primary reality. Among the old masters, he found that Hals, Velázquez, and Goya had come closest to this ideal. He admired their broad, open technique, their preoccupation with light and color values. Many of his canvases are, in fact, "pictures of pictures"—they translate into modern terms those older works that particularly challenged him. Yet he always filtered out the expressive or symbolic content of his models, lest the viewer's attention be distracted from the pictorial structure itself. His paintings have an emotional reticence that could easily be mistaken for emptiness unless we understand its purpose.

Courbet is said to have remarked that Manet's pictures were as flat as playing cards. Looking at *The Fifer* (colorplate 60) we can see what he meant. Done three years after the *Luncheon*, it is a painting without shadows (there are a few, but it takes a real

280. Auguste Renoir. *Le Moulin de la Galette*. 1876. Canvas, 51 1/2 × 69″. The Louvre, Paris

effort to find them), hardly any modeling, and no depth. The figure looks three-dimensional only because its contour renders the forms in realistic foreshortening; otherwise, Manet eschews all the methods devised since Giotto's time for transmuting a flat surface into a pictorial space. The gray background seems as near to us as the figure, and just as solid; if the fifer stepped out of the picture, he would leave a hole, like the cut-out shape of a stencil. Here, then, the canvas itself is no longer a "window," but a screen made up of patches of color. In retrospect, we realize that the revolutionary qualities of Manet's art already appear, less obviously, in the *Luncheon*; the three main figures form a unit almost as shadowless and stencil-like as the fifer. They would be more at home on a flat screen than they are in their Courbet-like landscape setting.

What brought about this "revolution of the color patch"? We do not know, and Manet himself surely did not reason it out beforehand. Perhaps he was impelled to create the

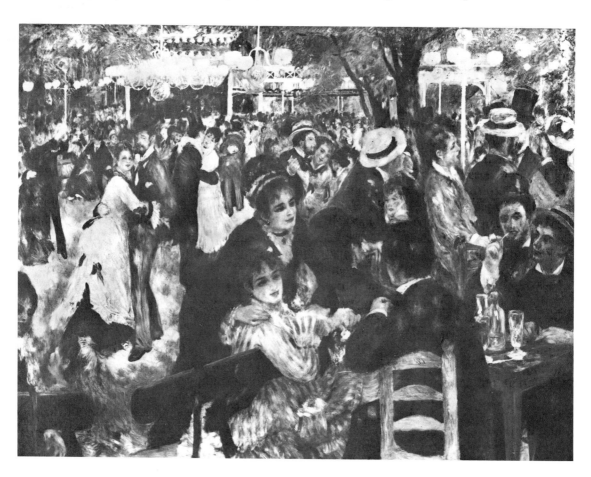

new style by the challenge of photography. The "pencil of nature" had vindicated the objective truth of Renaissance perspective (see colorplate 27), but it had also established a standard of representational accuracy that no handmade image could rival. Painting needed to be rescued from competition with the camera. This Manet accomplished by insisting that a painted canvas is, above all, a surface covered with pigments—that we must look *at* it, not *through* it. Unlike Courbet, he gave no name to the style he had created; when his followers began calling themselves Impressionists, he refused to accept that term for his own work. The word was coined in 1874, after a hostile critic had looked at a picture entitled *Impression: Sunrise* by Claude Monet—and it certainly fits Monet better than it does Manet. Monet had adopted Manet's concept of painting and applied it to landscapes done out of doors, such as *The River* (colorplate 61). It is flooded with sunlight so bright that conservative critics claimed it made their eyes smart. In this flickering network of color patches, the reflections on the water are as "real" as the banks of the river Seine. Even more than *The Fifer*, Monet's painting is a "playing card"; were it not for the woman and the boat in the foreground, the picture could hang upside down with hardly any difference of effect. This inner coherence sets *The River* apart from earlier "impressions" such as Corot's *Papigno* (see fig. 276), even though both share the same on-the-spot immediacy and fresh perception.

RENOIR; DEGAS

Scenes from the world of entertainment—dance halls, cafés, concerts, the theater—were favorite subjects for Impressionist painters. Auguste Renoir, another important member of the group, filled his with the *joie de vivre* of a singularly happy temperament. The flirting couples in *Le Moulin de la Galette* (fig. 280), under the dappled pattern of sunlight and shade, radiate a human warmth that is utterly entrancing, even though the artist permits us no more than a fleeting glance at any of them. Our role is that of the casual stroller, who takes in this slice of life as he passes. By contrast, Edgar Degas makes us look steadily at the disenchanted pair in his café scene (fig. 281), but, so to speak, out of the corner of our eye. The design of this picture, at first glance, seems as unstudied as a snapshot, yet the longer we look, the more we realize that everything has been made to dovetail precisely—that the zigzag of empty tables between us and the luckless couple reinforces their brooding loneliness. Compositions as boldly calculated as this set Degas apart from his fellow Impressionists. A wealthy aristocrat by birth, he had been trained in the tradition of Ingres, whom he greatly admired. Like Ingres, he was a masterful portraitist, although he portrayed only friends and relatives, people with whom he had emotional ties. His profound sense of human character lends weight even to seemingly casual scenes such as that in figure 281. A decade later, Degas again presents us with an oblique view in *The Tub* (fig. 282), but now the design has grown severe, almost geometric: the tub and the crouching woman, both vigorously outlined, form a circle within a square, and the rest of the rectangular format is filled by a shelf so sharply tilted that

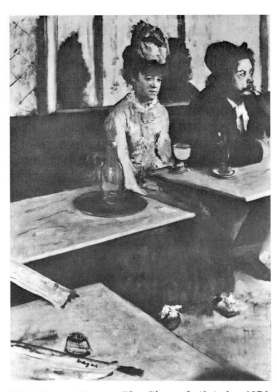

281. EDGAR DEGAS. *The Glass of Absinthe*. 1876. Canvas, 36 × 27″. The Louvre, Paris

it almost shares the plane of the picture; yet on this shelf Degas has placed two pitchers (note how the curve of the small one fits the handle of the other!) that are hardly foreshortened at all. Here the tension between "two-D" and "three-D," surface and depth, comes close to the breaking point.

The Tub is Impressionist only in its shimmering, luminous colors. Its other qualities are more characteristic of the 1880s, the first post-Impressionist decade, when many artists showed a renewed concern with problems of form (see the next chapter). Among the major figures of the movement, Monet alone remained faithful to the Impressionist view of nature. About 1890, he began to paint pictures in series, showing the same subject under various conditions of light and atmosphere. These tended increasingly to resemble Turner's "airy visions, painted with tinted steam" as Monet concentrated on effects of colored light (he had visited London, and knew Turner's work). But Monet never ventured into subjective fantasy, nor did he abandon the basic approach of his earlier work. His *Water Lilies, Giverny* (fig. 283) is a consistent sequel to *The River*, across a span of almost forty years. The pond surface now takes up the entire canvas, so that the effect of a weightless screen is stronger than ever; the artist's brushwork has greater variety and a more personal rhythm; the theme, however, is still the endlessly fascinating interplay of reflection and reality.

WHISTLER

Courbet, during his later years, enjoyed considerable fame and influence abroad; the Impressionists gained international recognition more slowly. Americans were among their first patrons, responding to the new style more readily than did Europeans. At a time when no French museum would have them, Impressionist works entered public collections in the United States, and American painters were among the earliest followers of Manet and his circle. James McNeill Whistler, who had settled in London in 1859 for the remainder of his life, was in close touch with the rising Impressionist movement in France during the 1860s. His best-known picture, *Arrangement in Black and Gray: The Artist's Mother* (fig. 284), reflects the influ-

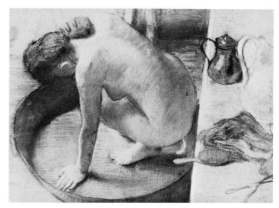

282. EDGAR DEGAS. *The Tub*. 1886. Pastel, 23 1/2 × 32 1/2″. The Louvre, Paris

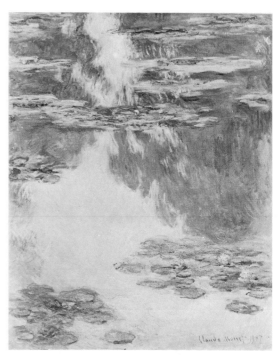

283. CLAUDE MONET. *Water Lilies, Giverny*. 1907. Oil on canvas, 36 1/2 × 29″. Collection Mr. and Mrs. David T. Schiff, New York

ence of Manet in its emphasis on flat areas. Its rise to fame as a symbol of our latter-day "mother cult" is a paradox of popular psychology that would have dismayed Whistler; he wanted the canvas to be appreciated for its formal qualities alone. A witty and sharp-tongued advocate of "art for art's sake," he thought of his pictures as analogous to pieces of music, often calling them "symphonies" or

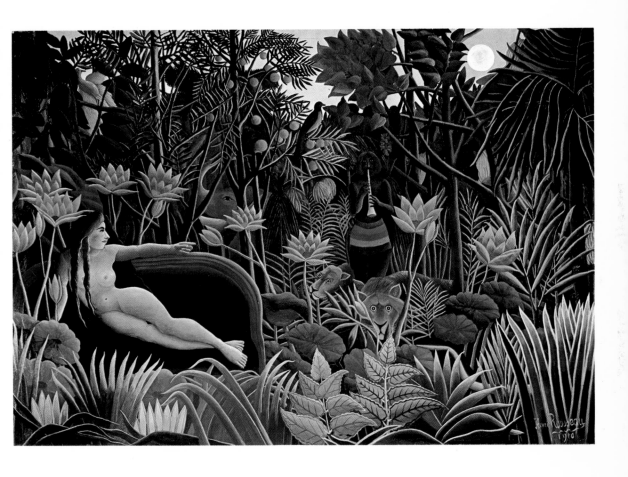

Colorplate 65. HENRI ROUSSEAU. *The Dream.* 1910. Oil on canvas, 6′ 8 1/2″ × 9′ 1/2″. The Museum of Modern Art, New York (Gift of Nelson A. Rockefeller)

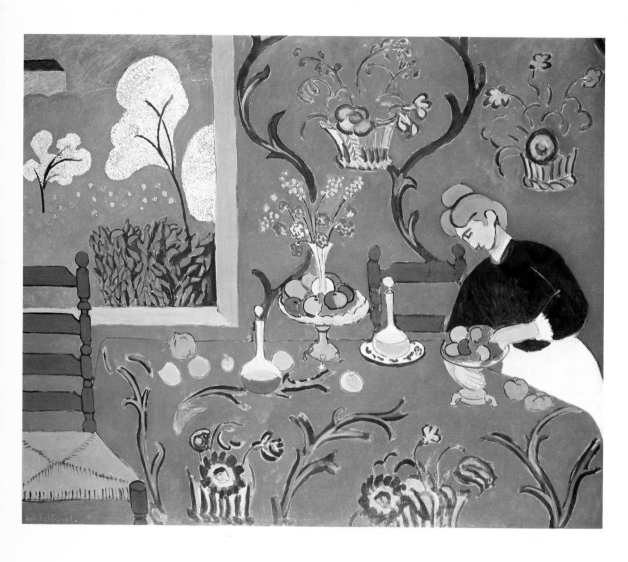

Colorplate 66. HENRI MATISSE. *Harmony in Red (Red Room)*. 1908–09. Oil on canvas, 71 1/4 × 96 7/8″. The Hermitage Museum, Leningrad

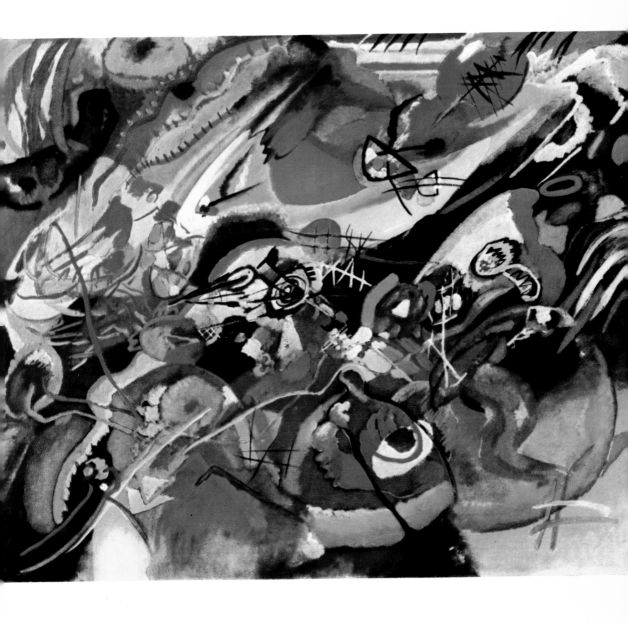

Colorplate 67. WASSILY KANDINSKY. *Sketch I for "Composition VII"*. 1913. Canvas, 30 3/4 × 39 3/8". Collection Felix Klee, Bern

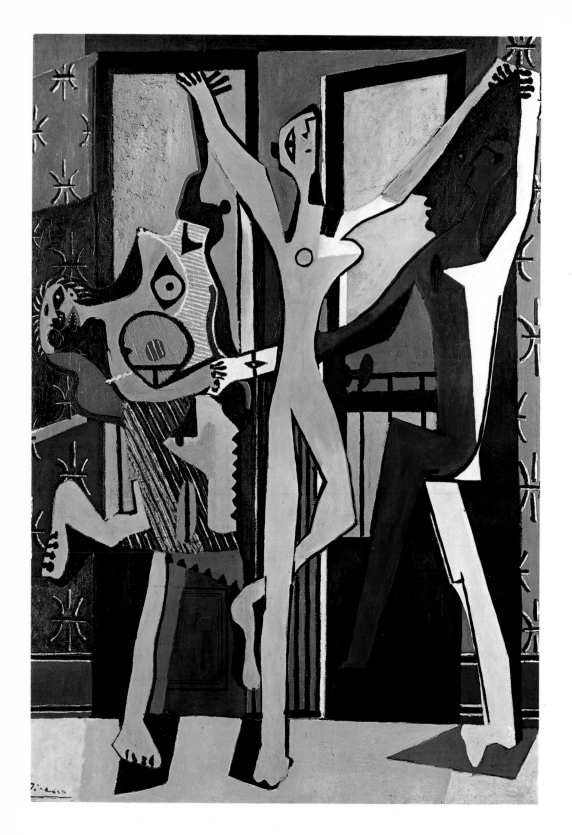

Colorplate 68. PABLO PICASSO. *Three Dancers*. 1925. Oil on canvas, 84 1/2 × 56 1/4″. Collection the Artist's Estate

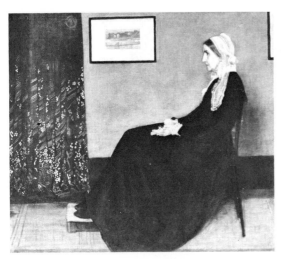

284. JAMES WHISTLER. *Arrangement in Black and Gray: The Artist's Mother*. 1871. 57 × 64 1/2″. The Louvre, Paris

285. JAMES WHISTLER. *Nocturne in Black and Gold: The Falling Rocket*. c. 1874. Panel, 23 3/4 × 18 3/8″. The Detroit Institute of Arts

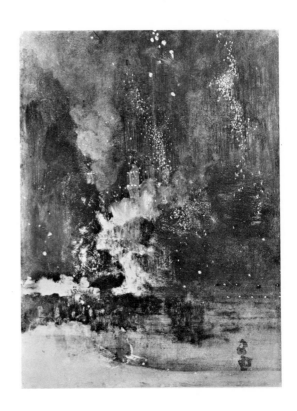

"nocturnes." The boldest of these is *Nocturne in Black and Gold: The Falling Rocket* (fig. 285); if it were not for the explanatory subtitle, we would have real difficulty figuring it out. No Frenchman had yet dared to produce a picture so "nonrepresentational," so reminiscent of Turner's "tinted steam" (see colorplate 59). It was this painting, more than any other, that prompted the British critic John Ruskin to accuse Whistler of "flinging a pot of paint in the public's face." Since Ruskin had highly praised Turner's *Slave Ship*, it would seem that what he really liked was not the "tinted steam" itself but the Romantic sentiment behind it. During the subsequent libel suit, Whistler stated his aims in words that fit *The Falling Rocket* especially well: "I have perhaps meant rather to indicate an artistic interest alone in my work, divesting the picture from any outside sort of interest. . . . It is an arrangement of line, form, and color, first, and I make use of any incident of it which shall bring about a symmetrical result." The last phrase is particularly significant, since Whistler acknowledges that in utilizing chance effects he does not look for resemblances but for a purely formal har-

mony. His statement reads like a prophecy of modern American abstract painting (see fig. 328).

HOMER; EAKINS

Whistler's gifted contemporary in America, Winslow Homer, also came to Paris as a young man, but left too soon to receive the full impact of Impressionism. He was a pictorial reporter throughout the Civil War and continued as a magazine illustrator until 1875. Yet he did some of his most remarkable paintings in the 1860s. Such a work is *The Morning Bell* (fig. 286); the fresh delicacy of the sunlit scene might be called "pre-Impressionist"—halfway between Corot and Monet (compare fig. 276, colorplate 61). But the picture has an extraordinarily subtle design as well: the dog, the center girl, and those at the right turn the footpath into a seesaw, its upward slant balanced by the descending line of treetops. Thomas Eakins arrived in Paris from Philadelphia about the time Homer painted *The Morning Bell;* he returned, four years later, with decisive impressions of Courbet, Manet, and Velázquez. Elements from these three artists are combined in *The*

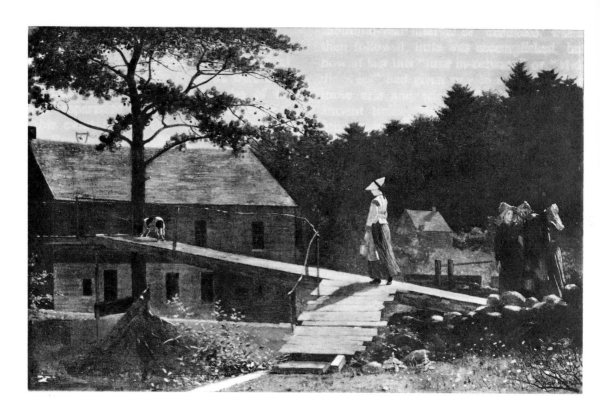

286. WINSLOW HOMER. *The Morning Bell.* c. 1866. Canvas, 24 × 38″. Yale University Art Gallery, New Haven (Stephen C. Clark Collection)

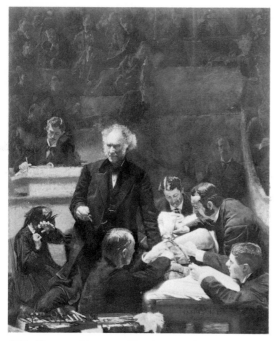

287. THOMAS EAKINS. *The Gross Clinic.* 1875. Oil on canvas, 96 × 78″. Jefferson Medical College, Philadelphia

Gross Clinic (fig. 287), the most imposing work of American nineteenth-century painting. A powerfully realistic canvas, it is a lifesize view of an operation in progress, glossing over none of the gruesome detail. Conservative critics denounced it as a "degradation of art," but to us it seems a splendid fulfillment of Baudelaire's demand for pictures that express the heroism of modern life.

CASSATT

Mary Cassatt's early training was very similar to Eakins', but she elected to settle in Paris, where she joined the Impressionists late in the 1870s. Although her family objected to her vocation, she was able to pursue her career as an artist at a time when it was frowned on as an occupation for women only because she was independently wealthy (like Berthe Morisot, another member of the group). A tireless champion of the Impressionists, Cassatt was instrumental in gaining early acceptance of their paintings in the United States through her social contacts with rich private collectors. Because or in spite of the fact that she never married, maternity provided the thematic material and formal focus for most of

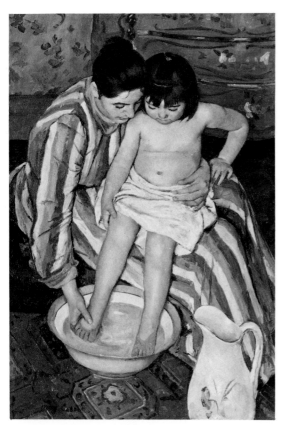

288. MARY CASSATT. *The Bath.* c. 1891. Canvas, 39 1/2 × 26″. The Art Institute of Chicago (Robert A. Waller Fund)

color? What Rodin did accomplish is strikingly visible in *The Thinker* (fig. 289), originally conceived as part of a large unfinished project called *The Gates of Hell*. The welts and wrinkles of the vigorously creased surface produce, in polished bronze, an everchanging pattern of reflections. But is this effect borrowed from Impressionist painting? Does Rodin dissolve three-dimensional form into flickering patches of light and dark? These fiercely exaggerated shapes pulsate with sculptural energy, and they retain this quality under whatever conditions the piece is viewed. For Rodin did not work directly in bronze; he modeled in wax or clay. How could he calculate in advance the reflections on the surfaces of the bronze casts that would be made from these models? He worked as he did, we must assume, for an entirely different reason: not to capture elusive optical effects, but to make emphatic the process of "growth"—the miracle of inert matter coming to life in the artist's hands. As the color patch, for Manet and Monet, is the primary reality, so are the malleable lumps from which Rodin builds his

her work, which reached its maturity around 1890. In its oblique view, simplified color forms and flat composition, *The Bath* (fig. 288) reflects Cassatt's debt to her mentors Degas (fig. 282) and Manet (colorplate 60), as well as her study of Japanese prints. These influences, however, have been assimilated into an individual and highly accomplished manner which, at its best, made her one of America's leading Impressionists.

SCULPTURE: RODIN

Impressionism, it is often said, revitalized sculpture no less than painting. This claim is at once true and misleading. Auguste Rodin, the first sculptor of genius since Bernini, redefined sculpture during the same years that Manet and Monet redefined painting; in doing so, however, he did not follow these artists' lead. How indeed could the effect of such pictures as *The Fifer* or *The River* be reproduced in three dimensions and without

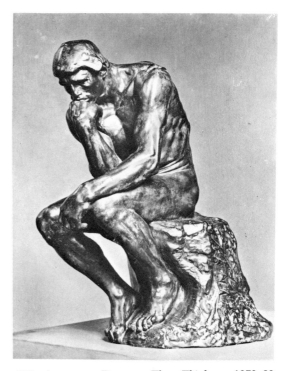

289. AUGUSTE RODIN. *The Thinker.* 1879–89. Bronze, height 27 1/2″. The Metropolitan Museum of Art, New York (Gift of Thomas F. Ryan, 1910)

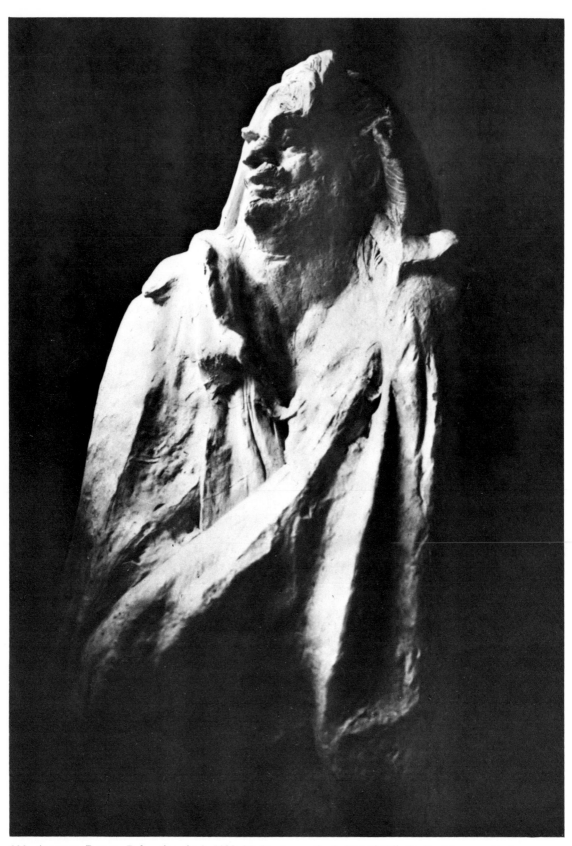

290. AUGUSTE RODIN. *Balzac* (portion). 1892–97. Plaster, entire height 9′ 10″. Rodin Museum, Paris

forms. By insisting on this "unfinishedness," he rescued sculpture from mechanical verisimilitude just as Manet had rescued painting from photographic realism.

Who is *The Thinker?* Partly Adam, no doubt, partly Prometheus, and partly the brute imprisoned by the passions of the flesh. Rodin wisely refrained from giving him a specific name, for the statue fits no preconceived identity. In this new image of man, form and meaning are one, instead of cleaving apart as in Carpeaux's *Dance.* Carpeaux produced naked figures that pretend to be nude, while *The Thinker*, like Michelangelo's superhuman bodies whose action-in-repose he shares, is free from subservience to the undressed model. But, despite his tremendous admiration for Michelangelo, Rodin was a modeler, not a carver. His works reveal their full strength only when we see them in plaster casts made directly from the clay originals, rather than in bronze. The *Balzac Monument* (fig. 290), his most daring creation, remained in plaster for many years, rejected by the committee that had ordered it. The figure is larger than life, physically and spiritually; it has the overpowering presence of a specter. Like a huge monolith, the man of genius towers above the crowd—he shares the "sublime egotism of the gods" (as the Romantics put it). Rodin has minimized the articulation of the body so that from a distance we see only its great bulk. As we approach, we become aware that Balzac is wrapped in a long, shroud-like cloak. From this mass the head thrusts upward with elemental force. When we are close enough to make out the features clearly, we sense beneath the disdain an inner agony that stamps *Balzac* as the kin of *The Thinker*.

Post-Impressionism

In 1882 Manet was made a Knight of the Legion of Honor by the French government. By that time Impressionism was gaining wide acceptance, but it had ceased to be a pioneering movement. The future belonged to the "Post-Impressionists." This colorless label designates a group of artists who had become dissatisfied with the limitations of Impressionism and ranged beyond it in various directions. It is difficult to find a more descriptive term for them, since they did not share a common goal. In any event, they were not "anti-Impressionists." Far from trying to undo the effects of the "Manet Revolution," they wanted to carry it even further; in essence Post-Impressionism is just a later stage—although a very important one—of the development that had begun with such pictures as Manet's *Luncheon on the Grass.*

CÉZANNE

Paul Cézanne, the oldest Post-Impressionist painter, was born in Aix-en-Provence, near the Mediterranean coast. He came to Paris in 1861, imbued with enthusiasm for the Romantics, especially Delacroix. But he soon discovered Manet as well, and by the early 1870s he had become an Impressionist. Toward the end of the decade, however, he set out "to make of Impressionism something solid and durable, like the art of the museums." What he meant by this can be seen in *Fruit Bowl, Glass, and Apples* (fig. 291): every brushstroke is like a building block, firmly placed within the pictorial architecture, and the colors are deliberately controlled so as to produce "chords" of warm and cool tones that reverberate throughout the canvas. Not since Chardin have simple everyday objects assumed such importance in a painter's eye. We also notice another aspect of Cézanne's mature style: the forms are deliberately simplified, and outlined with dark contours; and the perspective is "incorrect" for both the fruit bowl and the horizontal surfaces, which seem to slant upward. The longer we study the picture, the more we realize the rightness of these apparently arbitrary distortions. When Cézanne takes these liberties with reality, his purpose is to uncover the permanent qualities beneath the accidents of appearance (all forms in nature, he believed, are based on the cone, the sphere, and the cylinder). This order underlying the external world was the true subject of his pictures, but he had to interpret it to fit the separate, closed world of the canvas. One detail of our painting is particularly instructive in this respect—the stem of the fruit bowl is slightly off center, as

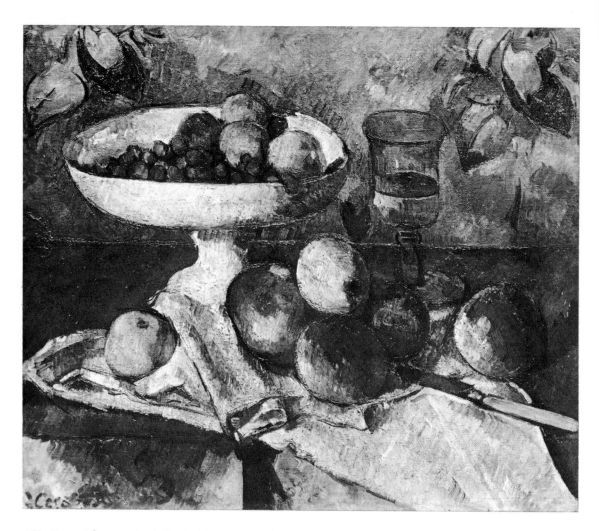

291. PAUL CÉZANNE. *Fruit Bowl, Glass, and Apples.* 1879–82. 18 × 21 1/2″. Collection René Lecomte, Paris

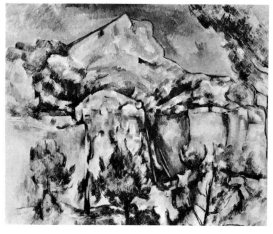

292. PAUL CÉZANNE. *Mont Sainte-Victoire Seen from Bibemus Quarry.* c. 1898–1900. Canvas, 25 1/2 × 32″. The Baltimore Museum of Art (The Cone Collection)

if the oval shape of the bowl, in response to the pressure of the other objects, were expanding toward the left.

To apply this method to landscape became the greatest challenge of Cézanne's career. From 1882 on, he lived in isolation near his home town, exploring its environs. One motif, the distinctive shape of a mountain called Mont Sainte-Victoire, seemed almost to obsess him; its craggy profile looming against the blue Mediterranean sky appears in a long series of compositions, such as the monumental late work in figure 292. There are no hints of man's presence here—houses and roads would only disturb the lonely grandeur of this view. Above the wall of rocky cliffs that bar our way like a chain of fortifications, the mountain rises in triumphant clarity, infinitely remote yet as solid and palpable as the shapes in the foreground. For all its architectural stability, the scene is alive with movement; but the forces at work here have been brought into equilibrium, subdued by the greater power of the artist's will.

SEURAT

Georges Seurat shared Cézanne's aim to make Impressionism "solid and durable," but he went about it very differently. His career was as brief as that of Masaccio, and his achievement just as astonishing. Seurat devoted his main efforts to a few very large paintings, for which he made endless series of preliminary studies. This painstaking method reflects his belief that art must be based on a system; but, as with all artists of genius, Seurat's theories do not really explain his pictures—it is the pictures, rather, that explain the theories. The subject of *A Sunday Afternoon on the Grande Jatte* (colorplate 62) is of the sort that had long been popular among Impressionist painters. Impressionist, too, are the brilliant colors and the effect of intense sunlight. Otherwise, however, the picture is the very opposite of a quick "impression"; the firm, simple contours and the relaxed, immobile figures give the scene a timeless stability that recalls Piero della Francesca (see fig. 169). Even the brushwork shows Seurat's passion for order and permanence; the canvas is covered by systematic, impersonal dots of intense color which were to merge in the beholder's eye and thereby produce intermediary tints more luminous than those obtainable from pigments mixed on the palette. This procedure he called Divisionism (others spoke of Neo-Impressionism, or Pointillism). The actual result, however, did not conform to the theory. Looking at the *Grande Jatte* from a comfortable distance, we find that the mixture of the colors in the eye is still incomplete; the dots are clearly visible, like the tesserae of a mosaic. Seurat must have liked this unexpected effect—otherwise he would have reduced the size of the dots—which gives the canvas the quality of a shimmering translucent screen.

VAN GOGH

While Cézanne and Seurat were converting Impressionism into a more severe, Classical style, Vincent van Gogh was moving in the opposite direction, believing that Impressionism did not provide the artist with enough freedom to express his emotions. He is sometimes called an Expressionist, but the term ought to be reserved for certain later painters (see p. 340). Van Gogh, the first great Dutch master since the seventeenth century, did not become an artist until 1880; since he died only ten years later, his career was even briefer than Seurat's. His early interests were in literature and religion. Profoundly dissatisfied with the values of industrial society, and imbued with a strong sense of mission, he worked for a while as a lay preacher among poverty-stricken coal miners. An intense sympathy for the poor pervades his early paintings. In 1886, however, he came to Paris and met Degas, Seurat, and other leading French artists. Their effect on him was electrifying: his pictures now blazed with color, and he even tried the Divisionist technique of Seurat. Although this Impressionist phase was vitally important for Van Gogh's development, he had to integrate it with the style of his earlier years before his genius could unfold fully. Paris had opened his eyes to the sensuous beauty of the visible world and taught him the pictorial language of the color patch, but painting continued to be a vessel for his personal emotions. To investigate this spiritual reality with the new means at his command, he went to Arles, in the South of France. It was there, between 1888 and 1890, that he produced his greatest pictures. Like Cézanne, he now devoted his main energies to landscape painting, but the sun-drenched countryside evoked a very different response in him: he saw it filled with ecstatic movement, not architectural stability and permanence. In his *Wheat Field and Cypress Trees* (colorplate 63), both earth and sky show an overpowering turbulence—the wheat field resembles a stormy sea, the trees spring flamelike from the ground, and the hills and clouds heave with a similar undulant motion. The dynamism that is in every brushstroke makes of each one not merely a deposit of color, but an incisive graphic gesture. Yet to Van Gogh himself it was the color, not the form, that determined the expressive content of his pictures. Although his desire "to exaggerate the essential and to leave the obvious vague" makes his colors look arbitrary by Impressionist standards, he neverthe-

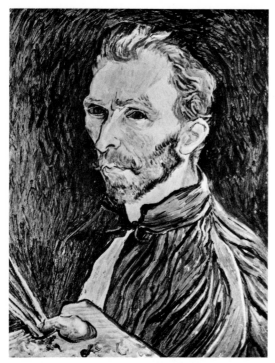

293. VINCENT VAN GOGH. *Self-Portrait*. 1889. Canvas, 22 1/2 × 17″. Private Collection

less remained deeply committed to the visible world. The colors of *Wheat Field* are stronger, simpler, and more vibrant than those in Monet's *The River* (compare colorplate 61) but in no sense "unnatural." They speak to us of that "kingdom of light" Van Gogh had found in the South, and of his mystic faith in a creative force animating all forms of life. Like Dürer before him (fig. 203), the missionary had now become a prophet. We see him in that role in the *Self-Portrait* (fig. 293), his emaciated, luminous head with its burning eyes set off against a whirlpool of darkness. At the time of this *Self-Portrait*, he had already begun to suffer fits of mental illness that made painting increasingly difficult for him. Despairing of a cure, he committed suicide a year later, for he felt that art alone had made his life worth living.

GAUGUIN

The quest for religious experience also played an important part in the work—if not in the life—of another great Post-Impressionist, Paul Gauguin. He began as a prosperous stockbroker in Paris, and an amateur painter and collector of modern art (he once owned Cézanne's *Fruit Bowl*, fig. 291). At thirty-five, however, he became convinced that he must devote himself entirely to art: he abandoned his business career and his family, and by 1889 he was the central figure of a new movement called Symbolism. His style, although less intensely personal than Van Gogh's, was an even bolder advance beyond Impressionism. Gauguin believed that Western civilization was "out of joint," having forced men into an incomplete life dedicated to material gain while their emotions lay neglected. To rediscover for himself this hidden world of feeling, Gauguin went to live among the peasants of Brittany in western France. Here religion was still part of everyday life, and in works such as *The Yellow Christ* (colorplate 64) he attempted to depict the simple, direct faith of country people. Here at last is what no Romantic painter had achieved: a style based on pre-Renaissance sources. Modeling and perspective have given way to flat, simplified shapes outlined heavily in black, and the brilliant colors are equally "unnatural." This style, inspired by folk art and medieval stained glass, is meant to re-create both the imagined reality of the Crucifixion and the trancelike rapture of the peasant women. Yet we sense that Gauguin did not share this experience: he could paint pictures *about* faith, but not *from* faith.

Two years later, Gauguin's search for the unspoiled life led him even farther afield. He voyaged to Tahiti as a sort of "missionary in reverse," to learn from the natives instead of teaching them. Yet none of his South Pacific

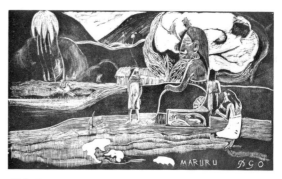

294. PAUL GAUGUIN. *Offerings of Gratitude*. c. 1891–93. Woodcut. The Museum of Modern Art, New York

canvases are as daring as those he had painted in Brittany. His strongest works of this period are woodcuts; *Offerings of Gratitude* (fig. 294) again presents the theme of religious worship, but with the image of a local god replacing Christ. In its frankly "carved" look and its bold white-on-black pattern, we can feel the influences of the native art of the South Seas and of other non-European styles. The renewal of Western civilization, and of Western art, Gauguin believed, must come from "the Primitives"; he advised his fellow Symbolists to shun the Greeks and to turn instead to Persia, ancient Egypt, and the Far East. This idea itself was not new. It stems from the Romantic myth of the Noble Savage, and its ultimate source is the age-old dream of an earthly paradise where Man had lived—and might live again—in a state of nature and innocence. But no one before Gauguin had gone so far in putting the doctrine of primitivism into practice. His pilgrimage to the South Pacific symbolizes the end of four hundred years of colonial expansion which had brought the entire globe under Western domination. The "white man's burden," once so cheerfully—and ruthlessly—shouldered, was becoming unbearable.

SYMBOLISTS

Gauguin's Symbolist followers, who called themselves Nabis (from the Hebrew word for "prophet"), were less remarkable for creative talent than for their ability to spell out and justify the aims of Post-Impressionism in theoretical form. One of them, Maurice Denis, coined the statement that was to become the First Article of Faith for twentieth-century painters: "A picture—before being a war horse, a female nude, or some anecdote—is essentially a flat surface covered with colors in a particular order." The Symbolists also discovered that there were some older artists, descendants of the Romantics, whose work, like their own, placed inner vision above the observation of nature. One of these was Gustave Moreau, a strange recluse who admired Delacroix yet created a world of personal fantasy. *The Apparition* (fig. 295) shows one of his favorite themes: the head of John the Baptist, in a blinding radiance of light, appears to the dancing

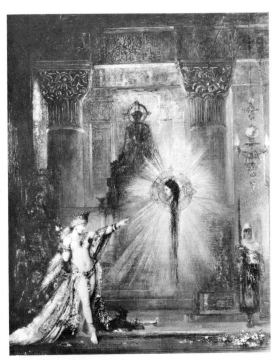

295. GUSTAVE MOREAU. *The Apparition (Dance of Salome)*. c. 1876. 21 1/4 × 17 1/2". Fogg Art Museum, Harvard University, Cambridge, Massachusetts (Grenville L. Winthrop Bequest)

Salome. Her odalisque-like sensuousness, the stream of blood pouring from the severed head, the vast, mysterious space of the setting—suggestive of an exotic temple rather than of Herod's palace—summon up all the dreams of Oriental splendor and cruelty so dear to the Romantic imagination, commingled with an insistence on the reality of the supernatural. Only late in life did Moreau achieve a measure of recognition; suddenly, his art was in tune with the times. During his last six years, he even held a professorship at the conservative Ecole des Beaux-Arts, the successor of the official art academy founded under Louix XIV (see pages 275–76). There he attracted the most gifted students, among them such future leaders as Matisse and Rouault.

How prophetic Moreau's work was of the taste prevailing at the end of the century is evident from a comparison with Aubrey Beardsley, a talented young Englishman whose elegantly "decadent" black-and-white drawings were the very epitome of that taste. They include a *Salome* illustration (fig. 296)

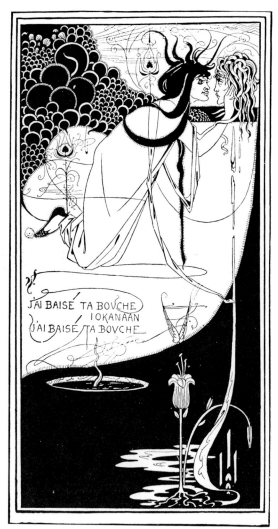

J'AI BAISÉ TA BOVCHE
IOKANAAN
J'AI BAISÉ TA BOVCHE

296. AUBREY BEARDSLEY. *Salome.* 1892. Pen drawing.
Princeton University Library, Princeton, New Jersey

of Japanese influence. Its affinity is to the work of the painter and poet Dante Gabriel Rossetti who in 1848 helped to found an artists' society called the Pre-Raphaelite Brotherhood. The basic aim of the Pre-Raphaelites was to do battle against the frivolous art of the day by producing "pure transcripts . . . from nature" and by having "genuine ideas to express." As the name of the Brotherhood proclaims, its members took their inspiration from the "primitive" masters of the fifteenth century; to that extent, they belonged to the Gothic revival, which had long been an important aspect of the Romantic movement. What set the Pre-Raphaelites apart from Romanticism pure and simple was an urge to reform the ills of modern civilization through their art. But Rossetti was not concerned with social prob-

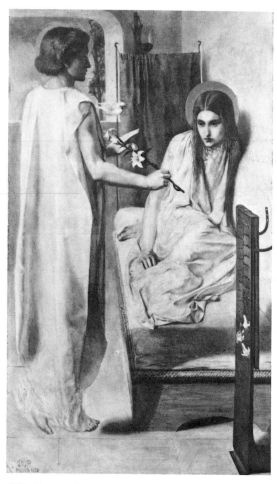

297. DANTE GABRIEL ROSSETTI. *Ecce Ancilla Domini.*
1850. 28 1/2 × 16 1/2". The Tate Gallery, London

that might well be the final scene of the drama depicted by Moreau: Salome has grasped that head and triumphantly kissed it. Whereas Beardsley's erotic meaning is plain—Salome is passionately in love with John and has asked for his head because she could not have him in any other way—Moreau's remains ambiguous: did his Salome perhaps conjure up the vision of the head? Is she, too, in love with John? Nevertheless, the parallel is striking, and there are formal similarities as well, such as the "stem" of trickling blood from which John's head rises like a flower. Yet Beardsley's *Salome* cannot be said to derive from Moreau's. The sources of his style are English, with a strong admixture

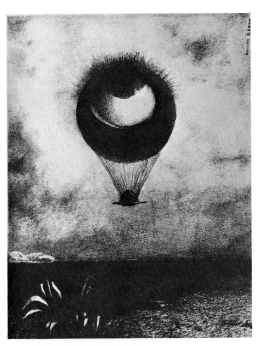

lems; he thought of himself, rather, as a reformer of aesthetic sensibility. His early masterpiece, *Ecce Ancilla Domini* (fig. 297), although realistic in detail, is full of self-conscious archaisms such as the pale tonality, the limited range of colors, the awkward perspective, and the stress on the verticals, not to mention the title in Latin. At the same time, this Annunciation radiates an aura of repressed eroticism that became the hallmark of Rossetti's work and exerted a powerful influence on other Pre-Raphaelites.

298. ODILON REDON. *The Balloon Eye*, from the series *À Edgar Poe*. 1882. Lithograph

299. HENRI DE TOULOUSE-LAUTREC. *At the Moulin Rouge*. 1892. Canvas, 48 3/8 × 55 1/4″. The Art Institute of Chicago (Helen Birch Bartlett Memorial Collection)

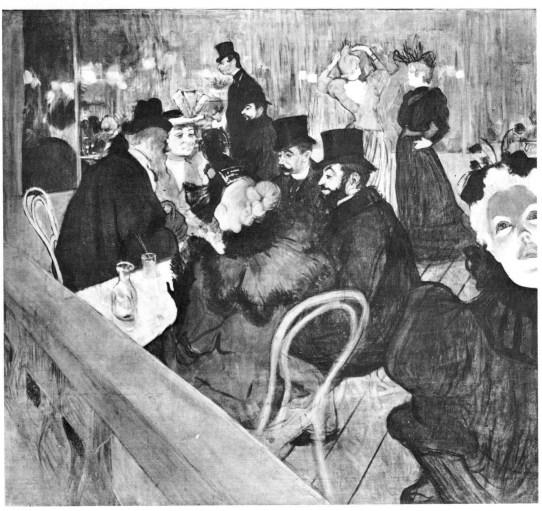

Another solitary artist whom the Symbolists discovered and claimed as one of their own was Odilon Redon. Like Moreau, he had a haunted imagination, but his imagery was even more personal and disturbing. A master of etching and lithography, he drew inspiration from the fantastic visions of Goya (see fig. 266) as well as Romantic literature. The lithograph shown in figure 298 is one of a set he issued in 1882 and dedicated to Edgar Allan Poe. The American poet had been dead for 33 years; but his tormented life and his equally tormented imagination made him the very model of the *poète maudit,* the doomed poet, and his works, excellently translated by Baudelaire and Mallarmé, were greatly admired in France. Redon's lithographs do not illustrate Poe; they are, rather, "visual poems" in their own right, evoking the macabre, hallucinatory world of Poe's imagination. In our example, the artist has revived a very ancient device, the single eye representing the all-seeing mind of God. But, in contrast to the traditional form of the symbol, Redon shows the whole eyeball removed from its socket and converted into a balloon that drifts aimlessly in the sky. Disquieting visual paradoxes of this kind were to be exploited on a large scale by the Dadaists and Surrealists in our own century.

TOULOUSE-LAUTREC

Van Gogh's and Gauguin's discontent with the spiritual ills of Western civilization was part of a sentiment widely shared at the end of the nineteenth century. A self-conscious preoccupation with decadence, evil, and darkness pervaded the artistic and literary climate. Even those who saw no escape analyzed their predicament in fascinated horror. Yet this very awareness proved to be a source of strength (the truly decadent do not realize their plight). The most remarkable instance of this strength was Henri de Toulouse-Lautrec; physically an ugly dwarf, he was an artist of superb talent who led a dissolute life in the nightspots of Paris and died of alcoholism. He was a great admirer of Degas, and his *At the Moulin Rouge* (fig. 299) recalls the zigzag composition of Degas' *The Glass of Absinthe* (see fig. 281). But this view of the well-known night club is no Impressionist "slice of life": Toulouse-Lautrec sees through the gay surface of the scene, viewing performers and customers with a pitilessly sharp eye for their character (including his own; he is the tiny bearded man next to the very tall one in the background). The large areas of flat color and the emphatic, smoothly curving outlines reflect the influence of Gauguin. Although Toulouse-Lautrec was no Symbolist, the Moulin Rouge that he shows us here has an atmosphere so joyless and oppressive that we can only regard it as a place of evil.

MUNCH; KLIMT

Something of the same macabre quality pervades the early work of Edvard Munch, a gifted Norwegian who came to Paris in 1889 and based his starkly expressive style on Toulouse-Lautrec, Van Gogh, and Gauguin. *The Scream* (fig. 300) was done in Berlin, where Munch settled after the controversy raised by his paintings had led to the Berlin Secession, but it still shows the influence of all three. The picture is an image of fear, the terrifying, unreasoning fear we feel in a nightmare. Munch visualizes this experience without the aid of frightening apparitions,

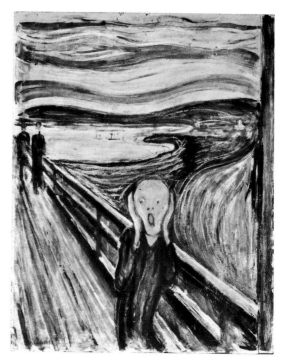

300. EDVARD MUNCH. *The Scream.* 1893. Canvas, 36 × 29″. National Museum, Oslo

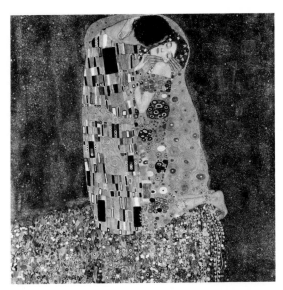

301. GUSTAV KLIMT. *The Kiss*. 1907–08. Oil on canvas, 70 7/8 × 70 7/8″. Österreichische Galerie, Vienna

and his achievement is the more persuasive for that very reason. The rhythm of the long, wavy lines seems to carry the echo of the scream into every corner of the picture, making earth and sky one great sounding board of terror. By the same token, the erotic anxiety in *The Kiss* (fig. 301) by Gustav Klimt, the most important member of the Vienna Secession, is more telling than in Beardsley's *Salome*. Engulfed in their mosaic-like robes, the angular figures steal a brief moment of passion, which emphasizes their joyless existence.

PICASSO

The young Pablo Picasso shared a similar sense of tragedy. Upon arriving in Paris in 1900, he came under the spell of the same artistic atmosphere that had generated the style of Munch. His so-called Blue Period (referring to the prevailing color of his canvases as well as to their mood) consists almost entirely of pictures of beggars and derelicts such as *The Old Guitarist* (fig. 302)—outcasts or victims of society whose pathos reflects the artist's own sense of isolation. Yet these figures convey poetic melancholy more than outright despair. The aged musician accepts his fate with a resignation that seems almost saintly, and the attenuated grace of his limbs reminds us of El Greco

(see colorplate 38). *The Old Guitarist* is a strange amalgam of Mannerism and the art of Gauguin and Toulouse-Lautrec (note the smoothly curved contours) imbued with the personal gloom of a twenty-two-year-old genius.

ROUSSEAU

A few years later, Picasso and his friends discovered a painter who until then had attracted no attention, although he had been exhibiting his work since 1886. He was Henri Rousseau, a retired customs collector who had started to paint in his middle age without training of any sort. His ideal—which, fortunately, he never achieved—was the arid academic style of the followers of Ingres. Rousseau is that paradox, a folk artist of genius. How else could he have done a picture like *The Dream* (colorplate 65)? What goes on in the enchanted world of this canvas needs no explanation, because none

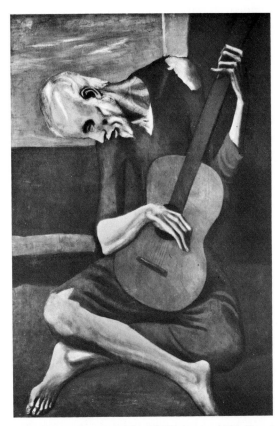

302. PABLO PICASSO. *The Old Guitarist*. 1903. Panel, 47 3/4 × 32 1/2″. The Art Institute of Chicago (Helen Birch Bartlett Memorial Collection)

is possible, but perhaps for that very reason its magic becomes unbelievably real to us. Rousseau himself described the scene in a little poem:

Yadwigha, peacefully asleep
Enjoys a lovely dream:
She hears a kind snake charmer
Playing upon his reed.
On stream and foliage glisten
The silvery beams of the moon.
And savage serpents listen
To the gay, entrancing tune.

Here at last is that innocent directness of feeling which Gauguin thought was so necessary for the age, and traveled so far to find. Picasso and his friends were the first to recognize this quality in Rousseau's work. They revered him, quite justifiably, as the godfather of twentieth-century painting.

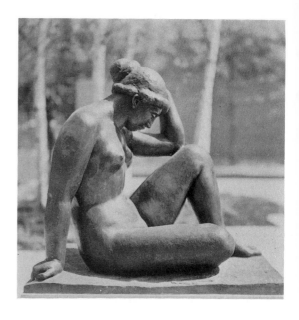

303. ARISTIDE MAILLOL. *Seated Woman (Méditerranée)*. c. 1901. Height 41″. Collection Dr. Oskar Reinhardt, Winterthur, Switzerland

SCULPTURE

Tendencies paralleling Post-Impressionism in painting appeared in sculpture around 1900, when younger men schooled by Rodin were ready to explore new paths. The finest sculptor of this generation was Aristide Maillol. A Symbolist painter at first, Maillol was less thoroughgoing than Gauguin in rejecting the European tradition. He took the early fifth century B.C. for his cutoff point, because he admired the simplified strength of the Archaic and Early Classical styles of Greek sculpture (see pages 52–56). The *Seated Woman* (fig. 303) evokes memories of early Greece. In its solidity, weight, and clearly defined volumes, it recalls Cézanne's statement that all natural forms are based on the cone, the sphere, and the cylinder. Maillol's ideas were the exact opposite of Rodin's. A statue, he believed, should be self-contained and at rest. No outside force should be able to disturb its harmonious repose. In this respect, the *Seated Woman* is the exact opposite of *The Thinker* (see fig. 289). Maillol later gave it the title *Méditerranée*—The Mediterranean—to suggest the source from which he drew the timeless serenity of his figure.

A state of brooding calm is also apparent in the *Standing Youth* (fig. 304) by the German sculptor Wilhelm Lehmbruck; here a Gothic elongation and angularity are conjoined with a fine balance derived from Maillol's art, and also with some of Rodin's expressive energy. The total effect is a looming monumental figure well anchored in space, yet partaking of that poetic melancholy we observed in Picasso's Blue Period. Ernst Barlach, another important German sculptor who reached maturity in the years before the First World War, seems the very opposite of Lehmbruck; he is a "Gothic primitivist," and more akin to Munch than to the Western Symbolist tradition. What Gauguin had experienced in Brittany and the tropics, Barlach found by going to Russia: the simple humanity of a preindustrial age. His figures, such as the *Man Drawing a Sword* (fig. 305), embody elementary emotions—wrath, fear, grief—that seem imposed upon them by invisible presences. When they act they are like somnambulists, unaware of their own impulses. Man, to Barlach, is a humble creature at the mercy of forces beyond his control; he is never the master of his fate. Characteristically, these figures do not fully emerge from the material substance (often, as here, a massive block of wood) of which they are made; their clothing is like a hard chrysalis that hides the body, as in medieval sculpture. Barlach's art has a range that is severely restricted in both form and emotion, yet its mute intensity within these limits is not easily forgotten.

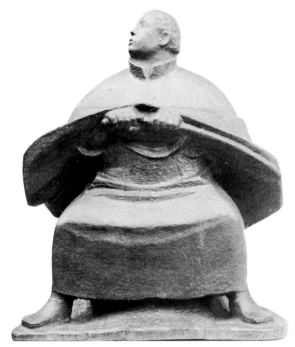

305. ERNST BARLACH. *Man Drawing a Sword*. 1911. Wood, height 31″. Museum, Cranbrook Academy of Art, Bloomfield Hills, Michigan

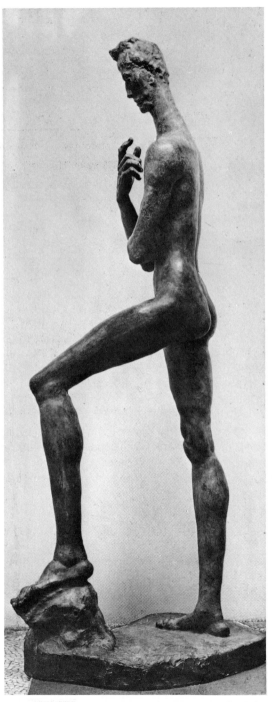

304. WILHELM LEHMBRUCK. *Standing Youth*. 1913. Cast stone, height 92″. The Museum of Modern Art, New York (Gift of Mrs. John D. Rockefeller, Jr.)

Art in Our Time

In our account of modern art we have already discussed a succession of "isms": Neoclassicism, Romanticism, Realism, Impressionism, Post-Impressionism, Divisionism, Symbolism. There are many more to be found in twentieth-century art—so many, in fact, that no one has made an exact count. These "isms" can form a serious obstacle to our understanding; they make us feel that we cannot hope to comprehend the art of our time unless we immerse ourselves in a welter of esoteric doctrines. Actually, we can disregard all but the most important "isms"; like the names for the styles of earlier periods, they are merely labels to help us put things in their proper place. If an "ism" fails the test of usefulness, we need not bother with it. This is true of many "isms" in contemporary art; the movements they designate either cannot be seen clearly as separate entities or have so little importance that they interest only the specialist. It has always been easier to invent a new label than to create a new movement that truly deserves one.

Still, we cannot do without "isms" altogether. Among the international trends of twentieth-century art, we find three main

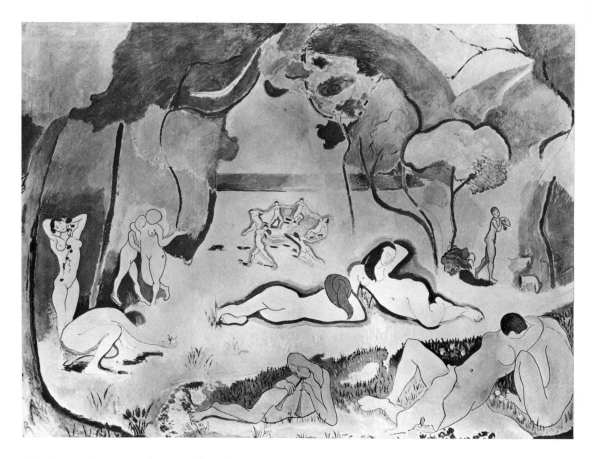

306. HENRI MATISSE. *The Joy of Life.* 1905–06.
68 1/2 × 93 3/4″. Copyright Barnes Foundation,
Merion, Pennsylvania

currents, each comprising a number of "isms," that began with the Post-Impressionists and have developed greatly since then: Expression, Abstraction, and Fantasy. The first stresses the artist's emotional attitude toward himself and the world; the second, the formal structure of the work of art; and the third explores the realm of the imagination, especially its spontaneous and irrational qualities. But we must not forget that feeling, order, and imagination are all present in *every* work of art: without imagination, it would be deadly dull; without some degree of order, it would be chaotic; without feeling, it would leave us unmoved. These currents, therefore, are not mutually exclusive. We shall find them interrelated in many ways, and the work of one artist may belong to more than one current. Moreover, each current embraces a wide range of approaches, from the realistic to the completely nonrepresentational (or nonobjective). Thus these three currents do not correspond to specific styles, but to general attitudes. The primary concern of the Expressionist is the human community; of the Abstractionist, the structure of reality; and of the artist of Fantasy, the labyrinth of the individual human mind.

EXPRESSIONISM

THE FAUVES

The twentieth century may be said, so far as painting is concerned, to have begun five years late. Between 1901 and 1906, several comprehensive exhibitions of the work of Van Gogh, Gauguin, and Cézanne were held in Paris. The young painters who had grown up in the "decadent," morbid mood of the 1890s were profoundly impressed, and some of them developed a radical new style, full of violent color and bold distortions. Their first public appearance, in 1905, so shocked the critics that they were dubbed the *Fauves* ("wild beasts"), a label they wore with pride. Actually, it was not a common program that brought them together, but their shared sense of liberation and experiment. Thus Fauvism comprised a number of loosely related individual styles, and the group dissolved after a few years.

MATISSE

Its leading member was Henri Matisse, the oldest of the founding fathers of twentieth-century painting. *The Joy of Life* (fig. 306), probably the most important picture of his long career, sums up the spirit of Fauvism better than any other single work. It obviously derives its flat planes of color, its heavy undulating outlines, and the "primitive" flavor of its forms from Gauguin (see colorplate 64); even its subject suggests the vision of Man in a state of Nature that Gauguin had pursued in Tahiti (see fig. 294). But we soon realize that these figures are not Noble Savages under the spell of a native god; the subject is a pagan scene in the Classical sense—a bacchanal, like Titian's (compare colorplate 35). Even the poses of the figures have for the most part a Classical origin, and in the apparently careless draftsmanship resides a profound knowledge of the human body (Matisse had been trained in the academic tradition). What makes the picture so revolutionary is its radical simplicity, its "genius of omission": everything that possibly can be, has been left out or stated by implication only, yet the scene retains the essentials of plastic form and spatial depth. Painting, Matisse seems to say, is the rhythmic arrangement of line and color on a flat plane, but it is not *only* that; how far can the image of nature be pared down without destroying its basic properties and thus reducing it to mere surface ornament? "What I am after, above all," he once explained, "is expression. . . . [But] . . . expression does not consist of the passion mirrored upon a human face. . . . The whole arrangement of my picture is expressive. The placement of figures or objects, the empty spaces around them, the proportions, everything plays a part." But what, we wonder, does *The Joy of Life* express? Exactly what its title says. Whatever his debt to Gauguin, Matisse was never stirred by the same ago-

nized discontent with the "decadence" of our civilization. He had strong feelings about only one thing—the act of painting: this to him was an experience so profoundly joyous that he wanted to transmit it to the beholder in all its freshness and immediacy. The purpose of his pictures, he always asserted, was to give pleasure.

The radical new balance Matisse struck between the "2-D" and "3-D" aspects of painting is particularly evident in his *Harmony in Red* (colorplate 66); he spreads the same flat blue-on-red pattern on the tablecloth and on the wall, yet he distinguishes the horizontal from the vertical planes with complete assurance. Cézanne had pioneered this integration of surface ornament into the design of a picture (see fig. 291), but Matisse here makes it the mainstay of his composition. Equally bold—but perfectly readable— is the view of a garden with flowering trees, seen through the window; the house in the distance is painted the same bright pink as the interior, and is thereby brought into relation with the rest of the picture. Likewise the blue of the sky, the greens of the foliage, and the bright yellow dots (for flowers) all recur in the foreground. Matisse's "genius of omission" is again at work: by reducing the number of tints to a minimum, he makes of color an independent structural element. It has such importance that *Harmony in Red* would be meaningless in a black-and-white reproduction.

ROUAULT; SOUTINE

Another member of the Fauves, Georges Rouault would not have used Matisse's definition of "expression." For him this had still to include, as it had in the past, "the passion mirrored upon a human face"; we need only look at his *Head of Christ* (fig. 307). But the expressiveness does not reside only in the "image quality" of the face. The savage slashing strokes of the brush speak equally eloquently of the artist's rage and compassion. (If we cover the upper third of the picture, it is no longer a recognizable image, yet the expressive effect is hardly diminished.) Rouault is the true heir of Van Gogh's and Gauguin's concern for the corrupt state of the world. He, however, hoped for spiritual renewal through a revitalized Catholic faith.

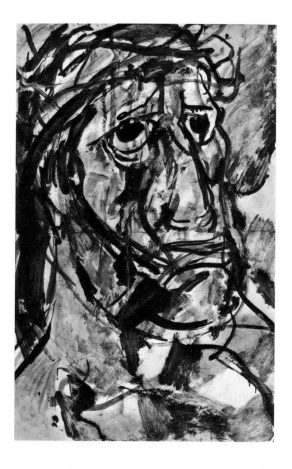

307. GEORGES ROUAULT. *Head of Christ*. 1905. Oil on paper, 45 × 31″. Walter Chrysler Museum, Provincetown

His pictures, whatever their subject, are personal statements of that ardent hope. Trained in his youth as a worker in stained glass, he was better prepared than the other Fauves to accept Gauguin's enthusiasm for medieval art. Rouault's later paintings—for example *The Old Clown* (figure 308), who acts as his Everyman—are made up of areas of glowing color outlined by heavy black borders in the manner of Gothic stained-glass windows (compare figure 137). Here the mood of resignation and inner suffering reminds us of Rembrandt and Daumier.

Rouault's Expressionism was unique among French painters. The only artist in Paris to follow his lead was Chaim Soutine, an immigrant from Eastern Europe. The tempestuous, violent brushwork in *The Dead Fowl* (fig. 309) clearly reflects the influence of the older master. Although the picture belongs conventionally to the class of still life, the dead bird is a terrifying symbol of death. As we look at the plucked, creamy-white body, we realize with sudden horror its close resemblance to a human shape. It evokes the earthward plunge of Icarus, or it is, perhaps, a cruelly direct image of Plato's definition of Man as a "featherless biped." For his power to transmute sheer anguish into visual form, Soutine has no equal among modern artists.

NOLDE; KOKOSCHKA; BECKMANN

It was in Germany that Fauvism had its most enduring impact, especially among the members of a society called *Die Brücke* (the bridge), a group of like-minded painters who lived in Dresden in 1905. One *Brücke* artist, Emil Nolde, stands somewhat apart; older than the rest, he shared Rouault's predilection for religious themes, although he was a far less articulate painter. The thickly encrusted surfaces and the deliberately clumsy draftsmanship of his *Last Supper* (fig. 310) make it clear that Nolde rejected all pictorial

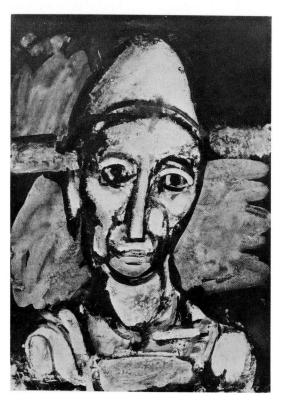

308. GEORGES ROUAULT. *The Old Clown*. 1917. Oil on canvas, 40 × 29 3/4″. Collection Mr. and Mrs. Stavros Niarchos, Paris

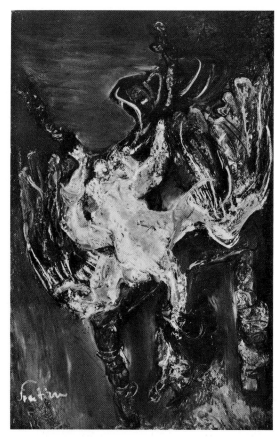

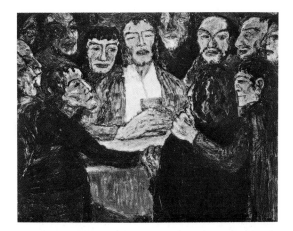

310. EMIL NOLDE. *The Last Supper*. 1909. Canvas. 32 1/2 × 41 3/4″. Stiftung Seebüll Ada und Emil Nolde, Neukirchen, Germany

309. CHAIM SOUTINE. *Dead Fowl*. c. 1926. Canvas, 38 1/2 × 24 1/2″. The Art Institute of Chicago (Joseph Winterbotham Collection)

refinement in favor of a primeval, direct expression inspired by Gauguin. Another artist of highly individual talent, related to *Die Brücke* although not a member of it, is the Austrian painter Oskar Kokoschka. His outstanding works are his portraits painted before World War I, such as his splendid *Self-Portrait* (fig. 311). Like Van Gogh, Kokoschka sees himself as a visionary, a witness to the truth and reality of his inner experiences (see fig. 293); the hypersensitive features seem lacerated by a great ordeal of the imagination. It may not be fanciful to find in this tortured psyche an echo of the cultural climate that also produced Sigmund Freud. A more robust descendant of the *Brücke* artists was Max Beckmann, who did not become an Expressionist until after he had experienced the First World War, which left him in deep despair at the state of modern

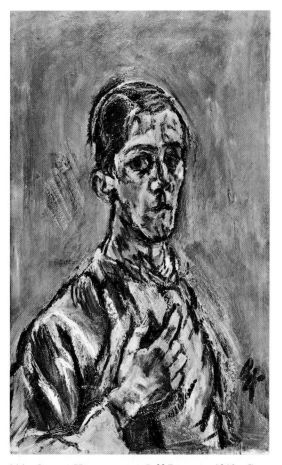

311. OSKAR KOKOSCHKA. *Self-Portrait*. 1913. Canvas, 32 × 19 1/2″. The Museum of Modern Art, New York

civilization. The wings of his triptych, *Departure* (fig. 312), completed when, under Nazi pressure, he was on the point of leaving his homeland, portray a nightmarish world crammed with puppet-like figures, as disquieting as Bosch's *Hell* (see right panel of fig. 155). Their symbolism, however, is even more difficult to interpret, since it is necessarily subjective, though no one would deny its evocative power. In the hindsight of today, the topsy-turvy quality of these two scenes, full of mutilations and meaningless rituals, seems to have the force of prophecy. The stable design of the center panel, in contrast, with its expanse of sea and its sunlit brightness, conveys the hopeful spirit of an escape to distant shores. After living through the Second World War in occupied Holland, under the most trying conditions, Beckmann spent the final three years of his career in America.

KANDINSKY

But the most daring and original step beyond Fauvism was taken in Germany by a Russian, Wassily Kandinsky, the leading member of a group of artists in Munich called *Der Blaue Reiter* (the Blue Horseman). After 1910,

Kandinsky abandoned representation altogether. Using the rainbow colors and the free, dynamic brushwork of the Paris Fauves, he created a completely nonobjective style. These works have titles as abstract as their forms: our example, one of the most striking, is called *Sketch I for "Composition VII"* (colorplate 67). Perhaps we should avoid the term "abstract," which is often taken to mean that the artist has analyzed and simplified the shapes of visible reality (remember Cézanne's dictum that all natural forms are based on the cone, the sphere, and the cylinder). This was not Kandinsky's method. Whatever traces of representation his work contains are quite involuntary—his aim was to charge form and color with a purely spiritual meaning (as he put it) by eliminating all resemblance to the physical world. Whistler, too, had spoken of "divesting his picture from any outside sort of interest"; he even anticipated Kandinsky's use of "musical"

312. MAX BECKMANN. *Departure*. 1932–35. Canvas: center panel 84 3/4 × 45 3/8", side panels each 84 3/4 × 39 1/4". The Museum of Modern Art, New York (Anonymous gift, by exchange)

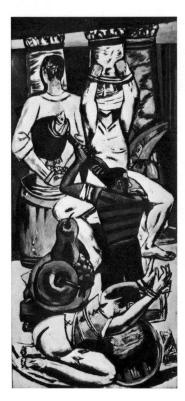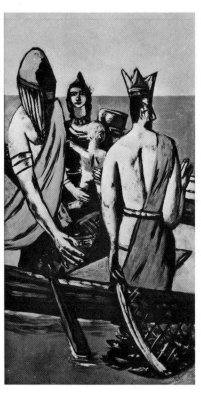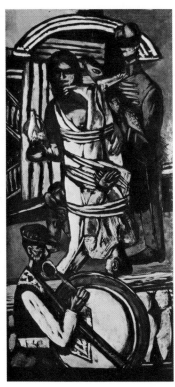

titles. But it was the liberating influence of the Fauves that permitted Kandinsky to put this theory into practice. The possibility was implicit in Fauvism from the start, as shown in our experiment with Rouault's *Head of Christ*: when the upper third of the picture is covered, the rest becomes a nonobjective composition strangely similar to Kandinsky's. How valid is the analogy between painting and music? When Kandinsky carries it through so strictly, does he really lift his art to another plane of freedom? Or could it be that his declared independence from representation now forces him instead to "represent music," which limits him even more severely? Kandinsky's advocates like to point out that representational painting has a "literary" content, and to deplore such dependence on another art. But why should the "musical" content of nonobjective painting be more desirable? Is painting less alien to music than to literature? The case is difficult to argue, nor does it matter whether this theory is right or wrong; the proof of the pudding is in the eating, not the recipe. Kandinsky's—or any other artist's—ideas are important to us only if we are convinced of the importance of his pictures. Did he create a viable style? Admittedly, his work demands an intuitive response that may be difficult for some of us, yet the painting reproduced here has density and vitality, and a radiant freshness of feeling that impresses us even though we are uncertain what exactly the artist has expressed.

ABSTRACTION

The second of our main currents is the one we called Abstraction. Literally, to abstract means to draw away from, to separate. If we have ten apples, and then separate the ten from the apples, we get an "abstract number," a number that no longer refers to particular things. But "apples," too, is an abstraction, since it places ten apples in one class, without regard for their individual qualities. The artist who sets out to paint ten apples will find no two of them alike, yet he cannot possibly take all of their differences into account: even the most painstaking portrayal of these particular pieces of fruit is

bound to be some sort of an abstraction. Abstraction, then, goes into the making of *any* work of art, whether the artist knows it or not. The process was not conscious and controlled, however, until the Renaissance, when artists first analyzed the shapes of nature in terms of mathematical bodies (see p. 180). Cézanne and Seurat revitalized this approach and explored it further; they are the direct ancestors of the abstract movement in twentieth-century art. Its real creator, however, was Pablo Picasso.

FACET CUBISM

About 1905, stimulated both by the Fauves and by the great Post-Impressionists, Picasso gradually abandoned the melancholy lyricism of his Blue Period for a more robust style. He shared Matisse's enthusiasm for Gauguin and Cézanne, but he viewed these masters very differently; in 1906–7, he produced a monumental canvas (fig. 313) so challenging that it outraged even Matisse. The title, *Les Demoiselles d'Avignon* ("The Girls of Avignon"), refers not to the town of that name but to Avignon Street in a notorious section of Barcelona; when Picasso started the picture, it was to be a temptation scene, but he ended up with a composition of five nudes and a still life. But what nudes! The three on the left are angular distortions of Classical figures, while the violently dislocated features and bodies of the other two have all the barbaric qualities of primitive art (see figs. 8, 9). Following Gauguin, the Fauves had discovered the aesthetic appeal of African and Oceanic sculpture, yet it was Picasso, rather than they, who used primitive art as a battering ram against the Classical conception of beauty. Not only the proportions, but the organic integrity and continuity of the human body are denied here, so that the canvas (in the apt words of one critic) "resembles a field of broken glass." Picasso, then, has destroyed a great deal; what has he gained in the process? Once we recover from the initial shock, we begin to see that the destruction is quite methodical: everything—the figures as well as their setting—is broken up into angular facets. These, we will note, are not flat, but shaded in a way that gives them a certain three-dimensionality. We cannot always be sure whether they are con-

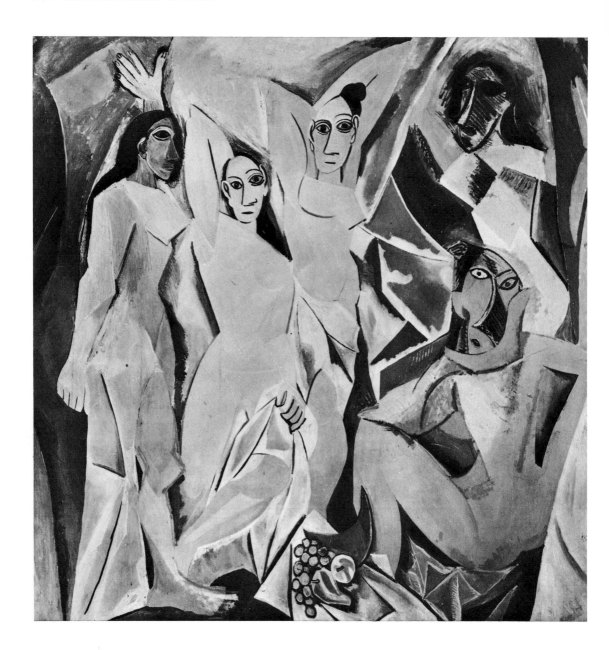

313. PABLO PICASSO. *Les Demoiselles d'Avignon.*
1906–07. Canvas, 96 × 92". The Museum of Modern
Art, New York (Acquired through the Lillie P. Bliss
Bequest)

cave or convex; some look like chunks of
solidified space, others like fragments of
translucent bodies. They constitute a unique
kind of matter, which imposes a new kind of
integrity and continuity on the entire canvas.
Unlike Matisse's *Harmony in Red,* the *Demoiselles* can no longer be read as an image
of the external world; its world is its own,
analogous to nature but built along different

principles. Picasso's revolutionary "building
material," compounded of voids and solids,
is hard to describe. The early critics, who saw
only the prevalence of sharp edges and angles, dubbed the new style Cubism.

That the *Demoiselles* owes anything to
Cézanne may seem hard to believe. Nevertheless, Picasso had studied Cézanne's late
work with care (see fig. 292), finding in its
abstract treatment of volume and space the
translucent structural units from which he
derived the facets of Cubism. The link is
clearer in Picasso's portrait of Ambroise
Vollard (fig. 314), painted four years later:

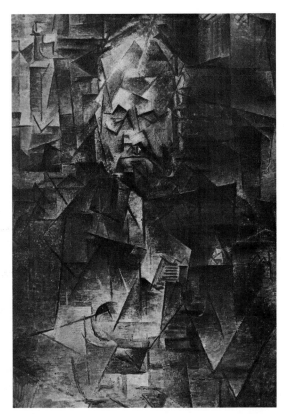

314. PABLO PICASSO. *Ambroise Vollard*. 1909–10. Canvas, 36 × 25 1/2″. Pushkin Museum, Moscow

the facets are now small and precise, more like prisms, and the canvas has the balance and refinement of a fully mature style. Contrasts of color and texture are reduced to a minimum, so as not to compete with the design. And the structure has become so intricate a web that it would seem wholly cerebral if the "imprismed" sitter's face did not emerge with such dramatic force. Cubism here has become an abstract style within the purely Western sense, as against the "barbaric" distortions of the *Demoiselles*. But its distance from observed reality has not significantly increased—Picasso may be playing an elaborate game of hide-and-seek with nature, but he still needs it to challenge his creative powers. The nonobjective realm held no appeal for him, then or later.

COLLAGE CUBISM

By 1910, Cubism was well established as an alternative to Fauvism, and Picasso had been joined by other artists—notably Georges Braque, with whom he collaborated so inti-

mately that their work at that time is hard to tell apart. Both of them initiated the next phase of Cubism, which was even bolder than the first, as evidenced by Braque's *Le Courrier* of 1913 (fig. 315). It is composed almost entirely of cut-and-pasted scraps of material, with only a few lines added to complete the design; we recognize strips of imitation wood graining, part of a tobacco wrapper with a contrasting stamp, half the masthead of a newspaper, and a bit of newsprint made into a playing card (the ace of hearts). This technique came to be known as *collage* (French for "paste-up"). Why did Picasso and Braque suddenly prefer the contents of the wastepaper basket to brush and paint? Because they had come to think of the picture surface as a sort of tray on which to "serve" the still life to the beholder, and they found the best way to explore this new concept was to put real things on the tray. The ingredients of a collage actually play a double role; they have been shaped and combined, then drawn or painted upon so as to give them a representational meaning, but they retain their original identity as scraps of material. Thus their function is both to *represent* (to be part of an image) and to *present* (to be themselves). In the latter role, they endow a collage with a self-sufficiency that no facet-Cubist picture could have. A tray, after all, is a self-contained area, detached from the rest of the physical

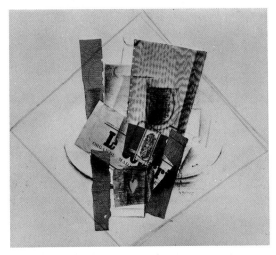

315. GEORGES BRAQUE. *Le Courrier*. 1913. Collage, 20 × 22 1/2″. The Philadephia Museum of Art (A.E. Gallatin Collection)

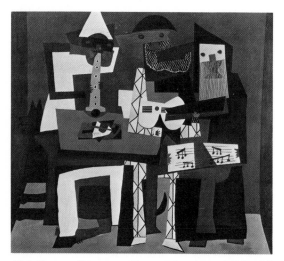

316. PABLO PICASSO. *Three Musicians*. 1921. Oil on canvas, 79 × 87 3/4″. The Museum of Modern Art, New York. (Mrs. Simon Guggenheim Fund)

world; unlike a painting, it cannot show more than is actually on it. The difference between the two phases of Cubism may also be defined in terms of picture space: facet Cubism retains a certain kind of depth, the painted surface acts as a window through which we still perceive remnants of the familiar perspective space of the Renaissance. This space lies behind the picture plane and has no visible limits; it may contain objects that are hidden from our view. In collage Cubism, on the contrary, the picture space lies in front of the plane of the "tray"; space is created not by illusionistic devices, such as modeling or foreshortening, but by the actual overlapping of layers of pasted materials. Collage Cubism, then, offers a basically new space concept, the first since Masaccio: it is a true landmark in the history of painting.

Before long Picasso and Braque discovered that they could retain this new pictorial space without the use of pasted materials; they had only to paint as if they were making collages. Picasso's *Three Musicians* (fig. 316) shows this "cut-paper style" so consistently that we cannot tell from the reproduction whether it is painted or pasted. It is, in any event, one of the great masterpieces of collage Cubism, monumental in size and conception. The separate pieces are fitted together as firmly as architectural blocks, yet the artist's primary concern is not with the surface pat-

tern (if it were, the painting would resemble a patchwork quilt), but with the image of the three musicians, traditional figures of the comedy stage. Their human presence, solemn and even sinister, may be sensed behind the screen of costumes and masks.

By now, Picasso was internationally famous. Cubism had spread throughout the Western world: it influenced not only painters, but sculptors and even architects. Picasso himself, however, was already striking out in a new direction. By 1920, he was working simultaneously in two separate styles: collage Cubism and a Neoclassic style of strongly modeled, heavy-bodied figures such as his *Mother and Child* (fig. 317). To many, this seemed a kind of betrayal, but in retrospect the cause of Picasso's double-track performance is evident: chafing under the limitations of collage Cubism, he needed to resume contact with the Classical tradition, the "art of the museums." The figures in *Mother and Child* have a mock-monumental quality

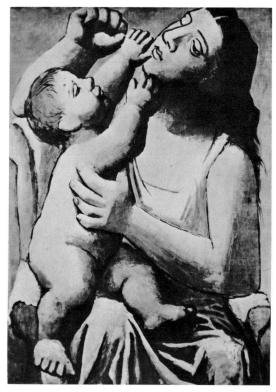

317. PABLO PICASSO. *Mother and Child*. 1921–22. Canvas, 38 × 28″. Collection the Alex L. Hillman Corporation, New York

that suggests colossal statues rather than flesh-and-blood human beings, yet the theme is treated with surprising tenderness. The forms, however, are carefully dovetailed within the frame, not unlike the way a collage is put together. A few years later the two tracks of Picasso's style began to converge, making an extraordinary synthesis that was the basis of his art thereafter. The *Three Dancers* of 1925 (colorplate 68) shows how he managed this seemingly impossible feat. Structurally, the picture is pure collage Cubism, even though, instead of cutting and pasting, the artist has imitated the appearance of collage with his brush; the canvas even shows painted imitations of specific materials—patterned wallpaper, and samples of various fabrics cut out with pinking shears. But the figures, a wildly fantastic version of a Classical dance, are an even more violent assault on convention than the *Demoiselles d'Avignon* (fig. 313). Human anatomy is here simply the raw material for Picasso's incredibly fertile inventiveness; limbs, breasts, and faces are handled with the same sovereign freedom as the fragments of external reality in Braque's *Le Courrier*. Their original identity no longer matters—breasts may turn into eyes, profiles merge with frontal views, shadows become substance, and vice versa, in an endless flow of transformations. They are "visual puns," offering wholly unexpected possibilities of expression—humorous, grotesque, macabre, even tragic.

FUTURISM

As originally conceived by Picasso and Braque, Cubism offered a formal discipline of subtle balance, used for traditional subjects—still life, portraiture, the nude. Other painters, however, saw in the new style a special affinity with the geometric precision of engineering that made it uniquely attuned to the dynamism of modern times. The short-lived Futurist movement in Italy exemplifies this attitude; in 1910 its founders issued a manifesto violently rejecting the past and exalting the beauty of the machine. At first they used techniques developed from Post-Impressionism to convey the surge of industrial society in otherwise static compositions still dependent upon representational images. But by adopting the simultaneous views of

facet Cubism in *Dynamism of a Cyclist* (fig. 318), Umberto Boccioni, the most original of the Futurists, was able to communicate furious pedaling across time and space far more tellingly than if he had actually depicted the human figure, which could be seen in only one time and place in traditional art. In the flexible vocabulary provided by Cubism, Boccioni found the means of expressing the twentieth century's new sense of time, space, and energy, as it was soon to be defined in Albert Einstein's theory of relativity. Moreover, Boccioni suggests the unique quality of the modern experience. With his pulsating movement, the cyclist has become an extension of his environment, from which he is now indistinguishable. Futurism literally died out in World War I; its leaders were killed by the same vehicles of destruction they had glorified only a few years earlier in their revolutionary manifesto. Strong echoes of Futurism appear, however, in *Brooklyn Bridge* (fig. 319), painted by the Italo-American Joseph Stella just before the end of the war. With its maze of vigorous luminescent cables, powerful diagonal thrusts and crystalline "cells" of space, it miraculously equals Walt Whitman's poem as a paean to that monument of modern technology. In a similar vein, *The City* (fig. 320), by the Frenchman Fernand Léger, is a beautifully controlled industrial landscape that is stable without being static, and its collage Cubism reflects the clean geometric shapes of modern machinery. Buoyant with optimism and

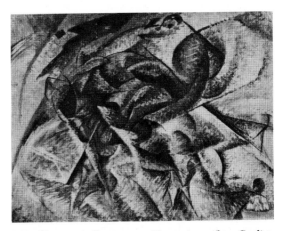

318. UMBERTO BOCCIONI. *Dynamism of a Cyclist.* 1913. Canvas, 27 5/8 × 37 3/8". Collection Gianni Mattioli, Milan

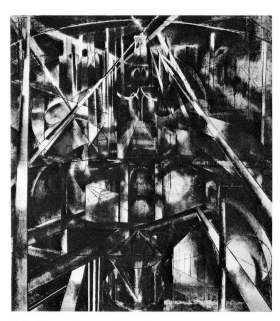

319. JOSEPH STELLA. *Brooklyn Bridge*. 1917. Canvas, 84 × 76″. Yale University Art Gallery, New Haven (Collection of the Société Anonyme)

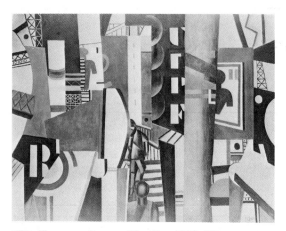

320. FERNAND LEGER. *The City*. 1919. Oil on canvas, 91 × 117 1/2″. The Philadelphia Museum of Art (A. E. Gallatin Collection)

pleasurable excitement, it conjures up a mechanized utopia. In this instance, the term "abstraction" applies more to the choice of design elements and their manner of combination than to the shapes themselves, since these (except for the two figures on the staircase) are "pre-fabricated" entities.

NEO-PLASTICISM: MONDRIAN

The most radical extension of Cubism, however, may be found in the work of a Dutch painter nine years older than Picasso,

Piet Mondrian. He came to Paris in 1912 as a mature Expressionist in the tradition of Van Gogh and the Fauves. Under the impact of Cubism, his ideas underwent a complete change, and within the following decade he developed a totally nonobjective style that he called Neo-Plasticism. *Composition with Red, Blue, and Yellow* (colorplate 69) shows Mondrian's style at its most severe: he restricts his design to horizontals and verticals and his colors to the three primary hues, plus black-and-white, thus eliminating every possibility of representation. Yet Mondrian sometimes gave his works such titles as *Trafalgar Square* or *Broadway Boogie-Woogie*, which hint at some degree of relationship with observed reality. Unlike Kandinsky, Mondrian did not strive for pure, lyrical emotion; his goal, he asserted, was "pure reality," and he defined this as equilibrium "through the balance of unequal but equivalent oppositions." Perhaps we can best understand what he meant if we think of his work as "abstract collage" that uses black bands and colored rectangles, instead of recognizable fragments of everyday materials. He was interested only in relationships, and wanted no distracting elements or fortuitous associations. But, by establishing the "right" relationship among his bands and rectangles, he transforms them as thoroughly as Braque transformed the snippets of pasted paper in *Le Courrier* (fig. 315). How did he go about discovering the "right" relationship? And how did he determine the shape and number of the bands and rectangles? In *Le Courrier*, the ingredients are to some extent "given" by chance; Mondrian, apart from his self-imposed rules, constantly faced the dilemma of unlimited possibilities. He could not change the relationship of the bands to the rectangles without changing the bands and rectangles themselves. When we consider his task, we begin to realize its infinite complexity. If we measure the various units in *Composition with Red, Blue, and Yellow*, we find that only the proportions of the canvas itself are truly rational, an exact square; Mondrian arrived at all the rest "by feel," and must have undergone agonies of trial and error. Strange as it may seem, Mondrian's exquisite sense of nonsymmetrical balance is so specific that critics well acquainted with his work have no difficulty telling fakes from genuine pictures. Designers who work with nonfigurative shapes, such as architects and typographers, are most likely to be sensitive to this quality, and Mondrian has had a greater influence among them than among painters (see figs. 357–359).

FANTASY

The third current, which we termed Fantasy, follows a course less clear-cut than the other two, since it depends on a state of mind more than on any particular style. The one thing all painters of fantasy have in common is the belief that imagination is more important than the outside world. And since every artist's imagination is his own private domain, the images it provides for him are likely to be equally private, unless he subjects them to a deliberate process of selection. But how can such "uncontrolled" images have meaning to the beholder, whose own inner world is not the same as the artist's? Psychoanalysis has taught us that we are not so different from each other in this respect as we like to think. Our minds are all formed according to the same basic pattern, and the same is true of our imagination and memory. They belong to the unconscious part of the mind where experiences are stored, whether we want to remember them or not. At night, or whenever conscious thought relaxes its vigilance, our experiences return and we seem to live through them again. However, the unconscious mind does not usually reproduce our experiences as they actually happened. They will often be admitted into the conscious part of the mind in the guise of "dream images"—in this form they seem less vivid, and we can live with our memories more easily. This digesting of experience is surprisingly alike in all of us, although the process works better with some individuals than with others. Hence we are always interested in imaginary things, provided they are presented to us in such a way that they seem real. What happens in a fairy tale, for example, would be very dull in the matter-of-fact language of a news report, but when it is told to us as it should be told, we are enchanted.

The same is true of paintings—we recall *The Dream* by Henri Rousseau (colorplate 65). But why does private fantasy loom so large in present-day art? There seem to be several interlocking causes: first, the cleavage that developed between reason and imagination in the wake of rationalism, which tended to dissolve the heritage of myth and legend that had been the common channel of private fantasy in earlier times; second, the artist's greater freedom—and insecurity—within the social fabric, giving him a sense of isolation and favoring an introspective attitude; and, finally, the Romantic cult of emotion that prompted the artist to seek out subjective experience, and to accept its validity. In nineteenth-century art, private fantasy was still a minor current. After 1900, it became a major one.

DE CHIRICO; CHAGALL

The heritage of Romanticism can be seen most clearly in the astonishing pictures painted in Paris just before World War I by Giorgio de Chirico, such as *Mystery and Melancholy of a Street* (fig. 321). This large and deserted square with its endless receding

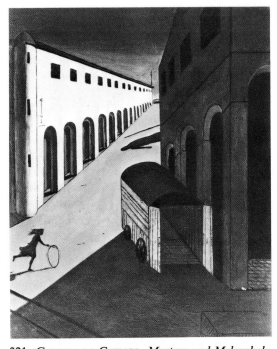

321. GIORGIO DE CHIRICO. *Mystery and Melancholy of a Street.* 1914. Canvas, 34 1/4 × 28 1/8." Collection Mr. and Mrs. Stanley R. Resor, New Canaan

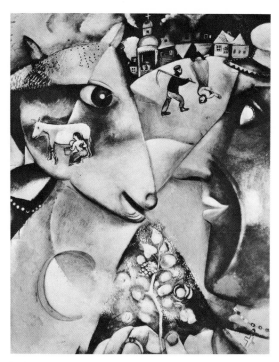

322. MARC CHAGALL. *I and the Village*. 1911. Canvas, 75 1/2 × 59 1/2″. The Museum of Modern Art, New York (Mrs. Simon Guggenheim Fund)

KLEE

The "fairy tales" of the German-Swiss painter Paul Klee are more purposeful and controlled than Chagall's, although at first they may strike us as more childlike. Klee, too, had been influenced by Cubism; but primitive art, and the drawings of small children, held an equally vital interest for him. During the First World War, he molded from these disparate elements a pictorial language of his own, marvelously economical and precise. *Twittering Machine* (fig. 323), a delicate pen drawing tinted with watercolor, demonstrates the unique flavor of Klee's art; with a few simple lines, he has created a ghostly mechanism that imitates the sound of birds, mocking our faith in the miracles of the machine age as well as our sentimental appreciation of bird song. The little contraption (which is not without its sinister aspect—the heads of the four sham birds look like fishermen's lures, as if they might entrap real birds) thus condenses into one striking invention a complex of ideas about

arcades, illuminated by the cold light of the full moon, has all the poetry of Romantic reverie. But it has also a strangely sinister air; it is "ominous" in the full sense of that term—everything suggests an omen, a portent of unknown and disquieting significance. De Chirico himself could not explain the incongruities in these paintings—the empty furniture van, the girl with the hoop—that trouble and fascinate us. Later on he adopted a conservative style and repudiated his early work, as if he were embarrassed at having put his dream world on public display. The power of nostalgia, so evident in *Mystery and Melancholy of a Street*, also dominates the fantasies of Marc Chagall, a Russian Jew who came to Paris in 1910. *I and the Village* (fig. 322) is a Cubist fairy tale that weaves dreamlike memories of Russian folk tales, Jewish proverbs, and the Russian countryside into one glowing vision. Here, as in many later works, Chagall relives the experiences of his childhood; they were so important to him that his imagination shaped and reshaped them for years without diminishing their persistence.

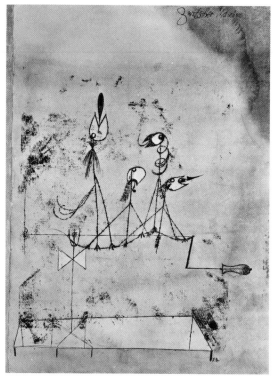

323. PAUL KLEE. *Twittering Machine*. 1922. Watercolor, ink, 16 1/4 × 12″. The Museum of Modern Art, New York

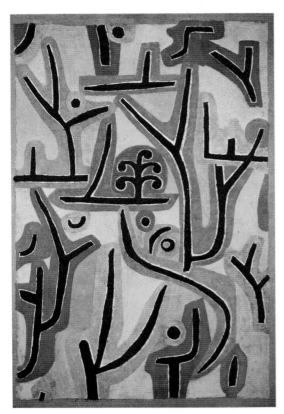

324. PAUL KLEE. *Park near L(ucerne)*. 1938. Oil on canvas, 39 1/2 × 27 1/2″. Klee Foundation, Bern

present-day civilization. The title has an indispensable role; it is characteristic of the way Klee works that the picture itself, however visually appealing, does not reveal its full evocative quality unless the artist tells us what it means. The title, in turn, needs the picture—the witty concept of a twittering machine does not kindle our imagination until we are shown such a thing. This interdependence is familiar to us from cartoons. Klee lifts it to the level of high art, yet retains the playful character of these visual-verbal puns. To him art was a "language of signs," of shapes that are images of ideas as the shape of a letter is the image of a specific sound, or an arrow the image of the command, "This way only." But conventional signs are no more than "triggers"; the instant we perceive them, we automatically invest them with their meaning, without stopping to ponder their shape. Klee wanted *his* signs to impinge upon our awareness as visual facts, yet also to share the quality of "triggers." Toward the end of his life, he immersed him-

self in the study of ideographs of all kinds, such as hieroglyphics, hex signs, and the mysterious markings in prehistoric caves— "boiled-down" representational images that appealed to him because they had the twin qualities he strove for in his own graphic language. This "ideographic style" is very pronounced in figure 324, *Park near L(ucerne)*; as a lyric poet may use the plainest words, these deceptively simple shapes sum up a wealth of experience and sensation: the innocent gaiety of spring, the clipped orderliness peculiar to captive plant life in a park.

DADA: DUCHAMP

In Paris, on the eve of World War I, we encounter still another painter of fantasy, the Frenchman Marcel Duchamp. After basing his early style on Cézanne, he had initiated a dynamic version of facet Cubism, similar to Futurism, by superimposing successive phases of movement on each other, as in multiple-exposure photography. Almost immediately, however, Duchamp's art took a far more disturbing turn. In *The Bride* (fig. 325) we will look in vain for any resemblance to the human form; what we see is a mechanism—part motor, part distilling apparatus; the opposite of Klee's twittering machine, it is beautifully engineered to serve no purpose whatever. Its title puzzles us (Duchamp has emphasized its importance by lettering it right onto the canvas). Did he intend to satirize the scientific view of man, by "analyzing" the bride until she is reduced to a complicated piece of plumbing? If so, the picture may be the negative counterpart of that glorification of the machine so stridently proclaimed by the Futurists.

It is hardly surprising that the organized mass killing during World War I should have driven Duchamp to despair. With a number of others who shared his attitude, he launched in protest a movement called Dada (or Dadaism). The term, French for "hobbyhorse," was reportedly picked at random from a dictionary, but as an infantile "all-purpose word" it perfectly fitted the spirit of the movement. Dada has often been called nihilistic, and its declared purpose was indeed to make clear to the public that all established values, moral or aesthetic, had been rendered meaningless by the catastrophe

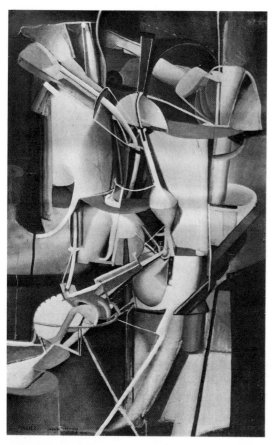

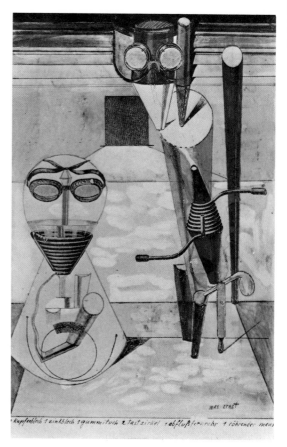

325. MARCEL DUCHAMP. *The Bride.* 1912. Canvas, 34 3/4 × 21 1/2″. The Philadelphia Museum of Art (Louise and Walter Arensberg Collection)

326. MAX ERNST. *1 Copper Plate 1 Zinc Plate 1 Rubber Cloth 2 Calipers 1 Drainpipe Telescope, 1 Piping Man.* 1920. Collage, 12 × 9″. Succession Arp, Meudon, France

of World War I. During its short life from 1916 to 1922, Dada preached non-sense and anti-art with a vengeance. Duchamp put his signature, and a provocative title, on ready-made objects such as bottle racks and snow shovels, exhibiting them as works of art. Not even modern art was safe from the Dadaists' assaults; one of them exhibited a toy monkey inside a frame, entitled *Portrait of Cézanne.* On the other hand, they adopted the technique of collage Cubism for their own purposes: figure 326, by the German Dadaist Max Ernst, an associate of Duchamp, is largely composed of cuttings from illustrations of machinery. The caption pretends to enumerate these ingredients, which include "1 piping man." Actually there are two figures made of piping, who stare at us blindly through their goggles, the one on the left a postwar version of Duchamp's *Bride.*

SURREALISM

Yet Dada was not completely negative. In its calculated irrationality there was also liberation, a voyage to unknown provinces of the creative mind. The only law respected by the Dadaists was that of chance, and the only reality that of their own imaginations. This is the message of Duchamp's Ready-Mades, which the artist created simply by shifting their context from the utilitarian to the aesthetic. Certainly they are extreme demonstrations of a principle. But the very principle—that artistic creation does not depend on manual craftsmanship—is an important discovery. Duchamp himself, having made his point, soon withdrew from artistic activity altogether; some of his fellow "chance-takers" founded, in 1924, Dada's successor, Surrealism. Led by the poet André Breton, they defined their aim as "pure psychic automatism . . . intended to express . . . the true process of thought . . . free from the exercise of reason and from any aesthetic or moral purpose." Surrealist theory is heavily larded with concepts borrowed from psychoanalysis, and its overwrought rhetoric is not always to be taken seriously. The notion that a dream can be transposed directly from the unconscious mind to the canvas, bypassing the conscious awareness of the artist, did not work out in practice; some degree of control was simply unavoidable.

DALI; ERNST; MIRO

We see this in *The Persistence of Memory* (fig. 327) by Salvador Dali, the most notorious of the Surrealists, who uses the meticulous verism of De Chirico to render a "paranoid" dream in which time, forms, and space have been distorted in a frighteningly real way. Nevertheless, the Surrealists devised several novel techniques for soliciting and exploiting chance effects. Max Ernst, the most inventive member of the group, often combined collage with "frottage" (rubbings from pieces of wood, pressed flowers, etc.— the process we all know from the children's pastime of rubbing with a pencil on a piece of paper covering a coin). In *Totem and Taboo* (fig. 328) he has obtained fascinating shapes and textures by "decalcomania" (the transfer, by pressure, of wet paint to the canvas from some other surface). Ernst has certainly found and elaborated upon an extraordinary wealth of images among his stains. The end result does have some of the qualities of a dream, but it is a dream born of a strikingly Romantic imagination.

Surrealism, however, has a more vigorously imaginative branch: such works by Picasso as the *Three Dancers* (colorplate 68) have affinities with it, and its greatest exponent is another Spaniard, Joan Miró, who produced the striking *Painting* (colorplate 70). His style has been labeled "biomorphic abstraction," since his designs are fluid and curvilinear rather than geometric. "Biomorphic concretion" might be a more suitable name, for the shapes in Miró's pictures have their own vigorous life. They seem to change before our eyes, expanding and contracting like amoebas until they approach human individuality closely enough to please the artist.

Their spontaneous "becoming" is the very opposite of abstraction, although Miró's formal discipline is no less rigorous than that of Cubism (he began as a Cubist).

NEWER TRENDS

Equally misleading is the term Abstract Expressionism, which is often applied to the style of painting that prevailed for about a dozen years following the end of World War II. The catalyst was direct contact with Surrealist émigrés, such as Max Ernst, who taught the Americans the principles of automatism. The theories of André Breton, however, were

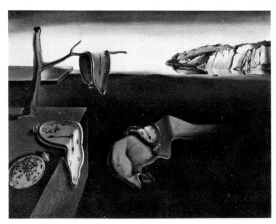

327. SALVADOR DALI. *The Persistence of Memory.* 1931. Oil on canvas, 9 1/2 × 13″. Collection The Museum of Modern Art, New York

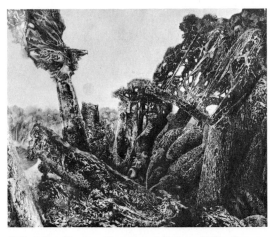

328. MAX ERNST. *Totem and Taboo.* 1941. Canvas, 28 × 36″. Collection William N. Copley, New York

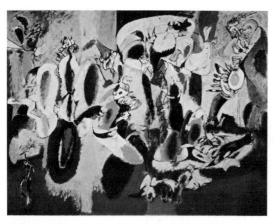

329. ARSHILE GORKY. *The Liver Is the Cock's Comb.*
1944. Canvas, 72 × 98." The Albright-Knox Gallery, Buffalo (Gift of Seymour H. Knox)

seen as too full of self-conscious symbolism.
Delving into the subconscious, the Abstract
Expressionists at first became myth-makers
who sought to evoke primeval images of universal, if elusive, meaning. After World War
II, the artistic decision-making process in
Abstract Expressionism became a direct
analogy to the resolution of the dilemmas
faced in real life and the anxiety they en-
gender. The act of painting thus became an
expression and affirmation of life, and at the
same time acquired an unparalleled creative
freedom.

330. JACKSON POLLOCK. *One (#31, 1950).* 1950.
Canvas, 8' 10" × 17' 5 1/2". The Museum of Modern Art, New York (Gift of Sidney Janis)

GORKY

Arshile Gorky, an Armenian who came to
America at sixteen, was the pioneer of the
movement and the single most important influence on its other members. It took him
twenty years—painting first in the vein of
Cézanne, then in that of Picasso—to arrive
at his mature style as we see it in *The Liver
Is the Cock's Comb* (fig. 329). The enigmatic
title suggests Gorky's close contact with André Breton, the Surrealist poet who found
refuge in New York during the war, as well as
his own experience in camouflage, gained
from a class he conducted earlier. Everything
here is in the process of turning into something else. The biomorphic shapes clearly
owe much to Miró, while their spontaneous
handling and the glowing color reflect Gorky's enthusiasm for Kandinsky (see color-
plates 70, 67). Yet the dynamic interlocking
of the forms, their aggressive power of attrac-
tion and repulsion, are uniquely his own.

ACTION PAINTING: POLLOCK

Had Gorky lived into the 1950s, he would
surely have been the leading figure among
the Abstract Expressionists. His principal
heir proved to be Jackson Pollock, who in
1950 did the huge and original picture entitled *One* (fig. 330) mainly by pouring and
spattering his colors instead of applying them
with the brush. The result, especially when
viewed at close range, suggests both Kandin-

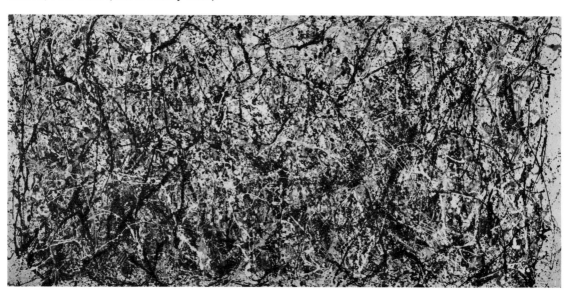

Colorplate 69. PIET MONDRIAN. *Composition with Red, Blue, and Yellow*. 1930. Canvas, 20 × 20″. Collection Mr. and Mrs. Armand P. Bartos, New York

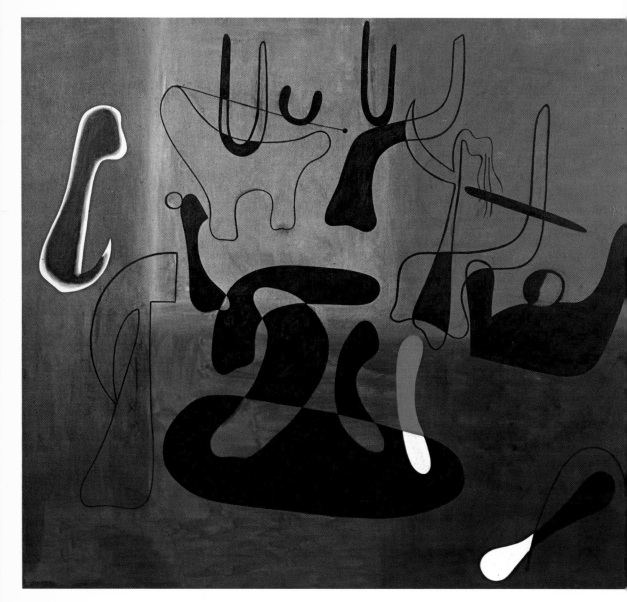

Colorplate 70. JOAN MIRÓ. *Painting*. 1933. 68 1/4 × 77 1/4″. The Museum of Modern Art, New York (Gift of Advisory Committee)

opposite: Colorplate 71. WILLEM DE KOONING. *Woman II*. 1952. 59 × 43″. The Museum of Modern Art, New York (Gift of Mrs. John D. Rockefeller, III)

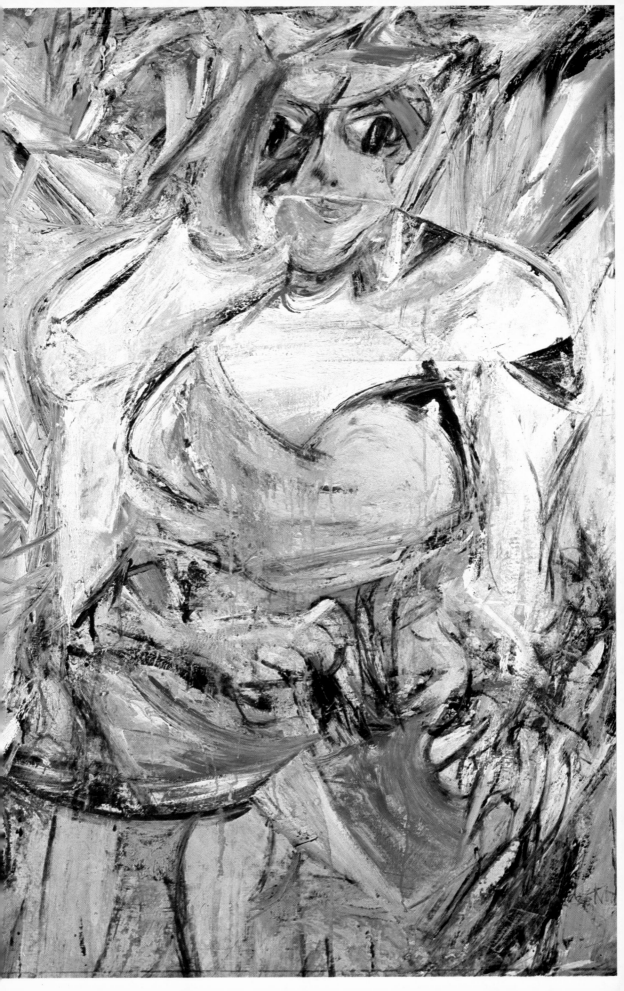

Colorplate 72. MARK ROTHKO. *Earth and Green*. 1955. 90 1/4 × 73 1/2″. Collection Gallery Beyeler, Basel

opposite: Colorplate 73. PAUL JENKINS. *Phenomena Astral Signal*. 1964. Acrylic on canvas, 9′ 8″ × 6′ 8″. Collection Mr. and Mrs. Harry W. Anderson, New York (Courtesy of the Martha Jackson Gallery, New York)

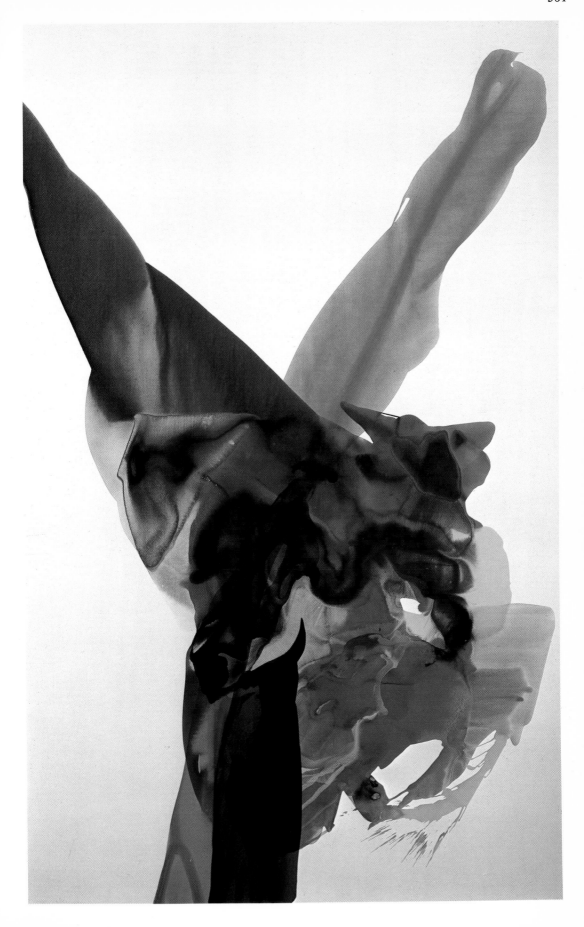

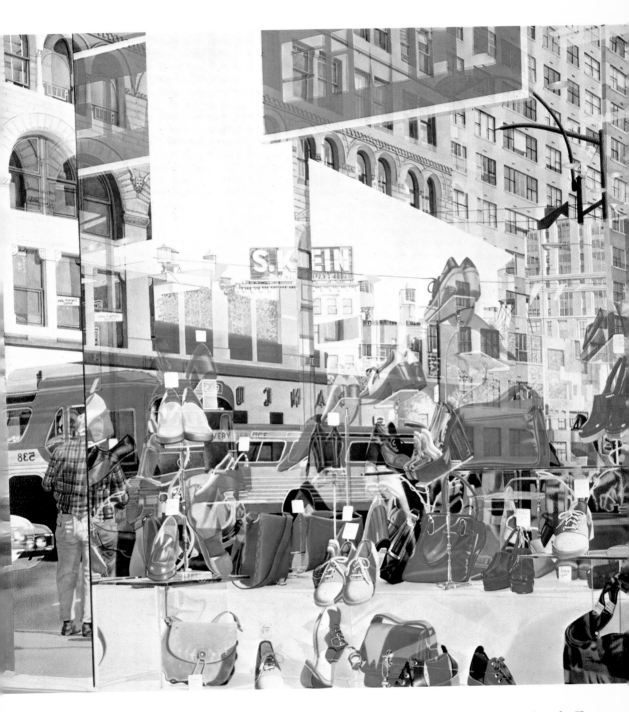

opposite: Colorplate 74. RICHARD ANUSZKIEWICZ. *Entrance to Green.* 1970. Acrylic on canvas, 108 × 72″. Collection Sidney Janis Gallery, New York

above: Colorplate 75. DON EDDY. *New Shoes for H.* 1973–74. Acrylic on canvas, 44 × 48″. The Cleveland Museum of Art (Purchased with a grant from the National Endowment for the Arts matched by gifts from members of The Cleveland Society for Contemporary Art)

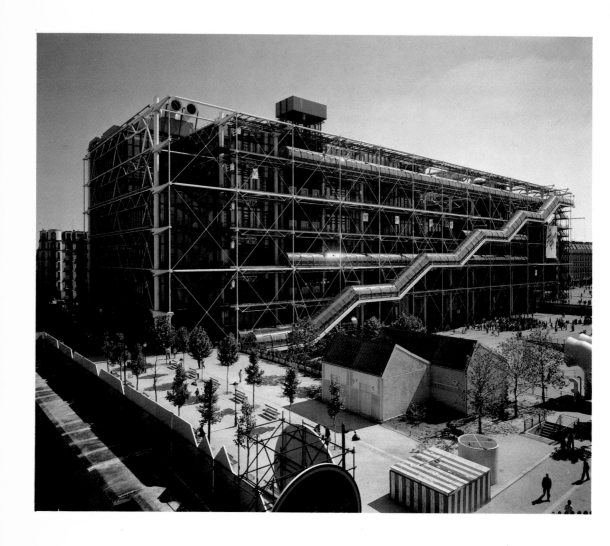

Colorplate 76. PIANO AND ROGERS. Georges Pompidou National Arts and Cultural Center. 1977. Paris. (Photograph Etienne Bertrand Weill)

sky and Max Ernst. Kandinsky's nonobjective Expressionism, and the Surrealists' exploitation of chance effects, are indeed the main sources of Pollock's work, but they do not sufficiently account for his revolutionary technique and the emotional appeal of his art. Why did Pollock "fling a pot of paint in the public's face" (as Ruskin accused Whistler of doing)? Not, surely, to be more abstract than his predecessors, for the strict control implied by abstraction is just what Pollock gave up when he began to dribble and spatter. A more plausible explanation is that he came to regard paint itself not as a passive substance to be manipulated at will but as a storehouse of pent-up forces for him to release. The actual shapes are largely determined by the internal dynamics of his material and his process: the viscosity of the paint, the speed and direction of its impact upon the canvas, its interaction with other layers of pigment. The result is a surface so alive, so sensuously rich, that all earlier painting looks pallid by comparison. But when he releases the forces within the paint by giving it a momentum of its own—or, if you will, by "aiming" it at the canvas instead of "carrying" it on the tip of his brush—Pollock does not simply "let go" and leave the rest to chance. He is himself the ultimate source of energy for these forces, and he "rides" them as a cowboy might ride a wild horse, in a frenzy of psychophysical action. He does not always stay in the saddle, yet the exhilaration of this contest, which strains every fiber of his being, is well worth the risk. Our simile, although crude, points up the main difference between Pollock and his predecessors: his total commitment to the *act* of painting. Hence his preference for huge canvases that provide a "field of combat" large enough for him to paint not merely with his arms but with the motion of his whole body. "Action Painting," the term coined some years ago for this style, conveys its essence far better than does Abstract Expressionism.

DE KOONING; DUBUFFET

Pollock's drip technique, however, was not in itself essential to Action Painting. Willem de Kooning, another prominent member of the group and a close friend of Gorky, never abandoned the brush although he is unmis-

takably an Action Painter. Whether or not De Kooning's work has a recognizable subject, it always retains a link with the world of images. In some paintings, such as *Woman II* (colorplate 71), the image emerges from the jagged welter of brushstrokes as insistently as it does in Rouault's *Head of Christ* (see fig. 307). What De Kooning has in common with Pollock is the furious energy of the process of painting, the sense of risk, of a challenge successfully—but barely—met.

Action Painting marked the international coming-of-age for American art. The movement had a powerful impact on European art, which in those years had nothing to show of comparable force and conviction. One French artist, however, was of such prodigal originality as to constitute a movement all by himself: Jean Dubuffet, whose first exhibition soon after the Liberation electrified—and antagonized—the art world of Paris. As a young man Dubuffet had received formal instruction in painting, but he responded to none of the various trends he saw around him nor to the art of the museums; all struck him as divorced from real life, and he turned to other pursuits. Only in middle age did he experience the breakthrough that permitted him to discover his creative gifts: he suddenly realized that for him true art had to come from outside the ideas and traditions of the artistic elite, and he found inspiration in the art of children and of the insane. The distinction between "normal" and "abnormal" struck him as no more tenable than established notions of "beauty" and "ugliness." Not since Marcel Duchamp (see pages 353–54) had anyone ventured so radical a critique of the nature of art. Dubuffet made himself the champion of what he called *l'art brut*, "art-in-the-raw." Compared with Paul Klee, who had first utilized the style of children's drawings (see page 352), Dubuffet's art is "raw" indeed; its stark immediacy, its explosive, defiant presence, are the opposite of the older painter's formal discipline and economy of means. Even De Kooning's wildly distorted *Woman II* (colorplate 71) seems gentle when matched against the shocking assault on our inherited sensibilities of *Le Metafisyx* (fig. 331). The paint is as heavy and opaque as a rough coating of plaster, and the lines artic-

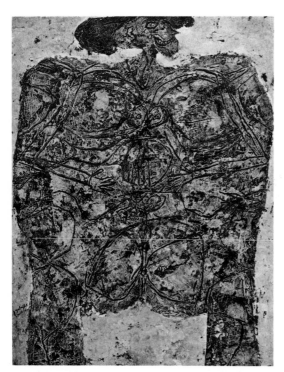

331. JEAN DUBUFFET. *Le Metafisyx (Corps de Dame)*. 1950. 45 3/4 × 35 1/4″. Collection Mr. and Mrs. Arnold Maremont, Winnetka, Illinois

ulating the blocklike body are scratched into this surface like graffiti made by an untrained hand. But appearances can be deceiving; the fury and concentration of Dubuffet's attack should convince us that his demonic female is not "something any child can do." In an eloquent statement the artist has explained the purpose of images such as this: "The female body . . . has long been associated with a very specious notion of beauty . . . which I find miserable and most depressing. Surely I am for beauty, but not that one. . . . I intend to sweep away everything we have been taught to consider—without question—as grace and beauty [and to] substitute another and vaster beauty, touching all objects and beings, not excluding the most despised. . . . I would like people to look at my work as an enterprise for the rehabilitation of scorned values, and . . . a work of ardent celebration."

ROTHKO

After the mid-1950s, Action Painting gradually lost its dominant position, but its force was far from spent. A number of artists

who had been in the movement transformed it into a style called color-field painting, in which the canvas is stained with thin, translucent color washes. Chief among these was Mark Rothko. In the mid-1940s he too had worked in a style derived from Gorky, yet within less than a decade he subdued the aggressiveness of Action Painting so completely that his pictures breathe the purest contemplative stillness. *Earth and Green* (colorplate 72) consists of two rectangles with blurred edges—one dark red, the other green—on a purplish-blue ground; the canvas is very large, over seven and one-half feet tall, and the thin washes of paint permit the texture of the cloth to be seen throughout. But to use such bare factual terms to describe what we see hardly touches the essence of the work, or the reasons for its mysterious power to move us. These are to be found in the delicate equilibrium of the two shapes, their strange interdependence, the subtle variations of hue (note how the dark blue "halo" around the upper rectangle seems to immerse it in the blue ground, while the green rectangle stands out more assertively in front of the blue). Not every beholder responds to the works of this withdrawn, introspective artist, but for those who do, the experience is akin to a trancelike rapture.

FRANKENTHALER; JENKINS

The stained canvas was also pioneered by Helen Frankenthaler, who was inspired by

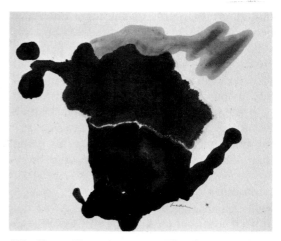

332. HELEN FRANKENTHALER. *Blue Causeway*. 1963. Oil on canvas. 57 3/4 × 74″. Collection the Artist. (Photograph by Rudolph Burckhardt)

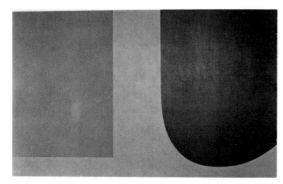

333. ELLSWORTH KELLY. *Red Blue Green*. 1963. 84 × 136." Collection Mr. and Mrs. Robert Rowan, Los Angeles

Rothko's example as early as 1952. Her achievement is symptomatic of a major development—during the twentieth century, for the first time in history, women have been recognized as the artistic equals of men (who nevertheless continue to enjoy the most success). In *Blue Causeway* (fig. 332) Frankenthaler uses the same biomorphic forms basic to early Action Painting but eliminates the personal handwriting found in the brushwork of Gorky and DeKooning, with results that are at once more lyrical and more decorative but no less impressive than theirs.

The stained canvas was soon adopted by many other artists. Among the most gifted of these is Paul Jenkins who has developed a distinctive variation on the theme of color-field painting. In *Phenomena Astral Signal* (colorplate 73) the liquid medium has been made to flow in currents of varying speed and density. The resulting veils of color may be gossamer-thin, or they may have the rich depth of stained glass. No spattering, no dribbling betrays the painter's "action"; the forces that give rise to these shapes seem to be of the same kind as those governing the cloud formations in a wind-swept sky and the pattern of veins in a leaf. Jenkins' staining technique is perfectly suited to his mystical belief (shared by many Abstract Expressionists) in the artist as a spiritual medium responding under supernatural guidance to invisible cosmic phenomena.

KELLY; STELLA

Many artists who came to maturity in the 1950s, however, turned away from Action Painting altogether in favor of hard-edge painting. *Red Blue Green* (fig. 333) by Ellsworth Kelly, an early leader of this tendency, abandons Rothko's impressionistic softness. Instead, flat areas of color are circumscribed within carefully delineated forms as part of a formal investigation of color and design problems for their own sake. The brilliant and precocious Frank Stella, having conceived an early enthusiasm for Mondrian, soon evolved a nonfigurative style that was even more self-contained; unlike Mondrian (see page 350 and colorplate 69), Stella did not concern himself with the vertical-horizontal balance which relates the older artist's work to the world of nature. Logically enough, he also abandoned the traditional rectangular format, in order to make quite sure that his pictures bore no re-

334. FRANK STELLA. *Empress of India*. 1965. Metallic powder in polymer emulsion, 6' 5" × 18' 8". Collection Irving Blum, Los Angeles

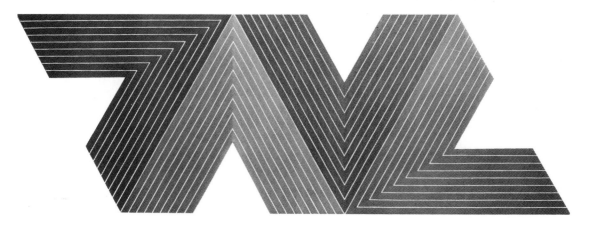

semblance to windows. The shape of the canvas now became an integral part of the design. In one of his largest works, the majestic *Empress of India* (fig. 334), this shape is determined by the thrust and counterthrust of four huge chevrons, identical in size and shape but sharply differentiated in color and in their relationship to the whole. The paint, moreover, contains powdered metal which gives it an iridescent sheen—yet another way to stress the impersonal precision of the surfaces and to remove the work from any comparison with the "hand-made" look of easel pictures. In fact, to speak of *Empress of India* as a picture seems decidedly awkward. It demands to be called an object, sufficient unto itself.

OP ART

Another direction can also be traced back to Mondrian: the trend—actually, a whole cluster of related trends—known as "Op Art" because of its concern with optics (that is, the physical and psychological process of vision). Despite the fact that it gathered force in the mid-1950s, Op Art is still in its infancy. There are several reasons for its slower development. Op Art does not have the topical impetus and the emotional appeal of Pop (see page 370); by comparison it seems overly cerebral and systematic, more akin to the sciences than to the humanities. On the other hand, its possibilities appear to be as unlimited as those of science and technology. Paradoxically, however, because of its very eagerness to take advantage of the new materials and processes constantly being supplied by science, Op Art does not seem fully in command of its own goals. Perhaps that is why so few of its creations have an air of finality about them.

When we use our eyes in everyday life, we take it for granted that the world around us is exactly the way it looks to us. Only when our eyes "deceive" us do we begin to realize that vision is a very complicated process, that our brain has to interpret the constant stream of information being transmitted from our eyes. Normally things work well, but they can go wrong by accident or intent and make us see a misleading image, one that differs from what we think is true: this is an optical illusion. Art has been making use of

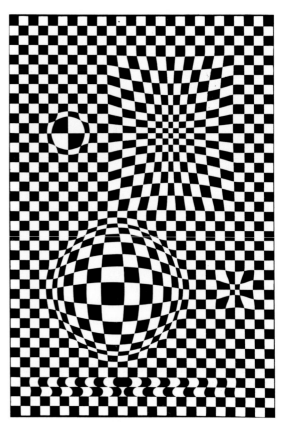

335. VICTOR VASARELY. *Vega.* 1957. 77 × 51″. Collection the Artist

optical illusion in one way or another since the Old Stone Age; without illusion, we would not find foreshortening so convincing, to take one example. What is new in Op Art is that it extends optical illusion to nonrepresentational art, and makes it work in apparently every conceivable way. Much of it consists of constructions or "environments" dependent upon light and motion for their effects. These cannot be reproduced in photographs, since they exploit those aspects of our visual apparatus that are least like the camera. We must confine ourselves in this book to the kind of Op Art which does not lose all of its essential qualities when illustrated.

VASARELY; ALBERS; ANUSZKIEWICZ

The present development of Op Art stems largely from the work of Victor Vasarely, a Hungarian long domiciled in France, who has been its chief theoretician as well as its most inventive practitioner. Many of his paintings, drawings, and constructions are in stark black-and-white, such as the large canvas, *Vega* (fig. 335), named after the brightest star in the constellation Lyra. It is a huge checkerboard whose regularity has been disturbed by bending the lines that make the squares. But such a description is no more than a list of ingredients—it does not tell us what we actually see. The size of the standard squares in relation to that of the entire field has been carefully chosen so as to tempt us to link the black squares into a network of diagonals when we view the picture from a certain distance (about 30 inches from our reproduction). But since many of these squares have been subjected to distortion, their sizes vary considerably, the largest having over ten times the area of the smallest. Consequently, no matter what our viewing distance, our eyes receive contradictory data: we read parts of the field in terms of diagonals, others in terms of verticals and horizontals. The picture thus practically forces us to move back and forth, and as we do so the field itself seems to move, expanding, undulating, contracting. If *Vega* were a three-dimensional object, the variety of effects to be observed as we move in relation to it would be greater still, for we would then receive different sets of contradictory data from each eye. In America Josef Albers, who came here after 1933, when Hitler closed the Bauhaus school at Dessau (see page 382), became the founding father of another, more austere kind of Op Art based on subtle color relations among simple geometric shapes. His gifted pupil Richard Anuszkiewicz paints in the same vein, but his self-imposed restrictions are less severe. In *Entrance to Green* (colorplate 74) the ever-decreasing series of rectangles creates a sense of infinite recession toward the center; this is counterbalanced by the color pattern which brings the center close to us by the gradual shift from cool to warm tones as we move inward from the periphery. Surely, Op Art has not yet reached its limits.

POP ART

Other artists who made a name for themselves in the mid-1950s rediscovered what the layman continued to take for granted despite all efforts to persuade him otherwise: that a picture is not "essentially a flat surface covered with colors" (as Maurice Denis had insisted) but an image wanting to be recognized. If art was by its very nature representational, then the modern movement, from Manet to Pollock, was based on a fallacy, no matter how impressive its achievements. The artists who felt this way seized upon those products of commercial art catering to "low-brow," popular taste: photography, advertising, magazine illustrations, and comic strips. Here, they realized, was an essential aspect of our present-day visual environment that had been entirely disregarded as vulgar and anti-aesthetic by the representatives of "highbrow" culture, and cried out to be examined. Only Marcel Duchamp and some of his fellow Dadaists, with their contempt for all orthodox opinion, had dared to penetrate this realm (see page 353). It was they who now became the patron saints of "Pop Art," as the new movement came to be called. Pop Art actually began in London in the mid-1950s, but from the very start its imagery was largely based on American mass media, which had been flooding England ever since the end of World War II. It is not surprising, therefore, that the new art had a special appeal for America, and that it reached its fullest development here during the following decade. Unlike Dada, Pop is not motivated by despair or disgust at present-day civilization; it views commercial culture as its raw material, an endless source of pictorial subject matter, rather than as an evil to be attacked. Nor does Pop share Dada's aggres-

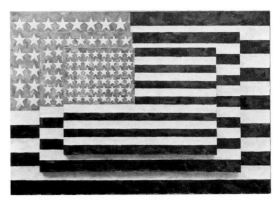

336. JASPER JOHNS. *Three Flags*. 1958. Encaustic on canvas, 30 7/8 × 45 1/4". Collection Mr. and Mrs. Burton Tremaine, Meriden, Connecticut

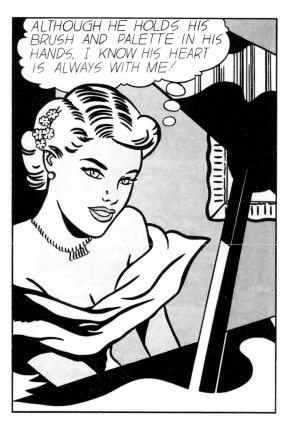

337. ROY LICHTENSTEIN. *Girl at Piano.* 1963. Magna on canvas, 68 × 48″. Harry N. Abrams Family Collection, New York

sive attitude toward the established values of modern art. It is not "anti-modern," then, but "post-modern."

JOHNS; LICHTENSTEIN; INDIANA

Among the pioneers of Pop Art in America perhaps the most important is Jasper Johns, who began by painting, meticulously and with great precision, such familiar objects as flags, targets, numerals, and maps. His *Three Flags* (fig. 336) presents an intriguing problem: just what is the difference between image and reality? We instantly recognize the Stars and Stripes, but if we try to define what we actually see here, we find that the answer eludes us. These flags behave "unnaturally" —instead of waving or flopping they stand at attention, as it were, rigidly aligned with each other in a kind of reverse perspective. Yet there is movement of another sort: the reds, whites, and blues are not areas of solid color but subtly modulated. Can we really say, then, that this is an image of three flags?

Clearly, no such flags can exist anywhere except in the artist's head. And we begin to marvel at the picture as a feat of the imagination—probably the last thing we expected to do when we first looked at it.

The artist who best represents Pop may well be Roy Lichtenstein. He has seized upon comic strips—or, more precisely, upon the standardized imagery of the traditional strips devoted to violent action and sentimental love, rather than those bearing the stamp of an individual creator. His paintings, such as *Girl at Piano* (fig. 337), are greatly enlarged copies of single frames, including the balloons, the impersonal, simplified black outlines, and the dots used for printing colors on cheap paper. These pictures are perhaps the most paradoxical in the entire field of Pop Art: unlike any other paintings past or present, they cannot be reproduced on the pages of this book, for they then become indistinguishable from the comic strip on which they are based. Enlarging a design meant for an area about six square inches to one no less than 3,264 square inches must have given rise to a host of formal problems that could be solved only by the most intense scrutiny: how, for example, to draw the girl's nose so it would look "right" in comic-strip terms, or how to

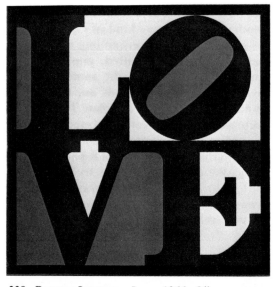

338. ROBERT INDIANA. *Love.* 1966. Oil on canvas, 71 7/8 × 71 7/8″. The Indianapolis Museum of Art (James G. Roberts Fund)

space the colored dots so they would maintain the proper weight in relation to the outlines. Clearly, our picture is not a mechanical copy, but an interpretation which remains faithful to the spirit of the original only because of the countless changes and adjustments of detail the artist has introduced. What fascinates Lichtenstein about comic strips—and what he makes us see for the first time—are the rigid conventions of their style, as firmly set and as remote from life as those of Byzantine art. Like an icon, his painting thus holds up a mirror to the ideals and hopes of our culture in ways that everybody knows how to "read."

Although it is sometimes referred to as "the new realism," Pop Art, while sharply observant of its sources, uses images which are themselves rather abstract. For example, Robert Indiana is obsessed with word images derived from signs, and he has devised a uniquely effective pictorial code for conveying them. *Love* (fig. 338) is a tribute to his faith in the power of what must be the most abused word in the English language. But in its formal precision, *Love* is as abstract as the hard-edge painting of Ellsworth Kelly. In fact, Pop Art soon became increasingly occupied with the same problems of color and design, and was thereby effectively absorbed into the mainstream of modern American painting.

PHOTO REALISM

A recent offshoot of Pop Art is the trend called Photo Realism because of its fascination with camera images. Photographs had been utilized by nineteenth-century painters soon after the invention of the "pencil of nature"—one of the earliest to do so, surprisingly, was Delacroix—but they were no more than a convenient substitute for reality. For the Photo Realists, on the other hand, the photograph itself is the reality from which they build their pictures. At its best, their work, as in *New Shoes for H* by Don Eddy (colorplate 75), has a visual complexity that challenges the most acute observer. In preparing *New Shoes for H*, Eddy took a series of pictures of the window display of a shoe store on Union Square in Manhattan. One photograph (fig 339) served as the basis

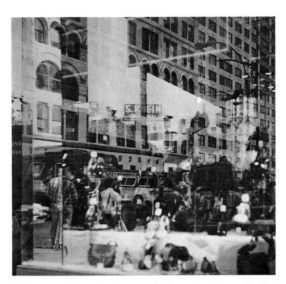

339. DON EDDY. Photograph for *New Shoes for H*. 1973. 6 1/4 × 6 1/2″ (see colorplate 75). The Cleveland Museum of Art (Gift of the Artist)

for the painting. What intrigued him, clearly, was the way glass filters (and transforms) everyday reality. Only a narrow strip along the left-hand edge offers an unobstructed view; everything else—shoes, bystanders, street traffic, buildings—is seen through two or more layers of glass, all of them at oblique angles to the picture surface. The combined effect of these panes—displacement, distortion, and reflection—is the transformation of a familiar scene into a dazzlingly rich and novel visual experience. Comparing the painting with the photograph, we realize that they are related in much the same way as Lichtenstein's *Girl at Piano* (fig. 337) is to the comic-strip frame from which it derives. Unlike Eddy's photograph, however, his canvas shows everything in uniformly sharp focus, articulates details lost in the shadows, and, most important of all, gives pictorial coherence to the scene through a brilliant color scheme whose pulsating rhythm plays over the entire surface. At the time he painted *New Shoes for H*, color had become newly important in Eddy's thinking; the H of the title pays homage to Henri Matisse and to Hans Hofmann, the latter a painter linked to Abstract Expressionism whom Eddy had come to admire.

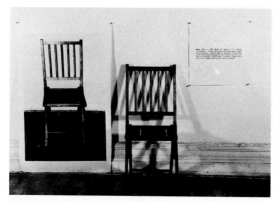

340. JOSEPH KOSUTH. *One and Three Chairs*. 1965. Installation view, The Museum of Modern Art, New York (Larry Aldrich Foundation Fund)

CONCEPTUAL ART

A later trend, Conceptual Art, has the same "patron saint" as Pop Art: Marcel Duchamp. It arose during the 1960s out of the Happenings staged by Alan Kaprow, in which the event itself became the art. Conceptual Art, however, challenges our definition of art even more radically by insisting that only the leap of the imagination, not the execution, is art. Thus, since works of art are incidental by-products, they can be dispensed with altogether, as can galleries and, by extension, even the artist's public. The creative process need only be documented in some way—usually in a verbal, sometimes in a photographic or cinematic form. This deliberately anti-art approach, which stems from Dada (see page 353), poses a series of stimulating paradoxes. As soon as the documentation achieves any visible form, it begins to come perilously close to more traditional forms of art (especially if it is placed in a gallery where it can be seen by an audience), since it is impossible to fully divorce the imagination from aesthetics. We see this, for example, in Joseph Kosuth's *One and Three Chairs* (fig. 340), which is clearly indebted to Duchamp's Ready-Mades: It "describes" a chair by combining in one installation an actual chair, a full-scale photograph of the same chair, and a printed dictionary definition of a chair. Whatever the artist's intention, this making, no matter how minimal, is as essential to the Conceptual artist as it was for Michelangelo. In the

end, all art is the final document of the creative process, because without execution, no idea can ever be fully realized. Without such "proof of performance," the Conceptual artist becomes like the emperor with his new clothes which no one else can see. And, in fact, Conceptual Art has embraced all media in one form or another.

SCULPTURE

BRANCUSI; MOORE

The sculptors of the twentieth century developed along much the same lines as the painters. Of the three currents we have traced, Expressionism had the least importance for sculpture. It is difficult to say why this should have been so, for the enthusiasm of the Fauves for primitive sculpture might be expected to have aroused even greater enthusiasm among sculptors. One important sculptor turned his gaze on primitive art: Constantin Brancusi, a Rumanian who came to Paris in 1904. The savage expressiveness of primitive carvings, however, interested

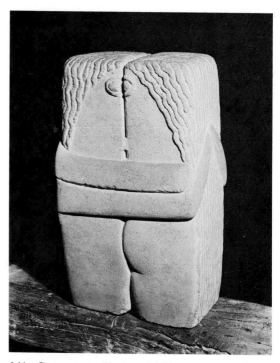

341. CONSTANTIN BRANCUSI. *The Kiss*. 1908. Height 22 3/4". The Philadelphia Museum of Art (Louise and Walter Arensberg Collection)

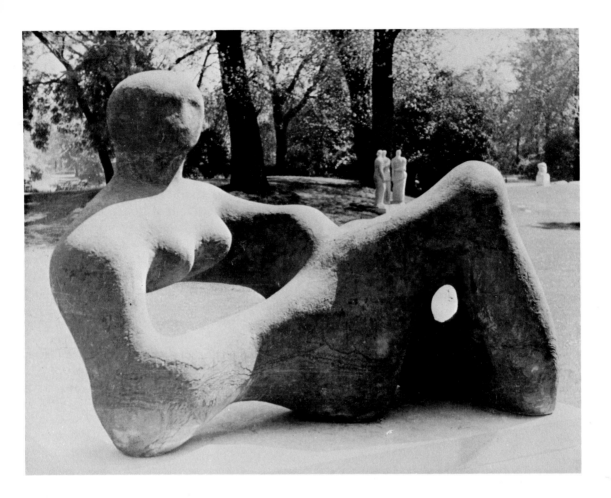

342. HENRY MOORE. *Recumbent Figure*. 1938. Green Horton stone, length about 54″. The Tate Gallery, London

Brancusi far less than their simplicity and directness. His *Kiss* (fig. 341) is compact and self-sufficient beyond anything even dreamed of by Maillol (compare fig. 303). The basic shape of the stone block has been disturbed as little as possible, and the embracing lovers have been distinguished from each other only enough so that we can identify them as man and woman. Rather than primitive, this work looks primeval, as though it came from the first age of creation.

Brancusi's "primevalism" was the starting point of a continuing sculptural tradition. It has appealed to English sculptors particularly, as we can see in Henry Moore's *Recumbent Figure* (fig. 342). More abstract than *The Kiss* and more subtly shaped, Moore's statue is also more human and more individual. And it seems, almost, to have been produced through the wearing away of stone by the winds and waters of the centuries, rather than by use of human tools and muscle power. Its design flows along in perfect harmony with the ridges and grooves of the natural layers of the stone.

Long before Moore carved this majestic and mysterious figure, Brancusi had taken his second daring step. Reserving his primeval style for works in wood or rough stone, he had begun to produce nonrepresentational pieces in metal or polished marble. They were even simpler in shape than *The Kiss*. *Bird in Space* (fig. 343) is not an abstract image of a bird. It is the trace of a bird moving through space—flight made visible. The metal of which Brancusi made this shape has a mirror polish, so that the surface reflects its surroundings. The entire object loses all suggestion of solidity and substance, and we see it as a gleaming piece of shaped space set within the free space that surrounds us also.

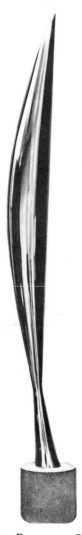

343. CONSTANTIN BRANCUSI. *Bird in Space*. 1919. Bronze, height 54″. The Museum of Modern Art, New York (Anonymous gift)

BOCCIONI; DUCHAMP-VILLON

Other sculptors at this time were tackling the problem of body-space relationships with the formal tools of Cubism. The running figure entitled *Unique Forms of Continuity in Space* (fig. 344), by the Futurist Umberto Boccioni, (see page 349), is as breathtaking in its complexity as *Bird in Space* is simple. Boccioni has tried to represent not the human form itself but the imprint of its motion upon the medium in which it moves; the figure remains concealed behind its "garment" of aerial turbulence. The statue recalls the famous Futurist statement that "the automobile at full speed is more beautiful than the Winged Victory," although it obviously owes more to the Winged Victory (fig. 57) than to the design of motor cars (in 1913, streamlining

was still to come). Raymond Duchamp-Villon, an elder brother of Marcel Duchamp, achieved a bolder solution in *The Great Horse* (fig. 345). He began with abstract studies of the animal, but his final version is an image of "horsepower," where the body has become a coiled spring and the legs resemble piston rods. Because of their very remoteness from the original anatomical model, these quasi-mechanical shapes have a dynamism that is more persuasive—if less picturesque—than that of Boccioni's figure.

Dada uncompromisingly rejected formal discipline in sculpture, as it did in the other arts—perhaps even more, since only objects in three dimensions could become Ready-Mades, the sculpture of Dada. Duchamp's examples consist in part of combinations of found objects; these "assisted" Ready-Mades approach the status of constructions, or three-dimensional collage. This technique, recently baptized "assemblage," has proved to have unlimited possibilities. It was taken

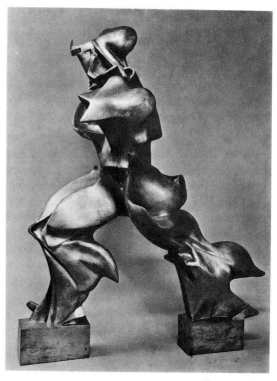

344. UMBERTO BOCCIONI. *Unique Forms of Continuity in Space*. 1913. Bronze, height 43 1/2″. The Museum of Modern Art, New York (Lillie P. Bliss Bequest)

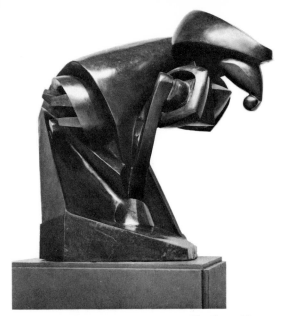

345. RAYMOND DUCHAMP-VILLON. *The Great Horse.* 1914. Bronze, height 39 3/8″. The Art Institute of Chicago (Gift of Miss Margaret Fisher)

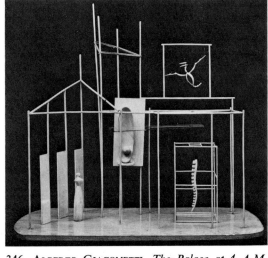

346. ALBERTO GIACOMETTI. *The Palace at 4 A.M.* 1932–33. Wood, wire, glass, and string, height 25″. The Museum of Modern Art, New York (Purchase)

up by Picasso in his *Bull's Head* (fig. 2); and numerous younger sculptors have explored it since World War II, especially in junk-ridden America. The Surrealist contribution to sculpture is harder to define: it was difficult to apply the theory of "pure psychic automatism" to painting, but still harder to live up to it in sculpture. How indeed could solid, durable materials be given shape without the sculptor being consciously aware of the process? Thus, apart from the devotees of the Ready-Made, few sculptors were associated with the movement.

GIACOMETTI; GONZALEZ

One of these was Alberto Giacometti, a Swiss sculptor and painter working in Paris. *The Palace at 4 A.M.* (fig. 346), an airy cage made of wood, glass, wire, and string, is the three-dimensional equivalent of a Surrealist picture; unlike earlier pieces of sculpture, it creates its own spatial environment that clings to it as though this eerie miniature world were protected from everyday reality by an invisible glass bell. The space thus trapped is mysterious and corrosive; it gnaws away at the forms until only their skeletons are left. Even they, we feel, will disappear before long. Surrealism may also have contributed to the astonishing sculptural imagination of Julio Gonzalez, a wrought-iron

craftsman from Catalonia who had come to Paris in 1900. Although he was a friend of Brancusi and Picasso, he produced no work of any consequence until the 1930s, when his creative energies suddenly came into focus. It was he who established wrought iron as an important medium for sculpture, taking

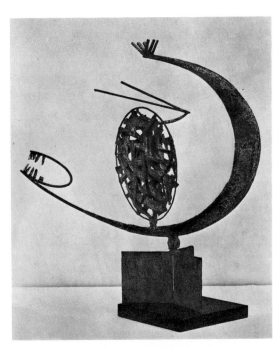

347. JULIO GONZALEZ. *Head.* c. 1935. Wrought iron, height 17 3/4″. The Museum of Modern Art, New York (Purchase)

advantage of the very difficulties that had discouraged its use before. The *Head* (fig. 347) combines extreme economy of form with an aggressive reinterpretation of anatomy that is derived from Picasso (see colorplate 68, especially the head of the dancer on the left): the mouth is an oval cavity with spikelike teeth, the eyes two rods that converge upon an "optic nerve" linking them to the tangled mass of the "brain." Similar gruesomely expressive metaphors have since been created by a whole generation of younger sculptors, in wrought iron and welded steel, as if the violence of their working process mirrored the violence of modern life.

CALDER

The early 1930s, which brought Giacometti and Gonzalez to the fore, produced another important development, the mobile sculpture —mobiles, for short—of the American Alexander Calder. These are delicately balanced constructions of metal wire, hinged together and weighted so as to move with the slightest breath of air. They may be of any size, from tiny tabletop models to the huge *Lobster Trap and Fish Tail* (fig. 348). At first, Calder had

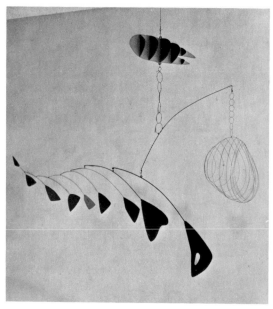

348. ALEXANDER CALDER. *Lobster Trap and Fish Tail*. 1939. Wire and aluminum, c. 8 1/2 × 9 1/2′. The Museum of Modern Art, New York (Gift of Advisory Committee)

349. DAVID SMITH. *Cubi* Series. Stainless steel. (left) *Cubi XVIII.* 1964. Height 9′ 8″. Museum of Fine Arts, Boston. (center) *Cubi XVII.* 1963. Height 9′. Dallas Museum of Fine Arts. (right) *Cubi XIX.* 1964. Height 9′ 5″. The Tate Gallery, London

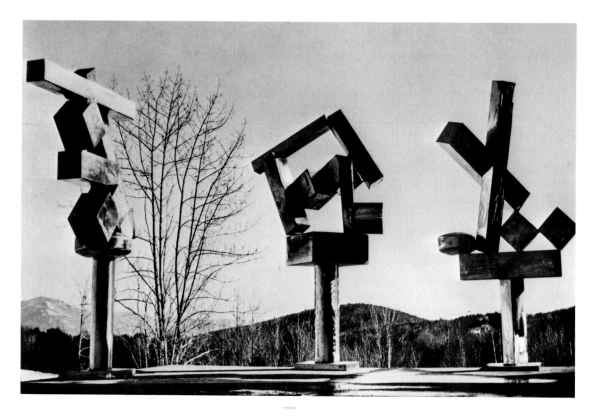

made motor-driven mobiles. It was his contact with Surrealism that made him realize the poetic possibilities of "natural" as against fully controlled movement; he borrowed biomorphic shapes from Miró, and began to think of mobiles as similes of organic structures—flowers on swaying stems, foliage quivering in the breeze, marine animals floating in the sea. Such mobiles are infinitely responsive to their environment. Unpredictable and ever-changing, they incorporate the fourth dimension, time, as an essential element of their structure. Within their limited sphere, they are more truly alive than any other man-made thing.

PRIMARY STRUCTURE: GOERITZ; SMITH

A recent sculptural movement extends the scope—indeed, the very concept—of sculpture in a fundamentally new direction. "Primary Structure," the most suitable name so far suggested for this type, conveys its two salient characteristics: extreme simplicity of shapes, and a kinship with architecture. Another term, "Environmental Sculpture" (not to be confused with the mixed-medium "environments" of Pop; see page 379), refers to the fact that many Primary Structures are designed to envelop the beholder, who is invited to enter or walk through them. It is this space-articulating function that distinguishes Primary Structures from all previous sculpture and relates them to architecture. They are, as it were, the modern successors, in structural steel and concrete, to such prehistoric monuments as Stonehenge (see figs. 6, 7). The first to explore these possibilities was Mathias Goeritz, a German working in Mexico City. As early as 1952–53, he established an experimental museum, The Echo, for the display of massive geometric compositions, some of them so large as to occupy an entire patio. His ideas have since been taken up on either side of the Atlantic. The American sculptor David Smith, for example, whose earlier work had been strongly influenced by the wrought-iron constructions of Julio Gonzalez (see fig. 347), evolved during the last years of his life a singularly impressive form of Primary Structure in his *Cubi* series. Figure 349 shows three of these against the open sky and rolling hills of the artist's farm at

Bolton Landing, New York (all are now in major museums). Only two basic components are employed—cubes (or multiples of them) and cylinders—yet Smith has created a seemingly endless variety of configurations. The units which make up the structures are poised one upon the other as if they were held in place by magnetic force, so that each represents a fresh triumph over gravity. Unlike the younger members of the Primary Structure movement, Smith executed these pieces himself, welding them of sheets of stainless steel whose shiny surfaces he finished and controlled with exquisite care. As a result, his work displays an "old-fashioned" subtlety of touch that reminds us of the polished bronzes of Brancusi.

BLADEN; SMITHSON

Often, these sculptors limit themselves to the role of designer and leave the execution to others, to emphasize the impersonality and duplicability of their invention. If no patron is found to foot the bill for carrying out these very costly structures, they remain on paper, like unbuilt architecture. Sometimes they

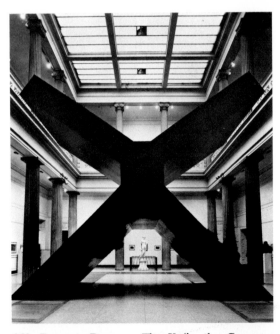

350. RONALD BLADEN. *The X* (in the Corcoran Gallery, Washington, D.C.). 1967. Painted wood, to be constructed in steel, 22′ 8″ × 24′ 6″ × 12′ 6″. Fischbach Gallery, New York

reach the mock-up stage, with painted wood substituting for metal, as in *The X* (fig. 350), by the Canadian Ronald Bladen, which was built for an exhibition inside the two-story hall of the Corcoran Gallery in Washington, D. C. Its commanding presence, dwarfing the Neoclassic colonnade of the hall, seems doubly awesome in such a setting. The ultimate medium for Environmental Sculpture is the earth itself, since it provides complete freedom from the limitations of the human scale. Some designers of Primary Structures have, logically enough, turned to "Earth Art," inventing projects that stretch over many miles. These latter-day successors to the mound-building Indians of Neolithic America have the advantage of modern earth-moving machinery, but this is more than outweighed by the problem of cost and the difficulty of finding suitable sites on our crowded planet. The few projects of theirs that have actually been carried out are mostly found—and the finding is itself often difficult enough—in the more remote corners of western America. *Spiral Jetty*, the work of Robert Smithson, juts out into the Great Salt Lake in Utah (fig. 351). Its appeal rests, in part, on the Surrealist irony of the concept: a spiral jetty is as self-contradictory as a straight corkscrew. But it can hardly be said to have grown out of the natural formation of the terrain like the Great Serpent Mound in Ohio, and one wonders if it will endure as long.

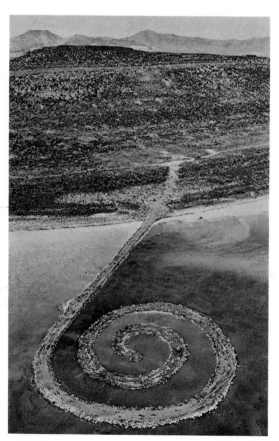

351. ROBERT SMITHSON. *Spiral Jetty*. 1970. Total length 1,500′; width of jetty 15′. Great Salt Lake, Utah

OLDENBURG

Primary Structures are obviously monuments. But just as obviously they are not monuments commemorating or celebrating anything except their designer's imagination. To the man in the street they offer no ready frame of reference, nothing to be reminded of, even though the original meaning of "monument" is "a reminder." Presumably, monuments in this traditional sense died out when contemporary society lost its consensus of what ought to be publicly remembered. Yet the belief in the possibility of such monuments has not been abandoned altogether. One artist, Claes Oldenburg, has proposed a number of unexpected and imaginative solutions to the problem; he is, moreover, an exceptionally precise and eloquent commentator on his ideas. All his monuments are heroic in size, though not in subject matter; all share one common feature, their origin in humble objects of everyday use. Oldenburg conceived and executed a monument shaped as a gigantic ice bag (fig. 352) with a mechanism inside to make it move—"movements caused by an invisible hand," as the artist described them. For a piece of outdoor sculpture he wanted a form that combined hard and soft and did not need a base. An ice bag met these demands, so he bought one and started playing with it. He soon realized, he says, that the object was made for manipulation, "that movement was part of its identity and should be used." He sent the *Giant Ice Bag* to the U.S. Pavilion at EXPO 70 in Osaka, Japan, where crowds were endlessly fascinated to watch it heave, rise, and twist like a living thing, then relax with an almost audible

collage, and stagecraft. George Segal, for example, creates lifesize three-dimensional pictures showing real people and real objects in everyday situations, such as *Cinema* (fig. 353). The subject is ordinary enough to be instantly recognizable: a man changing the letters on a movie theater marquee. Yet the relation of image and reality is far more subtle and complex than the obvious authenticity of the scene suggests. The man's figure is cast from a live model by a technique of Segal's invention, and retains its ghostly white plaster surface. Thus it is one crucial step removed from our world of daily experience, and the neon-lit sign has been carefully designed to complement and set off the shadowed figure. Moreover, the scene is brought down from its natural context, high above the entrance to the theater where we might have glimpsed it in passing, and presented at eye-level, in isolation, so that we grasp it completely for the first time.

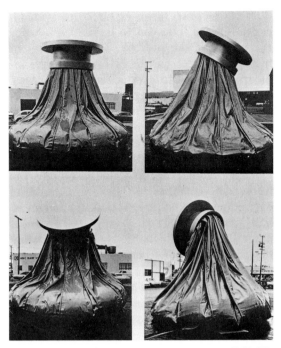

352. CLAES OLDENBURG. *Giant Ice Bag.* 1969–70. Plastic and metal, with interior motor, height 15′ 6″, diameter 18′

sigh. What do these monuments celebrate? What is the secret of their appeal? Part of it, which they share with Pop Art, is that they reveal the aesthetic potential of the ordinary and all-too-familiar. There is one dimension, however, that is missing in Oldenburg's monuments. They delight, astonish, amuse—but they do not move us. Yet they do have an undeniable grandeur. We might say, with Baudelaire, that they express "the heroism of modern life."

ENVIRONMENTS: SEGAL

Other artists associated with Pop embrace in their work the entire range of their physical environment, including the people. They usually find the flat surface of a canvas too confining; in order to bridge the gap between image and reality, they often introduce three-dimensional objects into their pictures, or they may even construct full-scale models of everyday things and real-life situations, utilizing every conceivable kind of material. These "environments" or "assemblages" combine the qualities of painting, sculpture,

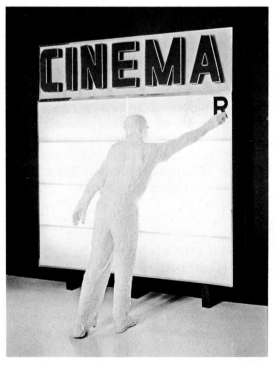

353. GEORGE SEGAL. *Cinema.* 1963. Plaster, metal, Plexiglass, and fluorescent light, 9′ 10″ × 8′ × 3′ 3″. The Albright-Knox Art Gallery, Buffalo (Gift of Seymour H. Knox)

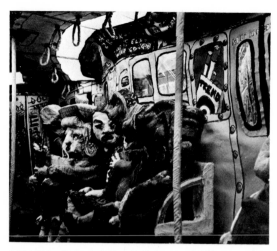

354. RED GROOMS AND THE RUCKUS CONSTRUCTION
Co. *Lexington Local* (detail) from *Ruckus Manhattan*. 1976. Mixed media, papier-mâché, 10′ × 9′ ×
36′. Courtesy Marlborough Gallery, New York
(Photograph by Richard L. Plaut, Jr.)

GROOMS

Perhaps the most ambitious environment
undertaken to date was *Ruckus Manhattan*,
created in 1975–76 by Red Grooms and his
"Ruckus Construction Company." The huge
installation (now dismantled) offered a riotous
tour of Manhattan, featuring a subway station complete with train (fig. 354). Bright and
colorful, it was truly popular art, for it was
intended to appeal to the man in the street.
People flocked to see the show, which became
a festive Happening in its own right. With
the zany humor of an underground comic,
Ruckus Manhattan held up a witty mirror
to New York and its denizens, who were
depicted as grotesque figures living in a
fascinating but crazy-quilt world.

TWENTIETH-CENTURY
ARCHITECTURE

For more than a century, from the mid-
eighteenth to the late nineteenth, architecture
had been dominated by a succession of "revival styles" (see p. 300). The use of this
term, we will recall, does not imply that
earlier forms were slavishly copied; the best
work of the time has both individuality and
high distinction. Yet the architectural wis-

dom of the past, however freely interpreted,
proved in the long run to be inadequate for
the needs of the present. The authority of
historical modes had to be broken if the industrial era was to produce a truly contemporary style. The search for such a style—
the analogue of Manet's achievement in
painting—began in earnest about 1880. It demanded more than a reform of architectural
grammar and vocabulary: to take full advantage of the expressive—not merely the
utilitarian—qualities of the new building
techniques and materials that the engineer
had placed at his disposal, the architect
needed a new philosophy. He had to redefine
the traditional concepts regarding form and
function, as well as the broader role of architecture in society. The leaders of modern
architecture have characteristically been vigorous and articulate thinkers, in whose
minds architectural theory is closely linked
with ideas of social reform. It is equally
significant that the movement began in commercial architecture (stores, offices, apartments), outside the range of traditional

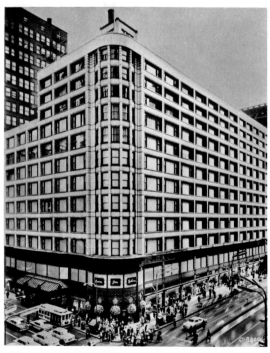

355. LOUIS SULLIVAN. Carson Pirie Scott & Company, Department Store. 1899–1904. Chicago

building types; that its symbol was the sky-scraper; and that its birthplace was Chicago, then a burgeoning metropolis not yet encumbered by any firm allegiance to the styles of the past.

SULLIVAN

Chicago was the home of Louis Sullivan, the first indisputably modern architect. His achievements are summed up in the department store of Carson Pirie Scott & Company (fig. 355), which he designed shortly before the turn of the century. If it is not a skyscraper by present-day standards, it is at least a potential one, for its structural skeleton, a steel frame, embodies the same principle on which the much taller skyscrapers of today are built. The Carson Pirie Scott store also illustrates Sullivan's dictum that "form follows function." The external walls do not pretend to support anything, since they no longer do; they have been reduced to a "skin" or sheathing over the steel beams, with most of the surface given over to huge windows. Yet Sullivan's dictum meant not

rigid dependence but a flexible relationship capable of a wide variety of expressive effects. Here the white terra-cotta sheathing emphasizes the horizontal continuity of the flanks as well as the vertical accent at the corner by subtle differences in spacing and detail.

WRIGHT

If Sullivan represents, as it were, the Post-Impressionist stage of modern architecture, his great disciple, Frank Lloyd Wright, represents its Cubist phase. This is certainly true of his brilliant early style, between 1900 and 1910, which had vast international influence. (His late work, beginning with the 1930s, will be omitted from this account.) During that first decade, Wright's main activity was the design of suburban houses in the Chicago area; these were known as "Prairie Houses," because their low, horizontal lines were meant to blend with the flat landscape around them. The last, and most accomplished, example is the Robie House (figs. 356, 357). Its "Cubism" is not merely a matter of the clean-cut rectangular elements

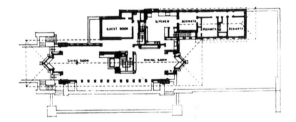

356. FRANK LLOYD WRIGHT. Plan of Robie House, Chicago. 1909

357. Robie House. Wright's brilliant early style became the basis for advanced architectural design everywhere between 1920 and 1950.

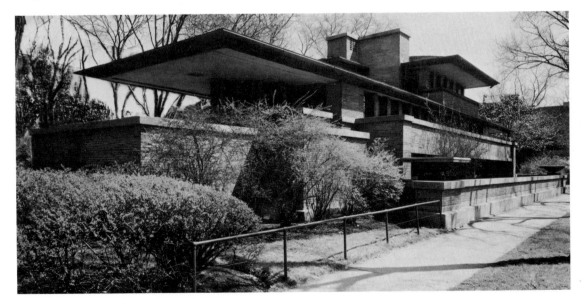

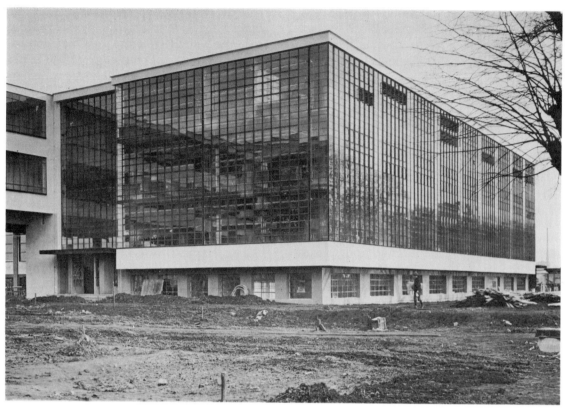

358. WALTER GROPIUS. Shop Block, the Bauhaus. 1925–26. Dessau

composing the structure, but of Wright's handling of space. It is designed as a number of "space blocks" grouped around a central core, the chimney; some of the blocks are closed and others are open, yet all are defined with equal precision. Thus the space that has been architecturally shaped includes the balconies, terrace, court, and garden, as well as the house itself: voids and solids are seen to be equivalent, analogous in their way to facet Cubism in painting, and the entire complex enters into active and dramatic relationship with its surroundings. Wright did not aim simply to design a house, but to create a complete environment. He even took command of the details of the interior, designing fabrics and furniture for it. The controlling factor here was not so much the individual client and his special wishes as Wright's conviction that buildings profoundly influence the people who live, work, or worship in them, so that the architect is really a molder of men, whether or not he consciously assumes this responsibility.

INTERNATIONAL STYLE: GROPIUS

Among the first Europeans to recognize Wright's importance were some Dutch architects who, at the end of World War I, joined forces with Mondrian. They found his principle of "the balance of unequal but equivalent oppositions" fully compatible with Wright's architecture. Their influence was so pervasive that the movement they represented soon became international. The largest and most complex example of this "International Style of the 1920s" is the group of buildings created in 1925–26 by the German architect Walter Gropius for the Bauhaus at Dessau (fig. 358), a famous art school whose curriculum embraced all the visual arts, linked by the root concept of "structure," *Bau.* The most dramatic is the shop block, a four-story box with walls that are a continuous surface of glass. This radical step had been possible ever since the introduction of the structural steel skeleton; Sullivan had approached it, but he could not yet free himself from the old notion of the

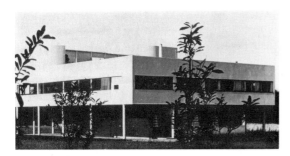

359. LE CORBUSIER. Savoye House. 1929–30. Poissy-sur-Seine

window as a "hole in the wall." Gropius frankly acknowledged, at last, that in modern architecture the wall is no more than a curtain or climate barrier, which may consist entirely of glass if maximum daylight is desired.

LE CORBUSIER; MIES VAN DER ROHE

In France, the most distinguished representative of the "International Style" during the 1920s was Le Corbusier. At that time he built only private houses—from necessity, not choice—but these are as important as Wright's "Prairie Houses." Le Corbusier called them *machines à habiter* (machines to be lived in), a term meant to suggest his admiration for the clean, precise shapes of machinery, not a desire for "mechanized living." Perhaps he also wanted to convey that his houses were so different from conventional ones as to constitute a new species. Such is indeed our impression as we approach the most famous of them, the Savoye House at Poissy-sur-Seine (fig. 359); it resembles a low, square box resting on stilts—pillars of reinforced concrete that form part of the structural skeleton and reappear to divide the "ribbon windows" running along each side of the box. The flat, smooth surfaces stress Le Corbusier's preoccupation with abstract "space blocks." To find out how the box is subdivided, we must enter it; we then realize that this simple "package" contains living spaces that are open as well as closed, separated by glass walls. Indoors, we are still in communication with the outside world (views of the sky and of the surrounding terrain are everywhere to be seen), yet we enjoy complete privacy, since an observer on the

ground cannot see us unless we stand next to a window. The functionalism of the Savoye House, then, is governed by a "design for living," not by mechanical efficiency.

America, despite its position of leadership at first, lagged behind in the 1920s. Not until the very end of the decade did the impact of the "International Style" begin to be felt on this side of the Atlantic. A few years later, the best German architects, whose work Hitler condemned as "un-German," came to this country and greatly stimulated the development of American architecture. Gropius, appointed chairman of the architecture department at Harvard University, had an important educational influence; Ludwig

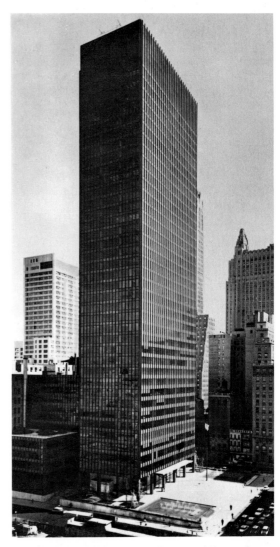

360. LUDWIG MIES VAN DER ROHE and PHILIP JOHNSON. Seagram Building. 1958. New York

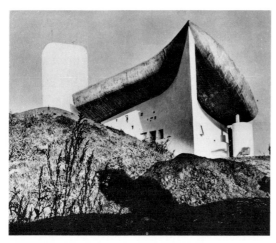

361. LE CORBUSIER. Notre-Dame-du-Haut, view from southeast. 1950–55. Ronchamp

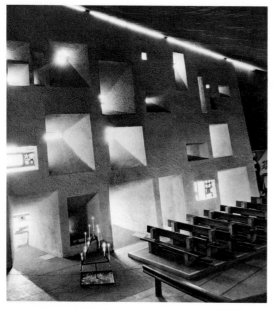

362. LE CORBUSIER. Interior, South Wall, Notre-Dame-du-Haut

Mies van der Rohe, his former colleague at Dessau, settled in Chicago as a practicing architect. His severely elegant Seagram Building in New York (fig. 360) exemplifies his dictum that "less is more." Mies van der Rohe is the great spiritual heir of Mondrian among recent designers, possessed of the same "absolute pitch" in determining proportions and spatial relationships.

Le Corbusier, in contrast to Mies van der Rohe, abandoned the geometric purism of the "International Style" in his later years.

Instead, he showed a growing preoccupation with sculptural, even anthropomorphic effects. His church of Notre-Dame-du-Haut at Ronchamp in southeastern France is the most revolutionary building of the mid-twentieth century. Rising like a medieval fortress from the crest of a mountain (fig. 361), it has a design so irrational that it defies analysis. The massive walls seem to obey an unseen force that makes them slant and curl like paper; and the overhanging roof suggests the brim of a huge hat, or the bottom of a ship split lengthwise by the sharp-edged buttress from which it is suspended. There is a conscious evocation of the dim, prehistoric past here; asked to create a sanctuary on a mountain top, Le Corbusier must have felt that this was the primeval task of architecture, placing him in a direct line of succession with the men who had built Stonehenge, the ziggurats of Mesopotamia, and the Greek temples. Hence, he also avoids any correlation between exterior and interior. The doors are concealed: we must seek them out like clefts in a mountainside, and to pass through them is much like entering a secret—and sacred—cave. Only inside do we sense the specifically Christian aspect of Ronchamp. The light, channeled through windows so tiny that they seem hardly more than slits or pinpricks on the exterior, cuts widening paths through the thickness of the wall, and thus becomes once more what it had been in medieval architecture—the visible counterpart of the Light Divine (fig. 362). There is true magic in the interior of Ronchamp, but also a strangely disquieting quality, a nostalgia for the certainties of a faith that is no longer unquestioned. Ronchamp thus mirrors the spiritual condition of Modern Man —which is a measure of its greatness as a work of art.

Le Corbusier belongs to the same heroic generation as Gropius and Mies van der Rohe; all were born in the 1880s. It was these men who in the course of their long, fruitful careers coined the language of twentieth-century architecture. Their successors continue to use it, adapting its vocabulary to new building types and materials but not questioning its fundamental logic. To younger architects today, the greatest challenge is not the individual structure but urban design: replacing the slums of our decaying cities with housing that will provide a socially healthful environment for very large numbers of people. Urban planning is probably as old as civilization itself (which, we recall, means "city life"). We have caught only a fleeting glimpse of it in this book (see fig. 141), since its history is difficult to trace by direct visual evidence: cities, like living organisms, are ever-changing, and to reconstruct their past from their present appearance is a laborious task. With the advent of the industrial era two centuries ago, cities began to grow explosively, and have continued to do so ever since. Much of this growth was uncontrolled beyond the laying out of a network of streets; housing standards were poor or poorly enforced. The unfortunate result can be seen in the overcrowded, crumbling apartment blocks that are the blight of vast urban areas everywhere. They were taken over by the poor, while those who could afford it fled to the dormitory towns of suburbia. This exodus, accelerated by the automobile, has produced the dangerous tensions that lend urgency to the cry for urban renewal today. Such renewal, needless to say, must involve the political, social, and economic forces of our entire society, rather than the architect alone. Yet the architect has an essential role in the process, for it is he—and only he—who will have to translate the schemes of the planning agencies into reality. One important problem engaging his attention is how to develop an alternative to the conventional high-rise apartment block in densely populated areas: a housing pattern that will be less deadeningly uniform (but no more expensive), and provide more light and air, safer access, and a multitude of other desirable features. One promising solution, by the Israeli architect Moshe Safdie and his associates (fig. 363), was demonstrated in the Habitat complex at the Montreal EXPO 67. The individual apartments consist of prefabricated "boxes" that can be combined into units of several sizes and shapes, attached to a zigzagging concrete framework which can be extended to fit any site. If the result looks a bit like a

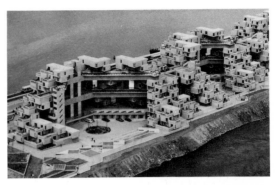

363. MOSHE SAFDIE and others. Habitat, EXPO 67, Montreal. 1967

Chinese puzzle, this impression disappears as we enter the complex and enjoy its openness, its fascinating variety of perspectives.

POST-MODERN

Spurred by more radical social theories, "post-modern" architecture—as its misleading name implies—pursues new approaches which repudiate the formal beauty of the International Style. Among the freshest, as well as most controversial, results is the recently opened Georges Pompidou National Arts and Cultural Center in Paris (colorplate 76). Selected in an international competition, the design by an English-Italian team looks like the Bauhaus (fig. 358) turned inside out. The architects have eliminated any trace of Le Corbusier's elegant façades (fig. 359) to expose the inner mechanics while disguising the underlying structure. The interior itself has no fixed dividing walls, so that it can be rearranged to meet any need. This stark utilitarianism reflects the populist sentiment current in France. Yet it is enlivened by eye-catching colors, each keyed to a different function. The festive display is as vivacious and imaginative as Léger's *The City* (fig. 320), which, with the Eiffel Tower, can be regarded as the Pompidou Center's true ancestor. It is in enterprises such as this and the Habitat that the architects of the future may well find their most fruitful fields of endeavor.

SYNOPTIC TABLE IV

POLITICAL HISTORY	RELIGION, LITERATURE	SCIENCE, TECHNOLOGY
1750	Gray's *Elegy* 1750 Diderot's *Encyclopedia* 1751–72 Johnson's *Dictionary* 1755 Edmund Burke (1729–97)	Watt perfects steam engine 1765–76 Priestley discovers oxygen 1774 Coke-fed blast furnaces for iron smelting perfected c. 1760–75
1775 American Revolution 1775–85; Constitution adopted 1789 French Revolution 1789–97; Reign of Terror under Robespierre 1793 Consulate of Napoleon 1799	Gibbon's *Decline and Fall* 1776–87 Paine's *The Rights of Man* 1790 Wordsworth and Coleridge, *Lyrical Ballads*, 1798	Power loom 1785; cotton gin 1792 Jenner's smallpox vaccine c. 1798
1800 Louisiana Purchase 1803 Napoleon crowns himself Emperor 1804; exiled to St. Helena 1815 Greeks declare independence 1822	Goethe's *Faust* (part I) 1808 Byron's *Childe Harold's Pilgrimage* 1812–18 Keats (1795–1821) Shelley (1792–1822) Sir Walter Scott (1771–1832)	First voyage of Fulton's steamship 1807; first Atlantic crossing 1819 Stephenson's first locomotive 1814 Faraday discovers principle of electric dynamo 1821
1825 Revolution of 1830 in France Queen Victoria crowned 1837 U.S. treaty with China opens ports 1844 U.S. annexes western land areas 1845–60 Revolution of 1848; fails in Germany, Hungary, Austria, Italy; France sets up Second Republic (Louis Napoleon)	Pushkin (1799–1837) Victor Hugo (1802–85) Dickens' *Oliver Twist* 1838 Thackeray's *Vanity Fair* 1847 *Communist Manifesto* 1848 Edgar Allan Poe (1809–49)	Erie Canal opened 1825 First railway completed (England) 1825 McCormick invents reaper 1831 Daguerreotype process of photography introduced 1839 Morse perfects telegraph 1844
1850 Louis Napoleon takes title of Emperor 1852 Perry's visit ends Japan's isolation 1854 Russia abolishes serfdom 1861 U.S. Civil War (1861–65) ends slavery Franco-Prussian War 1870–71 Disraeli British prime minister 1874–80	Melville's *Moby Dick* 1851 Whitman's *Leaves of Grass* 1855 Baudelaire (1821–67) Tolstoy's *War and Peace* 1864–69 Dostoyevsky's *Crime and Punishment* 1867 Marx's *Das Kapital* 1867–94	Darwin publishes *Origin of Species* 1859 Bessemer patents tilting converter for turning iron into steel 1860 Pasteur develops germ theory 1864 Mendel publishes first experiments in genetics 1865 Nobel invents dynamite 1867 First transcontinental railroad completed in America 1869 Suez Canal opened 1869
1875 Spanish-American War 1898; U.S. gains Philippines, Guam, Puerto Rico, annexes Hawaii	Mark Twain's *Tom Sawyer* 1876 Henrik Ibsen (1828–1906) Emile Zola (1840–1902) Oscar Wilde (1854–1900) Henry James (1843–1916) G. B. Shaw (1856–1950)	Bell patents the telephone 1876 Edison invents phonograph 1877. Edison invents electric light bulb 1879 First internal combustion engines for gasoline 1885 Roentgen discovers X-rays 1895 Marconi invents wireless telegraphy 1895 Edison invents motion picture 1896 The Curies discover radium 1898

NOTE:
Figure numbers of black-and-white illustrations are in (italics). Colorplate numbers are in (bold face).
Duration of papacy or reign is indicated by the abbreviation r.

ARCHITECTURE	SCULPTURE	PAINTING	
Soufflot, Panthéon, Paris (*251*)		Greuze, *Village Bride* (*254*) West, *Death of Wolfe* (*256*)	1750
Jefferson, Monticello (*252*) Langhans, Brandenburg Gate, Berlin (*253*)	Houdon, *Voltaire* (*257*)	David, *Death of Socrates* (**54**) Copley, *Watson and the Shark* (**55**) David, *Death of Marat* (*255*) Gros, *Napoleon at Arcole* (*268*)	1775
	Canova, *Pauline Borghese* (*262*)	Goya, *Family of Charles IV* (*265*) Géricault, *Mounted Officer* (*269*) Ingres, *Odalisque* (**57**) Goya, *Third of May, 1808* (**56**) Friedrich, *Polar Sea* (*274*)	1800
Barry and Pugin, Houses of Parliament (*259*) Labrouste, Bibliothèque Ste.-Geneviève, Paris (*261*)	Rude, *La Marseillaise* (*263*)	Corot, *Papigno* (*276*) Ingres, *Bertin* (*267*) Delacroix, *Frédéric Chopin* (*270*) Turner, *Slave Ship* (**59**) Bingham, *Fur Traders* (*275*) Courbet, *Stone Breakers* (*277*)	1825
Garnier, Opéra, Paris (*260*)		Daumier, *Third-Class Carriage* (*271*) Manet, *Luncheon on the Grass* (*278*) Homer, *Morning Bell* (*286*) Monet, *The River* (**61**) Whistler, *The Artist's Mother* (*284*)	1850
	Rodin, *The Thinker* (*289*)	Eakins, *Gross Clinic* (*287*) Renoir, *Moulin de la Galette* (*280*) Degas, *Glass of Absinthe* (*281*) Cézanne, *Fruit Bowl, Glass, and Apples* (*291*) Van Gogh, *Wheat Field and Cypress Trees* (**63**) Toulouse-Lautrec, *Moulin Rouge* (*299*) Munch, *The Scream* (*300*)	1875

	POLITICAL HISTORY	RELIGION, LITERATURE	SCIENCE, TECHNOLOGY
1900	T. Roosevelt (1901–09) proclaims Open Door policy; Panama Canal opened 1914 Internal strife, reforms in Russia 1905 Revolution in China, republic set up 1911 First World War 1914–18; U.S. enters 1917 Bolshevik Revolution 1917; Russia signs separate peace with Germany 1918 Gandhi agitates for Indian independence after First World War Irish Free State established 1921 Mussolini's Fascists seize Italian government 1922 Turkey becomes republic 1923	Marcel Proust (1871–1922) W. B. Yeats (1865–1939) André Gide (1869–1951) T. S. Eliot (1888–1964) James Joyce (1882–1941) Eugene O'Neill (1888–1953) D. H. Lawrence (1885–1930)	Planck formulates quantum theory 1900 Freud's *Interpretation of Dreams* 1900 Pavlov's first experiments with conditioned reflexes 1900 Wright brothers' first flight with power-driven airplane 1903 Einstein's theory of relativity 1905 Ford begins assembly-line automobile production 1909 First radio station begins regularly scheduled broadcasts 1920
1925	Stalin starts Five-Year Plan 1928 Hitler seizes power in Germany 1933 Roosevelt proclaims New Deal 1933 Mussolini conquers Ethiopia 1936 Spanish Civil War 1936–39; won by Franco Hitler annexes Austria 1938 Second World War 1939–45 Atomic bomb dropped on Hiroshima 1945 United Nations Charter signed 1945 Israel becomes independent 1948 Communists under Mao win in China 1949	Sinclair Lewis (1885–1951) William Faulkner (1897–1962) Ernest Hemingway (1898–1961) Thomas Wolfe (1900–1938) Berthold Brecht (1898–1956) André Malraux (1901–1976) Jean Paul Sartre (1905–1980) Albert Camus (1913–1960)	First regularly scheduled TV broadcasts in U.S. 1928, in England 1936 Atomic fission demonstrated on laboratory scale 1942 Penicillin discovered 1943 Computer technology developed 1944
1950	Korean War 1950–53 U.S. Supreme Court outlaws racial segregation in public schools 1954 Common Market established in Europe 1957 African colonies gain independence after 1957	Samuel Beckett (born 1906) Eugene Ionesco (born 1912) Jean Genêt (born 1910) Lawrence Durrell (born 1912)	Genetic code cracked 1953 First hydrogen bomb (atomic fusion) exploded 1954 Sputnik, first satellite, launched 1957
1960	John F. Kennedy assassinated 1963 Johnson begins massive U.S. intervention in Vietnam 1965 Martin Luther King assassinated 1968 Russia invades Czechoslovakia 1968		First manned space flight 1961 First manned landing on the moon 1969
1970	Civil war in Pakistan gains independence for People's Republic of Bangladesh 1972–73 Vietnam War ends 1973 Nixon resigns presidency 1974 Death of Franco 1975	First non-Italian pope elected since Adrian VI in 1522—Pope John Paul II (from Poland) 1978	First orbiting laboratory (Skylab) 1973 Viking I and II Space Probes land on Mars 1976 Voyager I Space Probe orbits Jupiter 1979

ARCHITECTURE	SCULPTURE	PAINTING	
Wright, Robie House (*356, 357*)	Maillol, *Méditerranée* (*303*) Brancusi, *The Kiss* (*341*) Barlach, *Man Drawing Sword* (*305*) Lehmbruck, *Standing Youth* (*304*) Duchamp-Villon, *The Great Horse* (*345*) Brancusi, *Bird in Space* (*343*)	Picasso, *Old Guitarist* (*302*) Rouault, *Head of Christ* (*307*) Matisse, *Joy of Life* (*306*) Picasso, *Demoiselles d'Avignon* (*313*) Klimt, *The Kiss* (*301*) Rousseau, *The Dream* (**65**) Chagall, *I and the Village* (*322*) Duchamp, *The Bride* (*325*) Kandinsky, *Sketch I for "Composition VII"* (**67**) De Chirico, *Mystery and Melancholy . . .* (*321*) Stella, *Brooklyn Bridge* (*319*) Léger, *The City* (*320*) Ernst, *1 Copper Plate . . .* (*326*) Picasso, *Mother and Child* (*317*) Klee, *Twittering Machine* (*323*)	1900
Gropius, Bauhaus (*358*) Le Corbusier, Savoye House (*359*)	Giacometti, *Palace at 4 A. M.* (*346*) Moore, *Recumbent Figure* (*342*) Calder, *Lobster Trap and Fish Tail* (*348*) Picasso, *Bull's Head* (*2*)	Picasso, *Three Dancers* (**68**) Dali, *The Persistence of Memory* (*327*) Miró, *Painting* (**70**) Klee, *Park near L(ucerne)* (*324*)	1925
Le Corbusier, Notre-Dame, Ronchamp (*361, 362*)		Dubuffet, *Le Metafisyx* (*331*) Pollock, *One* (*330*) De Kooning, *Woman II* (**71**) Rothko, *Earth and Green* (**72**) Vasarely, *Vega* (*335*) Johns, *Three Flags* (*336*)	1950
Mies van der Rohe and Johnson, Seagram Building (*360*)	Segal, *Cinema* (*353*) Bladen, *The X* (*350*)	Lichtenstein, *Girl at Piano* (*337*) Jenkins, *Phenomena Astral Signal* (**73**) Stella, *Empress of India* (*334*) Indiana, *Love* (*338*)	1960
Piano and Rogers, Georges Pompidou National Arts and Cultural Center (**76**)	Oldenburg, *Giant Ice Bag* (*352*) Smithson, *Spiral Jetty* (*351*) Grooms, *Lexington Local* (*354*)	Anuszkiewicz, *Entrance to Green* (**74**) Eddy, *New Shoes for H.* (*339*, **75**)	1970

GLOSSARY *Cross references are indicated by words in* SMALL CAPITALS.

ABSTRACT. Having little or no reference to the appearance of natural objects; pertaining to the non-representational art styles of the twentieth century.

AMBULATORY. A passageway, especially around the CHANCEL of a church. An ambulatory may also be outside a church.

AMPHORA. A Greek vase having an egg-shaped body, a narrow cylindrical neck, and two curving handles joined to the body at the shoulder and neck.

APSE. A large niche facing the nave of a church, usually at the east end. See BASILICA.

ARCADE. A series of ARCHES and their supports.

ARCH. A structural member, often semicircular, used to span an opening; it requires support from walls, PIERS, or COLUMNS, and BUTTRESSING at the sides.

ARCHAIC. A relatively early style, as Greek sculpture of the seventh and sixth centuries B.C.; or any style adopting characteristics of an earlier period.

ARCHITRAVE. The main horizontal beam, and the lowest part of an ENTABLATURE.

ASSEMBLAGE. Two or more accidentally "found" objects placed together as a construction. See READY-MADE.

ATMOSPHERIC PERSPECTIVE. A means of showing distance or depth in a painting by changing the tone of objects that are far away from the picture plane, especially by reducing in gradual stages the contrast between lights and darks.

BARREL VAULT. A semi-cylindrical VAULT.

BASE. The lowest element of a COLUMN, wall, DOME, etc.

BASILICA. In the Roman period, the word refers to the function of the building—a large meeting hall—rather than to its form, which may vary according to its use; as an official public building, the Roman basilica had certain religious overtones. The term was used by the Early Christians to refer to their churches. An Early Christian basilica had an oblong plan, flat timber ceiling, trussed roof, and an APSE. The entrance was on one short side and the apse projected from the opposite side, at the farther end of the building.

BAYS. Compartments into which a building may be subdivided, usually formed by the space between consecutive architectural supports.

BLACK-FIGURED. A type of Greek vase painting, practiced in the seventh and sixth centuries B.C., in which the design was painted mainly in black against a lighter-colored background, usually the natural clay.

BOOK OF HOURS. A book for individual private devotions with prayers for different hours of the day; often elaborately ILLUMINATED.

BUTTRESS, BUTTRESSING. A masonry support that counteracts the THRUST exerted by an ARCH or a VAULT. See FLYING BUTTRESS, PIER BUTTRESS.

CAPITAL. The crowning member of a COLUMN, PIER, or PILASTER, on which the lowest element of the ENTABLATURE rests. See DORIC COLUMN, IONIC COLUMN, CORINTHIAN COLUMN.

CARTOON. A preliminary SKETCH or DRAWING made to be transferred to a wall, a panel, or canvas as a guide in painting a finished work.

CASTING. A method of reproducing a three-dimensional object or RELIEF. Casting in bronze or other metal is often the final stage in the creation of a piece of sculpture; casting in plaster is a convenient and inexpensive way of making a copy of an original. See SCULPTURE.

CHANCEL. In a church, the space reserved for the clergy and CHOIR, set off from the NAVE by steps, and occasionally by a screen.

CHAPEL. A compartment in a church containing an altar dedicated to a saint.

CHOIR. See CHANCEL.

CLASSIC. Used specifically to refer to Greek art of the fifth century B.C.

CLASSICAL. Used generally to refer to the art of the Greeks and the Romans.

CLERESTORY. A row of windows in a wall that rises above the adjoining roof.

COLLAGE. A composition made by pasting cut-up textured materials, such as newsprint, wallpaper, etc., to form all or part of a work of art; may be combined with painting or drawing or with three-dimensional objects.

COLONNADE. A series of COLUMNS placed at regular intervals.

COLOR. The choice and treatment of the hues in a painting.

COLUMN. A vertical architectural support, usually consisting of a BASE, a rounded SHAFT, and a CAPITAL.

COMPOSITION. The arrangement of FORM, COLOR, LINE, etc., in any given work of art.

COMPOUND PIER. A PIER with COLUMNS, PILASTERS, or SHAFTS attached.

CORINTHIAN COLUMN. First appeared in fifth-century

Greece, apparently as a variation of the IONIC. The CAPITAL differentiates the two: the Corinthian capital has an inverted bell shape, decorated with acanthus leaves, stalks, and volute scrolls. The Corinthian ORDER was widely used by the Romans.

CORNICE. The crowning, projecting architectural feature, especially the uppermost part of an ENTABLATURE.

COUNTERPOISE (*contrapposto*). The disposition of the parts of the body so that the weight-bearing leg, or engaged leg, is distinguished from the raised leg, or free leg, resulting in a shift in the axis between the hips and shoulders. Used by the Greek sculptors as a means of showing movement in a figure.

CROSSING. In a cross-shaped church, the area where the NAVE and the TRANSEPT intersect.

CUPOLA. A rounded, domed roof or ceiling.

DOME. A large CUPOLA supported by a circular DRUM or square BASE.

DORIC COLUMN. The Doric COLUMN stands without a BASE directly on the top of the stepped platform of a temple. Its SHAFT has shallow FLUTES.

DRAWING. A SKETCH, design, or representation by lines. Drawings are usually made on paper with pen, pencil, charcoal, pastel, chalk, etc.

DRUM. One of several sections composing the SHAFT of a COLUMN; also a cylindrical wall supporting a DOME.

ENCAUSTIC. A method of painting in colors mixed with wax and applied with a brush, generally while the mixture is hot. The technique was practiced in ancient times and in the Early Christian period, and has been revived by some modern painters.

ENGAGED COLUMN. A COLUMN that is part of a wall and projects somewhat from it. Such a column often has no structural purpose.

ENGRAVING. A design incised in reverse on a copper plate; this is coated with printer's ink, which remains in the incised lines when the plate is wiped off. Damp paper is placed on the plate, and both are put into a press; the paper soaks up the ink and produces a print of the original.

ENTABLATURE. The upper part of an architectural ORDER.

ETCHING. Like ENGRAVING, etching is an incising process. However, the design is drawn in reverse with a needle on a plate thinly coated with wax or resin. The plate is placed in a bath of nitric acid; the etched lines are produced on the plate by the coating. The coating is then removed, and the prints are made as in engraving.

FAÇADE. The front of a building.

FLUTE, FLUTES. Vertical channels on a column SHAFT; see DORIC COLUMN, IONIC COLUMN.

FLYING BUTTRESS. An ARCH that springs from the upper part of the PIER BUTTRESS of a Gothic church, spans the aisle roof, and abuts the upper NAVE wall to receive the THRUST from the nave VAULTS; it transmits this thrust to the solid pier buttresses.

FORESHORTENING. A method of representing objects as if seen at an angle and receding or projecting into space; not in a frontal or profile view.

FORM. The external shape or appearance of a representation, considered apart from its color or material.

FREESTANDING. Used to refer to a work of SCULPTURE in the round, that is, in full three-dimensionality; not attached to architecture and not in RELIEF.

FRESCO. A technique of wall painting known since antiquity; the PIGMENT is mixed with water and applied to a freshly plastered area of a wall. The result is a particularly permanent form of painted decoration.

FRIEZE. In CLASSICAL architecture an architectural element that rests on the ARCHITRAVE and is immediately below the CORNICE; also, any horizontal band decorated with moldings, RELIEF sculpture, or painting.

GABLE. The triangular part of a wall, enclosed by the lines of a sloping roof. See PEDIMENT.

GALLERY. A roofed promenade. See AMBULATORY, COLONNADE.

GOSPELS, GOSPEL BOOK. Contains the four Gospels of the New Testament that tell the life of Christ, attributed to the Evangelists Matthew, Mark, Luke, and John. Often elaborately illustrated.

GROIN. The sharp edge formed by the intersection of two VAULTS.

GROIN VAULTS. A VAULT formed by the intersection at right angles of two BARREL VAULTS of equal height and diameter, so that the GROINS form a diagonal cross.

GROUND PLAN. See PLAN.

HIEROGLYPHICS. The characters and picture-writing used by the ancient Egyptians.

ICON. A panel painting of Christ, the Virgin, or saints; regarded as sacred, especially by Eastern Christians.

ILLUMINATION. A term used generally for manuscript paintings. Illuminated manuscripts may contain separate ornamental pages, marginal illustrations, ornament within the text, entire MINIATURE paintings, or any combination of these.

ILLUSIONISM, ILLUSIONISTIC. The effort of an artist to represent the visual world with deceptive reality.

ILLUSTRATION. The representation of an idea, scene, or text by artistic means.

IONIC COLUMN. The Ionic COLUMN stands on a molded BASE. The SHAFT normally has FLUTES more deeply cut than Doric flutes. The Ionic CAPITAL is identified by its pair of spiral scroll-like ornaments.

JAMB. The side of a doorway or window frame.

KORE. An ARCHAIC Greek statue of a draped maiden.

KOUROS. An ARCHAIC Greek statue of a standing nude youth.

LINE. A mark made by a moving tool such as a pen or pencil; more generally, an outline, contour, or silhouette.

LINEAR PERSPECTIVE. A mathematical system for representing three-dimensional objects and space on a two-dimensional surface. All objects are represented as seen from a single viewpoint.

MASS. The expanse of COLOR that defines a painted shape; the three-dimensional volume of a sculptured or architectural form.

MEDIUM. The material with which an artist works, such as marble, TERRA-COTTA, OIL PAINT, WATERCOLOR, etc.

METOPE. An oblong panel between the TRIGLYPHS on the ENTABLATURE of the Doric ORDER.

MINIATURE. A painting or drawing in an ILLUMINATED manuscript; also a very small portrait, sometimes painted on ivory.

MOBILE. A type of sculpture made of movable parts that can be set in motion by the movement of air currents.

MODELING. See SCULPTURE. In painting or DRAWING, the means by which the three-dimensionality of a form is suggested on a two-dimensional surface, usually through variations of COLOR and the play of lights and darks.

MONUMENTAL. Frequently used to describe works that are larger than lifesize; also used to describe works giving the impression of great size, whatever their actual dimensions.

MOSAIC. A design formed by embedding small pieces of colored stone or glass in cement. In antiquity, large mosaics were used chiefly on floors; from the Early Christian period on, mosaic decoration was increasingly used on walls and vaulted surfaces.

MOTIF. A distinctive and recurrent feature of theme, shape, or figure in a work of art.

MURAL. A wall painting. See FRESCO.

NAVE. The central aisle of a BASILICAN church, as distinguished from the side aisles; the part of a church between the main entrance and the CHANCEL.

OIL PAINTING. Though known to the Romans, it was not systematically used until the fifteenth century. In the oil technique of early Flemish painters, PIGMENTS were mixed with drying oils and fused while hot with hard resins; the mixture was then diluted with other oils.

ORDER. In architecture, a CLASSICAL system of proportion and interrelated parts. These include a COLUMN, usually with BASE, SHAFT, and CAPITAL, and an ENTABLATURE with ARCHITRAVE, FRIEZE, and CORNICE.

PAINTING MEDIUMS: see ENCAUSTIC, FRESCO, OIL PAINTING, TEMPERA, WATERCOLOR.

PASTEL. Powdered PIGMENTS mixed with gum and molded into sticks for drawing; also a picture or sketch made with this type of crayon.

PEDIMENT. In CLASSICAL architecture, the triangular part of the front or back wall that rises above the ENTABLATURE. The pediments at either end of a temple often contained sculpture, in high RELIEF or FREESTANDING.

PERISTYLE. A COLONNADE (or ARCADE) around a building or open court.

PERSPECTIVE. See ATMOSPHERIC PERSPECTIVE, LINEAR PERSPECTIVE.

PIER. A vertical architectural element, usually rectangular in section; if used with an ORDER, often has a BASE and CAPITAL of the same design.

PIER BUTTRESS. An exterior pier in Romanesque and Gothic architecture, buttressing the THRUST of the VAULTS within.

PIETÀ. In painting or sculpture, a representation of the Virgin Mary mourning the dead Christ whom she holds.

PIGMENT. Dry, powdered substances which, when mixed with a suitable liquid, or vehicle, give color to paint. See OIL PAINTING, FRESCO, ENCAUSTIC, TEMPERA, WATERCOLOR.

PILASTER. A flat vertical element having a CAPITAL and BASE, engaged in a wall from which it projects. Has a decorative rather than a structural purpose.

PLAN. The schematic representation of a three-dimensional structure, such as a building or monument, on a two-dimensional plane. A GROUND PLAN shows the outline shape at the ground level of a given building and the location of its various interior parts.

PORTAL. An imposing doorway with elaborate ornamentation in Romanesque and Gothic churches.

POST AND BEAM. A system or unit of construction consisting solely of vertical and horizontal elements.

PROPORTION, PROPORTIONS. The relation of the size

of any part of a figure or object to the size of the whole. For architecture, see ORDER.

PYLON. In Egyptian architecture, the entranceway set between two broad oblong towers with sloping sides.

READY-MADE. A manufactured object exhibited as being aesthetically pleasing. When two or more accidentally "found" objects are placed together as a construction, the piece is called an ASSEMBLAGE.

RED-FIGURED. A type of Greek vase painting in which the design was outlined in black and the background painted in black, leaving the figures the reddish color of the baked clay after firing. This style replaced the BLACK-FIGURED style toward the end of the sixth century B.C.

RELIEF. Forms in SCULPTURE that project from the background, to which they remain attached. Relief may be carved or modeled shallowly to produce low relief, or deeply to produce high relief; in very high relief, portions may be entirely detached from the background.

REPRESENTATIONAL. As opposed to ABSTRACT, means a portrayal of an object in recognizable form.

RHYTHM. The regular repetition of a particular form; also, the suggestion of motion by recurrent forms.

RIB. An ARCH or a projecting arched member of a VAULT.

RIBBED VAULT. A compound masonry VAULT, the GROINS of which are marked by projecting stone ribs.

SARCOPHAGUS. A coffin made of stone, marble, terra-cotta (less frequently, of metal). Sarcophagi are often decorated with paintings or RELIEF.

SCALE. Generally, the relative size of any object in a work of art, often used with reference to normal human scale.

SCULPTURE. The creation of a three-dimensional form, usually in a solid material. Traditionally, two basic techniques have been used: carving in a hard material, and modeling in a soft material such as clay, wax, etc. For types of sculpture, see FREESTANDING and RELIEF.

SHAFT. A cylindrical form; in architecture, the part of a COLUMN or PIER intervening between the BASE and the CAPITAL. Also, a vertical enclosed space.

SKETCH. A rough drawing representing the main features of a composition; often used as a preliminary study.

STAINED GLASS. The technique of filling architectural openings with glass colored by fused metallic oxides; pieces of this glass are held in a design by strips of lead.

STILL LIFE. A painting or drawing of an arrangement of inanimate objects.

TEMPERA. A painting process in which PIGMENT is mixed with an emulsion of egg yolk and water or egg and oil. Tempera, the basic technique of medieval and Early Renaissance painters, dries quickly, permitting almost immediate application of the next layer of paint.

TERRA-COTTA. Clay, modeled or molded, and baked until very hard. Used in architecture for functional and decorative parts, as well as in pottery and SCULPTURE. Terra-cotta may have a painted or glazed surface.

THRUST. The downward and outward pressure exerted by an ARCH or VAULT, and requiring BUTTRESSING.

TRANSEPT. In a cross-shaped church, an arm forming a right angle with the NAVE, usually inserted between the latter and the CHANCEL or APSE.

TRIGLYPH. A vertical block with V-cut channels, placed between METOPES on the ENTABLATURE of the Doric ORDER.

TYMPANUM. The space above the beam and enclosed by the ARCH of a medieval PORTAL or doorway; a church tympanum frequently contains RELIEF sculpture.

VAULT. An arched roof or covering, made of brick, stone, or concrete. See BARREL VAULT, GROIN VAULT, RIBBED VAULT.

VELLUM. Thin, bleached calfskin, a type of parchment on which manuscripts are written or printed.

WATERCOLOR. PIGMENTS mixed with water instead of oil or other mediums, or a picture painted with watercolor, often on paper.

WOODCUT. A printing process in which a design or lettering is carved in relief on a wooden block; the areas intended not to print off are hollowed out.

ZIGGURAT. An elevated platform, varying in height from several feet to the size of an artificial mountain, built by the Sumerians to support their shrines.

BOOKS FOR FURTHER READING

Asterisks (*) indicate that titles are available in paperback.

Part One: How Art Began

1. IMAGES AND IMAGINATION
*Arnheim, Rudolf, *Art and Visual Perception*, University of California Press, Berkeley, 1974
*Elsen, Albert E., *Purposes of Art*, 3rd ed., Holt, Rinehart and Winston, New York, 1972
*Gombrich, Ernst H., *Art and Illusion*, 4th ed., Pantheon Books, New York, 1972
*Panofsky, Erwin, *Meaning in the Visual Arts*, Anchor Books, Garden City, 1955
*Read, Herbert E., *Art and Society*, 2nd ed., Pantheon Books, New York, 1950
*Rosenberg, Harold, *The Anxious Object: Art Today and Its Audience*, 2nd ed., Horizon, New York, 1966

2. MAGIC AND RITUAL— THE ART OF PREHISTORIC MAN
*Boas, Franz, *Primitive Art*, new ed., Dover, New York, 1955
Leroi-Gourhan, André, *Treasures of Prehistoric Art*, Abrams, New York, 1967
*Wingert, Paul S., *Primitive Art: Its Traditions and Styles*, Oxford University Press, New York, 1962

3. EGYPTIAN ART
*Groenewegen-Frankfort, Henriette A., and Ashmole, Bernard, *Art of the Ancient World*, Abrams, New York, 1975
Lange, Kurt, and Hirmer, Max, *Egypt*, 4th ed., Phaidon, London, 1968
Smith, William Stevenson, *The Art and Architecture of Ancient Egypt*, reprinted with corrections, Pelican History of Art, Penguin Books, Baltimore, 1965
Woldering, Irmgard, *The Art of Egypt*, Greystone, New York, 1963

4. THE ANCIENT NEAR EAST
Akurgal, Ekrem, *Art of the Hittites*, Abrams, New York, 1962
*Frankfort, Henri, *The Art and Architecture of the Ancient Orient*, rev. ed., Pelican History of Art, Penguin Books, Baltimore, 1971

Strommenger, Eva, and Hirmer, Max, *5000 Years of the Art of Mesopotamia*, tr. by Christina Haglund, Abrams, New York, 1964

5. AEGEAN ART
Demargne, Pierre, *Aegean Art: The Origins of Greek Art*, tr. by Stuart Gilbert and James Emmons, Golden Press, New York, 1964
Marinatos, Spyridon N., and Hirmer, Max, *Crete and Mycenae*, Abrams, New York, 1960

6. GREEK ART
Beazley, John D., and Ashmole, Bernard, *Greek Sculpture and Painting to the End of the Hellenistic Period*, Cambridge University Press, London, 1966
*Boardman, John, *Greek Art*, rev. ed., Praeger, New York, 1973
*Carpenter, Rhys, *Greek Sculpture*, University of Chicago Press, 1971
Havelock, Christine M., *Hellenistic Art*, New York Graphic Society, Greenwich, 1970
*Lullies, Reinhard, and Hirmer, Max, *Greek Sculpture*, Abrams, New York, 1960
Pollitt, Jerry J., *The Art of Greece: Sources and Documents*, Prentice-Hall, Englewood Cliffs, 1965
Richter, Gisela M. A., *A Handbook of Greek Art*, 6th ed., redesigned, Phaidon, London, 1969
——, *The Sculpture and Sculptors of the Greeks*, 4th ed., rev., Yale University Press, New Haven, 1970

7. ETRUSCAN ART
Pallottino, Massimo, *Etruscan Painting*, Skira, Geneva, 1952
Richardson, Emeline, *The Etruscans: Their Art and Civilization*, University of Chicago Press, 1964

8. ROMAN ART
Andreae, Bernard, *The Art of Rome*, Abrams, New York, 1978
*Brilliant, Richard, *Roman Art: From the Republic to Constantine*, Phaidon/Dutton, New York, 1974
*Hanfmann, George M. A., *Roman Art*, New York Graphic Society, Greenwich, 1964
*L'Orange, Hans P., *Art Forms and Civic Life in the

Late Roman Empire, Princeton University Press, 1965

Maiuri, Amedeo, *Roman Painting*, Skira, Geneva, 1953

*Pollitt, Jerry J., *The Art of Rome and Late Antiquity: Sources and Documents*, Prentice-Hall, Englewood Cliffs, 1966

*Wheeler, Robert Eric Mortimer, *Roman Art and Architecture*, Praeger, New York, 1964

9. EARLY CHRISTIAN AND BYZANTINE ART

Demus, Otto, *Byzantine Art and the West*, New York University Press, 1970

Grabar, André, *The Beginnings of Christian Art, 200–395*, tr. by Stuart Gilbert and James Emmons, Thames and Hudson, London, 1967

————, *Byzantium: Byzantine Art in the Middle Ages*, tr. by Betty Forster, Methuen, London, 1969

*Krautheimer, Richard, *Early Christian and Byzantine Architecture*, Pelican History of Art, Penguin Books, Baltimore, 1965

*Mango, Cyril, *The Art of the Byzantine Empire, 312–1453: Sources and Documents*, Prentice-Hall, Englewood Cliffs, 1972

Morey, Charles Rufus, *Early Christian Art*, 2nd ed., Princeton University Press, 1953

*Rice, David Talbot, *Art of the Byzantine Era*, Praeger, New York, 1966

Zarnecki, George, *Art of the Medieval World*, Abrams, New York, 1976

Part Two: The Middle Ages

1. EARLY MEDIEVAL ART

*Conant, Kenneth J., *Carolingian and Romanesque Architecture, 800–1200*, 3rd ed., Pelican History of Art, Penguin Books, Baltimore, 1973

*Davis-Weyer, Caecilia, *Early Medieval Art: 300–1150: Sources and Documents*, Prentice-Hall, Englewood Cliffs, 1971

Grabar, André, and Nordenfalk, Carl, *Early Medieval Painting*, Skira, Geneva, 1957

*Pevsner, Nikolaus, *An Outline of European Architecture*, 6th ed., Penguin Books, Baltimore, 1960

2. ROMANESQUE ART

Demus, Otto, *Romanesque Mural Painting*, Abrams, New York, 1971

*Focillon, Henri, *The Art of the West in the Middle Ages*, ed. by Jean Bony, tr. by Donald King, 2 vols., Phaidon, New York, 1963

Zarnecki, George, *Romanesque Art*, Universe History of Art, Universe Books, New York, 1971

3. GOTHIC ART

*Branner, Robert, *Chartres Cathedral*, Norton, New York, 1969

Deuchler, Florens, *Gothic Art*, Universe Books, New York, 1973

Evans, Joan, *Art in Medieval France*, Oxford University Press, New York, 1952

*Frisch, Teresa G., *Gothic Art: 1140–1450: Sources and Documents*, Prentice-Hall, Englewood Cliffs, 1971

*Holt, Elizabeth Gilmore, ed., *A Documentary History of Art*: Vol. 1, *The Middle Ages and the Renaissance*, 2nd ed., Doubleday, Garden City, 1957

*Mâle, Emile, *The Gothic Image: Religious Art in France of the Thirteenth Century*, tr., by Dora Nussey, Harper, New York, 1958

*Meiss, Millard, *Painting in Florence and Siena after the Black Death*, Princeton University Press, 1951

*Panofsky, Erwin, *Gothic Architecture and Scholasticism*, Archabbey Press, Latrobe, Pennsylvania, 1951

Pope-Hennessy, John W., *Italian Gothic Sculpture*, 2nd ed., Phaidon, New York, 1970

Sauerländer, Willibald, *Gothic Sculpture in France*, Abrams, New York, 1973

*Simson, Otto G. von, *The Gothic Cathedral: Origins of Gothic Architecture and the Medieval Concept of Order*, 2nd ed., Princeton University Press, 1974

Part Three: The Renaissance

1. "LATE GOTHIC" PAINTING, SCULPTURE, AND THE GRAPHIC ARTS

*Cuttler, Charles D., *Northern Painting: From Pucelle to Bruegel*, Holt, Rinehart and Winston, New York, 1968

*Friedländer, Max J., *From Van Eyck to Bruegel: Early Netherlandish Painting*, Phaidon, New York, 1969

*Hind, Arthur M., *History of Engraving and Etching*, 3rd ed., rev., Houghton, Mifflin, Boston, 1923

————, *An Introduction to a History of Woodcut*, 2 vols., Houghton, Mifflin, Boston, 1935

*Ivins, William M., Jr., *How Prints Look*, Metropolitan Museum of Art, New York, 1943

*Panofsky, Erwin, *Early Netherlandish Painting*, 2 vols., Harvard University Press, Cambridge, 1958

2. THE EARLY RENAISSANCE
IN ITALY

*Berenson, Bernard, *Italian Painters of the Renaissance*, rev. ed., Phaidon, London, 1967

Borsook, Eve, *The Mural Painters of Tuscany*, Phaidon, London, 1960

Gilbert, Creighton, *History of Renaissance Art Throughout Europe: Painting, Sculpture, Architecture*, Abrams, New York, 1973

*Gombrich, Ernst H., *Norm and Form: Studies in the Art of the Renaissance*, Phaidon, London, 1966

Hartt, Frederick, *History of Italian Renaissance Art*, Abrams, New York, 1969

*Panofsky, Erwin, *Renaissance and Renascences in Western Art*, Humanities Press, New York, 1970

Pope-Hennessy, John, *Italian Renaissance Sculpture*, Phaidon, New York, 1971

*Turner, Almon R., *The Vision of Landscape in Renaissance Italy*, Princeton University Press, 1966

3. THE HIGH RENAISSANCE
IN ITALY

*Freedberg, Sydney J., *Painting in Italy, 1500–1600*, Pelican History of Art, Penguin Books, Baltimore, 1971

*————, *Painting of the High Renaissance in Rome and Florence*, 2 vols., Harvard University Press, Cambridge, 1961

*Klein, Robert, and Zerner, Henri, *Italian Art, 1500–1600: Sources and Documents*, Prentice-Hall, Englewood Cliffs, 1966

*Wittkower, Rudolf, *Architectural Principles in the Age of Humanism*, Random House, New York, 1965

*Wölfflin, Heinrich, *Classic Art: An Introduction to the Italian Renaissance*, 3rd ed., Phaidon, New York, 1968

4. MANNERISM AND
OTHER TRENDS

*Friedlaender, Walter F., *Mannerism and Anti-Mannerism in Italian Painting*, Columbia University Press, New York, 1957

*Shearman, John K. G., *Mannerism*, Style and Civilization, Penguin Books, Baltimore, 1967

5. THE RENAISSANCE
IN THE NORTH

*Benesch, Otto, *The Art of the Renaissance in Northern Europe*, rev. ed., Phaidon, London, 1965

————, *German Painting from Dürer to Holbein*, tr. by H. S. B. Harrison, Skira, Geneva, 1966

*Blunt, Anthony, *Art and Architecture in France,* *1500–1700*, 2nd ed., Pelican History of Art, Penguin Books, Baltimore, 1970

Leymarie, Jean, *Dutch Painting*, tr. by Stuart Gilbert, Skira, Geneva, 1956

*Panofsky, Erwin, *Albrecht Dürer*, 2 vols., 3rd ed., Princeton University Press, 1948

*Stechow, Wolfgang, *Northern Renaissance Art, 1400–1600: Sources and Documents*, Prentice-Hall, Englewood Cliffs, 1966

Waterhouse, Ellis K., *Painting in Britain, 1530–1790*, 3rd ed., Pelican History of Art, Penguin Books, Baltimore, 1969

6. THE BAROQUE IN ITALY,
FLANDERS, HOLLAND, AND SPAIN

Enggass, Robert, and Brown, Jonathan, *Italy and Spain, 1600–1750: Sources and Documents*, Prentice-Hall, Englewood Cliffs, 1970

*Friedlaender, Walter F., *Caravaggio Studies*, Princeton University Press, 1955

Held, Julius, and Posner, Donald, *Seventeenth and Eighteenth Century: Baroque Painting, Sculpture, Architecture*, Abrams, New York, 1971

*Rosenberg, Jakob, *Rembrandt, Life and Work*, rev. ed., Phaidon, London, 1964

*————, Slive, Seymour, and Ter Kuile, E. H., *Dutch Art and Architecture, 1600–1800*, rev. ed., Pelican History of Art, Penguin Books, Baltimore, 1972

*Waterhouse, Ellis K., *Italian Baroque Painting*, 2nd ed., Phaidon, New York, 1969

*Wittkower, Rudolf, *Art and Architecture in Italy, 1600–1750*, 3rd ed., Pelican History of Art, Penguin Books, Baltimore, 1973

————, *Gian Lorenzo Bernini, The Sculptor of the Roman Baroque*, 2nd ed., Phaidon, London, 1966

*Wölfflin, Heinrich, *Principles of Art History*, tr. by Mary D. Hottinger, Holt, New York, 1932

7. THE BAROQUE IN FRANCE
AND ENGLAND

Friedlaender, Walter F., *Nicolas Poussin, A New Approach*, Abrams, New York, 1966

Thuillier, Jacques, and Châtelet, André, *French Painting from Le Nain to Fragonard*, Skira, Geneva, 1964

Part Four: The Modern World

1. NEOCLASSICISM
AND ROMANTICISM

Brown, Milton W., *American Art to 1900*, Abrams, New York, 1977

*Eitner, Lorenz, *Neoclassicism and Romanticism, 1750–1850: Sources and Documents*, 2 vols., Prentice-Hall, Englewood Cliffs, 1970

*Friedlaender, Walter F., *From David to Delacroix*, Harvard University Press, Cambridge, 1952

Hamilton, George Heard, *Nineteenth and Twentieth Century Art: Painting, Sculpture, Architecture*, Abrams, New York, 1970

*Honour, Hugh, *Neoclassicism*, Style and Civilization, Penguin Books, Harmondsworth, 1968

*———, *Romanticism,* Harper and Row, New York, 1979

Rosenblum, Robert, *Transformations in Late Eighteenth Century Art*, Princeton University Press, 1967

*Vaughan, William, *Romantic Art*, Oxford University Press, New York, 1978

2. REALISM AND IMPRESSIONISM

Kelder, Diane, *The French Impressionists and Their Century*, Praeger, New York, 1970

*McCoubrey, John, *American Art, 1700–1960: Sources and Documents*, Prentice-Hall, Englewood Cliffs, 1965

*Nochlin, Linda, *Impressionism and Post Impressionism, 1874–1904: Sources and Documents*, Prentice-Hall, Englewood Cliffs, 1966

*———, *Realism and Tradition in Art, 1848–1900: Sources and Documents*, Prentice-Hall, Englewood Cliffs, 1966

*———, *Realism,* Style and Civilization, Penguin Books, Baltimore, 1971

*Pool, Phoebe, *Impressionism*, Oxford University Press, New York, 1967

Rewald, John, *The History of Impressionism*, 4th rev. ed., New York Graphic Society for the Museum of Modern Art, New York, 1973

3. POST-IMPRESSIONISM

Herbert, Robert L., *Neo-Impressionism,* New York Graphic Society, Greenwich, 1968

Rewald, John, *Post-Impressionism from Van Gogh to Gauguin*, 2nd ed., Museum of Modern Art, New York, 1962

Schmutzler, Robert, *Art Nouveau,* tr. by Edouard Roditi, Abrams, New York, 1962

4. TWENTIETH-CENTURY PAINTING AND SCULPTURE

Arnason, H. H., *History of Modern Art: Painting, Sculpture, Architecture*, 2nd ed., Abrams, New York, 1977

*Barr, Alfred H., Jr., *Matisse, His Art and His Public*, reprint of 1951 ed. of the Museum of Modern Art, Arno Press, New York, 1966

*Brown, Milton W., *American Painting from the Armory Show to the Depression*, Princeton University Press, 1955

*Cooper, Douglas, *The Cubist Epoch*, Phaidon, New York, 1971

Fry, Edward F., *Cubism*, McGraw-Hill, New York, 1966

*Goldwater, Robert J., *Primitivism in Modern Art*, rev. ed., Vintage Books, New York, 1967

*Gray, Camilla, *The Russian Experiment in Art, 1863–1922*, Abrams, New York, 1970

*Haftmann, Werner, *Painting in the Twentieth Century*, expanded ed., 2 vols., Praeger, New York, 1965

*Herbert, Robert L., ed., *Modern Artists on Art*, Prentice-Hall, Englewood Cliffs, 1965

Hunter, Sam, and Jacobus, John, *American Art of the Twentieth Century: Painting, Sculpture, Architecture*, Abrams, New York, 1973

Lippard, Lucy R., *Pop Art*, Praeger, New York, 1966

*Read, Herbert, *A Concise History of Modern Painting*, Oxford University Press, New York, 1974

*———, *A Concise History of Modern Sculpture*, Oxford University Press, New York, 1964

*Muller, Joseph-Emile, *Fauvism*, Praeger, New York, 1967

*Rose, Barbara, *American Art Since 1900*, rev. ed., Praeger, New York, 1975

*Rosenblum, Robert, *Cubism and Twentieth-Century Art*, Abrams, New York, 1966

Rubin, William, *Dada and Surrealist Art*, Abrams, New York, 1968

*Selz, Peter, *German Expressionist Painting*, University of California Press, Berkeley, 1957

Taylor, Joshua C., *Futurism*, Museum of Modern Art, New York, 1961

5. TWENTIETH-CENTURY ARCHITECTURE

*Hitchcock, Henry-Russell, *Architecture: Nineteenth and Twentieth Centuries*, Pelican History of Art, Penguin Books, Baltimore, 1971

*Pevsner, Nikolaus, *Pioneers of Modern Design*, 2nd ed., Museum of Modern Art, New York, 1949

Tafuri, Manfredo, and Dal Co, Francesco, *Modern Architecture*, Abrams, New York, 1979

INDEX

Aachen: 97; Palace Chapel of Charlemagne, 100, *fig. 93*

Abduction of the Sabine Woman (Bologna), 229–30, 274, *fig. 200*

Abraham, interior west wall, Reims Cathedral, 128, *fig. 130*

Abstract Expressionism, 355–56, 365

Abstraction, 340, 345–51

Abu, statue of, from the Temple of Abu, Tell Asmar, 28, *fig. 26*

Achilles Painter, 47; Attic white-ground vase, *fig. 40*

Acropolis, Athens: Parthenon, 50–51, *fig. 45;* Parthenon, sculptures, 56, *fig. 53;* Propylaea, 51, 296, *fig. 46;* Temple of Athena Nike, 51–52, *fig. 46*

Action Painting, 356–67

Adam and Eve, from *The Ghent Altarpiece* (Jan van Eyck), 166–67, 177, *fig. 145*

Adam and Eve Reproached by the Lord, from the Doors of Bishop Bernward for St. Michael's, Hildesheim, 105, *fig. 99*

Adoration of the Magi (Gentile da Fabriano), 155, *colorplate 21*

Adoration of the Magi (Leonardo da Vinci), 209, *fig. 176*

Aegean art, 41–43

Aegina: sculpture from pediment of Temple at, 54; *Dying Warrior, fig. 50*

African sculpture, 17

Agesander, Athenodorus, and Polydorus of Rhodes: *The Laocoön Group*, 59, *fig. 58*

Akhenaten (Amenhotep IV), Pharaoh, 25–26; relief portrait of, 26, *fig. 22*

Akkadians, 29

Albers, Josef, 369

Alberti, Leone Battista, 183–84, 192, 217, 230; Sant' Andrea, Mantua, 183, *fig. 167*

Alexander the Great, 31; see also *Battle of Issus*, mosaic from Pompeii

Altamira (Spain): cave painting, 12–13, *fig. 4*

Altdorfer, Albrecht, 235; *The Battle of Issus, colorplate 40*

Ambroise Vollard (Picasso), 346–47, *fig. 314*

Amen, temples of, 25

Amenhotep III, Colonnade and Court of, Luxor, *fig. 21*

Amenhotep IV, see Akhenaten

American architecture, 380–82,

383–84; see also Monticello (Jefferson)

American painting: Impressionist, 320–27; Neoclassical, 297–98; Romantic, 314; twentieth-century, 349, 355–72

American sculpture, 376–80

Ancestor worship, 16, 19, 66

Animal Head, from the Oseberg Ship-Burial, 98, *fig. 90*

Animal style, Celto-Germanic, 97–98, 99, 114

Annunciation, from the *Isenheim Altarpiece* (Grünewald), 232, *colorplate 39*

Annunciation, from the *Merode Altarpiece* (Master of Flémalle), 163–64, 165, 167, 168, 184, *colorplate 22*

Annunciation, west façade, Reims Cathedral, 127–28, 146, *fig. 129*

Anthemius of Tralles and Isidorus of Miletus, 85; Hagia Sophia, Constantinople, *figs. 85, 86*

Antwerp Cathedral, altarpiece (Rubens), 246, *fig. 219*

Anuszkiewicz, Richard, 369; *Entrance to Green, colorplate 74*

Apostle, St.-Sernin, Toulouse, 112–13, *fig. 108*

Apparition (Dance of Salome) (Moreau), 333, 334, *fig. 295*

April, from the *Very Rich Book of Hours of the Duke of Berry* (Limbourg Brothers), 154–55, *fig. 144*

Ara Pacis, Rome, relief on, 68, 127, *fig. 72*

Arc de Triomphe, Paris, *La Marseillaise* (Rude), 303, *fig. 263*

Arch, in Roman architecture, 63, 65, 80, 182

Arch of Titus, Rome, relief on, 68, *fig. 73*

Archaic Greek art, 44, 106; architecture, 50; sculpture, 52–54; vase painting, 44–46

Archangel Michael, The, ivory leaf of diptych, 83–84, 113, *fig. 82*

Arnolfo di Cambio: Florence Cathedral, *fig. 124*

Arrangement in Black and Gray: The Artist's Mother (Whistler), 320, *fig. 284*

Art academies, 276; see also French Royal Academy

Art collectors, in Holland, 251

"Art for art's sake," 317, 320

Artist: Early Renaissance view of, 174; High Renaissance view of, 192; in reign of Louis XIV, 276

Ashurnasirpal II Killing Lions, relief from Palace at Nimrud, 30–31, 45, *fig. 29*

"Assemblage," 374–75

Assumption of the Virgin (Correggio), 226–27, *fig. 195*

Assyrian art, 30–31, 48

At the Moulin Rouge (Toulouse-Lautrec), 336, *fig. 299*

Aten, religious worship of, 25

Athena Nike, Temple of, Acropolis, Athens, 51–52, *fig. 46*

Athens, 50, 56; see also Acropolis

Atmospheric perspective, 165

Attalus I, of Pergamum, 58

Audience Hall of Darius, Persepolis, 31–32, *fig. 31*

Augustus Caesar, 68

Aurignacians, 12

Austrian architecture, Late Baroque, 279

Automatism, 355

Autun Cathedral, west tympanum, *Last Judgment* (detail), 114, *fig. 110*

Avignon Pietà, The (Southern French Master), 170–71, *fig. 151*

Babylon: 29–30, 31; Ishtar Gate from, 31, *fig. 30*

Bacchanal (Titian), 220, 227, *colorplate 35*

Back from the Market (Chardin), 281–82, 283, *colorplate 52*

Balloon Eye, The (Redon), 336, *fig. 298*

Balzac (Rodin), 329, *fig. 290*

Baptismal Font (Renier of Huy), St.-Barthélemy, Liège, 114–15, *fig. 111*

Baptistery, Florence, see Florence

Barberini Palace, see Palazzo Barberini, Rome

Barlach, Ernst, 338–39; *Man Drawing a Sword, fig. 305*

Baroque art, 239–40; architecture, 243, 244–46; painting, 240–42, 246–56; sculpture, 243–44; see also Baroque Classicism; Late Baroque architecture

Baroque Classicism, 256, 273; architecture, 275–78, 283; painting, 273–75; sculpture, 278

Baroque Revival, see Neo-Baroque style

Barry, Charles, and A. Welby Pugin, Houses of Parliament, London, *fig. 259*

"Basilica," Paestum, 50, *fig. 44*
Basilica of Constantine, Rome, 64–65, 217, *fig. 65*
Basilicas, Early Christian, 80, 85
Bath, The (Cassatt), 327, *fig. 288*
Bathers (Fragonard), 281, 283, *colorplate 51*
Battle of Gods and Giants, north frieze, Treasury of the Siphnians, Delphi, 54, *fig. 49*
Battle of Hastings, from the *Bayeux Tapestry*, 117, *fig. 113*
Battle of Issus (Altdorfer), 235, *colorplate 40*
Battle of Issus, mosaic from Pompeii, 48, 69, 235, *fig. 41*
Battle of Ten Naked Men (Pollaiuolo), 187–88, *fig. 172*
Baudelaire, Charles, 315, 336
Bauhaus, Dessau (Gropius), 382–83, *fig. 358*
Bayeux Tapestry, 117; *The Battle of Hastings* from, *fig. 113*
Beardsley, Aubrey, 333–34; *Salome, fig. 296*
Beckmann, Max, 343–44; *Departure, fig. 312*
Bellini, Giovanni, 191, 220; *St. Francis in Ecstasy, colorplate 31*
Berlin: The Brandenburg Gate (Langhans), 296, *fig. 253*
Berlin Secession, 336
Bernini, Gianlorenzo, 243–45, 276, 280; *David*, 243, *fig. 214; The Ecstasy of St. Theresa*, 244, *fig. 215; Model for Equestrian Statue of Louis XIV*, 278, 280, *fig. 239;* St. Peter's, Rome, colonnade, 243, 244, *fig. 213*
Bernward, Bishop of Hildesheim, 104–5; Doors of, St. Michael's, 104–5, 112, 115, *fig. 99*
Berry, Duke of, 154
Bertin, Louis, portrait of (Ingres), 307–8, *fig. 267*
Bibles, illustrated, *see* Illumination
Bibliothèque Ste.-Geneviève, Paris (Labrouste), Reading Room, 302, *fig. 261*
Billy Goat and Tree, offering stand from Ur, 29, *colorplate 3*
Bingham, George Caleb, 314; *Fur Traders on the Missouri, fig. 275*
"Biomorphic Abstraction," 355
Bird in Space (Brancusi), 373, *fig. 343*
Birth of Venus (Botticelli), 188, 220, *colorplate 29*
Birth of the Virgin (Pietro Lorenzetti), 152, *fig. 140*
Black-figure vase painting, 45
Bladen, Ronald, 378; *The X* (in the Corcoran Gallery, Washington, D.C.), *fig. 350*
Blake, William, 305
Blaue Reiter, Der, 344
Blinding of Samson (Rembrandt), 252, *fig. 225*
Blue Causeway (Frankenthaler), 367, *fig. 332*

Boar Hunt, wall painting from the Palace at Tiryns, 43, *fig. 35*
Bobabilicon, from *Los Proverbios* (Goya), 307, *fig. 266*
Boccioni, Umberto, 349, 374; *Dynamism of a Cyclist*, 349, *fig. 318; Unique Forms of Continuity in Space*, 374, *fig. 344*
Boffrand, Germain, 280; Salon de la Princesse, Hôtel de Soubise, Paris, *fig. 243*
Bohemian Master: *Death of the Virgin*, 153, 164, *colorplate 19*
Bologna, Giovanni da, 229–30, 274; *The Abduction of the Sabine Woman, fig. 200*
Book illustration, *see* Illumination
Borghese, Pauline, statue of (Canova), 302–3, *fig. 262*
Borromini, Francesco, 244–46, 279, 280; San Carlo alle Quattro Fontane, Rome, 245, *fig. 217*
Bosch, Hieronymus, 173–74; *The Garden of Delights*, 173–74, 177, 238, *fig. 155, colorplate 26*
Botticelli, Sandro, 188, 220; *The Birth of Venus, colorplate 29*
Bourges Cathedral, stained-glass window, *Habakkuk*, 148, *fig. 137*
Bramante, Donato, 192, 215–18; St. Peter's, Rome, original design for, 217–18, 243, *figs. 185, 186; The Tempietto*, Rome, 215–17, 283, *fig. 184*
Brancusi, Constantin, 372–73; *Bird in Space, fig. 343; The Kiss, fig. 341*
Brandenburg Gate, Berlin (Langhans), 296, *fig. 253*
Braque, Georges, 347, 348; *Le Courrier*, 347, 350, *fig. 315*
Breton, André, 354, 355–56
Bride, The (Duchamp), 353, *fig. 325*
Broederlam, Melchior, 154; *Presentation in the Temple and Flight into Egypt, fig. 143*
Bronzino, Agnolo, 223–24, 237; *Eleanora of Toledo and Her Son Giovanni de' Medici, fig. 193*
Brooklyn Bridge (Stella), 349, *fig. 319*
Brücke, Die, 342–43
Bruegel, Pieter, The Elder, 237–38, 250, 256; *The Land of Cockayne*, 238, *colorplate 42; The Return of the Hunters*, 238, *fig. 209*
Brunelleschi, Filippo, 179, 181–83, 184; Florence Cathedral, dome, 124, 181–82, 218, *fig. 124;* San Lorenzo, Florence, 182, 217, *fig. 165*
Building of the Tower of Babel, portion of painted nave vault, St.-Savin-sur-Gartempe, 117, *fig. 114*
Bull's Head (Picasso), 10, 375, *fig. 2*
Burial of Count Orgaz (El Greco), 226, *colorplate 38*
Burnacini, Lodovico, 244, 277; Stage Design for "La Zenobia di Radamisto," *fig. 216*

Byzantine art, 78–79, 84, 104; architecture, 84–86; mosaics, sculpture, and painting, 86–88; *see also* Neo-Byzantine style of Italian painting
Byzantine Empire, 78, 88

Caen: St.-Etienne, 110, 120, *fig. 104*
Calder, Alexander, 376–77; *Lobster Trap and Fish Tail, fig. 348*
Calendar illustration, 154, 238
Callicrates, 52; Parthenon, Athens, *fig. 45*
Calling of St. Matthew (Caravaggio), 240–41, 243, *colorplate 43*
Campin, Robert, *see* Master of Flémalle
Canova, Antonio, 302–3; *Pauline Borghese as Venus, fig. 262*
Caradosso: Medal with Bramante's design for St. Peter's, *fig. 186*
Caravaggio, 240–41, 242, 246, 250, 251, 273, 297, 316; *The Calling of St. Matthew*, 240–41, 243, *colorplate 43*
Carolingian art, 100–103
Carpeaux, Jean-Baptiste, 303–5, 329; *The Dance*, Opéra, Paris, *fig. 264*
Carracci, Annibale, 241–42; Ceiling Fresco, Farnese Gallery, Rome, *fig. 212*
Carson Pirie Scott & Company, Chicago (Sullivan), 381, *fig. 355*
Cassatt, Mary, 326–27; *The Bath, fig. 288*
Castagno, Andrea del, 180, 186–87; *David, fig. 171*
Catacomb of SS. Pietro e Marcellino, Rome, painted ceiling, 79, *fig. 76*
Cathedrals, Age of Great, 118, 119; *see also* Churches and cathedrals
Catholic Church, *see* Roman Catholic Church
Cave paintings, 12–14
Ceiling frescoes, illusionistic, 226–27, 241–42, 280
Cellini, Benvenuto, 228–29, 239; *The Saltcellar of Francis I, fig. 199*
Celto-Germanic art, 97–100, 103, 116
Cemetery, The (Ruisdael), 254, *fig. 228*
Cézanne, Paul, 329–31, 340, 341, 345, 346; *Fruit Bowl, Glass, and Apples*, 329–30, 332, *fig. 291; Mont Sainte-Victoire Seen from Bibemus Quarry*, 330–31, *fig. 292*
Chagall, Marc, 352; *I and the Village, fig. 322*
Chardin, Jean-Baptiste Siméon, 281–82, 283; *Back from the Market, colorplate 52; Kitchen Still Life, fig. 245*
Charlemagne, 88, 97, 100, 103; Gospel Book of, *St. Matthew* from, 102, *fig. 95;* Palace Chapel of, Aachen, 100, *fig. 93*

Charles I, king of England, portrait of (Van Dyck), 250, 284, *fig. 222*

Charles IV, king of Spain, family portrait of (Goya), 306, *fig. 265*

Chartres Cathedral, 122; nave, *colorplate 16*; west portals, sculpture, 126–27, *figs. 127, 128*

Chefren, Pharaoh, 22; Pyramid of, Giza, *fig. 17*

Chellini, Giovanni, bust of (Rossellino), 179–80, *fig. 162*

Cheops, Pyramid of, Giza, *fig. 17*

Chiaroscuro, 209

Chicago: Carson Pirie Scott & Company (Sullivan), 381, *fig. 355*; Robie House (Wright), 381–82, *figs. 356, 357*

Chios, *Maiden* from, 54, *colorplate 6*

Chirico, Giorgio de, 351–52, 355; *Mystery and Melancholy of a Street, fig. 321*

Chopin, Frédéric, portrait of (Delacroix), 309, *fig. 270*

Christ Crowned with Thorns (Titian), 221, *fig. 190*

Christ Entering Jerusalem, from the *Maestà Altar* (Duccio), 150, 151, *fig. 139*

Christ in the House of Levi (Veronese), 228, *fig. 198*

Christ Preaching (Rembrandt), 254, *fig. 227*

Christ Washing the Feet of Peter, from the *Gospel Book of Otto III*, 105, *colorplate 14*

Christianity, 78–79, 88, 106; and Classical antiquity, 162–63, 188

Christ's Entry into Jerusalem (Giotto), 150, 151, *colorplate 17*

Churches and cathedrals: Baroque and Late Baroque, 243, 244–45, 279, 283; Byzantine, 84–86; Carolingian, 100–101; Early Christian, 79–80; Gothic, 118–25; Neoclassical, 295; Ottonian, 104–5; Renaissance, 181–84, 215–18; Romanesque, 107–12; twentieth-century, 384

Cinema (Segal), 379, *fig. 353*

City, The (Léger), 349–50, 385, *fig. 320*

Classic Greek art, 44, 106, 192; architecture, 50–52; sculpture, 55–58; vase painting, 46–48; wall painting, 46, 48, 70

Classic Greek orders (Doric and Ionic), 48–50, 51–52; in Neoclassical architecture, 296; in Renaissance architecture, 182, 183, 215, 239; in Roman architecture, 65

Classical mythology in European art, 188–89, 220, 227, 235, 241, 250, 281

Classicism: in Byzantine art, 87; in French seventeenth-century art, 256–78; in Gothic sculpture, 127, 145, 148; Palladian, 230–31, 283;

Raphaelesque, 242; Romanesque, 112, 114–15, 117; *see also* Neoclassicism

Claude Lorrain, 275, 314; *A Pastoral, fig. 235*

Clouet, Jean, 237; *Francis I, fig. 208*

Colbert, Jean Baptiste, 275–76, 280

Collage Cubism, 347–49, 354

Cologne Cathedral, *The Gero Crucifix*, 104, 112, 128, *fig. 97*

Color-field painting, 366

Colosseum, Rome, 63, *fig. 62*

Column: of Doric temple, 48, *fig. 42*; of Ionic temple, 52, *fig. 42; see also* Classic Greek orders

Comic strips, 370

Composition with Red, Blue, and Yellow (Mondrian), 350–51, *colorplate 69*

Conceptual Art, 372

Constable, John, 309, 311, 315; *Stoke-by-Nayland*, 311, *fig. 273*

Constantine the Great, 67–68, 78; head of statue of, *fig. 71; see also* Basilica of Constantine

Constantinople: 78, 150; Hagia Sophia, 85–86, *figs. 85, 86*

Contrapposto (counterpoise), 55, 174

Copley, John Singleton, 298; *Watson and the Shark, colorplate 55*

Corcoran Gallery, Washington, D.C., *The X* (Bladen), 378, *fig. 350*

Cornaro Chapel, *see* Santa Maria della Vittoria, Rome

Corot, Camille, 314–15; *Papigno*, 315, 319, *fig. 276*

Correggio, 226–27, 241; *The Assumption of the Virgin*, 226–27, *fig. 195; Jupiter and Io*, 227, 244, *fig. 196*

Cortona, Pietro da, 242; *Glorification of the Reign of Urban VIII, colorplate 44*

Cosimo, *see* Piero di Cosimo

Counter Reformation, 226, 240, 241

Courbet, Gustave, 315–16, 318, 320; *The Stone Breakers*, 316, *fig. 277*

Courrier, Le (Braque), 347, 350, *fig. 315*

Court and Pylon of Ramesses II, Temple of Amen-Mut-Khonsu, Luxor, 25, *fig. 21*

Coysevox, Antoine: Palace of Versailles, Salon de la Guerre, *fig. 237*

Cranach, Lucas, the Elder, 235; *The Judgment of Paris, fig. 206*

Creation of Adam (Michelangelo), 213–14, 241, *fig. 181*

Crete, Minoan art of, 41–42

Cross Page, from *Lindisfarne Gospels*, 99, *fig. 91*

Crossing of the Red Sea, from *Klosterneuburg Altar* (Nicholas of Verdun), 117, *fig. 115*

Crucifixion, The, bronze plaque, 99–100, *fig. 92*

Crucifixion, The, from the *Isenheim Altarpiece* (Grünewald), 231–32, *fig. 202*

Crucifixion, The, mosaic, Monastery Church, Daphnē, 87, *fig. 88*

Crucifixion: The Last Judgment (Hubert and Jan van Eyck), 165, *colorplate 23*

Cubi Series (Smith), 377, *fig. 349*

Cubism, 345–49, 353; in architecture, 381–82; in Dada, 354; in sculpture, 374

Da Vinci, *see* Leonardo da Vinci

Dada, 353–54, 369–70, 374

Dali, Salvador, 355; *The Persistence of Memory, fig. 327*

Dance, The (Carpeaux), 303–5, 329, *fig. 264*

Daphnē: Monastery Church, mosaic, 87, *fig. 88*

Darius I, king of Persia, Audience Hall of, Persepolis, 31–32, *fig. 31*

Darius III, king of Persia, see *Battle of Issus*

Dark Ages, art of, 97–100

Daumier, Honoré, 309–11; *Don Quixote and Sancho Panza, fig. 272; The Third-Class Carriage, fig. 271*

David, Jacques Louis, 297, 307, 308; *The Death of Marat*, 297, 307, *fig. 255; The Death of Socrates*, 297, *colorplate 54*

David (Bernini), 243, *fig. 214*

David (Castagno), 180, 186–87, *fig. 171*

David (Donatello), 177, 212, *fig. 158*

David (Michelangelo), 212, 243, *fig. 179*

David and Goliath, from the *Prayer Book of Philip the Fair* (Master Honoré of Paris), 150, *fig. 138*

De Chirico, *see* Chirico

De Kooning, *see* Kooning

De La Tour, Georges, 273; *Joseph the Carpenter, fig. 232*

De Prospectiva Pingendi (Piero della Francesca), illustrations from, 186, *fig. 170*

Dead Fowl (Soutine), 342, *fig. 309*

Death of General Wolfe (West), 297–98, *fig. 256*

Death of Marat (David), 297, 307, *fig. 255*

Death of Socrates (David), 297, *colorplate 54*

Death of the Virgin (Bohemian Master), 153, 164, *colorplate 19*

"Decalcomania," 355

Degas, Edgar, 319–20, 336; *The Glass of Absinthe, fig. 281; The Tub, fig. 282*

Delacroix, Eugène, 307, 309, 371; *Frédéric Chopin*, 309, *fig. 270; Greece Expiring on the Ruins of Missolonghi*, 309, *colorplate 58*

Delivery of the Keys (Perugino), 192, *fig. 175*

Demoiselles d'Avignon, Les (Picasso), 345–47, *fig. 313*
Denis, Maurice, 333
Departure (Beckmann), 344, *fig. 312*
Descent from the Cross (Rosso Fiorentino), 222, *colorplate 36*
Descent from the Cross (Van der Weyden), 168, 246, *colorplate 25*
Dessau: Bauhaus (Gropius), 382–83, *fig. 358*
Diderot, Denis, 297
Diocletian, 80; Palace of, Split (Yugoslavia), 65, *fig. 66*
Dipylon Vase, from Athens, 44, *fig. 37*
Discovery and Proving of the True Cross (Piero della Francesca), 185–86, *fig. 169*
Discovery of Honey (Piero di Cosimo), 188–89, *colorplate 30*
Divisionism, 331
Dome: of Florence Cathedral, 124, 181–82, 218; of Hagia Sophia, Constantinople, 85; of the Pantheon, Rome, 64; of St. Paul's Cathedral, London, 283; of St. Peter's, Rome, 217–18; of the Tempietto, Rome, 215
Domed, central-plan churches, 84–85, 183–84, 217
Don Quixote and Sancho Panza (Daumier), 310–11, *fig. 272*
Donatello, 174–77, 184, 190; *David*, 177, 212, *fig. 158; Equestrian Monument of Gattamelata*, 177, *fig. 159; Prophet (Zuccone)*, 175–77, *fig. 157; St. George*, 174–75, *fig. 156*
Doors, bronze, *see* "Gates of Paradise" (Ghiberti); St. Michael's, Hildesheim, bronze doors for
Dorians, 43
Doric order, 48–50, 51, *fig. 42; see also* Classic Greek orders
Dream, The (Rousseau), 337–38, 351, *colorplate 65*
Dubuffet, Jean, 365–66; *Le Metafisyx (Corps de Dame)*, *fig. 331*
Duccio, 150, 151; *Christ Entering Jerusalem*, from the *Maestà Altar*, *fig. 139*
Duchamp, Marcel, 353–54, 369, 372; *The Bride*, 353, *fig. 325*
Duchamp-Villon, Raymond, 374; *The Great Horse*, *fig. 345*
Dürer, Albrecht, 231, 233–34; *The Four Horsemen of the Apocalypse*, 233–34, *fig. 204; Knight, Death, and Devil*, 234, 254, *fig. 205; Self-Portrait*, 233, *fig. 203*
Durham Cathedral, 110–11, 119, 120, *fig. 105*
Dutch painting: Golden Age, 250–56, 281–82; Late Gothic, 169–70, 173–74
Dying Gaul (Roman copy), from Pergamum, 58, *fig. 56*
Dying Warrior, from pediment of Temple at Aegina, 54, *fig. 50*

Dynamism of a Cyclist (Boccioni), 349, *fig. 318*

Eakins, Thomas, 325–26; *The Gross Clinic*, *fig. 287*
Early Christian art, 78, 79; architecture, 79–80; manuscript illumination, 81–83; mosaics, 80–81; painting, 79; sculpture, 83–84
Early Renaissance art in Italy, 174; architecture, 181–84; painting, 184–92; sculpture, 174–81
Earth and Green (Rothko), 366, *colorplate 72*
Earth Art, 378
Eastern Orthodox Church, 78; central-plan churches of, 85, 108
Ebbo, Archbishop of Reims, Gospel Book of, *St. Mark* from, 102–3, 104, 114, *fig. 96*
Ecce Ancilla Domini (Rossetti), 335, *fig. 297*
Ecole des Beaux-Arts, 333
Ecstasy of St. Theresa (Bernini), 244, *fig. 215*
Eddy, Don, 371; *New Shoes for H*, *fig. 339, colorplate 75*
Egypt: New Kingdom, 22–26; Old Kingdom, 18–22
Egyptian art, 18–19; architecture, 21–22, 25; painting, 23–24, 71; sculpture, 19–21, 26, 53, 54
El Greco, *see* Greco, El
Eleanora of Toledo and Her Son Giovanni de' Medici (Bronzino), 223–24, 237, *fig. 193*
Embryo in the Womb (Leonardo da Vinci), 211, *fig. 178*
Empress of India (Stella), 368, *fig. 334*
English architecture: Gothic, 122–23, Gothic revival, 301; Romanesque, 110–11; *see also* Wren, Sir Christopher
English painting, 283–85, 311–13
Engravings, 172–73, 233, 234
Enlightenment, 294, 296, 299, 302
Entrance to Green (Anuszkiewicz), 369, *colorplate 74*
Environmental Sculpture, 377, 378
"Environments," 379–80
Equestrian Monument of Gattamelata (Donatello), 177, *fig. 159*
Equestrian Monument of Peter the Great (Falconet), 280, *fig. 244*
Equestrian Statue of Marcus Aurelius, 67, 177, 278, *fig. 69*
Equestrian statues of Louis XIV, models for (Bernini; Girardon), 278, 280, *figs. 239, 240*
Erasmus of Rotterdam, 234; portrait of (Holbein), 237, *fig. 207*
Eremitani, Church of, Padua, frescoes (Mantegna), 189–91, *fig. 174*
Ernst, Max: *1 Copper Plate 1 Zinc Plate 1 Rubber Cloth 2 Calipers 1 Drainpipe Telescope, 1 Piping Man*, *fig. 326; Totem and Taboo*, *fig. 328*

Eskimo mask, from southwest Alaska, 17, *fig. 11*
Etchings, 254, 307
Etruscan art, 60; architecture, 62–63; sculpture and painting, 61–62
Eve of St. Nicholas (Steen), 255, *fig. 230*
Ewer, from Meuse Valley, 115, *fig. 112*
Expressionism, 340–45, 372

Fabriano, *see* Gentile da Fabriano
Facet Cubism, 345–47, 348, 353
Faiyum, Egypt, *Portrait of a Boy* from, 71, *colorplate 10*
Falconet, Etienne Maurice, 280; *Equestrian Monument of Peter the Great*, *fig. 244*
Family of Charles IV (Goya), 306, *fig. 265*
Fantasy, 340, 351–55
Farnese Palace, *see* Palazzo Farnese, Rome
Fauves, 340–42, 344, 345
February, from the *Very Rich Book of Hours of the Duke of Berry* (Limbourg Brothers), 154, 155, 238, *colorplate 20*
Fêtes galantes, 281
Fifer, The (Manet), 318, *colorplate 60*
Fiorentino, *see* Rosso Fiorentino
Fischer von Erlach, Johann, 279; St. Charles Borromaeus, Vienna, *fig. 241*
Flamboyant Gothic, 122, 123
Flanders, 118, 163, 231, 250; *see also* Flemish painting
Flemish painting: Baroque, 246–50; Late Gothic, 163–69, 171, 172, 174, 191; *see also* Bruegel, Pieter; Limbourg Brothers
Flight into Egypt (Broederlam), 154, *fig. 143*
Florence: 163, 174; Baptistery, 111–12, *fig. 107;* Baptistery, bronze doors (Ghiberti), 177–79, *fig. 160;* Cathedral (Arnolfo di Cambio; Brunelleschi), 124, 175, 181–82, 218, *fig. 124;* Or San Michele, 174; Palazzo Medici-Riccardi (Michelozzo), 182–83, *fig. 166;* Palazzo Vecchio, 125, *fig. 126;* San Lorenzo (Brunelleschi), 182, 217, *fig. 165;* San Lorenzo, Medici tombs (Michelangelo), 215, 228, *fig. 183;* Santa Croce, 124, 182, *fig. 123; see also* Florentine painters; Florentine sculptors
Florentine painters, 184–89, 222, 223; *see also* Leonardo da Vinci
Florentine sculptors, 174–81; *see also* Cellini, Benvenuto; Michelangelo
Foundry Painter, 45–46; *Lapith and Centaur*, Attic red-figured kylix, *fig. 39*

Fountain of the Innocents, Paris, reliefs from (Goujon), 239, *fig. 211*
Four Horsemen of the Apocalypse (Dürer), 233–34, *fig. 204*
Fragonard, Jean-Honoré, 281, 283; *Bathers, colorplate 51*
France, 238, 256; *see also* French architecture; French painting; French sculpture
Francesca, *see* Piero della Francesca
Francis I, king of France, 223, 238–39; gold saltcellar for (Cellini), 228–29, *fig. 199;* portrait of (Clouet), 237, *fig. 208*
Frankenthaler, Helen, 366–67; *Blue Causeway, fig. 332*
Frankish kingdom, 88, 103
Frédéric Chopin (Delacroix) 309, *fig. 270*
Frederick II, Holy Roman Emperor, 145
French architecture: Baroque Classicist, 275–78; Gothic, 118–22; Neoclassical, 295; Renaissance, 238–39; Rococo, 280; Romanesque, 107–10; Romantic, 302; twentieth-century, 383, 384, 385
French painting: Baroque Classicist, 273–75; Gothic and Late Gothic, 146–50, 170–71; Impressionist, 319–20; Neoclassical, 296–97; Post-Impressionist, 329–31, 332–33; Renaissance, 237; Rococo, 280–83; Romantic, 307–11; *see also* Courbet, Gustave; Manet, Edouard
French Revolution, 278, 294, 297, 306
French Royal Academy, 276, 281, 333
French sculpture: Baroque, 278; Gothic, 126–28; Neoclassical, 299; Renaissance, 239; Rococo, 280; Romanesque, 112–14; Romantic, 303–5; *see also* Maillol, Aristide; Rodin, Auguste
Fresco, 69, 151; *see also* Ceiling frescoes, illusionistic
Friedrich, Caspar David, 313–14; *The Polar Sea, fig. 274*
"Frottage," 355
Fruit Bowl, Glass, and Apples (Cézanne), 329–30, 332, *fig. 291*
Fur Traders on the Missouri (Bingham), 314, *fig. 275*
Futurism, 349–50, 353, 374

Gainsborough, Thomas, 284–85; *Mrs. Siddons, fig. 249; Robert Andrews and His Wife, colorplate 53*
Galatea (Raphael), 220, 241, *fig. 188*
Garden of Delights (Bosch), 173–74, 177, 238, *fig. 155, colorplate 26*
Garden of Love (Rubens), 250, 281, *colorplate 45*
Garnier, Charles, 302, 303–5; Opéra, Paris, *fig. 260*
"Gates of Paradise" (Ghiberti), 177; *The Story of Jacob and Esau* from, 177–79, *fig. 160*
Gattamelata, equestrian monument of (Donatello), 177, *fig. 159*
Gauguin, Paul, 332–33; influence of, 336, 338, 340, 341, 342, 343, 345; *Offerings of Gratitude*, 333, *fig. 294; The Yellow Christ*, 332, *colorplate 64*
Geertgen tot Sint Jans, 169–70, 228, 273; *The Nativity, fig. 150*
Geneva Cathedral, altarpiece (Witz), 171
Genre painting, 255–56, 281–82, 296
Gentile da Fabriano, 155; *The Adoration of the Magi, colorplate 21*
Geometric form, in painting, 186; *see also* Cézanne, Paul
Geometric style, of Greek vase painting, 44
Georges Pompidou National Arts and Cultural Center, Paris (Piano and Rogers), 385, *colorplate 76*
Georgian architecture, 295
Géricault, Théodore, 309; *Mounted Officer of the Imperial Guard, fig. 269*
German architecture: Late Baroque, 279–80; Ottonian, 104–5; twentieth-century, 382–83
German painting: Expressionist, 342–44; Late Gothic (prints), 171–73; Ottonian (manuscripts), 105; Renaissance, 231–37; Romantic, 313–14
German sculpture: Gothic, 128; Ottonian, 104, 105
Germanic art of the Dark Ages, 97–98
Germany, 103–4, 171
Gero Crucifix, The, 104, 112, 128, *fig. 97*
Ghent Altarpiece (Hubert and Jan van Eyck), 165–67, *figs. 145, 146*
Ghiberti, Lorenzo, 146, 177–79, 181, 184; *The Sacrifice of Isaac*, 146, *fig. 136; The Story of Jacob and Esau*, from the "Gates of Paradise," 177–79, *fig. 160*
Ghirlandaio, Domenico, 189; *An Old Man and His Grandson, fig. 173*
Giacometti, Alberto, 375; *The Palace at 4 A.M., fig. 346*
Giant Ice Bag (Oldenburg), 378–79, *fig. 352*
Giorgione, 220; *The Tempest, colorplate 34*
Giotto, 150, 151, 163, 184; *Christ's Entry into Jerusalem*, 150, 151, *colorplate 17*
Giovanni Arnolfini and His Bride (Jan Van Eyck), 167–68, *fig. 148, colorplate 24*
Giovanni Chellini (Rossellino), 179–80, *fig. 162*
Girardon, François, 278; *Model for Equestrian Statue of Louis XIV, fig. 240*
Girl at Piano (Lichtenstein), 370–71, *fig. 337*
Girl Dancers and Musicians, tomb painting from Thebes, 24, *fig. 20*
Giza: The Great Sphinx, 22, *fig. 18;* Pyramids of Mycerinus, Chefren, and Cheops, 22, *fig. 17*
Glaber, Raoul, 107
Glass of Absinthe (Degas), 319, 336, *fig. 281*
Glorification of the Reign of Urban VII, Ceiling Fresco, Palazzo Barberini, Rome (Cortona), 242, *colorplate 44*
Gloucester Cathedral, 123, *fig. 122*
Goeritz, Mathias, 377
Goes, Hugo van der, 168–69; *The Portinari Altarpiece*, 169, 189, *fig. 149*
Goethe, Johann Wolfgang von, 313
Gold Drinking Horn (Persian), 32, *fig. 32*
Gonzalez, Julio, 375–76, 377; *Head, fig. 347*
Good Government (Ambrogio Lorenzetti), 152–53, *figs. 141, 142*
Gorky, Arshile, 356; *The Liver Is the Cock's Comb, fig. 329*
Gospel Book of Abbot Wedricus, St. John the Evangelist from, 115–16, *colorplate 15*
Gospel Book of Archbishop Ebbo of Reims, St. Mark from, 102–3, 104, 114, *fig. 96*
Gospel Book of Charlemagne, St. Matthew from, 102, *fig. 95*
Gospel Book of Otto III, Christ Washing the Feet of Peter from, 105, *colorplate 14*
Gothic art, 106, 118; architecture, 118–25; painting, 146–55; sculpture, 126–46; *see also* Late Gothic painting in Northern Europe
Gothic revival: in architecture, 301; in painting, 334
Goujon, Jean, 239; Reliefs from the *Fountain of the Innocents*, Paris, *fig. 211*
Goya, Francisco, 305–7, 318, 336; *Bobabilicon (Los Proverbios, No. 4)*, 307, *fig. 266; The Family of Charles IV*, 306, *fig. 265; The Third of May*, 307, *colorplate 56*
Great Circle, Stonehenge, 15–16, *figs. 6, 7*
Great Horse, The (Duchamp-Villon), 374, *fig. 345*
Great Sphinx, Giza, 22, *fig. 18*
Greco, El (Domenicos Theotocopoulos), 226; *The Burial of Count Orgaz, colorplate 38*
Greece Expiring on the Ruins of Missolonghi (Delacroix), 309, *colorplate 58*
Greek architecture, 48–52; *see also* Classic Greek orders
Greek Revival, 296
Greek sculpture, 52; Archaic, 52–54; architectural, 54; Classical, 55–57; Hellenistic, 58–59
Greek temple, typical plan of, 48, *fig. 43*

Greek vase painting, 44–48

Greek wall painting, 48, 69, 70

Greeks, ancient, 43–44

Greeks Battling Amazons (Scopas?), 56–57, *fig. 54*

Greuze, Jean-Baptiste, 296–97; *The Village Bride, fig. 254*

Grooms, Red, 380; *Ruckus Manhattan, fig. 354*

Gropius, Walter, 382–83, 384; Bauhaus, Dessau, *fig. 358*

Gros, Antoine-Jean, 308–9; *Napoleon at Arcole, fig. 268*

Gross Clinic, The (Eakins), 325–26, *fig. 287*

Grünewald, Matthias, 231–33; *The Isenheim Altarpiece,* closed *(The Crucifixion),* 231–32, *fig. 202; The Isenheim Altarpiece,* open *(The Annunciation, Virgin and Child with Angels, The Resurrection),* 232–33, *colorplate 39*

Guarini, Guarino, 246, 280; Palazzo Carignano, Turin, *fig. 218*

Habakkuk, stained-glass window, Bourges Cathedral, 148, *fig. 137*

Habitat, EXPO 67, Montreal (Safdie and others), 385, *fig. 363*

Hagia Sophia, Constantinople (Istanbul), 85–86, *figs. 85, 86*

Hals, Frans, 251, 318; *The Jolly Toper, colorplate 46; The Women Regents of the Old People's Home at Haarlem, fig. 224*

Hammurabi, 29–30; stone inscribed with law code of, 30, *fig. 28*

Happenings, 372, 380

Hard-edge painting, 367

Hardouin-Mansart, Jules, 277; Palace of Versailles, *figs. 237, 238*

Harmony in Red (Red Room) (Matisse), 341, *colorplate 66*

Harvest Scenes, tomb painting from Thebes, 23–24, *fig. 19*

Head (Gonzalez), 376, *fig. 347*

Head of Christ (Rouault), 341, 345, 365, *fig. 307*

Heda, Willem, 254–55; *Still Life, fig. 229*

Hellenistic art, 56, 58–59, 69, 212, 273

Henry VIII (Holbein), 237, *colorplate 41*

"*Hera,*" from Samos, 53–54, *fig. 48*

Hercules and Antaeus (Pollaiuolo), 180, 181, *fig. 163*

Hercules Strangling the Nemean Lion (Psiax), 45, *fig. 38, colorplate 5*

Hermes (Praxiteles), 57–58, *fig. 55*

High Renaissance art in Italy, 192; architecture, 215–18; painting, 209–11, 212–14, 218–21; sculpture, 211–12, 215

Hildesheim: St. Michael's, 104, *fig. 98;* bronze doors for, 104–5, 112, 115, *fig. 99*

Hofmann, Hans, 371

Hogarth, William, 284, 296; *The Orgy,* Scene III from *The Rake's Progress, fig. 248*

Holbein, Hans, the Younger, 235–37; *Erasmus of Rotterdam, fig. 207; Henry VIII, colorplate 41*

Holland, 237, 250–51; *see also* Dutch painting

Holy Roman Emperors, 103–4, 145

Holy Trinity, The (Masaccio), 184, 226, *colorplate 27*

Homer, Winslow, 325; *The Morning Bell, fig. 286*

Honoré, *see* Master Honoré of Paris

Hôtel de Soubise, Paris, Salon de la Princesse (Boffrand), 280, *fig. 243*

Houdon, Jean Antoine, 299; *Voltaire, fig. 257*

House of the Vettii, Pompeii, Ixion Room, 69, 145, *fig. 74*

Houses of Parliament, London (Barry and Pugin), 301, *fig. 259*

Humanism, 162–63, 234, 273

I and the Village (Chagall), 352, *fig. 322*

Iconoclastic Controversy, 86

Icons, 88

Ictinus and Callicrates, Parthenon, Acropolis, Athens, *fig. 45*

Illumination (manuscript painting), 81; Carolingian, 101–3; Early Christian, 81–83; Gothic, 147, 150, 154–55; Irish, 99–100; Ottonian, 105; Romanesque, 115–16

Illusionism: in Baroque art, 226, 241, 242, 243–44, 280; in Hellenistic-Roman art, 69, 79, 105, 150

Imhotep, 21–22

Imperial Procession, relief on *Ara Pacis,* Rome, 68, 127, *fig. 72*

Impressionism, 319–27; and Post-Impressionism, 329, 331

Indiana, Robert, 371; *Love, fig. 338*

Industrial revolution, 294, 302

Ingres, Jean-Auguste Dominique, 307–8, 309, 319; *Louis Bertin,* 307–8, *fig. 267; Odalisque,* 302, 307, 309, *colorplate 57*

Ink blot on folded paper, 10, *fig. 1*

International Style, of Gothic art: painting, 154–55, 163, 165, 169, 172, 184; sculpture, 146, 177

International Style, of twentieth-century architecture, 382–84

Ionians, 43–44; and Persians, 32

Ionic order, 48, 51–52, *fig. 42*

Irish manuscript illuminations, 99–100

Irish monasteries, 98–99

Isenheim Altarpiece (Grünewald), 231–33, *fig. 202, colorplate 39*

Ishtar Gate, from Babylon, 31, *fig. 30*

Isidorus of Miletus, 85

Islam, 78, 88

Istanbul, *see* Constantinople

Italian architecture: Baroque, 243, 244–46; Gothic, 123–25; Renaissance, 181–84, 215–18; Romanesque, 111–12; *see also* Palladio, Andrea

Italian painting: Baroque, 240–42; Early Renaissance, 184–92; Futurist, 349; Gothic, 150–53, 155; High Renaissance, 209–11, 212–14, 218–21; Mannerist, Proto-Baroque and Realist, 221–28; Northern Renaissance painting and, 231, 233, 237, 273

Italian sculpture: Early Renaissance, 174–81; Gothic, 145–46; High Renaissance, 211–12, 215; Mannerist, 228–30; *see also* Boccioni, Umberto; Canova, Antonio

Ivory panels and reliefs, Early Christian, 83–84

Ixion Room, House of the Vettii, Pompeii, 69, 145, *fig. 74*

Jacob Wrestling with the Angel, from *Vienna Genesis,* 82–83, *fig. 80*

Jamb Statues, west portals, Chartres Cathedral, 126–27, *fig. 128*

Jefferson, Thomas, 295–96; Monticello, *fig. 252*

Jenkins, Paul, 367; *Phenomena Astral Signal, colorplate 73*

Johns, Jasper, 370; *Three Flags, fig. 336*

Johnson, Philip: Seagram Building, New York, *fig. 360*

Jolly Toper, The (Hals), 251, *colorplate 46*

Joseph the Carpenter (De La Tour), 273, *fig. 232*

Joy of Life (Matisse), 341, *fig. 306*

Judgment of Paris (Cranach), 235, *fig. 206*

Judgment of Paris (Raimondi, after Raphael), *fig. 279*

Julius II, Pope, 212, 217, 218

Junius Bassus, sarcophagus of, 83, 102, 109–10, *fig. 81*

Jupiter and Io (Correggio), 227, 244, *fig. 196*

Justinian, 78, 84, 86

Justinian and Attendants, mosaic, San Vitale, Ravenna, 86, *fig. 87*

Kaisersaal, *see* Würzburg

Kandinsky, Wassily, 344–45, 356–65; *Sketch I for "Composition VII," colorplate 67*

Kaprow, Alan, 372

Kelly, Ellsworth, 367; *Red Blue Green, fig. 333*

Khorsabad: Palace of Sargon II, 30

Kiss, The (Brancusi), 373, *fig. 341*

Kiss, The (Klimt), 337, *fig. 301*

Kiss of Judas, choir screen, Naumberg Cathedral, 128, *fig. 131*

Kitchen Still Life (Chardin), 282, *fig. 245*

Klee, Paul, 352–53, 365; *Park Near L(ucerne)*, 353, *fig. 324; Twittering Machine*, 352–53, *fig. 323*

Klimt, Gustav, 337; *The Kiss, fig. 301*

Klosterneuburg Altar (Nicholas of Verdun), 117; *The Crossing of the Red Sea* from, *fig. 115*

Knight, Death, and Devil (Dürer), 234, 254, *fig. 205*

Knossos, Palace of Minos, 41–42, *fig. 33; "Toreador Fresco"* from, 42, *colorplate 4*

Kokoschka, Oskar, 343; *Self-Portrait, fig. 311*

Kooning, Willem de, 365; *Woman II, colorplate 71*

Kore statues, 53–54

Kosuth, Joseph, 372; *One and Three Chairs, fig. 340*

Kouros statues, 52–54

Kritios Boy (Standing Youth), 55–56, *fig. 51*

La Tour, *see* De La Tour, Georges

Labrouste, Henri, 302; Reading Room, Bibliothèque Ste.-Geneviève, Paris, *fig. 261*

Laestrygonians Hurling Rocks at the Fleet of Odysseus, wall painting, Rome, 69–70, *colorplate 9*

*Land of Cockayne (*Bruegel), 238, *colorplate 42*

Landscape painting, 153, 154, 171, 189; Dutch, 254; English, 284, 311–12; Flemish, 238, 250; French, 275, 314–15, 319, 330–31; German, 235, 313–14; Roman, 69–70; Venetian, 191, 220

Landscape with the Burial of Phocion (Poussin), 275, *fig. 234*

Landscape with the Château of Steen (Rubens), 250, *fig. 221*

Langhans, Karl: The Brandenburg Gate, Berlin, *fig. 253*

Laocoön Group (Agesander, Athenodorus, and Polydorus of Rhodes), 59, 66, 212, *fig. 58*

Lapith and Centaur (The Foundry Painter), 45–46, *fig. 39*

Lascaux (Dordogne, France): cave painting, 12, *fig. 3*

Last Judgment (Michelangelo), 213, 214, *figs. 180, 182*

Last Judgment (Hubert and Jan van Eyck), 165, *colorplate 23*

Last Judgment, west tympanum, Autun Cathedral, 114, *fig. 110*

Last Supper,. The (Leonardo da Vinci), 209–10, 218–20, 224, *fig. 177*

Last Supper, The (Nolde), 342–43, *fig. 310*

Last Supper, The (Tintoretto), 224–26, 228, *fig. 194*

Late Baroque architecture, 279–80

Late Gothic painting in Northern Europe, 163–74, 228, 231, 232, 233, 255

Le Corbusier, 383, 384; Notre-Dame-du-Haut, Ronchamp, *figs. 361, 362;* Savoye House, Poissy-sur-Seine, *fig. 359*

Le Nain, Louis, 273, 282, 310; *Peasant Family*, 273, *fig. 231*

Le Nôtre, André, 278; Palace of Versailles, gardens, *fig. 238*

Le Vau, Louis, 276, 277; Palace of Versailles, *fig. 238*

Lebrun, Charles, 276–77, 281, 285; Salon de la Guerre, Palace of Versailles, 277, *fig. 237*

Léger, Fernand, 349–50, 385; *The City, fig. 320*

Lehmbruck, Wilhelm, 338; *Standing Youth, fig. 304*

Leo X, Pope, 215

Leonardo da Vinci, 192, 209–11, 274; *Adoration of the Magi*, 209, *fig. 176; Embryo in the Womb*, 211, *fig. 178; The Last Supper*, 209–10, 218–20, 224, *fig. 177; Mona Lisa*, 210–11, *colorplate 32*

Lescot, Pierre, 239, 276; Louvre, Paris, Square Court, *fig. 210*

Letter, The (Vermeer), 256; *colorplate 48*

Lexington Local, from *Ruckus Manhattan* (Grooms), *fig. 354*

Liberal arts, 174, 276

Lichtenstein, Roy, 370–71; *Girl at Piano, fig. 337*

Liège: St. Barthélemy, Baptismal Font (Renier of Huy), 114–15, *fig. 111*

Limbourg Brothers, 154; *April* and *February*, from the *Very Rich Book of Hours of the Duke of Berry*, 154–55, 238, *fig. 144, colorplate 20*

Lindau Gospels, cover of, 103, 114, *colorplate 13*

Lindisfarne Gospels, Cross Page from, 99, *fig. 91*

Lion Gate, Mycenae, 43, 50, 54, *fig. 34*

Lions and monsters: in Greek art, 45; in Romanesque art, 113–14; *see also* Animal style; Assyrian art

Literature, and Romantic painting, 305

Lithographs, 336

Liver Is the Cock's Comb (Gorky), 356, *fig. 329*

Lobster Trap and Fish Tail (Calder), 376, *fig. 348*

Lombards, 88, 100

London: Houses of Parliament (Barry and Pugin), 301, *fig. 259;* St. Paul's Cathedral (Wren), 283, *fig. 247*

Lorenzetti, Ambrogio, 152–53; *Good Government, figs. 141, 142*

Lorenzetti, Pietro, 152; *The Birth of the Virgin, fig. 140*

Lorenzo the Magnificent, 188

Louis VI, king of France, 119

Louis XIV, king of France, 240, 256–73, 275–76, 280; models for

equestrian statues of (Bernini; Girardon), 278, 280, *figs. 239, 240*

Louis Bertin (Ingres), 307–8, *fig. 267*

Louvre, Paris, 239; East Front (Perrault), 276, 278, 283, *fig. 236;* Square Court (Lescot), 239, *fig. 210*

Love (Indiana), 371, *fig. 338*

Luncheon on the Grass (Manet), 316–18, *fig. 278*

Luther, Martin, 233, 234

Luxor: Temple of Amen-Mut-Khonsu, 25, *fig. 21*

Maderno, Carlo, 243; St. Peter's, Rome, nave and façade, *fig. 213*

Madonna (Giovanni Pisano), 146, *fig. 135*

Madonna and Angels (Luca della Robbia), 179, *fig. 161*

Madonna and Child with Saints (Veneziano), 185, *colorplate 28*

Madonna Enthroned, panel painting, 88, *colorplate 12*

Madonna with the Long Neck (Parmigianino), 223, 224, *colorplate 37*

Maestà Altar (Duccio), *Christ Entering Jerusalem* from, 150, 151, *fig. 139*

Magdalenians, 12, 13–14

Maiden, from Chios, 54, *colorplate 6*

Maids of Honor (Velázquez), 250, 306, *fig. 223*

Maillol, Aristide, 338, 373; *Seated Woman (Méditerranée), fig. 303*

Maitani, Lorenzo: Orvieto Cathedral, *fig. 125*

Male Figure Surmounted by a Bird, from the Sepik River (New Guinea), 16–17, *fig. 8*

Man Drawing a Sword (Barlach), 338–39, *fig. 305*

Man in a Red Turban (Self-Portrait?) (Jan van Eyck), 167, 222, 252, *fig. 147*

Man with the Glove (Titian), 220–21, *fig. 189*

Manet, Edouard, 316–19, 329; *The Fifer*, 318, *colorplate 60; Luncheon on the Grass*, 316–18, *fig. 278*

Mannerism, 221–22; painting, 222–26; sculpture, 228–30

Mantegna, Andrea, 189–91; *St. James Led to His Execution, fig. 174*

Mantua: Sant' Andrea (Alberti), 183, *fig. 167*

Manuscript painting, *see* Illumination

Marat, Jean Paul, see *Death of Marat* (David)

Marcus Aurelius, equestrian statue of, 67, 177, 278, *fig. 69*

Marie de' Medici, Queen of France, Landing in Marseilles (Rubens), 248, 273, *fig. 220*

Marseillaise, La (Rude), 303, *fig. 263*

Martini, Simone, 151–52; *The Road to Calvary, colorplate 18*

Masaccio, 184, 185, 220; *The Holy Trinity*, 184, 226, *colorplate 27*

Mask, from the Bamenda area, Cameroons, 17, *fig. 9*

Mask, from the Gazelle Peninsula (New Britain), 17, *fig. 10*

Mask (Eskimo), from southwest Alaska, 17, *fig. 11*

Master Honoré of Paris, 150; *David and Goliath* from the *Prayer Book of Philip the Fair, fig. 138*

Master of Flémalle (Robert Campin), 163–64, 165, 171; *Annunciation*, from the *Merode Altarpiece*, 163–64, 165, 167, 168, 184, *colorplate 22*

Matisse, Henri, 341, 345, 371; *Harmony in Red (Red Room)*, 341, *colorplate 66; The Joy of Life*, 341, *fig. 306*

Medici, Cosimo I de', 223

Medici, Lorenzo de', 188

Medici, Marie de', 248

Medici (family), 182, 210, 215

Medici Chapel, *see* San Lorenzo, Florence

Medici Palace, *see* Palazzo Medici-Riccardi, Florence

Melchizedek and Abraham, interior west wall, Reims Cathedral, 128, *fig. 130*

Merode Altarpiece (Master of Flémalle), see *Annunciation*, from the *Merode Altarpiece*

Mesopotamian art, 27–31, 43, 53

Metafisyx (Corps de Dame) (Dubuffet), 365–66, *fig. 331*

Meuse Valley, art of, 114–15

Michelangelo, 192, 211–15, 329; Ceiling Fresco, Sistine Chapel, Rome, 212–14, 218, 241, *figs. 180, 181; The Creation of Adam*, 213–14, 241, *fig. 181; David*, 212, 243, *fig. 179; The Last Judgment*, 213, 214, *figs. 180, 182;* St. Peter's, Rome, 217–18, 243, *fig. 187;* Tomb of Giuliano de' Medici, 215, 228, *fig. 183*

Michelozzo, 182–83; Palazzo Medici-Riccardi, Florence, 182–83, *fig. 166*

Middle Kingdom (Egypt), 22

Mies van der Rohe, Ludwig, 383–84; Seagram Building, New York, *fig. 360*

Milan, 210

Miniature painting, *see* Illumination

Minoan art, 41–42

Minos, Palace of, *see* Knossos

Miraculous Draught of Fishes (Witz), 171, *fig. 152*

Miró, Joan, 355, 377; *Painting, colorplate 70*

Mnesicles: Propylaea, Acropolis, Athens, *fig. 46*

Mobiles, 376–77

Model for Equestrian Statue of Louis XIV (Bernini), 278, 280, *fig. 239*

Model for Equestrian Statue of Louis XIV (Girardon), 278, *fig. 240*

Moissac: St.-Pierre, south portal (portion), 113–14, *fig. 109*

Mona Lisa (Leonardo da Vinci), 210–11; *colorplate 32*

Monasteries, Irish, 98–99

Monastery, Plan of, St. Gall, 100–101, 108, *fig. 94*

Mondrian, Piet, 350–51, 367, 368, 382, 384; *Composition with Red, Blue, and Yellow*, 350–51, *colorplate 69*

Monet, Claude, 319, 320; *The River*, 319, 332, *colorplate 61; Water Lilies, Giverny*, 320, *fig. 283*

Mont Sainte-Victoire Seen from Bibemus Quarry (Cézanne), 330–31, *fig. 292*

Monticello, Charlottesville, Virginia (Jefferson), 295–96, *fig. 252*

Montreal EXPO 67: Habitat (Safdie and others), 385, *fig. 363*

Moore, Henry, 373; *Recumbent Figure, fig. 342*

Moreau, Gustave, 333, 334; *The Apparition (Dance of Salome), fig. 295*

Morning Bell, The (Homer), 325, *fig. 286*

Mosaics, 80–81, 86, 87

Moses Well, The (Sluter), 145, 168, *fig. 133*

Mother and Child (Picasso), 348–49, *fig. 317*

Moulin de la Galette (Renoir), 319, *fig. 280*

Mounted Officer of the Imperial Guard (Géricault), 309, *fig. 269*

Mrs. Siddons (Gainsborough), 284–85, *fig. 249*

Mrs. Siddons as the Tragic Muse (Reynolds), 285, *fig. 250*

Munch, Edvard, 336–37; *The Scream, fig. 300*

Mycenae: Lion Gate, 43, 50, 54, *fig. 34*

Mycenaean art, 42–43

Mycerinus, Pharoah: pyramid of, Giza, *fig. 17;* statue of *(Mycerinus and His Queen)*, 20–21, 52–53, 54, *fig. 14*

Mystery and Melancholy of a Street (De Chirico), 351–52, *fig. 321*

Mythology, *see* Classical mythology in European art

Nabis, 333

Napoleon, 307, 308–9; portrait of (Gros), 308–9, *fig. 268;* statue of (Canova), 302

Napoleon at Arcole (Gros), 308–9, *fig. 268*

Narmer, king of Egypt, Palette of, 19–20, *fig. 13*

Nativity, The (Geertgen tot Sint Jans), 169–70, 228, 273, *fig. 150*

Nativity, The (Nicola Pisano), 145, *fig. 134*

Naturalism, of Caravaggio, 240–41, 310

Naumberg Cathedral, choir screen, *The Kiss of Judas*, 128, *fig. 131*

Navaho Sand Painting, Arizona, 18, *fig. 12*

Nebuchadnezzar, Ishtar Gate of, 31, *fig. 30*

Neo-Babylonians, 31

Neo-Baroque style: architecture, 301–2; painting, 306–7, 308–9, 310; sculpture, 303–5

Neo-Byzantine style of Italian painting, 150

Neoclassicism: architecture, 294–96; painting, 296–98; sculpture, 299, 302

Neo-Plasticism, 350

Neo-Platonism, 188, 211

Netherlands, 237; *see also* Dutch painting; Flemish painting

Neumann, Balthasar, 279–80; Kaisersaal, Episcopal Palace, Würzburg, *colorplate 49*

New Guinea, ancestor figure from, 16

New Kingdom (Egypt), 22–26

New Shoes for H (Eddy), 371, *fig. 339, colorplate 75*

New Stone Age, 14–16

New York: Seagram Building (Mies van der Rohe and Philip Johnson), 384, *fig. 360*

Nicholas of Verdun, 117, 148; *The Crossing of the Red Sea*, from *Klosterneuburg Altar, fig. 115*

Nike of Samothrace (Winged Victory), 58, 374, *fig. 57*

Nocturne in Black and Gold: The Falling Rocket (Whistler), 325, *fig. 285*

Nofretete, Queen, portrait bust of, 26, *fig. 23*

Nolde, Emil, 342–43; *The Last Supper, fig. 310*

Normans, 103, 110

North Italian Realist painting, 227–28

Northern painting: Gothic, 153–55; Late Gothic, 163–74, 228, 231, 232, 233, 255; Renaissance, 231–38

Northern Renaissance art, 231–39

Notre-Dame, Paris, 119–20, 122, *figs. 116–19*

Notre-Dame-du-Haut, Ronchamp (Le Corbusier), 384, *figs. 361, 362*

Notre-Dame-la-Grande, Poitiers, 109, *fig. 103*

Nudes, in European art: painting, 166–67, 307, 310, 345; sculpture, 177, 180, 212, 302–3, 305, 329

Odalisque (Ingres), 302, 307, 309, *colorplate 57*

Odo of Metz, 100

Odyssey Landscapes, wall painting, Rome, 69–70, *colorplate 9*

Offering Stand, from Ur, 29, *color-plate 3*

Offerings of Gratitude (Gauguin), 333, *fig. 294*

Oil painting, 164

Old Clown, The (Rouault), 342, *fig. 308*

Old Guitarist, The (Picasso), 337, *fig. 302*

Old Kingdom (Egypt), 18–22

Old Man and His Grandson (Ghirlandaio), 189, *fig. 173*

Old Stone Age, 12–14

Oldenburg, Claes, 378–79; *Giant Ice Bag, fig. 352*

One (#31, 1950) (Pollock), 356, *fig. 330*

One and Three Chairs (Kosuth), 372, *fig. 340*

1 Copper Plate 1 Zinc Plate 1 Rubber Cloth 2 Calipers 1 Drainpipe Telescope, 1 Piping Man (Ernst), 354, *fig. 326*

Op Art, 368–69

Opéra, Paris (Garnier), 302, *fig. 260; The Dance* (Carpeaux), 303–5, *fig. 264*

Or San Michele, Florence, *St. George* (Donatello), 174–75, *fig. 156*

Orders, architectural, *see* Classic Greek orders

Orgy, The, from *The Rake's Progress* (Hogarth), 284, *fig. 248*

Orthodox Church, 78, 85, 108

Orvieto Cathedral, 124–25, *fig. 125*

Oseberg Ship-Burial, *Animal Head* from, 98, *fig. 90*

Otto I, 103, 106

Otto III, Gospel Book of, illumination from, 105, *colorplate 14*

Ottonian art, 103–5

Padua: Arena Chapel, fresco (Giotto), *colorplate 17;* Church of the Eremitani, frescoes (Mantegna), 189–91, *fig. 174; Equestrian Monument of Gattamelata* (Donatello), 177, *fig. 159*

Paestum: "Basilica" and Temple of Poseidon, 50, *fig. 44*

Painted Ceiling, Catacomb of SS. Pietro e Marcellino, Rome, 79, *fig. 76*

Painting (Miró), 355, *colorplate 70*

Palace at 4 A.M. (Giacometti), 375, *fig. 346*

Palace Chapel of Charlemagne, Aachen, 100, *fig. 93*

Palace of Diocletian, Split (Yugoslavia), 65, *fig. 66*

Palace of Minos, *see* Knossos

Palace of Versailles, *see* Versailles

Palaces: Assyrian, 30; Italian, 125, 182–83; Minoan and Mycenaean, 41–42, 43; Persian, 31–32

Palazzo Barberini, Rome, Ceiling Fresco (Cortona), 242, *colorplate 44*

Palazzo Carignano, Turin (Guarini), 246, *fig. 218*

Palazzo Farnese, Rome, Ceiling Fresco, Gallery (Carracci), 241–42, *fig. 212*

Palazzo Medici-Riccardi, Florence (Michelozzo), 182–83, *fig. 166*

Palazzo Vecchio, Florence, 125, 212, *fig. 126*

Palette of King Narmer, from Hierakonpolis, 19–20, *fig. 13*

Palladio, Andrea, 230–31, 283; Villa Rotonda, Vicenza, *fig. 201*

Panthéon, Paris (Soufflot), 295, *fig. 251*

Pantheon, Rome, 63–64, 84, 111, 279, *figs. 63, 64*

Papigno (Corot), 315, 319, *fig. 276*

Papyrus Half-Columns, Funerary District of King Zoser, Saqqara, 22, 48, 52, *fig. 16*

Paris, 118, 256, 280; Arc de Triomphe, *La Marseillaise* (Rude), 303, *fig. 263;* Bibliothèque Ste.-Geneviève, Reading Room (Labrouste), 302, *fig. 261; Fountain of the Innocents,* reliefs from (Goujon), 239, *fig. 211;* Georges Pompidou National Arts and Cultural Center (Piano and Rogers), 385, *colorplate 76;* Hôtel de Soubise, Salon de la Princesse (Boffrand), 280, *fig. 243;* Louvre (Lescot; Perrault), 239, 276, 283, *figs. 210, 236;* Notre-Dame, 119–20, 122, *figs. 116–19;* Opéra (Garnier), 302, 303–5, *fig. 260;* Panthéon (Soufflot), 295, *fig. 251;* St.-Denis, royal Abbey Church of, 118–19, 122, 126

Park Near L(ucerne) (Klee), 353, *fig. 324*

Parliament, *see* Houses of Parliament, London

Parma Cathedral, dome fresco (Correggio), 226–27, *fig. 195*

Parmigianino, 222–23, 307; *The Madonna with the Long Neck,* 223, 224, *colorplate 37; Self-Portrait,* 222–23, *fig. 192*

Parry, Sir William Edward, 313

Parthenon, Acropolis, Athens: 50–51, *fig. 45;* sculptures from, 56, *fig. 53*

Parting of Lot and Abraham, mosaic, Santa Maria Maggiore, Rome, 81, 105, *fig. 78*

Pastoral, A (Claude Lorrain), 275, 314, *fig. 235*

Pauline Borghese as Venus (Canova), 302–3, *fig. 262*

Peasant Family (Le Nain), 273, *fig. 231*

Peloponnesian War, 44, 56

Pergamum, *Dying Gaul* from, 58, *fig. 56*

Perpendicular style, of English architecture, 123, 283

Perrault, Claude, 276, 278, 283;

Louvre, Paris, East Front, *fig. 236*

Persepolis: Audience Hall of Darius, 31–32, *fig. 31*

Persian art, 31–32, 115

Persistence of Memory (Dali), 355, *fig. 327*

Perspective (spatial depth): in ancient art, 68, 69, 81, 178; atmospheric, 165; in Gothic art, 146, 150, 151, 154; in Late Gothic art, 163–64, 165; in modern art, 319, 329, 348; in Renaissance art, 178–79, 184, 186, 233

Perugino, Pietro, 191–92; *The Delivery of the Keys, fig. 175*

Peter the Great, equestrian statue of (Falconet), 280, *fig. 244*

Petrarch, 162

Phenomena Astral Signal (Jenkins), 367, *colorplate 73*

Phidias(?): *Three Goddesses, fig. 53*

Philippus the Arab, 67, *fig. 70*

Photo Realism, 371

Photography, 307–8, 319

Piano and Rogers: Georges Pompidou National Arts and Cultural Center, Paris, *colorplate 76*

Picasso, Pablo, 337, 338, 345–49, 376; *Ambroise Vollard,* 346–47, *fig. 314;* Blue Period, 337; *Bull's Head,* 10, 375, *fig. 2; Les Demoiselles d'Avignon,* 345–47, *fig. 313; Mother and Child,* 348–49, *fig. 317; The Old Guitarist,* 337, *fig. 302; Three Dancers,* 349, 355, *colorplate 68; Three Musicians,* 348, *fig. 316*

Piero della Francesca, 185–86, 192, 234; *De Prospectiva Pingendi,* illustrations from, 186, *fig. 170; The Discovery and Proving of the True Cross,* 185–86, *fig. 169*

Piero di Cosimo, 188–89; *The Discovery of Honey, colorplate 30*

Pietà (Avignon), see *Avignon Pietà*

Pietà (Bonn), 128, 168, 231, *fig. 132*

Pilgrimage to Cythera (Watteau), 281, 283, *colorplate 50*

Pisa: Cathedral, Baptistery, and Campanile, 111, *fig. 106;* pulpit for Baptistery (Nicola Pisano), 145, *fig. 134*

Pisano, Giovanni, 146; *Madonna, fig. 135*

Pisano, Nicola, 145; *The Nativity,* from pulpit of Baptistery, Pisa, *fig. 134*

Pliny, 70

Poe, Edgar Allan, 336

Pointillism, *see* Divisionism

Poitiers: Notre-Dame-la-Grande, 109, *fig. 103*

Polar Sea, The (Friedrich), 313–14, *fig. 274*

Polish Rider, The (Rembrandt), 252–54, *colorplate 47*

Pollaiuolo, Antonio del, 180, 181, 187–88; *Battle of Ten Naked Men,* 187–88, *fig. 172; Hercules and*

Antaeus, 180, 181, *fig. 163*
Pollock, Jackson, 356–65; *One (#31, 1950), fig. 330*
Pompeii: House of the Vettii, Ixion Room, 69, 145, *fig. 74;* mosaic from, see *Battle of Issus;* Villa of the Mysteries, wall painting, 70, *fig. 75*
Pompidou Center, Paris (Piano and Rogers), 385, *colorplate 76*
Pontormo, 222; *Study of a Young Girl, fig. 191*
Pop Art, 369–71, 379
Pope, as head of Church, 78, 88–97; *see also* Julius II; Leo X; Urban II
Portinari Altarpiece (Van der Goes), 169, 189, *fig. 149*
Portrait Head, from Delos, 58, *colorplate 7*
Portrait of a Boy, from the Faiyum, Egypt, 71, *colorplate 10*
Portrait of Cézanne (Ready-Made), 354
Portrait of Charles I Hunting (Van Dyck), 250, 284, *fig. 222*
Portrait of a Roman, 65–66, *fig. 67*
Portrait painting: Cubist, 346–47; English, eighteenth-century, 284–85; Flemish and Dutch Baroque, 250, 251, 252; Flemish Late Gothic, 167–68; French Rococo, 282–83; Renaissance and Mannerist, 189, 220–21, 222–24, 233, 237; Roman, 70–71; Romantic, 306, 307–9
Portrait sculpture: Egyptian, 20–21, 26; Hellenistic, 58; Neoclassical, 299; Renaissance, 179–80; Roman, 65–68; Romantic, 302–3
Portraiture, *see* Portrait painting; Portrait sculpture
Poseidon: statue of, 56, *fig. 52;* Temple of, Paestum, 50, *fig. 44*
Post-Impressionism, 329–38
Post-modern architecture, 385
Poussin, Nicolas, 242, 273–75, 276, 281, 297; *Landscape with the Burial of Phocion,* 275, *fig. 234; The Rape of the Sabine Women,* 273–74, *fig. 233*
"Poussinistes," 281, 297
Prague, 153
Prairie Houses (Wright), 381
Prato: Santa Maria delle Carceri (Sangallo), 184, *fig. 168*
Praxiteles, 57–58; *Hermes, fig. 55*
Prayer Book of Philip the Fair (Master Honoré of Paris), *David and Goliath* from, 150, *fig. 138*
Pre-Raphaelites, 334–35
Presentation in the Temple and Flight into Egypt (Broederlam), 154, *fig. 143*
Primary Structures, 377–78
"Primevalism," 373
Primitive art, 16–18, 345, 372
Primitivism, 333, 338
Prince Rahotep and His Wife Nofret, 21, *colorplate 1*

Princesse de Polignac (Vigée-Lebrun), 283, 285, *fig. 246*
Printing, development of, 171–72; *see also* Engravings; Etchings; Lithographs; Woodcuts
Prophet (Zuccone) (Donatello), 175–77, *fig. 157*
Propylaea, Acropolis, Athens, 51, 296, *fig. 46*
Protestant Reformation, 214, 231, 234, 237
Proto-Baroque painting, 226–27
Proverbios, Los (Goya), *Bobabilicon* from, 307, *fig. 266*
Psiax, 45; *Hercules Strangling the Nemean Lion,* Attic black-figured amphora, *fig. 38, colorplate 5*
Purse Cover, from the Sutton Hoo Ship-Burial, 97, *fig. 89*
Putto with Dolphin (Verrocchio), 181, *fig. 164*
Pyramids, 21, 22; of Mycerinus, Chefren, and Cheops, Giza, *fig. 17;* of King Zoser, Saqqara, *fig. 15*

Queen Nofretete, 26, *fig. 23*

Rahotep, Prince, and his wife Nofret, statue of, 21, *colorplate 1*
Raimondi, Marcantonio: *The Judgment of Paris* (after Raphael), *fig. 279*
Raising of the Cross (Rubens), 246, 252, *fig. 219*
Rake's Progress, The (Hogarth), Scene III, *The Orgy,* 284, *fig. 248*
Ramesses II, Court and Pylon of, Luxor, *fig. 21*
Rape of the Sabine Women (Poussin), 273–74, *fig. 233*
Raphael, 192, 218–20, 223, 273, 276; *Galatea,* 220, 241, *fig. 188; The School of Athens,* 218–20, *colorplate 33*
Ravenna: San Vitale, 84–85, 100, *figs. 83, 84;* San Vitale, mosaics, 86, *fig. 87;* Sant' Apollinare in Classe, 80, 84, 108, 111, *fig. 77, colorplate 11*
Reading Room, *see* Bibliothèque Ste.-Geneviève, Paris
Ready-Mades, 354, 372, 374
Realism: of Courbet, 315–16; in Gothic and Late Gothic painting, 154, 163; in Gothic sculpture, 126, 128, 145, 146; *see also* North Italian Realist painting
Recumbent Figure (Moore), 373, *fig. 342*
Red Blue Green (Kelly), 367, *fig. 333*
Red-figure vase painting, 45–46
Redon, Odilon, 336; *The Balloon Eye, fig. 298*
Reformation, 214, 231, 234, 237
Reims Cathedral: west façade, center portal, *Annunciation* and *Visitation,* 127–28, 145, 146, *fig. 129;* west wall, interior, *Melchizedek and Abraham,* 128, *fig. 130*

Rembrandt, 241, 252–54, 285, 306; *The Blinding of Samson,* 252, *fig. 225; Christ Preaching,* 254, *fig. 227; The Polish Rider,* 252–54, *colorplate 47; Self-Portrait,* 252, *fig. 226*
Renaissance art, *see* Early Renaissance art in Italy; High Renaissance art in Italy; Northern Renaissance art
Renaissance revival, in architecture, 301, 302
Renier of Huy, 114–15; Baptismal Font, St.-Barthélemy, Liège, *fig. 111*
Renoir, Auguste, 319; *Le Moulin de la Galette, fig. 280*
Resurrection, from *The Isenheim Altarpiece* (Grünewald), 232–33, *colorplate 39*
Return of the Hunters (Bruegel), 238, *fig. 209*
Revival styles, 300
Reynolds, Sir Joshua, 285; *Mrs. Siddons as the Tragic Muse, fig. 250*
River, The (Monet), 319, 332, *colorplate 61*
Road to Calvary (Simone Martini), 151–52, *colorplate 18*
Robbia, Luca della, 177, 179; *Madonna and Angels,* 179, *fig. 161*
Robert Andrews and His Wife (Gainsborough), 284, *colorplate 53*
Robie House, Chicago (Wright), 381–82, *figs. 356, 357*
Rococo style, 280–83, 305–6
Rodin, Auguste, 327–29, 338; *Balzac,* 329, *fig. 290; The Thinker,* 327–29, *fig. 289*
Roman art, 62; architecture, 62–65, 108, 256, 279, 295; painting, 69–71, 79, 105, 145; sculpture, 65–68
Roman Catholic Church, 78, 88–97, 106; *see also* Counter Reformation
Roman emperors, portraits of, 66–68
Roman Empire, 62, 66–68, 78, 83, 106
Romanesque art, 105–6; architecture, 107–12; painting, 115–17; sculpture, 112–15
Romanticism, 299–300, 333, 351; architecture, 300–302; painting, 305–15; sculpture, 302–5
Rome, 58–59, 106, 191, 240, 256; *Ara Pacis,* relief on, 68, 127, *fig. 72;* Arch of Titus, relief on, 68, *fig. 73;* Basilica of Constantine, 64–65, 217, *fig. 65;* Catacomb of SS. Pietro e Marcellino, painted ceiling, 79, *fig. 76;* Colosseum, 63, *fig. 62; Equestrian Statue of Marcus Aurelius,* 67, 177, 278, *fig. 69;* Palazzo Barberini, Ceiling Fresco (Cortona), 242, *colorplate 44;* Palazzo Farnese, Ceiling Fresco, Gallery (Carracci), 241–42, *fig. 212;* Pantheon,

63–64, 84, 111, 279, *figs. 63, 64;*
St. Peter's (Bramante; Michelangelo; Maderno; Bernini), 217–18;
243, 244, *figs. 185–87, 213;* San
Carlo alle Quattro Fontane (Borromini), 245, *fig. 217;* Santa
Maria della Vittoria, Cornaro
Chapel (Bernini), 244, *fig. 215;*
Santa Maria Maggiore, mosaic,
81, *fig. 78;* Sistine Chapel, Ceiling
Fresco and *Last Judgment*
(Michelangelo), 212–14, 218, 241,
figs. 180–82; Sistine Chapel,
fresco (Perugino), 191–92, *fig.
175;* Tempietto (Bramante),
215–17, *fig. 184;* Vatican Palace,
frescoes (Raphael), 218–20, *colorplate 33;* wall painting, *Odyssey
Landscapes,* 69–70, *colorplate 9;
see also* Roman art
Ronchamp: Notre-Dame-du-Haut
(Le Corbusier), 384, *figs. 361, 362*
Rossellino, Antonio, 179–80; *Giovanni Chellini, fig. 162*
Rossetti, Dante Gabriel, 334–35;
Ecce Ancilla Domini, fig. 297
Rosso Fiorentino, 222; *The Descent
from the Cross, colorplate 36*
Rothko, Mark, 366, 367; *Earth and
Green, colorplate 72*
Rouault, Georges, 341–42; *Head of
Christ,* 341, 345, 365, *fig. 307;
The Old Clown,* 342, *fig. 308*
Rouen: St.-Maclou, 122, *fig. 120*
Rousseau, Henri, 337–38, 351; *The
Dream, colorplate 65*
Royal Academy of Painting and
Sculpture, Paris, 276, 281, 333
"Rubénistes," 281, 309
Rubens, Peter Paul, 246–50, 251,
281; *The Garden of Love,* 250,
281, *colorplate 45; Landscape
with the Château of Steen,* 250,
*fig. 221; Marie de' Medici, Queen
of France, Landing in Marseilles,*
248, 273, *fig. 220; The Raising of
the Cross,* 246, 252, *fig. 219*
Ruckus Manhattan (Grooms), 380,
fig. 354
Rude, François, 303; *La Marseillaise, fig. 263*
Ruisdael, Jacob van, 254; *The Cemetery, fig. 228*
Ruskin, John, 325

Sacrifice of Isaac (Ghiberti), 146,
178, *fig. 136*
Safdie, Moshe, 385; Habitat, EXPO
67, Montreal, *fig. 363*
St. Bernard of Clairvaux, 112
St. Charles Borromaeus, Vienna
(Fischer von Erlach), 279, *fig. 241*
St.-Denis, royal Abbey Church of,
Paris, 118–19, 122, 126
St. Dorothy, woodcut, *fig. 153*
St.-Etienne, Caen, 110, 120, *fig. 104*
St. Francis in Ecstasy (Bellini), 191,
220, *colorplate 31*
St. Gall, Switzerland, *Plan of a
Monastery,* 100–101, 108, *fig. 94*

St. George (Donatello), 174–75,
fig. 156
St. James Led to His Execution
(Mantegna), 189–91, *fig. 174*
St. John the Evangelist, from the
Gospel Book of Abbot Wedricus,
115–16, *colorplate 15*
St.-Maclou, Rouen, 122, *fig. 120*
St. Mark, from the *Gospel Book of
Archbishop Ebbo of Reims,*
102–3, 104, 114, *fig. 96*
St. Matthew, from the *Gospel Book
of Charlemagne,* 102, *fig. 95*
St. Matthew (Savoldo), 227–28, *fig.
197*
St. Michael's, Hildesheim, 104, *fig.
98;* bronze doors for, 104–5, 112,
115, *fig. 99*
St. Paul's Cathedral, London
(Wren), 283, *fig. 247*
St. Peter's, Rome (Bramante; Michelangelo; Maderno; Bernini),
217–18, 243, 244, 279, *figs.
185–87, 213*
St.-Pierre, Moissac, south portal
(portion), 113–14, *fig. 109*
St.-Savin-sur-Gartempe, portion of
painted nave vault, 117, *fig. 114*
St.-Sernin, Toulouse, 107–9, 110,
119, 120, *figs. 100–102; Apostle,*
112–13, *fig. 108*
Salisbury Cathedral, 123, *fig. 121*
Salome (Beardsley), 333–34, *fig.
296*
Salon de la Guerre, *see* Versailles,
Palace of
Salon de la Princesse, *see* Hôtel de
Soubise, Paris
Saltcellar of Francis I (Cellini),
228–29, *fig. 199*
Samos: Temple of Hera, *"Hera"*
from, 53–54, *fig. 48*
San Carlo alle Quattro Fontane,
Rome (Borromini), 245, *fig. 217*
San Lorenzo, Florence (Brunelleschi), 182, 217, *fig. 165;* Medici
Chapel, Tomb of Giuliano de'
Medici (Michelangelo), 215, 228,
fig. 183
San Vitale, Ravenna, 84–85, 100,
figs. 83, 84; mosaics, 86, *fig. 87*
Sand Painting (Navaho), Arizona,
18, *fig. 12*
Sangallo, Giuliano da, 184; Santa
Maria delle Carceri, Prato, *fig.
168*
Sant' Andrea, Mantua (Alberti),
183, *fig. 167*
Sant' Apollinare in Classe, Ravenna,
80, 84, 108, 111, *fig. 77, colorplate 11*
Santa Croce, Florence, 124, 182,
fig. 123
Santa Maria della Vittoria, Rome,
Cornaro Chapel, *The Ecstasy of
St. Theresa* (Bernini), 244, *fig. 215*
Santa Maria delle Carceri, Prato
(Sangallo), 184, *fig. 168*
Santa Maria Maggiore, Rome, mosaic, 81, *fig. 78*

Saqqara: Funerary District of King
Zoser, 21–22; Papyrus Half-Columns, 22, 48, 52, *fig. 16;* Step
Pyramid, *fig. 15*
Sarcophagus of Junius Bassus, 83,
102, 109–10, *fig. 81*
Sargon II, palace of, 30
Savoldo, Girolamo, 227–28; *St.
Matthew, fig. 197*
Savoye House, Poissy-sur-Seine (Le
Corbusier), 383, *fig. 359*
Scenes of a Dionysiac Mystery Cult,
Villa of the Mysteries, Pompeii,
70, *fig. 75*
Schongauer, Martin, 172–73, 233,
234; *The Temptation of St. Anthony, fig. 154*
School of Athens (Raphael), 218–20,
colorplate 33
Science, and art, 211, 240, 294
Scientific perspective, 178–79, 184,
186, 319
Scopas(?): *Greeks Battling Amazons,* 56–57, *fig. 54*
Scream, The (Munch), 336–37, *fig.
300*
Seagram Building, New York (Mies
van der Rohe and Philip Johnson),
384, *fig. 360*
Seated Woman (Méditerranée)
(Maillol), 338, *fig. 303*
Segal, George, 379; *Cinema, fig.
353*
Self-Portrait (Dürer), 233, *fig. 203*
Self-Portrait (Kokoschka), 343, *fig.
311*
Self-Portrait (Parmigianino),
222–23, *fig. 192*
Self-Portrait (Rembrandt), 252, *fig.
226*
Self-Portrait (Van Gogh), 332, *fig.
293*
Seurat, Georges, 331, 345; *A Sunday
Afternoon on the Grande Jatte,
colorplate 62*
She-Wolf (Etruscan), 61, *fig. 60*
Siddons, Sarah, portraits of (Gainsborough; Reynolds), 284–85,
figs. 249, 250
Siena, 151; Palazzo Pubblico, fresco
(Ambrogio Lorenzetti), 152–53,
figs. 141, 142
Sistine Chapel, Rome, 191; Ceiling
Fresco and *Last Judgment* (Michelangelo), 212–14, 218, 241,
figs. 180–82; fresco (Perugino),
191–92, *fig. 175*
Sketch I for "Composition VII"
(Kandinsky), 344–45, *colorplate
67*
Skyscrapers, 381
Slave Ship, The (Turner), 312–13,
325, *colorplate 59*
Sluter, Claus, 145, 168; *The Moses
Well, fig. 133*
Smith, David, 377; *Cubi* Series,
fig. 349
Smithson, Robert, 378; *Spiral Jetty,
fig. 351*
Soufflot, Jacques Germain, 295;

Panthéon, Paris, *fig. 251*
Soundbox of a Harp, from Ur, 28–29, 45, *fig. 27*
Soutine, Chaim, 342; *Dead Fowl, fig. 309*
Spain, 226; and Holland, 237; *see also* Spanish painting
Spanish painting, 226, 250, 305–7
Sphinx, Giza, 22, *fig. 18*
Spiral Jetty (Smithson), 378, *fig. 351*
Spoils from the Temple in Jerusalem, relief on the Arch of Titus, Rome, 68, *fig. 73*
Stage Design for *"La Zenobia di Radamisto"* (Burnacini), 244, 277, *fig. 216*
Stained canvas, 366–67
Stained glass, 147–50, 342; *see also* Chartres Cathedral
Standing Youth (Kouros), 50, 52–53, 55, *fig. 47*
Standing Youth (The Kritios Boy), 55–56, *fig. 51*
Standing Youth (Lehmbruck), 338, *fig. 304*
Steen, Jan, 255–56; *The Eve of St. Nicholas, fig. 230*
Stella, Frank, 367–68; *Empress of India, fig. 334*
Stella, Joseph, 349; *Brooklyn Bridge, fig. 319*
Step Pyramid, Funerary District of King Zoser, Saqqara, 21, *fig. 15*
Still Life (Heda), 254–55, *fig. 229*
Still-life painting, 254–55, 282, 342
Stoke-by-Nayland (Constable), 311, *fig. 273*
Stone Breakers, The (Courbet), 316, *fig. 277*
Stonehenge, *Great Circle,* 15–16, *figs. 6, 7*
Story of Jacob and Esau, from the "Gates of Paradise" (Ghiberti), 177–79, *fig. 160*
Strawberry Hill, Twickenham (Walpole, with Robinson and others), 301, *fig. 258*
Study of a Young Girl (Pontormo), 222, *fig. 191*
Suger, Abbot, 119, 121–22, 127, 146–47
Sullivan, Louis, 381, 382–83; Carson Pirie Scott & Company, Chicago, *fig. 355*
Sumerian art, 27–29
Sunday Afternoon on the Grande Jatte (Seurat), 331, *colorplate 62*
Surrealism, 354–55; in sculpture, 375, 377
Sutton Hoo Ship-Burial, purse cover from, 97, *fig. 89*
Symbolism (Symbolist Movement), 332, 333–36

Tell Asmar: Temple of Abu, statuettes from, 28, 30, *fig. 26*
Tempera, 164
Tempest, The (Giorgione), 220, *colorplate 34*
Tempietto, Rome (Bramante),

215–17, 283, *fig. 184*
Temple of Abu, Tell Asmar, statuettes from, 28, 30, *fig. 26*
Temple of Amen-Mut-Khonsu, Luxor, 25, *fig. 21*
Temple of Athena Nike, Acropolis, Athens, 51–52, *fig. 46*
Temple of Poseidon, Paestum, 50, *fig. 44*
Temples: Egyptian, 25, 48; Greek, 48–52; Roman, 63–65, 276, 295; Sumerian, 27–28
Temptation of St. Anthony (Schongauer), 172–73, 233, 234, *fig. 154*
Thebes (Egypt), 22
Thinker, The (Rodin), 327–29, *fig. 289*
Third of May (Goya), 307, *colorplate 56*
Third-Class Carriage (Daumier), 310, *fig. 271*
Three Dancers (Picasso), 349, 355, *colorplate 68*
Three Flags (Johns), 370, *fig. 336*
Three Goddesses, from east pediment of the Parthenon, 56, *fig. 53*
Three Musicians (Picasso), 348, *fig. 316*
Tiepolo, Giovanni Battista, 280, 281; Ceiling Fresco, Kaisersaal, Episcopal Palace, Würzburg, *fig. 242*
Tintoretto, 224–26, 228; *The Last Supper, fig. 194*
Tiryns, wall painting from Palace at, 43, *fig. 35*
Titian, 192, 220–21, 227, 248–50; *Bacchanal,* 220, *colorplate 35; Christ Crowned with Thorns,* 221, *fig. 190; Man with the Glove,* 220–21, *fig. 189*
Titus, Arch of, Rome, relief on, 68, *fig. 73*
Tomb of Giuliano de' Medici (Michelangelo), 215, 228, *fig. 183*
Tomb paintings: Early Christian, 79; Egyptian, 23–24; Etruscan, 61–62
"Toreador Fresco," from the Palace of Minos, Knossos, 42, *colorplate 4*
Totem and Taboo (Ernst), 355, *fig. 328*
Toulouse: St.-Sernin, 107–9, 110, 119, 120, *figs. 100–102; Apostle,* 112–13, *fig. 108*
Toulouse-Lautrec, Henri de, 336; *At the Moulin Rouge, fig. 299*
Tower of Babel, 28
Trajan, 66, *fig. 68*
Tub, The (Degas), 319–20, *fig. 282*
Turin: Palazzo Carignano (Guarini), 246, *fig. 218*
Turner, Joseph Mallord William, 311–13, 320; *The Slave Ship,* 312–13, 325, *colorplate 59*
Tutankhamen, coffin of, 26, *colorplate 2*
Twentieth-century architecture, 380–85

Twentieth-century painting, 339–40; Abstraction, 345–51; Expressionism, 340–45; Fantasy, 351–55; Newer Trends, 355–72
Twentieth-century sculpture, 372–80
Twittering Machine (Klee), 352–53, *fig. 323*
Two Dancers, wall painting, Tomb of the Lionesses, Tarquinia, 61–62, *colorplate 8*

Unique Forms of Continuity in Space (Boccioni), 374, *fig. 344*
Universities, 119
Ur: offering stand from, 29, *colorplate 3;* sound box of a harp from, 28–29, 45, *fig. 27*
Urban II, Pope, 106
Urban VIII, Pope, 242
Urban design, 384–85
Uruk (Warka): "White Temple," 28, *figs. 24, 25*

Van der Goes, *see* Goes, Hugo van der
Van der Weyden, *see* Weyden, Rogier van der
Van Dyck, Anthony, 250, 284; *Portrait of Charles I Hunting, fig. 222*
Van Eyck, Hubert, 165–66, 191; *Crucifixion: The Last Judgment,* 165, *colorplate 23; The Ghent Altarpiece,* 165–67, *figs. 145, 146*
Van Eyck, Jan, 165–68, 169, 171, 191; *Adam and Eve,* from *The Ghent Altarpiece,* 166–67, 177, *fig. 145; Crucifixion: The Last Judgment,* 165, *colorplate 23; The Ghent Altarpiece,* 165–67, *figs. 145, 146; Giovanni Arnolfini and His Bride,* 167–68, *fig. 148, colorplate 24; Man in a Red Turban (Self-Portrait?),* 167, 222, 252, *fig. 147*
Van Gogh, Vincent, 331–32, 340; *Self-Portrait,* 332, *fig. 293; Wheat Field and Cypress Trees,* 331–32, *colorplate 63*
Vaphio Cups, 43, *fig. 36*
Vasarely, Victor, 368–69; *Vega, fig. 335*
Vase painting, Greek, 44–48
Vatican Palace, Rome, frescoes (Raphael), 218–20, *colorplate 33*
Vatican Vergil, illumination from, 81–82, *fig. 79*
Vault: in Gothic architecture, 120–21; in Roman architecture, 63, 64–65; in Romanesque architecture, 108–9, 110–11
Vega (Vasarely), 369, *fig. 335*
Velázquez, Diego, 250, 318; *The Maids of Honor,* 250, 306, *fig. 223*
Venetian painting, 191, 220–21, 224–26, 228, 280
Veneziano, Domenico, 184–85; *Madonna and Child with Saints, colorplate 28*

Venus of Willendorf, 14, *fig. 5*

Vermeer, Jan, 256; *The Letter, colorplate 48*

Veronese, Paolo, 228; *Christ in the House of Levi, fig. 198*

Verrocchio, Andrea del, 181, 192; *Putto with Dolphin, fig. 164*

Versailles, Palace of (Lebrun; Le Vau; Hardouin-Mansart; Le Nôtre), 276–78, *fig. 238;* Salon de la Guerre, 277, *fig. 237*

Very Rich Book of Hours of the Duke of Berry (Limbourg Brothers), 154–55, 238, *fig. 144, colorplate 20*

Vicenza: Villa Rotonda (Palladio), 230–31, *fig. 201*

Vienna: St. Charles Borromaeus (Fischer von Erlach), 279, *fig. 241*

Vienna Genesis, illumination from, 82–83, *fig. 80*

Vienna Secession, 337

Vigée-Lebrun, Marie-Louise-Elizabeth, 282–83, 285; *Princesse de Polignac, fig. 246*

Vikings, 103

Villa of the Mysteries, Pompeii, wall painting, 70, *fig. 75*

Villa Rotonda, Vicenza (Palladio), 230–31, *fig. 201*

Village Bride, The (Greuze), 296–97, *fig. 254*

Vinci, *see* Leonardo da Vinci

Virgin and Child with Angels, from *The Isenheim Altarpiece* (Grünewald), 232–33, *colorplate 39*

Visitation, west façade, Reims Cathedral, 127, 145, 146, *fig. 129*

Vitruvius, 64

Vollard, Ambroise, portrait of (Picasso), 346–47, *fig. 314*

Voltaire (Houdon), 299, *fig. 257*

Walpole, Horace, 301; Strawberry Hill, Twickenham, *fig. 258*

Washington, D.C.: *The X,* in the Corcoran Gallery (Bladen), 378, *fig. 350*

Water Lilies, Giverny (Monet), 320, *fig. 283*

Watson and the Shark (Copley), 298, *colorplate 55*

Watteau, Antoine, 281, 283; *A Pilgrimage to Cythera, colorplate 50*

Wedricus, Abbot, Gospel Book of, *St. John the Evangelist* from, 115–16, *colorplate 15*

West, Benjamin, 297–98; *The Death of General Wolfe, fig. 256*

Weyden, Rogier van der, 168, 246; *The Descent from the Cross, colorplate 25*

Wheat Field and Cypress Trees (Van Gogh), 331–32, *colorplate 63*

Whistler, James McNeill, 320–25, 344; *Arrangement in Black and Gray: The Artist's Mother,* 320, *fig. 284; Nocturne in Black and Gold: The Falling Rocket,* 325, *fig. 285*

"White Temple," Uruk (Warka), 28, *figs. 24, 25*

William the Conqueror, 103, 110, 117

Winckelmann, Johann, 295

Winged Victory, see *Nike of Samothrace*

Witz, Conrad, 171; *The Miraculous Draught of Fishes, fig. 152*

Wolfe, James, see *Death of General Wolfe* (West)

Woman II (De Kooning), 365, *colorplate 71*

Women artists, 282–83, 326

Women Regents of the Old People's Home at Haarlem (Hals), 251, *fig. 224*

Woodcuts, 172, 233–34, 333

Wounded Bison, cave painting, Altamira (Spain), 12–13, *fig. 4*

Wren, Sir Christopher, 283; St. Paul's Cathedral, London, *fig. 247*

Wright, Frank Lloyd, 381–82; Robie House, Chicago, *figs. 356, 357*

Wrought-iron sculpture, 375–76

Würzburg: Episcopal Palace, Kaisersaal (Neumann), 279–80, *colorplate 49;* Ceiling Fresco, Kaisersaal (Tiepolo), 280, *fig. 242*

X, The (Bladen), 378, *fig. 350*

Yellow Christ, The (Gauguin), 332, *colorplate 64*

Youth and Demon of Death, Etruscan cinerary container, 62, *fig. 61*

Zeus (or Poseidon), statue of, 56, *fig. 52*

Ziggurats, 27–28

Zoroaster, 31

Zoser, king of Egypt, funerary district of, Saqqara, 21–22, *figs. 15, 16*

Zuccone (Donatello), 175–77, *fig. 157*

LIST OF CREDITS

The authors and publisher wish to thank the libraries, museums, and private collectors for permitting the reproduction in black-and-white and in color of paintings, prints, and drawings in their collections. Photographs have been supplied by the owners or custodians of the works of art except for the following, whose courtesy is gratefully acknowledged:

Alinari (including Anderson and Brogi), Florence (41, 56, 69, 72, 73, 74, 78, 87, 107, 124–126, 134–136, 140, 141, 156–159, 160–166, 168, 169, 173, 174, 176, 177, 179–183, 187–189, 192–195, 198, 200, 215, 217, 262); American Museum of Natural History (12); Andrews, Wayne, Grosse Point, Mich. (252); Copyright Archives Centrales Iconographiques, Brussels (111, 145, 146, 219); Archives Photographiques, Paris (3, 28, 109, 133, 137, 207, 231, 234, 237, 243, 254, 264, 280, 282); Copyright The Barnes Foundation, Merion, Pa. (306); Bildarchiv Oesterr. Nationalbibliothek, Vienna (80); Borsig, Arnold von, Berlin (123); Brassaï, Paris (2); Bruckmann, F., Munich (192); Bulloz, Paris (110, 211, 263, 264); Burckhardt, Rudolph, New York (337); Burstein, Barney, Boston, Mass. (307); Commissione Pontificale d'Archeologia Sacra, Rome (76); Copyright Country Life, London (258); Deutsche Fotothek, Dresden (277); Deutscher Kunstverlag, Munich (93, 253); Devinoy, Pierre, Paris (114); Dingjan, A., The Hague (224); Fleming, R. B. and Co., Ltd., London (283); Fotocielo, Rome (54, 213); Fototeca Unione, Rome (61, 62, 63); Frantz, Alison, Athens (34, 45, 46); Gabinetto Foto- grafico Nazionale, Rome (184, 212, 214, 239); German Archaeological Institute, Rome (24, 84); Giraudon, Paris (103, 113, 208, 236, 257, 260, 267, 268, 278, 281, 284); Gorgoni, Gianfranco, New York (351); Photo-Verlag Gundermann, Würzburg (242); Hahn, E., Berlin (9); Hervé, Lucien, Paris (358–60); Hirmer Fotoarchiv, Munich (15–18, 21, 23, 33, 40, 48, 50, 52, 55, 57, 58, 71, 81, 86); Hürliman, Martin, Zurich (244); Istituto Centrale del Restauro, Rome (139); Kersting, A. F., London (105, 122, 251); Kidder-Smith, G. E., New York (44, 65, 83, 85, 106, 117); Kühn, H., Mainz (4); Levy, Et., and Neurdein Réunis, Paris (120); Copyright London County Council (226); Foto-Marburg, Marburg/Lahn (36, 97, 127, 128, 130, 131, 261); Marlborough Gallery, New York (349); A. and R. Mas, Barcelona (223, 265); McKenna, Rollie, New York (167, 201); Ministry of Works, London, Crown Copyright (6); National Monuments Record, London (247, 259); Nickel, Richard, Park Ridge, Ill. (354); Oldenburg, Claes, Copyright, courtesy Gemini Gel, Los Angeles (352); Oriental Institute, University of Chicago (26, 31); Powell, Josephine, Rome (88, 142); Rabin, Nathan, New York (328); Rheinisches Bildarchiv, Cologne (132); Roubier, Jean, Paris (102, 104, 118, 129); St. Joseph, Dr. J. K. (7); Schmidt-Glassner, Helga, Stuttgart (241); Smith, Edwin, London (121); Sunami, S., New York (8, 321–323, 330, 343, 346); Vizzavona, Paris (220, 290); Ward, Clarence, Oberlin, Ohio (116, 119); Wehmeyer, Hermann, Hildesheim (98, 99); Yan Photo Reportage, Toulouse (101, 108); Yugoslav State Tourist Office, New York (66).